Trade Marks and Brands

Recent developments in trade mark law have called into question a variety of basic features, as well as bolder extensions, of legal protection. Other disciplines can help us think about fundamental issues such as: What is a trade mark? What does it do? What should be the scope of its protection? This volume assembles essays examining trade marks and brands from a multiplicity of fields: from business history, marketing, linguistics, legal history, philosophy, sociology and geography. Each part pairs lawyers' and non-lawyers' perspectives, so that each commentator addresses and critiques his or her counterpart's analysis. The perspectives of non-legal fields are intended to enrich legal academics' and practitioners' reflections about trade marks, and to expose lawyers, judges and policy-makers to ideas, concepts and methods that could prove to be of particular importance in the development of positive law.

LIONEL BENTLY is Herchel Smith Professor of Intellectual Property Law at the University of Cambridge, Director of the Centre for Intellectual Property and Information Law at the University of Cambridge, and a Professorial Fellow at Emmanuel College, Cambridge.

JENNIFER DAVIS is Newton Trust Lecturer and Fellow of Wolfson College, University of Cambridge.

JANE C. GINSBURG is the Morton L. Janklow Professor of Literary and Artistic Property Law at Columbia University School of Law. She also directs the law school's Kernochan Center for Law, Media and the Arts.

Cambridge Intellectual Property and Information Law

As its economic potential has rapidly expanded, intellectual property has become a subject of front-rank legal importance. *Cambridge Intellectual Property Rights and Information Law* is a series of monograph studies of major current issues in intellectual property. Each volume contains a mix of international, European, comparative and national law, making this a highly significant series for practitioners, judges and academic researchers in many countries.

Series editor
William R. Cornish
Emeritus Herchel Smith Professor of Intellectual Property Law, University of Cambridge
Lionel Bently
Herchel Smith Professor of Intellectual Property Law, University of Cambridge

Advisory editors
François Dessemontet, Professor of Law, University of Lausanne
Paul Goldstein, Professor of Law, Stanford University
The Rt Hon. Sir Robin Jacob, Court of Appeal, England

A list of books in the series can be found at the end of this volume.

Trade Marks and Brands

An Interdisciplinary Critique

Edited by

Lionel Bently,

Jennifer Davis

and

Jane C. Ginsburg

CAMBRIDGE
UNIVERSITY PRESS

CAMBRIDGE UNIVERSITY PRESS
Cambridge, New York, Melbourne, Madrid, Cape Town, Singapore,
São Paulo, Delhi

Cambridge University Press
The Edinburgh Building, Cambridge CB2 8RU, UK

Published in the United States of America by Cambridge University Press,
New York

www.cambridge.org
Information on this title: www.cambridge.org/9780521889650

First published 2008

Printed in the United Kingdom at the University Press, Cambridge

A catalogue record for this publication is available from the British Library

Library of Congress Cataloguing in Publication data
Trade marks and brands: an interdisciplinary critique / Lionel Bently,
Jennifer Davis and Jane C. Ginsburg (eds.)
p. cm.
Includes bibliographical references.
ISBN 978-0-521-88965-0
1. Trademarks – Law and legislation.   2. Trademarks (International law)
3. Brand name products – Law and legislation.   4. Intellectual property
(International law)   I. Bently, Lionel, 1964–
II. Davis, Jennifer, 1964–   II. Ginsburg, Jane C.
K1555.T733   2008
346.04′88 – dc22
                                                        2007052481

ISBN 978-0-521-88965-0 hardback

Contents

List of figures and tables

Notes on the contributors

JONATHAN ALDRED is a Fellow of Emmanuel College and a Newton Trust Lecturer in the Department of Land Economy, both in the University of Cambridge. An economist by training, his research interests are now interdisciplinary, spanning economics, philosophy, law and political theory. He has particular interests in the philosophical foundations of welfare economics and economic theories of rational choice. Recent publications have focussed on the scope and limitations of using monetary measures to value environmental impacts and public policy outcomes. He is currently working on an introductory book on the ethical assumptions behind popular economic arguments: *Ethical Economics*.

LIONEL BENTLY has been the Herchel Smith Professor of Intellectual Property Law and Director of the Centre for Intellectual Property and Information Law at the University of Cambridge since October 2004. He is also a Professorial Fellow of Emmanuel College, Cambridge. He is co-author (both with Brad Sherman) of *Intellectual Property Law* (2001; 2nd edn, 2004) and *The Making of Modern Intellectual Property Law – The British Experience, 1760–1911* (Cambridge, 1999). He is also the author of *Between a Rock and a Hard Place: The Problems Facing Freelance Creators in the UK Media Market-Place* (2002) and co-editor (with David Vaver) of *Intellectual Property in the New Millennium: Essays in Honour of Professor William Cornish* (Cambridge, 2004). With Martin Kretschmer, he is co-director of an AHRC-funded resource enhancement project developing a digital resource of primary documents relating to copyright history from five jurisdictions (the USA, UK, France, Germany and Italy).

JENNIFER DAVIS is a Newton Trust Lecturer in Intellectual Property Law and a member of the Centre for Intellectual Property and Information Law, University of Cambridge. She is also a Fellow of Wolfson College, Cambridge. She is the author of *Intellectual Property Law* (2008). She has a particular interest in trade mark law and unfair competition and has published extensively on these topics. Before joining the Faculty of Law, Dr Davis practised as a lawyer in the area of intellectual property litigation.

GRAEME B. DINWOODIE is a Professor of Law, Associate Dean, and Director of the Program in Intellectual Property Law, at Chicago-Kent College of Law. He also holds a Chair in Intellectual Property Law at Queen Mary College, University of London. He is the author of several articles and casebooks, including *Trademarks and Unfair Competition: Law and Policy* (2nd edn, 2007) (with M. Janis) and *International Intellectual Property Law and Policy* (with W. Hennessey and S. Perlmutter). Prior to teaching, Professor Dinwoodie had been an associate with Sullivan and Cromwell in New York. Professor Dinwoodie was the Burton Fellow in Residence at Columbia Law School for 1988–9, working in the field of intellectual property law, and a John F. Kennedy Scholar at Harvard Law School for 1987–8. He is a member of the American Law Institute.

ALAN DURANT is Professor of Communication at Middlesex University Business School, London, where his current research is into ways of adjudicating contested meanings in different areas of media law. As well as being author or co-author of a number of textbooks on English language and literature, his publications include *Conditions of Music* (1984), *Ezra Pound: Identity in Crisis* (1981) and (with Nigel Fabb, Derek Attridge and Colin MacCabe) *The Linguistics of Writing: Arguments Between Language and Literature* (1987).

DEV GANGJEE joined the London School of Economics as a lecturer in intellectual property law in 2005, after a period as a Rhodes Scholar at Oxford. While his research interests lie broadly in intellectual property, there is a special focus on regimes regulating signs, such as trade marks, geographical indications and domain names. He is a research associate of the Oxford Intellectual Property Research Centre and his doctoral work has focussed on geographical indications. He has published in the area as well as presented his work in the USA, UK, Japan and China. He is inured to the deluge of comments which inevitably follow, such as 'Oh! You research wine?'

JANE C. GINSBURG is the Morton L. Janklow Professor of Literary and Artistic Property Law at Columbia University School of Law, and Director of its Kernochan Center for Law, Media and the Arts. She has held the Arthur L. Goodhart Visiting Chair of Legal Science at the University of Cambridge, and is an Honorary Fellow of Emmanuel College, University of Cambridge. With Professor Sam Ricketson, she is the co-author of *International Copyright and Neighbouring*

Rights: The Berne Convention and Beyond (2006). With Professor
Rochelle Dreyfuss and Professor François Dessemontet, she was a
co-reporter for the American Law Institute project on Intellectual
Property: Principles Governing Jurisdistion, Choice of Law and
Judgments in Transnational Disputes (to be published in 2008).

ANDREW GRIFFITHS is a reader in law at the University of Manchester.
His teaching and research interests include trade mark law, company
law and law-and-economics. He is the author of *Contracting with
Companies* (2005).

DAVID M. HIGGINS is 40th Anniversary Reader in Business and
Economic History at the University of York. He was, previously, lecturer
and senior lecturer in economics at the University of Sheffield. His major
research interests are British industrial performance in the nineteenth
and twentieth centuries, aspects of interwar economic performance, and
the protection of intellectual property. His research has been funded by
grants from the Economic and Social Research Council (ESRC), the
Leverhulme Trust and the Nuffield Foundation. He was elected a
Fellow of the Royal Historical Society in 2007.

JAMES LEACH is Senior Lecturer in Social Anthropology at the University
of Aberdeen. He held a Research Fellowship at King's College
Cambridge while his contribution to this volume was being written.
James trained in Manchester between 1989 and 1997, and has undertaken long-term field research on the Rai Coast of Papua New Guinea,
as well as additional research on comparative material in the UK. His
publications include work on the topics of art, aesthetics, kinship,
ownership, intellectual and cultural property, interdisciplinary collab-
orations, free/open-source software communities and knowledge
production.

MIGUEL LEY-PINEDA is a Ph.D. student in the Faculty of Philosophy at
the University of Cambridge. He works in ancient Greek philosophy
but has interest in contemporary political philosophy, the philosophy of
organizations and intellectual property.

CELIA LURY is Professor of Sociology at Goldsmiths, University of
London. Her first book, *Cultural Rights: Technology, Legality and
Personality* (1993), identified the importance of regimes of intellectual
property rights in contemporary culture, a theme which she has continued to explore in more recent studies, including *Brands: The Logos of
the Global Economy* (2004) and *Global Culture Industry: The Mediation of
Things* (with Scott Lash) (2007).

CATHERINE W. NG joined the University of Aberdeen as a lecturer in law after having completed her D.Phil. – which included work as a Europaeum scholar at the Institut universitaire de hautes études internationales in Geneva – and after having completed her subsequent research fellowship at the Institut. Her D.Phil. thesis won the first British Brands Group Prize awarded for the best Oxford dissertation or thesis related to the law or practice of trade marks, unfair competition, or branding. An adaptation of it is being published in two parts in the *Intellectual Property Journal* (20 (2007)). She has published articles in the *European Intellectual Property Law Review* and Canada-wide intellectual property law journals on topics ranging from domain names to patent law to law governing copyright and comparative advertising. She is a research associate at the Oxford Intellectual Property Research Centre.

ALEX OLIVER is University Reader in Philosophy at the University of Cambridge and a Fellow of Gonville and Caius College. His research interests span metaphysics, ethics and logic, and include the nature of properties and sets, the ethics of organizations and the metaphysics of intellectual property. He has held a Mellon Fellowship at Yale University, a Research Fellowship at Gonville and Caius, and a Leverhulme Trust Major Research Fellowship for work on the logic of plurals. He has also advised public and private institutions on loyalty, educational strategy, corporate responsibility, the ethics of taxation, and trust in charities.

BRONWYN PARRY is a reader in cultural and economic geography at Queen Mary University of London. Prior to her arrival at Queen Mary in 2004, she researched and taught at the University of Cambridge for ten years. Her primary interests lie in investigating the way human–environment relations are being recast by technological, economic and regulatory change. She has undertaken large-scale research projects into the organization and operation of the bioprospecting industry and, more recently, on the legal and ethical implications of the expansion of human tissue and organ banking in the UK. Her work on benefit-sharing, bioprospecting and intellectual property rights has been published in international journals. She is the author of the widely acclaimed book *Trading the Genome: Investigating the Commodification of Bio-information* (2004). She has also written extensively on the emergence and regulation of the bio-economy, commodification of the body and bodily artefacts, and has developing interests in the global trade in reproductive services and post-humanism. She is a permanent member of the Nuffield Council on Bioethics and has acted as a consultant to the UK government in the drafting of the 2004 Human Tissue Bill, and in the development of their policies on travel, migration and infectious disease risk. She has also acted as an advisor to the UN on international compliance with genetic access and benefit-sharing regimes.

MEGAN RICHARDSON is an associate professor in the Law Faculty, The University of Melbourne, Australia. Her research interests span the fields of intellectual property and personality rights and lately have been particularly focussed on legal protection of traditional culture/folklore.

JONATHAN E. SCHROEDER is Professor of Marketing at the School of Business and Economics, University of Exeter. He is also a Visiting Professor in Marketing Semiotics at Bocconi University in Milan, and Visiting Professor in Design Management at the Indian School of Business, Hyderabad. His research focusses on the production and consumption of images, and has been widely published in marketing, organization, psychology, design and law journals. He is the author of *Visual Consumption* (2002) and co-editor of *Brand Culture* (2006). He is an editor of *Consumption Markets & Culture*, and serves on the editorial boards of the *Journal of Business Research*, the *European Journal of Marketing*, *Marketing Theory*, the *International Journal of Indian Culture, Business Management* and *Advertising and Society Review*.

DOMINIC SCOTT is Professor of Philosophy at the University of Virginia, Charlottesville. Although he works mainly in ancient Greek philosophy, his interests also include ethics, the philosophy of organizations, trust and intellectual property. Until 2007 he taught at the University of Cambridge where he helped set up the Forum for Philosophy in Business, a research centre devoted to investigating questions of practical life with a philosophical dimension.

MICHAEL SPENCE is Head of the Social Sciences Division of the University of Oxford and a Fellow of St Catherine's College, Oxford. He is a consultant to the law firm Olswang. Michael has a comparative perspective on the law of intellectual property. His work has a critical focus on suggested ethical and economic justifications of the existing regimes.

DAVID VAVER is Emeritus Professor of Intellectual Property and Information Technology Law in the University of Oxford, Director (since 2008) of the Oxford Intellectual Property Research Centre at St Peter's College, and Fellow of St Peter's College. Most recently he edited a five-volume compilation on *Intellectual Property Rights: Critical Concepts in Law* (2006).

Editors' preface

Recent developments in trade mark law have called into question a variety of basic features, as well as bolder extensions, of legal protection. Other disciplines can help us think about fundamental issues such as: What is a trade mark? What does it do? What should be the scope of its protection? The present volume assembles essays examining trade marks and brands from a multiplicity of fields. We believe the broad range of the contributions to this volume makes it unique. There are already works on trade mark law, works on branding and marketing, works on linguistics and marketing, and works on sociological aspects of commercial identity, but no attempt to bring these approaches together. Equally importantly, rather than offering a litany of discrete chapters each independently covering a different discipline, each part of this book pairs lawyers' and non-lawyers' perspectives, so that each commentator will address and critique his or her counterpart's analysis. Authors of the main papers and of the commentaries divide roughly evenly between lawyers and specialists from other disciplines.

The perspectives of non-legal fields are intended to enrich legal academics' and practitioners' reflections about trade marks, as well as to expose lawyers, judges and policy-makers to ideas, concepts and methods that could prove to be of particular importance in the development of positive law. For those who wish to explore further, an extensive bibliography collecting commentaries from all the fields here represented concludes the volume. We hope the volume will prove of interest as well to academics both in law and in other disciplines whose modes of analysis are brought to bear on the intellectual property issue in question.

The essays grow out of two successive workshops held at Emmanuel College, University of Cambridge, in July 2005 and July 2006. We are grateful to all the participants, including those who did not present papers, but whose questions and critiques helped the presenters sharpen or rethink their arguments. We would also like to thank Gaenor Moore, for her assistance in editing and the compilation of the bibliography and case-list. We express our appreciation as well to the Master and

Bursar of Emmanuel College for their support of this project. Both of the workshops were generously funded by the Herchel Smith bequest to Emmanuel College for the promotion of research into intellectual property law.

LIONEL BENTLY

JENNIFER DAVIS

JANE C. GINSBURG

Cambridge and New York, July 2007

Table of cases

Table of statutes

Part I

Legal and economic history

1   The making of modern trade mark law: the construction of the legal concept of trade mark (1860–1880)

*Lionel Bently**

Although some accounts of the history of trade mark law trace the origin of trade mark protection to Greek or Roman times,[1] and other accounts of the British history locate the origins of British trade mark law in the medieval guilds,[2] or the sixteenth-century case of *JG* v *Samford*,[3] British trade mark law did not really take anything like its modern shape until the latter half of the nineteenth century.[4] The period between 1860 and 1910 witnessed the development of many of the characteristic features of modern trade mark law: a legal understanding of a trade mark as a sign which indicates trade origin;[5] the establishment of a central registry in 1876; the conceptualization of the

---

* For comments on earlier drafts, my thanks to Robert Burrell, Dev Gangjee, Jane Ginsburg and David Higgins; for research assistance, to Doug McMahon.
[1] E.g. W. Robertson, 'On Trade Marks' (1869) 14 Jo Soc Arts 414–17; E. S. Rogers, 'Some Historical Matter Concerning Trade-Marks' (1910) 9 *Michigan Law Review* 29.
[2] Most famously, F. Schechter, *The Historical Foundations of the Law Relating to Trade-Marks* (New York: Columbia University Press, 1925).
[3] (1584). See J. H. Baker and S. F. C. Milsom, *Sources of English Legal History: Private Law to 1750* (London: Butterworths, 1986) 615–18; J. H. Baker, *An Introduction to English Legal History* (4th edn, London: Butterworths, 2004) 459. The *Samford* case was referred to in *Southern* v *How*, (1656) Pop R. 144, where it is stated that Doderidge J held that the action would lie, and it was this source that caused the cast to be later relied on. Schechter, *Historical Foundations*, 123, argues that *Southern* v *How* is a dubious authority for the modern law of passing off: 'the sole contribution of that case was at best an irrelevant dictum of a reminiscent judge that he remembered an action by one clothier against another for the mis-use of the former's trade-mark'.
[4] F. M. Adams, *A Treatise on the Law of Trade Marks* (London: George Bell and Sons, 1874) 3 (law of trade marks 'much more recent' than that of patents 'being almost exclusively the growth of the last seventy or eighty years'). See, to similar effect, E. M. Daniel, *The Trade Mark Registration Act* (London: Stevens and Haynes, 1876) 1; D. M. Kerly, *The Law of Trade-Marks and Trade Name, and Merchandise Marks* (London: Sweet and Maxwell, 1894) 2; H. Ludlow and H. Jenkins, *A Treatise on the Law of Trade-Marks and Trade-Names* (London: W. Maxwell and Son, 1873) 10; Wadlow, *The Law of Passing Off: Unfair Competition by Misrepresentation* (3rd edn, London: Sweet and Maxwell, 2004) 29.
[5] Kerly, *The Law of Trade-Marks* 5 (a 'symbol expressly adopted by the plaintiff to distinguish his goods and identify them with him').

trade mark as an object of property;[6] the recognition of a dual system
of protection: one based on registration, the other based on use in the
marketplace;[7] and the development of international arrangements for the
protection of marks in foreign territories.[8] Looking back from the early
twenty-first century, it is clear that, while there were significant developments
in trade mark law in the period before 1860 and the period after 1910, the
majority of the most salient features of the current trade mark regime were
developed (or if not developed, institutionalized) in this period of intense
legislative, judicial, diplomatic and scholarly activity. Although all these
developments were intertwined, time and space only permits this chapter to
attempt to chart one of these developments: the genesis of a legal conception
(or a number of conceptions) of 'a trade mark' in the first part of this period.

The situation in mid-century

At mid-century, as the law of designs, patents and copyright was crystal-
lizing,[9] there was no (coherent) law of trade marks. Giving evidence to
the Select Committee of 1862, solicitor Joseph Travers Smith complained of the 'very considerable' evils of the existing law:[10] 'They arise
from the fact that trade marks are not recognized as having any legal
validity or effect; that there is no written law on the subject of trade marks,
and we have consequently no definition by which we can try what a trade
mark is, nor consequently what particular symbol amounts to a trade
mark.' Indeed, while at this stage we see the publication of textbooks
on copyright, designs and patents,[11] there were no textbooks on 'trade

---

[6] See L. Bently, 'From Communication to Thing: Historical Aspects of the Conceptualisation
of Trade Marks as Property' in G. Dinwoodie and M. Janis (eds.), *Trademark Law
and Theory: A Handbook of Contemporary Research* (Cheltenham: Edward Elgar, 2008)
(describing tendency towards conceptualization of trade marks as property from
around 1860).

[7] Registration was provided for under the Trade Marks Act 1875, and the Office opened on
1 January 1876. For the first set of Rules, see (1875–6) Sol Jo 178 (1 January 1876).

[8] Following a period where recognition of British interests abroad largely turned on the
existence of bilateral treaties, in 1883 a multilateral agreement was adopted, the Paris
Convention for the Protection of Industrial Property, of 20 March 1883. Great Britain was
not an original signatory (they were Belgium, Brazil, Spain, France, Guatemala, Italy,
Holland, Portugal, Salvador, Serbia and Switzerland) but acceded on 17 March 1884.

[9] B. Sherman and L. Bently, *The Making of Modern Intellectual Property Law* (Cambridge:
Cambridge University Press, 1999) Chs. 5–7.

[10] *Select Committee on Trade Marks Bill and Merchandize Marks Bill, Report, Proceedings and
Minutes of Evidence* (1862) 12 *Parliamentary Papers* 431, Q. 2619 (Travers Smith).

[11] Textbooks on these areas emerged from the 1820s. Some of these covered both copyright
and patents (e.g. R. Godson, *A Practical Treatise on the Law of Patents for Inventions and of
Copyright* (London: Butterworth, 1823); others discussed one 'area' alone (e.g., on
patents, W. M. Hindmarch, *A Treatise on the Law Relating to Patent Privileges* (London:

marks'. Although the term 'trade mark' had been present in some cases,[12] there was no consensus as to what a trade mark was, nor on what a 'law of trade marks' would look like. In fact, we can probably say that, as of 1850, it made no sense to talk of 'a law of trade marks' in the UK.

To say there was no law of trade marks is not to say that there were no laws regulating misrepresentation in trade. However, the protection afforded to traders who found they were victims of the fraudulent imitation of their names and marks was fragmented, drawing on a variety of jurisdictional sources, some statutory and some based on judicial precedent, and lacked any abstract logic.[13] The statutory systems tended to be confined to specific trades: under this heading, there was the protection of the marks of makers of knives, sickles, shears, scissors and other cutlery wares in Hallamshire by registration with the Cutlers' Company of Sheffield;[14] the protection given over use of the sign LONDON under the Cutlery Trade Act;[15] the protection of marks woven into and fixed on linen;[16] protection of the names of

---

Stevens, 1846)); while yet others dealt with what today would be thought of as 'sub-categories' of law (e.g. E. M. Underdown, *The Law of Artistic Copyright* (London: John Crockford, 1863)).

[12] *Collins Co.* v *Brown* (1857) 3 K&J 423, 426 (Page-Wood V-C); *Dixon* v *Fawcus* (1861) 3 El & El 537, 546 (Crompton J); *Dent* v *Turpin* (1861) 2 J & H 139.

[13] Britain was not alone in this respect: Belgian law had special regimes for hardware and cutlery (1803), cloth (1820) and pipes (1838): *Reports Relative to legislation in Foreign Countries on the subject of Trade Marks* C-596 (1872) 54 *Parliamentary Papers* 585, 594–610; and the French law prior to 1857 was described as comprising provisions which were 'heterogeneous, incongruous and sometimes contradictory': ibid., 615.

[14] Act for the Good Order and Government of the Makers of Knives, Sickles, Sheers, Scissors and Other Cutlery Wares, 21 Jac. 1 c. 31 (1623); An Act for the Better Regulation of the Company of Cutlers within the Liberty of Hallamshire, 31 Geo. 3 c. 58 (1791); An Act for amending and rendering more effectual an Act passed in the Thirty-First Year of the Reign of His Present Majesty, for the Better Regulation and Government of the Company of Cutlers, 41 Geo. 3 c. 97 (1801) (local) (amending the provisions on testamentary disposition and widows' rights); An Act to Repeal certain Parts of An Act Passed in the Thirty-first year of his Present Majesty, for the Better Regulation and Government of the Company of Cutlers, 54 Geo. 3 c. 109 (1814) (local) (liberalizing trade in Sheffield, and entitling traders to register marks, as well as limiting those that could be granted); An Act for Amending the Acts Passed with Respect to the Masters, Wardens, Searchers, Assistants, and Commonalty of the Company of Cutlers in Hallamshire in the County of York, 23 & 24 Vict. c. 43 (1860) (local) (extending Act to all 'using or exercising the Arts or Trades of Manufacturers of Steel and Makers of Saws and Edgetools and other Articles of Steel or of Steel and Iron combined having a cutting Edge' and giving a statutory right to become a freeman of the company and be granted a Mark).

[15] Act to Regulate the Cutlery Trade in England (1819) 59 Geo. 3 c. 7, s. 3 (limiting the legitimate use of hammer symbols to hand-made cutlery; and prohibiting the use of the word LONDON other than on cutlery made within twenty miles of the City of London).

[16] An Act for Better Regulation of Linen and Hemper Manufactures in Scotland (1726) 13 Geo. 1 c. 26 s. 30 (authorizing weavers of linens to weave their name into wares and to fix 'some known mark' on pieces of linen manufacture, and punishing counterfeiting of such name or mark).

patentees;[17] protection of marks used in the hop trade;[18] of marks on gun barrels;[19] and of hallmarks on gold and silver wares.[20] In addition, there was regulation of the use of family crests and insignia under the law of heraldry and arms. In certain circumstances, there was the possibility of criminal action based on forgery,[21] cheat,[22] conspiracy to defraud[23] or obtaining benefits by false pretences.[24] Another possibility, attempted by some, was to try and register labels as designs or, after 1862, with the Stationers' Company, so as to claim copyright protection.[25] Most importantly, there were the general actions at common law and in equity: the action on the case for deceit at common law, which had, at least since *Sykes* v *Sykes* in 1824, been available for cases involving use of marks on goods with intent to

---

[17] Patent Law (Amendment) Act (1835) 5 & 6 Wm. 4 c. 83, s. 7 (prohibiting the marking of goods with the name, stamp, mark or other device of patentee, and use of the word PATENT).

[18] Hops (Prevention of Frauds) Act 1866, 29 & 30 Vict. c. 37 (repealing and replacing (1814) 54 Geo. 3 c. 123). The 1866 Act uses the term 'trade mark'. For a prosecution, see *R* v *Edward Swonnell*, *The Times*, 27 June 1868, p. 11e.

[19] An Act to Insure Proper and Careful Manufacture of Fire Arms in England (1813) 53 Geo. 3 c. 115, s. 9 (relating to unauthorized counterfeiting of 'mark' or 'stamp' on any gun, fowling piece, blunderbuss, pistol or other description of arms usually called small arms).

[20] Act to amend Laws in Force for Preventing Fraud and Abuses in the Making of Gold and Silver Wares in England (1844) 7 & 8 Vict. c. 22 (repealing and replacing (1798) 38 Geo. 3 c. 69, s. 7).

[21] *R* v *Closs* (1857) Dearsley & B 460, 27 LJMC 54; *R* v *Smith* (1858) Dearsley & B 566, 27 LJMC 225 (not forgery because baking powder wrappers were not documents or instruments). Forgery was placed on a statutory footing in the codification of 1861: 24 & 25 Vict. c. 98.

[22] *R* v *Closs* (1857) Dearsley & B 460, 27 LJMC 54 (per Cockburn CJ). (A copy of a painting by John Linnell, with forged signature, could be a cheat, describing the scope of 'cheat' as encompassing the placing of 'a false mark or token upon an article, so as to pass it off as a genuine one when in fact it was only a spurious one, and the article was sold and money obtained by means of that false mark or token'. On the facts, the prosecution had not demonstrated that the purchaser bought the painting on the basis of the signature.)

[23] *Select Committee* (1862), Q. 2273 (J. Dillon).

[24] An Act for Consolidating and Amending the Law in England Relative to Larceny and other offences Connected therewith (1827) 7 & 8 Geo. 4 c. 29, s. 53 (offence of obtaining money by false pretences); Larceny Act (1861) 24 & 25 Vict. c. 96, ss. 88–90. *R* v *Smith* (1858) Dearsley & B 566, 27 LJMC 225 (per Pollock CB, Willes J and Chanell B.: D's labelling of its product as BORWICK'S BAKING POWDERS was not a forgery but was obtaining money by false pretences); *R* v *Dundas* (1853) 6 Cox Crim Cas 30 (Erle J, Northern Circuit) (two years' imprisonment for obtaining money by false pretences where D had sold seventy-two bottles of blacking marked EVERETT'S PREMIER in labels imitating Everett's labels); *R* v *Suter & Coulson* (1867) 10 Cox Crim Cas 577 (pawning watch with false mark of Goldsmiths' Company was obtaining money by false pretences). Cf. *R* v *Bryan* (1857) 7 Cox Crim Cas 312 (representing that spoons were 'equivalent to ELKINGTON'S A' was exaggeration as to quality and not a false pretence). See also *Select Committee* (1862), Qs. 2747–8 (Travers Smith).

[25] Copyright of Designs Act 1842 (5 & 6 Vict. c. 100); Fine Art Copyright Act 1862 (25 & 26 Vict. c. 68); *Select Committee* (1862), Q. 2465 (Browning).

deceive;[26] and an action in equity ancillary to the common law action for deceit, under which the Court of Chancery would grant injunctive relief pending establishment of the claimant's rights at law.[27] From 1839, with the case of *Millington* v *Fox*,[28] the action in Chancery seemed to have made a tentative move towards an independent status, insofar as relief was made available without evidence of intent to deceive.

By the 1850s, the complex state of the law had become a real cause of inconvenience and expense to traders who wished to gain protection in the United Kingdom.[29] Moreover, the complexity of the law was also seen as an impediment to attempts to gain protection for British traders abroad. And there was certainly a sense that British traders needed protection abroad, as the markets for their goods, in the UK, the British colonies and elsewhere, were being penetrated by counterfeit goods originating outside the UK. If British traders were to get protection in other European countries, the United States or Russia – the countries where counterfeit goods originated or were sold – then some form of international arrangement was almost certainly necessary. And British traders foresaw that it would be difficult to base any arrangement of a principle of reciprocity when British law itself was so difficult to comprehend and expensive to apply.[30]

The development of a law of trade marks, 1860–1875

The period from 1860 to 1880 was one of particularly intense activity in relation to trade mark law. Although there had long been complaints about the prevalence of misleading use of trade marks,[31] little effort had

---

[26] E.g. *Morison* v *Salmon* (1841) 2 Man & G 385 ('Morison's Universal Medicine'); *Crawshay* v *Thompson* (1842) 4 Man & G 357 ('WC' in oval on iron); *Rodgers* v *Nowill* (1847) 5 CB 109, 136 ER 816 ('J. Rodgers & Sons' on pen-knives).

[27] *Motley* v *Downman* (1837) 3 My & Cr 1, 14 per Lord Cottenham LC.

[28] (1838) 3 Myl & Cr 338.

[29] On the expense of litigation see *Select Committee* (1862) Qs. 1681–3 (D. Sinclair); Qs. 1970, 1987 (Polson); Qs. 2450–3 (Morley); Qs. 2503, 2511 (Coxon); Q. 2613 (Joseph Travers Smith).

[30] See L. Levi, 'On Trade Marks' (1859) Jo Soc Arts 262, 265 (explaining that the French law of 1857 would only protect foreigners where a treaty existed between France and the relevant country affording reciprocal protection to French traders); *Select Committee* (1862), Q. 2619 (Travers Smith) ('the defective condition of the English law prevents foreign governments from giving any remedy, because there is no sufficient reciprocity in England').

[31] 'Instances of tradesmen endeavouring to obtain an advantage to themselves by the use of the name and reputation of others, have, unfortunately, of late become too common.' Lord Langdale MR in *Franks* v *Weaver* (1847) 10 Beav 297, 302 (medicine case). See also 'Proposed Alterations in the law of Trade Marks' (1861) Sol Jo & Rep 2; *Select Committee* (1862), Q. 2754–5 (Hindmarch); H. B. Poland, *The Merchandise Marks Act 1862* (London: J. Crockford, 1862) 5.

hitherto been made to develop the law.[32] This changed in the late 1850s, when the Chambers of Commerce around the UK started to involve themselves in an attempt to procure legislation.[33] The case was made for amendment of the law in arenas such as the Royal Society of Arts[34] and the National Association for the Promotion of Social Science,[35] as well as provincial law societies.[36] Having determined that some kind of reform was essential, the Chambers of Commerce engaged lawyers to draft legislation,[37] which was presented to the government. In 1861, the first Bill dealing with the matter was introduced by Lord Campbell into the House of Lords,[38] but ultimately was not proceeded with beyond the Committee stage in the Commons. By this point, the Government had

---

[32] But note F. Crossley's claim to the meeting of the Association of Chambers of Commerce on 6 Feb 1861, that 'deputation after deputation from Sheffield had been before the Government on that subject [trade marks], but without effect'. See 'Association of Chambers of Commerce', *The Times*, 7 Feb. 1861, p. 12f; 'Proposed Alterations' ('There have been numerous deputations upon the subject to the President of the Board of Trade ...').

[33] 'Trade Marks' (1858) 6 Jo Soc Arts 595 (20 August 1858) (reporting meeting of Birmingham Chamber of Commerce unanimously approving motion that improper use of trade marks was wrong and should be discouraged in every way by the Chamber). On the influence of Chambers of Commerce, see A. R. Ilersic and P. F. B Liddle, *Parliament of Commerce: The Story of the Association of British Chambers of Commerce, 1860–1960* (London: Association of British Chambers of Commerce and Newman Neame, 1960) Ch. 9 (explaining activities in field of patents and trade marks); G. R. Searle, 'The Development of Commercial Politics, 1850–70' Ch. 5 in *Entrepreneurial Politics in Mid-Victorian Britain* (New York: Oxford University Press, 1993) (analysing political activities of Association of Chambers of Commerce).

[34] Professor Leone Levi, an academic and barrister active in the Association of British Chambers of Commerce, gave a significant paper at the Fifteenth Ordinary Meeting of the Royal Society of Arts on 16 March 1859: see (1859) Jo Soc Arts 262.

[35] A. Ryland, 'The Fraudulent Imitation of Trade Marks', (1859) *Transactions of the National Association for the Promotion of Social Science* 229, with responses at 269. For background to the activities of the Social Sciences Association, see L. Goldman, 'The Social Science Association, 1857–1886: A Context For Mid-Victorian Liberalism, (1986) 101 *English Historical Review* 95–134, and L. Goldman, *Science, Reform and Politics in Victorian Britain: The Social Science Association, 1857–1886* (Cambridge: Cambridge University Press, 2002).

[36] See 'On Fraudulent Trade Marks', (1861) Sol Jo & Rep 820, reporting a paper by John Morris given to the Metropolitan and Provincial Law Association, Worcester; and 'The Registration of Trade Marks' (1861) Sol Jo & Rep 839, reporting a paper by Arthur Ryland to the same Association.

[37] 'State of Trade', *The Times*, 3 December 1860 p. 4f. (reporting a meeting of representatives of Sheffield and Wolverhampton Chambers of Commerce with the Birmingham Chamber and consequent resolution that the Sheffield Chamber should prepare a Bill to provide for the registration of trade marks at home, as well as to empower the Crown to conclude conventions with foreign powers for reciprocal protection).

[38] Bill 1861 (based on Bill by Travers Smith on behalf of Chambers of Commerce). Parl. Deb., vol. 161, col. 327, 12 February 1861; col. 1272, 4 March 1861; col. 1940, 14 March 1861; col. 2153, 18 March 1861; Parl. Deb., vol. 162, col. 543, 15 April 1861; 164 Parl. Deb., vol. 164, col. 1089, 18 July 1861.

decided that a Select Committee of the House should be convened to consider the matter carefully.[39] So, in February 1862, following the introduction of a Government Bill on 'merchandise marks',[40] and a private member's bill on 'Trade Marks' (drafted by solicitor William Smith on behalf of the Sheffield Chamber of Commerce and introduced by John Arthur Roebuck, MP for Sheffield),[41] a Committee was convened.[42]

The Select Committee, comprising 'lawyers and mercantile men of great experience and representing different interests',[43] met and heard evidence from a wide range of traders (file makers, edge tool manufacturers, cutlery manufacturers, gun makers, thread manufacturers, needle makers, button makers, lace makers, starch and confectionery makers, brewers, paper makers), merchants,[44] bureaucrats[45] and lawyers.[46] Following its deliberations, it was decided – not, it seems, unanimously – to pursue the Government Bill,[47] and this was done, so that in 1862 the Merchandise Marks Act was passed. This Act created criminal offences for uses of mis-descriptions in trade with intent to defraud, and specifically referred to misuse of trade marks, which were defined broadly to encompass 'any Name, Signature, Word, Letter, Device, Emblem, Figure, Sign, Seal, Stamp, Diagram, Label, Ticket or other Mark of any

---

[39] Parl. Deb., vol. 164, col. 1089, 18 July 1861; Parl. Deb., vol. 165, col. 274, 14 February 1862.

[40] Parl. Deb., vol. 165, col. 988, 3 March 1862.

[41] Parl. Deb., vol. 165, col. 442, 18 February 1862; col. 770, 26 February 1862.

[42] Parl. Deb., vol. 165, col. 1231, 7 March 1862; col. 1280, 10 March 1862; col. 1489, 13 March 1862. Roebuck resisted particularly the addition of Moffatt.

[43] Poland, *Merchandise Marks Act* 7. Chaired by Roebuck, the Committee comprised three barristers (Selwyn, Hugh Cairns and Sir Francis Goldsmid, a lawyer and MP for Reading), two members of the Government (Milner Gibson, President of the Board of Trade, and Sir William Atherton, the Attorney General), manufacturers (Sir Francis Crossley, a carpet manufacturer; Alderman William Copeland, a pottery manufacturer and MP for Stoke; Edmund Potter, a calico printer and MP for Carlisle); George Moffatt, a tea-broker and MP for Southampton; and Crum Ewing. Selwyn, who generally appeared before the Master of the Rolls, was counsel in *Hall* v *Barrows* (1863) 4 De G J & S 150, (1863) 32 LJ Ch 548; *Bury* v *Bedford* (1863) 32 LJ Ch 741; *In re Uzielli*; *Ponsardin* v *Peto* (1863) 33 LJ Ch 371.

[44] R. Smith and J. Dale of Westhead, and J. Dillon of Morrison, Dillon and Co.; H. Browning. W. H. Teulon and Adolphus Baker, hop merchants. Some of the merchants actually dissented from the dominant assumption that trade marks were of public benefit. Dillon, for example, was concerned about the proliferation of marks introducing 'obstructions to business': Select Committee (1862), Q. 2268 (Dillon, in response to a question from Moffatt).

[45] George Wilkinson, the master cutler of the Cutlers' Company; Bennet Woodcroft, Superintendant of Specifications in the Patent Office; and Lewis Edmunds, Clerk of the Patents.

[46] William Smith, Arthur Ryland, Joseph Travers Smith and William Hindmarch QC.

[47] Parl. Deb., vol. 167, col. 1418, 4 July 1862.

other Description lawfully used by any person to denote any chattel, to be the Manufacture, Workmanship, Production or Merchandise of such Person'.

While the 1862 Act was welcomed in many quarters as a great improvement,[48] it was recognized as being of limited value, particularly because liability was dependent on a demonstration of intent to defraud.[49] Moreover, the Act treated fraudulent use of trade marks as just one type of fraudulent trade practice, failing thus either to establish the trade mark as property, or even to recognize its specific characteristics. Not surprisingly, therefore, the Chambers of Commerce and Royal Society of Arts persisted in lobbying for a registration system.[50] This resulted in Bills being introduced into Parliament in 1869,[51] 1873[52] and finally – and successfully – in 1875.[53] The 1875 Act established a registration system for trade marks, and made the existence of such registration equivalent to public use. This, it was anticipated, would save traders the expense of establishing rights in the mark every time legal action was taken, as well as allowing all traders to know what marks had been protected.

---

[48] Vice-Chancellor Page-Wood had said that 'no-one rejoiced more than he had done at the passing of the Act ... in this branch of the Court he had been on all occasions most anxious to correct the mischiefs against which the Act was directed': *Farina* v *Meyerstein*, *The Times*, 1 February 1864, p. 10f. Even the President of the Association of Chambers of Commerce welcomed it as a 'valuable addition to the statute book': see Ilersic and Liddle, *Parliament of Commerce*, 94. See also Poland, *Merchandise Marks Act*; Robertson, 'On Trade Marks' 414, 415; E. Johnson, 'Trade Marks' (1881) 29 Jo Soc Arts 493, 505.

[49] J. S. Salaman, *A Manual of the Practice of Trade Mark Registration* (London: Shaw and Son, 1876) 3 (describing the Act as 'less useful than might have been expected'); *Special Report from the Select Committee on Merchandise Marks Act (1862) Amendment Bill 203* (1887) 10 *Parliamentary Papers* 357, 376, Qs. 17–18; Kerly, *The Law of Trade-Marks* 7. For an example of its limitations, see *R* v *Scotcher*, *The Times*, 24 March 1864, p. 11e. For some examples of sentencing, comparable to those under the provisions of the Trade Marks Act 1994, see (1865–6) 41 *Law Times* 126 (6 Jan. 1866) (reporting sentencing of defendant to two months' hard labour for making pianos bearing BROADWOOD & CO); (1866–7) 42 *Law Times* (22 Dec. 1866) (six months' imprisonment without hard labour for defendant who had applied BASS & CO to beer).

[50] 'Association in Birmingham' (1866) 14 Jo Soc Arts 131; 'Birmingham Chamber of Commerce' *The Times*, 2 August 1872, p. 12e; 'Associated Chambers of Commerce' *The Times*, 24 Sept. 1873, p. 12c.

[51] (1868–9) Bill No 126 (13 May 1869; withdrawn, July). *The Times*, 8 June 1869, p. 12e. Two years later it was said that the earlier Bill which represented the Board of Trade's views received 'a very cool reception in the House': Parl. Deb., vol. 204, col. 1387, 6 March 1871.

[52] (1873) Bill No 133. It received a first reading on 21 April 1873, and was withdrawn on 7 July 1873. Sampson Lloyd commented that 'the opposition of one member of the house was sufficient to prevent it being proceeded with': *The Times*, 24 September 1873, p. 12c.

[53] Introduced by Lord Cairns on 22 June, the Act received royal assent on 13 August. See Parl. Deb., vol. 225, col. 155, 15 July 1875; Parl. Deb., vol. 226, col. 703, 7 August 1875; *The Times*, 10 September 1875, p. 8a.

Although the two Acts and the Select Committee constitute key developments in the period, trade mark protection was being developed apace in other fora.[54] The 1860s witnessed a surge in case law on trade marks, with some fifty-nine reported cases, compared to twenty-five in the 1850s, fifteen in the 1840s and ten in the 1830s.[55] In part, this case law was driven by a growth in the use of marks and a sharp increase in advertising,[56] following the reduction in stamp duty on newspaper advertising in 1833 and its removal in 1855,[57] as well as the triumph of the spectacular Great Exhibition of 1851.[58] The desire to litigate may also have been facilitated by the progressive reforms of the judicial system (in particular, the procedural rules applicable in the courts of equity).[59]

[54] 'Lord Langdale, Lord Cranworth and Lord Justice Mellish had given ... recognition to the Law of Trade Marks, and Lord Westbury and Sir William Page-Wood, afterwards Lord Hatherley, had finally established the rights of owners of Trade Marks. The nature of this property being once established, the next step was to give it statutory recognition, and supply facilities for securing it protection, and this Lord Cairns undertook in the Trade Marks Act 1875, which for the first time established a system of Registration of Trade Marks in accordance with the practice of Foreign countries, in which perhaps English Trade Marks are, from the reputation of the English manufacturer, a property more important even than in the British dominions.' J. Lowry Whittle, 'The Late Earl Cairns' (1885–6) 11 Law Mag & L Rev (5th ser.) 133, 150. Whittle was Assistant Registrar of Trade Marks and Designs from 1876.

[55] The numbers are derived from an examination of the cases digested in Lewis B. Sebastian, *A Digest of Cases of Trade Mark, Trade Name, Trade Secret ... decided in the courts of the United Kingdom, India, the Colonies and the United States of America* (London: Stevens and Sons, 1879).

[56] The claimant in *Holloway* v *Holloway* (1853) 13 Beav 209, for example, spent £30,000 per annum on advertising, 'a sum equal to the entire revenue of many a German principality': see 'Advertisements' (1855) 97 *Quarterly Review* 183, 212. Nevett tells us that this increased to £40,000 in 1864, and £50,000 in 1883, the year of Thomas Holloway's death: T. R. Nevett, *Advertising in Britain: A History* (London: Heinemann / History of Advertising Trust, 1982) 71.

[57] One of the few histories of advertising focussed on Britain describes the period between 1855 and 1914 as the period of 'the great expansion' of advertising: Nevett, *Advertising in Britain* Ch. 5.

[58] T. Richards, *The Commodity Culture of Victorian England: Advertising and Spectacle, 1851–1914* (London: Verso, 1991). Aspects of Richards' argument are criticized by Roy Church in 'Advertising Consumer Goods in Nineteenth-Century Britain: Reinterpretations' (2000) 53(4) *Economic History Review* 621, 629–30. Church, at 633, suggests that in the 1850s manufacturers attempted to distance themselves from the excesses of hyperbolic advertising by adopting a minimalist approach announcing 'the products coupled with the name of the supplier and sometimes a message of no more than two or three words intended to associate name with product such as ... "Glenfield's Starch", "Colman's Mustard", ... "Pear's Soap"'. It was precisely these pithy designations that were involved in many trade mark cases.

[59] The Chancery Regulation Act 1862, usually known as Sir John Rolt's Act, required Chancery courts to determine issues of law and fact rather than, as was previously the practice, staying proceedings for equitable relief and requiring parties to have these matters determined in a court of law. This was clearly a significant development in

This flurry of cases not only led to an elaboration of the applicable principles and rules, but also produced a level of consistency and coherence that had, prior to that, been difficult to establish, with judgments of different courts and different personnel appearing very sporadically. A hugely significant figure during the 1850s and 1860s was Vice-Chancellor Page-Wood, who decided at least forty-five cases,[60] though Lord Westbury LC had an important impact in developing protection during his relatively short tenure of the office of Lord Chancellor from 1861 to 1865.[61] Counsel, too, remained remarkably stable, with Sir John Rolt, Hugh Cairns and Roundell Palmer having the majority of the trade

relation to trade mark matters, where the practice had been for Chancery courts to refuse relief in any situation of doubt. See, for examples of the previous practice, the series of actions in *Farina* v *Silverlock* (1855) 1 K&J 509, 517, 69 ER 560; (1856) 6 De G M & G 214, 43 ER 1214; 4 K & J 650, (1858) 70 ER 270, or *Rodgers* v *Nowill* (1857) 6 Hare 325, 67 ER 1191; (1847) 5 CB 109, 136 ER 816; (1853) 3 De G M & G 614, 43 ER 241.

[60] For the period from 1853 to 1868, Page-Wood was one of the three Vice-Chancellors, and later was briefly Lord Chancellor (Hatherley). The cases in which he was involved were: *Flavel* v *Harrison* (1853) 10 Hare 467; *Edelsten* v *Vick* (1853) 11 Hare 78; *Farina* v *Gebhardt* (1853) Seb. Dig (118) 64; *Hoffman* v *Duncan* (1853) Seb. Dig (122) 66; *Taylor* v *Taylor* (1854) 23 LJ Ch 255; *Farina* v *Silverlock* (1855) 1 K & J 509; *Welch* v *Knott* (1857) 4 K & J 747; *Collins Co.* v *Brown* (1857) 3 K&J 423; *Collins Co* v *Cohen* (1857) 3 K&J 428; *Ansell* v *Gaubert* (1858) Seb. Dig (163) 91; *Churton* v *Douglas* (1859) Seb. Dig (172) 96; *Mappin Bros.* v *Mappin & Webb, The Times*, 31 May 1860, p. 11a; *Henderson* v *Jorss, The Times*, 22 June 1861, p. 11b; *Dent* v *Turpin* (1861) 2 J & H 139; *Cartier* v *Westhead, The Times*, 12 July 1861, p. 11a; *Cartier* v *May, The Times*, 13 July 1861, p. 11a; *Young* v *Macrae* (1862) 9 Jur NS 322; *Woolam* v *Ratcliff* (1863) 1 H & M 259; *Batty* v *Hill* (1863) 1 H & M 264; *Braham* v *Bustard* (1863) 1 H & M 447; *Leather Cloth Co.* v *Hirschfield* (1863) Seb. Dig (214) 120; *Leather Cloth Co. Ltd* v *American Leather Cloth Co.* (1863) *Seb. Dig* (223) 127; *Leather Cloth Co. Ltd* v *Hirschfield (No. 2)* (1863) *Seb. Dig* (224) 130; *Browne* v *Freeman* (1864) 12 WR 305; *M'Andrew* v *Basset* (1864) 33 LJ Ch 561; *Farina* v *Cathery (No. 1), The Times*, 30 April 1864, p. 13c; *Montague* v *Moore* (1865) Seb. Dig (242) 141; *The Correspondent Newspaper Co. Ltd* v *Saunders* (1865) Seb. Dig (246) 143; *Williams* v *Osborne* (1865) 13 LT 498; *Leather Cloth Co. Ltd* v *Hirschfield (No. 3)* (1865) Seb. Dig (252) 148; *Harrison* v *Taylor* (1865) 11 Jur NS 408; *Southorn* v *Reynolds* (1865) 12 LTNS 75; *Beard* v *Turner* (1865) 13 LT 746; *Ainsworth* v *Walmsley* (1866) LR 1 Eq Cas 518; *Standish* v *Whitwell* (1866) 14 WR 512; *Morgan* v *M'adam* (1866) 36 LJ Ch 228; *Scott* v *Scott* (1866) 16 LT 143; *Liebig's Extract* v *Hanbury* (1867) 17 LTNS 298; *Blackwell* v *Crabb* (1867) 36 LJ Ch 504; *Graveley* v *Winchester* (1867) Seb. Dig (272) 162; *Field* v *Lewis* (1867) Seb. Dig (280) 167; *Stephens* v *Peel* (1867) 16 LT 145; *Farina* v *Cathery (No. 2), The Times*, 27 April 1867, p. 10d; *Lamplough* v *Balmer* (1867) WN 293. Page-Wood V-C was made Lord Chancellor in 1868 and in this capacity he presided in *Wotherspoon* v *Currie* (1871–2) LR 5 HL 508. For biographical background relating to Page-Wood, including an incomplete autobiographical sketch, see W. R. Stephens, *A Memoir of Lord Hatherley* (London: R. Bentley and Sons, 1883).

[61] Westbury gave decisions in *Edelsten* v *Edelsten* (1863) 1 De G J & S. 185, *Hall* v *Barrows* (1863) 4 De G J & S 150, *M'Andrew* v *Basset* (1864) 4 De G J & S 380, as well as in the House of Lords in *Leather Cloth* v *American Leather Cloth Co.* (1865) 11 HLC 523, and *Wotherspoon* v *Currie* (1871–2) LR 5 HL 508.

marks business.[62] During the 1870s, key figures in the judiciary were Mellish LJ, Romer MR and Lord Cairns. And in the period from 1862 to 1882, the House of Lords heard five cases on trade marks: *Leather Cloth*,[63] *Wotherspoon v Currie*,[64] *Singer Machine Manufacturers v Wilson*,[65] *Johnston v Orr-Ewing*;[66] *The Singer Manufacturing Company v Loog*.[67] By the time of the latter case, Lord Selborne LC could refer to 'the ordinary principles applicable to trade-marks and trade-names', and Lord Blackburn agreed that the relevant law was 'well-settled'.[68]

Alongside judicial activity, commentators were beginning to collect, organize and codify the decisions and statutes: beginning with Edward Lloyd's treatise in the early 1860s,[69] Harry Bodkin Poland's commentary on the 1862 Act, Leone Levi's *International Commercial Law*,[70] followed by more substantial treatises by Ludlow and Jenkins and Frank Mantel Adams in the early 1870s.[71] Following the 1875 Act, a number of texts were published commenting on the registration system: James Bryce offered a supplement to Ludlow and Jenkins' work,[72] and Adams re-issued his text with a copy of the Act;[73] J. Seymour Salaman, solicitor to the Trade Mark Protection Society, which had lobbied for the Act, issued *A Manual of the Practice of Trade Mark Registration*;[74] while John Bigland Wood,[75] Charles Drewry,[76] Lionel B. Mozley,[77] Edward Morton

---

[62] Cairns, a Tory, and Roundell Palmer, a Liberal, were later to be Lord Chancellors (Cairns, in 1868, and from 1874 to 1880; Palmer from 1872 to 1874, and 1880–5). In this capacity, Cairns introduced the 1875 Registration Bill into Parliament, and gave judgments in the House of Lords decision in *Singer v Wilson* (1877) LR 3 HL 376; Roundell Palmer, as Lord Selborne LC, was the leading judge in two House of Lords decisions: *Johnston v Orr-Ewing* (1882) 7 HL 219, and *The Singer Manufacturing Company v Loog* (1882) 8 HL 15.

[63] *Leather Cloth v American Leather Cloth Co.* (1865) 11 HLC 523.

[64] (1872) LR 5 HL 518.   [65] (1877) LR 3 HL 376.   [66] (1882) LR 7 HL 219.

[67] (1882) LR 8 HL 15.   [68] (1882) LR 8 HL 15, 17, 29.

[69] *The Law of Trade Marks* (1862). Note also the paper by Professor Leone Levi, of King's College, London, 'On Trade Marks'; and subsequent papers by E. M. Underdown, 'On the Piracy of Trade Marks' (1866) 14 Jo Soc Arts 370; and Robertson, 'On Trade Marks'.

[70] L. Levi, *International Commercial Law* (London: V. and R. Stevens, 1863) Ch. 20.

[71] Ludlow & Jenkins, *A Treatise*; F. M. Adams, *A Treatise* (1874).

[72] J. Bryce, *The Trade Marks Registration Acts 1875 and 1876* (London: William Maxwell & Sons, 1877).

[73] F. M. Adams, *A Treatise on the Law of Trade-Marks: with the Trade-Marks Registration Act of 1875 and Rules* (London: Butterworths, 1876).

[74] Salaman, *A Manual of the Practice*.

[75] J. B. Wood, *The Law of Trade Marks* (London: Stevens, 1876).

[76] C. S. Drewry, *The Law of Trade Marks* (London: Knight, 1878).

[77] L. B. Mozley, *Trade Marks Registration. A Concise View of the Law and Practice* (London: 1877).

Daniel[78] and Lewis Boyd Sebastian offered yet more texts, the latter establishing itself as the market-leader and going into five editions.[79]

Another environment in which trade mark law was coming under scrutiny was within the Foreign Office, which started to take a keen interest in the laws of foreign countries.[80] From as early as 1858, British traders had sought the assistance of the Government in gaining some sort of international recognition of their rights. The primary concern was preventing use of British trade marks abroad, especially in Germany. In a document submitted by various representatives of the Sheffield steel goods trade to the Secretary of State for the Foreign Office, the Earl of Malmesbury, the petitioners expressed the desire of securing for themselves and successors an honourable reputation and just rewards for their efforts.[81] The Foreign Office responded by conducting a detailed inquiry into the laws of foreign states through the network of consuls and embassies. The resulting picture was uneven, with most laws seemingly based in ideas of forgery, counterfeiting and deceit. The terms on which such protection was made available were unclear, and the Foreign Office decided to attempt to negotiate bilateral treaties protecting British traders, following the model of the existing copyright bilaterals.[82] The first such treaty was signed with Russia in 1859, and was

[78] Daniel, *The Trade Mark Registration Act.*
[79] L. B. Sebastian, *The Law of Trade Marks and their Registration* (London: 1878). Sebastian went into five editions: 1884, 1890, 1899 (with Harry Baird Hemming), 1911 (with Harry Baird Hemming and Skinner Raymond Sebastian). Note also Sebastian, *Digest*, and Sebastian's *The Law of Trade Mark Registration* (London: Stevens, 1906), issued in a second edition by F. E. Bray and J. Q. Henriques in 1922. Kerly, the leading practitioner text today, first entered the field in 1894: Kerly, *The Law of Trade-Marks* (with further editions in 1901, 1908, 1913, 1923 and 1927).
[80] As Leone Levi wrote, in the context of discussion of an international commercial code, 'we are constantly borrowing from one another': L. Levi, 'An International Commercial Code', *The Times*, 27 August 1878, p. 6f. The Colonial and India Offices were also significant. Note also the references to the Indian Penal code, (1861) Sol Jo & Rep 3, and the reproduction of the relevant provisions at 'Trade Marks and Property Marks' (1861) Sol Jo & Rep 14.
[81] Robert Jackson, Hobson Smith, William Matthews to Earl of Malmesbury, 13 May 1858, NA: FO 83/211.
[82] Emerson Tennant, Board of Trade, to Malmesbury, 13 July 1858, NA: FO 83/211 (approving Foreign Office's plans to negotiate bilateral treaties for mutual recognition of trade marks but rejecting suggestion of 'a regular system of mutual registration and publication in the territories of contracting parties'). Examples of such treaties were the Convention Between Her Majesty and the French Republic (Signed at Paris, 3 November 1851) (1852) 54 *British Parliamentary Papers* 103; Convention Between Her Majesty and the King of Prussia (Signed at London, 14 June 1855) (1856) 61 *British Parliamentary Papers* 263, Art. 3; Convention Between Her Majesty and the Queen of Spain, (Signed at Madrid, 7 July 1857) (1857–8) 60 *British Parliamentary Papers* 261. See C. Seville, *The Internationalisation of Copyright: Books, Buccaneers and the Black Flag* (Cambridge: Cambridge University Press, 2006) 49–56.

closely followed by agreements with France, Belgium, Italy, the Zollverein and Austria.[83] This interest in legal protection for trade marks in foreign countries continued and the findings started to be published in the *Parliamentary papers* (or 'blue books' as they were widely known): in 1872, there was published *Reports Relative to legislation in Foreign Countries on the subject of Trade Marks*,[84] along with a second Report on *Treaty Stipulations between Great Britain and Foreign Powers on the Subject of Trade Marks*.[85] Within a relatively short time, this activity would intensify further,[86] and consideration would be given to the formulation of a multilateral treaty, ultimately resulting in the Paris Convention on Industrial Property in 1883.[87]

It was in these four environments that the British legal system seems to have begun to develop its conception (and to contest various conceptions) of trade mark law. Of course, what was at stake differed significantly from domain to domain, but – importantly – none of these environments operated in isolation: appreciation of foreign law fed into calls for legislative change,[88] legislative reform fed into commentaries, commentaries into case law (and vice versa), and judicial opinion into legislative reform. Two examples of how these parallel developments were intertwined can be seen in the persons of two key figures: Lords Westbury and Cairns. Richard Bethell, then a barrister and MP, chaired an early meeting of the Royal Society of Arts at which Leone Levi gave a paper highlighting deficiencies in the protection of trade marks.[89] Bethell, later as Lord

---

[83] Treaty of Commerce and Navigation with Russia (St Petersburg, 12 January 1859); Treaty of Commerce with France (Paris, 23 January 1860); Treaty of Commerce and Navigation with Belgium (London, 23 July 1862); Treaty of Commerce and Navigation with Italy (Turin, 6 August 1863); Treaty of Commerce with the Zollverein (Berlin, 30 June 1865); Treaty of Commerce with Austria (Vienna, 16 December 1865); Treaty of Friendship, Commerce and Navigation with Columbia (London, 16 February 1866).

[84] C.–596. Setting out the laws of Austria, Belgium, Denmark, France, Germany, Netherlands, Portugal, Russia, Spain, Sweden, Switzerland, Turkey and the United States.

[85] Setting out treaties with Austria, Belgium, Colombia, France, Italy, Russia and the Zollverein.

[86] A further investigation of foreign laws resulted in another blue book: *Reports relative to Legislation in Foreign Countries on the Subject of Trade Marks Part I. European Countries*, C. 2284 (1879) 73 *Parliamentary Papers* 469. Note also *Extracts from Treaties and Declarations Now in Force* Between Great Britain and Foreign Powers Relating to Trade Marks, Designs and Industrial Property (C.-5554) (1888) 98 *Parliamentary Papers* 745.

[87] Although Great Britain was not originally a party, it joined in 1884.

[88] Parl. Deb., vol. 161, col. 327, 12 February 1861 (Lord Chancellor stating that 'In most other countries the forging of such marks was a crime'); Underdown, 'On the Piracy of Trade Marks'; E. Lloyd, 'On the Law of Trade Marks No. V' (1861) *Sol Jo & Rep* 614.

[89] 'Fifteenth Ordinary Meeting', (1859) Jo Soc Arts 262. Bethell made a number of comments at the end of Levi's talk emphasizing that counterfeiting 'is in effect theft ... The thief obtains at once the fruits, probably, of a life of labour, invention and industry'.

Chancellor Westbury, gave ground-breaking decisions widening and strengthening protection.[90] Lord Cairns, who, as Lord Chancellor, introduced the 1875 Trade Mark Registration Act into Parliament, had himself frequently appeared in trade mark litigation, first as a barrister and then as a judge, and had also been a member of the 1862 Select Committee.[91]

The debate over the nature of a trade mark

Rather like the situation with the concept of a 'brand' today, in 1860 there was no 'legal' conception of a trade mark. To the extent that the term had meaning, it was as a description of a particular commercial artefact or insignia: the legal system at this stage building its categories and actions either around more general notions, such as deceit, fraud, misrepresentation or cheat,[92] or around specific trades or products. This meant that the identification of what was a 'trade mark' was, at mid-century, of little consequence;[93] or, as barrister William Hindmarch explained to the Select Committee, the term 'trade mark' was 'an improper term, except in Hallamshire' (that is, within a six-mile radius of Sheffield).[94]

Over the next thirty years, as the legal system began to treat the concept of a 'trade mark' as a term of art, carrying legal consequences, the term became highly contested. This process of legal definition really began with the formulation of the Bills in 1861 and 1862, and the subsequent Select Committee. Virtually everyone agreed that the laws preventing the fraudulent use of 'trade marks' needed to be strengthened and the prevalent assumption seemed to be that some law – whether based on criminalization, registration or property – should apply to use of marks in all trades. Trade-specific legislation was seen as lacking in principle, irrational and productive of unnecessary and undesirable distinctions:

---

[90] The *Solicitors' Journal* welcomed Lord Westbury's contribution to the jurisprudence relating to trade marks, asserting that 'under his authority, the extent of the jurisdiction of courts of equity in granting injunctions has been defined in a broad and philosophical manner': 'Trade Names and Marks' (1864) Sol Jo & Rep 175, 177. Another key figure in the judicial development of trade marks was Page-Wood V-C, who was also President of the Jurisprudence Section of the Social Science Association in 1859, just when it was campaigning for trade mark reform. See Goldman, 'The Social Science Association, 1857–1886' 95, 127 n. 3.

[91] Though he does not appear to have attended a single meeting of its proceedings.

[92] Some opposed the shift from 'fraud' to 'trade mark': see Crauford, (1862) Parl. Deb., vol. 165, col. 770, 26 February 1862.

[93] One exception to this would have been when a trader sought to transfer its business and trade marks.

[94] *Select Committee* (1862), Q. 2757 (W. Hindmarch).

a modern law should be general and applicable to all trades.[95] In drafting laws regulating the use of 'trade marks' it was necessary to determine exactly what was meant by that term – as Milner Gibson, President of the Board of Trade, noted in the Commons, '[t]he question which, under the circumstances, naturally suggested itself was, *what was a trade mark* [?]' (emphasis added).[96]

For those proposing protection only with registration, significantly greater precision seemed to be required.[97] This was because certain assumptions were being made about the nature, role and effect of registration.[98] On the assumption that registration was going to delineate a field of exclusivity, then it was perceived to be important that the field be established with clarity and certainty through some form of representation. Such a representation necessarily involved decontextualization: the sign protected would have to be extracted from its usual environment (whether a wrapper, or stamped into a knife blade, or featured on the end of a piece of cloth) and re-presented in a register. In turn, registration required that the meaning and significance of the mark necessarily be inherent in the representation itself, rather than from its relation to other signs, images, shapes, or get-up. Accordingly, the definition of trade marks (or at least, registrable trade marks) had to be limited to matter that traders could identify *ex ante* as worth protecting, and which could be represented in a meaningful way.

[95] One commentator asked, rhetorically, whether 'the makers of pins or needles, powder or shot, hair-dye or Eau-de-Cologne are not entitled to precisely the same protection, and by the use of the same means, as the makers of knives and forks, or a ship's anchor?': 'Proposed Alterations in the Law of Trade Marks' 3. For this reason it was argued that the law must go beyond stamping or marking goods to encompass marking of labels and packages.

[96] Parl. Deb., vol. 165, col. 446.

[97] A broad definition of registrable trade marks might be problematic bureaucratically, and have undesirable legal consequences. Proponents of registration, such as Ryland, seemed to have thought the Registry would not work as well were it 'so very large': *Select Committee* (1862), Q. 737 (Ryland). See also Alfred Marten (for Mr Hermon), Parl. Deb., vol. 226, cols. 703–4, 7 August 1875 (stating 'he wished to call attention to the difficulty of getting a proper definition of the term "trade mark"' and arguing that 'it would be better for the purposes of registration not to undertake the difficult task of definition, but to simply use the term "trade mark" and leave the definition to the ordinary Courts of Law').

[98] Cf. the views of William Hindmarch, who opposed a registration system. Hindmarch observed that if rights were based on 'use' but registration was based on some sort of act of 'representation' then the necessary gap between 'representation' and 'reality' would mean that third parties could not rely on the representation. Alternatively, if, following registration, the trader's rights were to be based on the representation then it followed that the act of representing the mark would have altered the very nature of the subject matter that was protected: *Select Committee* (1862), Qs. 1881, 2997 (Hindmarch).

That said, the legislative arena was not the only one in which the process of defining trade marks was beginning to be important. In international negotiations, the question of what could be a trade mark, or receive protection, was critical – different governments needed to understand what each others' systems protected, and to find a vocabulary that could be used to designate what any treaty covered. An 1858 attempt by the Foreign Office to discover whether British traders were protected in Prussia immediately ran into confusion. The Prussian Penal code provided that:

> Whosoever shall forge the name or firm and the place of residence or place of manufacture of a native manufacturer, Producer or Merchant, on goods or bales, or knowingly bring into circulation goods thus fraudulently marked, shall be punished with a fine of fifty up to one thousand Marks and on repetition of the offence shall beside undergo a term of imprisonment not exceeding six months.[99]

Seemingly confining its own protection to the combination of name and place, the Prussian respondent queried what the British Foreign Office meant by the term 'trade mark', in particular inquiring whether the term included or excluded 'arbitrary signs not couched in words or letters'.[100]

Specific treaty provisions sought to overcome the question of definition in various rather inconsistent ways. The Austrian Treaty of 16 December 1865, for example, referred to 'trade marks and other distinctive marks',[101] a Treaty with the Zollverein in 1875 referred to 'marks or labels of goods, and of their packages',[102] while the US Treaty of 1877 gave subjects and citizens of the USA the same rights as British citizens 'in everything relating to property in trade marks and trade labels'.[103] An 1882 Convention with the French Republic, referred to protection of 'rights of property in trade-marks, names of firms, and other distinctive marks showing the origin or quality of goods', while a series of Conventions with Rumania (1880), Serbia (1882) and Montenegro (1882) referred to property in 'trade-marks and trade-labels or tickets'.[104] By the late 1870s, Edmund Johnson, Secretary to the London Trade

---

[99] Prussian Penal Code 1851, Art. 269.
[100] Baron Manteuffel to Augustus Paget, 1858, Berlin, in NA: FO 83/211.
[101] Treaty of Commerce between Her Majesty and the Emperor of Austria, Vienna, 4 January 1866, Art. 11 in *Treaty Stipulations Between Great Britain and Foreign Powers on the Subject of Trade Marks* (1872) (C. 633) 54 *Parliamentary Papers* 673, 675.
[102] *Declaration for extending to German Empire Stipulations in Commercial Treaty Between Great Britain and Zollverein, May 1865, for Protection of Trade Marks, London, April 1875* (C. 1207) (1875) 82 *Parliamentary Papers* 585.
[103] *Declaration between Great Britain and United States for Protection of Trade Marks* (C. 1901) (1878) 80 *Parliamentary Papers* 439. See also *Declaration between Great Britain and Denmark for the Protection of Trade Marks, Copenhagen, November 28, 1879* (C. 2463) (1880) 78 *Parliamentary Papers* 295 ('everything relating to property in trade-marks and trade-labels').
[104] *Extracts from Treaties and Declarations Now in Force* 745, 749–52.

Marks' Committee, identified the question of the definition of what is meant by a trade mark as the first key step towards any possible multilateral agreement for the protection of marks.[105] 'The initial difficulties which must encounter any attempt to establish an international trade mark law', Johnson asserted, 'will be found in the fact that each country has defined a trade mark according to its own prevalent ideas of what it should be, and not with the view of finding some definition which would be common to all countries'. It was of 'pressing importance' to unify at the earliest possible moment the definition of a trade mark.

The question of what was a 'trade mark' was also being discussed in the case law on equitable protection against misrepresentations in trade. In one case, Lord Westbury LC differentiated between 'a trade mark properly so called' and other insignia.[106] It is perhaps no coincidence that Lord Westbury should have been the first to distinguish between 'trade marks' and other misrepresentations in trade, because it was he who was advocating that trade marks be viewed as 'property'. As with registration, the proposal that certain signs be treated as 'property' seemed to require that there be an identifiable, distinct, autonomous object, and Lord Westbury gradually began to clarify what he understood to be the defining characteristics of trade marks.

However, judicial definition and categorization of signs was not necessarily tied to adoption of a proprietary understanding of (what we now call) passing off. The process of definition was also a predictable response to the sheer proliferation of cases: the judiciary were starting to elaborate rules from holdings in particular instances, and the type or form of the misrepresentation was treated as a relevant factor in developing such rules. Grappling for labels, the judiciary would refer to 'real trade marks', and even began to draw up a taxonomy of marks carrying different legal effects.[107] These processes of defining a trade mark were in turn aided by the work of commentators and textbook-writers. Many commentators felt it was necessary at least to define their subject and explain

---

[105] Johnson, 'Trade Marks' 493, 497–8.

[106] *Hall v Barrows* (1863) 4 De G J & S 150, 157. Note also *Leather Cloth v American Leather Cloth Co.* (1865) 11 HLC 523, where Lord Westbury described the plaintiff's symbol as 'in reality an advertisement of the character and quality of their goods', not something which had 'hitherto been properly designated by' the term 'trade mark' (546). Lord Kingsdown, at 538, said that what 'is usually meant by a trade mark' is a 'symbol or emblem' which has by use come 'to be recognised in trade as the mark of the goods of a particular person'.

[107] *Singer Manufacturing v Wilson* (1876) LR 2 Ch Div 434, 441–3 Jessel MR (dividing cases of false representations into two classes: true trade marks, that is, 'a mark which shews that the goods are made by some particular maker', and a second class where without using the plaintiff's mark there is a representation that the goods are those of the plaintiff). James LJ, on appeal, at 451 approved the analysis.

why it deserved its own treatment. As Underdown wrote: 'the accurate definition of a Trade Mark properly so-called, is of the highest importance to the due understanding of the subject and its difficulties'.[108] Likewise, Sebastian's text asked rhetorically 'with what class of objects is this branch of the law concerned?' and proceeded to attempt to distinguish 'true trade marks from other marks'.[109]

The meaning of trade mark

Over the next decades a number of possible conceptions of the nature and function of a trade mark were suggested. Amongst the contested issues were questions of the form of trade marks: whether they were confined to names or visual images and devices or encompassed words. There were also questions as to the manner in which trade marks were associated with goods – was a sign a trade mark only if it was impressed on goods, or could material associated with goods, such as labels, wrappers and bottles constitute trade marks? Finally, there were questions about which marks stamped on goods were trade marks and which were not; and whether trade marks functioned to indicate trade origin, geographical origin or quality (or something else). As we will see, these questions were not resolved by the 1875 Trade Marks Act, and the definition of trade mark (or registrable trade mark) continued to be debated well into the twentieth century – with statutory changes to the definition of registrable marks being made again in 1883, 1888 and 1905. Indeed, while aspects of the debates over the definition of 'trade marks' are in many ways different to those of today, many of the concerns remain the same. Here I want to confine my discussion to two questions concerning what types of matter could be marks, and two concerning the meaning conveyed by the mark.

Names

The first area of interest relates to names. It seems clear, at least from the submissions to the Select Committee of 1862, that many considered the name of a trader as the archetypal trade mark.[110] This is perhaps not surprising: the existing trade-specific statutory regimes which covered

---

[108] Underdown, 'On the Piracy of Trade Marks'.
[109] Sebastian, *The Law of Trade Marks* (1878), at 14, 16.
[110] This can be seen from the explanation of solicitor John Morris, that 'Trade marks are not confined to the name of the manufacturer or owner, but extend, ... to the use of signs and marks of every conceivable kind'. See 'On Fraudulent Trade Marks', reporting a paper by John Morris given to the Metropolitan and Provincial Law Association, Worcester.

linen, hops and patentees (referred to above) had provided protection against counterfeiting of names used on goods and sometimes even compelled the marking of goods with the manufacturers' names; while both the criminal law of forgery and civil law relating to trade misrepresentations had been invoked against misuse of (amongst others) BORWICK'S, VELNO'S,[111] EVERETT'S, SYKES', RODGERS', MORISON'S and HOLLOWAYS. As Salaman observed in his 1876 treatise, 'a man's name is still [a] stronger trade mark than any that can be devised'.[112]

What is more interesting about the perception of the name as the archetypal trade mark is that it points to a rarely noticed conception of trade mark protection as founded in personhood. While English law may have declined to recognize a right of personality (and continues to do so today),[113] the laws that were in the process of recognition in this period seem to have been informed by (even if they did not articulate) an idea of inherent right in a person's name. Indeed Potter, one of the members of the Select Committee, inquired of deponents whether they would 'grant a mark without a name',[114] and himself advocated that protection be confined to names and monograms accompanied by names.[115] Others were open to recognizing a broader notion of what could be protected, so as to include, for example, marks or devices, but largely on the basis that these were substitutes or proxies for names, signatures or addresses. As Arthur Ryland, a chief proponent of registration, indicated, '[w]hat a crest or coat of arms is to a gentleman the trade mark is to the manufacturer'.

If names were the archetypal trade marks, the question of their protection immediately pointed to two distinct difficulties. The first was the problem of reconciling the inherent right of one trader to gain protection for the use of his name on goods and the inherent right of a trader of the same (or a similar) name to use his or her name. The courts had already encountered exactly such problems in applying the extended law of deceit (which we now label 'passing off'), and had resolved that if the use was bona fide the court would not interfere,[116] but if there was evidence of

---

[111] *Canham* v *Jones* (1813) 2 V&B 218 (VELNO's vegetable syrup).
[112] Salaman, *A Manual of the Practice* 11.
[113] *Clark* v *Freeman* (1848) 11 Beav 112 (unsuccessful action by royal surgeon, Sir James Clark to prevent defendant selling its goods as 'Sir J. Clarke's Consumption Pills'); *Belisle Du Boulay* v *Jules Réné Herménégilde du Boulay* (1869) LR 2 PC 430 (holding no right to prevent a former slave using the Du Boulay name in St Lucia).
[114] *Select Committee* (1862) Q. 2684. Travers Smith responded that he would: while 'a mark with a name would be far better, because that would indicate origin ... many valuable existing marks are without names'.
[115] Ibid. Q. 2181 (Potter).
[116] *Burgess* v *Burgess* (1850) 3 De G M & G 896 (action by father who sold essence of anchovies under the name JOHN BURGESS AND SON against his son, William Harding

fraudulent intent the court would prevent further use of the name.[117] However, the recognition that other traders might legitimately use the same name as one already used by an existing trader was a problem for those who wanted trade marks to be seen as property, because the determination of the legitimacy of the use necessarily depended *upon its context*.[118] Either the proprietary regime would need to be carefully calibrated to accommodate the special position of names (as it is in today's law – section 11(2)(b) of the Trade Marks Act 1994), or names – the archetypal marks – would need to be excluded from registration as such. And it was the latter course that was adopted in the 1869 Bill which proposed the registration of marks that would be protected by law, other than 'a name of a person, firm, or company only unaccompanied by a mark sufficient to distinguish it from the same name when used by other persons'. Similarly, the definition of a trade mark successfully adopted in 1875[119] permitted only the registration of a name of an individual or firm 'printed, impressed or woven in some particular and distinctive manner', or 'a written signature or copy of a written signature of an individual or firm'.[120]

The perception that names were extensions of personhood threw up a second problem: that is, why such right should need to be based on registration. Indeed, there seems to have been quite widespread opinion that names were so special that a kind of inherent right existed warranting protection without formality, whereas other insignia such as emblems or

Burgess, for using name W. H. BURGESS, and label BURGESS'S ESSENCE OF ANCHOVIES failed, though Knight Bruce LJ recognized that the case would have been different had there been 'any circumstance of fraud'); *Mappin Bros.* v *Mappin & Webb, The Times*, 31 May 1860, p. 11a; *Dence* v *Mason* (1880) 41 LTNS 573 (preventing defendant using plaintiff's name 'BRAND' but permitting him to use as 'MASON AND BRAND'); *Dunnachie* v *Young* (1883) 10 Sess. Cas. (4th Ser.) 874, 885 (per Lord Craighill, stating that 'the name of a person may be a trade-mark' but observing that other manufacturers of the same goods with the same name may use that name as long as they make bona fide efforts to distinguish their goods and avoid deception).

[117] *Croft* v *Day* (1843) 7 Beav 84 (Day, surviving partner of Day and Martin, blacking manufacturers, successful against nephew, also called Day, who had joined with a friend called Martin in the manufacture of blacking); *Holloway* v *Holloway* (1853) 13 Beav 209 (protection of manufacturer of HOLLOWAY'S PILLS AND OINTMENTS at 244 Strand against Henry Holloway who had set up business as 'H. Holloway pills and ointments' at 210 Strand using similar boxes, pots, labels and wrappers to those of the plaintiff; while recognizing the defendant's right to constitute himself a vendor of Holloway's pills and ointments, Lord Langdale MR found there was clear evidence of fraudulent intent).

[118] The 1862 Merchandise Marks Act, which imposed criminal liability only where there was a demonstration of fraudulent intent, had little problem in including names within the scope of its definition of trade mark.

[119] Alfred Marten (for Mr Hermon), 226 Parl. Deb., vol. 226, col. 703–4, 7 August 1875.

[120] Rather startlingly, Sebastian in his 1878 text *Law of Trade Marks* asserted that 'a name is in its very nature generic, and is properly applied to designate, not one individual in the world, but, it may be, many thousands, to all of whom it is equally appropriate': 18–19.

devices should only be protected if used in trade or registered.[121] Accordingly, if a trade mark registry was to be employed, it should only cover emblems and symbols, not names, which should receive legal protection automatically.[122] The 1875 Act, as we have just noted, allowed only for protection of names in limited circumstances. However, in order to avoid prejudice to existing interests,[123] the Act also permitted the registration of 'any special and distinctive word or words or combination of figures or letters used as a trade mark before the passing of this Act'. The Act, unfortunately, left unclear the relationship between registration, non-registrability and other forms of protection. For some time, at least some commentators thought that the common law protection was abolished and that protection arose under the Act alone.[124] Had such a position been adopted by the courts, traders who chose to use their own names (unaccompanied by a distinctive device) would have been left with virtually no protection under the civil law.

Other indicia

Nearly all those involved in the processes of defining the concept of a 'trade mark' accepted that it must cover 'marks', 'symbols', 'emblems' and other visual 'devices'. Such signs were precisely what had been protected under the regime operated by the Cutlers Company of Sheffield,[125] which was in many ways the model relied on by those seeking recognition of trade marks as properties by registration. Such 'marks' had also been protected by the statutes relating to hallmarking, the marking of gun barrels, linens, and the protection of patentees.

---

[121] *Select Committee* (1862) Q. 725 (Ryland) ('I would have registered simply the trade mark; it appears to us unnecessary to register the names of those manufacturers who have not adopted a mark'); 732 ('no one can use the name of another, without authority, innocently'); 'The Registration of Trade Marks', reporting a paper by Arthur Ryland (prohibiting fraudulent use of a name or label was desirable, 'but the error was in including them under the term trade mark').

[122] Yet others thought that both names and marks were equally deserving of protection and should be susceptible to registration, if such a system were adopted: *Select Committee* (1862), Q. 1111 (J. Smith) ('the name in many instances might be a trade mark alone or in combination with a cipher').

[123] Alfred Marten (for Mr Hermon), Parl. Deb., vol. 226, cols. 703–4, 7 August 1875.

[124] See below.

[125] The two most famous such marks in this period were the Rodgers mark which comprised a Star and Maltese cross (originally granted to William Birks in 1682) and the I*XL mark used by George Wolstenholm & Sons, originally granted to William Smith in 1787: D. Higgins and G. Tweedale 'Asset or Liability? Trade Marks in the Sheffield Cutlery and Tool Trades' (1995) 37 *Business History* 1, 6.

Indeed, such insignia were uppermost in the minds of many of those who discussed trade mark matters in this period. For example, one commentator in the *Solicitors' Journal* identified 'what is popularly known as a trade mark' with 'a certain device representing some animal known to the actual or mythical world, which is impressed upon each article' – though few contemporaries would actually have limited the concept of marks to representations of animals.[126]

While there was no doubt that such emblems should be encompassed in the definition of a trade mark, contemporaries contested how much further a definition could – or should – go. The courts had indicated that the protection the law provided against fraudulent misrepresentation could extend to misrepresentation by use of any and all indicia,[127] and relief had been accepted as in principle available in relation to the fraudulent use of a particular name and livery for a bus service, as well as the use of cotton ties in a particular place on fabric.[128] John Polson, of the starch-maker Brown and Polson, giving evidence to the Select Committee, said he wanted a means of 'claiming property in trade marks, and in the general features of the packet, or style of getting up, and in the name of the article'.[129] And Adams, in his textbook on trade marks,[130] defined a trade mark as 'any symbol, or mark, or name, or other indication' including a 'mode of tying bundles of goods or of peculiarly shaped bottles or boxes exclusively associated with the plaintiff's manufacture or business'. However, as far as registration was concerned, little consideration seems to have been given to protection of shapes, get-up or what we now call 'exotic' marks. Perhaps those seeking protection were few, and the problems associated with representing such marks so transparent, that interested traders were content enough to rely on whatever protection the common law and criminal provisions provided in cases of real fraud.

However, controversy did surround the extent to which words could or should be protected as trade marks. Certainly, words had been protected at common law. In *Perry* v *Truefit*, Lord Langdale MR had considered the phrase MEDICATED MEXICAN BALM protectable in principle, and other cases recognized the possible protection of the words SOLID-HEADED

---

[126] 'Proposed Alterations in the Law of Trade Marks' 3.
[127] *Perry* v *Truefitt* (1842) 6 Beav 66, 73.
[128] *Knott* v *Morgan* (1836) 2 Keen 213 (imitation of overall trade dress of claimant's omnibus business, including livery of staff, gave rise to injunction, though this was confined to 'names, words or devices' on its buses which were colourable imitations of the claimant's); *Woollam* v *Ratcliff* (1863) 1 H & M 259 (tying of silk).
[129] *Select Committee* (1862) Q. 1971 (Polson).   [130] F. M. Adams, *A Treatise* (1874) at 8.

PINS,[131] THE EXCELSIOR WHITE SOFT SOAP,[132] COCOATINA,[133] PESSENDEDE, as well as geographical names such as GLENFIELD and ANATOLIA.[134] Some of the judges had begun to differentiate between protectable and unprotectable words, sketching taxonomies of marks. For example, when holding that 'COLONIAL LIFE ASSURANCE' was not the exclusive property of the first trader to employ the phrase, Sir John Romilly MR sought to categorize signs as 'distinctive marks', 'symbolical cases' and, unprotected, 'descriptive terms'.[135] In *Leather Cloth Co. v American Leather Cloth* (1865),[136] the claimant claimed protection of the court for a mark comprising a circle including the words 'CROCKETT INTERNATIONAL LEATHER CLOTH CO. EXCELSIOR. JR & CP CROCKETT & CO MANUFACTURERS, NEWARK HJ USA WEST HAM ENGLAND'. (The defendant's 'logo' was a semi-circle including the words 'AMERICAN LEATHER CLOTH COMPANY. SUPERIOR, LEATHER CLOTH MANUFACTURED BY THEIR MANAGER LATE WITH JR & CP CROCKETT 12 YDS OLD KENT ROAD, LONDON'.) Lord Kingsdown said that what 'is usually meant by a trade mark' is a 'symbol or emblem' (rather than words) which has by use come 'to be recognised in trade as the mark of the goods of a particular person'. Lord Westbury averred:

I ought to have regarded this affix to the Plaintiff's goods, which is here denominated a trade mark, as something which, according to the anterior usage and applications of the words 'trade mark', by no means resembles or comes within the description of anything that has hitherto been properly designated by that name ... My Lords, what is here called by the Appellants a trade mark, is, in reality, an advertisement of the character and quality of their goods.

While the judges may have made progress in gradually differentiating between the protection afforded to various words depending upon the meaning the words conveyed when used in specific (and known) contexts,[137] the proponents of property in marks faced a much more difficult task. If the registration of a word was to be permitted, and the consequence of such registration was to be that the registrant had the exclusive right to use the word on specified goods, it would be necessary to produce a mechanism of determining in advance (and without context) the meaning of any words for which registration was sought. Moreover, even with

[131] *Edelsten v Vick* (1853) 11 Hare 78.   [132] *Braham v Bustard* (1863) 1 H & M 447.

[133] *Schweitzer v Atkins* (1868) 37 LJ Ch. 847.

[134] *M'Andrew v Basset* (1864) 33 LJ Ch 561.

[135] *Colonial Life Assurance Co. v Home and Colonial Life Assurance Co.* (1864) 33 Beav 548.

[136] *Leather Cloth v American Leather Cloth Co.* (1865) 11 HLC 523, 538 per Lord Kingsdown.

[137] Including the idea of secondary meaning of terms whose primary meaning is descriptive: Lord Westbury in *Wotherspoon v Currie* (1871–2) LR 5 HL 508.

the benefit of a categorical scheme indicating which marks should be registrable, the operation of such a system would necessarily involve investing some low-level administrator with the power to accept or refuse registration. An additional worry was that such a broad system would lead to a proliferation of rights or properties. One merchant giving evidence to the Select Committee argued that protection should be limited to devices.[138] This reflected a real fear of a multiplication of protected marks which could render merchants liable, and a consequent desire that wholesalers and retailers need only be vigilant about the use of particular kinds of sign.[139] He objected to the 'net being too wide' and a 'flooding of the most ridiculous things'.[140]

Analysis of comparative laws confirmed to contemporaries that words might be a problem. The Austrian registration law of 1858, for example, covered 'special signs which serve to distinguish the productions and goods of one tradesman intended for the commercial market, from those of any other tradesman', specifically referring to 'devices, ciphers, vignettes and the like' but excluding marks 'which are commonly used in the trade in particular kinds of goods' as well as marks comprising 'merely of letters, words, or numbers, or of the arms of states and countries'.[141] Similar limitations were enacted in the Imperial German Statute for the Protection of Trade Marks, 30 November 1874 and the Dutch Act of 1880.[142]

Even proponents of a registration system, such as Arthur Ryland, seemed to recognize the legitimacy of some of these fears. He proposed that registration be limited to devices, so that terms such as 'medicated balm' and 'solid-headed pins' that had been protected in earlier case law would escape the registration system. He averred that 'it was just and wise

---

[138] *Select Committee* (1862), Qs. 2372, 2394, 2397 (S. Morley).

[139] See also ibid., Q. 2362 (Dillon).

[140] In this respect it is of interest that the 1869 Bill would have prohibited the registration of more than one trade mark for the same description of goods: Trade Marks Registration Bill (1868–9) *Parliamentary Papers*, 5 Bills, clause 12. The unsuccessful 1873 Bill which followed the 1869 Bill in many respects abandoned this limitation.

[141] Imperial Patent of 7 December 1858, issuing a Law for the Protection of Trade Marks and other Denotations, in *Reports Relative to Legislation in Foreign Countries* 585, 588–90.

[142] Article 3 ('registration is forbidden if the mark consists exclusively of numerals, letters, public words, armorial bearings, or scandalous designs'): *Reports Relative to Legislation in Foreign Countries* 469, 513–23. See also the Dutch Bill Laying Down Regulations Respecting Trade and Factory Marks (1879), in ibid. at 541. According to the Explanatory statement on the Dutch Bill, the exclusion of word marks explicitly drew on the German and Austrian laws, and the basis of the exclusion was to prevent appropriation of common property: 'Care must be taken in the public interest, that symbols which, from their very nature are common property, should not be appropriated by individuals for their exclusive advantage', ibid. at 551). The Dutch Bill became the Law of 25 May 1880, and remained in force until 30 September 1893.

to exclude all such names. It appears to me unfair and contrary to public policy to allow any one house the exclusive right to an adjective.'[143]

Ryland's approach was ultimately that adopted in the 1875 Registration Act. Section 10 allowed for registration of 'a distinctive device, mark, heading, label or ticket' to which there might be added 'any letters, words, or figures, or combination of letters, words or figures', but did not offer protection for words, as such – no matter whether they were invented, fancy or non-descriptive. As if to emphasize this, the saving for acquired rights permitted the registration of 'any special and distinctive word or words or combination of figures or letters used as a trade mark before the passing of this Act'. Many marks which were thus in fact distinctive (such as words that were adopted and became distinctive after 1875) could not be registered.[144] The limited definition became the subject of litigation,[145] and criticism.[146] Only six years later the view was widely held that 'a trade mark consisting of a fancy name [was] of far greater value than any device'.[147]

How did 'trade marks' differ from other markings on goods?

Perhaps the most interesting aspects of the debates over the development of a definition of 'trade mark' in this period related to how a trade mark could be differentiated from other signs, symbols and literature associated with products. As with 'the impressions upon a piece of gingerbread',[148] not all marks on products could be conceived as or understood as trade marks. But what criteria differentiated between those impressions on a piece of gingerbread that were accidental, those that were decorative, and those that were trade marks? Manchester traders, objecting to an early version of the Merchandise Marks Bill, had made the point that 'it is utterly impossible to ascertain in most cases, whether any trade mark, or the alleged trade mark is interfered

---

[143] 'The Registration of Trade Marks', reporting a paper by Arthur Ryland. Ryland observed that this was the law in Prussia too.

[144] J. E. Evans-Jackson, 'The Law of Trade Marks' (1899) 47 Jo Soc Arts 563, 565 ('the Act of 1875 contained one great defect in that it did not provide for the registration or protection of word marks ... The greatest dissatisfaction resulted from this').

[145] Ex parte Stephens (1876) 3 Ch. D 659 (AEILYTON case); Rose v Evans, The Times, 12 May 1879, p. 6b (LIMETTA, the botanical name of a lime tree, unregistrable). On whether words used before the passage of the Act were 'distinctive', see Reinhardt v Spalding, The Times, 11 December 1879, p. 4a (FAMILY SALVE was distinctive of medicines given eighteen years' use).

[146] Johnson, 'Trade Marks' 493.   [147] Ibid. 501.

[148] Select Committee (1862), Q. 1209 (J. Smith). The judiciary also struggled when dealing with material on goods that did not have the classic features of trade marks. See Leather Cloth v American Leather Cloth Co. (1865) 11 HLC 523, at 546.

with, or even whether the mark is intended as a trade mark or not'.[149] And at least one member of the 1862 Select Committee (who himself decided to give evidence), Edmund Potter, a calico printer, took the view that trade marks comprised 'all those things ... which embody some amount of design upon them'.[150] Questioned by Roebuck about the distinction between trade marks and designs (already protected under a registration system), he responded that he considered it 'all the same ... I cannot separate them'.[151]

Those who sought to distinguish between the various markings that could adorn products, so as to identify which were trade marks, tended to focus on the function of each mark: trade marks might be in the same (ontological) form (words, colours, etc.) as other signs, yet what made a sign a trade mark was how it functioned or how it was understood. For example, the Chairman of the Select Committee, John Arthur Roebuck, suggested to the witness George Wilkinson, Master Cutler of the Cutlers' Company, that a trade mark was an emblem 'impressed upon a manufacture *for the purpose of denoting* that the manufacture has been produced by a certain person'.[152] Four years later, the solicitor Underdown, likewise articulated his view of '[t]he accurate definition of a trade mark' as 'any mark, name, figure, letter or device employed *to denote* that any article of trade, manufacture, or merchandize, is of the manufacture, workmanship, production or merchandize of the person using it with or upon goods'.[153] While differing slightly as to detail, both these functional definitions would be familiar to trade mark lawyers today for whom the classical understanding of a trade mark is that it is a sign which operates (or is intended to operate) *to denote* trade origin.

While the definition of the function of trade marks in this period was in many ways not dissimilar to how such signs would be described today, two aspects are particularly worthy of note. The first relates to the specific content of the indication of trade origin: for it was contested whether trade marks were (or should be confined to) marks indicating workmanship or manufacture, or were indications of the entity that produced the goods, or just that the goods had been approved by whoever happened to be the trade mark owner.

---

[149] See 'On Fraudulent Trade Marks' 820, 821, quoting from a petition by the wholesale houses of Manchester against the Bill.
[150] *Select Committee* (1862), Q. 2183 (Potter).   [151] Ibid. Q. 2211, 2215 (Potter).
[152] Ibid. Qs. 1726–8 (G. Wilkinson).
[153] Underdown, 'On the Piracy of Trade Marks' 370.

The London merchant J. Dillon thought a trade mark was 'a mark that is affixed to goods, which identifies those goods as being *made by* a particular man'.[154] He said that a trade mark should not be used by a person other than the manufacturer because

> the trade mark is referred to as a mark implying a certain fact, that it is an established manufacture by certain man or firm, at a certain place. *If you alter …the person, that destroys the mark.* I have heard of people attempting to sell their trade marks, but I should as soon think of a soldier selling his medal.

Taking his analysis to its logical conclusion, he would have opposed even the use of the same mark by successors to a partnership.[155] Others had a broader idea of origin. Giving evidence to the 1862 Select Committee, William Smith, solicitor and Secretary of the Sheffield Chamber of Commerce, and John Smith, iron founder and President of the Sheffield Chamber of Commerce, took what we would recognize as the modern position: a trade mark 'shows that the goods are made by some particular person or by some other person whom he has authorised to make for him'.[156] Another lawyer, Underdown, was keen to emphasize that marks could be of value to the merchant or wholesale dealer so as to indicate 'care in their selection': he defined trade marks as marks denoting 'that any article of trade, manufacture, or merchandize, *is of the manufacture, workmanship, production or merchandize of the person using it with or upon goods*'.[157] Yet others suggested that a trade mark 'may signify no more than … that the article to which it is affixed has passed into the market through the hands of the person entitled to use the mark, and finally may come to be regarded by the public as a mere guarantee of quality'.[158]

Trade marks as indicators of geographic origin

A second aspect of the functional definitions employed in this period is of interest because it is one that seems very much to have been lost from

---

[154] *Select Committee* (1862), Q. 2286 (Dillon), Q. 2336 (Dillon, agreeing with Potter that a trade mark is 'a means of communicating to the buyer the name of the maker of the article').

[155] Ibid. Q. 2343 (Dillon).   [156] Ibid., Q. 616 (William Smith); Qs. 1225–35 (J. J. Smith).

[157] Underdown, 'On the Piracy of Trade Marks' 370. The 1862 Merchandise Marks Act defined the objects of trade mark protection broadly as any mark 'lawfully used by any person to denote any chattel, or (in Scotland) any Article of Trade, Manufacture or Merchandise to be … the Manufacture, Workmanship, Production or Merchandise of such Person … or … to be an Article or Thing of any peculiar or particular Quality or Description made or sold by such Person'.

[158] Ludlow and Jenkyns, *A Treatise*, 2.

today's trade mark law. While today commentators consider trade marks as indications of trade origin, those from the 1860s and 1870s seem to have thought that a trade mark also indicated *where* a product was made. Arthur Ryland described a mark as 'a device used by manufacturers to denote the person by whom, *or the place where*, the article bearing it was made' (emphasis added). Writing in 1874,[159] F. M. Adams described a trade mark as 'any symbol, or mark, or name, or other indication which when affixed to goods offered for sale in the market would convey to the minds of purchasers the impression that those goods were the manufacture of some person or form, *or some particular place*'. Lionel Mozley, solicitor, similarly defined a trade mark as indicating that an article or commodity 'is made by a particular firm or person, *at a particular place or manufactory*, or is of a particular quality or description'.[160] A similar definition had been adopted in the Indian Penal Code,[161] and in the Prussian law of 1851,[162] and had received judicial approval from Sir John Romilly in *Hall* v *Barrows* and Lord Cranworth LC in *Leather Cloth*.[163]

This tendency to link indications of trade origin with indications of geographical origin looks odd to a commentator in the twenty-first century. The emphasis being placed on trade marks as indications of geographical origin may, in part, have reflected the fact that many traders marked their goods with the name and address of the place where the goods were made. Associations, then, might rapidly have been formed between particular (non-geographic) trade names and places of geographical origin. Moreover, it also reflected the fact that many consumers

---

[159] F. M. Adams, *A Treatise* (1874). See also Levi, *International Commercial Law* 598.
[160] Mozley, *Trade Marks Registration* 1.
[161] Article 478 of the Indian Penal Code 1860 defined a trade mark as 'a mark used for denoting that goods have been made or manufactured by a particular person or *at a particular time or place*, or that they are of a particular quality': 'Trade Marks and Property Marks' 14.
[162] According to Levi's *International Commercial Law*, this prohibited the fraudulent marking of merchandise with 'the name of the firm, and with the dwelling or manufacturing place of a Prussian manufacturer, producer or tradesman'.
[163] (1863) 32 LJ Ch 548. Sir John Romilly MR considered whether the mark could be sold, and held it could not. He divided marks into two categories: those that 'denote the spot where certain articles are manufactured' which 'might possess peculiar local advantages for the manufacture of the article' and those that 'denote the persons by whom they are manufactured'. In *Leather Cloth* v *American Leather Cloth Co.* (1865) 11 HLC 523, Lord Cranworth LC defined the right to a mark as 'the exclusive right to use it for the purpose of indicating where, or by whom, *or at what manufactory*, the article to which it was affixed was manufactured' (emphasis added). See also *Dunnachie* v *Young* (1883) 10 Sess. Cas. (4th Ser.) 874 (GLENBOIG, being the name of the place from which the clay was dug, was a good trade mark for fire bricks) (Lord Craighill: 'names of places, or, as they have been called, geographical names, are also used as trade marks').

would have taken the geographical origin of the goods as an indication of
their likely quality: non-geographical marks, such as names, could thus in
the public mind be associated with the place where the goods were made
and that, in turn, with the quality of the goods. As Adams explained, a
trade mark 'should in fact be an assurance to the public that they are
reaping the benefit of some person's superior skill, or *the peculiar local
advantages of some place*'.[164] In contrast, while today one might associate
Terry's chocolate with York, or Cadbury's with Birmingham, a consumer
would not think that the quality of such manufactured goods depended
on the location of its manufacture. Today, most manufacturing businesses are assumed to be highly mobile, employees from different locations equally capable, and the quality (as opposed to cost) of production
not related to geographical location.

In the 1860s, the question of whether a trade mark indicated the place of
manufacture (as well as the trade origin) not only was relevant to the
definition of a mark, but also was seen to have potentially significant legal
implications. More specifically, in so far as a (non-geographic) trade mark
indicated geographic origin, the question arose whether it became misdescriptive to use the same mark in relation to any other geographical
source. This had potentially significant consequences, either if the proprietor wanted to re-locate, or if the business was to be sold to a manufacturer
in a different location.[165] Smith thought there was no misrepresentation by
sale of a mark, even if the public expected a particular sort of product. The
President of the Board of Trade, Milner Gibson, asked him about whether
he would object to a man who hitherto had manufactured cigars in Havana
selling the right to use its mark to another trader who might make cigars in

[164] F. M. Adams, *A Treatise* (1874), 60. In *Hall v Barrows* (1863) 32 LJ Ch 548, Sir John
Romilly MR explained that a 'mark or brand which denotes goods manufactured at a
particular place may be, and probably would be sold with the works themselves, and the
mark would be, as it were, attached to the spot, to denote which it was first adopted, and
which might possess peculiar local advantages for the manufacture of the article'.
[165] A related question of whether the key relationship was between mark and place had been
raised as early as *Motley v Downham* (1837) 3 My & Cr 1. There the dispute was over
whether the mark 'M.C.', which had been used to brand boxes of tin plates from a works
at Carmarthen, had been purchased, with the goodwill of the business, by a trader who
then moved the place of manufacture forty-four miles to Glamorganshire. A decade later
the defendant commenced business at the Carmathan works and marked their tin plates
'M.C. Carmarthan'. The Vice-Chancellor had granted an injunction, but the Lord
Chancellor, Lord Cottenham, discharged the order, giving the plaintiff leave to bring
the case at law. He did not seem to think the case would have been problematic, except
for the fact that the defendant was using a mark that had always been used by persons
carrying on manufacture of tin plates at that works. He thought the issue 'one of
considerable nicety' whether a mark associated with a particular place could continue
to be used by a person who operated out of that place.

Ipswich.[166] Smith responded that he did not see this as enabling a fraud. In contrast, solicitor Arthur Ryland, one of the chief figures in the Chamber of Commerce movement for trade mark registration, was more disturbed. He described a mark as 'a device used by manufacturers to denote the person by whom, *or the place where*, the article bearing it was made' (emphasis added). He did not think marks should be transferred other than with the trade, but had real difficulty with Milner Gibson's interrogation about whether a business in one geographical location should be permitted to sell its business and mark to a trader at a different location.[167] Others were more categorical: according to Wright, a Birmingham button manufacturer, 'the trade mark should not travel'.[168]

Towards a 'modern' definition of trade marks: 1875–1888

The passage of the 1875 Act was by no means the end of the debates over the definition of a trade mark.[169] In fact, the registration processes intensified the amount of discussion over what could be protected as a trade mark. With many thousands of applications, the registrars were required to make many thousands of decisions.[170] A large number of cases also made their way to court.[171] All this activity threw up

---

[166] *Select Committee* (1862), Q. 620 (Milner Gibson to W. Smith).
[167] Ibid. Q. 908 (A. Ryland).   [168] Ibid. Q. 1075 (J. S. Wright).
[169] In fact, the new system came in for considerable criticism, particularly from the Manchester cotton trade which sought immediate exclusion from the scope of the Act: D. Higgins and G. Tweedale, 'The Trade Marks Question and the Lancashire Cotton Industry, 1870–1914' (1996) 27 *Textile History* 207–28, esp. at 211. See also (1876) Sol Jo 402, 18 Mar. 1876; *Board of Trade Committee to Inquire into Duties, Organisation and Arrangements of Patent Office as relates to Trade Marks and Designs, Report, Minutes of Evidence, Appendices* (hereafter Herschel Committee) (C.-5350) (1888) 81 *Parliamentary Papers*, para. 15, Q. 172 (evidence of H. R. Lack), Q. 1252 (evidence of Mr Joseph Fry, head of the Manchester Department of the Patent Office).
[170] The registrars were assisted in their determinations by the Commissioners of Patents, the Lord Chancellor, Master of the Rolls, and Law Officers of the Crown: Trade Mark Rules, r. 68. In some fields and districts, such as Manchester and Redditch, the local Chambers of Commerce gave assistance to the registrars in determining what was common in the trade. See *Reports of the Commissioners of Patents for Inventions* (1878–9) 26 *Parliamentary Papers* 808, 817; Herschell Committee, Q. 1252 (Joseph Fry); Q. 2011 (L. Whittle); Johnson, 'Trade Marks' 500–3 (on Manchester Cotton Committee and Redditch Committee on needle labels). The decisions of the Comptroller could be appealed to the Board of Trade. The Manchester Committee of Experts was regarded by some as a 'tribunal of commerce': *In re Brook's Trade mark*, *The Times*, 15 July 1878, p. 4d (Hall V-C), but this view was criticized by Earl Cairns in *Orr Ewing* v *Registrar of Trade-Marks* (1879) LR 4 HL 479, 483.
[171] Trade Marks Registration Act 1875, s. 5. See, e.g., *Ex parte Stephens* (1876) 3 Ch D 659 (Jessel MR) (word mark AEILYTON not registrable); *In Re Barrows' Trade Marks* (1877) 5 Ch D 353 (Court of Appeal) (Jessel MR) (on form of registration in series of marks involving letters BBH); *In re Mitchell's Trade Mark* (1877) 7 Ch D 36 (refusing to rectify

inconsistencies of interpretation and exposed difficulties of application, eventually prompting statutory reform in 1883 and again in 1888. By the end of this period, trade mark law started to look much more like that in operation today than it had done in either 1850 or even 1875. The key developments were: the consolidation of various definitions of 'trade mark'; the clarification of the relationship between protection based on registration and that available despite the absence of registration; the extension of registration to word marks; the exclusion from registrability of descriptive and geographical marks; and the development of a multi-lateral arrangement for the mutual protection of marks overseas.

Consolidating the idea of a trade mark

As I have already suggested, in 1860 there was no such thing as a legal concept of 'trade mark'. By 1875 there were at least three legal conceptions of trade marks: the very broad notion adopted in section 1 of the Merchandise Marks Act 1862;[172] the tentative definition of trade mark being developed in the context of common law protection (later called

---

register to include twenty-three trade marks comprising single letters, A through to W, for steel pens, because the section referred to a 'combination of letters'); *In re Hyde & Co.'s Trade Mark* (1878) 7 Ch D 724 (Jessel MR) (expunging old trade mark BANK OF ENGLAND for sealing wax because it had been common name in trade for twenty years); *In re Leonardt* (1878) Seb. Dig 373 (Jessel MR) (registration of picture and word marks permitted with disclaimers); *In re Jelley, Son, & Jones' Application* (1878) 51 LJ Ch 639 n, 41 LTNS 332 (Jessel MR) (considering registrations of old marks in new classes); *In Re Rotherham's Trade-Mark* (1879) 11 Ch D 250 (Bacon V-C), (1880) 40 Ch D 585 (CA) (TOD in Arabic was distinctive device, per James LJ, or the name of an individual printed in a particular or distinctive manner, per Baggallay LJ); *In re J. B. Palmer's Trade Mark* (1883) 24 Ch D 505 (CA) ('BRAIDED FIXED STARS' expunged from register as descriptive of matches, whose heads did not fall off when lighted, that had been subject to patented process of braiding); *In Re Leonard & Ellis's Trade-Mark* (1883) 26 Ch D 290 (VALVOLINE expunged from register, because it had not been used in this country before the passing of the 1875 Act, or, if it had, it had not been used as a trade mark but as a description of an invented product) (CA); *In re Anderson's Trade Mark* (1884) 26 Ch D 409 (refusing registration of picture of Liebig and words 'BRAND BARON LIEBIG' for meat extract, even with disclaimer of words, because they formed essential part of mark); *Edwards v Dennis* (1885) 30 Ch D 454; *In re James's Trade Mark* (1885) 31 Ch D 344 (pictorial representation of goods themselves not 'distinctive device'), reversed (1886) 3 RPC 340.

[172] The 1862 Merchandise Marks Act defined the objects of trade mark protection broadly – as to the type of subject matter and its communicative content: 'the expression "Trade Mark" shall include any Name, Signature, Word, Letter, Device, Emblem, Figure, Sign, Seal, Stamp, Diagram, Label, Ticket or other Mark of any other Description ... lawfully used by any person to denote any chattel, or (in Scotland) any Article of Trade, Manufacture or Merchandise to be ... the Manufacture, Workmanship, Production or Merchandise of such Person ... or ... to be an Article or Thing of any peculiar or particular Quality or Description made or sold by such Person'.

'passing off'); and the very narrow definition inserted in the Trade Mark Registration Act 1875.[173] While the adoption of different definitions of trade mark by the legislature, not surprisingly, drew criticism,[174] it is easy to understand the desire to adopt a cautious approach to establishing rights over signs by registration. The adoption of registration would change the nature of trade mark protection, reinforcing emerging notions of the trade mark as the object of property, rather than as a component in a communicative context.[175] Limiting the initial coverage of the registration system to specific types of signs seemed sensible, given the impossibility of predicting confidently how the system would operate and what its impact would be. As Daniel explained in his treatise, 'it would seem to have been the object of the framers of the Act to define and restrict trade marks to within those limits which experience had proved to be the most generally useful and the most capable of protection'.[176]

In the period between 1875 and 1888 it became increasingly clear that it would be preferable if the different conceptions of what qualified as a trade mark could be aligned as far as possible. For some people, it made no sense that there could be criminal liability where there was no civil liability, so it was important that the definition of registrable trade mark be expanded to include those matters which would fall within the scope of the Merchandise Marks Act. The consolidation was effected in 1887, when, prompted by certain international developments and internal reform movements, two parallel committees considered reform of the Merchandise Marks Act of 1862 and the Trade Mark provisions of the Patents, Designs and Trade Marks Act 1883.[177] The resulting legislation created an offence of 'forging'

---

[173] In some respects the period is interesting because of the ideas that were mooted but not adopted. One of these was that 'trade marks' were identifiers, rather like ID codes or fingerprints. From this perspective, M. Henry in a paper to the Royal Society of Arts argued that marks be confined to letters and numbers (excluding devices), so that each trade mark was 'more distinctive, more substantial and therefore more secure; it would impart to it a sharply defined, and unmistakable idiosyncrasy'. Henry's conception was of marks such as 'A50' for beer: M. Henry, 'Trade marks' (1862) 10 Jo Soc Arts 255. For the same idea see (1875) Jo Soc Arts 567.

[174] Alfred Marten (for Mr Hermon), *Parl. Deb.*, vol. 226, cols. 703–4, 7 August, 1875 ('The definition in the Act of 1862 in reference to the fraudulent imitation of trade marks was a most extensive one; but in the Bill it was proposed that there should be a far less extensive definition. A good deal of difficulty must arise from having one definition in relation to fraudulent imitation and another in reference to registration.').

[175] Sherman and Bently, *The Making*, 197–8; Bently, 'From Communication', (suggesting that the stylization of trade marks as 'property' did not carry expansive consequences).

[176] Daniel, *The Trade Mark Registration Act* 40. Also noting that 'there were no legal restrictions in existence before upon what might be used as a trade mark'.

[177] The Select Committee chaired by Baron de Worms was established in April 1887 and concluded its proceedings at the end of June. The Departmental Committee, known as the Herschell Committee, had been established in February 1887, hearing evidence

or 'falsely applying' a trade mark,[178] and defined 'trade mark' as a mark registered under the 1883 Act.[179] The legislation also made it an offence to apply a 'false trade description',[180] which would cover descriptions as to 'the place or country in which any goods were made or produced' and 'the material of which any goods were composed'.[181] Importantly, as the concept of a 'trade mark' was consolidated, it was increasingly distinguished from indications of the place of manufacture.

In this same period, the courts clarified that marks that were not registrable could be protected if they had been used, and, in due course, it was accepted that (whatever the statutory wording may have implied) the registration system operated without prejudice to pre-existing rules giving protection against trade misdescriptions. The 1875 Act had provided that 'from or after' July 1, 1876, 'a person shall not be entitled to institute any proceeding for trade mark infringement of any trade mark as defined by this Act until and unless such trade mark is registered in pursuance of this Act'.[182] It would have been open to a bold court to hold that this meant that use-based protection had been abolished. Indeed, initially, most commentators indicated that they understood the impact of the Act to make registration essential.[183] Naturally, this prompted a rush to register for which the bureaucracy was ill prepared. Given the delays in the registration process that in fact ensued,[184] an amending Act put back the date to 1 July 1877 (and provision for further delay in relation to 'cotton marks' was introduced in 1877).[185] These deferments are evidence of a widespread belief that the 1875 Act took away existing remedies for 'trade

between March and June 1887, issuing an interim report in August 1887 and a final report in March 1888. Baron de Worms was a member of the Herschell Committee and a number of witnesses gave evidence to both committees.

[178] Merchandise Marks Act 1887 (50 & 51 Vict. c. 28), s. 2(1)(a), (b).

[179] Ibid. s. 3(1). It added that 'trade marks' included 'any trade mark which, either with or without registration, is protected by law in any British possession or foreign state to which the provisions of the one hundred and third section of the Trade Marks Act 1883, are, under Order in Council, for the time being applicable'.

[180] Ibid. s. 2(1)(d).   [181] Ibid. s. 3(1).

[182] Trade Mark Registration Act 1875, s. 1.

[183] Salaman, *A Manual of the Practice* 7 n (b) ('The clause renders registration virtually compulsory, and it would seem that all persons whose marks are of any value must register, otherwise their marks may be pirated with impunity'); Daniel, *The Trade Mark Registration Act* at 37 ('Henceforth it will be necessary for any person intending to claim the exclusive use of a trade mark to register it at the office established by the Act').

[184] In an article in 1881 Edmund Johnson states that by 1880 there had been 21,636 advertised marks and 18,764 registered ones. The Manchester Committee, established to examine the huge numbers of marks applied for in relation to cotton goods, examined over 40,000 marks, finding only 10 per cent capable of registration. See Johnson, 'Trade Marks'; see, also, (1879) 23 Sol Jo 819 (16 Aug. 1879).

[185] Trade-Marks Registration Amendment Act 1876 (39 & 40 Vict. c. 33); Trade Marks Registration Extension Act 1877 (40 & 41 Vict. c. 37).

mark infringement'.[186] Moreover, the 1876 Act implied that this effect related only to registrable marks, so that unregistrable, or at least *refused*, marks were still protected in some way.[187] This can be seen from the fact that it made provision for the issuance by the registrar of 'Certificates of Refusal' – the idea being that the holder of such a certificate could take advantage of whatever remedies the legal system provided for 'trade mark infringement'.[188] In so providing, the legislature acknowledged that at least these marks could receive protection without registration.

The implication of the 1875 and 1876 Acts was that, as regards registrable trade marks within the meaning of the 1875 Act, proceedings could only be brought where there was registration. The 1883 Act seemed to confirm this, again stating that a person was not entitled to institute proceedings to prevent or recover damage for trade mark infringement unless 'in the case of a trade mark *capable of being registered* under this Act, it has been registered'.[189] However, given the narrow notion of trade mark embodied in the 1875 and 1883 Acts, the prohibition did not appear to prevent a claimant bringing a number of actions simultaneously, some based on registration and the others based on the traditional protection afforded to unregistrable marks. Case law soon confirmed that a claimant could indeed bring an action based on traditional principles in relation to unregistrable 'get-up', and that this was so even where aspects of the total get-up could have been registered, but were not.[190] Later case law suggested that registration was required as a prerequisite to the action only where the claimant needed to rely on registration to establish use,[191]

---

[186] The 1876 Act replaces the words 'any proceeding for trade mark infringement' with 'any proceeding to prevent or to recover damages for the infringement of any trade mark'. This change might have been to allay concerns either that all the 1875 Act did was to remove the right to an injunction but not damages (as suggested by Lord Blackburn in *Orr Ewing* v *Registrar of Trade-Marks* (1879) LR 4 HL 479, 498) or that the Merchandise Marks Act 1862 was rendered inapplicable to trade marks that had not been registered: see Bryce, *The Trade Marks Registration Acts*, 16–17 (raising this question and arguing that the power to bring criminal proceedings under the 1862 Act in respect of the fraudulent imitation of an unregistered mark 'does not seem to be taken away by this section'). See, also, the Patents, Designs and Trade Marks Act 1883, s. 77.

[187] Section 1 provided that proceedings for trade mark infringement could only be brought were the mark registered or, in the case of marks in use before 13 August 1875, if it were refused.

[188] Trade-Marks Registration Amendment Act, s. 2; Patents, Designs and Trade Marks Act 1883, s. 77.

[189] Patents, Designs and Trade Marks Act 1883, s. 77.

[190] *Lever* v *Goodwin* (1887) 4 RPC 492; *Great Tower* v *Langford* (1888) 5 RPC 66 (injunction granted based on defendant's use of similar packaging and colours to those of claimant).

[191] *Faulder* v *Rushton* (1903) 20 RPC 477 (where SILVER PAN was expunged from the register as being words that referred to the character or quality of jam, but the claimant

leaving the possibility that a claimant might even rely on passing off in circumstances where the mark had been registered. Ultimately, the 1905 Act would fully establish the registration system as conferring specific statutory rights,[192] and clarified that nothing therein 'shall be deemed to affect rights of action against any person for passing off goods as those of another person or the remedies in respect thereof'.[193]

Extending protection to word marks

This consolidation of the definition of 'trade mark' in the criminal regime with that of the registration system was made possible, in some respects, by the expansion of the statutory definition of 'trade mark' in the latter. In particular, the 1883 Act expanded the definition of registrable trade marks to cover 'fancy words' or 'words not in common use'.[194] This extension, in turn, exacerbated the confusion over what, exactly, could be registered. Even the Comptroller of the Patent Office, Henry Reader Lack, admitted his inability to identify whether certain words were fanciful marks.[195] At first, the registry adopted a liberal approach to the interpretation of 'fancy',[196] only to receive contradictory instructions from the Board of Trade,[197] the law officers[198] and especially the courts,[199] which were more concerned to protect the public than to

established secondary meaning, and succeeded in its action for 'passing off', Vaughan Williams LJ stating that all s. 77 of the 1883 Act meant was that if a claimant wanted to rely on statute he or she must register).

[192] Trade Marks Act 1905 (5 Edw 7 c. 15), s. 39.

[193] See also Trade Marks Act 1938 (1 & 2 Geo. 6 c. 22), s. 2; Trade Marks Act 1994, s. 2.

[194] Patents, Designs and Trade Marks Act 1883, s. 64. 'The New Patents, Designs and Trade-Marks Bills II' (5 May 1883) Sol J 444, 446; *In re Price's Patent Candle Company* (1884) 27 Ch D 681 (NATIONAL SPERM not fancy words but ones in common use and known to trade; label not distinctive); *In re Hanson's Trade Mark* (1887) 37 Ch D 112 (red, white and blue coffee label was not distinctive).

[195] Herschell Committee, Q. 160, Q. 2986. According to Lack, in his evidence to the Herschell Committee Q. 17, registration of fancy words gave 'a great deal of trouble'. The use of the phrase 'fancy words' was also criticized as 'the source of all our trouble' by Edmund Johnson, the manager of the Trade Mark Protection Society, Qs. 888–903, 946–8. See also Qs. 82–3 (Courtenay Boyle, saying 'Word marks lead to endless litigation. They are very troublesome ... What is a fancy word is an extremely difficult question'). For a discussion of problems with word marks, even after the 1888 amendments, see 'Words as Trade-Marks' (1900) 44 Sol Jo 548–9 (23 June 1900); Evans-Jackson, 'The Law of Trade Marks'.

[196] Herschell Committee, Q. 2815 (J. L. Whittle).

[197] Ibid. Qs. 162–4 (H. R. Lack, explaining that Board of Trade had instructed the Comptroller not to register word marks in relation to classes 23, 24 and 25 but that the Comptroller had ignored them).

[198] Ibid. Q. 2815 (J. L. Whittle).

[199] See Ibid. Q. 200 (Lack, explaining that, having initially taken a liberal approach to what constituted a 'fancy word', the Law Officers and Courts demanded a more restrictive approach be taken). This is something of an oversimplification. Initially, the first

please applicants.[200] As Lord Justice Cotton explained: 'the intention of the Act was to benefit traders ... [but] the Act was also intended to protect the public ... by cutting down the numerous forms of words and other things, by the use of which traders tried to secure themselves exclusive rights'.[201] According to this jurisprudence, if a word *could* be seen as an indication of where the goods were produced or of their characteristics, the word was not a 'fancy' word.[202] Thus a mark that alluded to the qualities of the goods was unregistrable,[203] and it was irrelevant whether the word had acquired 'secondary meaning' through use.[204] In its attempt to comply with these judicial precedents, the Registry's own practices were altered and thus appeared to many observers to be hopelessly inconsistent.[205] 'The judges and solicitors are like blind men leading the blind', a manufacturer observed: 'our so called trade mark system is a thorough disgrace to us, ruinous to the man of small means, and not just to any of us'.[206]

---

instances judges, particularly Chitty J and Bacon V-C, had adopted a liberal interpretation of the concept of 'fancy words' in part influenced by the practice of the Registrar: *In re Trade-Mark 'Alpine'* (1885) 29 Ch D 877 (ALPINE registrable for cotton embroidery); *In re Leaf's Trade Mark* (1886) 3 RPC 289 (ELECTRIC registrable for cotton piece goods); *In re Van Duzer's Trade Mark* (1886) 3 RPC 240 (MELROSE regarded by Bacon V-C as fancy word for toiletries). This approach was reversed in *In re Van Duzer's Trade Mark* (1887) 34 Ch D 623 (CA).

[200] See *In re Van Duzer's Trade Mark* (1887) 34 Ch D 623, 634 (Cotton LJ), 641 (Lindley LJ). Contrast the views adopted in *Orr Ewing* v *Registrar of Trade-Marks* (1879) LR 4 HL 479, where, in considering whether certain labels were distinctive, the courts were substantially more liberal than the registrar and the Manchester Committee.

[201] *In re Van Duzer's Trade Mark* (1887) 34 Ch D 623, 634 (Cotton LJ).

[202] Ibid. 623; the Court of Appeal held neither ELECTRIC for cotton goods nor MELROSE for hair restorer to be 'fancy words'. The Court said that, while some words in the dictionary or in an atlas could be 'fancy words', they could only be so where there was obviously no reference to any description or designation of where the article is made, or of what its character is. Even though Melrose was a settlement of only 2,000 inhabitants, it was not obvious that it could not be taken to be describing the goods as made at Melrose. The Court of Appeal repeated the analysis in *In re Arbenz Trade Mark* (1887) 35 Ch D 248 (GEM held not to be fancy word for guns), and it was applied obediently by Chitty J in *Towgood* v *Pirie* (1887) 4 RPC 67 (JUBILEE unregistrable for paper) and *In re Ainslie & Co.'s Trade Mark* (1887) 4 RPC 212 (BEN LIDI, the name of a Scottish mountain, unregistrable for whisky).

[203] *In re Waterman's Trade Mark* (1888) 5 RPC 368 (CA) (REVERSI unregistrable for board game which involved turning over pieces of opponent).

[204] *In re Van Duzer's Trade Mark* (1887) 34 Ch D 623, 635 (Cotton LJ), 644 (Lopes LJ).

[205] For inconsistency in relation to geographical marks, see Herschell Committee, Q. 1924 (evidence of J. Imray). There are obvious parallels with the inconsistency of decision-making in Europe in the period since implementation of the First Council Directive 89/104/EEC of 21 December 1988 to approximate the laws of the Member States relating to trade marks.

[206] Quoted by E. Johnson in his evidence to the Herschell Committee, Q. 1161.

From positive to negative definition

Traders seemed to want to expand the range of registrable signs,[207] and those involved in the administrative process were largely sympathetic.[208] Positive definitions of what were trade marks – 'fancy words', 'distinctive labels', 'brands' and the like – were proving too difficult to apply with any consistency.[209] Influenced, in part, by foreign precedents, thought turned towards defining trade marks negatively – that is, by identifying those matters which should *not* be registrable, rather than specifying that which could be registered.[210] In a significant review by a committee appointed by the Board of Trade and chaired by Lord Herschell, witnesses identified situations where traders should not be able to register signs because other traders might need to use them. John Cutler, barrister and Professor of law at King's College, London,[211] argued that traders should not be able to register words 'which would interfere with the reasonable rights of the trading community at large'.[212] For example, with regard to 'geographical marks', witnesses testified that it would be wrong for one person to register such a mark so as to prevent another person manufacturing goods at that place from using the mark.[213] Similar principles justified excluding descriptions of the quality of goods and personal names. The

---

[207] Ibid. Q. 2639 (evidence of J. Cutler). In *In re Trade-Mark 'Alpine'* (1885) 29 Ch D 877, 880, Chitty J suggested that the 'English public' was 'not so ready ... to buy articles passing under an entirely new name, which may give rise to a suspicion of adulteration'.

[208] Herschell Committee Qs. 2934–6, 3006 (H. R. Lack).

[209] On 'brands' see ibid. Qs. 1733–43, 2023–7 (evidence of J. L. Whittle).

[210] Giving evidence to ibid. at Q. 263, Lack explained that he favoured registration of anything, 'Subject to a provision which is inserted in most acts abroad: that no property can be acquired by the registration of marks which are descriptive, or of common use in a trade, or contrary to morality, or things of that sort.' See also Q. 2982 (H. R. Lack); Q. 2865 (J. L.Whittle); Edmund Johnson, Q. 903, who would have permitted registration of 'any word or words ... provided that such word or words be not inherently in any way descriptive or qualitative of the goods themselves to which applied, or to be applied, or in common use in connexion with such goods'. See also Qs. 946–7 and Q. 1161, where Johnson draws on the work of Professor Max Muller to argue that there is an 'ample choice' of English word marks, and makes clear he sees the issue of the suitability of trade marks as one for traders not requiring 'the parental care of the courts'. For an analysis of trade mark practice as historically responsive to assumptions about language, see Megan Richardson, 'Trade Marks and Language' (2004) *Sydney Law Review* 193.

[211] Professor of English Law from 1864 to 1906, as well as Professor of Indian Jurisprudence, 1865–79. He was author of J. Cutler, *On Passing Off; Or Illegal Substitution of the Goods of One Trader for the Goods of Another Trader* (London, 1904).

[212] Herschell Committee, Q. 2639; Q. 2815 (J. L. Whittle) (word might be adopted if not likely to interfere with trade purposes); Q. 2877 (words should be allowed to be registered as long as there is 'no harm').

[213] Ibid. Q. 1919 (evidence of J. Imray, a patent agent); Qs. 2639–53 (J. Cutler) (arguing for exclusion of any city, town, village or district in the United Kingdom).

Committee reported that the 'expression "fancy word" is certainly not a
happy one, and has naturally given rise to considerable differences of
opinion as to its meaning' and recommended that invented and existing
words be registrable subject to limitations 'which at once suggest themselves'.[214] Following its recommendations,[215] the language of 'fancy
words' was abandoned and the definition of registrable trade mark was
again extended in 1888 to cover 'invented words' and 'a word or words
having no reference to the character or quality of the goods, and not being
a geographical name'.[216] Special protection for certain geographical designations associated with particular quality was left to the criminal law
relating to merchandise marks.[217]

Parallel processes of extension of the meaning of a trade mark occurred
in other European states: Austria dropped its refusal to register words as
trade marks in 1890, elaborating that the term 'mark' covered 'special
signs which serve to distinguish the productions and goods intended for
the commercial market from any other similar productions and goods'.
Extension of subject matter to 'words' also occurred in Denmark (1890),
Switzerland (1890), the Netherlands (1893), Germany (1894), Sweden
(1897) and Japan (1899). The same processes saw the demarcation of
excluded terms. In Austro-Hungary, the statute excluded from registration words which related exclusively 'to place, time, and manner of
production, and ... to quality, price, designation, quantity and weight',
and similar formulations were adopted in Germany and Denmark.[218]
The Swiss statute of 1890 explicitly recognized a special form of protection for geographical indications.[219]

Multilateral protection

Efforts to find a shared definition for international purposes continued.[220] However, in a period during which European countries were

[214] Ibid. para. 26.   [215] Ibid. paras. 25–8.

[216] Patents, Designs and Trade Marks Act 1888 (51 & 52 Vict. c. 50), s. 10 (inserting a new s. 64 in the 1883 Act).

[217] Merchandise Marks Act 1887, s. 3(1)(b) defining 'trade description' as including an indication 'as to the place or country in which goods are produced'. Following a review by a committee chaired by Baron Henry de Worms, the 1887 Act replaced the 1862 Act. See *Select Committee* (1887) 357; 'The Merchandise Marks Act, 1887' (5 November 1887) Sol Jo 3–4, 20–1, 40–1, 56.

[218] *Reports from Her Majesty's Representatives Abroad on Trade-Marks Laws and Regulations* (Cd. 104) (1900) 90 *Parliamentary Papers* 269, 272–80.

[219] Ibid.

[220] Particularly after 1887 through activities of the Association Internationale pour la Protection de la Propriété Industrielle: F.-K. Beier and A. Reimer, 'Preparatory Study for the Establishment of a Uniform International Trademark Definition' (1955) 45

still establishing their own definitions of trade marks, it was inevitably problematic to locate a common definition of 'trade mark' for international purposes. The Paris Convention for the Protection of Industrial Property, signed in 1883, came up with a partial solution, at least with respect to different views as to the suitable 'form' of trade marks: to require all member countries to recognize as protected, any items registered as trade marks in the country of origin.[221] According to traditional accounts the clause originated from discussion between the Russian and French delegates over certain requirements of the Russian system that registrations be in Cyrillic – a requirement waived in favour of the French, so that they, but not Russian applicants, could obtain registrations in Latin letters.[222] Coupled with a requirement relating to national treatment, this 'telle-quelle' clause seemed to reduce at least some of the urgency over the formulation of an international definition of 'trade mark'.[223] As it turned out, the creation of a definition of 'trade mark' at the international level would not occur until the 1994 WTO Agreement.[224]

Trademark Reporter 1266; S. P Ladas, *Patents, Trademarks and Related Rights: National and International Protection* (Cambridge, Mass.: Harvard University Press, 1975) vol. II, para. 569, 974–7.

[221] 'Every trade-mark duly registered in the country of origin shall be admitted for registration, and protected in the form originally registered in all the other countries of the Union' (Art. VI).

[222] L. A. Ellwood, 'The Industrial Property Convention and the "Telle Quelle" Clause', (1956) 46 *Trademark Reporter* 36, 37–8. In fact, the practice of accepting as registrable marks registered in a foreign territory, despite the fact that they would be unregistrable under domestic law, can be traced to the earlier practices of the Austrian Registry, described in a letter from Sir H. Eliot to the Marquis of Salisbury, 12 October 1878, in *Reports Relative to Legislation in Foreign Countries on the Subject of Trade Marks* 469, 473. This approach seems to have been terminated in 1890 when Austria–Hungary introduced a new law for the protection of trade marks: see letter from Sir H. Rumbold to the Marquess of Salisbury, 23 June 1899, in *Reports from Her Majesty's Representatives Abroad on Trade-Marks Laws and Regulations* 269, 273.

[223] For its influence on the recommendations of the Herschell Committee, see Herschell Committee (1888) para. 26 (rejecting suggestion that word marks not be allowed in relation to cotton goods on the basis that such marks were allowed by other countries so Britain would be obliged to protect them). See also para. 40, where the Committee state that the implications of Art. 6 of the Paris Convention demand 'serious and immediate attention'. See *In Re Californian Fig Syrup Company's Trade-Mark* (1888) 40 Ch D 626 (Stirling J stating that s. 103 did not seem to him to give effect to Art. 6 of the Paris Convention); *In Re Carter Medicine Company's Trade-Mark* (1892) 3 Ch 472 (attempt to register CARTER'S LITTLE LIVER PILLS under Patents, Designs and Trade Marks Act 1883, s. 103, based on application in United States, rejected North J, preferring the Attorney General's understanding of s. 103, that 'any trade-mark, the registration of which has been duly applied for in the country of origin, may be the subject of application for registration under this Act', to that of the applicant).

[224] Agreement on Trade-Related Aspects of Intellectual Property Rights 1994 Art. 15.

2 The making of modern trade mark law: the UK, 1860–1914. A business history perspective

*David M. Higgins**

Professor Bently has shown that between 1870 and 1913 important changes were introduced to British trade mark law.[1] The single most important piece of legislation during this period was the Trade Marks Registration Act (1875). The crucial provisions of this Act were that registration became prima facie evidence of the right of the registered proprietor to exclusive use of the trade mark and, from 1876, no person was allowed to institute proceedings to prevent infringement of a mark unless it was registered. These early developments, although of fundamental legal importance, did not occur *in vacuo*: in many respects they were the outcome of sustained pressure by commercial and industrial interests. This commentary complements Professor Bently's discussion in the following ways. First, it places the legal issues into a business history context in order to demonstrate that trade marks issues can enhance our understanding of the performance of British industry during this period. Second, I discuss the extent to which the Trade Marks Registration Act (1875) can be considered a success, by examining features of trade mark registration and litigation between 1875 and 1914. In the penultimate section of my commentary I discuss how pressure for protection of individual trade marks developed into a much broader campaign focussing on geographical indicia. Conclusions are presented in the final section.

Trade marks and business history

The principal reason why so much commercial pressure was exerted to secure trade mark legislation, both before and after 1875, was that trade marks were recognized as particularly valuable intangible assets. At a

* My thanks to Lionel Bently and Jane Ginsburg.
[1] L. Bently, Chapter 1 of this volume.

theoretical level, it is recognized that trade marks are important because they reduce search costs (thereby facilitating repeat purchases), they encourage product differentiation and they help reputable goods obtain price premiums.[2] All of these functions have long been recognized by business historians and it is useful to provide a brief survey of this evidence and the issues thereby generated.

Business historians have traditionally referred to trade marks when discussing the growth of particular firms and the marketing strategies adopted by their owners. Thus, for example, Sutton has demonstrated that branding and trade marks were an important component of Clark's product differentiation strategy.[3] Jones' study of Nettlefold showed that their quest for a recognizable trade mark resulted in the use of the 'castle' mark which represented 'an enduring solidity and reliability and at the same time was a typically British symbol'.[4] In the soap industry, the rapid growth of Lever Bros. during the late nineteenth century has been attributed to shrewd and aggressive marketing of distinctive trade marks: SUNLIGHT, MONKEY BRAND, VIM and LUX.[5] Staying with soap, by 1896 Crosfield's had registered over 300 marks, among the most important of which was PYRAMID.[6] In the cocoa and confectionery industry, branded consumer products were made universally recognizable through packaging, but the differential success of firms depended on the extent to which particular brands were marketed. Fitzgerald has argued that Cadbury's BOURNEVILLE, launched in 1906, rapidly overtook Rowntree's ELECT, which was launched in 1886.[7]

Because trade marks were an integral part of the marketing and product differentiation strategies of firms, the corollary was that valuable trade

---

[2] G. Akerlof, 'The Market for "Lemons": Quality Uncertainty and the Market Mechanism' (1970) 84 *Quarterly Journal of Economics* 488; W. M. Landes and R. A. Posner, 'Trademark Law: An Economic Perspective' (1987) 30 *Journal of Law and Economics* 265.

[3] G. B. Sutton, 'The Marketing of Ready Made Footwear in the Nineteenth Century: A Study of the Firm of C. & J. Clark' (1964) 6 *Business History* 97.

[4] E. Jones, 'Marketing the Nettlefold Woodscrew by GKN 1850–1939' in R. P. T Davenport-Hines (ed.), *Markets and Bagmen: Studies in the History of Marketing and British Industrial Performance, 1830–1939* (Aldershot: Gower, 1986) 136.

[5] C. Wilson, *The History of Unilever: A Study in Economic Growth and Social Change* vol. I (London: Cassell, 1954) 27–57.

[6] A. E. Musson, *Enterprise in Soap and Chemicals: Joseph Crosfield and Sons Ltd, 1815–1965* (Manchester: Manchester University Press, 1965) 104, 181.

[7] R. Fitzgerald, 'Rowntree and Market Strategy, 1897–1939' (1989) 18 *Business and Economic History* 47–8. It has also been suggested that Joseph Rowntree believed that, provided the mark was a reliable indicator of quality, there was no need to promote the mark through advertising: R. Fitzgerald, *Rowntree and the Marketing Revolution, 1862–1969* (Cambridge: Cambridge University Press, 1995) 69.

44   David M. Higgins

marks (or trade marks perceived to be valuable by their owners) had to be protected from any infringement, however slight or apparently inconsequential.[8] It has been recognized in the historiography that many prestigious firms frequently instigated court action to protect their marks from infringement. For example, Huntley & Palmer, whose biscuits were commonly known as READING BISCUITS launched a successful action for infringement against the Reading Biscuit Company.[9] In *Schweppes* v *Gibbens* (1904), the plaintiff initiated action claiming that the defendant's labels were calculated to deceive, but this action and the subsequent appeal were lost.[10] In *Wills* v *Watts* (1879), the plaintiff (one of England's premier cigarette manufacturers, W. D. & H. O. Wills) was granted a perpetual injunction against those who used the name BLACK JACK.[11] In another case, Lever Bros. successfully opposed the registration of PERFECTION by Crosfield on the grounds that this word was not distinctive but was a commendatory or descriptive word in common usage. This case, fought between 1907 and 1909, cost Crosfield's almost £13,000.[12]

Remaining with the pre-1914 period, the interest that business historians have traditionally shown in trade marks has slowly begun to change: instead of analysing the trade mark issues affecting specific firms, more attention has been devoted to understanding how these marks operated in the broader business and economic environment. Chandler's analysis of the growth and expansion of entrepreneurially successful firms operating across a wide range of consumer products – Cadbury Bros. in cocoa and chocolate confectionery, Huntley & Palmer and Peak Frean in biscuits, Lever Bros. in soap and cleaning products, Reckitt & Sons in starch and 'blue', and Schweppes in soft drinks – revealed the complex interaction between large-scale manufacturing, national and international distribution networks, and heavy advertising of packaged and branded products.[13] In a similar vein Wilkins argued that the separation between producer and consumer (a defining feature of the growth of the modern

---

[8] As I demonstrate later, the trade mark registration strategies of many entrepreneurs was to secure exclusivity of the mark originally registered and as many variants thereof as possible.
[9] T. A. B. Corley, *Quaker Enterprise in Biscuits: Huntley and Palmers of Reading, 1822–1972* (London: Hutchinson, 1972) 143–5; *Huntley & Palmer* v *The Reading Biscuit Company Ltd.* (1893) 10 RPC 277.
[10] D. A. Simmons, *Schweppes: The First 200 Years* (London: Springwood Books, 1983) 59.
[11] B. W. E. Alford, *W. D. & H. O. Wills and the Development of the UK Tobacco Industry, 1786–1965* (London: Methuen, 1973) 127.
[12] Musson, *Enterprise in Soap and Chemicals*, 190.
[13] A. D. Chandler, *Scale and Scope: The Dynamics of Industrial Capitalism* (Cambridge, Mass.: Harvard University Press, 1990) 262–8.

corporation) required that the name and reputation of the former obtain legal protection. In Wilkins' view, trade marks were an integral component of the growth of large-scale firms because this asset provided the means to realize economies of scale and scope.[14] Church's contributions to the history of advertising have emphasized the link between marketing and product development with particular importance being attached to branding strategies designed to encourage consumers to demand *specific* branded products.[15] Finally, in the alcoholic beverages industry, recent work has emphasized the relationship between brand protection and quality signals to consumers, and the importance of brands to different parts (producer, intermediary and retailer) of the supply chain.[16]

However, despite this volume of work, surprisingly little analysis of contemporary debates on trade mark issues has been conducted by business historians. Many of the legal issues covered in this evidence, for example the costs of obtaining relief pre-1875, the constituents of a trade mark, the signs and other indicia that could be registered as trade marks, and the relationship between passing-off and trade mark infringement, were of critical importance to the branding and advertising strategies of firms in the nineteenth century.[17] In the remainder of this section two topics covered in the contemporary evidence of particular interest to business historians are discussed. First, what insight is provided by the evidence given before the Select Committee of 1862[18] on the export performance of British firms? Second, how did the separation of production from distribution affect trade mark issues?

[14] M. Wilkins, 'The Neglected Intangible Asset: The Influence of the Trade Mark on the Rise of the Modern Corporation' (1992) 34 *Business History* 68, 92. For a dissenting view, see D. M. Higgins and G. Tweedale, 'Asset or Liability? Trade Marks in the Sheffield Cutlery and Tool Trades' (1995) 37 *Business History* 1.

[15] R. Church, 'New Perspectives on the History of Products, Firms, Marketing and Consumers in Britain and the United States Since the Mid-Nineteenth Century' (1999) 52 *Economic History Review* 405; R. Church, 'Advertising Consumer Goods in Nineteenth-Century Britain: Reinterpretations' (2000) 53(4) *Economic History Review* 621. Although Church is correct to emphasize the positive advantages of branding – for example, maintaining reputation and charging premium prices – he has overlooked the fact that these benefits can only be internalized when an individual firm has exclusive rights to a particular trade mark.

[16] J. Simpson, 'Selling to Reluctant Drinkers: The British Wine Market, 1860–1914' (2004) 57 *Economic History Review* 80; P. Duguid, 'Developing the Brand: The Case of Alcohol, 1800–1880' (2003) 4 *Enterprise and Society* 405.

[17] Aspects of the evidence given before various Select Committees are discussed later in this chapter. See also L. Bently, Chapter 1 of this volume, 3–41.

[18] *Report from the Select Committee on Trade Marks Bill, and Merchandize Marks Bill* (hereafter, *Select Committee*, 1862).

The export performance of British industry between 1870 and 1914 has generated a substantial literature.[19] It has been argued that poor export competitiveness in an increasingly hostile trading environment unduly affected Britain's rate of growth and a host of factors have been used to explain this poor performance. A common assumption has been that British manufacturers were immune from foreign competition until the industrialization of Germany and the USA. For example, in 2003 it was claimed: 'After all, in 1870 British industry still did not really face much strong competition in the international marketplace for manufactures.'[20] However, the evidence given before the Select Committee of 1862 makes it abundantly clear that many manufacturers experienced intense foreign competition prior to this date, much of which was 'unfair': that is, it involved the misappropriation of British trade marks. Many British marks were so highly valued abroad that they were subject to deliberate and wide-spread copying, often by the simple expedient of direct imitation, which resulted in lost sales.[21] The practice which generated most complaint was that foreign manufacturers placed reputable British marks on their lowest quality output and reserved their own marks for their best-quality productions. William Brittain, a commercial traveller for the Sheffield firm William Hall, stated of his journeys through Prussia and other German states, 'I have seen articles bearing the names of the most respectable Sheffield houses, and their corporate marks, and sold as genuine, which were of bad quality and which must inevitably injure the reputation of the manufacturers whose names they bore.'[22] Robert Bartleet, a needle manufacturer in Redditch, reported that,

our reputation has been considerably damaged in some markets: in fact, I may say utterly destroyed, in consequence of the German manufacturers putting our name and label, or precise imitations of them both, upon the very commonest goods they manufacture, although those names and marks of ours represented the very best quality that we made. The consequence was, that in some foreign countries purchasers concluded that they were buying our genuine manufactures, and they found them extremely bad, and we have entirely lost the trade in them.[23]

---

[19] For a recent evaluation, see, for example, C. Knick Harley, 'Trade, 1870–1919: From Globalisation to Fragmentation' in R. Floud and P. Johnson (eds.), *The Cambridge Economic History of Modern Britain*, vol. II: *Economic Maturity, 1860–1939* (Cambridge: Cambridge University Press, 2004) 168–76.

[20] A. Thompson and G. Magee, 'A Soft Touch? British Industry, Empire Markets, and the Self-Governing Dominions, c.1870–1914' (2003) 56 *Economic History Review* 711.

[21] *Select Committee*, 1862, Q.9; Q. 939; Q. 2461.

[22] Ibid. Q. 409.   [23] Ibid. Q. 939.

Consequently, British marks were no longer reliable as guarantors of quality, while the relative standing of foreign manufacturers was improved.[24] Matters were exacerbated by the high profit margins that could be earned from misrepresentation: premiums of between 20 and 400 per cent were reported.[25] Although only a limited number of firms were seriously affected by trade mark infringement in foreign countries, the evidence indicates that all of these firms were successful in establishing an unrivalled reputation for quality which was communicated by their trade marks.[26] It is also evident that when these firms lost markets or market shares prior to 1870, much of this appears to have been attributable to fraud, not necessarily lack of competitiveness.[27]

The separation between production and distribution of manufactures has also figured prominently in debates on the poor performance of British industry between 1870 and 1914. It has been recognized that the representative British firm was too small to be directly responsible for its own sales and marketing in foreign markets. Consequently, the majority of British firms were heavily reliant on independent merchants.[28] It has been alleged that this separation imposed a vertically disintegrated

---

[24] Ibid. Q.9; Q. 32; Q. 35; Qs. 295–6; Q. 409; Qs. 419–20; Q. 700; Q. 941; Q. 1935; Q. 2461. Thomas Coxon representing Bass reported that, in India, Bass's labels were placed on bottles containing inferior beers. Ibid. Q. 2535. Growing international competition in manufactures, first from Germany, and then from the United States, intensified British complaints about underhand practices. See, for example, R. J. S. Hoffman, *Great Britain and the German Trade Rivalry, 1875–1914* (New York: Russel and Russel, 1964); C. Bucheim, 'Aspects of XIXth Century Anglo-German Trade Rivalry Reconsidered' (1981) 10 J. European Economic History 273–89. Among contemporary works on Anglo-German trade rivalry which caught the public imagination, perhaps the most famous was E. E. Williams, *Made in Germany* (London: Heinemann, 1896).

[25] *Select Committee*, 1862, Q. 328; Q. 409; Q. 1936; Qs. 2467–8.

[26] James Coats of J. &. P Coats, thread manufacturers, reported that his company had secured over 100 injunctions in the United States against parties imitating their trade marks: ibid. Q. 1589.

[27] This is not to claim that Britain's loss of export markets generally was attributable to unfair competition. Evidence given before the Select Committee of 1862, indicates that, at least in the Sheffield trades, a distinction was made between fraudulent competition (based on false marking) and 'cheap competition' (foreign goods sold below British prices). The former practice was most feared by Sheffield manufacturers because they believed their products were unsurpassable in terms of quality. In other words, their products did not compete directly with lower-quality German products. In effect, protection of trade marks was thought to provide insulation against low-quality competition: ibid. Qs. 359–60; Q. 366; Qs. 418–20; Qs. 704–10. However, as Tweedale has noted, the extensive involvement of Sheffield manufacturers in trade and merchandise mark issues blinded them to the fact that 'German success was not so much due to their unscrupulous techniques as to more efficient production and marketing': G. Tweedale, *Steel City: Entrepreneurship, Strategy, and Technology in Sheffield, 1743–1993* (Oxford: Oxford University Press, 1995) 175–6.

[28] P. L. Payne, *British Entrepreneurship in the Nineteenth Century* (London: Macmillan, 1974) 54.

48   David M. Higgins

structure on British industry which meant that the maximum benefits of large-scale, high-throughput production were unobtainable. The effect of this was that unit costs of production were unnecessarily high with damaging consequences for the long-run competitiveness of British manufacturing.[29] However, important trade mark issues caused by this separation – all well documented in the contemporary official evidence – have been overlooked. As I demonstrate below, in the case of trade marks, there is ample evidence that independent merchants exercised a deleterious effect on the reputation of British manufacturers.[30]

One problem was that British merchants were undermining the reputation that particular manufacturers had established in their own marks by demanding that other British manufacturers stamp the established manufacturers' marks on their output.[31] It was claimed that merchants were, at best, indifferent to the quality of the manufactures they exported, or that they deliberately sought to undermine reputable marks by placing them on inferior products.[32] This automatically raised questions about the extent to which the name or mark of a dealer, compared to that of the manufacturer, acted as a quality guarantee.[33] Concern was expressed that by imposing their own marks on output merchants were acquiring some of the goodwill that would have been attributable to the manufacturer had his marks appeared on the goods it made.[34] This practice was thought to be particularly harmful to reputable manufacturers.[35] In the watch-making industry the viability of firms was threatened: here it was the custom for the retailer to insist that his name and address were marked, not those of the manufacturer.[36]

---

[29] Doubts remain about the extent to which the heterogeneity of British domestic and export markets permitted the adoption of mass-production methods.

[30] In the penultimate section I indicate that this separation prevented the introduction of legislation which might have prevented misleading geographical indications of origin.

[31] *Select Committee*, 1862, Q. 998; Q. 1003; Q. 1007; Qs. 2223–4; *Special Report from the Select Committee on Merchandise Marks Act (1862) Amendment Bill 203* (1887) 10 *Parliamentary Papers* 357 (hereafter, *Select Committee*, 1887), Qs. 2356–7.

[32] *Select Committee*, 1887, Qs. 2196–8. It was stated that merchants built up trade by placing reputable marks on output produced by quality producers. Once the trade in products bearing these marks was established, merchants would then contract new manufacturers to place the original marks on lower-quality output. Until this quality debasement was discovered, merchants made substantial profits. This practice was possible because merchants used 'blind' names and marks: *Select Committee*, 1887, Qs. 4745–54.

[33] *Select Committee*, 1887, Qs. 2246–8; *Report from the Select Committee on Merchandise Marks Act, 1887* (1890), (hereafter, *Select Committee*, 1890), Qs. 1306–9.

[34] *Select Committee*, 1862, Qs. 1094–5.   [35] *Select Committee*, 1887, Q. 664.

[36] Irrespective of the quality-debasement issues discussed above, this custom of retailers ensured that potential customers could not go direct to the manufacturer and it simultaneously increased their bargaining power over manufacturers: ibid. Qs. 1570–8.

If the manufacturer refused, he lost orders.[37] More generally it was feared that merchants were responsible for quality debasement of British manufactures, a direct result of the competitive structure of British manufacturing.[38] This latter problem was acutely felt by Manchester merchants in the Lancashire cotton textile industry. Manchester witnesses argued that the existing system allowed merchants to register marks which bore a close resemblance to reputable marks already on the Register. The practice developed by which unscrupulous merchants placed orders with Lancashire textile firms to export inferior wares bearing marks closely resembling the reputable mark.[39] A further problem arose when products did not bear a trade mark: what effect would be conveyed to the consumer if a merchant marked his UK name and address upon foreign manufactured products imported for sale in the UK?[40]

Was the Trade Marks Registration Act of 1875 a success?

The key provisions of the Trade Marks Registration Act 1875, relating to registration as a means of establishing property in a trade mark and as a precondition for instigating defence against infringement have already been discussed. Judging by the number of trade mark registrations which followed the 1875 Act, it does appear that businessmen responded enthusiastically. Data on total annual registration of trade marks, 1882–1914, are shown in Figure 2.1, from which a number of trends are apparent. First, there was a rapid increase in registrations between 1882 and 1890, when annual registrations increased from 2,563 to 6,014. Thereafter, there was an equally pronounced decline and trough. In fact the number of registrations achieved in 1890 (6,014) was not exceeded

---

[37] Ibid. Q. 1570; Q. 1578; Qs. 1627–8.
[38] Ibid. Qs. 4775–8; *Report of the Committee Appointed by the Board of Trade to Inquire into the Duties, Organisation, and Arrangements of the Patent Office*, C. 5350, 1888 (hereafter, *Report*, 1888), Q. 1598; Q. 1605.
[39] *Report*, 1888, Qs. 102–3; Qs. 202–3; Q. 1599; Q. 1605; Q. 1610; Q. 3274; Qs. 3255–7; Q. 4252; *Select Committee*, 1890, Q. 4171; Q. 4181; Q. 4188; Q. 4243; Q. 4248; Q. 4299.
[40] *Select Committee*, 1887, Qs. 2120–32. A number of possible factors can be used to explain this particular practice: for example, foreign manufacturers were persuaded by British import merchants not to mark their output; alternatively, foreign manufactures were marked and imported to Britain, but subsequently British marks or other British indicia were substituted for the original marks.

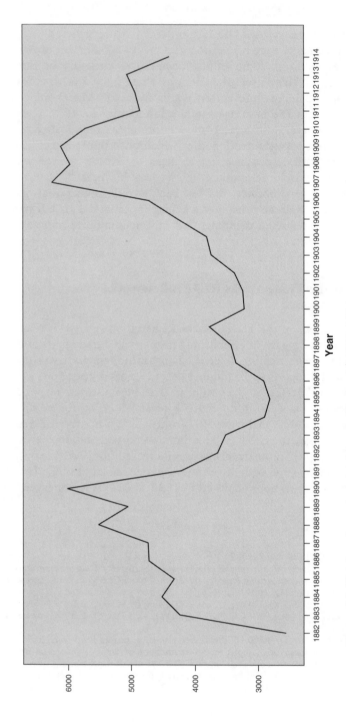

Figure 2.1 Total trade mark registrations in England,* 1882–1914.

* Includes registrations by foreign companies.

Source: calculated from *Reports of the Comptroller-General of Patents, Designs and Trade Marks* (various issues).

until 1907. Thereafter, the annual number of registrations, 1907–14, averaged 5,418.[41]

It is useful to examine the extent to which the fifty trade mark classes during our period varied in trade mark intensity because this provides evidence to business historians of the importance of trade marks to firms in these industries. Trade mark intensity is a measure of the extent to which the trade mark registrations of a particular class over a given period are greater or less than the mean registration for all classes over the same period. This is achieved by calculating the class means for the period 1882–1914. The class means are defined as: $\bar{TI}_i = \dfrac{\sum_t TI_{it}}{34}$, where $\bar{TI}_i$ is the mean number of registrations for a given class, 1882–1914, and where the term on the right-hand side is the mean registration for all classes over the same period.[42] The average trade mark intensity for all trade mark classes for the period 1882–1914 was 86.11. Those classes which can be considered most trade mark intensive (because their class means exceeded 86.11) are shown in Table 2.1.

Table 2.1 indicates that industries supplying consumer products were the most trade-mark-intensive during our period. It is well known that in this period significant changes occurred in retail and distribution and in the production of a wide range of consumer goods. Perhaps the classic statement of these trends was made by Wilson who commented: 'From machine to shop there flowed the branded, packaged, standardised, advertised products newly characteristic of this urbanised, industrialised

[41] The data used in this chapter are taken from the *Report of the Comptroller-General of Patents, Designs and Trade Marks*. Yearly data on registration begins in 1882. This series does not, therefore, include the rapid rise in registrations immediately following the 1875 Act. The trends in registrations shown in Figure 2.1 are not easily explained. The rapid rise, 1882–90, and decline, 1890–5, are perhaps to be expected given the pent-up demand for registration. Macroeconomic factors, such as the rate of growth of Gross Domestic Product (GDP), appear to be negatively correlated with the trends in registration. For example, between 1890 and 1895, when registrations declined precipitously, the rate of growth of GDP increased from 1.6 per cent p.a. during 1882–9, to 2.2 per cent p.a. during 1889–99. Between 1899 and 1906–7, when registrations increased rapidly, GDP growth rates declined from 2.2 per cent p.a., to 1.4 per cent p.a. Thereafter, registrations declined, but the rate of GDP growth increased to 1.7 per cent p.a.: N. Crafts, 'Long-run Growth' in R. Floud and P. Johnson (eds.), *The Cambridge Economic History of Modern Britain*, vol. II: *Economic Maturity, 1860–1939* (Cambridge: Cambridge University Press, 2004) 13. A negative relationship between registrations and the rate of growth of Gross National Product (GNP) has been observed for American data, although this relationship was not statistically significant: W. M. Landes and R. A. Posner, *The Economic Structure of Intellectual Property Law* (Cambridge, Mass.: Harvard University Press, 2003) 252.

[42] For a discussion of this methodology, see D. M. Higgins and T. J. James, *The Economic Importance of Trade Marks in the UK (1973–1992): A Preliminary Investigation* (London: The Intellectual Property Institute, 1996).

Table 2.1 *Highly trade-mark-intensive classes, 1882–1914*[1]

Class	Class mean	Industries covered by class
42	537	Substances used as food
45	313	Tobacco
3	262	Chemical substances for use in medicine, etc.
50	256	Miscellaneous goods
43	247	Fermented liquors and spirits
38	235	Articles of clothing
24	220	Cotton piece goods
13	174	Metal goods not included in other classes
48	165	Perfumery, etc.
39	138	Paper (except paper-hangings), stationery, etc.
1	136	Chemical substances used in manufactures, etc.
2	99	Chemical substances used in agriculture, etc.
23	93	Cotton yarn and sewing cotton
34	87	Cloths and stuffs of wool, Worsted or hair

[1] Refer to footnote 41.
Source: calculated from *Report of the Comptroller-General of Patents, Designs and Trade Marks* (various issues).

society that was setting itself new patterns and standards of social life.'[43] It should be apparent from Table 2.1 that *registered* trade marks played a crucial role in this consumer boom.

The evidence in Table 2.2 demonstrates that many of these trade marks had considerable longevity: 63.3 per cent of trade marks first registered between 1876 and 1900 were renewed after fourteen years, and 52.2 per cent of trade marks first registered between 1876 and 1886 were renewed after twenty-eight years.[44] Indeed, many of the most famous trade marks which are current were registered during this period, for example: BISTO, BOVRIL, CADBURY, GLENLIVET, GUINNESS, HOVIS, OXO, ROLLS ROYCE and WEDGWOOD.[45]

Another interesting feature of registrations during this period was the registration by the same proprietor of very similar marks in the same trade mark class, for example the registrations J. S. FRY & SONS, FRY,

[43] C. Wilson, 'Economy and Society in Late Victorian Britain' (1965) 18 *Economic History Review* 191.
[44] Unfortunately, no further data were published by the Comptroller-General on renewals.
[45] *Trade Marks Journal* (*TMJ*) 924 (11 December 1895) 1030; *TMJ* 1422 (28 June 1905) 818; *TMJ* 438 (18 August 1886) 816; *TMJ* 2 (10 May 1876) 48; *TMJ* 590 (17 July 1889) 535; *TMJ* 929 (15 January 1896) 63; *TMJ* 1483 (29 August 1906) 1201; *TMJ* 1561 (26 February 1908) 300; *TMJ* 14 (2 August 1876) 325.

Table 2.2 *Duration of registered trade marks*

Year of first registration	% renewed after 14 years		% renewed after 28 years	
1876	(1890)	70	(1904)	56
1878	(1892)	66.5	(1906)	50
1880	(1894)	60.5	(1908)	47
1882	(1896)	68	(1910)	56
1884	(1898)	65	(1912)	50
1886	(1900)	68	(1914)	54
1888	(1902)	66		
1890	(1904)	61		
1892	(1906)	60		
1894	(1908)	61		
1896	(1910)	58		
1898	(1912)	59		
1900	(1914)	60		

Source: calculated from *Report of the Comptroller-General of Patents, Designs, and Trade Marks* (various issues).

FRY & SONS and FRY'S MILK CHOCOLATE.[46] One company which was exceptionally prolific in this respect was Bass & Co. Consider the following registrations: BASS & CO'S PALE ALE; BASS & CO'S; BASS & CO'S BURTON ALE; BASS & CO'S NO.1 STRONG ALE; BASS & CO'S NO.2 STRONG ALE; BASS & CO'S NO.3 STRONG ALE; BASS & CO'S NO. 3B STRONG ALE; BASS & CO'S NO.4 BURTON ALE; BASS & CO'S NO.5 BURTON ALE; BASS & CO'S NO.6 BURTON ALE; BASS & CO'S STOUT; BASS & CO'S DOUBLE STOUT; BASS & CO'S EXTRA STOUT; BASS & CO'S PORTER.[47]

It is apparent from these examples that manufacturers sought jealously to avoid any possible infringement of their marks. The registration of very similar marks by the same proprietor can be viewed as a defensive strategy to prevent rival manufacturers acquiring the reputation established in a particular mark.[48] This strategy became especially important because, following the Trade Marks Registration Act 1875, registration provided prima facie evidence of exclusive rights to the mark. If a person succeeded

[46] The first three of these marks were advertised in *TMJ* 454 (8 December 1886) 1288, the last in *TMJ* 1849 (3 September 1913) 1408.
[47] *TMJ* 1 (3 May 1876) 24; *TMJ* 278 (25 April 1883) 233; *TMJ* 396 (28 October 1885) 1021.
[48] These registrations would have allayed concerns that another trader would use a similar mark and/or that they would register a similar mark. In the former case, the Trade Marks Registration Act (1875) made it easier for owners of registered marks to bring actions for infringement, and in the latter case, publication of marks prior to their registration allowed owners of registered marks to lodge a complaint with the Comptroller.

in registering a mark which *might* deceive consumers as to the true origin of the products, considerable harm would be done to those who had first registered the mark. Although the 1875 Act met many of the requirements demanded by businessmen, its enforcement was to generate considerable litigation. One topic which proved contentious was the extent to which trade marks denoted *geographical* origin. This topic is of particular interest to business historians because, although geographical indicia were not capable of registration as trade marks, the products of many firms were identified by geographical indicia or had geographical connotations.[49]

From a businessman's perspective it would have been a relatively easy exercise to begin manufacturing in a locality the reputation of which had already been established by incumbent firms.[50] By such means the new entrant could hope to sell his products with geographical indicia and thereby benefit from the reputation of the locality and its established firms. The fundamental legal issue here was not that a misleading use of a geographical name had been made by the new entrant but that the geographical appellation was calculated to deceive: that is, the new entrant represented his products as those of the established manufacturers in the locality.

Numerous cases exist of this practice between 1875 and 1914, and in all of these cases the incumbent firms had to establish that their use of a geographical appellation had acquired a secondary meaning: specifically, that use of the appellation was understood in the trade and by consumers as indicating their products alone. In cases where established firms were able to prove secondary meaning one important line of defence was to demonstrate that the reputation a locality had achieved for a particular product was due to the activities of one established firm. In the case of *Huntley & Palmer* v *The Reading Biscuit Company, Ltd* (1893), it was established that 'the only reputation of the town of Reading in the biscuit trade had been acquired by, and was in connection with, the trade of the Plaintiffs, and of no one else'.[51] In other successful cases it was not even necessary for the plaintiff to establish that his products were produced in a particular locality. In *C. T. Brock & Co. 's Crystal Palace Fireworks Ltd*

---

[49] The related theme, fraudulent use of geographical appellations, attracted sustained criticism by businessmen after the Trade Marks Registration Act 1875, and is discussed in the penultimate section of this chapter.

[50] In *Wotherspoon* v *Currie* (1871–2) LR 5 HL 508, the defendant had gone to Glenfield for the purpose of using that name. In *Braham* v *Beachim* (1878) LR 7 Ch D 848, the defendants were restrained from using the name 'Radstock Colliery Proprietors' until they acquired a colliery in Radstock.

[51] 10 RPC 277. Similarly, *Worcester Royal Porcelain Company* v *Locke & Co. The Same* v *Rhodes* (1902) 19 RPC 479, and *Montgomery* v *Thompson* (1891) 7 RPC 367.

v *James Pain & Sons* (1911), it was admitted that the plaintiff did not produce his fireworks in Crystal Palace. The plaintiffs were successful because they proved that as a result of having the exclusive right to give firework displays at the Palace between 1866 and 1910, the term 'Crystal Palace' as applied to fireworks, 'has acquired a secondary meaning, and has come to denote exclusively the fireworks manufactured and sold by the said firm of C. T. Brock & Co.'.[52] The principle of secondary meaning extended to export markets.[53]

Geographical Indications: from individual to community protection

The previous section has shown that businessmen responded enthusiastically to the Trade Marks Registration Act 1875. Registration of trade marks was important for facilitating legal action not only in the domestic market, but also abroad. As far as foreign infringement was concerned, international reciprocity of trade mark rights followed the Trade Marks Registration Act 1875. An International Convention for the Protection of Industrial Property (hereafter, Convention) was concluded in Paris on 20 March 1883. Belgium, Brazil, Spain, France, Guatemala, Italy, Holland, Portugal, Salvador, Serbia and Switzerland, were the first signatories to this Convention, followed by Britain in 1884.[54] Article II of the Convention provided that the citizens in each of the contracting states would enjoy the same rights in other contracting states as those states currently granted to their own subjects;[55] Article VI stated that 'Every trade mark duly registered in the country of origin shall be admitted for registration, and protected in the form originally registered in all the other countries of the Union',[56] and Article IX indicated that 'all goods illegally

---

[52] *C. T. Brock & Co.'s Crystal Palace Fireworks Ld v James Pain & Sons* (1911) 28 RPC, 462. The appeal was dismissed: *C. T. Brock & Co.'s Crystal Palace Fireworks Ltd v James Pain & Sons* (1911) 28 RPC 697.

[53] *Price's Patent Candle Company Ltd v Ogston and Tenant Ltd* (1909) 26 RPC 797. Where secondary meaning could not be established, the Plaintiffs were unable to prevent rival firms using similar geographical appellations to describe their products. See, for example, *Whitstable Oyster Fishery Company v Hayling Fisheries, Ltd, and George Tabor* (1900) 17 RPC 461, and 18 RPC 434; *Hopton Wood Stone Firms Ltd v Gething* (1910) 27 RPC 605; *Wolff and Son v Nopitsch and Others* (1900) 17 RPC 321 and (1901) 18 RPC 27.

[54] *International Convention for the Protection of Industrial Property*, C. 4043 (1884). Hereafter, *International Convention*. For a full discussion of the history of the international conventions, see S. P. Ladas, *Patents, Trade marks, and Related Rights: National and International Protection* (Cambridge, Mass.: 1975).

[55] *International Convention* 7.

[56] Ibid. By Art. VIII, however, trade names did not have to be registered to secure international protection.

bearing a trade mark or trade name may be seized on importation into those States of the Union where this mark or name has a right to legal protection'.[57] The Convention and its subsequent revisions – Brussels, 1900, and Washington, 1911 – reinforced international commitment to trade mark protection. Nonetheless, the effectiveness of these Conventions, and the Trade Marks Registration Act 1875, were undermined by the rapid growth of another type of infringement – misleading geographical indications of origin (hereafter, GIs) – which generated considerable official interest.[58]

Professor Bently has already indicated that within our period there was considerable uncertainty as to what features constituted a trade mark and what relationship, if any, existed between a mark and the name of the place in which a business was situated. One aspect of this relationship which proved particularly difficult to resolve during our period was whether GIs should be accorded international protection. Whereas infringement of a trade mark affected only the reputation of the registered owner, abuse of GIs affected entire industries and communities.

Contemporaries recognized that a trade mark could refer to the place of origin (as distinct from trade origin),[59] but the official evidence was far from unanimous on whether GIs could be registered as trade marks. One factor was that many GIs had become generic terms denoting a particular method or style of manufacture. Thus, for example, it was recognized that 'cardigan' jackets were made in Leicester, not Cardigan; Kidderminster carpets were no longer made in Kidderminster but in Scotland and Yorkshire; 'Wilton' carpets were made in Halifax, not Wilton; 'Dutch' tapes were made in Manchester, not Holland; and French cambrics were made in the North of Ireland.[60]

Practices such as these raised the obvious problem that labelling an article with a false *place* of origin was different from giving an article a name which was a proper *description* of the article. The Herschell Committee recognized that, for some British industries, registration of GIs as trade marks was vital: for example, the use of terms such as

---

[57] Ibid.
[58] In addition to the Select Committees appointed in 1862, 1887 and 1890, to consider the general problem of merchandise marks infringement, other Select Committees were appointed to consider the problem in specific industries. See, for example, *Report from the Select Committee on Marking of Foreign Meat* (1893), and *Report and Special Report from the Select Committee on the Agricultural Produce (Marks) Bill* (1897). For a discussion of the malpractice discussed in these Reports, see D. M. Higgins, 'Mutton Dressed as Lamb? The Misrepresentation of Australian and New Zealand Meat in the British Market, c. 1890–1914' (2004) 44 *Australian Economic History Review* 161–84.
[59] L. Bently, Chapter 1 of this volume, 3–41.   [60] *Select Committee*, 1887, Qs. 3288–305.

'Glen' and 'Loch', in the Scotch whiskey industry.[61] This Committee recognized other problems in using geographical terms as trade marks. For example, the simple use of a place *qua* trade mark could not prevent its legitimate use if it was used as part of the address of a manufacturer in the same class of products.[62] Recognizing that considerable problems would arise if geographical words descriptive of the place of manufacture were registered, the most this Committee was prepared to concede was that 'geographical names ought only to be permitted where they clearly could not be regarded as indicative of the place of manufacture or sale'.[63]

Two further complications had to be addressed: unregistered marks were ineligible for protection in those countries which were signatories to the Convention; and British trade mark law did not permit registration of geographic appellations until 1905. Each is considered below.

As far as international misuse of GIs was concerned, Article X of the Convention stated that the provision for seizure on importation of all goods illegally bearing a trade mark or trade name 'shall apply to all goods falsely bearing the name of any locality as indication of the place of origin, when such indication is associated with a trade name of a fictitious character or assumed with a fraudulent intention'.[64] However, the two restrictions imposed in this Article were thought to be very unsatisfactory from a British perspective because the Merchandise Marks Act 1887 provided that goods bearing false indications of origin *alone* would be seized.[65] The British Foreign Office, aided by the Cutlers' Company, exerted considerable diplomatic pressure to alter this weakness in Article X, but these were ultimately unsuccessful during our period.[66] The asymmetry generated by the passing of the Merchandise Marks Act 1887 was quickly recognized by British contemporaries. For example, in a Memorial to the Secretary of State for Foreign Affairs, the Cutlers' Company complained that 'while manufacturers, merchants and traders in this country are most properly prohibited from practices with reference to the marking of goods which before the passing of the Act of 1887 were

---

[61] *Report* 1888, Q. 1161.   [62] Ibid. Q. 905.   [63] Ibid. xi.
[64] *International Convention* 8.
[65] Merchandise Marks Act 1862, 25 & 26 Vict. c. 88, s. 7, s.; Merchandise Marks Act, 1887, 50 & 51 Vict. c. 28, s. 3(b).
[66] In fact, subsequent Conventions extended Art. X to cover 'dishonest competition', but no *specific* provision for misleading GIs was provided. Article X *bis* Treaty Series No. 15 (1902), *Additional Act Modifying the Industrial Property Convention of March 20, 1883*, Cd. 1084, 12; Article X *bis* Treaty Series No. 8 (1913), *International Convention for the Protection of Industrial Property Signed at Washington, Convention of March 20, 1883*, Cd. 6805, 113.

commonly adopted, their competitors are under no such restrictions, but can, and do, carry on such practices to the great detriment of the trade of this country'.[67]

One solution to these problems would have been to require that all imported products which had *no marking* were marked either with the indicia 'Made Abroad', or with a definite indication of origin,[68] but these suggestions were rejected. Indeed, such was the strength of feeling expressed on these points by merchants and manufacturers that the Select Committees of 1890 and 1897 reached opposite conclusions: the former Committee was not prepared to permit substitution of the term 'Made Abroad' in place of a definite indication of origin[69] but the latter Committee was prepared to recommend this change.

The reason why these Committees made different recommendations appears to be that attitudes towards protecting British interests hardened between 1890 and 1897. The Committee of 1890 was heavily influenced by Britain's obligations under the Convention, which had recently met at Rome in 1886, and Madrid in 1890. At these Conventions British delegates were urged to secure an amendment to Article X in order that false indications of origin alone became illegal. Although this proposal was generally well received, considerable diplomatic pressure continued to be applied,[70] and in these circumstances there was a reluctance unilaterally to introduce changes which threatened international agreement. It was recognized, for example, that use of 'Made Abroad' in place of a definite indication of origin would have been against the interests of each of the states which had acceded to the Convention.[71] Other witnesses believed that the imposition of compulsory marks of origin would jeopordize future international cooperation on misleading GIs.[72] In these circumstances, the Committee was keen to signal to other members of the Convention that British legislation had general applicability. Thus it was stated: 'your Committee would point out that the consumer is just as defrauded if he buys Swedish goods in the belief that they are German, or

---

[67] Inclosure No. 115, 7. *Miscellaneous No. 3* (1888), *Correspondence Relative to the Protection of Industrial Property*, C. 5521.

[68] *Select Committee*, 1890, Qs 2358–62; Q. 2382; Q. 3427; Q. 3432; Q. 3445; Q. 3507; Qs. 3692–3; Q. 3707; Qs. 3727–30; Q. 3738; Q. 3822; Q. 3856; Qs. 3887–9; Qs. 4496–8; *Report from the Select Committee on Merchandise Marks* (1897) (hereafter *Select Committee, 1897*), Qs. 58–9.

[69] *Select Committee*, 1890, iii–iv.

[70] For a further discussion of this activity, see D. M. Higgins, '"Made in Sheffield?": Trade Marks, the Cutlers' Company and the Defence of "Sheffield"' in C. Binfield and D. Hey (eds.), *Mesters to Masters: A History of the Company of Cutlers in Hallamshire*, (Oxford: Oxford University Press, 1997).

[71] *Select Committee*, 1890, iii–iv; Q. 4989.   [72] Ibid. Q. 846.

French wine in the belief that it is Spanish, as if he buys foreign goods in the belief that they are English'.[73]

However, seven years, later the desire to obey diplomatic niceties had waned considerably. The British proposal to amend Article X had still not been ratified, to the considerable irritation of the Board of Trade and the Foreign Office.[74] The Committee of 1897 recommended that the words 'Made abroad' should be substituted for a definite indication of origin. This Committee recognized that specification of a particular country of origin damaged the trade secrets of British merchants and dealers.[75] More fundamentally, though, this Committee was of the opinion that 'it is not right to fix British taxpayers with the cost of protecting the individual purchaser against possible deception as to the exact country of origin, other than the United Kingdom, and her Colonies and dependencies'.[76]

In any case, even if British attempts to alter Article X had succeeded, this would not have solved the problem of products being imported blank but subsequently falsely marked with misleading descriptions (often in the English language to convey the impression they were English).[77] Concern was also expressed that falsely marked products were being sent directly from Europe to third markets in which international reciprocity had not been agreed.[78] In other words, even if British legislation to permit registration of GIs (a vital prerequisite for protection under the Convention) had been introduced sooner, this would have had only a limited impact on the misuse of GIs.

---

[73] Ibid. iv. See also the evidence of Herbert Hughes, arguably Britain's leading authority on this topic, ibid, Qs. 4989–91.

[74] Inclosure No. 6, *Report of Departmental Committee of the Board of Trade and Foreign Office*: 'the Committee . . . recommend the British delegates be empowered, if they consider it desirable, to abstain . . . from taking any further part in the proceedings of the Conference in the event of the proposed British addition to Article X, coupled with an obligation to legislate, being rejected': (1890) *Papers and Correspondence Relative to the Recent Conference at Madrid on the Subject of Industrial Property and Merchandise Marks* C. 6023, 7.

[75] *Select Committee*, 1897, iv.

[76] *Select Committee*, 1897, iv.

[77] *Select Committee*, 1890, Q. 37; Q. 118; Q. 190; Q. 195; Q. 197; Q. 334; Qs. 530–4; Qs. 2311–13; Qs. 2369–76; Q. 3872; Q. 4561; Qs. 4708–1; *Select Committee*, 1897, Qs. 43–5; Q. 48; Q. 745; Q. 860; Q. 867; Q. 922.

[78] These delays were especially annoying to the Cutlers' Company because 'it is in Germany that so much of the piracy of the name of "Sheffield" takes place while the United States is the principal market to which the spurious goods are sent': Inclosure No. 12, *Correspondence Relative to the Protection of Industrial Property*, C. 5521 (1888), Cutlers' Company to the Earl of Iddesleigh.

A Select Committee was appointed in 1905 to consider a Bill introduced by Fletcher Moulton and others[79] in the same year to extend the provisions of the Trade Marks Registration Act 1875. This Committee agreed that there should be greater latitude in the words that could be registered as trade marks, especially as domestic registration was a vital prerequisite for international protection under the Convention.[80] In the case of GIs it was recognized that many geographical marks made good trade marks, provided that use of such marks did not 'prevent others from using them honestly and truly as geographical words indicating the place of origin'.[81] Accordingly, the Trade Marks Act 1905 provided that such marks could be registered.[82] After 1905, GIs could be registered as trade marks under the Certification Mark scheme and, by virtue of registration, they would have been afforded protection under the Convention. Nonetheless, from a British perspective during our period it appears that the Merchandise Marks Acts were the most suitable mechanism for protecting GIs.[83]

Conclusions

In this brief commentary it is impossible to discuss the myriad legal issues raised by Professor Bently. To this commentator, at least, it seems that misuse of trade marks and the ensuing legal remedies followed a predictable trajectory: attempts by individual firms to protect their own marks in domestic and foreign markets were quickly followed by a much broader campaign – involving industries and communities – to protect GIs. This progression is explained by the way in which the law governing trade marks evolved. As Professor Bently has demonstrated, during the nineteenth century the definition of a trade mark excluded geographical

[79] Bill 76, 'A Bill to consolidate and amend the Law relating to Trade Marks'. In addition to Moulton, the other sponsors of the Bill were: Messrs. Butchers, Cawley, Cripps, Eve and Robson, and Sir Albert Rollit. A number of other Bills to amend the Trade Marks Registration Act 1875 had been introduced around the same time, for example: Bill 79, 1901; Bill 128, 1902; Bill 174, 1903; Bill 53, 1904.
[80] *Report and Special report from the Select Committee on the Trade Marks Bill* (1905).
[81] Ibid. Q. 1446.
[82] 5 Edw. 7. c. 15, s. 62. By this Act, and subsequently, GIs became known as 'certification marks'. It should be emphasized that certification marks cover much more than geographic indicia and include, for example, material, mode of manufacture, quality, accuracy or other characteristics. The provisions for examination and certification contained in this section were relaxed by the Trade Marks Act 1919, 9 & 10 Geo. 5 c. 79.
[83] For example, describing alcoholic beverages as port or Madeira when they were not the produce of Portugal or Madeira was deemed to be a false trade description under the Merchandise Marks Act. I am grateful to Professor Bently for this observation.

names.[84] The consequence of this was that those trying to protect the reputation of particular regions from misrepresentation had to explore other avenues, principal among which was the International Convention for the Protection of Industrial Property. From a business history perspective, it is also apparent that demands for better trade and merchandise mark protection were influenced by the type of infringement. Given the rapidly changing economic environment within which business operated during the nineteenth century, it was inevitable that legal remedies for infringement were always one step behind.

[84] L. Bently, Chapter 1 of this volume, 3–41.

Part II

Current positive law in the EU and the USA

3   Between a sign and a brand: mapping
     the boundaries of a registered trade mark
     in European Union trade mark law

Jennifer Davis

In 2004, the easyGroup, best known for its airline, easyJet, announced the launch of a mobile phone service, easyMobile. The service was widely advertised using the colour orange, which had traditionally been associated with the Group's many other 'easy' products and services. In February 2005, Orange Personal Communications Ltd (Orange), which also provides a mobile phone service associated with the colour orange, initiated proceedings for passing off[1] and registered trade mark infringement against easyGroup. Orange is the proprietor of a large number of registered trade marks (both UK and Community trade marks) for a broad variety of goods and services.[2] Its registered marks include the word ORANGE, the colour orange and marks combining both word and colour. In the UK it had registered the colour orange to be used, *inter alia*, with electronic communications apparatus and instruments. Orange alleged that the association of the colour orange with easyMobile would confuse customers as to the source of the latter's service. But Orange made it clear that its concerns went beyond possible customer confusion. It was also concerned that by using the colour orange on its mobile service, easyMobile would damage the Orange 'brand'. According to a spokesman, 'Our brand, and the rights associated with it, are extremely important to us. In the absence of any firm commitment from Easy [not to use orange], we have been left with no choice but to start an action for trademark infringement and passing off.'[3] Orange has valued its brand as worth 6.6 billion Euros.[4] Little wonder that, as it told the press, it was 'prepared to "do what it has to" to protect its brand and

---

[1] Also known as the law of unregistered trade marks.
[2] E1079169. Including electrical and electronic communications and telecommunications apparatus and instruments, food and drink, cosmetics, clothing and financial services.
[3] J. Best, 'Orange and easyMobile go to war over colour', 21 February 2005. http://networks.silicon.com/mobile/0.39024665.39128035.00.htm.
[4] www.orange.com, 3 March 2006.

image'.[5] In the same year that Orange began its dispute with easyGroup, the world experienced the first 'orange revolution' in the Ukraine. Large numbers of Ukrainians hoping to unseat the Prime Minister Yanukovych took to the streets wearing orange and under orange banners.[6] Since the Ukrainian election, the colour orange and the idea of an 'orange revolution' have become widely associated with other 'people-led' opposition movements. Furthermore, orange has continued to be the preferred colour for identifying orange juice containers in retail outlets.

The registration of a trade mark endows the proprietor with a monopoly. Yet it is clear that registration entitles Orange to control the use of the word ORANGE and the colour orange only in certain situations. In other words, it has only a limited monopoly over these trade marks. It is the purpose of this chapter to examine how the law of registered trade marks has developed through both statute and case law to demarcate the boundaries of this monopoly. It will do so by examining registered trade marks as both signs and as brands. At its simplest, registration is designed to protect a trade mark when used in the course of trade as a badge of origin in relation to specified goods and services – such as, for example, the use of the colour orange for mobile phone services. But of course that same mark may have a host of other meanings. One concern of this chapter will be to examine how the present law of trade marks shapes the boundaries of protection by excluding certain meanings of the sign which is the subject of registration from falling within the registered trade mark monopoly. The question of which meanings should be excluded has been the subject of considerable controversy, both judicial and academic. It is fair to say, however, that the public interest behind such exclusions is that these are meanings which should be available for other traders to use. Thus, this chapter will seek to examine how the trade mark monopoly has been limited, in the interest not of the proprietor, but of his competitors.

A second concern of this chapter will be to examine the extent to which the trade mark monopoly has come to encompass not only the trade mark's role as a badge of origin but also wider brand values which the trade mark may embody, however defined. For example, in the case of Orange, it is clear that the company sees its use of the word ORANGE and the colour orange as conveying to the public something more than an indication of origin for its goods. Orange (embodied in both word and

---

[5] J. Day, 'Easy brand's future may not be orange', *Guardian*, 16 August 2004. Interestingly, according to the founder of easyGroup, Stelios Haji-Ioannou, its legal team, by what 'may be an oversight', had neglected to register its characteristic 'brand' colours (both orange and black) as a trade mark.

[6] Orange was the party colour of his opponent, Yushchenko, who subsequently was elected Prime Minister.

colour) is also its 'brand'. And, as a brand, it conveys a host of other meanings. Thus, according to its website, the brand ORANGE has become 'synonymous with making mobile communications an intuitive part of every day life'. It is 'friendly, honest, straightforward' and 'dynamic' and it is 'one brand that stands for the same things in every country in which we operate'.[7] This chapter will examine the extent to which the present trade mark monopoly protects brand values. The question of whether trade mark registration should protect those meanings of the mark which go beyond its role as a badge of origin has also been a subject of debate. In this case, however, the interests which lie behind such wider protection are not those of the public or his competitors, but rather of the trade mark proprietor.

Section 1 of this chapter will begin by looking at the registered trade mark as a sign. It will point out that the substantive law of trade marks[8] does not define 'a sign', as such, but does make clear that a trade mark must consist of a sign which is capable of acting as a badge of origin and of graphic representation. This section will examine both of these requirements. It will suggest that the way in which these requirements have been interpreted by the courts has meant that, potentially, a very broad spectrum of signs may be registered. Section 2 will then look at how the TM Directive has been interpreted to limit the category of registrable signs, by identifying those meanings of a sign which will be protected by registration and by defining those that will not. It will seek to locate the boundary which has been drawn by the courts between the trade mark as sign whose meanings remain in the public domain and the trade mark as a protected monopoly. Section 3 of this chapter will then go on consider the trade mark as a brand. It will suggest that, although widely used and understood in current marketing and indeed legal discourse, there is no agreed definition of a brand. Nonetheless, there has been pressure on the courts to expand the protection afforded by registration to encompass what are seen as brand values. This chapter will then go on to locate the boundary between a registered trade mark monopoly and a brand, and to suggest how it is changing. Finally, Section 4 of the chapter will suggest that the

[7] Apparently, Orange operates in seventeen countries and has 57 million customers.
[8] Trade mark law in the European Union is governed by the First Council Directive 89/104/ EEC of 21 December 1988 to approximate the laws of the Member States relating to trade marks (hereafter, TM Directive). There is also a community-wide trade mark, the Community Trade Mark (CTM). The CTM is governed by the Council Regulation (EC) No. 40/94 of 20 December 1993 on the Community Trade Mark (hereafter, TM Regulation). An application for a CTM is made to the Community trade mark office in Alicante (OHIM). The substantive law governing both national trade marks and the CTM is, in most important respects, the same. The final word in interpreting both the Directive and the Regulation lies with the European Court of Justice (ECJ).

manner in which the substantive law of trade marks has developed has failed to offer a positive definition of the registered trade mark monopoly. Rather, the courts have tended to proceed by identifying those meanings that registration excludes rather than includes. This chapter will conclude that it is both cause and consequence of this negative definition of the trade mark monopoly that, rather than being fixed by its legal definition, its shape has, in fact, changed over time and continues to do so. Not surprisingly, the direction of such change will reflect broader ideological shifts as to where the balance of the public interest lies between proprietors, competitors and the public more generally.

1   The registered trade mark as a sign

The TM Directive defines a trade mark. According to Article 2 of the Directive:[9] 'A trade mark may consist of any sign capable of being represented graphically particularly words, including personal names, designs, letters, numerals, the shape of goods or of their packaging, provided such signs are capable of distinguishing the goods of one undertaking from those of other undertakings.' The definition does not define a sign. It simply tells us what sorts of signs may be distinctive. It tells us that the sign must be capable of acting as a badge of origin. It also tells us that it must be capable of graphic representation and it sets out a range of signs which it will be assumed are capable of both.[10]

However, it is also important to note that the definition offered by Article 2 indicates what signs may constitute trade marks but not, necessarily, what trade marks will be registered. Article 3 of the Directive sets out grounds for refusal to register a trade mark.[11] Unsurprisingly, signs which cannot constitute a trade mark because they do not fulfil the requirements of Article 2

---

[9] Article 4 TM Regulation.

[10] From one point of view, the Directive's definition of a trade mark (rather than a sign) fits with the definition of a sign which was first suggested by Ferdinand de Saussure in his *Course in General Linguistics* (ed. C. Bally and A. Sechehaye with A. Riedlinger; trans. and annotated by R. Harris) (London: Duckworth, 1983) and which has become the basis for the development of semiotics. According to Saussure, a sign is made up of two components. The first is a signifier (which, in this case would be the subject of registration, whether it be a word, letter or shape of goods). A sign is also made up of the signified, which in the case of a registered trade mark would be the fact that we understand the signifier to mean that it is a badge of origin. We also know from semiotics that the relationship between the signified and the signifier may be arbitrary, that its meaning can change over time and that it can embody more than one meaning. See R. Harris and T. J. Taylor, *Landmarks in Linguistic Thought*, vol I: *The Western Tradition from Socrates to Saussure* (2nd edn, London: Routledge, 1997) 211–19.

[11] And also the grounds for finding a registered mark invalid.

will not be registered.[12] However, the Directive also recognizes a category of trade marks which, while capable of being represented graphically and of acting as a badge of origin, will only be registered if they are actually acting as a badge of origin in the marketplace. Thus, trade marks which are devoid of any distinctive character (Art. 3(1)(b)), trade marks which are descriptive (Art. 3(1)(c)),[13] and trade marks which are generic or customary in the trade (Art. 3(1)(d)) will not be registered unless through the use which is made of them they have acquired a distinctive character and are recognized by the public as a badge of origin.[14]

One preoccupation of the courts in interpreting the TM Directive has been to define those trade marks which are excluded from registration because they are descriptive or devoid of distinctive character. This issue will be examined in the following section. However, the courts have also found themselves faced with a precedent question: that is, what sorts of signs may be precluded from constituting trade marks because they do not fit the definition given in Article 2? In *Philips v Remington*,[15] the ECJ made it clear that no sign may be precluded from registration because it is, prima facie, incapable of acting as a badge of origin. It held that in principle all signs may either be distinctive *ab initio* and so registered or else be registered if they have acquired distinctive character through the use which is made of them.[16] The ECJ has also made it clear that what constitutes a sign which will be capable of distinguishing either inherently or because of the use made of it is an open-ended category. It held in *Sieckmann*[17] that the list of signs set out in Article 2 is 'not exhaustive'. It

---

[12] Article 3(1)(a) TM Directive; Art. 7(1)(a) TM Regulation.
[13] The actual wording is 'trade marks which consist exclusively of signs or indications which may serve, in trade, to designate the kind, quality, quantity, intended purpose, value, geographical origin, or the time of production of the goods or of rendering of the service; or other characteristics of the goods or service'.
[14] Article 7(1)(b)–(d) TM Regulation. There is a further category of signs and marks which will not be registered on public interest grounds even if they are acting as a badge of origin. These include functional shapes (Art. 3(1)(e)) and marks which offend against accepted principles of morality (Art. 3(1)(f)) and deceptive marks (Art. 3(1)(g)). For functional shape marks, see T. Hays, 'Distinguishing Use versus Functional Use: Three Dimensional Marks' in J. Phillips and I. Simons (eds.), *Trade Mark Use* (Oxford: Oxford University Press, 2005) 93.
[15] *Koninklijke Philips Electronics NV v Remington Consumer Products Ltd*, Case C-299/99 [2002] 2 CMLR 52, paras. 39–40. See J. Davis, 'European Trade Mark Law and the Enclosure of the Commons' (2002) 4 IPQ 362–3.
[16] Whether they will in fact go on to become distinctive may depend upon a number of factors including how likely it is that the average consumer for the goods will see them as a trade mark. This may be more difficult for signs which do not constitute 'traditional' trade marks such as the shape of the goods themselves. See discussion in Section 2 below.
[17] *Ralf Sieckmann v Deutsches Patent- und Markenamt*, Case C-273/00 [2003] CMLR 40 at paras. 44–5.

might also include signs, for example, 'which are not in themselves capable of being perceived visually, provided that they may be represented graphically'. Later, in *Libertel*,[18] the ECJ made it clear that single colours are also in principle capable of acting as a badge of origin although they may have little inherent capacity to do so.

Where a suggested mark has been deemed, by the ECJ, as not constituting a sign for the purposes of registration, this has been the case not because that mark was incapable of acquiring distinctive character but rather because it was not a 'sign' at all. The recent case of *Dyson* v *Registrar of Trade Marks* presents one of the very rare instances where the ECJ has considered this matter.[19] In this case, the vacuum cleaner manufacturer sought to register a mark in the UK which consisted of 'a transparent bin or collection chamber forming part of the external surface of the vacuum cleaner'. Dyson illustrated its application with a picture of two transparent bins, but made clear to the Trade Marks Registry that these illustrations were simply examples of their intended mark, which would in fact cover 'all conceivable shapes' of such bins.[20] According to the ECJ, the Dyson 'sign' was not a sign at all but a 'concept'. The ECJ defined a 'concept', unlike a sign, as not capable of being perceived by the five senses and appealing only to the imagination.[21] In this case, the ECJ held the subject matter of the application to be not a particular type of transparent collecting bin, but 'rather in a general and abstract manner', all the conceivable shapes of collecting bins.[22] It was a mere property of the product concerned rather than a sign. To allow the registration of such a concept would be to deprive other traders from competing in the same market using the same concept.

To date, more problematic for the courts than what constitutes a sign has been the second attribute of a trade mark, which is that it must consist of a sign which may be represented graphically. In *Sieckmann*,[23] the ECJ explained that the purpose of this provision is to achieve legal certainty. It is to ensure that the subject of registration is precisely defined both for the benefit of the authorities who will register the sign and also for other traders, in particular competitors of the proprietor, who will not wish to trespass upon the area of protection which has been endowed by registration. In order to fulfil these objectives, according to the ECJ, what constitutes the sign must be 'unambiguous'. The trade mark register must

[18] *Libertel Groep BV* v *Benelux-Merkenbureau*, Case C-104/01 [2003] 2 CLMR 45 at para. 40.
[19] *Dyson Ltd* v *Registrar of Trade Marks*, Case C-321/03 [2007] 2 CMLR 14. There, registration depended upon the Dyson sign having acquired distinctiveness through use.
[20] *Dyson* at para. 20.   [21] *Dyson* at para. 29.   [22] *Dyson* at para. 35.
[23] *Sieckmann*, paras. 46–55; see also Advocate General Colomer's opinion, *Ralf Sieckmann* v *Deutsches Patent- und Markenamt*, Case C-273/00, para. 53.

'avoid any element of subjectivity in the process of identifying and perceiving the sign. Consequently, the means of graphic representation must be unequivocal and objective.'[24] In general, both the registering authorities and the courts have assumed that two-dimensional signs and those that may be easily reduced to two dimensions, such as shapes, meet the criterion of being capable of graphic representation. Problems have arisen, however, with signs which must be represented by another sign in order to be represented graphically: these have included odours, sounds, and a single colour which, according to Advocate-General Leger in *Libertel*,[25] 'is always the attribute of something else', and, unlike 'words, designs, letters, numerals, the shape of goods or their packaging, has no independent existence'.[26]

The ECJ first addressed the graphic representation of such 'non-traditional' signs in *Sieckmann*, which concerned an application to register the odour 'balsamically fruity with a slight hint of cinnamon' as a trade mark. Shortly after the introduction of the CTM, the OHIM had allowed the registration of the smell of fresh cut grass, represented simply by the words, 'the smell of fresh cut grass'.[27] In *Sieckmann*, the ECJ confirmed that olfactory signs might be registered provided they were capable

---

[24] A postmodernist would argue that there might be no objective perception of a sign. Rather, signs may only be understood subjectively and hence their meanings will depend upon the observer. See, for example, J. Baudrillard, 'The Evil Demon of Images and the Precession of Simulacra' in T. Docherty (ed.), *Postmodernism: A Reader* (Hemel Hempstead, Herts.: Harvester, 1993), 194–9, and A. Easthope, 'Postmodernism and Critical and Cultural Theory' in S. Sim (ed.), *The Icon Dictionary of Postmodern Thought* (Cambridge: Icon Books, 1998), 15–27. The ECJ has neatly sidestepped this dilemma by assuming there will be only one observer for a sign, that is the 'average consumer' for the goods or services with which it is associated. The average consumer is assumed to be reasonably well informed, observant and circumspect: *Lloyd Schuhfabrik Meyer* v *Klijsen Handel BV*, Case C-342/97 [2000] 2 CMLR 1343; *Gut Springenheide and Tusky* v *Oberkreisdirektor des Kreises Steinfurt-Amt für Lebensmittelüberwachung*, Case C210/96 [1999] 1 CMLR 1383. In fact, I have argued the court will assume, under this formulation, that the average consumer will always be the same imagined individual, but, depending upon the nature of the goods or services, he will be more or less likely to understand the sign at issue to be acting as a trade mark. See J. Davis, 'Locating the Average Consumer: His Judicial Origins, Intellectual Influences and Current Role in European Trade Mark Law' (2005) IPQ 183.

[25] *Libertel Groep BV* v *Benelux-Merkenbureau*, Case C-104/01 [2003] 2 CMLR 45 at para. 67.

[26] In their article, 'Making Sense of Trade Mark Law' (2003) 1 IPQ 388, R. Burrell and M. Handler argue that the bureaucratic requirement of graphic representation is not suited to signs which are not capable of being reduced to a visual representation and that there is a necessity for different bureaucratic criteria when faced with non-traditional signs (390). Their argument is convincing. However, the concern here is rather to examine how the ECJ have set about defining the universe of signs which are deemed to be capable of graphic representation.

[27] *Vennootschap onder Firma Senta Aromatic Marketing's Application*, Case R 156/1998-2 [1999] ETMR 429.

of graphic representation, particularly by means of images, lines or characters. However, that representation had to be clear, precise, self-contained, easily accessible, intelligible, durable and objective.[28] *Shield Mark BV*[29] applied similar criteria to the graphic representation of sound marks. Here the application was to register two signs. The first was the sound of the first nine notes of Beethoven's 'Für Elise', which was represented *inter alia* by the notes graphically transcribed on the stave, and also by the sequence of musical notes which it was stated were played on a piano. The second was for the sound of a cock crowing which was represented *inter alia* by the sign 'Kukelekuuuuu' and the words, 'Sound mark, the trade mark consists of an onomatopoeia imitating a cockcrow'. In this case, the ECJ applied the *Sieckmann* criteria and held that, in the case of a sound mark, those requirements were satisfied 'where the sign is represented by a stave divided into measures and showing, in particular, a clef, musical notes and rests whose form indicates the relative value and, where necessary, accidentals'.[30] On the other hand, a simple written description would not suffice, nor, in relation to the cockcrow, would onomatopoeia, without more.[31] Finally, the *Sieckmann* criteria were applied to colours in *Libertel* where the Dutch mobile phone company sought to register a trade mark for the colour orange. It offered, as the graphical representation of its mark, an orange rectangle and, as a written description, the word 'orange'. It was held by the ECJ that the *Sieckmann* criteria may be satisfied by a sample of the colour together with a description in words of the colour; or, alternatively, by the designation of a colour using an internationally recognized identification code since such 'codes are deemed to be precise and stable'.[32]

It is possible to argue that criteria for the graphic representation of a sign – that it must be clear, precise, self-contained, easily accessible, intelligible, durable and objective – has limited the range of signs which may be monopolized through trade mark registration. Certainly, it was

---

[28] *Sieckmann* at para. 55. In the case of olfactory marks, the ECJ held (at para. 73) that 'the requirements of graphic representability are not satisfied by a chemical formula, by a description in written words, by the deposit of an odour sample or by a combination of those elements'.

[29] *Shield Mark BV* v *Joost Kist HODN Memex*, Case C-283/01 [2004] 1 CMLR 41.

[30] *Shield* at para. 64.

[31] *Shield* at para. 60. In the case of onomatopoeia, the ECJ was particularly concerned that there was insufficient legal certainty in a written description, 'because it is not possible for the competent authorities and the public, in particular traders, to determine whether the protected sign is the onomatopoeia itself, as pronounced, or the actual sound or noise. Furthermore, an onomatopoeia may be perceived differently, depending on the individual, or from one Member State to another.'

[32] *Libertel* at paras. 35–7.

widely argued after *Sieckmann* that it would be practically impossible for an odour to be represented graphically with sufficient legal certainty, and that for all intents and purposes the ECJ has accepted that olfactory signs cannot be registered.[33] The situation with regard to the graphic representation of sound marks is arguably more equivocal. Thus, it may again be posited that it would be extremely difficult to register natural sounds, such as those an animal might make, as they are not easily reduced to musical notation. However, the decision in *Shield* suggests that such difficulties do not extend to music itself or sounds which may be reduced to a combination of musical notes even though, as it has been convincingly argued, music (unlike the visual arts) is not static and each performance of a musical work will inevitably be a new process of creation.[34] Nonetheless, the assumption following *Shield* is that each performance of such music, provided it follows the musical notation, will fall within the registered trade mark's monopoly.

In the case of single colours, it may be argued that the ECJ has been even more permissive in the requirements for graphic representation. In effect, it has simply made registration contingent on the applicant identifying its mark by reference to an internationally accepted colour code. Once again this would overlook particular perceptual difficulties which might be presented by the graphic representation of single colours which, according to Advocate General Leger, are 'always the attribute of something else'.[35] Far from providing legal certainty, then, the registration of a colour mark per se would leave other traders with the difficulty of establishing in what ways they might use the same colour on their goods without infringement. This difficulty would be exacerbated because the same colour might be perceived differently depending upon the surface on which it is placed.[36]

---

[33] See, for example, Burrell and Handler, 'Making Sense', 394, and P. Turner-Kerr, 'Trade Mark Tangles: Recent Twists and Turns in EC Trade Mark Law' (2004) 29(3) E.L. Rev. 346. This view was confirmed when an application for a CTM consisting of the smell of ripe strawberries was recently rejected by the Court of First Instance, in part because the smell of ripe strawberries would differ with the variety of strawberries: *Eden SARL v Office for Harmonisation in the Internal Market*, Case T305/04 [2006] ETMR 14. In this case the graphic representation proffered was a picture of a red strawberry and the words 'smell of ripe strawberries'. In *Dyson*, the ECJ held that a 'concept' was not capable of graphic representation, because it 'is capable of taking on a multitude of different appearances and is not specific' (para. 37).

[34] A. Rahmatian, 'Music and Creativity as Perceived by Copyright Law', (2005) 3 IPQ 267, esp. 272–5.

[35] AG's opinion, *Libertel* at para. 67. As a result, he believed that it would be difficult for a competent authority faced with an application for a colour mark 'without shape or contour' to ascertain whether the other conditions required for registration, such as the need for distinctiveness, had been met.

[36] AG's opinion, *Libertel* at para. 75.

The requirement that a trade mark must be capable of graphic representation provides one boundary between signs which may be registered and signs which reside in the public domain. The TM Directive has been broadly interpreted so that even signs which are not directly visible and single colours may fall on the side of registrability. While the hurdle to registration is nonetheless high in relation to olfactory marks, it is considerably lower in relation to single colour marks and a wide variety of sound marks. Another boundary to registration is, as we have seen, provided by the requirements of Article 3, which are concerned with the meanings of trade marks. Signs which are capable of graphic representation may yet be excluded on grounds of meaning. It is to the meaning of signs which this chapter now turns.

2   Limiting the domain of registrable signs

Article 3 is designed to exclude from registration signs which are devoid of distinctive character and descriptive signs.[37] All registered trade marks should share at least one meaning: they act as a badge of origin for the consumer for the goods and services to which they attach. To that extent, it can be argued, all registered trade marks are descriptive. Some signs which are entirely invented, such as made-up words, may carry only this one meaning.[38] Other signs may have meanings which are so distant from the goods or services with which they are used that they are deemed to be sufficiently distinctive to be registered without evidence that the average consumer has come to see them as a badge of origin through use. An example of an inherently distinctive mark frequently proffered by the courts is the mark NORTH POLE for bananas.[39] By contrast, Article 3 of the TM Directive is designed to exclude, from the monopoly afforded by registration, signs which are either devoid of distinctive character without

---

[37] The Directive also excludes registration of generic signs and signs which are common in the trade. Article 3(1)(d) TM Directive; Art. 7(1)(d) TM Regulation.

[38] Although, through nurturing, they may acquire other attractive meanings, which are often referred to as 'brand values'. The extent to which these further meanings should be protected by registration will be addressed in Section 3 below. Alternatively, they may acquire further meanings which are derived precisely from their use as a trade mark, some of which may not be attractive, such as the prefix 'Mc', as in 'Mcjobs', for jobs which are badly paid and insecure: N. Klein, *No Logo* (London: Flamingo, 2000) 237. For further examples, see George Ritzer, *The McDonaldization of Society* (Boston: Pine Forge Press, 2000) 10, 210. In her piece, 'Expressive Genericity: Trademarks as Language in the Pepsi Generation' (1960) 65 *Notre Dame Law Review* 397, R. C. Dreyfuss argues that this 'expressive function of trade marks' should remain in the public domain.

[39] There are also signs whose meanings are allusive. For an interesting discussion, see J. Phillips, *Trade Mark Law: A Practical Anatomy* (Oxford: Oxford University Press, 2003), 98–102.

being used or signs whose meanings should, in any event, remain in the public domain. Thus, a sign which may be devoid of distinctive character, because the consumer on seeing it understands it to mean something other than that it is an indication of origin, will not be registered. Nor will a sign which is descriptive of the goods and services to which it is attached. However, these signs may become registrable if they go on to acquire a secondary meaning: that is if, because of the use that is made of them, consumers also come to see them as a badge of origin.

Among the signs which are assumed to be devoid of distinctive character are descriptive signs.[40] According to the ECJ a key reason for denying registration to descriptive signs which have not acquired a secondary meaning is not only their lack of distinctiveness but also that their descriptive meanings should be left free for other traders to use. The leading case, *Windsurfing* (1999), concerned the registration of a geographical name: in this case, the word CHIEMSEE, the name of a German lake, for clothing.[41] The ECJ held that geographical names which are associated by the average consumer with a certain class of goods or may be so associated in the future (whether or not they were manufactured in that location) should not be registered.[42] The public interest resided in ensuring that geographical names remain available,[43] not least because they may be an indication of the quality and other characteristics of the categories of goods concerned. They may also, in various ways, influence consumer tastes by, for instance, associating the goods with a place that may give rise to a favourable response.

Depending upon the context in which they are used, this public interest clearly does not apply to all geographical names, as the suggestion by the courts that NORTH POLE for bananas is inherently distinctive makes clear.[44] This same public interest which applied to geographical names was held, in later cases, to apply to all descriptive signs, or more precisely those signs which are deemed to be descriptive of the goods and services

---

[40] Most of the cases concerning descriptive marks which have reached the ECJ have been concerned with word marks. However, the Court has applied the same criteria to shape of goods marks – such as an application to register the shape of a forklift truck for forklift trucks – which are also deemed to be descriptive. See *Linde AG v Deutsches Patent- und Markenamt*, C-53/01 to C-55/01 [2003] 2 CMLR 44.

[41] There is a growing line of ECJ decisions which make this point, beginning with the decision in *Windsurfing Chiemsee Produktions- und Vertriebs GmbH v Boots- und Segelzubehör Walter Huber and Franz Attenberger*, Joined Cases C-108/97 and C-109/97 [1999] ETMR 585.

[42] *Windsurfing* at para. 37.   [43] *Windsurfing* at para. 26.

[44] This is the case even though it is precisely the public association between the North Pole and its descriptive meanings which gives it value as a trade mark for bananas.

against which registration is sought.[45] Of more difficulty for the courts has been drawing the boundary between those signs which are plainly descriptive and those signs which might be distinctive, although composed of descriptive elements.

Generally, the ECJ has taken an expansive approach to defining the category of signs which are descriptive and so should remain in the public domain. It is true that shortly after the *Windsurfing* decision, the ECJ held that the words BABY-DRY for diapers were not descriptive and could be registered, because, it held, their 'syntactically unusual juxtaposition is not a familiar expression in the English language, either for designating babies' nappies or for describing their essential characteristics'.[46] However, since BABY-DRY, it is generally accepted that the ECJ has become more willing to identify descriptive marks which should remain in the public domain.[47] Thus, it held that DOUBLEMINT might be refused registration as a CTM for chewing gum. This was so, even though it was not used descriptively by other traders at the time. It was sufficient that it could be used for such a purpose in the future and that at least one of its possible meanings was descriptive.[48] The approach taken in *Wrigley* was confirmed in later cases.[49] In *Koninklijke* v *Benelux-Merkenbureau* (2004),[50] the applicant sought to register the word POSTKANTOOR (Dutch for 'post office') for, *inter alia*, goods and services including paper, advertising, insurance, postage and stamps. The ECJ held that a descriptive sign could not be registered even if there were synonyms capable of designating the same characteristics of the goods or services. It also held that a mark consisting of descriptive elements is itself

---

[45] *OHIM* v *W. M. Wrigley Jr, Company*, Case C-191/01 P [2004] 3 CMLR 21.

[46] *Procter & Gamble Company* v *OHIM*, Case C-383/99 P [2002] ETMR 3 at para. 43. It was, according to the ECJ at para. 44, a 'lexical invention' which bestowed 'distinctive power on the mark'.

[47] At the time, the 'BABY-DRY' decision was controversial. See, for example, A. Griffiths, 'Modernising Trade Mark Law and Promoting Economic Efficiency: An Evaluation of the Baby-Dry Judgement and its Aftermath' (2003) 1 IPQ 2, which praised the judgment for giving certainty to trade mark proprietors, and also my own dissenting view in J. Davis, 'A European Constitution for IPRs? Competition, Trade Marks and Culturally Significant Signs' (2004) 41 CMLR 41, 1012. One explanation for this judgment may be that the ECJ applied the wrong public interest criteria to descriptive signs, suggesting that they should not be registered because they lacked distinctiveness rather than that they should remain in the public domain because others may wish to use them. See *Procter & Gamble* at para. 37.

[48] *Wrigley* at paras. 32–5.

[49] In *OHIM* v *Zapf Creation AG*, Case C-498/01 P [2004] ETMR 68, Advocate General Jacobs held that the proper approach to assessing whether or not a sign was descriptive, following *Wrigley*, was that taken in *Windsurfing* by the ECJ, rather than in *Procter & Gamble*.

[50] *Koninklijke KPN Nederland NV* v *Benelux-Merkenbureau*, Case C-363/99 [2004] 2 CMLR 10.

descriptive unless there is 'a perceptible difference' between the word and the sum of its parts, so that the word has acquired its own meaning independent of its components.[51] It went on to hold that even a neologism of two descriptive words would not be registrable, unless there was a perceptible difference between that word and the sum of its parts.[52] Finally, in a case which reached only so far as the Advocate General, Advocate General Jacobs held that the words NEW BORN BABY were descriptive of dolls, even though they were descriptive of what the toy represented rather than the toy itself, noting that: 'It seems clear that, where an essential characteristic of a product is to represent something else, a term consisting exclusively of elements which designate that something else may not be registered as a trade mark.'[53]

Signs which are devoid of distinctive character will not be registered. This is not to say that to be registrable a sign must reach a 'specific level of linguistic or artistic creativity or imaginativeness'.[54] The general public interest which lies behind this provision is that the registered trade mark should fulfil its essential function of enabling the end user to distinguish the goods or services to which it attaches from those which have a different origin.[55] As a result, any sign which reaches that level of distinctiveness, no matter how mundane, will be registrable. Signs which have been identified as devoid of distinctive character have carried a range of meanings, but have in common the fact that the average consumer would not, without education, expect one of those meanings to be that of trade origin. This category of signs has been held to include colours, slogans, shapes and people's names,[56] although obviously this too would be an open-ended list. In *Libertel*, the applicant sought to register the colour

---

[51] Although the ECJ at para. 5 recognized that this new meaning too might itself be descriptive of the goods, in which case the word could not be registered.

[52] *Campina Melkunie BV* v *Benelux-Merkenbureau*, Case C-265/00 [2005] 2 CMLR 9. In this case, the applicant sought to register BIOMILD as a CTM for mild-flavoured yoghurt.

[53] *Zapf* at paras. 28 and 29.

[54] *SAT.1 Satellitenfernsehen GMBH* v *OHIM*, Case C-329/02 P [2005] 1 CMLR 57 at para. 41, although a 'highly imaginative mark' will be held to be inherently more distinctive, as in *The Royal County of Berkshire Polo Club Ltd* v *OHIM*, Case T-214/04 [2006] ETMR 59 at para. 43. In this case the Court of First Instance was referring to Ralph Lauren's trade marks comprising the word POLO and a figurative mark of a polo player. The marks were held to be particularly distinctive because there was only an 'arbitrary' connection between the mark and the goods, which included perfumes and colognes.

[55] *SAT.1* at para. 23. The essential purpose was identified in *Hoffmann-La Roche*, Case 102/77 [1978] ECR 1139. The exception is colour marks. In relation to colour marks, the ECJ has held that the public interest in judging them devoid of distinctive character is that, since the number of colours is limited, it would be anti-competitive to allow an extensive monopoly of a single colour: *Libertel* at para. 54.

[56] For names, see *Nichols Plc* v *Registrar of Trade Marks*, Case C-404/02 [2004] ECR I-8499.

orange for telecommunications goods.[57] According to the ECJ, 'whilst colours are capable of conveying certain associations of ideas, and of arousing feelings, they possess little inherent capacity for communicating specific information, especially since they are commonly and widely used, because of their appeal, in order to advertise and market goods or services, without any specific message'.[58] Clearly, Orange Communications would endorse the first part of this statement but not the second. A similar approach has been taken to advertising slogans. The ECJ has taken the view that a slogan may promote a product and 'commend' its quality, but that the average consumer is 'not in the habit of making assumptions about the origin of products on the basis of such slogans'.[59]

Both colours and slogans have been found devoid of distinctive character because, although they are widely used in advertising for the messages they might convey, the courts have assumed that the average consumer, without education, would not understand that one of those messages concerned the origin of the goods. Another major category of signs which have been held to be devoid of distinctive character consists of three-dimensional shapes. According to the ECJ, all shape marks face an initial hurdle. In relation to three-dimensional shapes, the average consumer 'is not in the habit of making assumptions about the origin of products on the basis of their shape or the shape of their packaging in the absence of any graphic or word element and it could therefore prove more difficult to establish distinctiveness in relation to such a three-dimensional mark than in relation to a word or figurative mark'. This is particularly true because 'a word or figurative mark consisting of a sign is independent of the appearance of the products it denotes'.[60] Such an assumption seems apt in relation to applications to register three-dimensional marks which consist of the shape of the goods themselves, such as the shape of a forklift truck for a forklift truck.[61] Not only are they descriptive but, as has been noted, the average consumer would be unlikely to perceive the shape of goods as a trade mark.[62] A similar point might be made about the shape of packaging.[63] With regard to the shape of goods, the ECJ has held that only shape of goods marks

---

[57] At this time *Libertel* was not part of the Orange Communication Group.

[58] *Libertel* at para. 40.

[59] *OHIM v Erpo Mobelwerk GmbH*, Case C-64/02P [2004] ECR II-10031 at para. 35.

[60] *Mag Instrument Inc. v OHIM*, C-136/02P at paras. 30–1; see also *Henkel KGaA v OHIM*, T393/02 [2004] ECR II-4115.

[61] *Linde.*   [62] *Mag Instrument* at para. 30.

[63] *Eurocermex SA v OHIM*, Case C-286/04P [2005] ECR I-5797, concerning the three-dimensional shape of a long-necked bottle with a slice of lemon plugged in the neck for, *inter alia*, beer, at para. 30.

which depart significantly from the norm or customs of the sector and
thereby fulfil their essential function of indicating origin could be registered.[64] Similarly with regard to packaging, the Court has held that, to be
registrable, the shape of the container must 'differentiate itself materially'
from the ordinary shapes of containers for the same products.[65] However,
it is submitted that it is less apt to draw such a conclusion about shape
marks which have only a random relationship with the product. Such was
the case in *Bongrain*,[66] where the applicant sought to register a 'six-lobed'
or flower shape with some 'superficial ridging' as a UK trade mark for
cheese. The application was refused on the basis that the mark was devoid
of distinctive character. In the Court of Appeal, Lord Justice Jacob held
that the average consumer would be 'astonished' to discover that the
shape of a cheese functioned as a trade mark without established use.
He noted: 'Consumers do not expect to eat trade marks or part of
them.'[67] Yet, arguably, it is difficult to differentiate the inherent distinctiveness of a random shape for a cheese from the use of the sign NORTH
POLE for bananas.[68]

Once a trade mark which is initially devoid of distinctive character or is
descriptive has acquired distinctiveness as a consequence of the use which
has been made of it, it may be registered.[69] Although in relation to both
descriptive marks and colour marks, the ECJ has held that there is a
public interest in leaving these signs free for others to use, the ECJ has
also held that no stricter criteria can be applied, when assessing the
acquired distinctiveness of such marks, than would be applied to any
other trade marks.[70] In other words, once such marks have acquired
distinctiveness, they cross the boundary which marks out the public
domain and are encompassed within the monopoly accorded to trade
marks through registration. There is, however, a major caveat. This is not

[64] *Mag Instrument* at para. 30. In this case, the shape of the Mag torch was held not to be
sufficiently distinctive without use.
[65] *Eurocermex* at para. 30.
[66] *Bongrain SA's Trade Mark Application* [2005] ETMR 472.   [67] *Bongrain* at para. 28.
[68] To argue otherwise would be to maintain that it would never be possible to register a
shape of goods mark without acquired distinctiveness. Yet in *Mag Instrument* at paras.
31–2, the ECJ recognized the category of marks 'which departs significantly from the
norm or customs of the sector' and contrasted these marks with those which are a mere
'variant' of a common shape and would therefore need acquired distinctiveness for
registration.
[69] Article 3(3) TM Directive; Art. 7(3) TM Regulation.
[70] *Linde* at para. 41. See also A. Folliard-Monguiral, 'Distinctive Character Acquired
through Use: The Law and the Case Law' in J. Phillips and I. Simon (eds.), *Trade
Mark Use* (Oxford: Oxford University Press, 2005), 49–70, and A. Carboni,
'Distinctive Character Acquired through Use: Establishing the Facts' in Phillips and
Simon (eds.), *Trade Mark Use*, 71–92.

true for all the meanings of the registered mark. Registration does not entitle the proprietor to prohibit third parties from using the mark descriptively or to indicate the intended purpose of the goods or services.[71] In other words, the descriptive meaning of the trade mark remains in the public domain, even if its meaning as a badge of origin (also arguably descriptive) does not. Thus, a third party may continue to use descriptively a sign which was initially descriptive but has also come to be seen as a badge of origin and has been registered as a trade mark, such as the word TREAT for food.[72] A third party may also use a trade mark which was not initially descriptive, as long as the third party's use of it is descriptive, such as the use by the third party of the trade mark BON JOVI to describe the contents of a compact disc.[73] It could be further argued that, once colours and slogans acquire distinctiveness, they continue to carry those other meanings, be they feelings or advertising values, that they had before they acquired distinctiveness.[74] In the latter case, as we have seen, it is precisely such further meanings that Orange has claimed for its brand. This chapter now goes on to examine the extent to which trade mark law will protect these additional 'brand values'.

3   Protecting the trade mark as a brand

Despite its ubiquity in contemporary discourse, there is no agreed definition of 'a brand'. This is true even if one looks only at literature concerned with branding.[75] Generally, however, a brand is understood to have a value which transcends the product with which it is associated. According to one observer, '[t]he difference between products and brands is fundamental. A product is something made in a factory; a brand is something bought by a consumer. A product can be copied by a competitor; a brand is unique. A product can be quickly outdated; a

---

[71] Article 6(1)(b) & (c) TM Directive; Art. 12(b) & (c) TM Regulation.

[72] *British Sugar Plc* v *James Robertson & Sons Ltd* [1996] RPC 281 – although, in this case, the claimant's trade mark TREAT for ice-cream toppings was found to be invalidly registered as it had not acquired distinctiveness through use.

[73] *R* v *Johnstone* [2004] ETMR 2; see also *Holterhoff* v *Freiesleben*, C-2/00 [2002] ECR I-4187.

[74] And, no doubt, containers would continue to be perceived as containers as well as trade marks. A notable example would be the Jif Lemon lemon-shaped container for lemon juice, which is also descriptive, but which has been registered as a trade mark because of distinctiveness acquired through use.

[75] For a full overview of this issue, see J. Davis, 'The Value of Trade Marks: Economic Assets and Cultural Icons' in Y. Gendreau (ed.), *Intellectual Property: Bridging Aesthetics and Economics – Propriété intellectuelle: entre l'art et l'argent* (Montreal: Éditions Themis, 2006) 97–125.

successful brand is timeless.'[76] As a result, brands are often deemed to
have a quality of 'transferability', in that they 'have the ability to transfer
consumer loyalty between products, services and categories over time and
to separate it [*sic*] from tangible production'.[77] Similarly, brands are
regarded as constituting something more than a trade mark *as it is legally
defined*. As we have seen, Orange refers to their brand '*and the rights
associated with it*' (my emphasis). It has been argued that 'a useful way to
conceptualise a brand is as an aggregation of assets which *includes, but is
not limited to* a trade mark'.[78] These other assets might include a visual
identity or identifying trade-dress or a particular marketing or advertising
strategy.[79] Alternatively, brands may be 'a combination of legal rights,
together with the culture, people, and programs of an organization within
which the specific logo and associated visual elements plus the larger
bundle of visual and marketing intangibles' and the 'associated goodwill
are deployed'.[80] Nonetheless, it is also the case that trade marks may be
seen as a key vehicle for brand values.[81] Thus, according to Advocate
General Colomer in the *Arsenal* v *Reed* case, 'it is simple reductionism to
limit the function of trade marks to an indication of origin'. Trade marks
might also indicate quality, reputation or the renown of the producer, or
they may be used for advertising purposes.[82] As we have seen in the case
of Orange, the visual embodiments of its trade marks and of its brand
coincide.

Thus far we have considered the justifications for leaving certain meanings of a trade mark in the public domain. In the case of the brand values
which attach to certain trade marks, it is possible to argue that these have

---

[76] S. King quoted in D. Haigh, *Brand Valuation: Understanding, Exploiting and
Communicating Brand Values* (London: Financial Times, 1998), 8; see also AG
Colomer in *Arsenal Football Club plc* v *Matthew Reed*, Case C-2006/01 [2002] ECR
I-10273 at para. 46, who noted: 'Experience teaches that, in most cases, the user is
unaware of who produces the goods that he consumes. The trade mark acquires a life of
its own, making a statement, as I have suggested, about quality, reputation and even, in
certain cases, a way of seeing life.'

[77] Haigh, *Brand Valuation*, 1; see also D. Aaker and E. Joachimsthaler, *Brand Leadership:
The Next Level of the Brand Revolution* (New York: The Free Press, 2000), 48.

[78] G. V. Smith, *Trade Mark Valuation* (New York: J. Wiley & Sons, 1997), 42. Other aspects
of brands may be protected, in the UK, by other intellectual property (IP) rights such as
copyright and confidentiality, and by the tort of passing off.

[79] G. V. Smith, *Trademark Valuation*, 42; T. Allen and J. Simmons, 'Visual and Verbal
Identity' in R. Clifton and J. Simmons (eds.), *Brands and Branding* (Princeton, N.J.:
Bloomberg, 2003) 114–15.

[80] D. Haigh and J. Knowles, 'Don't waste time with brand valuation', 5 October 2004,
Marketing NPV, www.brandfinance.com.

[81] This point was made as early as 1925 by F. I. Schecter in his seminal essay, 'The Rational
Basis of Trade Mark Protection' (1926–7) 40 Harv. Law Rev. 824, at 831.

[82] *Arsenal* v *Reed* at para. 44.

not been appropriated from the public domain. Rather they have been nurtured by the proprietor and, as such, the question is not whether they belong in the public domain, but to what extent they may be protected through trade mark registration from use by third parties.[83] In particular, the question arises of the extent to which registration will protect a trade mark against use of a sign which may conflict with it in such a way as to undermine these brand values either through 'dilution' or 'tarnishment'.[84] The law relating to registered trade marks has demarcated the protection accorded to trade marks as brands in two key areas. The TM Directive offers protection to trade marks with a reputation[85] against registration[86] or use[87] by a third party of an identical or similar mark on similar or dissimilar goods without due cause where such use would take unfair advantage of, or be detrimental to, the distinctive character or repute of the earlier trade mark. More contentiously, the ECJ has interpreted the Directive as offering protection for a registered trade mark against non-trade mark use by a third party.[88]

Conflict between a registered trade mark with a reputation and the use by a third party of an identical or similar sign will occur even if the average consumer is not confused as to the origin of the goods and services sold under the conflicting sign.[89] It is sufficient if the consumer associates the registered mark and the sign, in such a way that the value of the former is

---

[83] It may of course be argued that the consumer is complicit in shaping both the meaning and value of brands. See, for example, D. B. Holt, *How Brands Become Icons: The Principles of Cultural Branding* (Boston: Harvard Business School Press, 2004). More commonly, however, the value of trade marks beyond their distinguishing role is held to be the property of the proprietor; see, for example, S. Casperie-Kerdel, 'Dilution Disguised: Has the Concept of Trade Mark Dilution Made its Way into the Laws of Europe?' (2001) EIPR 185 at 188, and M. Richardson, 'Copyright in Trade Marks? On Understanding Trade Mark Dilution' (2000) 1 IPQ 67. See also J. Davis, 'To Protect or Serve? European Trade Mark Law and the Decline of the Public Interest' (2003) 25 EIPR 180 at 184–5.

[84] Conflict may arise either at the point of registration or later by the use by a third party of an infringing mark. According to AG Jacobs in *Adidas-Salomon AG v Fitnessworld Trading Ltd* Case C408/01 [2003] ETMR 91, dilution means that a mark is no longer capable of arousing an immediate association with the goods for which it is registered or used. The concept of detriment, often referred to as 'tarnishment', describes the situation where the goods for which the infringing sign is used appeal to the public's senses in such a way that the mark's power of attraction is affected. See also *Premier Brands UK Ltd v Typhoon Europe Ltd* [2000] FSR 767. For a discussion of the concept of dilution as used in American and EU trade mark law, see I. Simon, 'Dilutive Trade Mark Applications: Trading on Reputations or Just Playing Games' (2004) EIPR 26(2), 67–74.

[85] For the criteria for assessing reputation, see *General Motors Corpn v Yplon SA*, C375/97 [2000] RPC 572 (ECJ).

[86] Article 4(4)(a) TM Directive; Art. 8(5) TM Regulation.

[87] Article 5(2) TM Directive; Art. 9(1)(c) TM Regulation.

[88] See discussion of *Arsenal v Reed* below.

[89] *Sabel BV v Puma AG and Rudolf Dassler Sport*, Case C-251/95 [1998] 1 CMLR 445 at para 16.

undermined. Following the passage of the TM Directive, the issue of whether a third party used an identical or similar mark without due cause was viewed as fundamental to whether or not such an association might arise. Thus, in early cases, conflict was more likely to be found where a third party used a sign whose meaning had no natural association with its own goods or services since, in such circumstances, consumers would be more likely to make an association between that sign and the registered mark. This point was neatly illustrated by two early cases, both concerning condoms, which came before the UK Trade Mark Registry. In the first the applicant sought to register the mark EVEREADY for condoms.[90] The application was opposed by Ever Ready, the maker of batteries, *inter alia* because of the undesirable associations which might be made by the public. The opposition was unsuccessful. The Registrar took the view that the public would not make an association between two such different products. In the second case,[91] the applicant sought to register the word VISA, also for condoms, and was opposed by the proprietor of VISA for financial services. In this case, the Appointed Person found for the opposition, believing that there would be 'cross pollination' between the applicant's use of VISA and the opponent's use, to the detriment of the latter. It has been convincingly argued that the difference between these two situations is that, in the first case, the consumer might make a natural connection between the descriptive meaning of 'ever ready' and condoms; in the latter case, there was no such natural association and hence the public would be more likely to associate VISA with the credit card.[92] However, in more recent cases, the courts have been willing to find a likelihood of conflict simply on the basis that use of the later sign will free-ride on the reputation of the earlier mark and that there is no over-riding compulsion for the third party to use the sign. Thus, in *Intel v Sihra*,[93] although the applicant, who produced toys, claimed that it had chosen the mark INTEL-PLAY because it 'stood for' intelligent play, this was held to conflict with the opponent's INTEL mark for microprocessors. The High Court held that the use of the INTEL-PLAY mark would dilute the strength of the INTEL mark and would also tarnish its distinctive character as its reputation was based on its use with 'high-quality, technologically-based' products, while INTEL-PLAY would be used on

---

[90] *Oasis Stores Ltd's Application* [1999] ETMR 531.

[91] *Sheimer (CA) (M) Sdn Bhd's Trade Mark Application* [2000] RPC 484.

[92] J. Rawkins, 'Entry Denied: Visa for Condoms Rejected in the UK' [2002] *Trade Mark World* 22. This was so even though the counsel for the applicant argued that VISA was a 'humourous allusion to the concept of "permission to enter"'.

[93] *Intel Corp. Inc. v Sihra* [2003] ETMR 44.

'unsophisticated' goods.[94] In this case, it may be argued that the latter sign had a naturally descriptive meaning, but in effect this was held to have been swamped by the meaning which INTEL had accrued as a brand. As a result, the descriptive meaning was no longer available to third parties.[95]

A key question which was effectively sidestepped in each of these decisions[96] is exactly what sort of association made by consumers will be deemed by the court to affect the distinctiveness of a mark with a reputation, if the same or a similar sign (or mark) is used by a third party. In *Adidas-Salomon* v *Fitnessworld*, the ECJ said of Article 5(2) TM Directive, 'It is sufficient for the degree of similarity between the mark with a reputation and the sign to have the effect that the relevant section of the public establishes a link between the sign and the mark'. The Court did not, however, go on to explicate the nature of this 'link'.[97] Certainly, in this case and earlier ECJ decisions, the Court had determined that the link in question need not be one where the average consumer was confused as to the origins of the goods or services sold under the respective marks.[98] In that situation, provided the goods or services are the same or similar, there will in any event be infringement. On the other hand, if any link is presumed to affect the distinctiveness of a mark with a reputation, then clearly 'brand values' will be given very wide protection indeed.

Recently, in another case involving the Intel mark,[99] precisely these issues were raised by the Court of Appeal (CA). In this case, Intel Corp.

---

[94] *Intel* v *Sihra* at para. 24. See also Simon, 'Dilutive Trade Mark Applications'.

[95] In *Quorn Hunt's Application* v *Opposition of Marlow Foods Ltd*, Case O-319–04 [2005] ETMR 11, the Trade Mark Registrar held that registration of the mark QUORN HUNT for, *inter alia*, goods to do with fox hunting would be detrimental to the registered trade mark QUORN for a vegetarian meat-substitute, because 'bearing in mind in particular the nature of the opponent's goods and the fact that vegetarians formed its core market, the association with hunting would damage the distinctive character of the QUORN mark to a material extent'.

[96] And other UK decisions such as *Premier Brands* v *Typhoon Europe* [2000] FSR 767 and *Electrocoin Automatics* v *Hitachi Credit* [2005] FSR 7.

[97] In *Addidas-Salomon* v *Fitnessworld* at para. 31, itself, the claimant who had a trade mark consisting of a three stripe motif used on its sportswear sued the defendant who also sold sports clothes which carried a double-stripe motif. The Court found that, provided the average consumer saw the double-stripe motive purely as an embellishment, there would be no infringement of the claimant's mark. However, the finding would be different if the use of the double-stripe motif as an embellishment nonetheless established a 'link' in the consumer's mind with the registered mark: A. Carboni, 'Two Stripes and You're Out: Added Protection for Trade Marks With a Reputation' [2004] 5 EIPR 229.

[98] See footnote 87.

[99] *In the matter of UK Trade Mark No. 2122181 Intelmark in Class 35 in the name of CPM United Kingdom Ltd and In the Matter of Request for Invalidity thereof by No. 81496 by Intel Corporation (Intel Corporation Inc.* v *CPM United Kingdom Ltd)* [2007] EWCA Civ. 431.

sought to have a community trade mark, INTELMARK, which had been registered by CPM UK, declared invalidly registered on the basis that it infringed their own INTEL mark. CPM was using its mark for marketing and telemarketing services. There was agreement that Intel's mark had a reputation, that it was not used by any other enterprise (although arguably unique use need not equate to distinctiveness), that the marks were being used on dissimilar goods and that there was no question that the public would be confused as to origin. If the court were to find that that the CPM mark infringed the Intel mark, and hence should be declared invalidly registered, it would have to be on the basis that the public made a 'link' between the marks, which would affect the distinctiveness of Intel's mark. It was argued by counsel for Intel, following *Adidas* v *Fitnessworld*, that a material link would arise with any use of the CPM mark which 'brought to mind' the Intel mark; and that, where the earlier mark was unique and highly distinctive, detriment would be caused by the use of the later mark on any other goods or services. The CA was not inclined to accept such a broad definition and addressed the question of what constituted the necessary link to the ECJ. In Jacob LJ's own opinion, however, to accept that any 'link' would be sufficient would have the effect of making trade mark law 'oppressive and all powerful'. Indeed, he opined that if 'a trade mark for particular goods and services is truly inherently and factually distinctive it will be robust enough to withstand a mere passing bringing to mind when it or a similar mark is used for dissimilar goods or services'.[100] His own view was that the boundary of trade mark protection should be drawn to include links where the average consumer would consider there was an economic connection between the owners of the marks and where the distinctiveness of the earlier mark is 'really likely' to be affected if the later mark is used on other goods.[101]

The protection afforded to marks with a reputation extends beyond their meaning as a badge of origin. Such marks are protected even when they are used on goods or services which do not lie within the ambit of the goods or services claimed at registration: that is, the goods and services which are supplied by the proprietor under the mark. To that extent, it may be argued that what is being protected are wider 'brand values', rather than the trade mark's meaning as an indicator of origin. In particular, these provisions of the TM Directive recognize that certain trade marks have the quality of transferability, which has been identified as a key brand attribute. Recently, the ECJ seemed also to offer protection for trade marks against use by third parties which was not itself trade mark

---

[100] *Intel Corporation Inc.* v *CPM United Kingdom Ltd* at para. 29.
[101] *Intel Corporation Inc.* v *CPM United Kingdom Ltd* at para. 35.

use, thus further recognizing the brand values which might be embodied in a trade mark.

In *Arsenal* v *Reed*,[102] the 'brand values' at issue were the brand's 'emotional' or 'irrational' attraction for the consumer and also its ability to be exploited through licensing or merchandising, that is its transferability.[103] In this case, which originated in the UK, the defendant, Reed, had sold merchandise carrying the registered marks of Arsenal Football Club. The Club sued for trade mark infringement. In the High Court, Reed argued that the marks were understood not as a badge of origin but as a mark of support, loyalty or affiliation.[104] The question posed to the ECJ was whether such use was non-trade mark use, and, if so, whether nonetheless it was infringing.[105] In effect, the ECJ was being asked whether the infringement provisions of the TM Directive could be used by proprietors to prevent the use of signs which undermined their mark's appeal, beyond their role as a mere indicator of origin. This was certainly the view of Advocate General Colomer, who as we have seen accepted that trade marks might embody advertising values as well as act as a badge of origin. As a result, he concluded that non-trade mark use of a sign should be sufficient to infringe a registered mark, if the result of such use was to exploit the commercial potential of the registered mark beyond its narrow role as a badge of origin.[106]

In the event, the ECJ took a more cautious approach. The ECJ held that non-trade mark use, such as the use of the Arsenal trade marks by Reed simply to mean a badge of allegiance or loyalty, could constitute infringing use. But it also found that such use would only be infringing if it affected the essential function of the mark, which, in this case, it recognized as the mark's ability to act as a guarantee of origin for the consumer.[107] The judgment in *Arsenal* v *Reed* suggests that the attitude of the ECJ towards trade mark protection and wider brand values remains equivocal. It is certainly the case that, throughout the judgment, the ECJ referred to the 'functions' of trade marks, in the plural, which leaves open the possibility that, on a different set of facts, the ECJ might have

[102] *Arsenal Football Club Plc* v *Matthew Reed*, Case C-206/01 [2003] 1 CLMR 12.
[103] See Davis, 'To Protect or Serve?' in particular 184–7; R. Sumroy and C. Badger, 'Infringing "Use in the Course of Trade": Trade Mark Use and the Essential Function of a Trade Mark,' in Phillips and Simon (eds.), *Trade Mark Use*, 164–5.
[104] *Arsenal Football Club plc* v *Matthew Reed* [2001] RPC 922.
[105] The relevant provision of the TM Directive is Art. 5, which provides that 'the proprietor shall be entitled to prevent all third parties not having his consent from using in the course of trade: (a) any sign which is identical with the trade mark in relation to the goods or services which are identical with those for which the trade mark is registered'.
[106] Advocate General, *Arsenal* v *Reed* at para. 42.   [107] *Arsenal* v *Reed*, ECJ, paras. 60–1.

been willing to recognize other protected meanings for a trade mark, such as those which are also commonly seen as embodied in a brand.[108] However, in the event, the ECJ appeared to identify the trade mark's function as an indicator of origin, as the key 'brand value' which should be protected against infringement.[109]

Commentators on the *Arsenal* v *Reed* case have generally welcomed it as a victory for brand owners, particularly those who wish to license their trade marks or are involved in merchandising.[110] This is so, even if there is some disagreement as to whether or not, following *Arsenal* v *Reed*, infringing use need no longer be trade mark use.[111] Thus, according to one observer, the rise in the value of brands at the end of the twentieth century, and the need to protect them through trade mark registration, meant that there needed to be a wider definition of a sign and a trademark as well as the definition of infringement. In the event, the ECJ reasoning in *Arsenal* v *Reed*, which eschewed trade mark use for infringement, 'is consistent with modern commercial activity'.[112] Elsewhere, the decision

[108] *Arsenal* v *Reed*, paras. 42, 51, 54. Davis, 'To Protect or Serve?' fn. 73.
[109] The equivocal nature of the ECJ judgment led to subsequent confusion as to the extent to which brand values are now protected by trade mark registration. When the case returned to the High Court, Mr Justice Laddie concluded that the ECJ had held that only trade mark use could infringe, since where the public did not understand the use of the mark as denoting origin there could be no damage to the mark's essential function: *Arsenal Football Club Plc* v *Matthew Reed* [2003] ETMR 36 at para. 20. He then went on to find that the ECJ had exceeded its jurisdiction by finding, on the facts, that Reed had infringed the Arsenal marks. He found for the defendant. However, in the Court of Appeal, Aldous LJ concluded that the ECJ had held that any use which affected the origin function of a mark was infringing: *Arsenal Football Club plc* v Matthew *Reed* [2003] 2 CMLR 25. Aldous LJ also found that, as a matter of fact, Reed had used the Arsenal marks in a trade mark sense, that is as a badge of origin.
[110] In the UK, the extent to which *Arsenal* v *Reed* could be viewed as heralding a new age for brand owners was somewhat muddied by the near simultaneous judgment of the House of Lords in *R* v *Johnstone* [2004] ETMR 2, in which their Lordships appeared to hold that, in order to be infringing use, use of a mark must be use as a badge of origin. It has been suggested that this apparent contradiction may arise from the fact that *Johnstone* was a criminal case and therefore the Court was concerned to make the barrier to infringement a high hurdle to cross. (See, for example, Sumroy and Badger, 'Infringing "Use in the Course of Trade"' 178.) Another, perhaps more convincing, interpretation is that their Lordships were concerned to draw a distinction between infringing use and descriptive use which was not infringing (see R. Calleja, 'R. v Johnstone' [2003] UKHL 28: 'Bootlegging and Legitimate Use of an Artist's Trade Mark' (2003) 14(7) Ent.L.R. 186). Whatever their intentions, there is no doubt that their Lordships' judgment in *Johnstone* has left the question of use in some disarray in the UK.
[111] For example P. Dryberg and M. Skylv, in their article 'Does Trade Mark Infringement Require that the Infringing Use be Trade Mark Use and if so, what is "Trade Mark Use"?' (2003) 5 EIPR 229, appear to take the position that it does.
[112] A. Poulter, 'What is "Use": Reconciling Divergent Views on the Nature of Infringing Use' (December 2003 / January 2004) 163 *Trademark World* 23.

in *Arsenal* v *Reed* is portrayed as offering 'broad' protection for trade marks in their role as 'brands', which is defined as 'a wider concept intended to attract consumer loyalty by virtue of values, including lifestyle messages, associated with that brand'.[113] However, it is submitted that the ECJ in fact took a rather more cautious approach to locating the border which might be drawn around protected 'brand values' than these commentators suggest. By finding that, on the one hand, the essential meaning of a trade mark remains its meaning as an indicator of origin, but, on the other, that non-trade mark use can compromise this meaning, the ECJ has taken a nuanced approach to the extent to which 'brand values' should be protected by trade mark registration. It may have recognized the importance of the transferability of trade marks (*qua* brands), but it has remained cautious as to the extent to which a trade mark's 'emotional' values might also be protected. Indeed, an excellent illustration of this nuanced approach is to be found in its recent judgment in *Adam Opel* v *Autec* (2007).[114] In this case, the car manufacturer Opel sued Autec, a toy manufacturer, which had put Opel's registered trade mark on scale models of the Opel Astra. Opel had registered its trade mark for both cars and toys. The ECJ found that this was non-trade mark use which would not affect the origin function of the mark, because the average consumer would not assume the toys originated from Opel.[115] But the ECJ also held out the possibility that Autec's use of the Opel mark might nonetheless infringe under the dilution provision of the TM Directive,[116] as such use might 'tarnish' the Opel mark, especially if the toys were of poor quality.

4   Between a sign and a brand

In her article 'Objects of Property and Subjects of Politics: Intellectual Property Laws and Democratic Dialogue', Rosemary Coombe argues that, by registering their trade marks, proprietors have 'the ability to

---

[113] Sumroy and Badger, 'Infringing "Use in the Course of Trade"' 164. See also H. Norman, 'Time to Blow the Whistle on Trade Mark Use' (2004) 1 IPQ 1, who believes that the value of trade marks, not least as merchandising and licensing tools, suggests that they deserve to be protected beyond their role as a badge of origin. From this perspective, she views the *Arsenal* decision as a promising development. See also J. Tumbridge, 'Trade Marks: The Confusion of "Use"' (2004) 9 EIPR 431.

[114] *Adam Opel AG* v *Autec AG*, Case C-48/105 [2007] ETMR 33.

[115] The ECJ distinguished this case from *Arsenal* v *Reed*. In *Opel* v *Autec*, the toy manufacturer's trade mark was also placed on the model car. Whereas, once Reed's goods had been purchased, there was nothing to distinguish them from official Arsenal merchandise, and hence the origin function of the Arsenal marks might be compromised.

[116] Article 5(2) TM Directive.

restrict and control meaning' because they 'own' the sign.[117] What has been suggested here, however, is that a registered trade mark may embody a variety of meanings, only some of which will fall within the monopoly afforded by registration. In addition, these meanings may change over time.[118] A descriptive sign may become distinctive through use or alternatively a trade mark may become available to be used descriptively by third parties. Since the passage of the TM Directive, the boundaries which are drawn around the protected meanings of registered trade marks have been contested. On the one hand, there has been a movement in case law to protect a generous public domain of unregistrable signs; on the other, the protection which has been given to trade marks as brands has grown stronger. It may be suggested that the reason for the shifting protection which is given to trade marks lies precisely in the intangible nature of what is protected. The protection afforded to a registered trade mark cannot be calculated by what sign appears on the Trade Mark Register, nor by what goods or services it is registered against. The protection afforded by registration is defined only at points of overlap, either with the public domain or with third parties' use of the registered trade mark. To that extent, proprietors cannot 'own' their signs

[117] R. Coombe, 'Objects of Property and Subjects of Politics: Intellectual Property Laws and Democratic Dialogue' (1991)69 *Texas Law Review* 1853 at 1876. For Coombe this has led to the restriction of democratic dialogue at a time when 'mass media imagery and commodified cultural texts provide the most important cultural resources for the articulation of identity and community in Western societies' (1864). Conversely, S. Carter in 'Does it Matter Whether Intellectual Property is Property?' (1993) 68 *Chicago-Kent Law Review* 715 at 720, agues that a trade mark is not property in the Lockean sense, such as a copyright, or is property, because it is the intellectual creation of the owner. By contrast, a trade mark 'is protected only to the extent that it distinguishes the owner's goods'. He further argues that the failure to view trade marks as 'property' stems from their intangible nature (that is, in contrast to a copyright which might reside in a painting) (723). M. A. Lemley, in 'Property, Intellectual Property, and Free Riding' (2005) 83 *Texas Law Review* 1031 at 1071, argues that it is dangerous to treat intellectual property as 'property' because that may be understood as implying both a fixed meaning and 'an absolute right to exclude'. This appears to be Coombe's understanding of trade mark registration but it is contested here.

[118] It is also the case that the public may themselves add meanings to trade marks which are not intended by their proprietors, such as, for instance, the adoption of the Burberry brand by soccer 'hooligans', and more recently of the Lonsdale clothing brand by neo-Nazis, which has led one multinational mail order company based in Germany to refuse to carry its products. According to a spokesman for the company, Quelle, 'Quelle wants to distance itself clearly from all tendencies associated with extremism ... We want to counter any suggestion that we are supporting right-wing extremists through the sale of these goods': *Independent*, 27 March 2006. Apparently, the letters 'NSDA' in the brand's name are taken to be close to the initials of the Nazi Party. A ban against individuals wearing the Lonsdale brand is already in place in many nightclubs, bars and schools in Holland. Lonsdale has begun an advertising campaign in Holland with the slogan 'Lonsdale loves all colours.'

because, until their boundaries are tested by law, it is unclear exactly what falls within their monopoly.

It is submitted that it is the intangible nature of the protection afforded to trade marks that allows it to accommodate some meanings and exclude others. This is true both at the bureaucratic and at the conceptual levels. As to the former, Burrell and Handler have convincingly argued that it is wrong to equate the visual representation of a mark as delimiting what is protected by registration, as was the assumption of the ECJ in *Sieckmann*.[119] For example, it is possible to infringe a registered mark through the use of a similar mark. Thus, although, following *Libertel*, Orange will give a precise Pantone colour code to identify the colour orange it wishes to register, nonetheless the use by another trader (for example easyGroup on its phones) of any other shade of orange will potentially fall within Orange's monopoly.[120] Similarly, the range of goods and services covered by registration are not determinative. We have seen that a trade mark with a reputation will be infringed by use of an identical or similar mark on dissimilar goods, suggesting that, despite the requirements of the Registry to identify the goods and services against which a mark is registered, the law has recognized the 'transferability' of trade marks as brands.

At a conceptual level too, the protection afforded by registration is unclear. We have seen how registered marks may carry a number of meanings: they may be descriptive of the goods against which they are registered and, if they have acquired distinctiveness through use, they may also be a badge of origin. Only the latter meaning will be protected through registration. Trade marks may also carry 'brand values', such as the Orange brands' qualities of being 'friendly, honest, straightforward, dynamic'. But the extent to which these advertising qualities will be protected by trade mark registration, following the decision in *Arsenal* v *Reed*, is by no means clear. Certainly, it is clear that Orange does not have a monopoly over these 'orange' qualities *tout court*. It may well be that the Ukrainians who campaigned with orange banners did so, in part, because they too saw the colour orange as, 'honest, straightforward and dynamic'. As David Lange has observed:[121] 'unlike real estate or personality, intel-lectual property is subject to unlimited recreation in the mind of each

[119] Burrell and Handler, 'Making Sense' at 405.
[120] For a similar point, see ibid. at 405. They also argue that whether, in infringement actions, a judge will find that a mark has been infringed, because the average consumer will be confused as to origin, may depend upon not just how the mark looks on the register but also how it has been in practice used in the marketplace (406–7).
[121] D. Lange, 'Recognizing the Public Domain' (1981) 44 *Law and Contemporary Problems* 147 at 150.

observer. This causes trouble enough in the task of establishing recognizable boundaries. But the real difficulty arises from the fact that more than
one person sensibly may assert a proprietary interest in what looks like the
same property.' We have argued here that this difficulty certainly holds
true in relation to trade marks. Far from there being a fixed legal definition of a trade mark, the most that can be said about a registered trade
mark is that it lies somewhere between a sign and a brand.

4 "See me, feel me, touch me, hea[r] me" (and maybe smell and taste me too): I am a trademark – a US perspective*

Jane C. Ginsburg

The preceding chapter, "Between a sign and a brand," addresses the current law in the UK and the EU regarding which signs can be a registered trademark, and the scope of protection a trademark receives. Jennifer Davis also considers the extent to which that scope does or should cover the more ineffable subject matter of "brand values." This comment from the perspective of United States trademark law will follow a similar plan. It first will address what is (and is not) a trademark, focusing on the extensions of trademarks beyond traditional word marks and design marks (logos; trade dress [get-up]) to the more controversial categories of product shape, colors, sounds, smells, tastes and touch. It then will explore the scope of protection, particularly with reference to recent legislation concerning "dilution," representing Congress' latest attempt to provide greater legal security to the "commercial magnetism"[1] of famous marks, while recognizing the free speech interests in the parodies, critiques and comparisons those marks also attract.

In US trademark law, state common law and federal statutory regimes cohabitate: statutory protection under the Lanham Federal Trademarks Act[2] adds to but does not fully supersede the underlying common law rules and rationale for trademark protection. Thus, for example, carrying forward the common law rule that "There is no such thing as a property in a trade-mark except as a right appurtenant to an established business"[3] a mark will not be registered unless it has been "used in commerce."[4] But a mark that has been used does not have to be registered to be protected

---

* Apologies to The Who.
[1] *Mishawaka Rubber & Woolen Mfg Co. v S. S. Kresge Co.* (1942) 316 US 203, 205.
[2] 15 USC §§ 1051 ff., first enacted 1946.
[3] *United Drug Co.v Theodore Rectanus Co.* (1918) 248 US 90, 97.
[4] See Lanham Act §§ 1(a)(1) and (d), 15 USC § 1051(a)(1) and (d).

either under the Lanham Act,[5] or at common law.[6] By the same token, given the broad inclusiveness of federal statutory subject matter, it is unlikely any sign capable of signaling a single source of origin would not be recognized under both the federal statute and state common law. The ensuing discussion will concentrate on the Lanham Act, but the analysis would apply to state law as well.

What is (and is not) a trademark?

The Lanham Act, section 2, establishes that, so long as a term is distinctive, it shall not be refused registration "on account of its nature."[7] Thus, rather than prescribing the kinds of marks that may be registered, the statute proceeds from the premise that the mark is protectable, and then provides a list of unless-es – bases on which a mark may be denied registration.[8] The key question thus becomes whether, to the relevant public, the mark "identifies and distinguishes" the goods or services of a particular producer;[9] do "buyers merely underst[an]d that the word [or sign means a kind of good or service in general, or does] it mean ... that and more than that; i.e., that it came from the same single, though if one please anonymous, source from which they had got it before?"[10]

The Supreme Court emphasized the statute's sweeping welcome in a case concerning the registrability of a single color applied to an ironing board presspad, a shade of green-gold unappealing in the abstract, but attractive enough to a competitor who allegedly sought to lure away customers who had come to identify the color with the plaintiff.[11] The lower court had applied an unwritten rule barring the registration of single colours, and the Supreme Court reversed. If, as the facts suggested, the colour had achieved secondary meaning, there was no per se reason to exclude it from the subject matter of trademarks. The defendant had contended that the color was "functional," and that registering it would disable other merchants from employing a product characteristic necessary to effective

---

[5] § 43(a) of the Lanham Act, 15 USC § 1125(a), which protects, *inter alia*, against "false designations of origin," has come to be interpreted to protect unregistered marks of all kinds.

[6] There are, however, several advantages to federal trademark registration; see Jane C. Ginsburg, Jessica Litman, Mary L. Kevlin, *Trademark and Unfair Competition Law* (4th edn., New York: Foundation Press, 2007) 177–9.

[7] "No trademark by which the goods of the applicant may be distinguished from the goods of others shall be refused registration on the principal register on account of its nature."

[8] This echoes the approach taken in the 1888 Amendment of the Patent, Designs and Trade Marks Act 1883; see Lionel Bently, Chapter 1 of this volume, 3–41.

[9] Lanham Act § 45; 15 USC § 1127 (definition of a trademark).

[10] *Bayer Co.v United Drug Co.* 272 F. 505, 509 (SDNY 1921)(Learned Hand, J).

[11] *Qualitex Co.* v *Jacobson Prods. Co. Inc.* (1995) 514 US 159.

competition in the goods. Functionality is indeed a longstanding doctrine in US trademarks law, precluding protection (at common law or by statute[12]) for a product feature "'if it is essential to the use or purpose of the article or if it affects the cost or quality of the article,' that is, if exclusive use of the feature would put competitors at a significant non-reputation-related disadvantage."[13] For example, in its celebrated "Shredded Wheat" decision,[14] the Supreme Court in 1938 declined to protect the pillow shape of the breakfast cereal because the form followed the functioning of a patent-expired device. Once competitors were free to copy and use the machine, its output must be equally free; to prohibit making cereal in the same shape would mean that competitors would have to incur the cost of designing around the shape by devising a different machine.[15] In *Qualitex*, however, while the court acknowledged that *some* color for a presspad was functional – because color hides the ironing stains – there was no competitive need for the plaintiff's *particular* color: a variety of somber shades would do.

Colors, even single colors, however, are visual marks, and come within a well-recognized category. What about marks directed at other senses? If, as the statute states, trademark protection extends to "any word, name, symbol, or device" used to indicate the source of goods, how broad is a "symbol or device," and how inviting is the "any?" The legislative history of the 1988 amendments to the Lanham Act suggests that the accommodation is vast indeed. The United States Trademark Association Trademark Review Commission's report to Congress had recommended that "the terms 'symbol, or device' ... not be deleted or narrowed to preclude registration of such things as a color, shape, smell, sound, or configuration which functions as a mark," and its suggestion was followed.[16] The *Qualitex* court similarly emphasized the statute's catholicity: "It is the source-distinguishing ability of a mark – not its ontological status as color, shape, fragrance, word, or sign – that permits it to serve these basic purposes [of identifying source]." Thus, for example, the flower-shape of the *Bongrain* cheese,[17] could well be registered in

---

[12] See Lanham Act § 2(e)(5) (functionality as a basis for denial of registration).
[13] *Qualitex* at 165, citing *Inwood Laboratories, Inc. v Ives Laboratories, Inc.* (1982) 456 US 844, 850, n. 10.
[14] *Kellogg Co. v National Biscuit Co.* (1938) 305 US 111 (Brandeis, J).
[15] The court also held the term "shredded wheat" generic for that type of cereal, see discussion below, text at notes 29–30.
[16] "The United States Trademark Association Trademark Review Commission Report and Recommendations to USTA President and Board of Directors" (1987) 77 *Trademark Rep.* 375, 421; see also (1987) 133 Cong. Rec. 32812 (statement of Sen. DeConcini) ("The bill I am introducing today is based on the Commission's report and recommendations").
[17] *Bongrain SA's Trade Mark Application* [2005] ETMR 472; see discussion in Davis, Chapter 3 of this volume, 65–91.

the USA, assuming secondary meaning were shown.[18] That does not mean the *taste* of the cheese could be a trademark, too. While taste marks and smell marks are at least theoretically registrable, it is important to ensure that the alleged mark does not collapse into the product itself. Bongrain cheese does not have to be flower-shaped to taste the same. But the taste (and perhaps the texture) *is* the cheese, so no matter how gastronomically distinctive (which may be highly debatable in fact), the taste is not "distinctive" in the trademark sense. The US Patent and Trademark Office's skeptical reception of flavor marks underscores the problem. For example, in upholding the Examiner's denial of registration to an orange flavor for antidepressants in quick-dissolving tablets and pills,[19] the Trademark Trial and Appeal Board (TTAB) recently held:

[W]e are not blind to the practical considerations involved in the registration of flavor marks. Flavor perception is very subjective; what applicant considers to be a unique and distinctive orange flavor may be considered by patients as simply an orange flavor ... Further, it is not clear how taste would as a practical matter function as a trademark ... [I]t is difficult to fathom exactly how a flavor could function as a source indicator in the classic sense, unlike the situation with other nontraditional trademarks such as color, sound and smell, to which consumers may be exposed prior to purchase.[20]

It is noteworthy that the TTAB appears to have taken the registration of sound and smell marks as a fait accompli. Like taste marks, smell marks present a risk of merging with the product, and the TTAB has accordingly cautioned that registration should be excluded for "scents or fragrances of products which are noted for those features, such as perfumes, colognes or scented household products."[21] Where, however, the nontraditional sign is more than a mere "pleasant feature of the goods,"[22] and does symbolize source, it is registrable. So it is only fitting that the Trademark Office has recently added another sense to the Principal Register's roster of sensory marks; it has accepted a trademark application for a "sensory, touch mark," consisting of a "velvet textured covering on the surface of a bottle of wine."[23]

---

[18] In *Wal–Mart Stores, Inc.* v *Samara Brothers, Inc.* (2000) 529 US 205, the Supreme Court held that a showing of secondary meaning was a prerequisite to protecting product designs (as opposed to packaging).

[19] *In re Organon, NV*, 79 USPQ.2D (BNA) 1639, 2006 TTAB LEXIS 206 (TTAB 2006) (also holding orange flavor functional for masking the unpleasant tastes of certain medicines). See also *Perk Scientific, Inc.* v *Ever Scientific, Inc.*, WL 851078 (ED Pa. 2005) (lack of carbonation and flavor selection held functional for glucose-tolerant beverage products).

[20] *Organon* at 2006 TTAB LEXIS 206 *41.

[21] *In re Clarke*, 17 USPQ.2d 1238, 1990 TTAB LEXIS 53 *7 (TTAB 1990).

[22] Id. at 1990 TTAB LEXIS 53 *5.

[23] See Registration Number 3155702 (17 October 2006).

Whatever the sense engaged by the mark, the mark must be "distinctive" of a single producer's goods or services. In other words, the purchasing public must recognize it as a trademark. In the case of nontraditional marks, including product shape, demonstrating that the public perceives the alleged mark as a mark is not always easy. For example, an appellate court rejected an assertion of trademark rights in the appearance of the Rock and Roll Hall of Fame Museum in Cleveland, Ohio.[24] While the museum was well known, and the I. M. Pei building was famous as a work of architecture, the Court was not persuaded that the public had come to see the overall shape of the building as a symbol for museum services. In the context of more conventional signs, however, trademark law has developed a framework for analyzing a mark's degree of distinctiveness; this in turn affects the availability and scope of protection.

At the top of the scale are "technical trademarks," terms which are "inherently distinctive," and thus qualify for protection or registration without demonstration of secondary meaning.[25] These include coined terms and "arbitrary" terms (words used completely out of lexicographic context, such as "apple" for computers) and "suggestive" terms (words which convey some information about the product, its attributes or its benefits, but do not fully describe it, such as "Ivory" for soap). Terms which are "merely descriptive" may be protected or registered, but must in effect earn their way to public recognition, through acquisition of "secondary meaning." Although developing secondary meaning obviously entails costs, proprietors nonetheless tend to favor descriptive terms because adopting descriptive terms for a trademark saves on communication costs: the mark will convey to potential consumers the key characteristics of the goods or services (that, of course, is why the trademark law declines to protect such marks *ab initio*, for fear of disabling competitors from deploying such indicative terms).

Generic terms, by contrast, may not be protected, and if they have been registered, they are subject to cancellation "at any time."[26] The ghosts haunting the US "trademarks graveyard"[27] include such former marks as "aspirin," "escalator," "nylon," and "linoleum." These are terms that lost their source-identifying significance, or as the Xerox Corporation's trademark-awareness advertisement cautioned, "They were once proud trademarks, now they're just names."[28] The public's (and competitors')

---

[24] *Rock & Roll Hall of Fame and Museum* v *Gentile Productions* 134 F.3d 749 (6th Cir. 1998).
[25] See, generally, *Abercrombie & Fitch Co.* v *Hunting World Inc.* 537 F.2d 4, 9–10 (2nd Cir. 1976).
[26] 15 USC § 1064(a); Lanham Act § 14(3).
[27] See Ginsburg *et al.*, *Trademark and Unfair Competition Law* 279.   [28] Ibid.

right to call the article by "the name by which it had become known"[29] will always take precedence over the former trademark proprietor's investment in the mark or the goods to which the mark was affixed. As Justice Brandeis emphasized in addressing Nabisco's claim to trademark rights in the term SHREDDED WHEAT, competition policy requires this result. This is true even, or perhaps especially, when the former trademark proprietor was first to market the goods for which its mark has become synonymous. Thus, Justice Brandeis endorsed the second-comer's free-riding: "Kellogg Company is undoubtedly sharing in the goodwill of the article known as 'Shredded Wheat'; and thus is sharing in a market which was created by the skill and judgment of plaintiff's predecessor and has been widely extended by vast expenditures in advertising persistently made." In other words, Nabisco and its predecessor *created* the market for the cereal; they fostered the demand for the product.[30] Then Kellogg, having expended no resources to make the public want to buy the cereal, came along to reap the benefits of Nabisco's assiduous cultivation of customers. "But that is not unfair," emphasized Brandeis. Kellogg is fully entitled to "shar[e] in the goodwill of [the] article," so long as it takes precautions not to deceive the public as to the source.

Scope of protection

If the principles and consequences of genericism (or "genericide") have remained fairly constant, US trademark law has in other ways evolved considerably since the simpler times of SHREDDED WHEAT. This may be most true with respect to the scope of trademark protection. Traditionally, "the trademark is treated as merely a protection for the goodwill, and not the subject of property except in connection with an existing business,"[31] and goodwill derived only from the specific goods sold or services offered in the specific locations where the trademark owner was doing business. The mark thus had no purchase as against different goods or in different places. Or, as summed up with character-istic eloquence by Judge Learned Hand in 1928:

The law of unfair trade comes down very nearly to this – as judges have repeated again and again – that one merchant shall not divert customers from another by

---

[29] *Kellogg*, above, note 14, 305 US at 118.
[30] As Graeme Dinwoodie recounts, inspiring this demand was no small task: initial public reaction to the cereal derided it as "shredded doormat," see Graeme B. Dinwoodie, "The Story of *Kellogg Co. v National Biscuit Co.*: Breakfast with Brandeis" in Jane C. Ginsburg and Rochelle Cooper Dreyfuss (eds.) *Intellectual Property Stories* (New York: Foundation Press, 2005) 222.
[31] *Hanover Star Milling Co. v Metcalf*, (1916) 240 US 403, 414.

representing what he sells as emanating from the second. This has been, and perhaps even more now is, the whole Law and the Prophets on the subject, though it assumes many guises. Therefore it was at first a debatable point whether a merchant's good will, indicated by his mark, could extend beyond such goods as he sold. How could he lose bargains which he had no means to fill? What harm did it do a chewing gum maker to have an ironmonger use his trade-mark? The law often ignores the nicer sensibilities.[32]

Even then, however, courts had begun to recognize that closely related goods could come within the ambit of the trademark. The "Aunt Jemima Doctrine," so-called from the decision holding that the seller of "Aunt Jemima" pancake syrup infringed the AUNT JEMIMA trademark for pancake flour, recognized that

goods, though different, may be so related as to fall within the mischief which equity should prevent. Syrup and flour are both food products, and food products commonly used together. Obviously the public, or a large part of it, seeing this trade-mark on a syrup, would conclude that it was made by the complainant. Perhaps they might not do so, if it were used for flatirons. In this way the complainant's reputation is put in the hands of the defendants. It will enable them to get the benefit of the complainant's reputation and advertisement.[33]

But what about the "flatirons?" Self-rising flour and flatirons, albeit both domestic articles, are so distant that it is unlikely the public would confuse one purveyor with the other, and no infringement would be found. Where the trademark is very famous, however, its market appeal may not be limited to the specific goods that it produces or closely related ones, and the ironmonger may derive unfair commercial advantage from the generalized goodwill the mark enjoys, at the cost of the diminution of that goodwill. Or so Frank Schechter contended in 1927 in a classic article titled "The Rational Basis of Trademark Protection":

[T]oday the trademark is not merely the symbol of good will but often the most effective agent for the creation of good will, imprinting upon the public mind an anonymous and impersonal guaranty of satisfaction, creating a desire for further satisfactions. The mark actually sells the goods. And, self-evidently, the more distinctive the mark, the more effective is its selling power . . . The real injury in all such cases [in which the mark is used on remote goods] can only be gauged in the light of what has been said concerning the function of a trademark. It is the gradual whittling away or dispersion of the identity and hold upon the public mind of the mark or name by its use upon non-competing goods. The more distinctive or unique the mark, the deeper is its impress upon the public

---

[32] *Yale Electric Corp.* v *Robertson* 26 F.2d 972, 973–4 (2nd Cir. 1928).
[33] *Aunt Jemima Mills Co.* v *Rigney & Co.* 247 F. 407, 409–10 (2nd Cir. 1917) (Learned Hand did not write the opinion, but sat on the panel).

consciousness, and the greater its need for protection against vitiation or dissociation from the particular product in connection with which it has been used.[34]

The harm Schechter described came to be known as "dilution," and, over time, many states began to enact "anti dilution" statutes.[35] In 1995, Congress adopted a federal anti-dilution act,[36] which it amended at the end of 2006.[37]

By the time Congress federalized dilution, however, courts had already so expanded the concept of "confusion" as to bring even many remote exploitations within the ambit of the owner of a famous trademark. Starting with the Second Circuit's 1961 decision in *Polaroid* [cameras] v *Polarad* [microwave receiving devices and television studio equipment],[38] courts addressing infringement claims concerning goods or services that were not identical to the plaintiff's inquired how similar the marks were, how close the goods or services were, and whether the plaintiff was likely (or perceived to be likely) to "bridge the gap" between its goods and the defendant's.[39] As trademark owners diversified the goods to which they affixed the mark, the zones of "proximate" products, and potential gap-bridging, expanded accordingly. In the 1980s and 1990s, with the increase in "merchandizing properties," goods that once seemed remote, such as beverages and clothing, now came within the tentacular embrace of famous marks, such as COCA-COLA. Indeed, as Schechter predicted, the mark sold the goods, no matter what they were, and – on beyond Schechter – the most famous marks came to sell not just goods, but an associated life style (usually connected with vigor, youth and beauty).

The judicial history of sports team merchandising illustrates the trajectory of trademarks from brand (in the sense of a proprietor's mark on a

---

[34] Frank I. Schechter, "The Rational Basis of Trademark Protection" (1927) 40 Harv L. Rev 813.

[35] These statutes and their federal counterparts arguably redefined the concept to encompass a far broader range of marks than Schechter intended. See Sara K. Stadler, "The Wages of Ubiquity in Trademark Law" (2003) 88 Iowa L. Rev 731.

[36] Federal Trademark Dilution Act of 1995, Pub. L. No. 104–98, 4, 109 Stat. 985, 986 (1995), *amending* 15 USC 1125 (2000).

[37] Trademark Dilution Revision Act of 2006, *amending* 15 USC 1125 (2006).

[38] *Polaroid Corp.* v *Polarad Elects. Corp.* 287 F.2d 492, 495 (2nd Cir.) (1961). The "*Polaroid* factors" are: "the strength of his mark, the degree of similarity between the two marks, the proximity of the products, the likelihood that the prior owner will bridge the gap, actual confusion, and the reciprocal of defendant's good faith in adopting its own mark, the quality of defendant's product, and the sophistication of the buyers." The Second Circuit did not in fact apply the factors to analyze infringement because it held that laches barred Polaroid's claim. The District Court had found no likelihood of confusion because the parties' goods did not overlap: 182 F. Supp.350 (EDNY 1960).

[39] Each of the federal circuits has its own version of the "*Polaroid* factors," many of them adding a "channels of trade" inquiry. See generally Ginsburg *et al.*, *Trademark and Unfair Competition Law* at 334–5.

particular good) to branding (in the sense of the progressive irrelevance of particular goods relative to the market power of the mark they bear). In the early 1980s, courts could still decline to find that the purveyor of unlicensed T-shirts bearing the name and insignia of a sports team was likely to cause confusion as to the origin or sponsorship of the unauthorized goods. Moreover, courts held that there was no legal support for an exclusive property right in the name and insignia.[40] By the end of the 1980s, however, the proposition that the sports team or event organizer enjoyed exclusive T-shirt rights appeared well established on either or both of two grounds: a rather credulous likelihood of confusion theory, or a more forthright, but legally frail, theory of a right to control "promotional goods" independently of proof of likely confusion.[41] So well settled, in fact, that Judge Alex Kozinski, who is a trenchant critic both of intellectual property (IP) and of popular culture, could in a 1993 article provocatively titled "Trademarks Unplugged"[42] (in homage to Eric Clapton,[43] but he might just as well have termed it "Trademarks Unmoored"), deplore the paucity of legal or moral justifications for giving sports teams control over fan loyalty goods, while recognizing that the positive law achieved that result. More broadly, Judge Kozinski observed "a growing tendency to use trademarks not just to identify products but also to enhance or adorn them, even to create new commodities altogether,"[44] and (*à la* Schechter) that "'ideograms that once functioned solely as signals denoting the source, origin, and quality of goods, have become products in their own right, valued as indicators of the status, preferences, and aspirations of those who use them.'"[45]

Trademark owners (or at least certain trademark owners) achieved this level of protection while nominally remaining within the framework of likelihood of confusion. Trademarks were not, at least not formally, a "right in gross" entitled to exclusivity even in the absence of a risk of

---

[40] *University of Pittsburgh* v *Champion Products* 566 F. Supp.711 (WD Pa. 1983) ("We have considerable sympathy for the plaintiff, University of Pittsburgh ('Pitt'). The notion that a university's name and insignia [for its football team] are its own property, to do with as it chooses, has a certain common-sense appeal. An examination of the law and the facts in this case has convinced us, however, that neither Congress, nor the Pennsylvania Legislature, nor the common law has created the property right that Pitt asserts here. We believe that were we to rule in favor of Pitt, we would be creating a new substantive right in an area of the law in which Congress and the states have legislated extensively. The relief sought by Pitt is not minor; it amounts to a judicially created, perpetual monopoly on a product, Pitt-insignia soft goods, which many people wish to purchase").
[41] *Boston Athletic Ass'n* v *Sullivan* 867 F.2d 22 (1st Cir. 1989).
[42] "Trademarks Unplugged" (1993) 68 NYUL Rev 960.   [43] See Ibid., n.*
[44] Ibid. at 961.
[45] Ibid. at 965, *quoting* Rochelle Cooper Dreyfuss, "Expressive Genericity: Trademarks as Language in the Pepsi Generation" (1990) 65 Notre Dame L. Rev 397, 397–8.

deceit. Congress changed that with the Federal Trademark Dilution Act of 1995, which protected "distinctive" famous marks even in the absence of likelihood of confusion or of competition. Thus, there would now be a clear federal right against the kinds of free rides that Schechter lamented, such as "Kodak" bicycles and "Rolls Royce" radio parts.[46] But this reinforcement of trademark protection coincided with increased public appropriation of trademarks as figures of speech. Already in 1990, Professor Rochelle Dreyfuss had proclaimed:

Trademarks have come a long way. Originating in the stratified economy of the middle ages as a marketing tool of the merchant class, these symbols have passed into popular culture . . . Some trademarks have worked their way into the English language; others provide bases for vibrant, evocative metaphors. In a sense, trademarks are the emerging lingua franca: with a sufficient command of these terms, one can make oneself understood the world over, and in the process, enjoy the comforts of home.[47]

The commercial ubiquity some trademarks enjoyed had come to permeate popular and even political speech,[48] sometimes ridiculing the trademark proprietor or its goods or services, sometimes using the trademark as a vehicle for a broader social point. For example, in *MasterCard International Inc.* v *Nader 2000 Primary Committee, Inc.*, at issue were the well-known MasterCard advertisements which the court described as follows:

"Priceless Advertisements." These advertisements feature the names and images of several goods and services purchased by individuals which, with voice overs and visual displays, convey to the viewer the price of each of these items. At the end of each of the Priceless Advertisements a phrase identifying some priceless intangible that cannot be purchased (such as "a day where all you have to do is breathe") is followed by the words or voice over: "Priceless. There are some things money can't buy, for everything else there's MasterCard."

---

[46] Schechter, "Rational Basis" 825.
[47] Dreyfuss, "Expressive Genericity" at 397–8. See also Robert C. Denicola, "Trademarks as Speech: Constitutional Implications of the Emerging Rationales for the Protection of Trade Symbols" (1982) Wis. L. Rev 158; Pierre N. Leval, "Trademark: Champion of Free Speech" (2004) 27 Colum. J. L. & the Arts 187.
[48] See, e.g., *Lucasfilms* v *High Frontier*, 622 F. Supp.931 (DDC 1985) (group critical of President Reagan's missile shield program dubbed it "Star Wars" and incurred – unsuccessful – lawsuit by producer of *Star Wars* films); *MasterCard International Inc.* v *Nader 2000 Primary Committee, Inc.*, 70 USPQ 2D (BNA) 1046, 2004 US Dist. LEXIS 3644 (SDNY 2004), discussed below; *American Family Life Insurance Company* v *Hagan, et al.*, 266 F. Supp.2d 682 (ND Ohio 2002)(political advertisement for gubernatorial candidate appropriated cartoon character symbol of plaintiff life insurance company to ridicule opponent).

Third-party presidential candidate Ralph Nader reworked the message to
his own purposes:

That political ad included a sequential display of a series of items showing the
price of each ("grilled tenderloin for fund-raiser; $1,000 a plate"; "campaign ads
filled with half-truths: $10 million"; "promises to special interest groups: over
$100 billion"). The advertisement ends with a phrase identifying a priceless
intangible that cannot be purchased ("finding out the truth: priceless. There are
some things that money can't buy").[49]

If trademarks now were to be enforceable against remote and non-
competing uses, did they threaten expressive uses in works of politics, art,
literature or even music? The 1995 legislation exempted comparative
advertising, news reporting and non-commercial uses, but it was not
clear (at least, not clear to the plaintiff trademark owners) that expressive
works that their creators offered for sale, or through which they sought
political donations, would qualify as "non-commercial." The case law,
however, came to interpret "non-commercial" broadly to encompass not
only political speech,[50] but also artistic, and even entertainment, exploitations. Judge Kozinski authored the leading decision, *Mattel* v *Universal
Music*.[51] In that case, the song "Barbie Girl" by the Danish one-hit (at
least in the USA) group Aqua in 1997 foisted on the airwaves lyrics like
the following, nasally sung to a catchy refrain: "I'm a Barbie girl, in a
Barbie world. Life in plastic, it's fantastic. You can brush my hair,
undress me everywhere. Imagination, life is your creation ... I'm a
blond bimbo girl, in a fantasy world. Dress me up, make it tight, I'm
your dolly." To which the bass in the group would interject in a froggish
croak (Aqua's album was, after all, called "Aquarium"): "C'mon Barbie,
let's go party!"

Holding that "the trademark owner does not have the right to control
public discourse whenever the public imbues his mark with a meaning
beyond its source-identifying function,"[52] the Ninth Circuit rejected
both the likelihood of confusion and the dilution claims urged by the
producers of the BARBIE doll. Following Second Circuit precedent, the
Ninth Circuit balanced the "public interest in free expression" against
the "public interest in avoiding consumer confusion," and accorded the
former decisive weight unless the song title's appropriation of BARBIE

---

[49] *MasterCard*, 2004 US Dist. LEXIS 3644 at *3.
[50] In ruling against MasterCard, the court pointed to legislative history distinguishing political from commercial speech, and affirming that political speech was "non-commercial"
under the dilution Act: ibid. at *24, *citing* 134 Cong. Rec. H. 1297 (daily edn. 13 April
1989) (statement of Wisconsin Rep. Kastenmeier).
[51] *Mattel, Inc.* v *Universal Music International* 296 F.3d 894 (9th Cir. 2002).
[52] Ibid. at 900.

"has no artistic relevance to the underlying work whatsoever, or, if it has some artistic relevance, unless the title explicitly misleads as to the source or the content of the work."[53] Observing that the BARBIE doll was the target of the song, the court held the group was entitled to identify the butt of its joke, and had done nothing to mislead the public into thinking that Mattel authorized the song. The Court dismissed the dilution claim on the ground that the 1996 Federal Trademark Dilution Act's exception for "non-commercial uses" should be construed to include parodies.

Congress has now endorsed this approach, by making explicit exceptions for parodying and criticizing or commenting on the trademark or its proprietor.[54] One of the first decisions to apply the 2006 amendments rejected the dilution claims brought by Louis Vuitton against a pets' novelty items company calling itself "Haute Diggity Dog." According to the court, HDD sells 'a line of pet chew toys and beds whose names parody elegant high-end brands of products such as perfume, cars, shoes, sparkling wine and handbags. These include – in addition to Chewy Vuiton (Louis Vuitton) – Chewnel No. 5 (Chanel No. 5), Furcedes (Mercedes), Jimmy Chew (Jimmy Cheo), Dog Perignonn (Dom Perignon), Sniffany & Co. (Tiffany & Co.) and Dogior (Dior). The chew toys and pet beds are plush, made of polyester, and have a shape and design that loosely imitate the signature product of the targeted brand. They are mostly distributed and sold through pet stores, although one or two Macy's stores carry Haute Diggity Dog's products. The dog toys are generally sold for less than $20."[55] Not exactly high (or even low) art, but a healthy recognition that humor can puncture even today's armor-clad trademark

---

[53] Ibid. at 902, citing *Rogers* v *Grimaldi* 875 F.2d 994, 999 (2nd Cir. 1989).
[54] Lanham Act § 43(c)(3) Exclusions. The following shall not be actionable as dilution by blurring or dilution by tarnishment under this subsection:
(A) Any fair use, including a nominative or descriptive fair use, or facilitation of such fair use, of a famous mark by another person other than as a designation of source for the person's own goods or services, including use in connection with –
(i) advertising or promotion that permits consumers to compare goods or services; or
(ii) identifying and parodying, criticizing, or commenting upon the famous mark owner or the goods or services of the famous mark owner.
[55] *Louis Vuitton Malletier SA* v *Haute Diggity Dog*, 507 F. 3d 252 (4th Cir. 2007). The appellate court held that the Trademark Dilution Revision Act's parody exception did not apply to Haute Diggity Dog because the defendant was using the altered famous trademarks as trademarks for its own goods; Section 43(c)(3)(A) exempts "fair use . . . of a famous mark by another person *other than as a designation of source for the person's own goods or services* . . ." (emphasis supplied). The court nonetheless found no violation of the revised dilution Act because the parodistic character of the defendant's use made blurring or tarnishment of the plaintiff's mark unlikely.

law.[56] That said, there remain speech-relevant ambiguities in the 2006 Anti-Dilution amendments. The parody and commentary exception applies to "identifying and parodying, criticizing, or commenting upon the famous mark owner or the goods or services of the famous mark owner."[57] What about uses, such as the Nader advertisement's, employing the trademark as a springboard to criticize something else? There is an arguable connection between Nader's lambasting of the insidious influence of money on politics and the MasterCard messages celebrating lavish expenditures, but one has to work at it to extract from the Nader advertisement an oblique critique of MasterCard.[58] On the other hand, even if the Nader advertisement is not a parody of MasterCard, its broader social critique might entitle it to be deemed a "fair use." The US copyright law has recently proved more welcoming than in the past of fair use defenses involving uses more satirical than strictly parodistic.[59] If the trademark law follows copyright's lead in this respect, as it has with respect to parody defenses,[60] then the trademarks "fair use" defense should encompass satire as well. Moreover, if, courts continue to interpret the general exception for "Any noncommercial use of a mark"[61] as generously as they did before the 2006 amendments, then we can hope that the trademark owner's rights will stop where third party artistic and political speech begins.

---

[56] For more extensive discussion of this proposition, see Jane C.Ginsburg, "Of Mutant Copyrights, Mangled Trademarks, and Barbie's Beneficence: The Influence of Copyright on Trademark Law" in Graeme Dinwoodie and Mark Janis (eds.), *Trademark Law and Theory: A Handbook of Contemporary Research* (Cheltenham: Edward Elgar, forthcoming 2008) (hereafter Ginsburg, "Mutant, Mangled").

[57] Lanham Act, § 43(c)(3)(A)(ii).

[58] For a similar exercise reconciling the South African dilution statute with constitutional guarantees of free speech, see *Laugh it Off Promotions CC* v *South African Breweries Int'l., Constitutional Court of S. Africa* (27 May 2005) CCT 42/04 ("Black Labour" t-shirt emulating logo of "Carling Black Label" beer and altering slogan "America's Lusty Lively Beer" to "Africa's Lusty Lively Exploitation"; it is not apparent that the Carling brewery was especially associated with apartheid; – rather, the T-shirt's message seems to have targeted a broader social problem).

[59] See, e.g., *Blanch* v *Koons* 467 F.3d 244 (2nd Cir. 2006) (incorporation of substantial copy of plaintiff's photograph in artistic collage satirizing modern mass consumption held fair use).

[60] For a discussion of the influence of copyright fair use case law on the evolving defense of fair use in trademark law, see Ginsburg, "Mutant, Mangled".

[61] Lanham Act § 43(c)(3)(C).

Part III

Linguistics

5 'How can I tell the trade mark on a piece of gingerbread from all the other marks on it?' Naming and meaning in verbal trade mark signs

Alan Durant

Introduction

The law of trade marks has evolved, in different jurisdictions, by addressing two interconnected sets of questions. The first set consists of questions regarding the degree of protection against confusion and deception that should be offered to consumers and traders, over and above traditional passing-off arrangements, in cases where names are used as trade badges or signatures of commercial personae. The second set, less prominent in the literature, are more abstract questions about how names and descriptions achieve their functions of denoting and referring to things in the world. Current legal argument is concerned to find a satisfactory route through these two, intertwined sets of difficulties. This chapter argues that the question voiced in no-nonsense Victorian fashion in my title (which, as Lionel Bently shows elsewhere in this volume,[1] encapsulates a developing nineteenth-century concern with precisely what it is about a sign that allows it to function as a trade mark) resists a definitive answer as much now as during the Victorian period, and continues to have legal significance.

Understandably in legal studies the main emphasis in relation to these two questions falls on how signs function as badges of origin in changing markets, rather than how signs function in principle. In this chapter, in a way that I intend to be complementary, I consider questions about trade mark signification from a broadly linguistic rather than legal perspective. Drawing on relevant published work,[2] I first revisit, as a matter of

---

[1] Lionel Bently, Chapter 1 of this volume. Among other topics, Bently explores how criteria evolved for differentiating between marks on a product that might be understood as 'trade marks'. Nineteenth-century discussion of gingerbread focussed especially on how trade marks differ from accidental and decorative signs.

[2] The most comprehensive and useful account of trade marks from a linguistic point of view is Roger Shuy, *Linguistic Battles in Trademark Disputes* (Basingstoke: Palgrave, 2002). As well as providing an introduction to linguistics for lawyers, and an introduction to trade

vocabulary, the canonical contrast in trade mark law between 'distinctive' and 'descriptive' signs.[3] In doing so, I explicate what might be called 'ordinary language confusion' surrounding the two terms[4] but go on to explore their divergent, technical meanings in trade mark law and in linguistics. My account of the two words shows how the 'distinctive'/ 'descriptive' threshold is made particularly important by how problematic entanglements at the border between the two categories become entangled. Linguistic formulation of this point strengthens an already established legal view: that the border zone between the two categories, both in terms of eligibility for registration and as regards enforcement of trade mark rights, should be judged on the basis of criteria to do with *use* of verbal signs in a given context as much as in terms of differing, but essentially stable *kinds* or *types* of sign.

The capability for meaning of verbal signs that overspills the canonical binary categorization – and which therefore calls for sharpened focus on types of use – may shed light on trade mark enforcement issues where 'trade mark use' is contrasted with other kinds of permissible use. To introduce this topic, I outline the established scale of different conceptual strengths of possible trade mark signs commonly used to show relative eligibility for protection (in the United States often referred to as the 'Abercrombie scale'[5]): from new coinages, through associative and

marks for linguists, Shuy reports a series of US cases in which he acted as an expert witness. In each, he shows how detailed evidence about how language works can be brought to bear on decisions to be made in trade mark litigation. The most ambitious account of trade marks from a legal-semiotic perspective, with thorough introductions to semiotic concepts as well as analyses of how those concepts relate to legal doctrines, is Barton Beebe, 'The Semiotic Analysis of Trademark Law' (2004) *UCLA Law Review* 621–704.

[3] See Graeme B. Dinwoodie and Mark Janis, *Trademarks and Unfair Competition: Law and Policy* (New York: Aspen Publishers, 2004), Ch. 2.

[4] Among the main achievements of 'ordinary language philosophy' (usually associated with the philosophers Gilbert Ryle, J. L. Austin, Paul Grice and John Searle) are not only the development of general concepts that laid the foundations for modern linguistic pragmatics (e.g. speech acts, the importance of inference in meaning) but also an approach to analysing concepts in terms of how they are commonly understood (e.g. Austin's 'A Plea for Excuses' in his *Philosophical Papers*, ed. J. O. Urmson and G. J. Warnock (Oxford: Oxford University Press, 1979), 175–204. For a collection of key papers, see Charles E. Caton (ed.), *Philosophy and Ordinary Language* (Urbana: University of Illinois Press, 1970). For a general introduction to 'ordinary language philosophy', from a linguistic perspective, see Siobhan Chapman, *Philosophy for Linguists* (London: Routledge, 2000), Ch. 4. In dealing with lay understanding of *general* rather than specifically legal concepts, such work differs from recent forensic linguistic analysis of frameworks of meaning underpinning statutory or constitutional terms.

[5] See Dinwoodie and Janis, *Trademarks and Unfair Competition* 51–5; the 'spectrum of distinctiveness' referred to as 'Abercrombie' is the result of clarification made during judgment in *Abercrombie & Fitch Co v Hunting World Inc.* 537 F.2d 4 (2nd Cir. 1976). For further discussion of sign types, see J. Phillips, *Trade Mark Law: A Practical Anatomy* (Oxford: Oxford University Press, 2003), and the points of view collected in J. Phillips and

descriptive words, to generic terms. By showing the dependence of different sign-types on communicative strategies for their meaning in a given setting, I argue that notions such as 'use in a context' and correspondingly 'comprehension in a context' are as relevant in analysing trade mark problems as an abstract, semiotic scale. Commercial signs require trade mark protection when used in particular discourse contexts (or when contested by others because of use in a given context), rather than in the abstract. What they mean, what effects they have, and how far they infringe particular rights, all depend on how they are used as much as on the inherent meaning potential of the signs themselves.

This much may be uncontroversial. But shifting from 'potential meaning' towards 'meaning in use' has another significance. Differing understandings of how verbal signs work affect how we are likely to view conflicts over interpretation that arise in balancing trade mark proprietor interest on the one hand and public rights in language and communication on the other: what is often characterized in legal discussion as the question of enclosure of an intellectual common.[6] The consequences of such enclosure become acute where trade mark owners gain protection for signs close to (or in cases of acquired secondary meaning, formerly beyond) the 'descriptive'/'distinctive' border: that is, where rights are conferred in signs that continue to do other, everyday work of meaning-making beside their specialized trade mark use. In such cases, the source-denotative, or commercially identifying, name in which the proprietor gains rights scoops up a cluster of features of descriptiveness from general usage. For the commercial enterprise, this brings a benefit: that the source-identifying function is enriched by other, value-adding evocative functions; a rich, affective means of expression becomes to some extent the proprietor's monopoly. At the same time, however, any such right cuts into the pool of expressive resource available in the language at large, because the risk is created of infringement claims against users who include not only direct commercial competitors but possibly traders in other areas (e.g. in some actions for trade mark dilution) and non-trade

I. Simons (eds.), *Trade Mark Use* (Oxford: Oxford University Press, 2005). For a clear linguistic account of different sorts of sign that is specifically aimed at 'teaching the jury', see Shuy, *Linguistic Battles* 64–6.

[6] In English law, the most famous and often quoted statement of such enclosure is that of Sir Herbert Cozens-Hardy MR, from 1909: 'Wealthy traders are habitually eager to enclose part of the great common of the English language and to exclude the general public of the present day and of the future from access to the enclosure.' For detailed historical discussion of this issue from 1909 onwards, as well as analysis of the current position in European law, see Jennifer Davis, 'European Trade Mark Law and the Enclosure of the Commons' (2002) 4 IPQ 342–67.

third parties (e.g. in dilution and tarnishment actions, for example against parodic imitation).[7]

By way of conclusion, I urge that the functioning of trade marks should be viewed less as a matter of freestanding individual trade mark signs – all trade-dressed up with nowhere to go – than (as they do inevitably turn out to be in problematic cases and are already recognized as being, if possibly more in American than in European law[8]) as a specialized, commercial kind of communicative expression, or *language in use.*

My conclusion invites speculation about future directions. To that end, I briefly consider linguistic questions that arise in a narrow but possibly symptomatic kind of infringement action: actions where 'non-trade mark use' (alternatively in the United States, 'fair use') might be argued in defence.[9] Such cases reverse the border zone conflict that arises when trade mark owners encroach on descriptive powers of language. Whereas trade mark proprietors sometimes borrow expressive resources in language (and relatedly in other semiotic systems) to enhance the evocative power of their protected marks, in the contrasting 'non-trade mark use' or 'fair use' cases the issue is how far language users can go safely into 'distinctive' naming uses without falling foul of trade mark law. There may be problems, I suggest, in this latter class of cases, with precisely what 'descriptive' means. The modifier 'descriptive' seems to take on a slightly different legal meaning when combined with 'use' than it does when combined with 'sign'. Cases on this horizon of trade mark law are importantly ones in which issues beyond the 'source and goodwill' value that trade mark law has traditionally protected – issues currently more associated with brands – will largely be settled.

The distinctive/descriptive contrast

Central to the development of trade mark law has been the concept of a sign's 'distinctiveness'. For a registered trade mark, distinctiveness is an

---

[7] The increased semiotic role of trade marks in relation to brand-building is a major theme of contemporary trade mark discussion, resulting in a series of recent and further forthcoming revisions of policy.

[8] Trade mark systems involve a balance between established use, registration of signs, and enforcement of rights in the face of alleged infringement. The balance differs between jurisdictions, with the US system more focussed on use than registration, in comparison with European law. The systems also relate in slightly different ways to the tort of passing-off, which is clearly use-based.

[9] EU law provides a general defence of 'non-trade mark use' (see Art.6(1)(b) & (c) First Council Directive 89/104/EEC of 21 December 1988 to approximate the laws of the Member States relating to trade marks (hereafter TM Directive). The closest equivalent concept in US law is 'fair use' (see Lanham Act, 15 USC § 1115(b)(4)).

indispensable property: it will need distinctiveness, or an association that consumers make with the mark as a designator of unique source,[10] if it is to be registered in the first place. It will then need to retain that distinctiveness, by aggressive action if necessary, for registration not to lapse. Although there are various kinds of non-distinctiveness for signs in trade mark law, 'distinctiveness' contrasts particularly with signs judged to be 'descriptive', or 'merely descriptive'. In the latter case, the 'descriptive' or 'merely descriptive' sign is normally ineligible for trade mark protection. But it may be capable of *acquiring* distinctiveness, if prominently used and advertised, and in due course recognized as a commercial name in addition to being a descriptive expression. For this chapter, what is of most interest is how the distinction between the two categories, which has ramifications as regards not only protectability but also possible future extensions of protectability, depends on two professional terms of art that are not completely clear as to the precise linguistic use they govern.

As with many key binary oppositions, the words employed to establish the distinction between 'descriptive' and 'distinctive' are not straightforward, either individually or as a contrasting pair. This is the case even if we restrict consideration to English, leaving aside difficulties with equivalents for the two words in other languages (e.g. in the EU Trade Mark Directive, 1988). Firstly, 'distinctive' and 'descriptive', like their equivalents in other languages, are not only legal terms but also words in everyday use. The two words are also deployed, in differing technical senses (and enter into different patterns of apparent synonymy and contrast), in other specialized fields. Significantly, those other specialized fields include linguistics and the philosophy of language, which are cognate disciplines that also address the questions of naming and description with which trade mark law is concerned. We should therefore consider complexities involved in use of each of these terms, as a way first into the categories and then into the border disputes between them.

Risk of 'ordinary language confusion'

For people not immersed in trade mark law, vocabulary problems with 'distinctive' and 'descriptive', in their everyday ordinary senses, begin more or less straightaway, even if the two terms seem at face value self-evident.

---

[10] The notion of source has been subject to historical modification, reflected in a series of different source doctrines; for discussion of semiotic implications of the different notions of source, see Beebe, 'Semiotic Analysis', 677–84.

In general use, 'distinctive' in English typically signifies some characteristic that makes perceptible, or marks, a difference between two or
more things. As with many other words (e.g. 'quality', 'intelligence' or
'special'), however, 'distinctive' allows a shift – recognizable in context
though not acknowledged as a separate sense in the *Oxford English
Dictionary* (*OED*) entry[11] – from neutral differentiation to something
preferred or approved: something considered 'distinctive' is often something judged to be remarkable, conspicuously excellent or in some other
way special. This expressive resonance of the word – which, if not a sense,
may be thought part of the word's semantic prosody[12] – is found with
different degrees of fixity in a cluster of words concerned with establishing
distinctions, especially (though not only) when used of people: consider
'distinguished', for instance, or the phrase 'person of distinction' – or the
complex shift towards both ends of the value spectrum that comes with
related 'discrimination'. When a trade mark sign is described as 'distinctive' in English, accordingly, it is important to keep in mind that it is the
neutral sense – with no colouring of approval or preference – that is at
stake, despite the fact that the 'distinctive' sign will be put forward as
something special and worth protecting . What is needed for 'distinctive'
is a special (or, more precisely, 'specialized') sense: namely, one signalling
origin rather than quality or creativity in the mind of an average
consumer.[13]

Complications arise similarly with 'descriptive'. 'Descriptive' is typically used to signify the recognizable or observable features of something.
It signals a property of the representation of (or process of representing)
characteristic marks or details of something. But the word can also convey
a more specific focus on what *is* the case rather than what ought, might or

[11] *Oxford English Dictionary*. For a detailed guide to working with *OED* entries, see Donna
Lee Berg, *A Guide to the Oxford English Dictionary* (Oxford: Oxford University Press,
1993). A detailed, corpus-based approach to contemporary word meaning is Michael
Stubbs, *Corpus Studies of Lexical Semantics* (Oxford: Blackwell, 2002).
[12] 'Semantic prosody' remains a slightly obscure and under-theorized term, but describes
how use of a word may typically carry an evaluative loading (e.g. in current English the
word 'fundamentalist' often signals disapproval, even though this is not part of its core
meaning). In *The Structure of Complex Words* (London: Chatto and Windus, [1951]
1979), William Empson sought to account for such properties in a different way: by
developing the concepts of 'appreciative pregnant sense' and 'depreciative pregnant
sense'; sometimes semantic prosody is subsumed in the notion of connotation.
[13] For discussion of the concept of the average consumer's perceptions as the accepted test
for measuring a trade mark's distinctiveness, see Jennifer Davis, 'Locating the Average
Consumer: His Judicial Origins, Intellectual Influences and Current Role in European
Trade Mark Law' (2005) IPQ 2 183–203. An interesting comparison with the notion of
'a reasonable man', from a semantic perspective, can be found in Anna Wierzbicka,
English: Meaning and Culture (Oxford: Oxford University Press, 2006) Ch. 4.

must be the case. This second use draws attention less to the particularities of something than to a choice to avoid expressions of feeling or valuation in commenting on it (so creating a contrast with words like 'prescriptive', 'polemical' or 'evaluative'). Or again – with judgment creeping back in, creating another sense – the word can suggest concern with richness of detail, or vividness in evoking something: the quality that contributes to a notably graphic or detailed account and results in a clash, for this sense, in the trade mark collocation 'merely descriptive'. As any lawyer will quickly point out, in trade mark law descriptive terms are *not* expressions to be considered essentially non-judgmental, or especially vivid and evocative; they are simply expressions that, while purporting to name an enterprise, in fact denote characteristics of a field of trade or goods in which that enterprise operates (as is confirmed by the way that a 'misleading', or in narrower US usage 'misdescriptive', sign is still viewed as 'descriptive' because it characterizes properties of the goods, albeit inaccurately). It is true that judgmental terms in trade mark law – laudatory terms such as 'superb' in *Superb* Software or 'top-quality' in *Top-Quality* Tarmac – *are* considered descriptive (as, incidentally, are 'software' and 'tarmac', too, in that they denote a field of trade, and so would be categorized as either descriptive or generic). But a sign that is especially evocative or vivid might just as easily be contributing to its being distinctive as to its being descriptive: the distinction just does not map onto the individual cases that way.

Specialized, technical senses: trade mark law

The game of everyday senses could continue. But it can also be brought abruptly to a halt. You just insist that the verbal complications illustrated here are extraneous: the two terms in trade mark law may seem intuitive (differing in this respect from the more opaque terminology of copyright or patent law); but they have specialized, technical rather than everyday meanings that kick in for a legal setting.

There is a cost in calling time on common parlance like this, of course. This is that legal terminology and categories are weakened in any claim to reflect how consumers actually think. But, accepting this limitation, we might say that meanings for the two terms are spontaneously calibrated when encountered in a legal context – as they would be, incidentally (though differently in the detail), in any other context or kind of discourse. Sense narrowing in comprehension contributes significantly to our understanding of any topic; and difficulties with the technical, trade mark senses of 'distinctive' and 'descriptive' will normally only arise for people from outside the field (including, not insignificantly, sometimes the legal protagonists in an action themselves) or when, in an interdisciplinary context, a particular sense cannot be taken for granted across disciplines. Being at cross purposes may in those circumstances create a problem if value-neutral and value-laden senses of the two words become tangled up. Unless the ground is cleared in advance of any particular argument, however, we only know whether misunderstandings are occurring if meaning is suddenly exposed as a problem.

Distinctive

According to Article 2 of the EU Trade Mark Directive, a trade mark is 'any sign capable of being represented graphically which is capable of distinguishing goods or services of one undertaking from those of other undertakings'. Similar definitions exist for other jurisdictions. What is 'distinguishing' here (note the move from 'distinctive' to 'distinguishing', illustrating the scope I have noted for slightly different meanings) concerns identification of a reference: the goods are distinguished in respect of whether they originate with one undertaking or another dealing in similar goods. Subject to historical qualifications to do with different doctrines of source, this is what lawyers refer to as the 'source-identifier' function of the trade mark.

In accurately identifying the source of goods, trade marks have traditionally been thought to serve a cluster of economic purposes: to act as a guarantee of quality (by preventing deception by competitors); to prevent confusion in the mind of the consumer; and to repay commercial investment in building business goodwill, including by means of advertising and other forms of promotion. More detailed taxonomies are also possible of the benefits that distinctive names are believed to bring. What is notable, however, is that, of the functions usually identified, only that of denoting or referring is a communicative function. The rest are commercial or mercantile functions. What makes a sign 'distinctive' for the purpose of trade mark law, from the language point of view, is essentially that it operates as a name conventionally does: it attempts to make unique, unambiguous reference, without elaboration or description, in a manner that will be successfully recognized in a given context by the sign's addressee (for trade mark law, the average consumer).

Descriptive

Descriptive expressions are interesting because, as has been said, although they cannot normally be registered as trade marks (or, if registered, are liable to be contested and declared invalid), they can nevertheless be registered if they are thought to have acquired secondary meaning. Such secondary meaning is acquired by the sign gradually taking on the function of use as a name *for* a specific enterprise as well as continuing to describe some property or characteristic *of* that enterprise. In general, descriptive signs (it is believed) should be kept available for use by other traders to describe competing products they may wish to offer in the same field of trade.

But what exactly is 'description' in this context? Typically a descriptive expression denotes an area of trade, by designating at least some of its features. As Article 3(1) of the Trade Mark Directive provides, a descriptive sign (that is, one devoid of any 'distinctive' character) is one which 'consists of signs or indications which may serve, in trade, to designate the kind, quality, quantity, intended purpose, value, geographical origin . . . or other characteristics of the goods or service'. Description here, then, is the delineation or depiction of properties or aspects of the trade being undertaken, rather than the naming of a particular enterprise (since a name identifies but does not tell you *about* an enterprise). Describable properties may be contextually clear, or they may be indicated in other promotional material, but they cannot be incorporated verbally into the registered trade mark sign itself without turning it from a name into a description and so normally forfeiting the right to trade mark protection.

As a sign, therefore, a trade mark is a combination of (or specified relation between) at least two elements: a signifier (the word or phrase, in its particular design get-up: the tangible symbol) plus a specified context in which it will be used: the designated market field in which the sign will be construed as a name – hence the common name–field registration formula: {protected name X} *for* {trade category Y}. Building on distinctions introduced in linguistics and semiotics by Ferdinand de Saussure and C. S. Peirce, recently Barton Beebe has provided an insightful analysis of three, rather than two, aspects of the sign (a three-legged stool that echoes Ogden and Richards' symbolization triangle).[14] Beebe emphasizes that the logo or verbal mark is the signifier (*not* the whole sign); the referent is the particular goods that the signifier points to (or more precisely the source which in turn points to the goods); and the signified is the sign's accumulated meaning.

Analysing a trade mark sign into its components in this way is helpful in seeking to account for textbook puzzle-cases like the descriptive geographic indicator NORTH POLE being registrable for bananas (where it

[14] See Beebe, 'Semiotic Analysis', 626–42. The 'Ogden & Richards triangle' account of the linguistic sign can be found in C. K.Ogden and I. A. Richards, *The Meaning of Meaning* (London: Routledge and Kegan Paul, 1923) Ch. 1.

serves as a name, no descriptive connection) but probably not for sledges (where it would be a descriptor of origin that other North Pole sledge manufacturers might also wish to use). More importantly the analysis makes possible Beebe's ambitious account of the historical shift in trade mark use from narrow source-identifier function towards richer reservoirs of associative meaning. This shift, Beebe argues, has been brought about by various kinds of collapsing between the three dimensions of the sign, as trade marks have increasingly been used without any specific relation to a given field of goods, or even to any good at all, only to the value conveyed by the logo itself.[15]

Secondary meaning

Arguably what makes descriptive signs in trade mark law particularly interesting (but also especially problematic) is that, as has been noted, they can have rights conferred in them if, over time, the sign is judged to have taken on the function of naming a particular trader rather than indicating properties or circumstances of a trade. This can be either because of the period of its use as a name or alternatively through active promotion (typically demonstrated by market research showing association of the mark with the producer on the basis of actual purchases, sales volume and advertising – processes euphemistically described as 'nurture'). Where a naming use is shown to have been established, then the sign is said to have acquired a 'secondary meaning': an extra meaning – a 'distinct' as well as 'distinctive' meaning – alongside its earlier (and continuing) descriptive meaning. So, with a case like AMERICAN AIRLINES, a descriptive expression becomes salient over time as the name of a commercial enterprise (and so the services they offer) but in different contexts continues to denote simply airlines which are American. The sign with acquired distinctiveness still appears in its conventional meaning to be 'descriptive', if we judge on the basis of the meaning of its component words, which designate a form of trade. But the sign is now also construed as 'distinctive' for a given commercial context, in being held to identify the source of the goods or service rather than telling a consumer about them.

The naming sense is 'secondary' in that it develops out of an already existing, descriptive sense (which was almost certainly the basis for choosing the sign in the first place). We might say that repeated use or nurture has brought about a semantic shift from whatever the sign's

---

[15] See Beebe, 'Semiotic Analysis', 656–67.

common lexical meaning might be to a more specific source-identifying, naming function. People perceiving the sign are assumed no longer to process its component meanings, and by doing so to discover (or strengthen previous knowledge regarding) relevant trade characteristics; instead they short-circuit any process of meaning-making and search directly for the referent, as they might do with a proper name in a contextually clear referring situation of use.

Generic

Completing the established typology of signs, a verbal sign is 'generic' when it names a class or set of things: a type (or genus). A textbook example might be 'animal', which is generic by being up a taxonomic level from 'dog' or 'cat'. A dog and a cat are both kinds of animal; and an animal must be either one or the other, or any of the other co-taxonyms at the same taxonomic level, but it cannot be both at the same time. Generic words are commonly encountered in dictionary definitions, where words are often defined, *genus et differentiae*, by means of a generic category to which the word to be defined belongs coupled with specifics that characterize it within that category (so a robin is 'a small thrush, native mainly to Europe, the adult male of which has a reddish-orange breast and head').[16]

In trade mark law, a 'generic' expression is a sign that designates a class of goods or services: beer, toothpaste, garden furniture. Such expressions have even less claim to protection than descriptive ones (with which to some extent they overlap, since part of descriptiveness, according to Article 3(1), is to designate the 'kind' of trade, a clear member–class relation). Since a generic term is in effect a superordinate, or hyperonym, for a number of more specialized sub-classes of goods, then almost directly by virtue of being generic (and so designating a class of products undifferentiated according to origin) it cannot be inherently distinctive of provenance. Such a term can become distinctive only on the basis of acquired secondary meaning, as above, or if applied fancifully or whimsically to an altogether different category of product (despite the seeming commercial drawback of, for example, a name like 'Beer' being adopted for a make of screwdriver, toothpaste or garden furniture).

---

[16] For discussion of how dictionaries construct definitions, see Sidney Landau, *Dictionaries: The Art and Craft of lexicography* (Cambridge: Cambridge University Press, 1984) Ch. 4, and Howard Jackson, *Lexicography: an introduction* (London: Routledge, 2002) Chs. 8 and 9.

Understood in this way, verbal signs recognized as being generic should be uncontroversial, being routinely beyond protection except where secondary meaning is established.[17] There are, nevertheless, circumstances in which generic terms become important. A new generic word may be created where previously a sign was held to be distinctive, if persistent use of the trade mark name, perhaps on account of its reputation, spreads into language use more widely and is perceived by customers as denoting all goods of the same kind regardless of whether they originate with the same producer or source (well-known examples of this process include KLEENEX, THERMOS and JEEP).

Specialized, technical senses: the study of language

As must already be clear, if the categories 'distinctive' and 'descriptive' feature at all in linguistic analysis, they will function differently there. The kinds of tests, for example, that determine whether a verbal sign fits a linguistic category are significantly different from whether a sign fits a trade mark class: linguists look for evidence not in periods of use in trade, or in advertising spend or evidence of consumer perception, but in the distribution and constraints on combination of linguistic elements, and/ or their correlation with social factors related to language user or context of use, and/or the nature of choices that guide their selection.[18] We should not therefore expect that whether something is judged to be 'descriptive' in trade mark law will have much bearing on whether it would be called 'descriptive' in linguistics.

In fact, 'distinctive' and 'descriptive' do both feature in linguistic work. To help clear a way for further interdisciplinary work between the fields, it may therefore be useful to note here what 'distinctive' and 'descriptive' typically mean in linguistic terminology.

Distinctive

The main, general use of the word 'distinctive' in linguistics is to describe features of speech or writing which allow a contrast to be made between linguistic units, whether those units are to do with sound structure,

---

[17] Note that EU and US law do not coincide on this point. See Art. 3(1)(d) TM Directive. For discussion of the impossibility of generic marks gaining secondary meaning under the Lanham Act, see Dinwoodie and Janis, *Trademarks and Unfair Competition* 52–3.

[18] Different methods and tests are of course appropriate for studying different aspects of linguistic structure. For a practical introduction, see Alison Wray, Kate Trott and Aileen Bloomer, *Projects in Linguistics: A Practical Guide to Researching Language* (London: Arnold, 1998).

sentence structure, or meaning. The term has been most commonly used in phonology, as part of the phrase 'distinctive feature' (where a distinctive feature is a minimal contrastive unit – an aspect of the representation of a sound – that can contribute to explaining how the sound system of a language is organized).[19] No collision with trade mark use of 'distinctive' seems likely, especially because the word 'contrastive' is often used rather than 'distinctive' for the general sense, except in the case of phonological distinctive features where 'distinctive' has become customary. One minor exception to the separateness of use does arise, even so. This is when distinctive features theory from linguistics is invoked in legal cases as a way of showing precisely how, and by how much, two contested expressions differ in sound structure. However, as Roger Shuy has noted,[20] use of this linguistic concept has met with only limited success in the courts, possibly due to confusion created precisely by the same word being used in different technical senses in two different fields, as judges and juries search in vain for relevant links between different understandings of 'distinctive'.

Descriptive

Rather more than is the case with 'distinctive', 'descriptive' in linguistics overlaps with trade mark usage in complicated ways, being used in at least three different contexts.

In its most general sense, 'descriptive' characterizes a generally acknowledged aim of the discipline: namely 'to develop a comprehensive, systematic and objective account of the patterns in use of a particular language or dialect, at a given point in time'.[21] 'Descriptive' accordingly contrasts with other ways of investigating language that are either prescriptive (like most traditional grammar), or historical (charting language change over time), or theoretical (where the aim is to make general statements about language as a whole, rather than to characterize in detail a particular state of language at a given time). Interestingly, this value-neutral sense of 'descriptive' may appear at least superficially relevant to

[19] See Roger Lass, *Phonology: An Introduction to Basic Concepts* (Cambridge Textbooks in Linguistics) (Cambridge: Cambridge University Press, 1984).
[20] Shuy, *Linguistic Battles*, reports how the linguist Jerrold Sadock presented evidence in a trade mark case using distinctive feature analysis to show that the sounds of 'Little Dolly' were only 13 per cent different from those of 'Little Debbie' (75); but Shuy also notes considerable scepticism from lawyers as regards presenting evidence along similar lines in one of his own cases, about the contraceptive B-Oval (110–15).
[21] David Crystal, *A Dictionary of Linguistics and Phonetics* (5th edn, Oxford: Blackwell, 2003) 107.

trade mark discussion of how far trade mark law should reflect public thinking about commercial communication and how far it should be normative in relation to use of signs (as part of commercial regulation and governance).

Alongside this general sense to do with the aims of linguistics there is a more particular sense to do with meaning. When different kinds of meaning potential or meaning effect are classified, sometimes the word 'descriptive' (alternatively 'propositional') is used to characterize a particular type of meaning that 'allows language to be used to make statements which are either true or false according to whether the propositions they express are true or false'.[22] The contrast here is with so-called 'non-descriptive' meaning, which consists of all the various other kinds of meaning that are often viewed as less systematic and less important in how language communicates information. Such non-descriptive kinds of meaning include expressive meaning (sometimes known as affective, attitudinal or emotive meaning), which is what is conveyed when speakers embody their beliefs, attitudes and feelings in emotive words (or particular kinds of intonation or other forms of expressivity) rather than talking about them in propositions. Linguists have emphasized in particular how the contrast between 'descriptive' and 'non-descriptive' meaning is relevant in judgments of synonymy. Two expressions may appear to have the same meaning, in the sense that if something is described as one or the other you could not say that one description is true but the other false, even though the two expressions differ in the feeling or attitudes they express.[23]

'Descriptive' has a third, still more specialized sense, in what has been called the 'description theory of names'.[24] Debates in this area have focussed on canonical proper names (e.g. names for people, such as Napoleon or Aristotle) and what are called 'definite descriptions' (typically phrases that take the form 'the + Noun Phrase', such as 'the old lady who lives next door'). Interest centres on how such expressions refer to entities in the world and on what limits such reference is subject to. In philosophical debates which run from J. S. Mill, through Frege, Russell

[22] John Lyons, *Linguistic Semantics: An Introduction* (Cambridge: Cambridge University Press, 1995) 44.
[23] Some examples with which to explore this notion are 'sociable' and 'friendly'; 'scoff' and 'jeer'; and 'throng' and 'crowd'. Massively more complex and debatable cases include, e.g., 'a terrorist was killed' and 'a freedom fighter was killed'.
[24] For a collection of key papers on this topic, see Gary Ostertag (ed.), *Definite Descriptions: A Reader* (Cambridge, Mass.: MIT Press, 1998). For the more general concept of linguistic 'definiteness', see Christopher Lyons, *Definiteness* (Cambridge: Cambridge University Press, 1999) Ch. 1.

and Strawson, to contemporary philosophers like Saul Kripke, this tradition of work presents alternative explanations of how proper names and
definite descriptions refer to their presumed bearers in the external world,
including bearers who do not exist (frequently debated examples include
Santa Claus, Hamlet and the present King of France) or bearers about
whom we have variable and sometimes only limited social knowledge
(e.g. Aristotle).

Bertrand Russell in particular separated what he proposed are logically
proper names, such as indexicals (to the non-philosopher not 'names' at
all: words like 'this' and 'that', which serve to point to things rather than
describe them), from ordinary proper names, which Russell characterized
as 'abbreviated definite descriptions'.[25] These other, seemingly proper,
names may appear to be names that refer directly, without any extra
apparatus of descriptive information; but for Russell – controversially
within subsequent philosophy – they only denote because of a cluster of
descriptions of the bearer activated in the mind, for which the name acts
as a kind of shorthand. Any distinction along these lines between strict
source identification and description will of course seem suggestive in
relation to trade mark terminology, not just because the notion 'description' is central but because the distinction seems to allow investigation of
whatever uniquely denoting capability underpins a trade mark's distinctiveness. Even with this third area of use, however – despite the inviting
parallels – caution needs to be exercised in going beyond perception of
general affinity to any claim to greater congruity of either purpose or
approach.

Names and their capabilities

It would be reassuringly simple, looking at differences between usage in
trade mark law and in linguistics, to conclude that there is just no overlap
between the two fields, despite prominent use of what appear to be
the same terms. That assessment would in my view be largely correct.
A doubt nevertheless persists: that ways of investigating naming and
meaning in linguistics and philosophy – however different the approach –
do tackle similar core questions regarding what the distinctiveness of the
'source-identifier function' claimed for trade mark signs must actually *be*.
Instead of simply contrasting the approaches, therefore, we would do well
to address questions of naming and meaning drawing on both fields,

---

[25] For relevant details in Russell's account, see the two chapters by Russell included in
Ostertag (ed.), *Definite Descriptions*.

linking notions of linguistic meaning and use with legal issues of how signs are used in the marketplace.

In trade mark thinking, 'distinctive' and 'descriptive' appear as two different kinds, or categories, of sign. Nobody (I think) really believes they are. The notion that signs are either 'distinctive' or 'descriptive' is shorthand. If signs were fixed in either class, then trade mark registration would be easy: just hand out a list (a Comprehensive Lexicon of Distinctive Trade Mark Signs) or a grammar (Rules for Creating Well-formed Trade Mark Signs). But whatever value such works might have as registration primers, they would not help as regards infringement: trade mark enforcement issues are not about *kinds* of sign, since the protection against which infringement is alleged only extends to signs that have already got over the bar of distinctiveness. Infringement issues are about use.

One reminder of this – and a way of seeing how the issue of use versus sign-type affects registration as well as infringement – is that the different classes of sign outlined in trade mark law are not so much a matter of inherent lexical properties as of words used and understood *'on the market'*. Verbal expressions are raw materials: letters and sounds, carrying baggage from the language system in terms of what they usually denote, along with an open-ended and exploitable assortment of associations or connotations. These signs – not blank sheets, each a marker for an area within conceptual space – are put to work in different ways. While the default for the word 'beer' may be for it to be viewed as generic, as a class of drink, it is still possible for 'beer' to be deployed as a distinctive mark if applied to the product class of garden furniture. Because this would be an act of naming, it would not be like Humpty Dumpty *referring to* things using whichever words he chooses from an existing vocabulary;[26] naming differs from referring in allowing a sort of creative baptism, to be ratified in subsequent social use. After a period of time, the name 'beer' might catch on, and be gradually adopted as a generic term for some kind of garden furniture. If it did so – and stranger things have happened in the history of the language – then there would be two senses for 'beer': 'beer' (1), a type of drink; and 'beer' (2), a type of garden furniture. However

---

[26] The relevant section of dialogue between Alice and Humpty runs, ' "I don't know what you mean by 'glory,'" Alice said. Humpty Dumpty smiled contemptuously. "Of course you don't – till I tell you. I meant 'there's a nice knock-down argument for you!'" "But 'glory' doesn't mean 'a nice knock-down argument,' " Alice objected. "When *I* use a word," Humpty Dumpty said, in rather a scornful tone, "it means just what I choose it to mean – neither more nor less." "The question is," said Alice, "whether you *can* make words mean so many different things" ': Lewis Carroll, *Through the Looking Glass* Ch. 6. When creating new names for things, you can.

extravagant this particular example, the general point holds: that the combination of signifier and signified as conventional semiotic sign, for trade marks as for all signs, *underdetermines* use.

Further evidence of a need to investigate relations between sign and use can be found in the tendency that the 'beer' example illustrates: that verbal expressions can *change* class within trade mark law, in one of several ways. They can change when a sign is deployed in a different context (as we saw with the 'beer' example). They can also change if a particular sign that has been judged to be distinctive ceases to be, and is demoted to descriptive because its distinctiveness has been successfully contested by a competitor. Or, in the case of acquired 'secondary meaning', the sign gains a new mode of use as a directly referring name. Or a sign shifts into 'generic' use, as a result of sense-widening: the naming use (HOOVER) broadens to description of a class ('hoover'), with an accumulation, around what was once a rigid naming device, of productive processes at work in the vocabulary at large, including conversion to other word classes ('let's hoover up'), use with determiners ('my hoover'), etc.[27]

The semantic changes at stake in such reclassification are examples of more general language processes (including sense narrowing, sense widening, pejoration, amelioration, etc.).[28] But to the trade mark owner they appear less as part of the flow of language use and semantic change than as fluctuations in a sign's commercial worth, equivalents of a racehorse winning the Derby or breaking its leg. When a descriptive term gains trade mark status, for instance through acquired secondary meaning, the trade mark proprietor gains rights in some part of a commonly created language system of meanings. A way of describing something that may be laden with cultural perception (such as overtones of value, approval, class or trendiness built up over a long period) is part-converted into property. Conversely, if a trade mark name becomes generic the trade mark proprietor's rights evaporate in a verbal expression that falls, by means of such 'genericide', into unrestricted public use.

---

[27] Shuy examines the processes by which an expression becomes generic in a case involving the phrase 'hospitality management' (*Linguistic Battles* 46–55); his account emphasizes as diagnostic the related characteristics of flexibility (moving readily across grammatical functions) and recency (being new in the use in question, and so still active or dynamic, often reflected in abrupt changes in an expression's frequency of usage).

[28] Another area of instruction to juries outlined in ibid. 60. A more detailed account of semantic change is Elizabeth Closs Traugott and Richard Dasher, *Regularity in Semantic Change* (Cambridge: Cambridge University Press, 2002); see also, from a cognitive linguistic perspective, Eve Sweetser, *From Etymology to Pragmatics: Metaphorical and Cultural Aspects of Semantic Change* (Cambridge: Cambridge University Press, 1990).

Calculating signs for meaning 'on the market'

The potential of signs, then, is activated in different ways for different contexts (taking 'context' here as both the sign's surrounding linguistic environment in an utterance or text, and also the social situation in which it is used). Such activation is an essential process in how signs function, and was introduced above to help explain why the words 'distinctive' and 'descriptive' themselves have different meanings in different situations. To grasp the significance of such processes for trade mark law, however, we need a further shift of emphasis: from signs *matched to* categories in a way that is fixed by the two-part formula 'X for Y' towards how a sign *is likely to be construed* on a given occasion of use.

Communication by means of signs is a matter of intentions, linguistic choices and active interpretation as well as of semiotic raw materials; the signs themselves function as symbolic counters within a larger sphere of communicative action. To see more clearly how lexical semantic properties relate to such communicative action, we can consider the sort of informal reasoning a prospective trade mark proprietor goes through in choosing a commercial name. Trade mark choices are revealed in such an account less as a selection of ready-made verbal signs with off-the-shelf meanings than as a process of strategic calculation in relation to variable interpretive as well as commercial circumstances.

Surveying the pool of available verbal signs (or sound and letter components that might be combined to make a new verbal sign), the would-be trade mark owner faces two levels of choice. The first is whether to build up use of a name that the product already has, helping that name to acquire secondary meaning, or whether to baptize the enterprise with a new name. The second of these choices requires anticipation of how that name will function in the marketplace and taking the precaution of making sure the baptized infant is formally registered. Strategic thinking is needed either way, perhaps more obviously with the new-name option (because of having to anticipate how the sign will play on the market) but also these days because of the high cost to the parent of bringing up a sign through 'nurture'.

Consider, then: you are a trader and you need a name. What kind of informal reasoning do you go through?

(A) To maximize distinctiveness without risk of descriptiveness, your obvious choice is to invent: you make up a word, legible and pronounceable within the prevailing language system but free from associations (including in other languages likely to be sufficiently accessible). But there is a disadvantage. Your verbal sign will have little or no recognition when first encountered, until its salience is built up in relation to the particular product it will now designate – a situation rather like secondary meaning but without a primary meaning. Your sign may well have sound symbolism that can convey associations (especially when linked to its given field of use) but it will have few if any connotations, except for those that will begin to accumulate from now on. Nor is your chosen sign yet part of any semantic field; so it won't be activated in memory if a potential customer thinks of some cognate term in broadly the same area of trade: your sign is not part of any 'mental thesaurus entry'. Your sign has what a distinctive mark *must* have: clear water all around it in a lexical field, with no similar name being used for a similar product.[29] But it lacks something you *want*: when used, your sign will not have an automatically spreading effect, activating other related terms and concepts in an established mental space. Being brand new, the signifier allows instant distinctiveness. But there is no conventional link with established meaning or associations – no meaning-making work already going on for language users – and therefore no chance to piggy-back on values and modes of perception with which expressions in a language are normally imbued. In short, your name will lack an essential value that trade mark law makes it odd to feel is missing: descriptiveness.

(B) Distinctiveness without descriptiveness can be achieved another way: by choosing an existing word or words with only an arbitrary relation to your field of trade. In this case, the signifier itself is not new: there *is* conventional meaning, but that meaning is in a different semantic field from the trade context for which you wish to register. Nothing should be activated in the mind for *your* context. In processing the sign in this context addressees will revert to the 'name-without-description' function (hence the strong distinctiveness). Helpfully, because arbitrary expressions of this kind have no connection with your specified trade, nobody in that trade should feel deprived of the same expression to describe their own product (thus lessening the likelihood of challenge). However, the processing jump to the naming function will not be instant: our orientation towards meaning and relevance makes us perceive all signs contrived to attract our

---

[29] In an impressive account of the significance of semantic fields within a language, Barton Beebe presents a striking graph for any given trademark, plotting form-variants against product-type variants. The graph shows visually how much elbow room any given trade mark sign has for a given area of trade. The notion of 'what is in the vicinity' for any given sign is an important part of Beebe's account of the Saussurean idea of 'value', and serves to establish his concept of 'differential distinctiveness'. See Beebe, 'Semiotic Analysis', 653–6.

attention as potentially meaningful; and we will strain to find some link between sign and product category if we can (as can be seen in the complex cases of APPLE and ACORN for computers, where some commentators suggest the relation is arbitrary while others chart symbolic connections; or with NORTH POLE for bananas where it might be said that opposites attract).

(C) Where we *can* find an inferable link or source of relevance for the sign, then the chosen sign is no longer arbitrary. Rather it falls into the category known as suggestive or associative. Suggestive or associative expressions evoke properties and qualities – and so appear descriptive – but only if you use your imagination and infer the connection. For that reason, the description is held to be of your own making, not something inherent in the sign itself (*that* would make the sign merely descriptive). Descriptiveness is avoided, accordingly, in proportion to the complexity of the inferential route. Your best choice is therefore an expression that relates figuratively to your own goods or services and in doing so somehow comments on or recommends them, but in the form of an expression that requires a series of processing steps to make the connection. As a sign-type, within a semiotic view, associative signs are figurative; but it is important to remember that what makes such signs figurative is active transference of meaning brought about inferentially when signs are used and understood.[30] For the business choosing a sign, suggestive or associative verbal expressions are arguably the most rewarding, because with them you get associations, connotation, resonance – collectively a sort of positive glow – that you have not had to build up painstakingly in the world of commerce but that is in effect donated, as a sort of feelgood 'corona' (to borrow an image of meaningful radiance used by Wittgenstein to describe a similar verbal effect[31]), from the existing stock of imagery in the language.

---

[30] For an overview of cognitive approaches to metaphor and other kinds of figurative language, see William Croft and D. A. Cruse, *Cognitive Linguistics* (Cambridge Textbooks in Linguistics) (Cambridge: Cambridge University Press, 2004) Ch. 8.

[31] The later writing of Wittgenstein is usually thought important for linguistics because of the notion of 'language games' it develops: the open-ended array of acts and functions that language serves, beyond just referring. The notion of 'language games' provided an important inspiration for ordinary language philosophy, and so pragmatics. Throughout *Philosophical Investigations*, however, Wittgenstein also emphasizes another verbal resource: the resonant power of individual words – 'Uttering a word is like striking a note on the keyboard of the imagination' (para. 6, 4e); or, 'Every familiar word ... carries an atmosphere with it in our minds, a "corona" of lightly indicated uses' (181e). See Ludwig Wittgenstein, *Philosophical Investigations*, trans. G. E. M. Anscombe (Oxford: Blackwell, 1953).

Choosing such a sign involves a balancing act, gambling on the average consumer's knowledge-base and inferential appetite: too little work of inference and the result is a descriptive sign for which you will get no protection; but choose an inferential link that is insufficiently reliable and you will not get impact or memorability – you are back to a comparatively empty, arbitrary sign, canonically source-denotative but with no associated poetic value added.

(D) You might just choose an openly descriptive expression. But if you do, your registration prospects are bleak, and you must take the 'secondary meaning' route to distinctiveness. Common descriptors, including characterization of ingredients, appearance, function or quality, require little or no work of inference to relate name and product. Nor do personal names, ironically being legally inherently non-distinctive (despite being socially the most established source-identifying verbal device there is). Nor do place or regional names, unless the place you choose has only indirect, mythical or poetic links to the trade rather than being an actual source (in which case there may be current or future competing providers whose interest will be damaged if you are granted rights in the geographic name).

(E) You might value plain speaking, and prefer to call yourself exactly what you do: what you see is what you get; it does what it says on the tin. But your name is then like a Yellow Pages entry or Google subject search term, rather than your own, unique trade name. You have no claim to inherent distinctiveness, since the name applies to a whole class of products, not just your own. Such a generic name choice might be helpful to a consumer who, when faced with a particular need, performs a general search for traders; but such names are not effective in identifying you as a specific provider, and like narrower descriptive expressions allow you only (under Art. 3(1)(d) of the Directive) the secondary meaning route to distinctiveness.

(F) Or finally, to get attention in a crowded marketplace, you can shout. You might do this by choosing a shocking or taboo name, achieving distinctiveness to the extent that your chosen expletive – 'Hallelujah', 'fcuk', etc – has an arbitrary or weak link with your trade area, even if it has shock-value and so memorability by other means. The commercial risk to be weighed up – beyond possibly failing to gain registration for an excluded category of sign[32] – is that of unpredictable public attitude. As FCUK and HALLELUJAH both illustrate,

---

[32] It is not possible to register taboo or offensive signs as trade marks, though of course the boundary as regards what is permissible is not static.

128   *Alan Durant*

taboo and risqué terms exist in a complex social field of variable associations and reactions, subject to rapid shifts of impact and acceptability.

The 'avoid descriptive' imperative

The different *choices* as regards sign-type outlined here, I have suggested, are commonly presented as inherently different types of sign (cf. the 'Abercrombie' list). Such lists imply stable meanings for signs if conjoined with a given commercial context. In order to draw attention to active work involved in meaning-making, rather than fixed semantic properties, I have presented the sign-types differently, as taking on meanings because their use is linked to anticipated practices of interpretation. In some cases, there may be little scope for misunderstanding (e.g. 'sportbetting.com' used for online sport betting); in other cases, the link between signifier and trade will be arguable (c.f. APPLE or ACORN for computers). In others again, it may be missed or misunderstood (c.f. JEHANGIR or KASHMIR for a garden centre). What I am suggesting is that sign lists reflect not so much a typology of fixed semiotic properties as patterns or tendencies in use and interpretation in given contexts. It is such kinds of use and understanding which determine meaning, as trade mark law commonly recognizes but must square with its longstanding core terminology of 'distinctive' and 'descriptive' signs.

Even now, however, the signifying choices I have described are still only half the picture; they exist in a world of *potential* utterances or communicative actions. I have looked at them as a would-be trade mark proprietor, thinking aloud, might consider choices within a system that is simultaneously linguistic and commercial. What do prospective trade mark proprietors actually do? Empirical data on this, sorted by conventional linguistic type, would almost certainly be interesting but is not readily available.[33] It is possible, nevertheless, to get closer to communicative practice in trade mark registration and litigation another way: by linking the communicator's intention introduced above to aspects of their commercial interest. Trade marks indicate source: but what is it, beyond source identification, that the modern trade mark proprietor wants?

---

[33] Even just classifying and counting entries on the 'Trade Marks Journal' pages of the UK Intellectual Property Office website (www.ipo.gov.uk) might provide a rough-and-ready measure. Difficulty arises, however, in sifting through the classes for which a mark may be simultaneously registered, since these represent different proportions of any given business and may relate *differently* to the name.

'Descriptive', we have seen, is something to be avoided if you want to register and protect a sign, because your sign will be judged not to have inherent distinctiveness. So prospective trade mark proprietors might be expected mostly to look for signs that steer as safely as possible away from linguistic markers of description (unless they opt for the 'acquired meaning' route). To maximize the strength, or 'muscularity', of their sign, they would typically select new coinages, or transpose existing words from one context to another in order to ensure that their chosen sign has only novel, inferable connections with the area of trade designated in the registration. Such strategies would incidentally help to avoid future slippage into descriptiveness. Yet it seems that would-be trade mark owners do not typically do this. Instead, their behaviour creates a surface contradiction: they want and need 'distinctive' but they choose 'descriptive' as far as they can. In effect, would-be trade mark proprietors cruise as close to the line as is likely to be permitted.

Since trade mark proprietors are sophisticated and of course not necessarily innocent agents, it is likely that in seeking a descriptive dimension for their chosen sign they pursue a strategy which reflects modern business realities (which in turn reflect a trend over the last century away from the classic 'marketplace trader' model towards the building-up of semiotic brand-value). For many modern businesses, while a trade mark may still be primarily a source identifier, solidifying name recognition, the aim is also to achieve something more: what Alex Kozinski has called a power to 'enhance or adorn' products.[34] Pursuing this aim, businesses try to smuggle direct or inferable description into the protected sign – including the laudatory dimension of self-praise, in whatever style is suitable for the particular field of trade – despite this being what trade mark registration in its classical form is there to prevent. Such a strategy is worthwhile for the would-be trade mark proprietor not because the devil has all the good words. That is unlikely to be the motivation because there is ample scope for verbal creativity on both sides of the border, as much in neologism as in oblique or associative description.[35] Rather, it is because the devil in this case is in the detail, in descriptiveness. The extra value available to the trade mark proprietor with a descriptive or near-descriptive sign lies in the richness of evocation that inferably descriptive expressions allow. Modern trade marks, in this sense, aspire less to the condition of a directly

[34] Alex Kozinsky, 'Trademarks Unplugged' (1993) 68 *New York University Law Review* 960, 961–75.
[35] For discussion (and extensive illustration) of the pervasiveness of verbal creativity, see Ronald Carter, *Language and Creativity: The Art of Common Talk* (London: Routledge, 2004). Analysis of a wide range of linguistic techniques common in advertising can be found in Greg Myers, *Words in Ads* (London: Arnold, 1994).

referring cipher – a name without a meaning, like Russell's indexicals – than to communicate as condensed, almost poetic, images. They seek protection not only in respect of origin but also for their quality of creative expression: protection more along the lines of copyright in creative work, or protection of commercial reputation against tarnishment or disparagement.

Pushing at the edge of description, then, rather than going for a more naked naming strategy, appears a way for trade mark owners to overcome restrictions imposed on protection of descriptive signs. Such symbolic opportunism is possible because inferably descriptive signs – as well as slogans such as 'making life taste better' or 'a good deal better' that may be protected on account of acquired secondary meaning – are given protection on the basis that, whatever their descriptive sense is, it can be partitioned off for legal purposes from the protected act of naming. Giving trade mark rights in the naming sense, as a result, is held not to confer exclusive rights in general usage. But this arrangement only leads out of one problem into another. It is only by analysing a particular instance of use that you can distinguish which sense is activated: name or description? In effect, the sense-partition assumption shifts the burden in showing infringement from sign-type to use-type: not what sort of sign something is, but what function the sign performs in its contested discourse context.

Senses in action

There is no intuitive way of separating out a distinctive (secondary) meaning from a descriptive (primary) meaning for a given use of an 'acquired secondary meaning' trade mark. All that is certain is that there is a naming use *as well as* a meaning. What seems likely, if anything, is that the naming use in any given context will simultaneously evoke, rather than be an alternative to, the descriptive sense: a shower gel called QUICKWASH that has acquired secondary meaning through nurture will not lose its implication of speedy efficacy just because 'quick wash' has become a name; nor will a clothing supplier called WICKED RAGS lose its style overtones of youth and fashion because the stylistically marked colloquial expression 'wicked rags' is now a name, not a description. Indeed, the capability of the sign to have more than one dimension of meaning – to operate on more than one level at once, like a poetic image – is almost certainly what the trade mark owner wanted it to do.

The precise mechanisms involved in poetic evocation by trade mark signs, which often function without being surrounded by other verbal discourse to set extra meanings off, are to some extent obscure. But then, how people engage in a mental search for words and concepts, and what penumbral effects they activate as they do so, is not fully understood either.[36] There is reason to believe, however (e.g. on the basis of evidence from speech error data, jokes and poetry), that the mental lexicon is spontaneously searched in more than a single way, sometimes for words beginning with the same sound, sometimes for words with the same number of syllables and stress pattern, sometimes for words with similar meaning, and sometimes for words existing in the same semantic field and stored close by in the lexicon – or some combination of all of these. The mental lexicon is networked in complex ways. When a word is used, because other associated words are activated in a sort of spreading effect, then filtered out in our search for relevance by constraints of collocation and context, encountering one word will make other words and concepts around it more accessible or salient. Where a trade mark sign simultaneously is, or approximates to, a descriptive term, then related words, concepts and images are more likely to be retrieved and used in thought, alongside the name, than for signs (including arbitrary or invented signs) that are mentally stored with fewer or no established connections. Significantly as regards styles in trade marks, this will be still more the case for idioms and echoic phrases used as slogans, which are allusive to social values, attitudes and everyday ways of speaking. The descriptive or near-descriptive sign has accordingly a kind of condensed power: it triggers mental effects that, if suitably guided, significantly enrich its resonance and make it more effective as a means of communication.

This general point about words in the mind can now be connected to the arguments over naming and meaning outlined above. The 'descriptive' or evocative sense of a trade mark is not separate from the naming sense, in the way that tests for 'sense autonomy' of polysemous words in lexical semantics can sometimes show that one word-sense precludes another.[37] Rather, the descriptive sense remains grafted onto the secondary, naming use – something like the sort of 'abbreviated description'

---

[36] An especially illuminating and clear account can, however, be found in Jean Aitchison, *Words in the Mind: An Introduction to the Mental Lexicon* (3rd edn, Oxford: Blackwell, 2003). For a more developed theoretical account, see also Walter Kintsch, *Comprehension: A Paradigm for Cognition* (Cambridge: Cambridge University Press, 1998).

[37] An example would be how, when you activate the 'river' sense of 'bank' in a given context, you simultaneously close off the 'financial institution' sense. See the extended discussion of linguistic evidence for sense boundaries in polysemous words and how they affect meaning construal in Croft and Cruse, *Cognitive Linguistics* Ch. 5. Note that the example of 'bank' would be described in many studies as a case of homonymy rather than polysemy, a distinction which is largely irrelevant to the Croft and Cruse account (for their discussion of this point, see 111).

Russell thought may be active with proper names for which we activate fragments of information to underpin the naming function (such that 'Aristotle' names a mental construct which functions as the bearer of various ideas the speaker or hearer has about Aristotle). Now, if this is broadly what happens, then protection granted to acquired meaning will encroach into descriptive properties of a sign in which there is a legitimate public interest, as an 'intellectual common', unless clear boundaries govern precisely what 'trade mark use' (as opposed to more general, public use of protected verbal signs) will be.

Trade mark meaning and use

My discussion so far questions whether problems in how trade mark signs are used and contested can be adequately worked through at the level of a sign-focussed semiotic model. My arguments are based on what is an established premise of linguistic pragmatics: that signs create meanings differently in different texts or utterances because the meaning-making processes involved go beyond inherent meanings of words or phrases, considered in an imagined default context.[38] This general view was presented above as the occasionally used slogan: meaning underdetermines use.

If linguistics is to contribute to our understanding of issues in trade mark law, then in my view that contribution is most likely to come from those branches of linguistics that investigate language in use, such as pragmatics or discourse analysis. Such approaches typically take as their starting point the idea that speakers provide evidence of intention to communicate, and choose signs conventionally suited to making their intended meaning accessible against a background of what the addressee believes, including about the situation in which the communication takes place. Addressees, in turn, construct interpretations for the given context rather than finding meaning in some fixed or stable form in the signs in front of them.[39]

Significantly for trade mark law, the discourse 'setting' in which interpretations are constructed involves more than just the topic area to which the sign is related at registration (for trade marks, the designated area of

---

[38] For discussion of pragmatic approaches in linguistics, see Jenny Thomas, *Meaning in Interaction: an introduction to pragmatics* (London: Longman, 1995); Stephen Levinson, *Pragmatics* (Cambridge Textbooks in Linguistics) (Cambridge: Cambridge University Press, 1983); and Louise Cummings, *Pragmatics: an interdisciplinary perspective* (Edinburgh: Edinburgh University Press, 2005).

[39] For a detailed (and extensively illustrated) account of the role played by intention and inference in interpretation, that ranges across a number of fields including literary criticism, art appreciation and also law, see Raymond Gibbs Jr, *Intentions in the Experience of Meaning* (Cambridge: Cambridge University Press, 1999).

trade: the Y that goes with X, such as the domain of shower gel for QUICKWASH). That 'more' includes dimensions of communication that have received some attention in trade mark law but are arguably less clearly articulated than the sign's semiotic properties. These communicative dimensions include: what genre the trade mark is embedded in (e.g. conventional editorial, such as a news story; name or slogan of an advert; text used in labelling, etc.); the level and type of cultural knowledge assumed on the part of the average consumer, as addressee (assumptions about commerce and communication, as well as general-knowledge assumptions that sponsor interpretive inferences); and the adopted mode of address (how the addressee is invited to view the discourse, including the presumed identity of its author or speaker-persona). How signs work in a given context of use also depends on intention and attribution of intention, as well as on the receiver's interpretive strategy. Enforcement must accordingly be similarly concerned with such aspects of use, if use considerations are not to be some sort of return of the repressed in relation to the semiotic framework that underpins trade mark law.

Questions of use are especially problematic in relation to descriptive aspects of trade mark signs. This can be either where secondary meaning has been established or where aspects of description are inferentially activated by associative signs. Difficulty arises because, as has been suggested, associative words and expressions – unlike bespoke, new-word or new-phrase trade marks – continue to have other roles in which people use them, and are therefore more likely to come up in different discourse contexts. ENTREPRENEUR, MOVIE BUFF and VCR may all have become protected trade mark names for given products; but they continue to be also used in their pre-existing, descriptive meanings. Some of the contexts in which such use continues will be conversational, some more formally editorial, some commercial; and within commercial contexts, there will be various, more localized styles as well as differing discourse functions served by the particular words. Some of those uses may constitute infringement while others will be permissible (and defensible as 'non-trade mark use' or US 'fair use'). But exactly *which* will depend on how trade mark law establishes standards, thresholds and exemptions in relation to different modalities of use, rather than of sign-meaning.[40]

---

[40] Although not specifically related to trademark law – the book is more concerned with general problems of constitutional principle – one of the best accounts of different ways of analysing language use within a legal framework that I am familiar with remains Kent Greenawalt, *Speech, Crime and the Uses of Language* (Oxford: Oxford University Press, 1989). Starting from a general interest in speech act theory, Greenawalt discusses a wide range of legally problematic communicative acts (agreements, threats, fraudulent

The frequency and significance of the word 'describe' in 'non-trade mark use' or 'fair use' defences is notable. This is despite the oddity of the word 'describe' in this context, since it can hardly be to do with specific properties of the goods. More likely in this context is one of the other senses of 'describe' and 'descriptive' outlined above: that of asserting something that may be true or false, or in some other way commenting rather than naming. The defendant's use of the plaintiff's mark is said to 'describe' the plaintiff's product or to 'describe' their own product, rather than being an infringing use. This is a sense closer to 'general communicative use', and contrasts with specifically 'naming' use. By implication, 'distinctive' and 'descriptive' are shifted up, in parallel, from sign-level to utterance level, even if the resulting four-way homology – between distinctiveness and descriptiveness, and trade mark use and description – begs questions about precisely what it is that is changing between the different levels. Such questions are complicated, too, by use of related contrasts to achieve the same distinction: between 'trade mark use' and 'non-trade mark use', between 'trade mark use' and 'fair use', and between 'trade mark use' and the catch-all 'permissible use'.

Infringement and 'non-trade mark use' as a defence

Whatever the terminology, in some circumstances legal stipulations regarding use can seem straightforward. For instance, blanket protection offered to editorial, non-commercial unauthorized use of trade marks provides a safeguard against a dystopian future in which verbal creativity is muzzled by commercial ownership of the means of communication. Such exemption reflects a policy imperative of encouraging rather than seeking to restrict discussion of trade marked goods and services in editorial contexts such as news reporting, commercial journalism and analysis, and comparative advertising. Such discussion is held to be socially beneficial, and to contribute to the effective functioning of markets as well as reflecting a more general freedom-of-expression rationale (however that rationale is legally represented). As regards trade marks in particular, positively valuing discussion and commentary requires that people should be allowed to make 'descriptive', non-trade mark use of otherwise protected forms of expression.

utterances, offensive expressions, etc.), and sets his analysis of each within a framework of rationales for freedom of speech. A complementary work, focussing on practical issues in presenting linguistic evidence in cases that turn on acts such as offering bribes, threatening, admitting and perjury, is Roger Shuy, *Language Crimes: The Use and Abuse of Language Evidence in the Courtroom* (Oxford: Oxford University Press, 1993).

Because of the complexity of distinctions here, however, complications seem inevitable when judgment in a given case is required to work through competing claims and counterclaims, each constructed from the detailed facts of a specific situation. One such complication that has special relevance to the problem of distinctiveness is whether there can be non-commercial uses that are still defensible as 'non-trade mark use' or 'fair use' within what is, nevertheless, overall, a commercial context. The equivocal English case of *Arsenal* v *Reed* (2003) raises such issues, in ways that are analysed in detail in this collection by Jennifer Davis.[41]

Equally interesting are cases where the alleged infringing use of a trade mark name – i.e. the naming use – is not presented *as a* name.[42] In the US 'The Joy of Six' case, for instance,[43] the alleged infringing use took the form of a newspaper headline: a sort of contemporary cultural allusion used over a news report about a basketball game. An entrepreneur, Diana Packman, had obtained trade mark rights in the name THE JOY OF SIX for football and basketball entertainment. When a Chicago Bulls victory in the National Basketball Association Championship was then reported as a front-page story in the *Chicago Tribune*, the headline prominently used above the story was 'The Joy of Six'. Subsequently, the front page was reprinted on posters, T-shirts and other memorabilia. An action against the newspaper for infringement failed, on the combined grounds that, although a protected trade mark was prominently and exactly presented, it did not appear in a trade mark (source-denotative) use; that the newspaper had exploited in good faith expressive rather than trade mark qualities of the phrase as a sort of recognizable idiom; and that the selling of reproductions on T-shirts was a regular spin-off for the newspaper which had not sought to benefit from the wording of this headline in particular.

This robust decision displays broad freedom-of-expression values that depend on careful assessment of modalities of language use. The judgment was made that even precise use of the trade mark wording would not be confusing to consumers as to source (the canonical basis of an infringement claim). Despite the trade mark wording undoubtedly

<hr />

[41] *Arsenal Football Club Plc* v *Matthew Reed*, Case C-206/01 [2003] ETMR (73) 895 19. For different interpretations of the outcome and issues raised, see Jennifer Davis, Chapter 3 of this volume.

[42] My discussion of cases here emerges out of discussion with Graeme Dinwoodie. Each of the three cases chosen to illustrate my points is comprehensively analysed, for slightly different purposes, in Dinwoodie and Janis, *Trademarks and Unfair Competition*. My comments should be checked against the fuller accounts they present of the relevant legal arguments (Ch. 9).

[43] *Packman* v *Chicago Tribune Co.* 267 F.3d 628 (7th Cir. 2001).

forming part of commercial copy, nor was the alleged infringing use construed as acting as a name or source indicator for a *different* product, in some other field of trade (the canonical basis of a dilution claim, if for instance the T-shirts had been sold as fashion items under the name THE JOY OF SIX rather than as *Chicago Tribune* front-page T-shirts). Use of the mark was taken instead to function as an allusion to the trade mark name, not exploited for its commercial value but functioning as the typical wordplay of newspaper headlines, in which echoing one voice in a different, novel context is common practice.

Despite a number of caveats, the alleged infringing use of the trade mark was held not to be trade mark use. Rather, 'The Joy of Six' was viewed as being, in effect, a kind of quotation, the sort of echoic effect that a linguist might classify as 'mention' (or 'interpretive use') rather than mainstream 'use'. What distinguishes 'mention' from 'use' in linguistics is that, in mention (or interpretive use), the speaker utters something as if with inverted commas round it, or quotes specific wording or seems to attribute chosen words to another voice. In doing so, the speaker seems to stand aside from the utterance, disclaiming or distancing him/herself from, rather than affirming or certifying *in propria persona*, what is said.[44] In everyday conversation, language users tend to make great play of, and respond easily to, interpretive use in a variety of forms, including irony. Sometimes the echoic aspect of interpretive use is signalled linguistically (for instance by stylistic shifts before and after the expression in question); but sometimes it is triggered only by what the speaker and hearer already mutually know or believe.

In 'The Joy of Six', as also in other cases based on an equivalent claim (despite lack of success for this particular plaintiff), the risk clearly arises of possible enclosure of the intellectual common. Although seen off in this case by a US 'fair use' defence, the question remains whether, and if so under precisely what conditions, a trade mark owner's right *could* encroach beyond directly naming use into so-called interpretive uses of an expression that draw on or in some other way echo general currency or meaning in the culture. If infringement actions develop a tendency to succeed in such cases, which are at a border between social comment and commercial use, then arguably expressive use of the form of a trade mark (including ironic or humorous uses) would become in principle contestable in almost any context from which a commercial benefit could be

---

[44] For exposition and further discussion of 'interpretive use', see Diane Blakemore, *Understanding Utterances: An Introduction to Pragmatics* (Oxford: Blackwell, 1992) 102–10. See also the diagram provided by Dan Sperber and Deirdre Wilson to show the different kinds of relationship that can exist between the propositional form of an utterance and the thought that the utterance is used to represent (*Relevance: Communication and Cognition* (2nd edn, Oxford: Blackwell, 1995) 232).

derived, even indirectly. Even if verdicts mostly went against the complaining trade mark proprietor, the mere fact of litigation (even the threat of litigation) would have a chilling effect by opening up a new frontier of protective action against allusive use, analogous to proprietors fending off potentially generic use of their trade mark.

Interpretive use and parody

From a linguistic point of view, related issues seem to arise in actions against trade mark parody. Whereas a trade mark owner may seek to build goodwill in what they do, including by means of connotations accumulated around the trade mark itself as brand associations, the parodist seeks (for expressive purposes of their own) to undermine that reputation by deflating the claimed authority of the trade mark owner's voice. Mimicry and impersonation are essential for this purpose, because a common target of parody is the mismatch – sometimes tantamount to hypocrisy – believed to exist between the target organization's or person's action and their public style of self-presentation. Parody enacts this by linking the recognized style of expression to the parodist's own, critical view of the 'real state of affairs'. A simultaneously comic and critical effect is achieved that depends on incongruity between apparent seriousness or authenticity of form and excess or absurdity of content.

Two recent US cases – not typical but possibly symptomatic – illustrate how use considerations arise in relation to parody. In each, parody is achieved by discourse which appears to be in the voice of, and so ostensibly endorsed or sponsored by, the trade mark proprietor. In 'Michelob Oily',[45] a mock advert was published on the back cover of a humour magazine called *Snicker*. The mock advert had been closely modelled on a campaign for MICHELOB beer and directly incorporated trade mark material from at least one of their adverts. The intention appeared to be to undermine the company's proclaimed sensitivity to environmental pollution by putting forward an alternative claim: 'One taste and you'll ... drink it oily'. Close similarity between the original advert and the simulation, except for the alternative message (but including exactly reproduced trade mark material), might arguably have given rise to the suggestion that the parody was an authentic Michelob advert. In another case, concerning the Aqua song 'Barbie Girl' (1997),[46] the

---

[45] *Anheuser-Busch, Inc.* v *Balducci Publications*, 28 F.3d 769 (8th Cir. 1994), *cert. denied*, 513 US 1112 (1995).
[46] *Mattel, Inc.* v *MCA Records Inc.* 296 F.3d 894 (9th Cir. 2002), *cert. denied*, 123 S. Ct 993 (2003).

chorus lyric of the contested song began: 'I'm a Barbie girl, in my Barbie world ...'. Not only was the trade mark name BARBIE used as part of the song's title, but the female singer sings throughout in the first person, naming herself as Barbie and so at face value appearing to speak *as* the trade mark figure, effectively representing the trade mark proprietor as a kind of mouthpiece.

In each of these cases therefore, there seems at least a prima facie possibility of confusion being created as to source (in both cases arguments were also made for dilution, and for tarnishment in 'Barbie' because of the song's alleged inappropriateness for young girls: 'You can brush my hair, undress me everywhere ... hanky-panky ...'). However, in each case what is said and shown also presents a kind of dissonance between content and form, potentially undermining or cancelling out the *in propria persona* effect created by stylistic imitation. The 'Michelob Oily' advert could be argued to be uninterpretable as an advert, given the bizarre nature of its promotional claim for a beer ('drink it oily'), if it were not perceived as parody of an earlier advert (even if the reader were unfamiliar with the precise advert used as the parody vehicle). If the Aqua song is not interpreted as parody, the listener is merely left wondering what significance attaches to a female singer repeatedly claiming she is a 'Barbie girl' while being repeatedly addressed by name as 'Barbie' by her male co-singer; the resulting song interpretation has gaps in that would inevitably prompt the interpreter to search for a different meaning. In each case we might accordingly say that (as with 'The Joy of Six') use of the trade mark is signalled as a kind of interpretive use, or imitative dramatic monologue or fantasized speech. This function of the contested material is signalled by dissonance between 'use' of the trade mark and the surrounding context, conveying that the mock advert and song do not originate with, and are not sponsored or endorsed by, the original manufacturer.

There is no easy judgment to make in either case, especially given that in an adversarial setting competing readings will not be argued in a disinterested way. Each case allows considerable complexity of plausible argument as to use, reflecting the continuing challenge of understanding how consumers comprehend a multi-layered piece of text. In such difficult cases, analysis of trade mark 'use' is forced to leave behind confident distinctions between sign-types and begins to resemble the more open-ended interpretive practices of literary criticism or hermeneutics. In litigation, interpretive use rather than plain assertion confers no automatic exemption from trade mark liability. 'Michelob Oily' in particular appears a knife-edge case as regards how far the parodist can go into trade mark territory with impunity. Beyond the particular case, the more general risk also arises of a chilling effect if publishers' advice to the social commentator or humorist – in contrast with Forster's to the novelist – becomes increasingly 'tell, don't show'.

Conclusion

In developing my argument from sign-type to communicative use, I have inevitably trodden roughly over carefully worked legal doctrines. My comments about types of use need to be hedged and modified accordingly. What is surprising in my discussion is the conceptual distance it is necessary to travel, both in linguistics and in the development of ways of doing business. The intuitive notion persists that we should be able to tell the trade mark on the gingerbread apart from other types of labelling or design, or from pieces of burnt crust, because of what it looks like, where it is, or what type of sign it is. It is as if we are looking for a wax seal, author's signature or certificate of authenticity. As we shift, however, from gingerbread for sale on a Victorian baking tray to a global media environment of online sales promotion, brand building and anti-corporate parody, efforts to ring-fence the canonical source-denotative sign typically believed to constitute a trade mark increasingly have to yield to other ways of understanding signs and their meanings. To develop those other ways further, lawyers and their collaborators in other disciplines must continue to refine their understanding of (and their ways of describing) communicative events and genres within which the gingerbread, along with its accompanying trade mark, is presented for sale.

6 What linguistics can do for trademark law

*Graeme B. Dinwoodie**

Introduction

In his contribution to this volume, Alan Durant provides legal scholars with both a rich understanding of how linguists view terms that are part of the basic argot of trademark law and a potentially vital explanation of the different social functions that word marks might serve.[1] Both aspects of his analysis introduce the complex variable of reality into trademark law. Trademark law must decide whether and when to take account of that complex reality, and what weight to afford such reality, no matter how enriched an account linguists offer about the actual meaning of signs. In this response, I suggest that, while trademark law should not become beholden to linguistics, the lessons of Durant's linguistic analysis are to some extent already accommodated in the practice of trademark law, and could be important guides in the further development of a number of legal principles.

Section 1 of this chapter explains why linguistics should matter to trademark law. Traditionally, and still most typically, words comprise the largest group of trademark subject matter. Trademark law is structured around protecting the meanings of those words, at least as understood by consumers, in order (classically) to prevent consumer confusion. I suggest some reasons why trademark law might ignore the precise reality of consumer understanding. However, the *starting point* (if not always the end point) of trademark law in many contexts is an understanding of how signs actually work in context, and linguistics is one way of establishing that starting point for words. I explain how trademark law (despite some superficial departures) does in large part take into consideration Durant's observation that legal analysis would comport more with the reality of how words function if it focused on marks *as they are used*.

* Thanks to Alan Durant for broadening my horizons on this subject, and to Jennifer Davis, Tom Lee and Brian Havel for comments on a draft of this chapter.
[1] See Alan Durant, Chapter 5 of this volume.

Section 2 of the chapter focuses on Durant's exploration of the concepts of "distinctiveness" and "descriptiveness," as understood by lawyers and linguists, respectively. Durant highlights a divergence between linguistic and legal understandings of these core parts of trademark terminology. One could attenuate the significance of this divergence simply by recognizing that the legal usage reflects technical terms of art. Instead, I argue that Durant's analysis should reinforce important lessons for legal scholars. In particular, it helps us to understand that these terms are, to *some* extent, vehicles for more complex policy prescriptions than either exoteric usage or current technical understandings would suggest. Current trademark law fails to acknowledge adequately the other-than-supposedly-ordinary meaning of these key parts of trademark terminology, undermining the transparency of trademark lawmaking.

Finally, in Section 3, I argue that particular insights developed by Durant from the field of linguistics may prove valuable in illuminating several points of contention in contemporary trademark law. For example, Durant argues that there is less inherent meaning to words than commonly assumed, even in conjunction with particular goods – a coupling on which trademark law focuses in deciding whether to recognize trademark rights without proof of actual distinctiveness. The assessment of this relation, sometimes described as a test of conceptual strength, nominally determines[2] whether a term is treated as inherently distinctive and hence immediately protectable.[3] Instead, Durant emphasizes that what words mean and what effects they have "depend on how they are used as much as on the inherent meaning potential of the signs themselves." International policymakers increasingly focus on lubricating the system of international registration, which tends to favor the adoption of marks that are treated as inherently distinctive. Durant's work suggests that this is the wrong focus, or at least that we need to defend the emphasis on trademark registration as pursuing more discrete goals of economic policy.

[2] As I discuss in Section 1, below, this rule which ostensibly operates as an assessment of the relation between the sign and the goods in practice is informed by a number of considerations that make the analysis even more contextual.
[3] Conceptual strength is also relevant to questions of infringement, although the weight that courts attach to that factor in their infringement analysis is uncertain. See Barton Beebe, "An Empirical Study of the Multifactor Tests for Trademark Infringement" (2006) 94 Cal. L. Rev. 1581, 1633–6 (concluding that "in opinions that do address the issue of trademark strength, and inherent strength in particular, there is a surprisingly good correlation between inherent strength and success in the multifactor test" but also noting that "in those opinions in which the court's assessment of the mark's inherent strength was at odds with its assessment of the mark's acquired strength, a finding of acquired strength (or weakness) almost invariably trumped a finding of inherent weakness (or strength)").

Likewise, Durant's analysis of the different functions of words may be of great help in the development of the "fair use" or "descriptive, non-trademark use" defense, the latter of which is becoming one of the most contested parts of trademark law in a number of countries.[4] Fair use is one doctrinal setting in which trademark law tries to separate the protectable and unprotectable meaning that a term might simultaneously carry. Yet, according to Durant, linguistic theory suggests that it is difficult to separate the descriptive understandings of a word from its source-identifying character. Instead, linguistics may offer a number of concepts that can help delineate the types of permissible uses of a trademark in a more refined fashion than the current legal concepts of "descriptive use" or non-trademark use.

1   The limits of reality: trademark law and linguistic meaning

A   Signs functioning in principle

Durant argues that the main emphasis in legal studies is on how signs function in changing markets rather than how signs function in principle. This is surely correct, and appropriate. Trademark law is at bottom a mercantile law, concerned with actual marketplace effects. But trademark law has developed rules that on their face purport to reflect how signs function in principle. For example, it is standard black-letter law that "descriptive" terms will not immediately operate as source identifiers; trademark law assumes that consumers will not use such types of signs to identify and distinguish the goods of one producer from those of another.[5] To receive trademark protection for a descriptive term, a producer must show that the term has acquired a secondary meaning in the marketplace.[6]

---

[4] See generally Graeme B. Dinwoodie and Mark D. Janis, "Confusion over Use: Contextualism in Trademark Law" (2007) 92 Iowa L. Rev. 1597; Graeme B. Dinwoodie and Mark D. Janis, "Lessons from the Trademark Use Debate" (2007) 92 Iowa L. Rev. 1703; see generally Jeremy Phillips and Ilanah Simon (eds.), *Trade Mark Use* (Oxford: Oxford University Press, 2005).

[5] See *Abercrombie & Fitch Co.* v *Hunting World Inc.* 537 F.2d 4 (2nd Cir. 1976); First Council Directive 89/104/EEC of 21 December 1988 to approximate the laws of the Member States relating to trade marks, 1989 OJ (L 40) 1, Art. 3 (hereinafter "Trademark Directive").

[6] Similar rules of law apply to non-word marks. Thus, in the United States, recent case law mandates that product design marks be protected only upon proof of secondary meaning, because, according to the Supreme Court, consumers ordinarily do not identify the source of a product by its shape or design. See *Wal-Mart Stores, Inc.* v *Samara Brothers, Inc.* 529 US 205 (2000).

One might surmise that such rules of law say, or assume, something about how signs function in principle.[7] But it is important to recognize that many of these rules have been induced over time from the reasoned outcomes in individual cases, where the outcome to some extent has been informed by how language *has* been used and understood in the marketplace. On the whole – and this is an important prudential consideration, as discussed below – it is probably true that terms that are descriptive fail immediately to act as source identifiers in the marketplace.

Moreover, the classification of a term as de iure descriptive, although nominally a question of fact in a trademark suit,[8] might also be understood simply as a legal conclusion about whether or not a term should immediately be reserved to the exclusive use of a single producer in the field in question. This broader understanding of the classification of a term as descriptive is bolstered if one examines some of the ways in which courts make a determination of whether a term is descriptive or distinctive. For example, in *Zatarain's, Inc.* v *Oak Grove Smokehouse, Inc.*, the Court of Appeals for the Fifth Circuit identified four considerations that bore on this question: the dictionary meaning of the term; whether it requires imagination, thought and perception to reach a conclusion as to the nature of the goods based on the term used; the extent of third party usage of the term; and whether competitors needed the term in order to compete.

To be sure, the first two factors – dictionary meaning, and the extent of imagination required to understand the nature of the goods from the term used – appear to look at inherent meaning. But looking at third party usage of the term, and whether competitors needed the term in order to compete, allow a court to have regard to the use of the mark in the marketplace whilst making a nominally conceptual determination. Certainly, much judicial analysis in this area appears essentially intuitive and unreasoned, as was the case in *Zatarain's* itself, but the legal determination at least appears to proceed from more than merely an assessment of how the term in question functions in principle.[9]

---

[7] See Durant, Chapter 5 of this volume, 107–39.
[8] See *Zatarain's, Inc.* v *Oak Grove Smokehouse, Inc.* 98 F.2d 786 (5th Cir. 1983). Likewise, the European Court of Justice has developed rules about how to determine distinctiveness or confusion, but has left it to national courts to make factual determinations about how signs actually operate. Of course, the line between EU-wide legal rules and national factual assessments of consumer understanding is not always clear. See *Arsenal Football Club plc* v *Matthew Reed* [2003] ETMR 73 895 (Court of Appeal).
[9] In addition, as discussed below, the classification of the mark on the spectrum of distinctiveness reflects parallel, but related, realities. Thus, the factors allow courts to consider not only how the term will function in use for consumers, but whether its reservation

Finally, to the extent that rules regarding different *types* of signs have not been consolidated into statutory form, but instead operate as a presumption or rule of thumb, those rules may on occasion give way to empirical reality. Thus, in *Peaceable Planet* v *Ty, Inc.*,[10] Judge Richard Posner explored the rationales behind another rule that appears to operate on assumptions about how certain signs function in principle: namely, that personal names should not be protected as trademarks, absent secondary meaning.[11] These include the assumption that "some names are so common – such as 'Smith,' 'Jones,' 'Schwartz,' 'Wood,' and 'Jackson' – that consumers will not assume that two products having the same name therefore have the same source, and so they will not be confused by their bearing the same name." (Like the rule on descriptive terms, the personal name exclusion also reflects economic or competitiveness concerns: namely, allowing a person to use his own name in his own business and ensuring that owners of businesses are not prevented from communicating useful information to the consuming public.)

However, despite the assumptions about how personal names function in principle, Judge Posner argued that the scope of a rule is often limited by its rationale and concluded that in the case before him (NILES for stuffed toy camels), the reality of how NILES would operate in the marketplace should prevail over routinized application of the "rule" on personal names. He explained that:

rules of law are rarely as clean and strict as statements of them make them seem. So varied and unpredictable are the circumstances in which they are applied that more often than not the summary statement of a rule – the terse formula that judges employ as a necessary shorthand to prevent judicial opinions from turning into treatises – is better regarded as a generalization than as the premise of a syllogism. The "rule" that personal names are not protected as trademarks until they acquire secondary meaning is a generalization, and its application is to be guided by the purposes that we have extracted from the case law. When none of the purposes that animate the "personal name" rule is present, and application of

to one producer would generate competitive costs. See Graeme B. Dinwoodie, "Reconceptualizing the Inherent Distinctiveness of Product Design Trade Dress," (1997) 75 North Carolina L. Rev. 471, 503–4 (explaining the dual lenses through which distinctiveness is assessed). See below, Section 2. Likewise, the Supreme Court's assimilation of product design marks with descriptive terms, while justified in terms of the function of a product designed for consumers, was in large part intended to pursue other goals such as preservation of competition. See *Samara*, above.

[10] 362 F.3d 986 (7th Cir. 2004).

[11] Judge Posner explained that "[a]lthough cases and treatises commonly describe personal names as a subset of descriptive marks, . . . it is apparent that the rationale for denying trademark protection to personal names without proof of secondary meaning can't be the same as the rationale just sketched for marks that are 'descriptive' in the normal sense of the word. Names, as distinct from nicknames like 'Red' or 'Shorty,' are rarely descriptive": ibid.

the "rule" would impede rather than promote competition and consumer welfare, an exception should be recognized. And will be; for we find cases holding, very sensibly – and with inescapable implications for the present case – that the "rule" does not apply if the public is unlikely to understand the personal name as a personal name.

Thus, even where trademark law may seem to adopt rules reflecting beliefs about how signs function in principle, the derivation of such rules, their practical implementation and their interpreted scope often allow legal analysis to reflect marketplace realities. As a result, much of trademark doctrine fits quite well with Durant's linguistic conclusion that, as regards both eligibility for protection and enforcement of rights, the meaning of signs should be judged on the basis of criteria concerning the use of the signs in a given context.[12]

B   Departures from reality or more complex reality

On occasion, however, trademark law departs from Durant's principle, and ignores the precise social reality of consumer understanding of words as used. In this section, I suggest some of the reasons why trademark law might do so, and discuss what those departures from reality might mean for the relevance of linguistics to trademark law.

(i)   *Competing goals* Trademark law may seek to pursue prescriptive goals that over-ride protecting the sanctity of actual consumer understanding. For example, most trademark laws permit third parties to make unauthorized use of a protected term otherwise than as a mark, in order fairly and in good faith to describe the qualities or characteristics of the goods of that third party.[13] In a recent case, *KP Permanent* v *Lasting Impressions*,[14] the United States Supreme Court recognized that the policy objectives underlying the so-called "classic fair use" defense might on occasion trump the classic concern of trademark law with

---

[12] See Durant, Chapter 5 of this volume at 107–39 (noting that "what [signs] mean, what effects they have, and how far they infringe particular rights, all depend on how they are used as much as on the inherent meaning potential of the signs themselves").

[13] § 33(b)(4) of the Lanham Act provides that it shall be a defense to an action for infringement of any mark "that the use of the name, term, or device charged to be an infringement is a use, otherwise than as a mark, of the party's individual name in his own business, or of the individual name of anyone in privity with such party, or of a term or device which is descriptive of and used fairly and in good faith only to describe the goods or services of such party, or their geographic origin."

[14] See *KP Permanent Make-Up, Inc.* v *Lasting Impression I, Inc.* 543 US 111 (2004) (recognizing that not all forms of confusion are actionable under trademark law, and thus holding that a third party may be permitted to engage in some uses of a mark notwithstanding that such uses cause confusion).

avoiding a likelihood of confusion. That is, the competitive gains that flow from enabling rival producers to make use of essential descriptive terms may exceed the reduction in search costs that would be achieved by prohibiting the competitors' somewhat confusing use. Likewise, the greater latitude sometimes afforded those who make unauthorized use of a trademark for parodic purposes might simply reflect a concern for free speech values that is more fundamental than solicitude for the integrity of consumer understanding.[15]

In some instances, these competing considerations appear incommensurable, requiring courts confronted with infringement claims to muddle through, trying as best they can to optimize competing social objectives. For example, in 1938 the United States Supreme Court held that rivals of the original producer of SHREDDED WHEAT pillow-shaped biscuits were entitled to use that term (which the Court deemed generic) in part because of competition considerations and concerns attendant to the integrity of the patent system.[16] But the Court also required the rivals to use the term in ways that paid due regard to whatever consumer association of the term with the original producer in fact remained.

On other occasions, the limit on trademark rights can be explained as fully concordant with the affirmative purposes of trademark law. For example, one can reconceptualize the parody defense, if such an autonomous defense exists, as recognition of the relatively small likelihood that a parodic use of a mark would cause confusion on the part of consumers.[17] Similarly, some scholars have aligned the fair use defense with the core objectives of trademark law by arguing that a non-trademark use will not cause confusion in the first place.[18] Indeed, even if the objectives are truly competing – such as free speech and avoidance of consumer confusion in some instances – it might be inaccurate to characterize these additional objectives as departures from linguistic reality. To be sure, they represent a reduction in the solicitude typically shown by trademark law for the preservation of

---

[15] See, e.g., *Mattel, Inc* v *Walking Mountain Productions* 353 F.3d 792, 807 (9th Cir. 2003) (permitting the use of BARBIE in the titles of photographs that displayed BARBIE dolls in "various absurd and often sexualized positions," where "the public interest in free and artistic expression greatly outweighs its interest in potential consumer confusion about Mattel's sponsorship of [defendant] Forsythe's works").

[16] See *Kellogg Co.* v *National Biscuit Co.* 305 US 111 (1938); see also Graeme B. Dinwoodie, "The Story of Kellogg v. National Biscuit Company: Breakfast with Brandeis" in J. C. Ginsburg and R. C. Dreyfuss (eds.), *Intellectual Property Stories* (New York: Foundation Press, 2005) 220.

[17] See, e.g., *Jordache Enterprises* v *Hogg Wyld, Ltd* 828 F.2d 1482, 1488 (10th Cir. 1987); see also Gary Myers, "Trademark Parody: Lessons From the Copyright Decision in Campbell v Acuff-Rose Music, Inc." (1996) 59 J. Law. & Contemp. Probs. 181, 207.

[18] See, e.g., Stacey L. Dogan and Mark A. Lemley, "Trademark and Consumer Search Costs on the Internet" (2004) 41 Hous. L. Rev. 777.

one marketplace function of words – namely, to identify source. But one might equally regard the decision of trademark law to temper its regard for the source-identification function of the word in question as respect for a more complex reality, namely that the word is also serving other (associative or communicative) functions that likewise warrant respect.

Thus, one could view these additional considerations as competing or complementary; one could regard the tempering of protection for actual consumer association as a sign either that trademark law is unconcerned with that reality, or that trademark law is paying due regard to the multiple functions that the term is serving. Historically, as a matter of trademark practice, linguistic understandings have been used most directly within the rubrics of consumer association and consumer confusion, such that decisions to derogate from full protection of the source-identifying function are not always evident. But as the multiple uses of trademarks become better understood, and perhaps as those other uses become more economically significant, linguistics may provide the tools to help us better incorporate competing functions that words are in fact serving.[19] Realities matter under either explanation; thus, as regards the protection of word marks, so do the insights that linguistics may have to offer.

(ii)   Efficiency calculations Alternatively, efficiency calculations common to operation of administrative or judicial schemes may suggest that the law operate with a less calibrated view of reality.[20] The costs incurred in order for administrative and judicial institutions to make finely grained, accurate assessments of consumer understanding might surpass the social gains that such accurate assessments would capture.

Those costs consist in part of the expense involved in adjudicating questions of consumer understanding. In order to contest the issue of secondary meaning, for example, litigants are likely to commission costly surveys of consumer understanding of words. The same is true of the primary enforcement question in trademark litigation: namely, the likelihood of consumer confusion. Although courts have been careful to deny that these studies are *required* in order to make out a trademark case, the existence of a survey is extremely strong evidence on both issues. Indeed, black-letter law in the United States suggests that the absence of a study demonstrating confusion would badly hamper a trademark infringement claim.[21]

---

[19] See below, Section 3.
[20] See generally Robert G. Bone, "Enforcement Costs and Trademark Puzzles" (2004) 90 Va. L. Rev. 2099.
[21] In the European Union in general, and in the United Kingdom in particular, the courts tend to shy away from surveys. See Jennifer Davis, "Locating the Average Consumer: His

If trademark law required courts to make assessments of understandings of words that varied from one group of consumers to another, as detailed linguistic analysis might enable it to do, the costs of litigating infringement suits would become prohibitive. Likewise, if in reflection of such detailed studies of marketplace reality, courts imposed relief requiring producers to use marks differently across different groups of consumers, the costs of doing business would skyrocket. Thus, on the whole, trademark law deals with a rough reality. Classic trademark infringement analysis enjoins third party uses that would confuse an "appreciable number of ordinarily prudent purchasers."[22] Indeed, the ordinarily prudent purchaser is in large part a legal fiction that implements a vision of the degree of consumer protection regulation that Congress and the courts think appropriate without rendering commerce inefficient.

To be sure, at some relatively high level of generality, trademark law might tailor relief to the realities of a more refined marketplace analysis. Thus, courts have recognized terms as generic in the consumer retail market but acting as a source identifier in the wholesale market.[23] And the territorial scope of trademark rights means that courts might offer relief in one part of the country (or one country) and not another. But, on the whole, considerations of efficiency require that trademark law make less semantically precise judgments about the function of words than linguistics might be able to venture.

That said, the starting point of trademark law is an understanding of how words (or other signs) actually work in context. If we can neither prove nor predict that a term will act as a source identifier for consumers, there is no reason for trademark law to be in play. Linguistics is thus (along with other disciplines, such as marketing or cognitive psychology) one way of establishing the starting point. Indeed, to make calculations about whether the costs of ascertaining precise pictures of reality outweigh the gains of efficient, rougher justice, one needs to know more about how linguists would find the answer and what form (e.g. how certain, how nuanced, how helpful) that answer would take.

Judicial Origins, Intellectual Influences and Current Role in European Trade Mark Law" (2005) IPQ 183. Moreover, recent empirical studies of the multifactor test for likely confusion employed by US courts to determine infringement suggest that, surveys are less important than doctrinal statements imply. See Beebe, "An Empirical Study" at 1640–2.

[22] See *Thompson Medical Co., Inc.* v *Pfizer, Inc.* 753 F.2d 208, 213 (2nd Cir. 1985).

[23] See *Bayer Co.* v *United Drug Co.* 272 F.S 505 (SDNY 1921); see also *Dawn Donut Co.* v *Hart Food Stores, Inc.* 267 F.2d 358 (2nd Cir. 1959).

2   Linguistics reinforcing lessons for legal scholars

The notions of descriptiveness and distinctiveness are both crucial to trademark law. As suggested above, the terms have become legal terms of art. But both terms are words in everyday use. Durant persuasively demonstrates that the terms "descriptive" and "distinctive" can carry a number of quite different meanings when used in their ordinary everyday senses. In particular, both words could imply either value-neutral or value-laden understandings; trademark law, on the whole, would purport not to be making any value judgment about the term for which protection is sought, other than that it serves a particular function.

As Durant acknowledges, this might all mean nothing. After all, one can simply treat the legal understandings as terms of art quite apart from everyday understandings about which linguistics can inform. However, the divergence between common and legal understandings of terms such as "descriptive" and "distinctive" is important because trademark law (through its use of terms that do not *obviously* seem to be terms of art, and its superficially simple consumer protection rationale) is often thought to be quite intuitive. Copyright and patent law are far less intuitive and, to the extent that they use key phrases that might seem to be capable of common-sense interpretation, the more extensive statutory definitions make clearer that these concepts are terms of art implementing a range of prescriptive choices.[24]

Showing the *different* understandings of terms such as "descriptive" is important precisely because it highlights that these are, to *some* extent, terms of art carrying more than a common meaning (if there is such a thing). In particular, courts often define the concept of distinctiveness in what might simply be described as "reactive" terms: courts are merely measuring what understanding exists, as one everyday meaning of the term "descriptive" would suggest. Of course, as noted above, much more is going on when a court labels a term "descriptive," and that determination reflects a number of prescriptive policy choices. Highlighting that even the everyday use of the term "descriptive" is not necessarily value-neutral helps to reinforce a lesson that trademark law badly needs to take on board.[25]

---

[24] Moreover, trademark law often resorts to repositories of common understanding, such as dictionaries, to inform its application and interpretation of the legal term of art. For application, see *Zatarain's*, above. On interpretation, see *Dastar Corp.* v *Twentieth Century Fox Film Corp.* 539 US 23 (2003), in which Justice Scalia offered an interpretation of the term "origin" that purported to be informed by everyday linguistic understandings of that term. Of course, perhaps the textualist philosophy of the current Supreme Court may make this concern more acute in a number of areas.

[25] See Graeme B. Dinwoodie, *Trademark Law and Social Norms* (Working Paper, March 2007), available at www.ssrn.com.

3   Linguistics informing the further development of trademark thought

A   The role of registration systems

One of the lessons that linguistics could teach lawyers and which is developed in Durant's chapter is that there is less inherent meaning to words than commonly assumed by trademark law, even when coupled with goods or services. Context of use is required to get a grasp on meaning. As Durant neatly puts it, "the combination of signifier and signified as conventional semiotic sign, for trademarks as for all signs, significantly *underdetermines* use." Trademark law does, of course, already give great weight to context. But perhaps there are still lessons to be learned from heeding Durant's admonition that the functioning of trademarks should be seen as a form of "language in use."

For example, this observation might suggest that the tort-based passing off model of preventing consumer confusion is more likely to mesh closely with real consumer understanding, with any analysis of consumer understanding at registration prior to use being too speculative to be useful. A broad reading of Durant's conclusion might question the wisdom of a registration system. A narrow, and better, reading might simply conclude that Durant's observation emphasizes the need to understand the development of registration systems as a function of other social and economic objectives.[26]

Taking that lesson forward, international lawmakers increasingly focus on lubricating the system of international registration, which tends to favor the adoption and protection of marks that are claimed to be inherently distinctive. (Registration is needed to take advantage of the international protection systems, with the exception of the protection of well-known marks.) But debates about the wisdom of registration systems should perhaps be conducted with candid reference to broader economic policy rather than under cover of enhanced protection of consumer understanding.

B   Permissible uses

Another area of trademark law where linguistics may offer insights is with respect to permissible uses. Unlike copyright law, trademark law has historically included very few affirmative defenses. Most permissible uses could be justified because they did not create likely confusion, or

---

[26] See Lionel Bently, Chapter 1 of this volume.

(in countries such as the United Kingdom) were not uses in the course of trade. Yet, explicit development of permissible uses is a topic that is beginning to command the attention of courts and legal scholars. And it is likely to continue to do so given expansion in trademark subject matter, broader interpretation of the types of actionable confusion, and the widespread adoption of dilution law. In short, as trademark rights get stronger, the clamor for defenses to permit the continuation of behavior previously outside the scope of trademark law will become greater.

New business models will also make certain referential uses of marks more significant. Increasingly – and this is especially true online – many innovators are seeking to generate profits not by asserting rights in the primary content that they generate and distribute, but by offering free content and instead building business models around the provision of complementary or affiliated goods and services. Complementary products and services will be one of the keys in the economy of the next few years. The ability of competitors to make reference to the mark affixed to primary products and thus to compete in those complementary and service markets will depend upon whether the scope of trademark rights will extend to preclude even very loose senses of affiliation that consumers might develop between the respective goods. But it will also depend on whether trademark law will directly and expressly privilege certain uses that enable competition in those complementary markets.

Moreover, as so much of online activity comes to be framed by the use of search engines that use trademarks rather than content to structure targeted advertising, the regulation of such practices will shape consumer shopping habits and the availability of information about complementary products. It is in this context, in particular, that the purported trademark use requirement (or non-trademark use defense) is being most heavily litigated.

Again, Durant's analysis offers interesting lessons for legal scholars. The function that producers and consumers *want* marks to serve has changed. The mark VIRGIN applied to a telephone may tell consumers that the phone manufacturer in question is striving to appeal to, and values, hip, young tech-savvy consumers. It might also say to other members of the public that the person using the VIRGIN phone is a hip, young tech-savvy consumer (even if he is not). Neither function is a classic naming function (as linguists would understand it). But the consumer understanding that has been engendered and that has been embodied in the term VIRGIN clearly comports with what some would call the "modern" notion of a mark, which is moving closer to what the marketing literature would call "brands."

This evolution might, as Barton Beebe suggests, have come about as a result of the practice of using marks as properties in and of themselves detached from any goods in particular.[27] But it might also reflect that consumers no longer value information about the source of goods or even about the physical characteristics or quality of the goods for which the name of the source vouches. Instead, consumers crave the emotive or associative understandings with which the mark has become imbued. Consumers want to buy "cool NIKE shoes," not "sturdy NIKE shoes," let alone "NIKE shoes made by Nike, Inc." (Sometimes, "sturdy" and "made by Nike, Inc." can be cool, of course, so these are not bright lines.)

Durant astutely observes that, despite the attractions of securing a legally strong mark by adopting a term that is wholly arbitrary or coined, producers have a tendency to select marks at the margin of descriptiveness. They do so because they would like to appropriate not only the source-identifying capacity of the term, but any evocative power that the term might also provide. And, Durant explains, this is best achieved by selecting a mark close to the line between descriptive and suggestive marks. He analogizes the operation of such marks to the "abbreviated description" that Bertrand Russell thought may be active in the case of proper names, "which only denote because of a cluster of descriptions of the bearer activated in the mind, for which the name acts as a kind of shorthand." As a result, Durant concludes that, when those marks are protected, "protection granted to acquired meaning will encroach into descriptive properties of a sign in which there is a legitimate public interest, as an 'intellectual common,' unless clear boundaries govern precisely what 'trade mark use' (as opposed to more general, public use of protected verbal signs) will be."

Some might propose, as a result, that descriptive terms should never be protected by trademark law.[28] Others might bemoan the strong reading given to the notion of incontestability in US law.[29] What trademark law has in fact done, in different ways, is to begin to strengthen defenses to claims of infringement. Indeed, Durant's conclusion about the operation of marks protected on the basis of secondary meaning supports the decision of the United States Supreme Court in *KP Permanent* that the fair use defense must encompass uses where some confusion is likely.[30]

---

[27] See Barton Beebe, "The Semiotic Analysis of Trademark Law" (2004) 51 UCLA L. Rev. 704.

[28] See Lisa P. Ramsey, "Descriptive Trademarks and the First Amendment" (2003) 70 Tenn. L. Rev. 1095 (arguing that the First Amendment prohibits protection or registration of descriptive terms).

[29] See *Park 'N Fly, Inc. v Dollar Park & Fly, Inc.* 469 US 189, 201 (1985).

[30] There is no identical fair use defense as such in EU law. To some extent, any requirement that a plaintiff must allege that a defendant has made a "trademark use" of the plaintiff's mark in order to mark out a trademark infringement claim under the Trademark

The justification for the fair use defense can easily be expressed in the vernacular of law and economics, the dominant contemporary rationale for US trademark protection: use by a third party of the non-source-identifying (descriptive) aspects of a mark will not increase consumer search costs because such use will not interfere with the mark's source-identifying capacity.[31] Thus, the fair use defense is intended to ensure that the trademark owner obtains protection not for the word in gross, but only for the source-identifying aspect of the term. This argument operates on the proposition that trademark law is able to separate the source-identifying aspects of the term from its other aspects. However, while Durant appears to endorse this overall view, he nevertheless queries how easily the different aspects of the term can effectively be separated. It might thus be better to acknowledge, as the Supreme Court implicitly did in *KP Permanent*, that "descriptive uses" of trademarks by third parties might interfere with consumer understandings of the term as a mark, but that such uses are still warranted for the competitive benefits they secure in light of the minimal confusion they cause.[32]

Directive might result in similar outcomes. However, it is not clear that the Trademark Directive mandates that the defendant make a trademark use. See *Anheuser-Busch, Inc.* v *Budejovicky Budvar*, Case C-245/02 [2004] ECR I-10989 (ECJ); *Arsenal Football Club plc* v *Reed*, Case C-206/01 [2002] ECR I-10273 (ECJ); *Hölterhoff* v *Freiesleben*, Case C-2/00 [2002] ECR I-4187 (ECJ). In its most recent judgment, the European Court of Justice did not squarely address the argument that infringement depended on a trademark use and held instead that there is a prima facie case of infringement if the defendant's use "affects or is liable to affect the functions of [the plaintiff's] trademark." *See Adam Opel* v *Autec AG*, Case C48/05 [2007] ETMR (33) 500 (ECJ 2007) at paras. 22–5. But to the extent that this does state a trademark use requirement, the Court effectively subsumed the trademark use analysis within the broader question of confusion (or antecedent notions of consumer association) by holding that the answer to that question depends upon whether "the relevant consumer perceive[d] the sign identical to the [plaintiff's] logo appearing on the [defendant's products] ... as an indication that those products come from ... [plaintiff] or an undertaking economically linked to it." As a result, the European Court appears less willing to sanction permissible uses that cause confusion. Of course, even confusion determinations themselves reflect policy choices regarding permissible levels of confusion. See Dinwoodie, *Trademark Law and Social Norms*; Davis, "Locating the Average Consumer." If the European courts were willing to acknowledge that reality, then EU law could, under the rubric of actionable confusion, approximate the position reached by US law in *KP Permanent*. Alternatively, the European Court could develop a more vibrant version of the defense based on the defendant's use of the mark in accordance with honest commercial practices. See Trademark Directive, Art. 6. But, here too, the *Adam Opel* Court may suggest little room for judicial development, preferring instead a strict textual interpretation of Art. 6 of the Directive. See *Adam Opel*, above (offering relatively limited scope to Art. 6 defenses in interpreting the Trademark Directive).

[31] See Dogan and Lemley, "Trademark and Consumer Search Costs" at 810–11.
[32] See Dinwoodie & Janis, "Confusion Over Use" at 122, 127–8.

Durant's conclusion about the inevitable intermingling of a word's descriptive and naming capacities suggests that the goal of ensuring continued public and competitor access to the functions of a term that do not implicate the legitimate purposes of trademark protection will have to be pursued aggressively. The most aggressive efforts to guarantee these permissible uses have taken the form, in several countries, of the argument that only a defendant's use of the plaintiff's mark "as a trademark" can give rise to prima facie liability.[33] Alternatively, some courts have begun to question whether certain forms of confusion currently giving rise to liability should be actionable.[34]

Affording greater scope to affirmative defenses (such as fair use) will also be potentially important.[35] This may involve courts articulating more clearly the types of third party uses that should be permitted, either because they only marginally implicate trademark interests or because they substantially affect other important communicative interests. Durant stresses that determining whether a defendant's use has evoked the source-identifying aspect of the plaintiff's mark, as opposed to the descriptive properties of that term, can only be done by analyzing the "discourse 'setting' in which interpretations are constructed." He concludes that this involves more than examining the relationship between the sign and the plaintiff's goods; analyzing descriptive "uses" is a more complex assessment than whether a term is "descriptive." More particularly, Durant suggests that attention must be paid to:

dimensions of communication that have received some attention in trade mark law but are arguably less clearly articulated than the sign's semiotic properties. These communicative dimensions include: what genre the trade mark is embedded in (e.g. conventional editorial, such as a news story; name or slogan of an

---

[33] See ibid.; see also *1–800 Contacts, Inc.* v *WhenU.com, Inc.* 414 F.3d 400 (2nd Cir. 2005); *Arsenal Football Club plc* v *Reed* [2003] ETMR (73) 895 (EWCA) (on remand from European Court of Justice) (merchandising); *T* v *Dr R.*, LG Dusseldorf, No. 2a O 198/02 (26 Mar. 2003) (Germany) (contextual advertising); *Nation Fittings (M) Sdn Bhd* v *Oystertec plc* [2006] FSR (40) 740 (Singapore HC 4 Jan. 2006) (product design trade dress claim); *Verimark (Pty) Ltd* v *BMW (AG)*, (2007) SCA 53 (Republic of South Africa, Court of Appeal, 17 May 2007); *Adam Opel* v *Autec AG*, Case C48/05 [2007] ETMR (33) 500 (ECJ); (TA) 506/06 *Matim Li* v *Crazy Line Ltd*, OM (2006) (Dist. Ct Tel Aviv, 31 July 2006) (Israel); *R* v *Johnstone* [2004] ETMR (2) 18 (HL); *Dyer* v *Gallacher* (2006) Scot SC 6 (Glasgow Sheriff Ct Scot.), available at www.bailii.org/databases.html#scot. Whether a trademark use is required as an element of an infringement case is far from settled. See generally Dinwoodie and Janis, "Confusion Over Use" (discussing US and EU law).

[34] See *Lamparello* v *Falwell* 420 F.3d 309 (4th Cir. 2005); *Gibson Guitar Corp.* v *Paul Reed Smith Guitars, LP*, 423 F.3d 539 (6th Cir. 2005).

[35] See *KP Permanent*, above; see also Dinwoodie and Janis, "Lessons," above, footnote 4 (discussing expansive reading of the fair use defense).

advert; text used in labelling, etc.); the level and type of cultural knowledge assumed on the part of the average consumer, as addressee (assumptions about commerce and communication, as well as general-knowledge assumptions that sponsor interpretive inferences); and the adopted mode of address (how the addressee is invited to view the discourse, including the presumed identity of its author or speaker-persona). How signs work in a given context of use also depends on intention and attribution of intention, as well as on the receiver's interpretive strategy. Enforcement must accordingly be similarly concerned with such aspects of use, if use considerations are not to be some sort of return of the repressed in relation to the semiotic framework that underpins trade mark law.

That is to say, the type of use will be relevant to infringement, but it must be a highly contextualized analysis of use type.

The trademark use requirement – one popular doctrinal candidate for ensuring socially useful third party uses – would deny such analysis, making the entire question (for other reasons, such as the belief that the rule would bring certainty) turn on whether the defendant used the plaintiff's mark "as a mark." For reasons that I have written about at length elsewhere, this is at once too blunt and too uncertain, given contested notions of what is a mark.[36] Resolving the extent of permissible uses within the rubric of confusion would offer such context, but current modes of analysis might be inadequate absent adaptation to guarantee permissible uses thought desirable, because courts are often reluctant to acknowledge the prescriptive choices bundled up in confusion analysis.[37]

This leaves the descriptive fair use defense.[38] At present, despite the opening provided by the United States Supreme Court in *KP Permanent*, courts have offered a very narrow reading of the defense.[39] Trademark lawyers have very little real understanding of what is a "descriptive use" because the issue has in the past been rarely litigated. Durant offers us a linguistic analysis that again might prove extremely useful. He explains that:

The frequency and significance of the word "describe" in "non-trade mark use" or "fair use" defences is notable. This is despite the oddity of the word "describe" in this context, since it can hardly be to do with specific properties of the goods. More likely in this context is one of the other senses of "describe" and "descriptive" outlined above: that of asserting something that may be true or false, or in

---

[36] See Dinwoodie and Janis, "Confusion Over Use."
[37] See Dinwoodie, *Trademark Law and Social Norms*; Davis, "Locating the Average Consumer."
[38] See Trademark Directive, Art. 6; 15 USC (2004) § 1115(b)(4).
[39] See *KP Permanent Make-Up, Inc.* v *Lasting Impression I, Inc.* 408 F.3d 596 (9th Cir. 2005) (calling for courts to analyze, among numerous other contextual factors, "the degree of likely confusion . . . "); see also *Adam Opel*, above.

some other way commenting rather than naming. The defendant's use of the plaintiff's mark is said to "describe" the plaintiff's product or to "describe" their own product, rather than being an infringing use. This is a sense closer to "general communicative use," and contrasts with specifically "naming" use.

This is a much broader reading of the term "descriptive" than courts have offered. Courts in the USA and EU have read fair use or descriptive use defenses quite literally. But, as Durant stresses, the term "descriptive" is an odd choice. That ambiguity allows room for the type of broad interpretation that Durant advances, building also on our earlier observation about the complex linguistic understanding of the term in the context of establishing rights.[40]

Indeed, Durant concludes with discussion of linguistic classification that might provide focus to the more general approach suggested above. In particular, the divide in linguistics between "use" and "mention" or "reference" might be really helpful as we begin to develop an understanding of the types of use that should be permitted; our current legal vocabulary is very unhelpful. Interpreting the successful arguments of the defendant in the *The Joy of Six* case, Durant suggests that:

> "The Joy of Six" was viewed as being, in effect, a kind of quotation, the sort of echoic effect that a linguist might classify as "mention" (or "interpretive use") rather than mainstream "use." What distinguishes "mention" from "use" in linguistics is that, in mention (or interpretive use), the speaker utters something as if with inverted commas round it, or quotes specific wording or seems to attribute chosen words to another voice. In doing so, the speaker seems to stand aside from the utterance, disclaiming or distancing him/herself from, rather than affirming or certifying *in propria persona*, what is said.

This concept may be valuable because the concept of "mention" subsumes a number of ordinary everyday conversational uses of marks that we assume to be properly outside the the control of trademark owners, as well as parodic uses that have been vindicated in prior case law.

Conclusion

Linguistics has a lot to teach trademark law. It is surely a discipline relevant to the practice of trademark law. But, perhaps more importantly,

---

[40] It is important for the full vitality of defenses under US law that courts can find a broad reading of descriptive uses, because the descriptive fair use defense is one of only a few defenses preserved after a plaintiff's mark becomes incontestable. See Dinwoodie and Janis, "Lessons"; see also *Adam Opel*, above (offering a narrow reading of Art. 6 of the Trademark Directive).

linguistic understanding of key terms of art in trademark law illustrates the inevitably prescriptive content of supposedly descriptive assessments of trademark claims. And concepts that linguists have developed to classify and explain the use of language may prove helpful in providing a framework in which trademark law can grapple with developing rules that address the multiple functions that trademarks now serve.

Part IV

Marketing

7 Brand culture: trade marks, marketing and consumption

*Jonathan E. Schroeder**

Visual images constitute much corporate communication about products, economic performance and social responsibility, and also inform governmental efforts to create positive attitudes for citizens, consumers and organizations. Brand image, corporate image, advertising images and images of identity all depend upon compelling visual imagery. Variously referred to as the attention economy, the aesthetic economy and the experience economy, this visual turn in marketing may call for rethinking traditional approaches to brands and trade marks. Branding's reliance on visual rhetoric brings up a host of interdisciplinary questions. How do images function within marketing communication? What does the production and consumption of images mean for marketing, law and society? How does the handling of images in the allied fields of visual studies, art history, film theory, design management and corporate identity shed light on the relationships between visual images, brands and consumption?

This chapter discusses methodological and theoretical issues of visual images as they pertain to brands, via interdisciplinary research examples and exemplars. I place visual issues within a broader theoretical perspective of *brand culture* – the cultural dimensions or codes of brands (history, images, myths, art, theatre) that influence brand meaning in the marketplace. Visual consumer research cuts across methodological and topical boundary lines – the possibilities and problems of visual approaches encompass experimental and interpretive realms, and include such varied topics as information processing, image interpretation and research techniques.

* Thanks to David Vaver for his energetic, playful and intellectually rich response to this chapter, and also to Jennifer Davis, Graeme Dinwoodie, Lionel Bently, Jane Ginsburg and Bronwyn Parry for comments and encouragement. Thanks to Steven Chan at VeriSign and Eileen Lynch at Merrill Lynch for kind permission to reproduce their brand images, and Emma Gregg for her picture research. I also acknowledge financial support from the Jan Wallanders and Tom Hedelius Foundation.

Visual consumption

Visual images exist within a distinctive socio-legal environment that invokes several legal approaches, as discussed by David Vaver in his response to this chapter. The visual rhetoric of contemporary brand communication, suggests Vaver, makes claims that 'no reasonable person would take seriously'. Yet advertising clearly works. However, unlike textual or verbal statements, such as product claims or political promises, pictures cannot generally be held to be true or false. Images often elude empirical verification.[1] Thus, images are especially amenable to helping strategists avoid being held accountable for false or misleading claims. For example, cigarette manufacturers have learned not to make text-based claims about their products, relying instead on visual imagery such as the lone cowboy in the American West.

Vaver places trade mark law and practice within the context of expanding protection for trade marks, and invokes the rational consumer that forms the basis for so much trade mark law, questioning the notion that 'consumers choose products or services on price, quality and service'. Of course, much brand communication emphasizes attributes other than price, quality and service, focussing instead on psychological, social and cultural connections between product and person, often via sophisticated visual images. As Vaver argues, 'in this atmosphere, brands and trade marks come into their own'.

Contemporary branding's reliance on visual images implies rethinking legal perspectives on trade marks. Many battles of the brands take place within the visual domain. The World Wide Web mandates visualizing almost every aspect of corporate strategy, operations and communication – web design has brought visual issues into the mainstream of strategic thinking, and spurred research and thinking about how images work strategically. Images – including brand images, corporate images and websites – constitute much corporate communication about products, economic performance and corporate identity, within what can be called *visual consumption*.[2]

---

[1] See Judith Lynne Zaichowsky, *The Psychology behind Trademark Infringement and Counterfeiting* (Mahwah, N. J.: Lawrence Erlbaum, 2005), for a marketing-based perspective on trade mark issues.

[2] 'Image' has often been opposed to 'substance' in marketing theory, as in wider intellectual discussions. For emerging notions about the role of the image in the economy and marketing, see, for example, Scott Lash and John Urry, *The Economies of Sign and Space* (London: Sage, 1994); Jonathan E. Schroeder, 'The Artist and the Brand' (2005) 39 *European Journal of Marketing* 1291–1305; and Barbara B. Stern, George M. Zinkhan and Morris Holbrook, 'The Netvertising Image: Netvertising Image Communication Model (NICM) and Construct Definition' (2002) 31 *Journal of Advertising* Fall 15–28.

From the consumer perspective, visual experiences dominate information technologies of the Internet, as they navigate through a computer-
mediated environment almost entirely dependent upon their sense of
sight. Photography remains a key component of many information technologies – digital incorporation of scanned photographic images helped
transform the Internet into what it is today. Photography, in turn, was
heavily influenced by the older traditions of painting in its commercial
and artistic production, reception and recognition, and now dominates
how consumers think about identity.[3]

Research on visual consumption has gone through several phases. In
the first phase, sociologists such as Erving Goffman and Howard Becker
deployed photographs as data, evidence and illustrations within research
projects and scholarly reports documenting visual aspects of society. In
the second phase, visual images in advertising, branding and corporate
identity were seen to reveal and reflect strategic as well as social issues
as researchers began to focus on the representational power of images via
visual analysis, consumer-generated images and photo-elicitation techniques.[4] In the current phase, visual images themselves have assumed
central importance, drawing from cultural studies and visual studies
disciplines that emerged to interrogate popular cultural forms, and later
visual culture. Within this phase, a typical study might investigate how the
television sports channel ESPN covers the Olympics, emphasizing the
visual technologies that structure information and ideology, or bring a
visual perspective to consumer identity, utilizing an interdisciplinary
approach beyond the interests of aesthetics or visual studies.[5]

---

[3] I argue that photography – encompassing film, video, still and digital photography – plays
a key role in consumption and branding processes, albeit one that is underestimated in
marketing scholarship: Jonathan E. Schroeder, *Visual Consumption* (London: Routledge,
2002).

[4] Visual analysis refers to a systematic method for studying visual culture and visual images.
There are various perspectives and schools involved, analogous to differing traditions of
literary criticism. Consumer-generated images refer to 'amateur' or 'personal' photographs and videos often posted on websites such as flickr, Facebook and fotolog. Photo
elicitation is a research technique wherein people respond to photographs, thus eliciting
data that may support more traditional interviewing methods. See Theo van Leeuwen and
Carey Jewitt (eds.), *Handbook of Visual Analysis* (London: Sage, 2001); Matthew Rampley
(ed.), *Exploring Visual Culture: Definitions, Concepts, Contexts* (Edinburgh: Edinburgh
University Press, 2005); and Jonathan E. Schroeder, 'Critical Visual Analysis' in Russell
W. Belk (ed.), *Handbook of Qualitative Research Methods in Marketing* (Cheltenham:
Edward Elgar, 2006) 303–21.

[5] See, e.g., Janet L. Borgerson and Jonathan E. Schroeder, 'Identity in Marketing
Communications: An Ethics of Visual Representation' in Allan J. Kimmel (ed.),
Marketing Communications: Emerging Trends and Developments (Oxford: Oxford
University Press, 2005), 256–77; and Eric Guthey and Brad Jackson, 'CEO Portraits
and the Authenticity Paradox' (2005) 42 *Journal of Management Studies* July 1057–82.

Each phase contains several streams of research, including those that focus on image interpretation from various perspectives, such as psychoanalysis or semiotics.[6] Others emphasize image-making as a social psychological act of representing and communicating, drawing on traditional anthropological and sociological theories and methods. Another approach utilizes photographs, or other visual artefacts, as stimuli for research, for photo-elicitation, akin to projective measures within psychology that investigate deeper meanings and associations that people bring to images. An additional related research practice concerns visual presentation of data, documentary films and videos as well as more filmic treatments of consumption topics such as rituals, subcultures or tourism. In the next section, I present some brief examples of visual analysis of advertising, websites and corporate communication to illustrate the shifting ground of contemporary branding.

The transformative mirror of consumption

A major 'claim' that advertisements make concerns consumer transformation. In short, if you purchase the advertised product, somehow you will be transformed – happier, more successful or more attractive. These branding efforts draw upon cultural materials – history, myths and popular figures – to propose meaning and value for consumers. In a recent paper, Schroeder and Zwick[7] argue that advertising imagery helps consumers resolve cultural contradictions. This study focussed on masculine identity. Within the feminized consumption realm, how might men be represented as consumers, without diminishing their power? How might the male body function to represent consumer goals, such as success, attractiveness or the good life? We assessed three contemporary advertising exemplars that articulate this set of contradictions, providing illustrative examples for reflecting on masculinity, ontology and desire. We do not claim that they are representative; rather we argue that they are meaningful, compelling images worthy of close analysis. In this way, we follow interpretive work that focusses on a limited range of materials in order to make broader points about representation and identity in visual materials.[8]

[6] See Stuart Hall (ed.), *Representation: Cultural Representation and Signifying Practices* (London: Sage, 1997), for a concise introduction to visual representation in social science.
[7] Jonathan E. Schroeder and Detlev Zwick, 'Mirrors of Masculinity: Representation and Identity in Advertising Images' (2004) 7 *Consumption Markets and Culture* 1, 21–51.
[8] This approach calls for an interdisciplinary imagination, like one expressed by art historian Ernst Gombrich in *The Uses of Images: Studies in the Social Function of Art and Visual Communication* (London: Phaidon, 1999).

Figure 7.1 COLOMA advertisement, c. 1999.

'She was impressed that he ordered their Mudslides with Coloma. Which did wonders for his self-confidence' states a recent print ad for Coloma '100% Colombian Licor de Cafe'. This ad features a black-and-white photograph of a white man and woman at a bar or restaurant table with a superimposed colour photograph of a COLOMA bottle next to a lowball glass that presumably contains a Mudslide drink.

The action takes place in an oval, gilt-framed mirror hanging to the left of the couple. The bespectacled man gazes at his reflection, which has curiously transformed him into a much more classically attractive visage. In the mirror's reflection, the man appears to be in his mid to late twenties, tall, dark, a rakish curl of hair falling seductively down his forehead. He has lost 'his' eyeglasses, pointed nose, unstylish hair, and oversized chin – he might be said to resemble Pierce Brosnan as James Bond. The woman – not caught in the reflection that we see – seems to be peering across her companion to look at his rugged reflection. She models a low-cut cocktail dress, which reveals a thin frame, a conservative, shoulder-length haircut, and make-up that exaggerates her facial expression – one of bemusement. She appears to be enjoying herself – her right arm reaches over and grasps the man's right arm. His right hand curls around his COLOMA Mudslide, maintaining its fetish-like powers of transformation.

We suggested that the ad represents a portrait of a male–female couple with the addition of another male peering in on them from behind the mirror. This mirrored image may be read in several ways: as the sage from whom the man learned the ways of ordering impressive drinks, or the self transformed by demonstrating taste. To order and consume the right product (even the choice of the restaurant) expresses the man's cultural capital in the field of middle-class consumer culture. Thus, the ornamental femininity of his date further enhances his capital accumulation, and her apparent pleasure at his beverage brand reaffirms his masculinity, attractiveness and taste in one go. Perhaps more attractive mirror-man admires less attractive man's drinking partner, thus conferring male status on the latter's ability to attract a desirable date? The alchemical mirror embodies contradictions of the consuming male; one must be vain and attractive, as well as rational and sophisticated.

Furthermore, the tropes of alcohol involve taste, the pleasures of imbibing, the ability to 'control one's liquor', and, at a more fundamental level, a ritual of adulthood, especially the male variety. In social theorist Pierre Bourdieu's theory of symbolic capital, the conversion of one form of capital into another in different social fields is precisely what makes it so valuable. Here, we see the conversion of cultural capital into social capital by virtue of acquiring a more desirable 'body-for-others'.[9] Either way, we have a provocative message of physicality and product use.

The 'homely' man seems caught, Narcissus-like, gazing at his more handsome reflection, looking away from his date. Mirrors are a traditional trope of vanity, narcissism, lust and pride in Western art. Usually, mirrors are linked to women, revealing, reflecting and reinforcing feminine attributes of beauty and vanity. In this ad, the mirror plays a double role – casting a reflection of the newly self-confident man, and echoing the

[9] Pierre Bourdieu, *Distinction – A Social Critique of the Judgment of Taste* (Cambridge, Mass.: Harvard University Press, 1984) 207.

female role of mirroring male identity. Thus, the feminine mirrors the masculine, reflecting back self-confidence, consumer expertise and embodied transformation. Furthermore, the woman stands in as a mirror. He looks to her to gain a flattering conception of himself – *She was impressed . . . Which did wonders for his self-confidence.* This ad stands out for its representation of the male gaze, and suggests a reordering of limits within the male discourse. The image appears to invert, or perhaps expand, the object of gaze; the man seems quite concerned with himself as an object of beauty, as he vainly pays more attention to his image than to his date. His self-doubts fade – thanks to the woman's positive impression – his masculinity reaffirmed. However, one might read this ad in other ways, as men to men, perhaps the striking man in the mirror attracts the gaze of the homely man, doubly disrupting the gaze, and transforming the ad into a potentially gay image.[10] This queer perspective finds homoerotic overtones in the gaze between the two men – one reflecting, one reflected – who wink at themselves while wooing others.

A similar visual theme occupies an early 2000s print ad for Gateway computers, 'The Way Things Should Be'. In this example, another apparently unattractive man gazes into a mirrored wall to see a more conventionally good-looking 'reflection', transformed, in this case, by his 'smart, sexy, and always on the go' GATEWAY notebook computer. His 'improved' reflection has more hair, a more conventionally masculine face, complete with a 'strong' jaw, and his clothes seem to fit him better. As in the COLOMA ad, he grasps the talismanic product with his right hand, as he straightens his necktie with his left, perhaps signalling grooming rituals that underlie contemporary notions of masculine regimes of appearance. Here, however, the modernist office environment provides the setting, subtly suggesting that looks count on the job as well as on the make. The classic visual analysis technique of comparing and contrasting helps to uncover themes common across product categories and brand campaigns, helping to shift our focus to broader cultural concerns than market-focussed studies, and opening up consumer research to interdisciplinary inquiry.

[10] For more on what is known as 'gay vague' branding strategy, which helps illustrate the malleability of brand images, see Barbara B. Stern and Jonathan E. Schroeder, 'Interpretive Methodology from Art and Literary Criticism: A Humanistic Approach to Advertising Imagery' (1994) 28 *European Journal of Marketing* 114–32; and Janet L. Borgerson, Jonathan E. Schroeder, Britta Blomberg and Erika Thorssén, 'The Gay Family in the Ad: Consumer Responses to Non-traditional Families in Marketing Communications' (2006) 22 *Journal of Marketing Management* 955–78.

Figure 7.2 Classical architectural imagery from Danske Bank, Copenhagen (photo by Jonathan E. Schroeder).

Architectural expression in the electronic age

In a *visual genealogy* of contemporary marketing communication and branding efforts, I analysed banking websites, corporate reports and marketing communication to reveal the staying power of classicism for transmitting certain key values about banks and for building brand images for global financial institutions.[11] This type of study requires interdisciplinary sources, and often a good introductory book from an implicated field offers a useful start – for example, Hazel Conway and Rowan Roenisch's wonderfully concise *Understanding Architecture*.[12]

[11] See Jonathan E. Schroeder, 'Architectural Expression in the Electronic Age' in Linda M. Scott and Rajeev Batra (eds.), *Persuasive Imagery: A Consumer Response Perspective* (Mahwah, N. J.: Lawrence Erlbaum, 2003) 349–82.

[12] Hazel Conway and Rowan Roenisch, *Understanding Architecture* (London: Routledge, 2005).

I studied bank websites, financial institutions' brand campaigns, credit card advertising and investment banks' corporate reports, and found that the classical language of architecture remains central, despite massive changes in banking and the financial sector. Although space and time are transfigured within the information-based electronic world of contemporary commerce, classical architecture remains a viable method for communicating consumer values.

Architecture has played a key role in persuading consumers about the merits of banks:

Created by private capital to serve a pragmatic function for its owners, bank architecture at the same time turns a public face to its community in a vigorous attempt to communicate, persuade, assure, impress, and convince ... Contemporary attitudes regarding money, respectability, security, and corporate aesthetics are reflected ... bank architecture thus communicates the importance of banks as institutions, assuring us of their stability, prosperity, and permanence and inviting us inside to do business.[13]

Architecture provided a strategic method for banks to communicate key attributes of stability, strength and security. The classical form visually generates 'a sense of longevity, stability, rectitude, even stable power'.[14] Customers entrust banks with their savings – this distinguishes banking from most other business concerns. Although most consumers are aware that banks do not delegate space to store their particular money – money is represented by computer databases now – the physical attributes of the bank have played an important role in projecting a proper image, including stability over time, financial and material strength, and financial and physical security. Classicism helped legitimize banking in the USA, since its inception as a sovereign nation:

Classicism, like language, is precise but flexible. It can suggest commercial probity, as we see in the classical architecture of bank buildings and above all, in the New York Stock Exchange. It can radiate culture, as in the neoclassical art museum in Philadelphia and many another city. In the early nineteenth century, the Greek temple form pledged allegiance to the democratic principles that America traced back to ancient Athens.[15]

Each of these strategic banking values – stability, strength and security – has a psychological dimension as well as a material solution. Stability,

---

[13] Robert Nisbet, 'Men and Money: Reflections by a Sociologist' in Robert Nisbet, Susan Wagg and Anne W. Tucker (eds.), *Money Matters: A Critical Look at Bank Architecture* (New York: McGraw Hill, 1990) 7–14 at 8.
[14] James F. O'Gorman, *A B C of Architecture* (Philadelphia: University of Pennsylvania Press, 1998) 94.
[15] Ibid. 95.

expressed in visual form by a sturdy structure, provides a metaphor for long-term endurance – 'this is why the posts, pillars, and columns which have assured people in many cultures of the buildings' structural stability have been just as critical in resolving other uncertainties and anxieties'.[16] Colossal columns, heavy materials and symmetrical form contribute to a building's appearance of strength. Of course, bank customers also desire financial strength, and an ability to withstand economic cycles. Security, for so long largely dependent on architectural fortresses, walled cities and massive structures, also relates to psychological anxiety about financial matters. The closed form of most banks was meant to signal protection – a secure institution to entrust with one's future. Furthermore, the use of the temple form created a visual of a special building protecting its valuables, allowing only certain people access to the interior space, and promoting a ritual element to the bank visit. Banks are not just depositories of money; they are repositories of hopes, dreams and anxieties – a modern temple.

Information technology drove many changes in the banking industry – money and financial matters are no longer confined to pieces of paper that must be sorted and stored in ways that leave a ledger and an audit trail. Instead, they are electronic entries, generated via computers, and disconnected from particular spaces or buildings. This transformation was instrumental in overhauling the US banking system from a loose network of numerous small local banks interacting with the Federal Reserve System to the current deregulated arrangement of mega-banks, online banking and international markets. The small town bank of the past, where customers knew the tellers, and met personally with the loan officer to discuss his or her mortgage, is gone, replaced by ATM machines, computerized forms and secondary markets for mortgages. More efficient, certainly, but possibly less human. This points to the continuing significance of classical architecture – perhaps it alone remains to symbolize banking's connection with the past by tapping into classicism as a powerful referent system. Although the premises of banking have changed, the promises of the banking industry have not.

A fourth banking attribute emerged along with the electronic revolution – *speed*. Now banks need to communicate the four Ss: Stability, Strength, Security and Speed, as customers expect quick and efficient transactions supported by computerized operations. However, the other values remain, and basic relationships between the consumer and the bank continue to require symbolic association. The giant Wells Fargo Bank's 1999 annual report announced that 'the basic financial needs of

[16] John Onians, *Bearers of Meaning: The Classical Orders in Antiquity, the Middle Ages, and the Renaissance* (Princeton, N.J.: Princeton University Press, 1988) 3.

Figure 7.3 Merrill Lynch advertisement, *c.* 1998. Reproduced courtesy of Merrill Lynch.

our customers, however, do not change that much. They want to borrow, invest, transact, and be insured. They want convenience, security, trust and dependability.'[17] What role does the classical form play today? Certainly, banks are no longer primarily physical places – they are name brands that occupy space in the consumer's mind. I am not concerned here with recently built banks, or general architectural trends. Rather, I am interested in how the classical form resides in contemporary marketing communication – advertising, corporate reports, websites and the ephemera of electronic banking – for these are the crux of brand building and meaning-making.

Merrill Lynch, one of the world's largest investment banking firms, created one of the most visually striking examples of the uses of classicism in contemporary bank advertising. One version of their late 1990s corporate image-building campaign features four Ionic columns in the background of a stylized Grecian amphitheatre. A circular, futuristic-looking podium sits at the centre of the amphitheatre, echoing its rounded form. Each architectural element appears as a separate photograph, morphed together to create a pastiche of classicism, resembling an ancient site that has been restored by Disney, or assembled for a film set. The golden columns are not supporting anything – they appear to float in the frame, hovering above the marble amphitheatre's circular steps. Strict classical form demanded an even number of columns – so even these detached,

---

[17] *Wells Fargo Bank 1999 Annual Report* (San Francisco: Wells Fargo, 2000) 4.

decontextualized columns nod to tradition. On the left side of the two-page spread, a quote from Merrill Lynch's CEO asserts, 'we believe that a more vibrant marketplace of ideas will make a difference in addressing the critical challenges of our day'. This somewhat ambiguous statement refers to that decade's deregulation of the finance industry, opening up new markets for banking firms.

The classical elements, abstracted and stylized, appear almost as if they have been cut and pasted from a graphics program, in what architectural historians Alexander Tzonis and Liane Lefaivre castigate as 'citation-ism'.[18] The image vaguely resembles an ancient site, but the Ionic columns show no signs of age, nor do the amphitheatre steps – they have been taken out of context and harnessed for Merrill Lynch's strategic communication. The podium clashes with the columns, its sleek form jars the image into the present. Of course, debate flows from the podium, thus the speaker is assumed to be from the current epoch, discussing ideas in a time-honoured tradition, within the classical forum of the amphitheatre. However, the podium also signifies a special position from which to speak, quite different from the open marketplace.

Merrill Lynch's quote refers to the classical marketplace – the *agora* – as an ideal for the open discussion of ideas. However, the image shows an amphitheatre – the domain of actors and plays – in which only certain people speak. Merrill Lynch portrays itself within the foundation of free society, equating open markets with open dialogue, freedom with financial freedom, and democracy with capitalism, but a close analysis of this ad reveals misplaced agency, confusing the scripted world of the theatre with the *agora*. Furthermore, the classical motifs help Merrill Lynch project a stable, strong and secure image – yet one that is flexible, adaptive to new environments and able to accommodate new forms, as the contemporary podium attests.

Using the shorthand of architectural language, which refers to classical forms, the Greek ideal, the marketplace of ideas, and the roots of Western democracy, Merrill Lynch produced a complex advertising image, simply realized. Their business, then, is not limited to financial matters – they deal in ideas, which require testing via dialogue and debate. Architecture functions as a heuristic for consumers in a cluttered marketplace of images. It is not necessary for viewers to identify columns as 'Ionic' or 'Doric', or know much about the history of classicism, for this ad to work as a reference to tradition, dialogue and debate, and the classical past. By

[18] Alexander Tzonis and Liane Lefaivre, *Classical Architecture: The Poetics of Order* (Cambridge, MA: MIT Press, 1986).

juxtaposing old and new styles, Merrill Lynch sets up an implicit contrast as well as an allusion to the passage of time.

Traditionally, consumers have valued three qualities in a bank: stability, strength and security. Banks adopted classical architectural form to persuade the public. In the electronic age, architecture no longer confines banking, nor do most consumer banking transactions take place within a bank's headquarters. Therefore, a change might be expected in communicative tools; classical motifs might seem outmoded or old-fashioned for the information society. However, banks have shifted the symbolic domain from the building to the marketing message, adopting architectural symbols for use in digitized images that carry on the communicative tradition of classical forms. Advertising, Internet sites and ATM banking still incorporate abstracted architectural symbols, and buildings continue to provide many metaphors for the banking industry. VeriSign, a digital infrastructure services company that provides online security to financial firms, echoes these architectural themes in their brand communications, which include classical buildings. Furthermore, the ad copy refers to the brand promise of stability, strength and security:

You trust that the ravages of 400 years have not weakened the bases.
You trust the granite bases to support the 24-foot high Corinthian columns.
You trust nothing more than eight columns to sustain a 15,000-ton dome above
    your head.
Yet you're wary of using a credit card online?

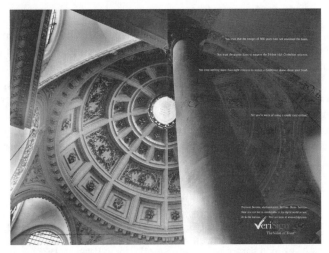

Figure 7.4 Architectural referents from VERISIGN, c. 2003. Reproduced courtesy of VERISIGN.

Thus, the high-tech, electronic VERISIGN brand invokes the legacy of the classical form in a neat comparative statement that marries the old and the new, placing an Internet business within the long legacy of architectural signification.

Banks today are in the business of building brands as much as physical structures. Consumer researcher Benoît Heilbrunn argues that brands are transformative devices which allow contradictory principles to coincide, such as nature and culture, the real and the imaginary, the past and the present, and the very distant and the here and now.[19] Classicism reinforces this notion, linking an ancient past to the present via rhetorical devices perfected during the classical era. Of course, these persuasive visual rhetorical tools are augmented via marketing information technology, selling the past to the future.[20]

Classicism remains a central cultural referent structure. Architecture provides spatial, historical and psychological images easily appropriated by visual media. Furthermore, architecture is a basic metaphorical structure for perception and cognition – indeed, it 'presents embodiments of thought when it invents and builds shapes'.[21] These shapes, translated into two dimensions, abstracted and isolated, are the building blocks of meaning-making. By tracing visual genealogies such as classicism, we gain an appreciation of the complex composition of current branding strategies.

Conclusion. Interdisciplinary insights into brand culture

Greater awareness of the associations between the traditions and conventions of visual history and the production and consumption of images helps to position and understand marketing communication as a global representational system, rather than a mere information conduit, as it is often treated by regulatory authorities. Research that extends previous work on visual representation into past, cultural and art historical realms may provide an essential bridge between visual meaning residing within producer intention and meaning wholly subsumed by individual

---

[19] See Benoît Heilbrunn, 'Cultural Branding between Utopia and A-topia' in Jonathan E. Schroeder and Miriam Salzer-Mörling (eds.), *Brand Culture* (London: Routledge, 2006) 103–17.

[20] As discussed by John Berger in *Ways of Seeing* (London: Penguin, 1972).

[21] Rudolf Arnheim, *The Dynamics of Architectural Form* (Berkeley: University of California Press, 1977), 274.

Brand Dimensions

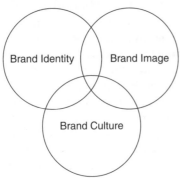

Figure 7.5 Dimensions of brand culture.

response, and between aesthetics and ethics.[22] In other words, along with brand identity and brand image, the realm of brand culture serves as a necessary complement to understanding brand meaning.[23]

To understand brands more fully, researchers must investigate the cultural, historical and representational conventions that shape consumption. If brands exist as cultural, ideological and political objects, then brand researchers require tools developed to understand culture, ideology and politics, in conjunction with more typical branding concepts, such as equity, strategy and value. Brand culture refers to the cultural influences and implications of brands in two ways. First, we live in a branded world: brands infuse culture with meaning, and brand management exerts a profound influence on contemporary society. Second, brand culture provides a third leg for brand theory – in conjunction with brand identity and brand image, brand culture provides the necessary cultural, historical and political grounding to understand brands in context. Future consumer research on visual issues must acknowledge images' representational and rhetorical power both as cultural artefacts and as engaging and deceptive bearers of meaning, reflecting broad societal, cultural and ideological codes.

---

[22] See, for example, Steve Charters, 'Aesthetic Products and Aesthetic Consumption: A Review' (2006) 9 *Consumption Markets and Culture* 3, 235–55; Daragh O'Reilly, 'Cultural Brands/Branding Cultures' (2005) 21 *Journal of Marketing Management* 573–88; and Alladi Venkatesh and Laurie Meamber, 'Arts and Aesthetics: Marketing and Cultural Production' (2006) 6 *Marketing Theory* March, 11–39.

[23] Brand culture represents one interdisciplinary framework for understanding how brands create value and meaning. For further discussion, see Schroeder and Salzer-Mörling (eds.), *Brand Culture*.

Brand research focussed on the legal, social and economic implications of images, fuelled by an understanding of the historical conditions influencing their production and consumption may require interdisciplinary training and collaboration. Furthermore, the consumer's perspective helps illuminate how brands (seemingly) attain so much value – consumers embrace, negotiate and adopt brands into their lives. This 'brand image', as referred to in Vaver's discussion of the *O2* mobile phone case, helps distinguish one brand from another. Branding's reliance on images, and the implicit claims that images make, often elude regulatory understandings of brand advertising, which typically focus on text-based matters, such as false claims, misleading statements, improper labelling, puffery and deceptive pricing.[24] Moreover, traditional theories of brand management consistently overemphasize functionality, product information and persuasive mechanisms of brand communication, neglecting the powerful roles that visual representation plays in brand strategy.

Key questions remain about the relationships between vision and value – why certain images are successful, superfluous or scandalous. Understanding the role that visual consumption plays in consumer preference, cultural production and representation signals a step towards understanding how aesthetics, images and vision inform and influence basic consumer issues of attention, branding, identity and meaning-making. From the consumer perspective, the brand overwhelms the trade mark, as Vaver points out in his response to this chapter. Thus, from the marketing and consumer research perspective, brands subsume trade marks – brands represent a heady combination of strategy, culture and consumer imagination.

---

[24] See Jonathan E. Schroeder and Janet L. Borgerson, 'An Ethics of Representation for International Marketing' (2005) 22 *International Marketing Review* 578–600; and, for a general introduction to social issues in brand communication, William Leiss, Stephen Kline, Sut Jhally and Jacqueline Botterill, *Social Communication in Advertising: Consumption in the Mediated Marketplace* (New York: Routledge, 2005).

8 'Brand culture: trade marks, marketing and consumption' – responding legally to Professor Schroeder's paper

*David Vaver**

Professor Schroeder's chapter on 'Brand culture' states that '[i]mages – including brand images, corporate images and websites – constitute much corporate communication about products, economic performance and corporate identity'.[1] It concludes that 'we live in a branded world: brands infuse culture with meaning, and brand management exerts a profound influence on contemporary society'.[2]

To make those points, Schroeder focuses on one sort of image: the photograph. He discusses how advertising uses images, often scanned and altered photographs, to give the advertised product a positive message with which especially adult male consumers can identify and which ultimately persuades them to buy. The ads he presents fall into familiar patterns. They show that a computer is not just a computer, liquor does not just make you drunk, and banks do not just steal your money through the various euphemisms by which your credit with them is progressively reduced. No, just carrying a laptop makes you a man (if you are one genetically; if you're not, then this ad is not for you); liquor makes any nerd attractive to women; and banks and other financial houses are solid citizens who spread democracy worldwide, and who among us would not want to donate our money to them so they could go on doing such good works on our behalf?

Part of the culture in which advertising and brands operate is law. Academic lawyers considering these ads might approach them in various ways, depending on their theoretical interests. One conventional approach might be to ask some questions such as the following:

(A) Are the ads legal in the countries in which they are likely to circulate? May advertisers present such messages with impunity and without

* My thanks to Dr Catherine Ng and Christopher G. Moore for helpful comments on earlier drafts.
[1] Jonathan E. Schroeder, Chapter 7 of this volume at 162.   [2] Ibid. 175.

178   *David Vaver*

verifying evidence, as against the state (representing the public) or
other traders (representing themselves)?
(B) Should the ads be legal? Why might one be concerned?
(C) If there are concerns, is legal intervention justified?
  – What is the history of the field?
  – If intervention is justified, what is the right mechanism or mech-
    anisms? E.g., criminal law, civil law, regulation through trade
    mark offices or other regulatory bodies?
  – If the jurisdiction is European, how does EC law affect matters?
A full-scale analysis such as this is a major research project. It is not
attempted here. This chapter is instead preliminary and selective. The
focus is the UK, with sorties abroad.

I

Are the advertisements legal? May advertisers present such messages with
impunity and without verifying evidence? Who can complain?

Schroeder suggests the ads are legal; and, on their face at least, they seem
inoffensive to someone raised in an English-speaking common law tradition. They seem to be American in origin and presumably comply with
American laws but they seem, again on their face at least, equally to comply
with UK law. The details of US and UK laws obviously differ, especially on
who can complain and sue, and for what. Otherwise, Schroeder's point
about brand culture transcending any one territory is generally supported
by US and UK legal norms on branding and advertising.

Schroeder's claim that brand culture is global suggests a tendency rather
than a fact. He does not (and presumably would not) claim that brands
mean the same for the inhabitants of New Caledonia as they do for those of
New York. Nor does he imply that the particular ads (translated if necessary) or brands would have the same effect on people of different cultures in
different jurisdictions, or even that using the same material beyond the USA
or the UK would be a good idea. It is a truism that an ad or brand that is
culturally meaningful, acceptable and effective in one jurisdiction may not
be so in another. Legal acceptance may equally vary among jurisdictions.

One reason the ads look legal to US or UK eyes is how little they actually
say about the product or service on offer. Objective facts that might affect a
decision to engage with the offering are suppressed in favour of 'nonbrand
facts', e.g. ideas that 'relate a brand to a certain lifestyle or problem or
motivation'.[3] So a PEPSI ad that associates the drink with youthfulness

---

[3] Ivan L. Preston, *The Tangled Web They Weave: Truth, Falsity and Advertisers* (Madison:
University of Wisconsin Press, 1994) 89.

does not say that drinking lots of sugared water rots your teeth and makes you fat, and you would do better to drink tap water. An aged analytical reader with a positive mindset might react to the ad thus:

Objectively, the relationship of Pepsi to my motivation towards youthfulness is nonexistent ... [T]he relationship doesn't exist physically. What I buy is a can or bottle of liquid containing certain ingredients – nothing more. I receive noth᠁ from Pepsi that has any natural relationship to any characteristics of ᠁

Nonetheless, I can see a relationship if I want to. I am free, a᠁ decide in my own perception that Pepsi *reflects* my motivation᠁ ical or social needs. If I say it does, then the relationship is ᠁᠁e, not about Pepsi. And from that relationship I receive a value that I appreciate and enjoy – and might not receive from any other soft drink. These benefits are real in a very important way, not as physical realities, but as the realities of my own mind.[4]

As an autonomous human being, I may choose to accept or reject the suggestion. Free speech ideals favour letting the advertiser plant the thought in my head if I choose to let it be planted. How much real choice I have is an interesting question. Whether or not I am harmed by feeling youthful in swigging from a bottle of brown, fizzy, sugared water, instead of sipping merely H_2O, is also debatable. Whether or not the economy needs to function on such 'fraudlets'[5] is another larger question.

Not all fraudlets are relatively harmless. Consider the following reaction to a CLAIROL television ad that asked 'Isn't it amazing that a little thing like hair coloring can change your whole outlook!':

[P]sychological or social motivations will loom larger as legitimate reasons for buying hair coloring than for buying a soft drink ... Clairol involves enhancing in consumers' minds the fear that a problem exists. The advertisers would probably protest that there is no harm in such a mental manipulation, because we don't have to be bothered by any psychological concerns if we don't want to be. But is unnecessary worry not a harm? Or wasted money? The possibility of objective reasons against buying loom[s] somewhat larger for Clairol than Pepsi.[6]

These approaches treat ads as a matter between advertiser and consumer. They say nothing of how the advertising affects other traders. Law too is concerned with the dyadic consumer v trader/advertiser relationship.[7] Likely consumer harm caused by an ad may be a reason for state intervention by prosecutors or (in the USA) a federal or state trade commission. Law is, however, as (perhaps more) often concerned with

[4] Ibid. 90.   [5] The late Arthur Leff's coinage.
[6] Preston, *The Tangled Web* 93.
[7] The advertiser/trader is sometimes the same entity, as is the case with the GATEWAY advertiser or the banks and financial service providers that figure in Professor Schroeder's chapter. The advertiser/trader may also involve different entities. Thus, the placer of the COLOMA ad (see section II below) is presumably the liquor manufacturer or

a triadic relationship: how the advertiser's acts affect not only the consumer but also other traders, particularly competitors. The consumer's actual or likely reaction becomes the measure of legal relations between traders struggling for market share. Legal standards may differ depending on whether two or three parties are nominally involved.

,   Take the consumer *v* advertiser/trader perspective: no octogenarian who does not feel a jot younger after drinking a bottle or a case can get a refund on his PEPSI from his corner store or from the Pepsi manufacturer. Applying CLAIROL to his few wisps may or may not indeed 'change [his] whole outlook!', but not in any way that lets him complain legally to the advertiser or anyone else. Law does sometimes interest itself in psychological harm and can compensate those who suffer it by the action of another who breaks a contract with, or commits a civil wrong against, them. But law's view of harm does not extend to what it would regard as the trivial concerns of the aggrieved PEPSI or CLAIROL consumer.[8] Law's ; ʳᵉ are more stoic than epicurean.

ᵉrspective to trader *v* trader, and the consumer piggy-in-the-m.. ᵉs more epicure than stoic. Schroeder's first example, dealing . ᵉd COLOMA,[9] coincidentally deals with a class of product that n.. ich in the law books everywhere. Competition in alcoholic drinks is fierce and traders push law hard in their quest for market share. Consider the five-year battle over 'advocaat' in England in the 1970s. In 1974 English drinkers started forsaking WARNINK'S ADVOCAAT in droves when cheaper KEELING'S OLDE ENGLISH ADVOCAAT first hit the market. KEELING'S was made from egg and fortified wine, and had till then been called 'egg flip'. WARNINK'S was a Dutch liquor made from egg and grain- or molasses-based spirit. (More about these ingredients later: see section V, below.) WARNINK'S was dearer than KEELING'S because spirit was taxed higher than fortified wine. Nobody bought KEELING'S thinking it was Dutch or WARNINK'S. Yet Warnink said Keeling lied when it called its drink 'advocaat': it was still just 'egg flip'. Warnink claimed Keeling had harmed it economically because the lie hurt the 'real' advocaat brand. Warnink shared in the goodwill of the

---

local distributor, which is not the same entity as the retailer from whom the consumer buys the liquor. Legal liabilities of advertiser and trader to the state or the consumer often differ.

[8] See Phillips, *Trade Mark Law: A Practical Anatomy* (Oxford: Oxford University Press, 2003) para. 2.48: 'Small and relatively harmless lies are all part and parcel of advertising and marketing in a free-market economy, where consumers must learn at an early age not to believe everything they read or hear.'

[9] Schroeder, Chapter 7 of this volume at 165.

brand and so had standing to have Keeling stopped and to get compensation for lost custom.

Warnink's problem was that only regular WARNINK'S drinkers or experts could tell the two beverages apart. Most consumers could not: there was 'no such gross difference of taste, colour, or other qualities, as would lead the inexperienced or casual customer to regard them as different species of drink'.[10] So were consumers really fooled? Keeling argued they were not. Those who cared paid more and stuck with WARNINK'S. Those who thought KEELING'S good enough, counted their pennies or just liked buying British (another mistake since Warnink was then also owned by a British company, Allied Breweries Ltd) went for KEELING'S. Keeling's lawyers pitched its case thus:

The issue is rather one of social policy than of law, viz., whether the court should protect the manufacturer or the general public which is benefited by competition promoting consumer progress. The contentions of [Warnink] produce ossification. Thus ice cream was originally made from cream but under the impact of social and manufacturing changes, it is now made from vegetable fats, a thing which on the arguments for [Warnink] could not have happened.[11]

The court was unpersuaded: this was 'a case of unfair, not to say dishonest, trading of a kind for which a rational system of law ought to provide a remedy to other traders whose business or goodwill is injured by it', even though:

in an economic system which has relied on competition to keep down prices and to improve products there may be practical reasons why it should have been the policy of the common law not to run the risk of hampering competition by providing civil remedies to every one competing in the market who has suffered damage to his business or goodwill in consequence of inaccurate statements of whatever kind that may be made by rival traders about their own wares. The market in which the action for passing off originated was no place for the mealy mouthed; advertisements are not on affidavit; exaggerated claims by a trader about the quality of his wares, assertions that they are better than those of his rivals even though he knows this to be untrue, have been permitted by the common law as venial 'puffing' which gives no cause of action to a competitor even though he can show that he has suffered actual damage in his business as a result.[12]

Times had changed. Keeling might have got away with it in the nineteenth century but no more: contemporary markets demanded higher standards of honesty.

---

[10] *Erven Warnink BV* v *J. Townend & Sons (Hull) Ltd* [1978] FSR 1, 11 (Ch).
[11] *Erven Warnink BV* v *J. Townend & Sons (Hull) Ltd* [1979] AC 731, 737, Griffiths QC arguing for the defendants.
[12] Ibid. 742, by Lord Diplock, with majority agreement.

Warnink is just one case among now many where, typically, Old World producers of food, wine and spirits have, through courts, legislatures, government departments and international fora, managed to get a legal monopoly over their product names and have prevented imitators from free-riding on their heavily promoted brands. Champagne, scotch and sherry producers have been among the most persistently aggressive, but everyone is in on this game. Parma ham, Swiss chocolate and feta cheese are just random recent examples where a trade sector has been protected under the guise of protecting the consumer.

For guise it is. The consumer pays more for the protected product even though he may have been just as happy with the cheaper one.[13] As the court that banned the marketing of Spanish sparkling wine in England as 'Spanish champagne' pointed out nearly a half-century ago:

> [T]he law in this respect has been concerned with unfair competition between traders rather than with the deception of the public which may be caused by the defendant's conduct, for the right of action known as a 'passing-off action' is not an action brought by the member of the public who is deceived but by the trader whose trade is likely to suffer from the deception practised on the public but who is not himself deceived at all.[14]

The ban on 'Spanish champagne' occurred even though the importer had, just before civil proceedings were started, been found not guilty, after a six-day hearing at the Old Bailey, on criminal charges of misleading the public with his labelling.[15] So under a consumer protection law passed by Parliament, a trader can be found not to be misleading consumers; but under a rule developed by the judges to protect traders, he can indeed be found to be misleading consumers, and can be stopped by an injunction and made to pay a good part of the other trader's usually enormous legal costs as well.

So when Schroeder focusses on the effect of the ads on 'the consumer', a lawyer might ask: what consumer are you looking at, and why? Is the purpose to help advertisers refine their tactics of persuasion? Is it to protect consumers from being misled? Is it to seek to protect a competitor's trade? The analysis may differ, depending on the purpose. In law,

---

[13] A point made long ago by Frank J in his extended essay on how far judges should protect trade marks: *Standard Brands Inc.* v *Smidler* 151 F.2d 34 (2nd Cir. 1945), demonstrating unease with the majority's conclusion that v8 vitamins must change their name because consumers might be fooled into believing the product was somehow connected with v8 vegetable juice.

[14] *Bollinger* v *Costa Brava Wine Co. Ltd* [1960] Ch 262, 274.

[15] As noted in passing in *Bollinger* v *Costa Brava Wine Co. Ltd (No. 2)* [1961] 1 WLR 277, 281 (Ch).

the standard to be adopted is often unclear. Just a few years before *Warnink*, a court had said, in allowing a comparative advertising suit to go to trial:

[I]n the kind of situation where one expects, as a matter of ordinary common experience, a person to use a certain amount of hyperbole in the description of goods, property or services, the courts will do what any ordinary reasonable man would do, namely, take it with a large pinch of salt . . . [I]n order to draw the line, one must apply this test, namely, whether a reasonable man would take the claim being made as being a serious claim or not.[16]

But, like negligence law's reasonable person, trade mark and passing-off law's reasonable consumer is a mass of contradictions. He or she may be, for example, simultaneously a rational sovereign and a gullible fool. As one legal commentator notes:

The sovereign consumer . . . serves one master, namely, the trademark apologist, in theoretical disputes over the basis of trademark protection and another, the restrictionist, in disputes over the scope of that protection. The rational consumer may justify the protection of trademarks for their informational content, but, in his perspicacity, he also justifies a narrow scope of protection as against other similar marks. The consumer as fool is a similarly double-edged construct. His susceptibility to the persuasive content of trademarks undermines the basis of trademark protection, but his lack of discernment also recommends a wide scope of protection when protection is given. The result is that trademark apologists – and plaintiffs – tend to adduce the sovereign when they speak of the basis of protection and the fool when they speak of the scope. Trademark restrictionists – and defendants – do the reverse. They adduce the fool when they speak of the basis, and the sovereign when they speak of the scope . . .

These tensions . . . continue to muddle outcomes in the courts because trademark law lacks a well-developed theory of the consumer and, specifically, of consumer sophistication.[17]

To which one might add: nor is there a well-developed theory of consumer sophistication that spans the laws that are designed to protect consumers from false or misleading advertising and the laws that protect traders from 'unfair' interferences with their trade and trade marks.[18]

---

16 *De Beers Abrasive Products Ltd* v *International General Electric Co. of New York Ltd* [1975] 1 WLR 972, 978 (Ch.). See further Ng, 'The Limits of Comparative Advertising in Civil Actions: Just When you Dare to Compare' (1998) 15 Can. I.P. Rev 143, (1999) 16 Can. I.P. Rev 149.
17 Barton Beebe, 'Search and Persuasion in Trademark Law' (2005) 103 Mich. L. Rev 2020, 2025.
18 See David Hoffman, 'The Best Puffery Article Ever' (2006), Temple University Legal Studies Research Paper No. 2006–11.

184   *David Vaver*

II

Let us now look at one of the ads in Professor Schroeder's chapter: that for COLOMA coffee liqueur.[19] A conventional interpretation of the text and picture might go something like this: the unnamed woman (a universal 'she') is said to be impressed that the man (a universal 'partner') ordered 'their' mudslides[20] with COLOMA. The male is clearly in charge: he is doing the ordering. The mere act of ordering is not enough for him to feel self-confident – about what, we're not told, but presumably something to do with his chances with the woman. This we are to assume from the puerile *double-entendre* under the COLOMA mark: 'the smoother way to stir things up'. It is the woman's validation of his ordering COLOMA that boosts his self-confidence. She may have said something, but that is not important: her sideways smiling glance, together with the placing of her arm on his, does the trick. Her arm is the wand that transforms the bespectacled nerd with his goofy grin into the smoother cocky-looking Don Juan character in the mirror, ready to 'stir things up'.[21]

A lawyer, asked by the advertiser or its agency to pass on the legality of this message, would spend little time on it. She might ask whether or not COLOMA was a registered mark and breathe a sigh of relief if it was; presumably it would then have passed the challenge that KAHLÙA, the market leader in coffee liqueur, might have posed because of the similarity between how the two marks look and sound.[22] The lawyer would also nod approvingly at how COLOMA was spelt with a capital 'C' in the text, and how the letterpress alongside the neck of the bottle read '100% Colombian Licor de Café' and not, e.g., 'Colombian kahlua'. She would feel comforted by these indications that COLOMA was being used distinctively as a trade mark and not just to describe any coffee liqueur – the danger of genericism KAHLÙA may face in some markets where the public increasingly calls all coffee liqueurs 'kahlua'.[23] The lawyer might then ask whether or not the claim found alongside the picture of the

[19] Schroeder, 'Brand Culture' 165.
[20] An alcoholic cocktail apparently made with vodka, coffee liqueur, Irish cream liqueur, and cream. The ad is clearly not directed to unsophisticates who, till now, associated mudslides only with natural disasters.
[21] For a Lacanian analysis of how mirrors function in ads, see Judith Williamson, *Decoding Advertisements: Ideology and Meaning in Advertising* (rpt, London and New York: Marion Boyers, 2002) 60ff.
[22] To compare COLOMA with KAHLÙA: the combination of the use of 'C' instead of 'K' and 'O' instead of 'Ù', the insertion of 'M', and the suggestion of Colombian origin probably saves COLOMA from being found confusingly similar to KAHLÙA and so being either unregistrable or an infringement.
[23] Sung In, 'Death of a Trademark: Genericide in the Digital Age' (2002) 21 *Review of Litigation* 159, 186, where KAHLÙA is given as an example of a term with the dual

bottle – '100% Colombian' coffee liqueur – was true and verifiable.[24] She might inquire how the ad came to be composed, to ensure that no copyright was infringed along the way. She would not be bothered that similarly themed ads were common in the drinks business, so long as this ad did not lift or imitate any large chunk of letterpress or artistry off another ad or work.[25]

As for the rest of the text and picture, the lawyer would argue that it should all be treated as metaphor, a vignette that would be understood as harmless puffery by the reasonable reader, whether before or after the mudslides. Such a reader – certainly the rational consumer, and probably even the gullible fool – would understand that a mudslide, even with COLOMA as ingredient, would not in itself turn him from nerd to knight, or his companion from sceptic to swooner. It might provide the occasion; what he did with it would be up to him and, no doubt, the woman. The lawyer would be unconcerned with the gender stereotypes the ad portrays and reinforces. Feminists and other critics have long despised this sort of advertising. Yet it has continued as the stock-in-trade of liquor (and much other) advertising for decades, and the law has left it alone. So too, unsurprisingly, have advertising codes that industry has established to regulate itself.

Schroeder inferentially makes the case that there are lies, damn lies, and advertising; for any advertiser who wrote anything as inane as the ads imply would be ridiculed, a fate probably worse than being cited for false or misleading advertising. But Schroeder shows one reason why

meaning of a trade mark coffee liqueur and any caffeine-based liqueur used to make coffee-flavoured alcoholic drinks; so it is susceptible to 'genericide', i.e., invalidation as a trade mark.

[24] Whether it is the liquor or the coffee that is supposed to be '100% Colombian' is unclear. The safest course would be to insist that the coffee is grown or blended in Colombia and that the liquor is also made there, unless the statement of origin is to be qualified. Geographic identity can be pretty dilute and yet still claim protection. MELTON MOWBRAY PORK PIE producers are currently seeking a European 'geographical indication' even though they are located in Nottinghamshire, Northamptonshire, Lincolnshire and everywhere else in Leicestershire other than Melton Mowbray where the pies originated. The application is proceeding over objections from a producer based in Wiltshire and Shropshire who feels excluded. Some consumers continue to believe the pies still come from Melton Mowbray but that apparently does not matter – all the law requires is that historically the pies once did: *Northern Foods plc v Department for Environment, Food & Rural Affairs* [2005] EWHC 2971 (Admin.) paras. 21, 28 and 30. (Why does the title of Arthur Leff's classic *Swindling and Selling* (New York: Free Press, 1977) come to mind?)

[25] Copyright law permits copying of advertising ideas and slogans and gimmicks unless discrete artistry or substantial letterpress is taken: *Norowzian v Arks Ltd (No. 2)* [2000] FSR 363 (CA), allowing similar style of advertising video; *GMG Radio Holdings Ltd v Tokyo Project Ltd* [2005] EWHC 2188 (Ch), allowing similar style of compact disc covers; *Sinanide v La Maison Kosmeo* (1928) 139 LT 365 (CA), holding no copyright in short advertising slogan.

advertisers use images rather than words to convey such messages: images do not actually 'tell' lies. The viewer discerns the message subconsciously. A picture here really is worth a thousand words, but what exactly those words are or mean cannot accurately be pinned down as if they were words in a contract or conveyance. In short, it is easier to lie through pictures than through words; it is also easier to get away with it legally.

In one sense, of course, the camera never lies; that is what Naomi Campbell, Michael Douglas, Catherine Zeta-Jones, randy footballers and motley royals complain about when the press publishes unapproved and often unflattering photographs of them. For them, image – their version of what the public is supposed to get when it sees them – is everything; it is what makes or breaks their earning power or popularity. So too with trade marks or brands. By themselves they may have little image or intrinsic meaning. It is for their owners to create and surround them with meanings that attract, retain and expand custom. This creation is not at all one way: viewers create their own meaning from messages directed at them. The advertiser hopes the viewer's construction of meaning is close to what he means to convey and that the result is positive: if the reader is a potential customer, that he is persuaded to identify with the message and then buy; if he is already a customer, that he will remain on message and keep buying the advertiser's product over others. The idea is to *manage* meaning. Managing means keeping others from interfering with the full impact of the message, especially if those others are rival advertisers.

III

Notably, Schroeder talks of 'brand' culture, not 'trade mark' culture. Trade marks do figure in the ads presented – COLOMA for liquor, GATEWAY for computers, UBS for a bank, OLDE for a brokerage, the stylized bull symbol for Merrill Lynch, VERI for an online financial security firm – but only enough to indicate the identity of the business involved. The marks do not dominate the ads: the pictures do, together with some anodyne letterpress or (possibly also trademarked) slogans. The 'brand' to which Schroeder refers is clearly something bigger than and different from the trade mark. It may encompass, but is more than, the image that surrounds the mark.

These notions and the distinction between brands and trade marks have long fitted into English legal discourse. They surfaced recently in a case where the O2 mobile phone company, which owned some registered marks depicting bubbles in various forms, tried to stop a rival from running comparative advertising using bubbles to refer to O2 and its prices. O2 claimed their trade marks had been infringed. The claim failed because the advertising strictly complied with the EU comparative advertising directive (97/55 EC). The court therefore held that the rival had a complete defence to trade mark infringement.[26]

O2 viewed bubbles as more than just trade marks. Images of bubbles served to present a positive image of O2 and its products to existing and potential consumers. O2's management wanted a monopoly on bubble imagery to promote any sort of business or venture. Here is the familiar egoist mindset at work. In business, egoist translates into monopolist: whatever I have created or bought is mine to own and control to the exclusion of everyone else. The vocabulary of creation and ownership is manipulated to downgrade prior art and inputs, and to emphasize the overwhelming importance of my additions. If all firms behaved in this pathologically self-absorbed way, everyday moderately honest commerce would grind to a halt.

O2 could not achieve its object of world domination, but it wanted to get as close as possible. It failed. Its rival had used the bubbles honestly to refer to O2's pricing, not to take unfair advantage of O2's trade marks. The judge prefaced his judgment in this way:

> Brands are big business. They can be worth many millions of pounds. The value of the Coca Cola brand has been said to be worth sixty per cent of the market capitalisation of the Coca Cola Corporation. Defining a brand is not easy. A lawyer would tend to think of goodwill, trade marks and so on. But a brand includes more elements; such as image and reputation; the values that the brand owner tries to inculcate in the buying public. A brand is what customers choose to buy. Many decisions about brands are made by customers emotionally or intuitively rather than rationally. Successful brands create a relationship of trust between the customer and the brand.
>
> Important to all this is the overall idea of the 'brand image'. The brand image can be created in a variety of ways: personal experience; word of mouth; how the brand is presented in stories in the media; packaging; point of sale display; retail staff; and, of course, advertising. The value of a brand lies in brand awareness; perceived quality; brand association and brand loyalty. The distinctiveness of a brand is of particular importance where the product offered by competitors in a given field of activity has few substantive differences.[27]

But the judge then went on to make the following point:

> English law does not ... protect brands as such. It will protect goodwill (via the law of passing off); trade marks (via the law of trade mark infringement); the use of particular words, sounds and images (via the law of copyright); shapes and

---

[26] *O2 Holdings Ltd* v *Hutchison 3G Ltd* [2006] EWHC 534 (Ch), questions referred to the ECJ [2006] EWCA Civ 1656.
[27] Ibid. paras. 4–6, by Lewison J.

configurations of articles (via the law of unregistered design right) and so on. But to the extent that a brand is greater than the sum of the parts that English law will protect, it is defenceless against the chill wind of competition.[28]

This viewpoint is constantly under pressure,[29] although it has been around a while. Nearly thirty years ago, a passing-off case originating in Sydney and ending up in London also involved marketing to boost the fragile masculinity on which ads such as COLOMA'S are premised. Whereas Coloma pushes alcohol as a way for men really to be men, the Australian case involved pitching a soft drink in a way that Australian he-men did not think they were sissies for consuming it. Cadbury Schweppes is a firm which (like O2) aggressively polices perceived assaults on the integrity of its marketing schemes.[30] In 1977 it sued a rival which mimicked the branding strategy Cadbury had introduced to launch a lemon squash drink to compete with colas.[31] Cadbury's marketing plan was for the drink:

> to be presented as a man's drink, fit for, and a favourite with, rugged masculine adventurers. The advertising campaign was to stress its masculinity and at the same time to awake happy memories of the sort of squash hotels and bars in the past used to make. The two themes of manliness and pubs were reflected in the name of the product and its get-up. [Cadbury] named it Solo and designed a medallion type of label very similar to the labels on beer sold in Australia. It was to be put up in cans and bottles, but especially cans, for which they chose a distinctive greenish yellow colour.[32]

A mass advertising campaign featured television and radio commercials. The initial television advertising:

> was devoted to action shots (accompanied by dramatic background music) of a rugged lone male canoeist shooting the rapids in a single kayak, attention being focussed on the potential dangers, such as rocky outcrops, bends, eddies and the like, on the run down the rapids. At the conclusion of the run, the canoeist pushes his kayak ashore. He then reaches into a portable icebox and, having taken out and

---

[28] Ibid. para. 7.

[29] *L'Oréal SA* v *Bellure NV* [2005] EWHC 269 (Ch), unenthusiastically allowing a claim that mere damage to goodwill can be actionable to go to trial; but the claim was dismissed at trial, although the claimant succeeded on more conventional grounds: *L'Oréal SA* v *Bellure NV* [2006] EWHC 2355 (Ch) at paras. 165–7 affd on this point [2007] EWCA Civ 968.

[30] It recently lost another suit in Australia for a monopoly on purple wrappers for chocolate although the case went to retrial for procedural error: *Cadbury Schweppes Pty Ltd* v *Darrell Lea Chocolate Shops Pty Ltd (No. 4)* [2006] FCA 446 (Fed. Ct, Aust.) revd [2007] FCA 1245 (Full fed. ct).

[31] *Cadbury Schweppes Pty Ltd* v *Pub Squash Co. Pty Ltd* [1981] 1 WLR 193 (PC), affirming the New South Wales Supreme Court.

[32] Ibid. 196.

opened a can of Solo, gulps it down. While he is drinking, a 'voice-over' announcer says: 'You've never tasted a lemon drink like Solo before . . . unless it was one of those great lemon squashes that pubs used to make . . . extra tang . . . not too many bubbles . . .' As he drinks, the canoeist spills some of the liquid down his chin. He finishes his drink with a smile and wipes his chin with the back of his hand. The 'voice-over' announcer says, and, as well, there is flashed on the screen, the words: 'Solo, a man's drink.'. . .

As the national campaign developed, the theme of the lone male adventurer was further elaborated. Viewers were introduced to a lone sailor fighting his way through boiling surf in a catamaran, and two virile men battling it out in a squash court. Lone masculine endeavour was the theme supporting the name Solo. Meanwhile the 'audio' in television and the radio broadcasts maintained the other theme, nostalgia for 'those great lemon squashes the pubs used to make'.[33]

Seeing SOLO'S market success, a competitor introduced its PUB SQUASH lemon soda squash. It deliberately copied the product and advertising themes of SOLO. So its advertising evoked masculinity and nostalgia, and had its hero swigging a PUB SQUASH after his endeavours. The cans were the same size and yellow shade as Solo and had a medallion label, but PUB SQUASH was clearly written on them in bold red letters. Both firms' trade marks were registered but clearly differed from each other. The rival certainly dented SOLO'S market, but had it passed-off its product as SOLO, as Cadbury claimed?[34]

Twenty-six hearing days before an Australian judge resulted in the claims being dismissed, and a direct appeal to the Privy Council was also dismissed. The trial court decided that buyers were not confused or deceived into buying PUB SQUASH believing it was SOLO. On the few occasions they selected PUB SQUASH by mistake, they either ultimately did not care or corrected the mistake by the time they came to pay for their purchase. The appeal court said it would not interfere with these findings since the evidence amply supported them and the trial judge was better placed to evaluate it. The court, however, indicated that it was willing to protect distinctive advertising campaigns against imitators who tried to use them to mislead consumers:

The tort [of passing-off] is no longer anchored, as in its early nineteenth century formulation, to the name or trade mark of a product or business. It is wide enough to encompass other descriptive material, such as slogans or visual images, which

---

[33] Ibid. 196–7, by Powell J, the trial judge.
[34] As well as unsuccessfully attacking the trade mark registration of PUB SQUASH, Cadbury sought an injunction and monetary relief for both unfair competition and passing-off. Both claims failed. The Australian High Court later held there is no such tort as unfair competition (*Moorgate Tobacco Co. Ltd* v *Philip Morris Ltd* (1984) 156 CLR 415); nor is there in England (*Hodgkinson & Corby Ltd* v *Wards Mobility Services* [1994] 1 WLR 1564 (Ch); *L'Oréal* [2006] EWHC, and [2007] EWCA, above, footnote 29.

radio, television or newspaper advertising campaigns can lead the market to associate with a plaintiff's product, provided always that such descriptive material has become part of the goodwill of the product. And the test is whether the product has derived from the advertising a distinctive character which the market recognises.

Caution was nevertheless advised:

> But competition must remain free; and competition is safeguarded by the necessity for the plaintiff to prove that he has built up an 'intangible property right' in the advertised descriptions of his product, or, in other words, that he has succeeded by such methods in giving his product a distinctive character accepted by the market. A defendant, however, does no wrong by entering a market created by another and there competing with its creator. The line may be difficult to draw; but, unless it is drawn, competition will be stifled.[35]

The imagery in *Cadbury* was conveyed through print, audio and the moving visual images of television ads. Professor Schroeder concentrates on one sort of visual image, the photograph, but the range of images that help build a brand is much wider. The imagery may partly come from product packaging. So, for example, in a case that contrasts sharply with *Cadbury*, Reckitt & Colman protected the look of its product packaging, a plastic imitation lemon that contained lemon juice. Packaging can imitate nature as art may imitate life; and here Reckitt claimed that buyers in supermarkets were so used to its distinctively packaged product that neither the proposed new entrant Borden nor, it seems, any other competitor could launch a similarly packaged lemon juice, even if it clearly put its own non-confusing trade mark on its product. After a 22-day trial, the trial court agreed and the law lords upheld the judgment. Only one seemed much concerned that a trader was being awarded a common law marketing monopoly for its product beyond what was likely to be available under intellectual property legislation.[36]

So a legal reading of these cases suggests at best two cheers for competition. What new entrant is going to imitate the market leader's selling strategy unless it has prepared an enormous war chest and summoned the persistence to wage its campaign up to the highest court? Large firms notoriously use or threaten expensive litigation to force smaller fry to steer wide of them. True, courts do offer more streamlined legal procedures today than they used to. Maybe only trials involving fake lemon will run for a month or more, if *Cadbury* and *Reckitt* are anything to go by. The more recent O2 trial ran for just a week. Still, expensive silks were involved there, much interlocutory skirmishing occurred, the case went

---

[35] *Cadbury*, above, footnote 31, 200.
[36] *Reckitt & Colman Products Ltd* v *Borden Inc.* [1991] 1 WLR 419 (HL).

off to appeal, and a partial reference to the ECJ has been ordered. Law is
not for those of faint heart or modest means.

IV

Let us return to Professor Schroeder's claim that there is nothing legally
wrong with the ads he presents. He is probably right, but it's worth taking
a moment to understand why.

Much of our law is based on the theory that, in a competitive market,
consumers choose products or services on price, quality and service. If this
premise is true, then the ads Schroeder portrays dismally fail the consumer.
There is a statement about price in the Gateway ad – 'notebooks . . . starting
from $799' – but otherwise nothing else but meaningless generalities about
price, quality or service.[37] Unless one assumes, perversely, that advertisers
are irrationally throwing away good money on their ads, the standard story
must be untrue or seriously incomplete.

And so it is. In practice, nothing much distinguishes most competing
products or services from one other. If COLOMA was truly different in
some significant way for the consumer, one would expect the advertiser to
say so. Those who believe Colombian coffee products are better are told
the product is Colombian; but this must be a marginal point, because it is
only marginally made. The advertiser tells us nothing else significant
about the product. The obvious inference is that there is nothing to tell.
COLOMA and KAHLÙA are probably much the same, certainly where
either is tossed into a cocktail. Similarly, we may infer that a GATEWAY
laptop is not much different from other brands; one bank or stockbroker
is much the same as another, and so on. There's no point in a mature
market in competing on price; diminishing margins do little for share
market prices or executive pay and bonuses. What quality and service
come with a product is not discovered till much later.

It was not always so. In 1976, full-page ads in *Time* magazine averaged
195 words; in 2000 they averaged 100. If cigarette ads are omitted, the
figures are even starker: the 2000 ad used just a third of the verbiage of its
1976 counterpart. On the American market, soap powder rarely now
touts how much cleaner it washes than Brand X: rather, ads show pictures
of snowy mountains surrounded by flowers, with some accompanying

---

[37] Anyway, the $799 statement is pretty irrelevant: whoever as 'smart, sexy, and always on
the go' as the man in the ad would head for the low end of the market? Presumably, as a
corporation man, he would be getting the machine on the company account; so the more
expensive machine he can persuade his employer to get, the smarter, sexier and more
permanently mobile would be his validated feeling.

text like: 'Crisp mountain air, bright sunshine and cool breezes, spring water'. Substitute aspirin, deodorant or beer for soap powder, and the ad would make as much sense. As ads proliferate and attention spans shorten, research suggests that the more information an ad contains the less effective it is. Infantilism rules for both children and adults. More than two cues – e.g. colour or picture – and the pre-schooler tunes out; much more than that for an adult, and he or she glazes over. Even worse: research suggests that 'consumers are annoyed by product claims and actually prefer to make decisions based on less mentally-taxing factors'.[38]

In this atmosphere, brands and trade marks come into their own. It is the recognized attractive trusted brand that customers turn to and are prepared to pay a premium for, even if the product is identical to a rival's. For the buyer is not really buying a thing; he is buying a vague expectation; and it is the brand that provides the expectation. As Revlon's founder said: 'In the factory we make cosmetics; in the store we sell hope.'[39] The ads may identify what the advertiser thinks is his potential consumer's problem, which the ad purports to solve. Male insecurity is what COLOMA perceives to be its target audience's problem; its remedy, a shot of alcohol for both man and woman, is utterly bogus; but for men who have tried everything else – including mudslides with KAHLÙA – and failed, here is one more (not necessarily last) hope to try. (Maybe flashing a GATEWAY laptop may help?) Of course, the problem may be non-existent or may be solved by something not involving COLOMA, but why would the advertiser spend money to tell you that?

If the hope is dashed, the disappointed consumer plainly has (as noted in section I above) no recourse against the trader from whom he bought the product. This puffery contains no legally binding promise or representation. Some puffery – especially when applied to expensive items such as motor vehicles[40] – can be prosecuted by English trading standards officers for contravening the Trade Descriptions Act 1968, if it is false or misleading about the product's 'fitness for purpose, strength, performance, behaviour or accuracy'.[41] However, nothing in these ads seems objectionable under that head. Even if it were, underfunded trading

---

[38] S. C. Haan, 'The "Persuasion Route" of the Law: Advertising and Legal Persuasion' (2000) 100 Columbia L.Rev 1281, 1305, summarizing here and earlier the research on which much of this paragraph is based.

[39] Quoted in T. Levitt, *The Marketing Imagination* (expanded edn, New York: Free Press, 1986) 128.

[40] 'Thus, such descriptions as "excellent condition throughout", "mechanically superb", "immaculate", and "showroom condition" have been held to amount to false descriptions in circumstances where the car has any serious mechanical or body defect': R. Bragg, *Trade Descriptions* (Oxford: Clarendon Press, 1991) 27 (omitting footnotes).

[41] Trade Descriptions Act 1968, ss. 1, 2(1)(d) and 3.

standards officers act only in egregious cases, and competitors cannot use the Act to take civil action.[42] The position differs from that in the USA, where not only may the Federal Trade Commission or its state counterparts proceed against similar offenders, but so too may competitors, who can have the advertising stopped and recover damages for lost trade.[43]

V

May the way a product or service is advertised have any negative legal effect on its trade mark? In theory it can. A trader cannot get legal protection for a business that is founded on lies: nobody should benefit from his own wrong. Sometimes the courts deny that any right exists; other times, they admit the right but refuse full enforcement for reasons of equity.

Quack medicines were among the major offenders from the mid nineteenth century through the early twentieth century. Their American promoters were among the first 'to recognize the power of the catchphrase, the identifiable logo and trademark, the celebrity endorsement, the appeal to social status, the need to keep "everlastingly at it".'[44] They and their UK counterparts often went to law, sometimes successfully, sometimes not. At the turn of the twentieth century, the US trade mark owner of CALIFORNIA SYRUP OF FIGS was perhaps surprised to be turned away in his suit against an imitator because his own laxative's active ingredient was senna, and the public did not know that all but an irrelevant *soupçon* of fig had been eliminated from the original recipe. Discussing eighty years' worth of US and UK case law, the US Supreme Court concluded that no protection would extend to a trade mark that was 'so plainly deceptive'.[45]

At the same time, across the Atlantic, the UK produced its own sensational 'Bile Bean' case. It involved a Leeds partnership that was selling great quantities of 'Bile Beans' on the fantastic story that they were made of a natural vegetable substance discovered by an eminent scientist, one Charles Forde, as the secret for the well-being of Australian aborigines.

---

[42] *Bollinger (No. 2)*, above, footnote 15. The false description may sometimes give rise to a passing-off action: *Erven Warnink*, above, footnote 11, 742–3.
[43] Lanham Act 1946, § 43(a) (15 USC § 1125), as am. in 1988; see R. Schechter and J. Thomas, *Intellectual Property: The Law of Copyrights, Patents and Trademarks* (St Paul, Minn.: Thomson West, 2003) 684ff.
[44] Mark Pendergrast, *For God, Country and Coca-Cola* (revised updated edn, New York: Thomson Texere, 2000), 11.
[45] *Worden & Co. v California Fig Syrup Co.* 187 US 516, 539–40 (1903); see generally Note, 'The Besmirched Plaintiff and the Confused Public: Unclean Hands in Trademark Infringement' (1965) 65 Columbia L. Rev 109.

194   David Vaver

The firm sued an Edinburgh chemist who was alleged to be passing off his own brand of 'Bile Bean' as the claimant's real thing. The falseness of the Australian story came out as the witnesses were examined. The Scottish courts dismissed the case.[46] They said that an advertiser could exaggerate the effects of his product but could not build his market on lies. There was no scientific research, nor any scientist called Charles Forde (a corruption of the name of one of the partners, Charles Fulford, who knew nothing about science but lots about huckstering). The medicine came from an American drug company, and no aborigine had been anywhere near it. These claims were so connected with the 'Bile Bean' name that no court should protect the trade associated with it.

The *Bile Bean* principle of denying relief applies to registered and unregistered marks and to passing-off and infringement.[47] It derives from a wider rule that activities built on deceit or other wrongs cannot expect legal protection. So in South Africa, a passing-off claim failed for a swimming pool chlorination system that was falsely claimed to be a successful Australian system that had sold well worldwide; and in Hong Kong, a local distributor of rice wine could not claim copyright in a product label against his mainland supplier so as to appropriate the latter's goodwill in the territory.[48] The wider principle was applied in England against Scientologists who failed to prevent a former member from revealing aspects of their creed because the tenets were not only falsely said to be scientifically provable but were also, according to the court, 'utterly absurd'; it also applied against a former MI5 spy who found he could not claim copyright in his *Spycatcher* exposé because he broke obligations of confidentiality to his ex-employer in writing and publishing it.[49] Similarly, in Hong Kong, it was suggested that copyright in photographs could be denied if the subject was coerced into posing.[50] But in its full width *Bile Bean* does not travel well. For example, in the USA, for free speech or other instrumental reasons, deceptive or other offensive matter

[46] *Bile Bean Mfg Co.* v *Davidson* (1905) 22 RPC 560, aff'd (1906) 23 RPC 725 (Ct Sess., IH).
[47] *Ford* v *Foster* (1872) LR 7 Ch. App. 611; *Sterling-Winthrop Group Ltd* v *Farbenfabriken Bayer AG* [1976] RPC 469 (HC Ire.).
[48] *Scott & Leisure Research and Design (Pty) Ltd* v *Watermaid (Pty) Ltd* 1985 (1) SA 211 (CPD), relying on equivalent South African case law; *Guangdong Foodstuffs Import & Export (Group) Corp.* v *Tung Fook Chinese Wine (1982) Co. Ltd* 1998 HKCU Lexis 1385 (HK HC), citing *Bile Bean*.
[49] *Church of Scientology of California* v *Kaufman* [1973] RPC 635 (Ch.), unsuccessfully alleging breach of confidence; *A-G* v *Guardian Newspapers Ltd (No. 2)* [1990] 1 AC 109, 224 (HL).
[50] *Mak Hau Shing* v *Oriental Press Group Ltd* [1996] 3 HKC 12 (HKCA) although the defence failed on the facts.

is not barred from copyright or patenting. Courts sometimes mark down the relief; otherwise it is for regulators to act against offending claimants.[51]

Even within trade mark and passing-off law, *Bile Bean* operates weakly for a number of reasons. First, the rule now has little *Lebensraum*. Detailed regulations everywhere today prescribe content and labelling standards for many goods, particularly food and drugs, backed by summary offences and strict liability. If seriously enforced, such laws create few occasions for *Bile Bean* to work its magic. The USA and the UK also now apply the rule quite narrowly in trade mark and advertising cases. In *Bile Bean* itself the court accepted that even 'gross' exaggeration of a product's virtues was all right.[52] Oddly, however, while standards of commercial honesty expected from defendants in passing-off and infringement claims have expanded, standards demanded of claimants have not. Statements extrinsic to the mark are often brushed aside as 'collateral' and irrelevant. Claimants who overstep the line are treated sympathetically if they step back before suing,[53] even as late as during the proceedings, since the court's decision to grant an injunction can take account of everything up to the time of judgment. The English 'advocaat' monopolists, who appeared in section I above, benefited from this indulgence. Over the years that they had the market to themselves, they helped create a widespread misconception (innocently, so the courts held) that 'real' advocaat contained brandy instead of lowly spirits. They, however, repented a few years before they sued. Although the climate of confusion persisted, the courts decided the monopolists' case against Keeling was unaffected.[54] Similarly, prematurely claiming that one's mark is registered does not affect the claim for a later injunction for its infringement.[55] Over time, indeed, a mark can shake off initially false connotations, gain

---

[51] *Belcher* v *Tarbox* 486 F.2d 1087 (9th Cir. 1973), copyright; *Juicy Whip Inc.* v *Orange Bang Inc.* 85 F.3d 1364 (Fed. Cir. 1999), further proceedings 382 F.3d 1367 (Fed. Cir. 2004), upholding validity of patent and awarding damages. Cf. Canada: *Aldrich* v *One Stop Video Ltd* (1987) 39 DLR (4th) 362 (BCSC), enjoining copyright in smut (following US law) but denying substantial damages or costs; similarly, *Fraserside Holdings* v *Venus Adult Shops* [2005] FMCA 997 at paras. 36ff. (Fed. Mag. Ct, Aust.); Note, 'Fraudulent Material is Entitled to Copyright Protection in Action for Injunctive Relief and Damages' (1974) 74 Columbia L.Rev 1351, 1359, arguing for validity and enforcement 'unless the infringer establishes that public policy will clearly be furthered by a denial of relief'.

[52] *Bile Bean*, above, footnote 46, 23 RPC at 736.

[53] Ibid.; *J. H. Coles Pty* v *Need* [1934] AC 82 (P.C.).

[54] *Erven Warnink*, above, footnote 10. The argument also failed in the Court of Appeal and was abandoned before the Lords: above, footnote 11.

[55] *Compaq Computer Corp.* v *Dell Computer Corp. Ltd* (1991) 21 IPR 433 (Ch.).

a secondary meaning and emerge untainted by its origins: witness COCA-COLA (more of which in a moment).

Secondly, applying the rule creates odd results, which in turn helps keep its ambit restricted. For when a court declares 'A pox on both your houses' and refuses relief, marketing by both suppliers may continue unabated and consumers can now be tricked by every market entrant. This result did not initially deter the US appeals court which in 1919 found that some consumers bought COCA-COLA believing it contained cocaine (as it did till 1903). Disapproving of the Coca-Cola company's neglect, the Court let KOKE continue to be passed off as COCA-COLA. But on appeal the US Supreme Court differed. Balancing wrongs, it decided that stopping the swindler was better than denying the claimant relief against 'a palpable fraud because possibly here and there an ignorant person might call for the drink with the hope for incipient cocaine intoxication'.[56] Intermediate courses are, of course, possible: enjoin both parties, or give the claimant what he wants only if he first cleans up his act. But few courts are this radical. Most see their job as dealing with the interests of parties before them, not those of the unrepresented public.

Thirdly, one might think that court rulings, with their attendant publicity, would bring the offensive trade to a halt. But this need not be so. Indeed, CALIFORNIA SYRUP OF FIGS was registered as a UK trade mark in 1910;[57] it still sells over the counter, with senna as its active ingredient in a syrup that, among other ingredients, includes extract of figs.[58] Media which benefited from carrying advertisements for quack medicines saw little profit in simultaneously running stories denouncing the trade. The bile bean sellers dropped their Australian story after losing the Scottish litigation but nonetheless continued to market the product as a panacea. Apparently no worse than other tonic-*cum*-laxatives, bile beans were selling a million a day by 1930 and disappeared only in the mid-1980s when people abandoned their 'obsession with purgation and inner cleanliness'.[59]

---

[56] *Coca-Cola Co.* v *Koke Co. of America* 254 U.S. 143, 147 (1920) by Holmes J, rev'ing 255 F. 894 (9th Cir. 1919).

[57] *Re Joseph Crosfield & Sons Ltd; Re California Fig Syrup Co.; Re Brock & Co. Ltd* [1910] 1 Ch. 130 (CA).

[58] A California company was the original registrant, but no limitation on the register compels such figs as it contained to be grown, or the syrup to be made, in California. It is unknown whether consumers then believed, or now believe, that: (1) the product had or has some association with California; or (2) 'California' was or is just as arbitrary as 'Epsom' is for salts. In the former case, the registration may be vulnerable. But see the MELTON MOWBRAY PIE case, above, footnote 24.

[59] R. C. Rowe, 'Bile Beans: For Inner Health' (2003) 17 (3–4) Int. Jo. Pharm. Medicine 137, 140.

Ultimately, the *Bile Bean* rule is ineffective because current advertising practice sidesteps it. The COLOMA and GATEWAY ads, for example, say and imply virtually nothing except hope. The law lets hope be peddled: it gives *spes* its space. None of the other ads Professor Schroeder discusses seems legally amiss either. The argument that no reasonable person would take their claims seriously would prevail.

On current theory, only continuous community pressure against objectionable ads has any chance of being effective. The law is uninterested. A citizen challenge to the registration of FCUK as a UK trade mark for being 'contrary to public policy or accepted principles of morality'[60] was recently dismissed. Swear words and other crudities may sometimes be unregistrable but this mark escaped even that rule. The tribunals hearing the case thought that 'the best barometer of public perception is evidence resulting from actual use in the market'.[61] Most people, far from objecting to the mark, flocked to buy the merchandise associated with it; so how could the mark be considered seriously offensive to anyone, bar the occasional crank or prude?

What goes for marks probably also goes for brands and the advertising associated with them. In ruling around the time of the *Bile Bean* case that posters advertising a circus were works of fine art, Holmes J famously said: 'if they command the interest of any public, they have a commercial value – it would be bold to say that they have not an aesthetic and educational value – and the taste of any public is not to be treated with contempt'.[62] The perceived democracy of the market is a hard ideal to shake. The public may not fully know or understand how it is manipulated by nonfact advertising but has become inured to it. Attempting to micro-regulate would no doubt attract the usual tirades about the state's nannying of its citizenry. Industry and its advertising agency proxies know how to pitch their freedom-to-advertise case to governments. Politicians are a receptive audience. They hardly need to be told, especially around election time, of the importance of keeping earnest hands off advertising.

Yet the question whether trade mark law or practice needs rethinking in the light of modern advertising practices persists. In an allied field, American researchers have argued that product liability law is largely premised on consumers acting rationally to assess risks on the basis of warnings contained in ads or labels. But if advertising is deliberately

---

[60] Trade Marks Act 1994, s. 3(3)(a).
[61] *Woodman's App'n for declaration of invalidity of FCUK trade mark* (R. Arnold QC, LCAP, 17 May 2006) para. 90.
[62] *Bleistein* v *Donaldson Lithographing Co.* 188 US 239, 252 (1903), holding the posters to be protected by copyright.

pitched to minimize or negate risks that nevertheless still remain, a stricter liability rule that accepts consumers for the gullible fools they are, rather than the rational sovereigns they ideally might be, seems more appropriate.[63] So in trade mark law, the current trend is to protect an ever-increasing range of marks ever more intensively, forever. One underlying justification may be that consumers use trade marks to choose rationally among products and services. If this justification is suspect, is it not relevant to ask if expansionism deserves support – if so, in what respects? if not, in what respects? – now that advertising has become a largely information-free zone?

---

[63] E.g. J. Hanson and D. A. Kysar, 'Taking Behavioralism Seriously: Some Evidence of Market Manipulation' (1999) 112 Harv L. Rev 1425.

Part V

Sociology

9 Trade mark style as a way of fixing things

Celia Lury

Introduction

This chapter will focus on the implications of recent developments in trade mark law for branding. It will address how the logo, as a sign of the brand, is legally constituted as a trade mark – that is, as a kind of intellectual property[1] – and how this legal constitution as property supports the valuation and exploitation of the brand as a commercial asset. The focus will be on the role of trade mark law in the organization of relations between firms in producer markets rather than on the relations between firms and final consumers that has been the focus of my own and much other previous work on brands.[2] It will be argued that the law contributes to the action of the brand as a new market modality or market cultural form, helping to organize the rise of a trade mark style of management. It will thus be suggested that trade mark law is a significant actor in the organization of producer markets, operating so as to consolidate and legitimate the use of branding as an object or mode of capital accumulation in a mediated economy.

What is a market?

There are many kinds of markets, but the concern here will be with what have been called producer markets. As the sociologist Harrison White[3] points out, an increasing number of markets are more than sites for direct

---

[1] The chapter relies on a number of legal texts for its understanding of trade mark law, notably S. Panesar, *General Principles of Property Law* (Harlow: Pearson Education, 2001); J. Davis, *Intellectual Property Law* (2nd edn, London: Butterworths, 2003); and P. Torremans, *Holyoak and Torreman's Intellectual Property Law* (4th edn, Oxford: Oxford University Press, 2005). The author would also like to thanks the editors for their very helpful comments, especially Lionel Bently.

[2] C. Lury, *Brands: The Logos of the Global Economy* (Oxford: Routledge, 2004); A. Arvidsson, *Brands: Meaning and Value in Media Culture* (London: Routledge, 2006).

[3] H. White, *Markets from Networks: Socioeconomic Models of Production* (Princeton and Oxford: Princeton University Press, 2002).

transactions between buyers and sellers. White proposes that firms continuously and jointly construct a market interface to provide a measure of shelter from the uncertainties of business. What he calls 'producer markets' are mobilizers of production in networks of continuing flows. It is producer firms which have to commit their facilities in advance to obtain a level of production for a period; both a firm's peers in the market and various possible occupants of the other roles up- and downstream go on to adapt their choices to this commitment. The market interface that emerges from this process in turn coordinates the commitments of producer firms to pumping downstream product flows into which procurements from upstream have been incorporated. Resulting streams of differentiated goods or services from the market get split among diverse buyers. In this understanding of markets, White does not presume that the buyer is necessarily the final consumer; rather, he locates firms within a chain of producers and buyers. Network ensembles of such markets constitute what he calls 'ecologies', with firm, market and sector levels.

White further proposes that the mechanism by which production markets work – that is, by which markets emerge from dispersed and heterogeneous networks of relations – is their self-reproduction by virtue of some form of signalling between firms. He believes that producers are not just *embedded in* a market, as Mark Granovetter[4] would argue; instead, 'they *actually constitute the market's interface in, and as, the set of their perceptions and choices.* They constitute the interface vis-à-vis the direction in which risk is perceived to originate.'[5] Flows of information are thus central to the mechanism that steers and reproduces a production market for White, and commitment and uncertainty are the twin themes in their processes of dynamic organization. He writes: 'Packaging as an industry offers producer firms long-term positions in niches, positions that help to mitigate the vital uncertainties that surround commitment and evaluation in a competitive environment. If we regard firms as atoms, the market is a molecule.'[6] It is the shared interface or frame of perception that organizes producers' strivings to maximize the gap between procurement costs and sales revenue, vis-à-vis buyers who hold out for equally good deals across producers with differentiated outputs, and thus organizes market discipline. And, in the case of producer markets, market discipline centres on *product quality*, of which more below.

White further suggests that the strategies for control of markets developed by firms are derived from and point towards devolution into other organizational forms, subject to the activities of additional institutions of

---

[4] M. Granovetter, 'Economic Action and Social Structure: The Problem of Embeddedness' (1985) 91(3) *American Journal of Sociology* 481–510.
[5] H. White, *Markets from Networks* 8; my emphasis.   [6] Ibid. 7.

finance and ownership. Thus, for example, he suggests that the multi-divisional firm has emerged as a hybrid between market and firm, drawing on and in turn shaping the production market mechanism and frame of perception. This chapter will suggest that brands may be understood in the same manner as a market form that is derived from, and contributes to, a distinctive organization of producer markets: that is, branding is – amongst other things – a specific form of market signal, framing the perception not just of consumers as is commonly argued, but also of other firms in the making of a market and, sometimes, as I will go on to describe, the making of a sector. Branding, however, does not contribute to the emergence of a single organizational form such as the multidivisional firm but rather to an inter-linked set of management strategies, collectively described here as a trade mark style. Indeed, this style and the development of branding have gone hand-in-hand in the last few years.

Let me give some examples of these management strategies and their organization of new or newly important forms of market exchange to illustrate this argument. Perhaps the most obvious (and longstanding) use of trade mark names to organize production is trade mark licensing. This is the commercial practice of allowing others to use a firm's trade marks on approved goods or services under terms that allow that firm to control the quality of the goods or services covered by the licence. Its most common form historically has been the licensing of third parties to produce or offer to supply more or less the same goods as those produced by the trade mark owner. In the United Kingdom, for example, Whitbread (a brewery with its own-brand beer) holds the licence to brew and distribute HEINEKEN beer. But while there is a long tradition of licensing of technological know-how and patents in industry, licensing of trade marks has only been systematically developed in recent years in conjunction with a growth in branding. For example, though many of the brands acquired as part of the take-over of Rowntree by Nestlé are sold only in Britain (for example, QUALITY STREET, AFTER EIGHT), they are owned by the Swiss company and licensed back to a British subsidiary. This exploitation of licensing agreements not only with third parties but also with a firm's own subsidiaries is relatively recent. It is argued by marketers and others that making a financial charge for the use of a trade mark focusses the user (whether they be a subsidiary or not) on the value of the asset and the need to both protect and exploit that value.[7] In addition, higher royalty rates than was the case before are now being demanded, and stricter conditions to ensure the proper use and maintenance of trade marks – both in legal and in marketing terms – are also evident.

[7] This practice often also has tax advantages for the parent company.

The last twenty or thirty years have also seen the rapid growth of franchising[8] as a business strategy, a strategy once again widely linked to the exploitation of brands as they are protected by trade mark. Franchised business
now accounts for over 38 per cent of all retail sales in the USA and originates
12 per cent of the Gross National Product.[9] Franchising is a 'distinctive form
of capital formation; one which permits flexible accumulation but eschews
flexible specialization. For the franchisee it offers entrepreneurship in a
package, ambition-by-numbers, capitalism in kit form; for the franchiser it
gives access to capital without ceding control, reconciles integrated admin-
istration with entrepreneurial motivation.'[10] Examples of brands developed
through the use of franchising include MCDONALD'S, HOLIDAY INN,
INTERFLORA, DYNO-ROD drain and pipe cleaning, PRONTAPRINT print-
ing and copying shops, HERTZ rental cars, CLARKS shoe shops and the
global airline BA. The ex-CEO of BA, Robert Ayling, writes:

Franchising has also proved an effective way of developing our business.
Franchising at British Airways dates back to 1993 and is central to our growth
strategy. We tend to franchise where we don't have the right size of aircraft, or
expertise in a particular market, or legal rights to fly. For example, we cannot fly
from Johannesburg to Durban for these reasons, so Connair flies it as a franchise.
 ... Our franchising agreement allows other airlines to use British Airways'
intellectual property – logo, style, trademark and service standards – provided
they deliver product consistently to our specifications.[11]

As indicated here, franchising typically involves the granting of not only
rights to use trade marks as discussed above but also rights to use the
business system developed by the licensor, typically in exchange for a
royalty or turnover related payment.[12] In this respect, it involves the

[8] See T. Royle, *Working for McDonald's in Europe: The Unequal Struggle?* (London:
Routledge, 2000). He notes that the origin of the word 'franchise' dates back to the
Middle Ages. In Norman England, barons were granted territories by the king in return
for the payment of royalties and provided they met many other requests made by the
monarch. The original meaning of the word comes from the French 'affranchir', meaning
'releasing from servitude or restraint'. However, he goes on to show, the modern franchise is absolutely not about release 'from restraint or servitude'.
[9] R. E. Caves and W. F. Murphy, 'Franchising: Forms, Markets and Intangible Assets' in
F. Hoy and J. Murphy (eds.), *Franchising: An International Perspective* (London:
Routledge, 2003) 82.
[10] N. Perry, *Hyperreality and Global Culture* (London: Routledge, 1998) 51.
[11] R. Ayling, 'British Airways brand leadership results from being true to our long-term
vision' in F. Gilmore (ed.), *Brand Warriors: Corporate Leaders Share Their Winning
Strategies* (London: HarperCollins Business, 1999) 43–4.
[12] There has been a shift in the last twenty or so years in Europe and the USA from what is
sometimes referred to as 'first-generation' franchising, in which the franchisee acquires
the business identity of the franchisor through the trade mark but conducts business as an
independent distributor, to 'format' franchising. In the latter, it is not just a trade mark
but a whole way of doing business – a business format – that is supplied to the franchisee.

sharing between firms – often at different points in the production process – of a number of intangible assets, only one of which is the trade mark. The arrangements may cover not only the look and design of the business, but also staff training, specialized accountancy and business control systems, criteria for staff selection and so on.

A key commercial issue in franchising is the management of the relationship between franchisor and franchisee. This is because the characteristics of the intangible assets that are shared between them – the trade mark and related intellectual property – are defined and maintained by the mark's mode of use.[13] In other words, in commercial practice as in the legal understanding of a trade mark, it is use that defines the value of the intangible asset at issue. And it is interesting to note here that although franchises are sometimes run as a loose confederation of independent operators, it is not uncommon, as in the case of McDonald's, for the franchises to function as 'little more than subsidiaries of the corporation'. In other words, the relationship between franchisor and franchisee can 'just as easily represent a strengthening as much as a weakening of corporate control'.[14] This strengthening of control typically operates through the regulation of the brand afforded by trade mark law. A UK franchisee of McDonalds comments:

the one thing I've learnt in the last two years, is that the brand is everything, they won't let you do anything without it being checked, tested and quality tested so many times ... having a McDonald's franchise there is a frustration factor ... changes that are made company-wise you have to go along with, they are foisted upon you, you have no say in what happens ... we are an extension of the company.[15]

In the case of McDonald's (an example of what is called a 'format franchise'), franchisees are economically dependent on the corporation as a consequence of extremely rigid and detailed rules and procedures, a paternalistic management style and what Royle terms 'recruited acquiescence'.[16] However, their legal 'independence' allows many of the

See A. Felstead, *The Corporate Paradox: Power and Control in the Business Franchise* (London: Routledge, 1993); and F. Hoy and J. Stanworth (eds.), *Franchising: An International Perspective* (London: Routledge, 2003).
[13] Caves and Murphy, 'Franchising'.
[14] Royle, *Working for McDonald's* 13 and 54.   [15] Ibid. 45.
[16] 'In most European countries, as in the USA and elsewhere, the average age of the McDonald's workforce is young. In the UK, for example, approximately two-thirds of the workforce are under 21 ... In Germany and Austria, very few under-18s are employed, largely because their employment is strictly regulated by national legislation. In addition, a large proportion of these workforces consists of foreign workers, particularly *Aussiedler* economic migrants from Eastern Europe ... The findings suggest that all of these workers have something in common; they are unlikely to resist or effectively oppose managerial control. McDonald's is able to take advantage of the weak and marginalised sectors of the labour market, what we have termed *recruited acquiescence*': Ibid. 198.

corporation's activities to slip through a variety of regulatory loopholes. In short, the separation between McDonald's and its franchise is 'a legal rather than an economic distinction,'[17] enabling the corporation to exercise control, and accrue licence fees, while restricting liability.

The exertion of economic control in conditions that minimize corporate risk and accountability is described by Naomi Klein[18] as a commercial race towards weightlessness. It is taken to its limit in the case of those companies that have been established on or are being developed through the exploitation of trade mark licensing arrangements alone. Thus, for example, the fashion clothing company Tommy Hilfiger is run entirely through licensing deals. Hilfiger commissions all its products from a group of other companies: Jockey International make HILFIGER underwear; Pepe Jeans London, HILFIGER jeans; Oxford Industries make TOMMY shirts; the Stride Rite Corporation makes its footwear.[19] Companies such as Hilfiger, and, to a lesser extent, Ralph Lauren, Calvin Klein and others, are thus able to acquire virtual (or 'weightless') production capacities through an extensive network of licensing agreements. These agreements function on the basis of an exchange between the designer, who provides the product design and permission to use the brand name, and the licensee, who pays to make, distribute and sometimes advertise and sell the branded product on the designer's behalf. As their reward for the deal, the designers obtain a specific proportion of sales[20] as well as guaranteed minimum payments each season. The licensee obtains the exclusive right to manufacture and distribute for a brand that has an established reputation and appeal among consumers.[21]

The scope of this practice was radically extended by the Trade Marks Act (TMA) 1994 which included the removal of the prohibition on 'trafficking' in trade marks contained in the 1938 Act, and thus made multi-class applications much easier. The earlier Act had forbidden trade mark proprietors from trafficking in their marks.[22] In effect, this Act prevented merchandisers from registering famous names or characters as trade marks if their intention was to deal in marks primarily as commodities *in their own right*, rather than to identify or promote merchandise in which they were interested in trading.[23] As Jane Gaines notes, the

---

[17] Ibid. 197.   [18] N. Klein, *No Logo* (London: Flamingo, 2000).   [19] Ibid.
[20] In the case of the Ralph Lauren Corporation that cut is 6 per cent: S. Caminiti, 'Ralph Lauren: The Emperor has Clothes' (11 November 1998) 137(9) *Fortune* 80–9.
[21] C. Moore, 'Streets of Style: Fashion Retailing within London and New York' in P. Jackson, M. Lowe, D. Miller and F. Mort (eds.), *Commercial Cultures: Economies, Practices, Spaces* (Oxford: Berg, 2000) 269.
[22] Trade Marks Act 1938 (1 & 2 Geo. 6 c. 22), s. 28(6).
[23] The leading case was the House of Lords' decision *Re American Greeting Corporation's Application ('Holly Hobbie')* [1984] 1 All ER 426.

lifting of this restriction on the licensing of marks seems to indicate an internal reversal within trade mark law: 'While unfair competition law is based on the prohibition against palming off one's goods as the goods of another, licensing itself is essentially a "passing off".'[24] She goes on to note that the unlimited transference, so fundamental to licensing, was anticipated and aptly described by a provision in the 1938 Trade Marks Act against 'trafficking in trade mark'. Here it was held that licensing helps companies dispose of reputation 'as though it were a marketable commodity'. It is this 1938 provision that was removed in the 1994 Act.

Indeed, such licensing arrangements are not necessarily made with only one licensee. To use the example of Ralph Lauren again, more than thirty companies are licensed to manufacture, distribute and advertise ranges of products, which include jeanswear, underwear, jewellery, cutlery (flatware) and furniture in over one hundred countries.[25] Many of Lauren's licensees are well-established brands in their own right. They include Rockport/Reebok who manufacture the RALPH LAUREN footwear ranges, and Westpoint Stevens who make RALPH LAUREN sheets, towels and bedding, while Clairol, the international cosmetics conglomerate, hold the licence for the production and distribution of RALPH LAUREN perfumes worldwide. The partnership with Clairol has been especially lucrative for the Ralph Lauren Corp., and in 1997 earned the company in excess of $20 million in brand payments alone.[26]

Even the responsibility for funding the continuing advertising support of the brand does not always remain with the brand or designer's company. Instead it may be transferred to licensed partners. A senior executive responsible for licensee relations in his organization explains the transfer of financial responsibility in the following way:

The licensees are initially attracted to the company because we have a strong brand. They commit to production, and distribution and they start to realise that the success they enjoy through us depends upon the continued success of the brand. So we take advantage of that dependence and shift the responsibility of maintaining and supporting the brand, by that I mean in the form of advertising costs, to them.[27]

As an example of this shift in responsibility, the advertising budget of $20 million for the POLO jeans brand was paid for entirely by Sun Apparel, the licensee responsible for the manufacture, distribution and promotion of

[24] J. Gaines, *Contested Culture: The Image, the Voice and the Law* (London: bfi Publishing, 1991) 214.
[25] Moore, *Streets of Style* 278–80.   [26] Caminiti, 'Ralph Lauren'.
[27] Ibid. quoted in Moore, *Streets of Style* 270.

208   Celia Lury

the jeans brand worldwide.[28] Sun Apparel's financial support of the POLO brand is by no means unique within the sector. Indeed, one company that participated in a survey conducted by Moore[29] indicated that all their brand and promotional costs were met by their licensee partners. Nevertheless, while the design companies mentioned above delegate the responsibility for manufacturing and distributing diffusion brands to their licensee partners, they nevertheless retain control over all aspects of designing, manufacturing and distributing their couture and ready-to-wear ranges. These collections are not as financially significant as the diffusion or lifestyle ranges. Arguably, however, they are the most important in terms of the development of the overall brand 'image', since these are the garments that are featured in their twice-yearly fashion shows, and receive extensive media coverage. In these and other ways, the legal control of brand image gives brand owners a defining influence over licensing, and many of the economic benefits accruing from the organization of production markets by the brand.

But the implications of the protection offered by trade mark law for the organization and coordination of markets are not only to do with the direct exploitation of trade marks in licensing deals. To begin to consider the implications of trade mark law more widely we need to consider the relationship between quality profiles and market identity, and thus it is worth considering what White has to say about quality in more detail. He notes that the term 'quality' suggests judgments of products in themselves, judgments made even of each product separately. However, as noted above, and in contradistinction to this, he himself proposes that the production market mechanism relies on standings that emerge from interaction between producers and buyers. He writes:

[28] Caminiti, 'Ralph Lauren'. On the other hand, the law supports the right of the trade mark owner to restrict the movement of goods. The supermarket chain Tesco obtained genuine LEVI 501 Jeans from suppliers outside the European Economic Area (EEA) and sold them in their UK stores at almost half the price of jeans sold in authorized Levi stores. Levi Strauss had always refused to sell jeans to Tesco, in part because the sale of Levi jeans alongside groceries was held to undermine the image of the brand. Levi Strauss therefore commenced proceedings in the UK High Court of Justice claiming that the import into, and subsequent sale of jeans within, the EEA constituted an infringement of their trade mark rights. The judgment, following earlier decisions of the European Court of Justice in *Silhouette International Schied* v *Hartlauer Handelsgesellschaft*, Case C-355/96 [1998] CMLR 953, and *Zino Davidoff* v *A & G Imports*, Cases C-414, 415 and 416/99 [2001] ECR 8691, [2002] 1 CMLR 1, [2002] Etml (9) 109 was that the mark holder – Levi Strauss in this case – must give explicit consent to importation before it can be considered that it has renounced its rights. Implied consent cannot be inferred merely from silence of the trade mark proprietor. This judgment thus gives mark holders greater control over the distribution of their goods in Europe and over maintaining the reputation of their brands. See *Levi Strauss & Co.* v *Tesco Stores Ltd* [2002] 3 CMLR 281.
[29] Moore, *Streets of Style*.

In actual business life, quality meanings become jointly imputed to properties that have gotten bundled together as a 'product', even though these properties may seem to an observer various and somewhat arbitrary. This bundle is perceived with respect to the product market as a whole, the source to which everyone turns for that bundle. Particular producers seek and realize differentiation in appreciation – the quality index – for their particular versions of that market product. And indeed, there often will be a cluster of variants by size, color, and so forth of that firm's products shipments, so that there is bundling at the firm level also.[30]

This is the aetiology of quality as a subtle economic and social construction rather than an evident attribute of products.[31] For White, it is dual notions of *differential* quality, referent both to product and to producer, that become established as the core around which a set of market footings for producers can reproduce itself in a joint market profile. He further suggests that the two sides, buyers and producers, exert contending pressures on the shape of this profile, pressures that correlate with their respective discriminations of quality. Choices interact to influence and calibrate the repeated commitments of flows in production and in payment. White concludes: 'Reputation in invidious array is the coin of discipline for production markets.'[32] What is important about this account for the argument being developed here is that it suggests that rather than one emanating from the other, quality and market identity co-produce each other across the set of firms in interaction: the way in which a quality profile develops establishes the identity and organization of a production market, and vice versa.

Let me illustrate some aspects of this claim – that quality and market identity produce each other – in relation to the signals produced in branding, and the implications of trade mark protection of logos for the markets that emerge. As noted above, White argues that producers and buyers or consumers continually make judgments as to the quality of products. And it might be thought that, in relation to brands, consumer judgments have a special importance. But what I will suggest is that consumer judgments of quality are subordinated to producer judgments in the implementation of trade mark law as it is applied to brands. I have argued elsewhere[33] that production organized in relation to brands may be described in terms of the simulation of innovation.[34] By this is meant that product innovation does not derive or emerge from innovation in the

---

[30] H. White, *Markets from Networks* 10.
[31] See also M. Callon, C. Meadel and V. Rabehariosa, 'The Economy of Qualities' (May 2002) 31(2) *Economy and Society* 194–217.
[32] H. White, *Markets from Networks* 10.   [33] C. Lury, *Brands*.
[34] My use of the term 'innovation' is descriptive; it refers to changes that market actors evaluate (in different ways) as changes that make a difference.

production process. Instead it is produced in practices of simulation or behaviour modelling – that is, through qualification trials[35] in which products (often prototypes) are experimentally tested in relation to the goal or aim of reaching a target consumer market.[36] In short, innovation does not originate in the production process, but rather emerges in relation to meeting the 'needs' of the market, where those 'needs' are interpreted in terms derived from marketing information about the consumer. The commercial value of innovation by simulation more generally is that it provides a mechanism for the organization of production for 'increasing returns'.[37] At the most basic level, relatively small differences in brand preference – if shared widely among a significant group of consumers – can lead to large differences in product choice across a range of product markets, and therefore in the value of a brand to a firm. In other words, 'a brand need not be "powerful" (in the sense that consumers believe it dramatically superior and refuse all substitutes) to be extremely valuable to the business'.[38] There is no direct proportionality between causes (innovation) and effects (increasing returns or profit) here; instead, an economic calculus of statistical probability is at work. The potential for (disproportionately) capitalizing on differences in preference is multiplied in the case of the brand insofar as it provides a mechanism for the exploitation of product differentiation within and across product markets, providing brands with the potential to transform market ecologies. The amplification of (sometimes slight) transformations in the design, styling, promotion and delivery of a particular product (or service) has the potential consequence of non-linear increases in returns as it is exploited in the multiple relations between products within and across product markets that comprise the brand: 'The key here is that wealth comes not from scarcity, as in conventional economics, but from abundance.'[39]

It might be thought from this that branding elevates the importance of judgments by consumers in the creation of quality profiles. But what is suggested here, by contrast, is that trade mark law is supporting the use of branding as a market signal *to producers rather than to consumers*, albeit with the qualification that the judgments that producers make about each

---

[35] Callon *et al.*, 'The Economy of Qualities'.
[36] Although this mode of innovation does not derive from innovation in the production process, it may of course require it.
[37] J. Urry, *Global Complexity* (Cambridge: Polity, 2003); M. Waldrop, *Complexity* (London: Penguin, 1994).
[38] P. Barwise, A. Dunham and M. Ritson, 'Ties that Bind: Consumers and Businesses' in J. Pavitt (ed.) *Brand.new* (London: V&A Publications, 2000) 89.
[39] Urry, *Global Complexity*, 53.

other are made in response to signals which involve the use of (marketing) information about consumers. Of particular note here are a series of changes in the law that are a part of the Trade Mark Act 1994 and some of the judicial responses to this Act. First, the general threshold of registrability has been set lower, so that, with a small number of exceptions, any sign, including shapes, may now be registered. TMA 1994 allows registration in many cases where previously an applicant would have had to establish 'acquired distinctiveness'.[40] Second, multi-class applications were made much easier, as noted above, facilitating the use of trade marks across previously distinct markets. Third, a trade mark may now be infringed by the non-trade mark use of the sign that is protected. The 1938 Act gave the proprietor of a registered trade mark the exclusive right to use the mark, and trade mark use was required to infringe.[41] However, in the rewording of this provision in the 1994 Act,[42] the exclusive rights are held to be infringed by 'use of a sign' in the course of trade without consent. This raised the question whether this change in wording to refer to use of a sign, as opposed to a trade mark, was significant. The case of *Arsenal Football Club plc v Matthew Reed*[43] suggests that it is. In this case, it was held that trade mark use is not necessary for infringement, only a use prejudicing the trade mark as an indicator of origin. Here then, the use of the sign may be held to infringe a trade mark, even when that use – as, in this case, as a badge of allegiance – is not trade mark use. These three shifts represent legal support for the freeing-up of the use of trade marks as signals between firms in the creation and changing organization of producer markets.

Fourth, there has also been a growing judicial acceptance – partial and uneven, but recognizable nonetheless – of more expansive trade mark rights over the last twenty or thirty years. In very general terms, this expansion comprises a judicial movement away from a 'confusion' definition of infringement (as to the origin of the product) towards a broader 'dilution' definition, which precludes all unauthorized uses that would lessen (or take advantage of) the mark's distinctiveness.[44] Thus it used to be the case that trademark infringement would only be found where the use of a protected mark by someone (X) other than its owner (Y) was likely to cause consumers to be *confused* as to the origin of the product to

[40] J. Davis, 'To Protect or Serve? European Trade Mark Law and the Decline of the Public Interest' (2003) 25(4) EIPR 180–7.
[41] D. Kitchin, D. Llewelyn, J. Mellor, et al., *Kerly's Law of Trade Marks and Trade Names* (14th rev. edn, London: Sweet and Maxwell, 2005).
[42] Trade Marks Act 1994, s. 10.   [43] Case C-206/01 [2002] ECR I-10273.
[44] Davis, *Intellectual Property Law* 220–9.

which the mark was attached.[45] The issue was whether consumers would think that X's product actually came from Y. Now it is increasingly being suggested – with varying degrees of success – that if X's use of Y's signs on its product causes consumers to be reminded of Y on seeing X's product, even while knowing that X and Y are distinct traders, infringement has occurred.[46] In other words, *creating associations between products is becoming established as the exclusive prerogative of the trade mark owner*; associations created by other producers can be legally prevented if they *dilute* the first mark. This is a significant shift insofar as it puts increasing importance on distinctions in quality created in what might be termed the horizontal axis between firms, at the expense of those emerging along the vertical axis linking producers to consumers.

This shift in legal practice is explicitly interpreted to be linked to the question of how the law should respond to recent changes in the commercial role of trade marks in markets. On the one hand, the role of the trade mark as a guarantor of (minimum) quality or standards for the consumer is held to be less crucial to a wide range of goods and services now than it was in the past. One impetus for early trade mark legislation was to enable the consumer to choose between products of a certain quality which carried a well-known mark and others of lesser or unknown quality. However, consumer legislation has ensured that, in many countries, the public can expect a certain minimum quality for a wide range of goods and services, whether a mark attaches to them or not. Instead, it is held that the competition between goods and services has come to reside more and more in what is called their 'publicity value', 'reputation' or 'brand image'.[47] On the other hand, changes in the organization of production mean that the origin of the thing that is the foundation of the property right is itself increasingly uncertain. For example, the ownership of many well-known brands is concentrated in a relatively few

---

[45] Although it should be noted that comparative advertising was previously prohibited under the 1938 legislation under a provision that prohibited 'importing a reference' to another trader's mark: Trade Marks Act 1938, s. 4.

[46] Such an interpretation of Art. 5(1) of the Trade Marks Directive was rejected in *Sabel BV v Puma AG and Rudolf Dassler Sport* Case C-251/95 [1997] ECR I-6191, but such 'links' are recognized as essential to dilution claims brought under Art. 5(2): *Adidas-Salomon AG and Adidas Benelux BV* v *Fitnessworld Trading Ltd* Case C-408/01 [2003] ECR I-12537.

[47] To this extent then, there is a convergence between the law of trade mark and that of passing-off, although of course there still remain a number of important differences. Goodwill is personal (not private) property, and it is the claimant's goodwill which is the property right protected by passing-off action. But while goodwill can be assigned or licensed it cannot be separated from the business that generated it. By contrast, trade marks are able to be assigned and licensed by their proprietors separately from the business to which they attach, so long as they do not become deceptive.

companies, many of which operate across international borders. It has been reckoned that just three (multidivisional) companies account for the ownership of nearly one-third of all branded products sold in UK supermarkets.[48] A trademark X on a soft drink may thus not mean that it is produced by X Soft Drinks Ltd but by its brand owner, a large multinational, which may also produce a number of competing brands, as well as the supermarket's 'own brand' product. Conversely, there are a few brands whose ownership is divided among a number of companies. So, for example, the BENSON & HEDGES cigarette brand is owned by three companies: Gallagher, BAT and Philip Morris, each owning the brand in different parts of the world.[49] The implications of brand identity – as protected by trade mark law – for the quality of products are thus not easily established by the average consumer, no matter if s/he be reasonably well informed, reasonably observant and circumspect as the legal test assumes. In short it seems that, while the changes described above make the legal role of the trade mark in signalling quality by protecting the consumer from confusion as to the origin of the mark increasingly outdated and inappropriate, these changes simultaneously make the role of logo as a signal of a firm's commitment of more significance to its competitors, and the ability of firms to exercise this role has been supported and extended by recent legislation and legal judgment.

To summarize all the legal changes described here then: there is now a wider range of signs that may be subject to use as trade marks, and thus a wider range may be used by firms as indicators or signals of future commitments by a firm; multi-class applications have been made significantly easier, thus providing the conditions for the use of logos as signals not only within markets but across them; the use of the sign registered as a logo is protected even when not used as a trade mark, simultaneously minimizing potential signalling confusion between firms in a market and dis-embedding market signals from the wider set of social relations in which consumers might situate their judgments as to quality; and conditions for the exclusive use of a sign as a market signal are increasingly determined in relation to a notion of distinctiveness that emerges along a horizontal axis of association established between firms[50] rather than in relation to the vertical axis between producers and consumers. Together these legal changes have a profound significance for the emergence and organization of producer markets.

First, trade mark law is contributing to a relatively greater authority being given to judgments by producers in the establishment of a quality

---

[48] Davis, *Intellectual Property Law* 205.
[49] G. Lury, *Brandwatching* (Dublin: Blackhall Publishing, 1998) 128.
[50] C. Lury, *Brands*.

214   *Celia Lury*

profile; and second, the quality profile so established is one in which
innovation by simulation is supported. What is at issue is legal support
for a particular mode of innovating (the simulation of innovation), linked
to constructions of producer markets framed by information *about* the
consumer, but rendered increasingly opaque *to* the consumer. Further,
the use of a legally protected logo as a signal is being extended across
previously distinct markets, providing the conditions for the organization
of production for the increase of (specifically non-linear) returns. In other
words, it is not just that particular judgments of quality are changing, but
that the mechanisms and criteria for judging quality are changing, transforming market ecologies, and these changes are supported and extended
by trade mark law. In White's terms, as the appreciation of the quality
index changes so does the organization of producer markets and vice versa.

Here it is worth noting that the rise of brands has contributed to the
emergence of a market environment in which the costs of new product
development have developed so that they are more or less prohibitive of
entry of new firms in many cases. Thus, while around 16,000 new
products are launched in the USA every year, 95 per cent of them are
launched as extensions of existing brands.[51] Moreover, the framing of
markets as fast-moving that is a characteristic of the introduction of
branding is both an innovation itself and the basis of further innovation,
not only at the level of the product but also at that of the market ecology.
It was at the heart of many of the strategies of the 1980s and 1990s in
which marketing experts systematically and repeatedly re-categorized
and fragmented target markets, combining, cross-tabulating and elaborating previously standard demographic variables to create multiple new
market permutations, market niches or lifestyles. The activities of targeting provided a constantly changing set of goals or tasks for producer
firms, intensifying the pace of design activity and multiplying the possibilities for (the simulation of) innovation. However, this activity did not
encourage the entry of new firms into markets, indeed perhaps the
reverse, as firms which were brand owners adopted strategies of brand
growth – brand differentiation, brand families, super-brands and sub-
brands – to manage the simulation of innovation, while the increasingly
disproportionate costs of marketing prohibited the entry of new firms.[52]

---

[51] J. Murphy, 'What is Branding?' in S. Hart and J. Murphy (eds.), *Brands* (Basingstoke:
Macmillan, 1998) 5.
[52] The probabilities of benefiting from increasing returns are improved by the exploitation
of a number of linked brands by a firm, although this is typically organized in different
ways in different industries. Many industries (industrial products, industrial services,
consumer services, frequently bought consumer products) market largely under a single
corporate or umbrella brand, often with sub-brands or other detailed product

One conclusion to be drawn is thus that this use of branding enabled firms that were brand owners to establish dominant positions within and across production markets, and restrict the entry of new firms, since the new firms were typically unable to afford the expenditure required for this mode of market signalling.

So-called 'diffusion' fashion brands provide an example of the kind of shift in market ecology made possible by the exploitation of trade marks across a dynamically changing set of producer markets. As described by Smith and Moore,[53] successful American designers such as Ralph Lauren and Calvin Klein have been adept in the development of a portfolio of brands, each of which is promoted using a distinct brand name, while still retaining some connection with the designer's name.[54] Each of the brands has a distinct visual identity, registered as trade marks, and is manufactured, managed and distributed using quite separate channels to distinct customer groups. Moore emphasizes the exploitation of a set of related distribution techniques to reach the middle retail market:

Where previously a fashion designer's store typically offered between two and three hundred product lines a season, the introduction of a diffusion brand at Ralph Lauren has swelled that company's product range to more than 6,000 lines per season. And where previously the fashion designer's ranges were distributed through a small number of company-owned stores in the fashion capitals of Paris, London, Milan and New York, as well as select department stores world-wide, the desire to attract the middle retail market has required that they adopt less narrow distribution methods. A more extensive market coverage has been achieved largely through the development of wholesale distribution to third party stockists. Through the extensive use of wholesaling, the Polo Ralph Lauren brand is now sold in over 1,600 department and speciality stories, as well as through 200 Polo Ralph Lauren shops and outlet stores world-wide, the majority of which are operated under franchise arrangements with local partners in over twenty countries.[55]

He further notes that many diffusion brands have become lifestyle brands, and some diffusion stores carry ranges which extend beyond

descriptions. But more expensive, infrequently bought consumer goods are more often marketed by a company as two or more product lines at very different price ranges. These are often separately branded. Examples here include the car companies Toyota, Nissan and Honda, who have all launched luxury-car ranges under separate brand names to their volume car ranges. Another current example of this kind of car-brand portfolio is VW's four-brand strategy (Audi, VW, Seat, Skoda) using a limited number of manufacturing platforms shared across the brands, as described by Barwise *et al.*, 'Ties that bind' 91–2.
[53] Moore, *Streets of Style*; P. Smith, 'Tommy Hilfiger in the Age of Mass Customization' in A. Ross (ed.), *No Sweat: Fashion, Free Trade, and the Rights of Garment Workers* (New York: Verso, 2000) 249–62.
[54] This is a strategy that enables brand exclusivity to be reconciled with wide availability.
[55] Moore, *Streets of Style* 267.

clothing and include jewellery, perfume, eyewear (spectacles), luggage, furniture, paint, fabrics, sheets, towels and bedding. He writes: 'The primary aim of this product line extension is to allow a greater number of customers access to the brand, be it through a $5 candle, a $3 bottle of (branded) mineral water, or a $500 suit.'[56] Similarly, the analysis presented here would suggest that the quality profile that emerges in a production process such as this is the quality which emerges from the simulation of innovation – what might be called distinctiveness – rather than the quality of individual products themselves. In commercial terms too, what emerges from the exploitation of such relations is also significant. In the case of diffusion or lifestyle brands, their commercial value may not be measured as the sum of the exchange of individual products but is a consequence of specific system effects when one or more of the products becomes successful. Such effects do not stand in direct or proportional relation to specific causes. Thus, while diffusion ranges account for between 50 and 60 per cent of companies' sales turnover, their contribution to gross profit may be as high as 90 per cent.[57]

The suggestion here then is that brands as they are protected by trade mark law allow markets to be organized in new ways. Successful brands (for example, MICROSOFT, COCA-COLA, HEINZ) provide the basis for longstanding monopolies or dominance of certain markets and afford protection of long-term investment against risk; they also restrict the entry of new competitors because of associated marketing costs. In addition, there are many examples of the use of a brand's strong position in one market in order to enter (and dominate) others. In short, a trade mark style of management enables firms to operate within and across markets in new ways. Of course, the exploitation of trade marks is not the only mechanism at work here, but it is integral to a range of market practices. Perhaps one of the clearest examples of this is Microsoft, whose operating-system software is used to run between 80 and 90 per cent of the world's computers.[58] Microsoft also controls nearly the same market share for applications such as word processors, spreadsheets, presentation graphics programs and relational databases – the components of the suite of office applications that the company 'bundles' together to consumers. The company's practices have been the subject of a long and bitterly fought anti-trust case in both the USA and Europe (type in 'Microsoft' and 'anti-trust' to your preferred search engine and read!). In an attempt to gain control of linked markets, Microsoft is said to have used its strong brand identity and control over the PC Operating System (OS) to eliminate or

---

[56] Ibid. 269.   [57] Ibid. 267.
[58] The adoption of the principle of store-clustering by Starbucks is another example.

dominate a number of rivals in markets for desktop applications. Allegations typically accuse Microsoft of, for example, selectively disseminating information about the OS's current and future functionality, thus requiring other companies to enter into unequal relations with the company if they are to be able to design functional products; giving away copies of its proprietary browser, Microsoft Internet Explorer (MTIE), to undermine its main rival, Netscape (MSIE is now included in the Microsoft basic operating system); pre-announcement of non-existent products to discourage consumer purchase of rival products (sometimes described as 'vaporware'); and predatory pricing of products to deprive rivals of revenue. The effect of such strategies, it is argued, is to drive rivals out of the market; deter future entrants; control a wide range of operating standards; play too large a part in the regulation of the Internet in relation to issues such as surveillance, copyright, personal privacy and the ability of Internet users to avoid commercial content. Supporters of Microsoft argue that the effect of its strategies is to reduce prices and reduce consumer uncertainty (this latter being the historical justification of trade marks), while its critics believe it has stifled invention and reduced choice. While the case of Microsoft is unusual, it does seem that branding organizes 'a certain structuration of competition, which acts both as a constraint and a resource for the collective qualification–requalification of products'.[59] And trade mark law enables it to do so in such a way as to extend the forms of market control exercised by large firms, both within and across previously distinct producer markets.

A further element of what is called here a 'trade mark style of management' is the use of a brand as a commercial asset. From the late 1980s onwards, brands became conspicuous in company mergers and acquisitions. This visibility was closely linked to the emergence of formal accountancy practices of brand valuation and the recognition of brand equity that occurred in the late 1980s, a significant boost to the ability of brands to function as market signals. A study of acquisitions in the 1980s showed that, whereas in 1981 net tangible assets represented 82 per cent of the amount bid for companies, by 1987 this had fallen to just 30 per cent.[60] This growth in the commercial importance of intangible assets became a public issue when, in 1988, Nestlé paid £2.5 billion (more than five times the book value) to win control of the Rowntree group, while Philip Morris purchased Kraft for $12.6 billion, six times what the company was worth on paper. In the same year, Interbrand (a branding

[59] Callon *et al.*, 'The Economy of Qualities' 201; M. Strathern, *Property, Substance and Effect: Anthropological Essays on Persons and Things* (London: Athlone Press, 1999).
[60] T. Blackett, *Trademarks* (London: Macmillan Business and Interbrand, 1998) 89.

consultancy that is now a part of Omnicom Group Inc.[61]), in collaboration with the London Business School, conducted the first 'whole portfolio' valuation for the UK foods group, Rank Hovis McDougall (RHM). In 1989, the London Stock Exchange endorsed the concept of brand valuation as used by RHM and a number of major branded goods companies now formally recognize the value of brands as intangible assets on their balance sheets.[62] In the UK, these include Cadbury Schweppes, Grand Metropolitan, Guinness, Ladbrokes and United Biscuits; in France, Pernod Ricard and Groupe Danone; while in Australia and New Zealand, companies include Pacific Dunlop, News International and Lion Nathan.

The brand consultancy Interbrand works on the principle that the value of a brand, like that of any other economic asset, is the worth *now* of the benefits of *future* ownership.[63] They argue that in order to calculate brand value it is necessary to identify clearly:

the actual benefits of future ownership; that is, the current and future earnings or cash flows of the brand;

their security and predictability and, therefore, the multiple (of profits) or discount rate (to cash flows) which can with confidence be applied.[64]

Interbrand provide criteria for the assessment of both brand strength[65] and the discount rate or the multiple to apply to brand-related profits, and argue that these criteria can be applied in a consistent, logical and verifiable manner. They produce tables of the world's most valuable brands, most of which are American-owned, on an annual basis. Thus, for example, in 1999, the top ten companies were all American-owned, with NOKIA (Finland) making it to eleventh place, MERCEDES (Germany) to twelfth, and NESCAFÉ (Switzerland) to thirteenth. COCA-COLA, the most valuable brand, was estimated to be worth $84 billion (59 per cent

---

[61] INTERBRAND is itself a brand, with the tagline 'Creating and managing brand value[TM]'.

[62] There are a number of parties who have an interest in the valuation of brands, including chief executives (wanting to unlock shareholder value); bankers (wanting to establish an agreed value for brands as part of their security); brand managers (wanting to develop and extend the equity of their brands); advertising agencies (wanting to demonstrate that a reduction of ad-spend can reduce the value of a brand); marketing directors (wanting to demonstrate the benefits of their management of brand portfolios); accountants (wanting business); finance directors (establishing royalty rates): J. Sampson 'Brand Valuation Today and Tomorrow' in R. Perrier (ed.), *Brand Valuation* (London: Interbrand, 1997) 175–99, quoted in G. Lury, *Brandwatching* 118.

[63] Blackett, *Trademarks* 91.   [64] Ibid. 91–92.

[65] The model of brand strength in the Interbrand valuation model has seven components: stability of market in which the brand performs (10%); stability or longevity of brand itself (15%); market leadership (25%); long-term profit trend (10%); consistent investment and support (10%); geographic spread (25%); legal protection under trade mark and copyright law (10%).

of the stated company value of $142 billion). In 2003, COCA-COLA was still top, NOKIA had risen to sixth place, and MERCEDES to tenth, while NESCAFÉ had fallen to twenty-first. US brands claimed sixty-two places in the top hundred, including eight out of ten of the top ten spots. There was no UK-owned brand in the top twenty in 1998, while, in 2003, the top British brand was HSBC at thirty-seventh. However, it is still not possible to recognize the value of brands on balance sheets in the USA and many other places. There is also only a very limited acceptance of the usefulness of brand accounting within many companies. Nevertheless, it is increasingly possible for companies to treat the brand as they do any other form of valuable asset. Thus, companies dispose of unwanted brands in much the same way as they dispose of a subsidiary, and acquire others to repair deficiencies in their brand portfolios – as, for example, was the case with the Unilever acquisition of CHESEBOROUGH PONDS and Ford's purchase of JAGUAR. Once brand value is recognized, it also becomes possible to mortgage or lease brands and thus to use them as a form of security.

The growth of the company Virgin provides an example of the radical use of the brand as a financial asset, and demonstrates further possible links between the use of the brand as a financial asset, the legal constitution of the trade mark as an intellectual property right, and the organization of producer markets. The Virgin CEO Richard Branson writes:

> We are in essence an unusual venture capital organization: a branded one. Whereas most venture capitalists are a financial resource, backing management teams and their ideas, we offer a powerful branding and management resource. We are also well placed to get any additional financial backing that may be required. As part of the deal we control how the brand – which we now know to be our greatest asset – is used. We therefore retain at minimum 51 per cent control of most Virgin branded businesses and are highly selective about what we invest in. Nine out of ten projects we look at are potentially very profitable but if they don't fit with our values we reject them.[66]

Initially a record label, the Virgin company now comprises a portfolio of companies providing goods and services in a diversity of product and service markets. The company's origins in the music industry are important to Branson, giving him experience in a business in which rights to properties are often shared through complex arrangements.[67] Thus he claims that it is as a consequence of the company's origin in the music

---

[66] R. Branson, 'Virgin: The Virtues of a Diversified Brand' in F. Gilmore (ed.), *Brand Warriors: Corporate Leaders Share Their Winning Strategies* (London: HarperCollins Business, 1999) 235.

[67] C. Lury, *Cultural Rights: Technology, Legality and Personality* (London: Routledge, 1993).

industry that 'we have the kind of management mind-set that regards partnership with other companies as a perfectly natural way of doing business ... We are a federation of businesses.'[68] The flexibility of the VIRGIN brand across markets is in part a consequence of the fact that it is not constrained by product category. As Branson puts it, 'we've never been constrained by the "what business are we in?" question'.[69] This in turn is a consequence of the exploitation of a core competence: the ability to manage high growth through alliances, joint ventures and outsourcing. The diversified group is said to be bound together by five core values – quality, value for money, competitiveness, innovation and fun – which together comprise the brand. The idea, Branson says, is to, 'build brands not around products but around reputation. The great Asian names imply quality, price and innovation rather than a specific item. I call these 'attribute' brands: They do not relate directly to one product – such as a Mars bar or a Coca-Cola – but instead to a set of values.'[70] While the wholesale adoption of the Virgin model is rare, it is associated with a more widespread transformation in the organization of production among producer markets. This involves a shift in the locus of control such that firms that might once have understood themselves as manufacturing firms come to see themselves as marketing firms, or, rather, as companies in which skills in market signalling involving the use of information about consumers becomes the defining attribute. For example, Nike does not itself manufacture the goods that bear its name: manufacturing is sub-contracted to factories in shifting locations in South and East Asia. As is true of Virgin, what is important to the success of the company is the creation, maintenance and exploitation of rights to use the company trade marks and associated logos. Nevertheless, Nike, like many other companies, retains a great deal of control of certain aspects of production, not only providing designs, but specifying materials, requiring standards of production and enforcing certain kinds of quality control, while not actually owning production capabilities themselves.[71] But while many companies continue to seek to control much of the production process (even if they do not own their own manufacturing plants or service outlets), this is not normally true in Virgin's case. Branson writes: 'As in the music business, third parties have always been responsible for much of the operation. Only the customer-facing activities [in Virgin

[68] Branson, 'Virgin' 235–6.   [69] Ibid. 232.   [70] Quoted in Klein, *No Logo* 24.
[71] Of course, many of the political campaigns targeted at Nike have sought to make them take responsibility not only for the standards of products being produced, but also for the human and environmental conditions in which their products are manufactured; see Klein, *No Logo*.

airlines] are Virgin branded or trained. Our cost base is therefore far lower than our main competitors' on most routes.'[72] Or, once again drawing parallels with the music industry:

Our culture is one of corporate artists: challenging conventions is proving to be one of the best ways to bring about success. Our approach to managing each business is based on our roots. Instead of musicians, the artists Virgin now manages are the individual companies and, of course, the Virgin brand. Virgin Management is fully involved with launching new companies, reviewing the opportunity, setting up the business, and providing a creative team of managers who are seconded to new Virgin companies for as long as they are needed. Fledgling Virgin ventures thus acquire the trademark management style plus unique skills and experience from all parts of the group. After the business has been set up, however, it is the responsibility of the individual company's management.[73]

The result is a virtual brand that is 'regenerated rather than extended in the conventional sense, by each business we become involved in'.[74] This is a radical statement of the use of a brand to manage a process of non-linear production across conventional trade categories, indicating a profound shift in the dynamics of market ecology. Growth is here not simply a consequence of brand extension *within* a market, but of regeneration *across* markets. This is the multiplication of brand origins, or, perhaps better, the management of a network of relations in which each new origin has the potential to provide the basis for further growth, acting as a signalling device that is able to communicate within and across markets. As the interview quoted above shows, it is Branson himself who describes this as a 'trade mark management style'.[75]

What has been argued here is that the terms of ownership afforded the mark owner by trade mark law have commercial significance in relation to co-operative and competitive relations between firms. The use of branding – as it is protected in trade mark law – plays a key role in the relationship between quality profiles and market identity, contributing to the establishment of networks and alliances within and between firms in ways that organize producer markets in particular ways and support particular forms of market exchange and capital accumulation. Those outlined here include trade mark licensing, franchising, the simulation of innovation, and the use of the brand as a commercial asset, and are collectively described as a trade mark style of management. This style

---

[72] Branson, 'Virgin' 230.   [73] Ibid. 237–8.   [74] Ibid. 235.
[75] For a discussion of trade mark style in the art world, see C. Lury, 'Portrait of the artist as a brand' in D. McClean and K. Schubert (eds.), *Dear Images: Art, Copyright and Culture* (London: Ridinghouse and ICA, 2002) 87–102.

marks the emergence and consolidation of trans-market cultural forms, changing the ecology of producer markets, enabling firms to introduce and consolidate forms of hierarchy, ownership and control that operate within and across individual producer markets. It is a highly flexible yet resilient market mechanism, setting the terms by which quality may be used to signal innovation. The recent changes in trade mark law described here have thus contributed to making branding an increasingly important means by which capital may not only build monopolies but also have investments in the ownership of the simulation of innovation within and across markets. Trade mark management style – as it is enabled by trade mark law – does more than protect the mark owner from unfair forms of competition; it makes it possible for mark owners to exploit new forms of production and exchange, to establish new kinds of market-cultural forms and to frame perception.

10 The irrational lightness of trade marks: a legal perspective

*Catherine W. Ng**

Professor Lury's thought-provoking chapter 'Trade Mark Style as a Way of Fixing Things' asserts that, in addition to their role as facilitators of transactions between manufacturers and consumers, trade marks have become a commercial asset in their own right. They have acquired an ability to exploit new forms of production and exchange,[1] and a value as 'an object or mode of capital accumulation'.[2]

A rear-view mirror perspective

This commentary will complement her paper by offering a rear-view mirror perspective, in time and in the chain of commerce, to demonstrate how developments in UK trade mark laws have accommodated traders as they extend their personae through trade marks to organize production and exchange. In trade mark laws, trade marks are consistently attributed a source distinguishing function: to identify the traders responsible for putting the trade marked goods[3] on the market, and to distinguish the traders' goods from those of other traders. Trade marks are defined by this source-distinguishing function.[4] In the market, however, trade marks serve as identifiers of brands and play a role in organizing the consumer market thereby.[5] In her chapter, 'Trade

---

* I am very much indebted to Professor L. Bently and Professor D. Vaver for their generous comments on earlier drafts of this chapter, and also wish to thank Professor P. Beaumont and Mr T. Burns for their helpful suggestions, and Ms Y. Marinova for her research assistance.
[1] C. Lury, 'Trade Mark Style as a Way of Fixing Things', Chapter 9 of this volume, 201.
[2] Ibid. 201.
[3] For simplicity, in this chapter, all references to goods are to goods and services unless the context suggests otherwise.
[4] Agreement on Trade-related Aspects of Intellectual Property Rights 1994 Art. 15; First Council Directive 89/104/EEC of 21 December 1988 to approximate the laws of the Member States relating to trade marks, Art. 2; Trade Marks Act 1994, s. 1.
[5] C. Lury, *Brands: The Logos of the Global Economy* (London: Routledge, 2004); C. Ng, 'The Dilution of the Law of Passing-off: Toward a Rational Basis for Irrational Trade Mark Protection' D. Phil. thesis, University of Oxford (2004) – an adaptation is published as 'A Common Law of Identity Signs' Part I (2007) 20 IPJ 177, Part II (2007) 20 IPJ 285.

Mark Style as a Way of Fixing Things', Professor Lury has demonstrated that trade marks also play a role in organizing the producer market.

This chapter supports her observations by showing that the consumer protection rationale in trade mark laws is not consistently reflected in the legal mechanisms. These mechanisms, however, facilitate the extension of commercial identities which organize the producer market. The three rationales often cited to justify trade mark protection are: (1) the protection of consumers – trade marks lower consumer search costs by distinguishing the desired goods of a desired trader from other goods and goods of other traders, and trade mark laws discourage others from making counterfeits; (2) the promotion of fair competition among traders – trade marks and trade mark laws allow traders who offer desired goods to attract and secure their clientele; and (3) with lower consumer search costs and fair competition among traders, the advancement of economic efficiency – trade marks identify the goods in demand and help direct resources towards the production of those goods with the economic votes consumers cast by their patronage. This chapter will show that the consumer protection rationale has been illusory. While the illusion of the consumer protection rationale lends a balanced appeal to the law, the hollowness of this rationale destabilizes the other rationales and leaves the boundaries of trade mark law wanting in rationalization. Beyond the consumer protection rationale, in the market where certain trade marks themselves are in demand and are driving the production of incidental goods which bear the marks, is economic efficiency as conceived in (3) being achieved? How should 'fair competition' in (2) be adjudicated between traders then, especially where the demand for some marks is largely created or buoyed by the consumers themselves?

This chapter exposes the illusory nature of the consumer protection rationale and urges a re-evaluation of the bases for trade mark laws in this light. In trade mark laws, the prevention of public confusion of the goods of one trader with those of other traders merely serves as an occasional demarcation of rights among business interests in trade marks.[6] Confused consumers have no recourse against counterfeiters under

---

[6] *Phones4U Ltd* v *Phone4u.co.uk Internet Ltd* [2006] EWCA Civ. 244 at para. 21, per Jacob LJ: 'In this discussion of "deception/confusion" it should be remembered that there are cases where what at first sight may look like deception and indeed will involve deception, is nonetheless justified in law. I have in mind cases of honest concurrent use and very descriptive marks. Sometimes such cases are described as "mere confusion" but they are not really – they are cases of tolerated deception or a tolerated level of deception'; on trade mark dilution: *Adidas-Salomon AG* v *Fitnessworld Trading Ltd*, Case C-408/01 [2004] Ch. 120 at 139: 'the protection conferred by article 5(2) of the [First Council] Directive [89/104/EEC] is not conditional on a finding of a degree of similarity between the mark with a reputation and the sign such that there exists a likelihood of confusion between

trade mark laws: the common law of passing-off and, for registered marks, the Trade Marks Act 1994.

Individual consumers and businesses alike favour certainty in their search in the marketplace. Individual consumers search for goods for personal or household consumption; businesses seek human, material and financial resources to produce goods, to access resources and markets for this production, and to market goods for distribution. Trade mark laws are justified in part by virtue of their role in facilitating such searches by enforcing the perceived distinction among the sources and qualities of the goods as expressed through trade marks. When a consumer, whether business or individual, is satisfied with the goods, the consumer may rely on the trade mark in an effort to return to the trade source for further purchase; such further purchase endows the source-supplier with financial resources to produce more of the same desired goods,[7] be they hamburgers by a McDonald's restaurant or by a Michelin-starred restaurant, or any other goods consumers would purchase. Efficiency in the market distribution of economic resources may thus be achieved. In practice, trade mark laws also enable traders to build a reputation, whether or not deserved. Consumers and trade sectors which develop, produce, distribute or contribute human, material and financial resources for the production and distribution of goods often organize their trade relationships based on this reputation.

Individuals often commence businesses as the source-supplier of goods under their own names. This practice predates trade mark laws as they are known today.[8] Many early trade mark cases were pursued for goods bearing the names of their initial proprietors. Businesses can be construed as extensions of these proprietors' public personae. The fast-food franchise of McDonald's Corporation, for example, began with brothers Dick and Mac McDonald at their McDonald's Restaurant in San Bernardino, California.[9]

Company law, however, has long permitted proprietors to seek economic and legal security by incorporating their businesses and becoming

them on the part of the relevant section of the public. It is sufficient for the degree of similarity between the mark with a reputation and the sign to have the effect that the relevant section of the public establishes a link between the sign and the mark.' The Trade Marks Act 1994, ss. 5(3) and 10(3), implement Art. 4(3) and (4)(a), and Art. 5(2) of the First Council Directive 89/104/EEC, respectively.

[7] Under-Secretary of State for Trade, *Report of the Committee to Examine British Trade Mark Law and Practice*, Cmnd 5601 (1974) 5, 20.

[8] E.g. *Hogg* v *Kirby* (1803) 8 Vesey Junior 215, 32 ER 336; *Sykes* v *Sykes* (1824) 3 Barnewell and Cressell 541, 107 ER 834; *Morison* v *Salmon* (1841) 2 Manning and Granger 385, 133 ER 795; *Perry* v *Truefitt* (1842) 6 Beav 66, 49 ER 749 (the term 'pass off' was first used in the headnote of this case).

[9] http://mcdonalds.com/corp/about/mcd_history_pg1.html (28 June 2007).

226   *Catherine W. Ng*

shareholders, delegating management responsibilities and thereby shielding themselves from corporate liabilities. By incorporation, companies assume legal personalities distinct from their constituent members[10] and become potentially perpetual. Shares in these companies may be issued, diluted, bought and sold. Corporate structures are often opaque and corporate management often unknown to the general public.[11] This public consists of actual and prospective consumers and traders who develop, produce, distribute or contribute human, material and financial resources for the production and distribution of goods: investors, employees, suppliers and purchasers. Many in their direct and indirect interactions with a company may be influenced by the reputation of the company.[12] This reputation may attract or repel them and thereby play a role in organizing the market of exchange. Few who are employed by, supply to or purchase from McDonald's Corporation and its franchisees are likely familiar with their corporate or management structure, yet many engage with them based on the reputation of MCDONALD'S.

At the consumer interface, the law of passing-off has also long tolerated such opacity in the trade mark source. The general proposition of the law is that 'no man may pass off his goods as those of another'.[13] In 1897, the House of Lords held it unnecessary for the public to know the exact source of a trade mark for that mark to attract common law protection against passing-off.[14] The relevant public is only required to know that goods (e.g. hamburgers) which bear the same mark (MCDONALD'S) emanate from the same source (McDonald's restaurants), though that source may be unknown to the

---

[10] *Salomon* v *Salomon & Co.* [1897] AC 22; Companies Act 1985, s. 13(3), to be replaced by Companies Act 2006, s. 16(2) effective 1 October 2008.
[11] *Royal British Bank* v *Turquand* (1856) 6 Ellis and Blackburn 327 at 332, 119 ER 886 at 888, per Jervis CJ: 'We may now take for granted ... that the parties dealing with [companies] are bound to read the statute and the deed of settlement. But they are not bound to do more.' Companies Act 1985, ss. 35 A and 35B, to be restated in Companies Act 2006, s. 40 effective 1 October 2008: s. 40(1) 'In favour of a person dealing with a company in good faith, the power of the directors to bind the company, or authorise others to do so, is deemed to be free of any limitation under the company's constitution.'
[12] D. B. Turban and D. W. Greening, 'Corporate Social Performance and Organisational Attractiveness to Prospective Employees' (1996) 40(3) *Academy of Management Journal* 658; M. J. Dollinger, P. A. Golden and T. Saxton, 'The Effect of Reputation on the Decision to Joint Venture' (1997) 18(2) *Strategic Management Journal* 127; D. M. Cable and M. E. Graham, 'The Determinants of Job Seekers' Reputation Perceptions' (2000) 21 *Journal of Organisational Behaviour* 929; V. Fleischer, 'Brand New Deal: The Branding Effect of Corporate Deal Structures' (2006) 104 *Michigan Law Review* 1581.
[13] *Reckitt & Colman Products Ltd* v *Borden Inc.* [1990] 1 WLR 491 at 499.
[14] *Birmingham Vinegar Brewery Company, Limited* v *Powell* [1897] AC 710; *GE Trade Mark* [1969] FSR 186 at 214 affirmed [1972] WLR 729 at 743. This was statutorily recognized as regards registered trade marks in s. 68 of the Trade Marks Act 1938, as amended by the Trade Marks (Amendment) Act 1984 for service marks.

public. A mark attracts common law protection against passing-off where: (1) this goodwill connecting the goods with a trade mark source in the public eye through marketing and sales is present; (2) a misrepresentation is made by the defendant to the public leading or likely to lead the public to believe that the goods offered by him are the goods of the plaintiff; and (3) this misrepresentation causes damage or likelihood of damage.[15] Neither specific damage to the plaintiff nor intent harboured by the defendant is necessary to constitute the tort.[16] Although, to establish the cause of action, the misrepresentation must confuse or be likely to confuse a substantial portion of the public, such confusion or its likelihood alone is not sufficient; damage or likelihood of damage to the plaintiff trader's goodwill is also required.

Trade marks may be further protected by registration. The UK registry system introduced in 1875[17] has changed the nature of trade mark laws. Unlike under the law of passing-off where the right is personal against a counterfeiter, registered trade mark rights are *in rem*, good against the world. This change of character is arguably a result of the legal system at the time. The roots of early plaintiff success in an action for passing-off in the courts of equity trace at least as far back as 1803;[18] and in the common law courts, as 1769.[19] The term 'pass off' first appeared in the headnote of an 1842 case.[20] The action proved expensive, not least because of the

[15] *Reckitt & Colman Products Ltd* v *Borden Inc* [1990] 1 WLR 491 at 499.
[16] In respect of special damage: *Blofeld* v *Payne* (1833) 4 Barnewall and Adolphus 410, 110 ER 509. In respect of the defendant's intent: *Millington* v *Fox* (1838) 3 Mylne and Craig 338, 40 ER 956.
[17] Trade Marks Registration Act 1875 (38 & 39 Vict. c. 91).
[18] In *Hogg* v *Kirby* (1803) 8 Vesey Junior 215 at 221, 32 ER 336 at 339, Lord Chancellor Eldon commented: 'The resemblance is such, that the books must have been bought and read, before it could have been discovered, that they were not the same [as the plaintiff's]. The argument in support of the injunction has occupied the several grounds of copyright, fraud, and contract; which satisfies me, that it was not distinctly ascertained, which in particular was to be occupied' (injunction was granted to restrain the defendant from publishing and selling any work as a continuation or a part of the plaintiff's work); *Day* v *Day* (1816) is an early case cited in *Eden on Injunctions* (1821) 314.
[19] E.g. in the *London Chronicle* (14 December 1769) 575: 'On Saturday last [9 December] ... [t]he action was brought against the defendant for having counterfeited a certain medicine for coughs, hoarsenesses, &c, invented by the plaintiff called Pectoral Lozenges of Told, and selling the same with Mr. Greenough, the plaintiff's name, affixed thereto; when the jury, which was special, brought in a verdict for the plaintiff, with fifty pound damages, and full costs of suit. It is hoped that this will prevent such gross impositions for the future, which, before the jury withdrew, the plaintiff declared in court, was his motive for bringing the action, and not the measure of damages.' The case is *Greenough* v. *Dalmahoy* as cited in J. Oldham, *English Common Law in the Age of Mansfield* (Chapel Hill: University of North Carolina Press, 2004) 196; *Sykes* v *Sykes* (1824) 3 Barnewell and Cressell, 541, 107 ER 834, is often cited as the first reported common law case. See F. I. Schechter, *The Historical Foundations of the Law Relating to Trade-Marks* (New York: Columbia University Press, 1925) 137.
[20] *Perry* v *Truefitt* (1842) 6 Beav 66, 49 ER 749.

228 Catherine W. Ng

complex relationship that then existed between the courts of law and equity. The case of *Rodgers v Nowill*,[21] in 1847, reportedly cost the plaintiff 2,211*l* in legal fees and took five years to establish the plaintiff's exclusive right to the trade mark.[22] Under the law of passing-off, plaintiffs must in each case prove their entitlement to an exclusive right against a trade mark use.[23] A registry system was intended to allow the plaintiffs to prove their right to the mark only upon registration and upon challenges for non-use. Proponents for the introduction of a registry system in the UK argued that the cost of passing-off litigation made difficult negotiations for reciprocal protection of UK trade marks in jurisdictions such as Prussia, France, Belgium and some states of the USA, which already enjoyed a registry system at least for some sectors.[24]

Initially, the introduction of a registry system would not appear to have changed the position of those with an interest in a mark. The early cases often cited for precedent are cases where the use of identical[25] marks or marks with minor variants[26] on apparently identical merchandise was alleged. The plaintiffs' cases were compelling. By 1833, even if the defendant's act did not occasion any specific damage to the plaintiff, 'it was still, to a certain extent, an injury to [the plaintiff's] right'.[27] The need to prove specific damage was dismissed. By 1838, the need to show the defendant's intent was eliminated as an element of the tort in the courts of equity.[28] The courts of equity were favoured by plaintiffs because only these courts could issue the most desired remedy of injunctive relief. Authorities saw the role of the courts of equity as upholding and reinforcing legal rights, especially of a proprietary nature.[29] Claims without the

---

[21] (1853) 3 De Gex Macnaughten and Gordon 614, 43 ER 241.
[22] *Minutes of Evidence of the Select Committee to whom the Trade Marks Bill, and the Merchandise Marks Bill were Referred* (1862) XII s. 431, s. 458.
[23] Under-Secretary of State for Trade, *Report*, 20.
[24] *Minutes of Evidence of the Select Committee* XII §431: Minutes of Evidence by Mr Robert Jackson (a partner in the firm of Spear & Jackson in Sheffield mfg saws, files etc) 20th March 1862.
[25] *Singleton v Bolton* (1783) 3 Douglas 293, 99 ER 661; *Sykes v Sykes* (1824) 3 Barnewell and Cressell 541, 107 ER 834; *Motley v Downman* (1837) 3 Mylne and Craig 1, 40 ER 824; *Millington v Fox* (1838) 3 Mylne and Craig 338, 40 ER 956; *Morison v Salmon* (1841) 2 Manning and Granger 385, 133 ER 795.
[26] *Day v Binning* (1831) 1 CP Coop 489, 47 ER 611; *Blofeld v Payne* (1833) 4 Barnewall and Adolphus 410, 110 ER 509; *Knott v Morgan* (1836) 2 Keen 213, 48 ER 610; *Crawshay v Thompson* (1842) 4 Man and G 357, 134 ER 146; *Rodgers v Nowill* (1847) 5 CB 109, 136 ER 816.
[27] *Blofeld v Payne* (1833) 4 Barnewall and Adolphus 410 at 411, 110 ER 509 at 510.
[28] *Millington v Fox* (1838) 3 Mylne and Craig 338, 40 ER 956.
[29] *Motley v Downman* (1837) 3 Mylne and Craig 1, 40 ER 824; J. Adams *The Doctrine of Equity* (London: William Benning & Co, 1850) 207; J. Indemaur, *A Manual of the Principles of Equity* (2nd edn, London: Geo Barber 'Law Students' Journal' Office, 1890) 339.

requirements of defendant's intent and specific damage to the plaintiff appeared consistent with those of a proprietary nature.[30] A registered trade mark is now incorporeal movable property in Scotland and personal property in the rest of the UK.[31] It can be owned, licensed,[32] assigned and subject to security interests. It is 'so transmissible either in connection with the goodwill of a business or independently'.[33]

To sustain the consumer protection rationale of trade mark protection, that of enabling the public to distinguish the unique sources of goods by their marks, the law restricted the trafficking of trade marks:[34] 'Trafficking in a trade mark context conveys the notion of dealing in a trade mark primarily as a commodity in its own right and not primarily for the purpose of identifying or promoting merchandise in which the proprietor of the mark is interested.'[35] In 1914, the House of Lords proclaimed:

The object of the law is to preserve for a trader the reputation he has made for himself, not to help him in disposing of that reputation as of itself a marketable commodity, independent of his goodwill, to some other traders. If that were allowed, the public would be misled, because they might buy something in the belief that it was the make of a man whose reputation they knew, whereas it was the make of someone else.[36]

The marks in that case were expunged. Once expunged, the marks were free to be used by anyone. The public would not have notice of this change in the marks' status beyond a note in the registry which few would access. Potential public confusion might result. The public protection argument with which the Lords justified the result thus appears

[30] See L. Bently, 'From Communication to Thing: historical aspects of the conceptualisation of trade marks as property' in G. Dinwoodie & M. Janis (eds.), *Trademark Law and Theory: A Handbook of Contemporary Research* (Cheltenham: Edward Elgar, 2008), which describes a tendency towards conceptualization of trade marks as property from around 1860.
[31] Trade Marks Act 1994, ss. 2 and 22. [32] Ibid. ss. 28ff. [33] Ibid. s. 24.
[34] Trade Marks Registration Act 1875 (38 & 39 Vict. c. 91), s. 2; Patents, Designs, and Trade Marks Act 1883 (46 & 47 Vict. c. 57), s. 70; and Trade Marks Act 1905 (5 Edw. 7 c. 15), s. 22 – all required that a registered trade mark be assigned and transmitted only in connection with the goodwill of the business concerned in the goods for which the mark had been registered, and that the mark be determinable with that goodwill. Trade Marks Act 1938 (1 & 2 Geo. 6 c. 22), s. 28, relaxed this position but retained the doctrine by permitting the use of a mark by a registered user, and by deeming such use to be use by the trade mark registrant. Under s. 28(6) of that Act, the Registrar must refuse an application for registration as a registered user if it appeared to him that the grant would tend to facilitate trafficking in a trade mark. The registrar did so in respect of the proposed character merchandising under the HOLLY HOBBIE mark; the decision was upheld by the House of Lords in *Re American Greetings Corp's Application* [1984] 1 All ER 426.
[35] *Re American Greetings Corp's Application* [1984] 1 All ER 426 at 433.
[36] *Bowden Wire Ltd* v *Bowden Brake Co. Ltd* (1914) 31 RPC 385 at 392.

strained. The remedy they imposed against the use of a mark by more than one source permitted all to use the mark.

Moreover, by this time, this 'man whose reputation they knew' could have been a company whose controlling shares and substantial assets could have been traded, and whose directing management could have been replaced, all with little impact on trade mark rights.[37] Yet each of these occasions can fundamentally affect the trade mark source. The concept of the source, to which a trade mark performing its source-distinguishing function under the law would point, appears paper-thin, potentially consisting of only the name and its attending public perception. Company law allows companies to be shielded by a corporate veil which is sometimes lifted to accommodate the public perception of a trade mark.[38]

In 1915, the House of Lords declared that, to attract common law protection for a mark, the goodwill protected under the law need not necessarily relate to the source of the mark, but might also be built upon the quality of the goods bearing the mark.[39] In that case, the defendant sold goods of the plaintiff's manufacture bearing the plaintiff's trade mark. However, those goods, having been found substandard by the plaintiff, had earlier been sold to waste-rubber merchants. The defendant purchased the goods from the merchants and resold those goods for their initial intended use under the plaintiff's original mark. Even though there was no misrepresentation as to the source of the goods, passing-off was found because the quality of the goods otherwise on the market had changed and the defendant's remarketing of earlier goods would cause confusion about the quality of the goods.[40] Meanwhile, a trader may at will alter the quality, manufacture, manufacturer and/or marketer of its

---

[37] *Salomon* v *Salomon & Co.* [1897] AC 22; *Bach Flower Remedies* [1999] RPC 1 at 28–9 *in obiter*: 'While I see the force of, and indeed to a substantial extent agree with, the argument that the attitude of those at the Bach Centre, who put themselves forward as the successors to Dr Bach, is pretty different from that of Dr Bach and his immediate successors, I do not see the applications to register or the attempts to maintain the registration of, the instant marks can be said to be in bad faith.' The decision was affirmed [2000] RPC 513.

[38] *Radiation Trade Mark* (1930) 47 RPC 37; *Revlon Inc.* v *Cripps & Lee Ltd* [1980] FSR 85; *Scandecor Developments AB* v *Scandecor Marketing AB* [2001] UKHL 21 paras. 52–3; Wadlow, *Passing Off* 204ff.

[39] For an earlier example of the court's protection of a trade mark's capacity to distinguish the quality of its underlying goods, see *Henderson* v *Jorss*, *The Times*, 22 June 1861, 11b, where the court found two types of injury which might result from the passing off: 'There was, first, the injury from loss of custom through an inferior article being sold more cheaply; and there was, secondly, the loss of the character of the trade-mark through the inferiority in quality of the goods sold under the imitation of it.'

[40] *A. G. Spalding & Bros.* v *A. W. Gamage Ltd* (1915) 32 RPC 273.

own goods underlying a mark and retain legal protection in the mark.[41] Neither consumers, competitors nor any other trade sectors have redress under trade mark laws for the market uncertainty that results from such potential alteration.

This goodwill protected under the law can spread with the range of goods bearing a mark. Trade mark laws facilitate this in three ways. First, the law of passing-off protects a mark from third party use not only on confusingly similar goods, but also on related goods which may be attributed to or connected with the mark claimant by confusion.[42] This reserves for trade mark claimants room to diversify and extend their activities into related markets. As Professor Lury explained, 'many diffusion brands have become lifestyle brands, and some diffusion stores carry ranges which extend beyond clothing and include jewellery, perfume, eyewear (spectacles), luggage, furniture, paint, fabrics, sheets, towels and bedding'.[43] The greater the diversification, the broader the selection of goods and their related goods, the broader therefore the protection under trade mark laws which reserve room for the development of an even greater range of goods to generate even greater reputation. A few companies may thereby dominate a market, subject to competition laws intended to protect public interest from the negative effects of such dominance.[44] When a company diversifies its business into a sector new to the company, the protection of its known mark in the new sector – of goods whose quality is unknown to consumers – again suggests that the consumer protection rationale in trade mark protection is strained. Such use of a mark does not assist the consuming public in discerning the quality of the underlying goods in the new sector. In any event, the Trade Marks Act 1994 not only protects trade marks from the

---

[41] *Warwick Tyre Company, Ltd* v *New Motor and General Rubber Company, Ltd* [1910] 1 Ch 248; *J. H. Coles Proprietary, Limited* v *J. F. Need* [1934] AC 82; *Bostitch Trade Mark* [1963] RPC 183 at 197; *Scandecor Developments AB* v *Scandecor Marketing AB* [2001] UKHL 21 at para. 21–2.

[42] *The Eastman Photographic Materials Company, Ltd* v *The John Griffiths Cycle Corporation, Ltd* (1898) 15 RPC 105; *Alfred Dunhill Ltd* v *Sunoptic SA* [1979] FSR 337; *Lego System Aktieselskab* v *Lego M Lemelstrich Ltd* [1983] FSR 155; *Mirage Studios* v *Counter-Feat Clothing Company Ltd* [1991] FSR 145; *Harrods Ltd* v *Harrodian School Ltd* [1996] RPC 697; Wadlow, *Passing Off* 267, 470.

[43] Chapter 9 of this volume, 215.

[44] D. Kitchin, D. Llewelyn, J. Mellor, *et al.*, *Kerly's Law of Trade Marks and Trade Names* (14th edn, London: Sweet and Maxwell, 2005) 569 ff.; R. Sumroy and C. Badger, 'Infringing "Use in the Course of Trade": Trade Mark Use and the Essential Function of a Trade Mark' in J. Phillips and I. Simon (eds.), *Trade Mark Use* (Oxford: Oxford University Press, 2005) 163, 179; P. Torremans, *Holyoak and Torremans Intellectual Property Law* (4th edn, Oxford: Oxford University Press, 2005) 429 ff.; N.J. Wilkof and D. Burkitt, *Trade Mark Licensing* (2nd edn, London: Sweet and Maxwell, 2005) 297 ff.

use and registration of identical or similar marks on confusing goods, but also protects trade marks with a reputation from dilution irrespective of the goods bearing them.[45] No public confusion is required to attract the latter protection.[46] Furthermore, as Professor Lury points out, no prior use of a mark is required to gain registration.[47]

Second, the law is not concerned when a trade mark is diluted, or when a business carried on using different trade marks for different market segments merges those segments to carry on business under one trade mark, or when a business segments its market sectors using different trade marks, if these acts are done by or with the consent of the trade mark source. An example of trade mark dilution by the trade mark source is the use of VIRGIN on a wide range of goods. The reputation of the mark is built on the trader's selection of goods and target markets which the trader wishes to associate or 'bundle'[48] with that mark. As Professor Lury notes, 'firms that might once have understood themselves as manufacturing firms come to see themselves as marketing firms'.[49] A trader may also merge its business in different market segments carried on under different trade marks into one segment carried on under one trade mark. After almost seventy years, all DIXONS UK High Street stores, starting May 2006, became known as CURRYS.DIGITAL, with no apparent accompanying change in corporate structure.[50] DIXONS' market segment will merge with CURRYS'. A trader may also segment a market by using different marks. 'VW's four-brand strategy (Audi, VW, Seat, Skoda)'[51] is one example. No recourse is available to the public as a result of any confusion which may arise from such change in the use of a trade mark by, or with the consent of, the trade mark source.

Third, the Trade Marks Act 1994 recognizes trade mark licensing, though common law rights under trade mark licensing remain problematic.[52] Trade mark licensing permits trade mark owners to extend sales beyond their reach, and to extend product lines beyond their core competence. Trade mark licensing was initially viewed under common and statute law as contrary to the legal rationale for trade mark protection: that trade marks serve to distinguish the unique sources of their underlying goods. 'Licensing' by definition permits co-existence of multiple sources for one trade mark. Trade mark licensing was recognized by statute[53] hesitantly and belatedly to accommodate industrial and

---

[45] Trade Marks Act 1994, ss. 5(3) and 10(3). See Lury, Chapter 9 of this volume, 211–12.
[46] *Adidas-Salomon AG* v *Fitnessworld Trading Ltd*, Case C-408/01 [2004] Ch. 120, see above note 6.
[47] Lury, Chapter 9 of this volume, 211.   [48] Ibid. 216.   [49] Ibid. 220.
[50] www.dsgiplc.com (28 June 2007).
[51] Lury, Chapter 9 of this volume, 211 footnote 43.
[52] Wilkof and Burkitt, *Trade Mark Licensing* 45.   [53] See above, footnote 34.

professional interests in business expansion.[54] The 'golden thread' found running through successful pre-1994 licences was the central control held by the licensor over the use of the mark, where such licences did not lead to confusion or deception.[55] This control is no longer required under Trade Marks Act 1994.[56] The Act relies on the licensors to control the use of their marks in order to maintain the commercial value in the mark and their legal interest in the mark, by not rendering it non-distinctive or generic.[57]

Successful licensors may negotiate favourable franchise arrangements with their franchisees and achieve 'commercial . . . weightlessness'[58] while performing the quality control required under common law.[59] After considering the definition of 'franchise' by the British Franchise Association, the International Franchise Association, and the Code of Ethics of the European Franchise Association, legal scholars found all involved a mutual agreement between the franchisor and the franchisee under which:

1. the franchisor licenses the franchisee to carry on business under a name, etc., owned or associated with the franchisor;
2. the franchisor controls the way in which the franchisee carries on that business;
3. the franchisor provides assistance to the franchisee in running the business;
4. the businesses are, however, separate: the franchisee provides and risks its own capital.[60] (The franchisor may nonetheless be held liable for third party liabilities incurred by the franchisee.[61])

A reputation cultivated under the shield of trade mark laws may, through franchising, be multiplied with relative ease and profit for the franchisor. The franchisor generally does not provide goods to the public in competition with the franchisees. Yet the goodwill engendered by the franchisees' businesses may accrue to the franchisor.[62] With each successful franchise, the prospective franchisees' desire for the franchise and the

---

[54] Board of Trade, *Report of the Departmental Committee on the Law and Practice Relating to Trade Marks*, Cmd 4568 (1934) para. 118.
[55] *Aktiebolaget Manus* v *R. J. Fullwood & Bland, Ltd* (1948) 65 RPC 329 affirmed [1949] Ch. 208; *Bostitch Trade Mark* [1963] RPC 183.
[56] *Scandecor Developments AB* v *Scandecor Marketing AB* [2001] UKHL 21; J. Davis, 'To Protect or Serve? European Trade Mark Law and the Decline of the Public Interest' (2003) 25(4) EIPR 180; Wilkof and Burkitt, *Trade Mark Licensing*, 130ff.
[57] The Secretary of State for Trade and Industry, *White Paper on Reform of Trade Marks Law*, Cm 1203 (1990) 25–6.
[58] Lury, Chapter 9 of this volume, 206.   [59] Wilkof and Burkitt, *Trade Mark Licensing* 47–8.
[60] J. N. Adams and K. V Prichard Jones, *Franchising* (4th edn, London: Butterworths, 1997) 21.
[61] Ibid. 33 ff.   [62] Wadlow, *Passing Off* 476–7.

234   *Catherine W. Ng*

franchisor's command of the market gain momentum. Reputation begets further reputation.

Trade mark laws also protect the marks of persons with reputation. Businesses such as McDonald's may have begun as an extension of public personae such as those of brothers Dick and Mac McDonald. One may also found businesses based on another's celebrity. Professor Lury's quotation from Richard Branson is apt: 'build brands not around products but around reputation'.[63] The CHANEL trade mark lives on despite the death of its eponymous founder. Its reputation has spread well beyond the initial medium (fashion) bearing the mark,[64] and signifies more than the initial source of the mark, the designer Gabrielle 'Coco' Chanel herself. The mark is owned and controlled by Chanel Limited. Company law permits the ownership and management of the business to change hands. A change in corporate ownership changes the constitution of the trade mark source; a change in corporate management may vary the quality of the goods. Nonetheless, the protection of the mark under trade mark laws remains. The reputation of the name or the mark continues to organize the ecology of production and consumption markets.

However, trade mark registrations of the names of famous persons have been refused, on the ground that:

where a famous name is concerned (other than names which are famous as indicators of trade source, as in these examples [of LAURA ASHLEY, HARRY RAMSDEN and DOROTHY PERKINS]) there is the possibility that the name will serve to signify not the trade source of the goods/services but merely the subject matter. The Elvis case is an example of this.[65]

As a result of the *Elvis* case mentioned, the ELVIS mark (though not recognized as a trade mark under the Trade Marks Act 1994) may nonetheless continue to be used to command and organize its market in toiletries as it has since the 1980s by a party unrelated to the singer Elvis Presley or his core competence in goods (records) or services (concerts).[66] However, neither this party nor the singer's estate may do so exclusively. Others may also trade on Elvis Presley's celebrity: 'In addressing the critical issue of distinctiveness there should be no a priori assumption that only a celebrity or his successors may ever market (or

[63] Lury, Chapter 9 of this volume, 220.
[64] Registered in the UK as Trade Mark 866556 for Class 25 'articles of clothing for women and girls', among registrations for the word mark in over thirty classes of goods and services (28 June 2007).
[65] *Executrices of the Estate of Diana, Princess of Wales' Application* [2001] ETMR 25.
[66] *Elvis Presley Trade Marks* [1999] RPC 567.

license the marketing of) his own character. Monopolies should not be so readily created.'[67]

From this glance at trade mark laws through to company law in the rear-view mirror, it appears that trade mark ownership and business ownership can be fragmented, commodified and traded as tools for organizing the production and consumption markets. Businesses, whether or not founded and operated as extensions of their proprietors' personalities, may have their shares bought, sold and mortgaged. Trade marks, with or without having established any goodwill through use, may now be owned, licensed and assigned in part or in full, and subject to security interests. The production and consumption markets of actual and prospective investors, employees, suppliers and purchasers of goods bearing trade marks – all traders and/or consumers through the portals of brand and corporate identities – are organized by these identities and their reputation, weightless as their trade marks may be, and irrational as such organization may seem. Trade mark laws have facilitated the extension of these identities and the proliferation of their reputation. The courts,[68] however, continue to insist on the source-distinguishing function of trade marks for registration, as intended for Trade Marks Act 1994.[69]

Objects in the mirror are closer than they appear[70]

The law of passing-off appears poised to facilitate further extensions of business and personal reputation. It protects an individual's personality (e.g., recently, of a sports-car racer) from being used in a false appearance of endorsement (in this case, of a sports radio station).[71] The intermediary of trade marks or other trade representation was bypassed to protect the reputation of the individual from certain uses of his personality. The use of a trade or personal mark or representation for endorsement or sponsorship is one example of a long-practised strategy of placing a mark

---

[67] *Elvis Presley Trade Marks* [1999] RPC 567 at 598.

[68] E.g. *Elvis Presley Trade Marks* [1999] RPC 567; *Executrices of the Estate of Diana, Princess of Wales' Application* [2001] ETMR 25.

[69] Secretary of State for Trade and Industry, *White Paper on Reform of Trade Marks Law* 11; H. Norman, 'Trade Mark Licences in the United Kingdom: Time for Bostitch to be Re-evaluated' (1994) 16(4) EIPR 154; a recital to the First Council Directive 89/104/EEC which forms the principal basis for Trade Marks Act 1994: 'Whereas the protection afforded by the registered trade mark, the function of which is in particular to guarantee the trade mark as an indication of origin, . . .'.

[70] The warning on passenger-side (convex) mirrors on motor vehicles in North America.

[71] *Irvine* v *Talksport Ltd* [2003] EWCA Civ. 423, [2003] 2 All ER 881 affirming [2002] 2 All ER 414 on this point.

beyond the mark owner's goods to extend the mark's reputation.[72] Individuals with a reputation may, as a licensing business, endorse or sponsor others' goods which are beyond the known core competence of these individuals. In the cultivation of this reputation, individuals may also bypass the initial intermediary of exchange rationalized in trade mark laws: the underlying trade-marked goods. Reputation and celebrity may be born not of trade-marked goods, but of the status of birth (e.g. from being children of well-known families), of life (e.g. from World Cup media attention on footballers' wives) or of the pursuit of celebrity itself (e.g. from an appearance on a reality television programme). With endorsed and sponsored goods as billboards, the celebrity (not necessarily built on trade) of the endorser or sponsor spreads further. The application of the law of passing-off in this context would appear rational if the law protects reputation, including, though not exclusively, the traditionally cited reputation which accrues from the production of goods demanded by consumers. It was perhaps this reputation which inspired the tradition of individuals venturing in businesses under their own names, and the protection of this reputation which solicited sympathy for trade mark protection. However, it is at times the reputation alone which sparks and fuels consumer demand, not vice versa. The trade mark registry continues to refuse registration of personal names or images where they serve no source-distinguishing function.[73] Where they may serve such a function,[74] again as Professor Lury points out, no prior use of the marks is required to gain registration.[75]

Are trade mark laws shedding their consumer protection mantel? After all, trade mark laws are justified for the three rationales of preventing consumer confusion as to the source or quality of trade-marked goods, promoting fair competition among traders and, as a result, advancing economic efficiency in resource distribution. Or are these oft-cited rationales for trade mark laws the emperor's clothes whose fictitious character is exposed in reflection? This chapter has argued for the latter. The reflection has revealed the *faux* foundation for the consumer protection

---

[72] E.g. F. I. Schechter, *Historical Foundations* 23: 'It would appear that very early in the history of medieval commerce, merchants, as soon as they had arrived at any degree of prominence or substance, were anxious to perpetuate the marks which they had used to designate their products. They – especially the wealthy wool-staplers – signified their recognition of the Divine source of their prosperity by the erection or restoration of churches, and in those churches they or the grateful recipients of their benefactions placed the same marks that they used upon their bales and their goods.'

[73] D. Vaver, 'Does Intellectual Property have Personality?' in R. Zimmerman and N. Whitty (eds.), *Rights of Personality in Scots Law: A Comparative Perspective* (Dundee: University of Dundee Press, 2007 forthcoming) 18–19.

[74] *Linkin Park LLC's Application* [2006] ETMR 74.   [75] Lury, Chapter 9 of this volume, 211.

rationale. Without a secure consumer protection rationale and a consistent application of the consumer confusion requirement in the legal mechanism which also serves as a demarcation of fairness in determining competing traders' interests in a mark, the rationale of promoting fair competition among traders needs to be reconsidered. While a registered trade mark is property in the UK,[76] and while the law of passing-off recognizes property in goodwill,[77] in both cases the property is awarded to and defended for its trader based on a distinctiveness assessed by reference to the relevant consumers' view of the underlying goods.[78] Beyond this distinctiveness, on what basis should the boundary for this 'property' be drawn, and how should this 'property' be apportioned (if at all) and awarded, to achieve what social aim? How should the role of the consumers who have participated in the proliferation and sustenance of this 'property' be taken into account in this award? Without a secure consumer protection rationale which presumes that consumer demand is trained more on the desirability of the goods than the desirability of their marks, the rationale of advancing efficient distribution of economic resources also needs to be reconsidered. Where a mark is desired by and its goods incidental to the consumer, the consumer's economic votes may favour promoting the mark more than producing the goods which fulfil material needs. Without any clear boundaries for trade mark protection that can be established from these rationales, trade mark laws, such as those against taking 'unfair' advantage of the repute of an earlier mark without due cause,[79] facilitate extensions of business personae and the protection of their reputation. This reputation influences businesses and individuals: consumers and trade sectors which develop, produce, distribute or contribute human, material and financial resources for the production and distribution of goods – investors, employers, suppliers and purchasers. Through such influence, this reputation organizes, at least in part, the production and consumption markets.

In the light of Professor Lury's observations, the role of trade mark laws in their commercial contexts can be better appreciated. The need for the rationales for trade mark protection to be reassessed and the boundaries for the protection to be re-rationalized becomes more apparent.

---

[76] Trade Marks Act 1994, ss. 2 and 22.
[77] *A. G. Spalding & Bros.* v *A. W. Gamage Ltd* (1915) 32 RPC 273.
[78] In respect of trade mark registration: *Linde AG's Trade Mark Application* [2003] RPC 45; in respect of the law of passing-off: *A. G. Spalding & Bros.* v *A. W. Gamage Ltd* (1915) 32 RPC 273.
[79] First Council Directive 89/104/EEC, Arts. 4(3), 5(2); Trade Marks Act 1994, ss. 5(3), 10(3).

Part VI

Law and Economics

11   A Law-and-Economics perspective on trade marks

Andrew Griffiths

1   The aims and scope of this chapter

The school of analysis that has come to be known as 'Law-and-Economics' involves the use of economic concepts and reasoning in the analysis of legal rules and institutions.[1] It includes both normative analysis, in which the law is evaluated in terms of its contribution to economic efficiency, and positive analysis of the development of the law and of proposals for reform.[2] Some scholars of Law-and-Economics have argued that common law rules have an underlying economic logic and achieve greater economic efficiency than rules imposed through legislation.[3] This chapter will suggest that trade mark law provides some vindication of this view when the traditional limits on the property rights of trade mark owners, which reflected the common law of passing-off, are compared to the trend towards giving them much broader protection against misappropriation and free-riding.

Trade marks play an important role in the organization of economic activity.[4] They are the means through which undertakings compete with each other.[5] Thus, after registering a sign as a trade mark for designated

---

[1] See generally R. Cooter and T. Ulen, *Law and Economics* (4th edn, London: Pearson Addison Wesley, 2004); N. Duxbury, *Patterns of American Jurisprudence* (paperback edn, Oxford: Clarendon Press, 1997) 301–419; N. Mercuro and S. Medema, *Economics and the Law: From Posner to Postmodernism* (Princeton: Princeton University Press, 1997); and R. Posner, *Economic Analysis of Law* (6th edn, New York: Aspen Publishing, 2002).

[2] See A. Ogus, 'Economics and Law Reform: Thirty Years of Law Commission Endeavour' (1995) 111 LQR 407.

[3] See in particular Posner, *Economic Analysis*. See also the discussion of this view in Mercuro and Medema, *Economics and the Law* 61–6, and in S. Deakin, 'Private Law, Economic Rationality and the Regulatory State' in P. Birks (ed.), *The Classification of Obligations* (Oxford: Clarendon Press, 1997) 284–8.

[4] This chapter will focus on registered trade marks, registered under the Trade Marks Act 1994 ('the 1994 Act') and equivalent legislation elsewhere, unless the context requires otherwise.

[5] The term 'undertaking' is not defined and refers to any kind of firm or unit for conducting business, regardless of its legal nature. It can include a collaborating group of legally separate entities. See *Scandecor Development* v *Scandecor Marketing* [2001] ETMR 800 (HL), [2002] FSR (7) 122 (HL), paras. 51–3.

goods or services (or 'products'),[6] an undertaking can use it to confer a distinctive identity on its products when they are ready for marketing and presentation to consumers. Such a distinctive identity enables consumers to recognize the undertaking's products and distinguish them from others and to make choices on this basis. For many products, such an identity provides the main reference point for consumers and defines the subject matter of their transactions.

The European Community Trade Mark Directive ('the EC Directive'),[7] which is the basis of trade mark law throughout the European Union, suggests in its preamble that an overriding objective of harmonizing this law is to ensure that the trade mark system helps achieve an effective and undistorted system of competition within the single market.[8] And, in ruling on the meaning of various provisions in the EC Directive, the European Court of Justice (or 'ECJ') has noted that 'undertakings must be able to attract and retain customers by the quality of their products or services, which is made possible only by distinctive signs allowing them to be identified'.[9]

To facilitate competition between undertakings and its consequential economic benefits, the law should provide a reliable system whereby undertakings can obtain the exclusive right to use a particular sign as a trade mark for products of the designated kind so that the distinctive identity it confers is under its control. The law should therefore entitle a trade mark's owner to prohibit unauthorized third parties from using the same sign or a confusingly similar sign to confer an identity on products of the designated kind that the owner does not wish to be identified in this way. The exclusivity of the identity that the trade mark signifies and confers means that it can provide a focal point for a reputation and thus for 'goodwill'.[10]

---

[6] This chapter will use the term 'products' to refer to goods or services unless the context requires otherwise.
[7] First Council Directive 89/104/EEC of 21 December 1988 to approximate the laws of the Member States relating to trade marks.
[8] The first recital in the preamble states: 'Whereas the trade mark law at present applicable in the Member States contain disparities which may impede the free movement of goods and the freedom to provide services and may distort competition within the common market; whereas it is therefore necessary, in view of the establishment and functioning of the internal market, to approximate the laws of Member States.'
[9] See *Loendersloot* v *George Ballantine*, Case C-349/95 [1998] ETMR 10, para. 22. See also *SA Cnl-Sucal* v *Hag*, Case C-10/89 ('*Hag II*') [1990] 3 CMLR 571, para. 13; and *Bristol-Myers Squibb* v *Paranova*, Case C-427/93 [1996] ETMR 1, para. 43.
[10] Lord Macnaghten gave what has come to be regarded as a classic description of goodwill, capturing its elusive quality, in his judgment in *Commissioners of Inland Revenue* v *Muller & Co.'s Margarine* [1901] AC 217, 223–4: 'What is goodwill? It is a thing very easy to describe, very difficult to define. It is the benefit and advantage of the good name,

As well as facilitating competition, trade marks have a further economic role as structuring devices in the organization of production and distribution. As is shown elsewhere in this book,[11] a trade mark is said to signify the source or 'origin' of products, but this term has acquired a special meaning in trade mark law. The sale of products under a particular trade mark indicates no more than that the trade mark's owner has authorized its use for this purpose. The owner need not have had any direct role in their production, though it should be in a position to vouch for their condition and quality. And a trade mark does not have to be linked to one specific undertaking or even remain linked to the same undertaking. For this reason, a trade mark has flexibility and versatility as a structuring device, which has provided a basis for the evolution of organizational structures such as franchising and sub-contracting.[12] However, this capacity to constitute a discrete component in a business organization depends on the fact that consumers attach significance to the distinctive identity that a trade mark signifies, such that it can be a source of value to its owner.

This chapter will examine the economic role of trade marks and consider how their legal protection might improve economic efficiency. Section 2 will analyse the nature of trade marks as an intangible resource, namely signs that are supposed to convey a particular piece of information. Section 3 will consider why such signs can become a source of value. Section 4 will then examine the law protecting trade marks and the economic case for extending this protection beyond that necessary to ensure the reliability of the information that they are supposed to convey.

2   Trade marks as signs

Law-and-Economics is concerned with how legal rules can improve and increase social welfare or 'wealth'.[13] Such improvements can be static or dynamic or both. Static improvements relate to the allocation and use of resources and are judged in terms of 'allocative efficiency' or 'productive efficiency'. Allocative efficiency measures social welfare according to how far economic resources are allocated to those who value them most or can

reputation, and connection of a business. It is the attractive force that brings in custom. It is the one thing which distinguishes an old-established business from a new business at its first start. The goodwill of a business must emanate from a particular centre or source.' See S. Lane, 'Goodwill Hunting: Assignments and Licenses in Gross after *Scandecor*' [1999] IPQ 264.
[11] See Jennifer Davis, Chapter 3 of this volume.
[12] See generally N. Klein, *No Logo* (London: Flamingo, 2000).
[13] See Duxbury, *Patterns of American Jurisprudence* 398–406, on the evolution of the concept of 'wealth-maximization' in Law-and-Economics.

derive the greatest return from them,[14] whereas productive efficiency measures a firm's effectiveness as a transformer and producer of economic resources.[15] Dynamic improvements relate to the size and quality of society's overall stock of resources over time and are judged in terms of 'dynamic efficiency'.[16]

One major contribution that Law-and-Economics has made to the analysis of law is to recognize that property rights protecting assets such as land can have a bilateral impact and that this affects their contribution to achieving the most efficient use of resources overall. A right that at first glance simply appears to protect the owner of a resource from a neighbour's 'wrongdoing' can instead be analysed as regulating incompatible or conflicting uses of resources.[17] From this perspective, there is not necessarily a case for entitling one owner to prohibit the other's activities. Instead, the law should be judged according to its effectiveness at achieving the most efficient use of the affected resources. Moreover, there is no economic case for extending the rights of property owners against perceived wrongdoing where the effect is to restrict the activities of others, at least not unless the resulting benefit to the property owner were to exceed the resulting costs for others.[18]

The rights of trade mark owners can be analysed as regulating the use of a resource, namely signs that can be used to indicate the origin of products, though this resource is intangible. The trade mark system enables undertakings to register and thereby appropriate signs from the public domain and to use them to guarantee that products of the designated kind have a specific origin. In order for a trade mark to convey this information, it is necessary for its owner to have the exclusive right to use it (or to

[14] Law-and-Economics makes use of two standards to evaluate the impact of law in terms of allocative efficiency, namely 'Pareto efficiency', which requires at least one party to benefit from a reallocation of resources and no party to lose, and 'Kaldor-Hicks efficiency', which requires the resulting benefits to exceed the resulting costs or losses: see Cooter and Ulen, *Law and Economics* 16–17 and 48, and A. Ogus (1994), *Regulation: Legal Form and Economic Theory* (Oxford: Clarendon Press, 1994) 23–8.
[15] According to this standard, social welfare can be improved through producing a given output with a lower-cost combination of inputs or through producing more output with the same combination of inputs: see Cooter and Ulen, *Law and Economics* 16.
[16] This standard identifies improvement as the introduction of new products or the improvement of existing products through innovation and entrepreneurship: see ibid. 286–7, and S. Deakin and A. Hughes, 'Economic Efficiency and the Proceduralisation of Company Law' [1999] *The Company Financial and Insolvency Law Review* 169, 173–4.
[17] See R. Coase, 'The Problem of Social Cost' (1960) *Journal of Law & Economics* 1. See further Cooter and Ulen, *Law and Economics* 74–114, and G. Calabresi and D. Melamed, 'Property Rules, Liability Rules and Inalienability: One View of the Cathedral' (1972) 85 *Harvard Law Review* 1089.
[18] This would be an improvement in terms of Kaldor-Hicks efficiency, though not Pareto efficiency: see above, footnote 14.

authorize its use) to confer an identity upon products of the relevant kind and, in effect, to determine their origin. This exclusive right is the basis of the legal function of a trade mark and is inherent in the legal meaning of 'origin'.[19] From this perspective, the use of signs as trade marks is competitive or 'rivalrous', at least in relation to the category of products for which it is registered, since allowing two or more undertakings to use the same sign as a trade mark would undermine its capacity to perform this function.

Once a sign has been registered as a trade mark, it acquires a new meaning, namely that products legitimately bearing it (or sold under it) have a particular origin. It also provides a convenient means of identifying or referring to products. From this perspective, a trade mark is like other signs or descriptors that have an accepted or sanctioned meaning. Using a trade mark nominatively, that is as a descriptor or reference point, is non-competitive or 'non-rivalrous' since such use does not affect or undermine its meaning as a trade mark, regardless of who uses it for this purpose or how often it is used.

In order for a trade mark to perform the economic roles that are dependent on its providing a reliable indication of a specific origin, it is necessary for its owner to have the right to prohibit unauthorized third parties from using the same sign or a confusingly similar sign to confer an origin-related identity upon products of the designated kind. What is not clear is how far the owner's rights should extend beyond what is necessary to underpin this function. In this regard, it is not self-evident that a trade mark's owner should have the right to prohibit others from using it nominatively or in other ways that derive from and do not contradict the specific meaning a sign acquires as a trade mark. To consider whether there might be an economic case for extending the property rights of trade mark owners, it is first necessary to consider why trade marks can become valuable assets and how they might be vulnerable to damage and exploitation.

3   The economic role of a trade mark

The importance that undertakings attach to registering and protecting trade marks suggests that they can add substantial value to products. There are a number of possible reasons for this, which are not mutually exclusive and might overlap in a particular case. One reason is that a trade

---

[19] *Major Bros.* v *Franklin* [1908] 1 KB 712; *Primark* v *Lollypop Clothing* [2001] ETMR 334; *Zino Davidoff* v *A & G Imports* and *Levi Strauss* v *Tesco Stores* and *Levi Strauss* v *Costco UK* (Joined Cases C-414/99 to C-416/99) [2002] ETMR 109.

mark somehow reduces the transaction costs that consumers would otherwise incur.[20] A second reason is that a trade mark links a product to something else that consumers might find attractive, such as an image, a set of values or a celebrity, and this linkage increases the product's appeal to consumers. In effect, the trade mark confers an additional intangible attribute upon the product. A third reason is that a trade mark leads consumers to perceive a product in a way that makes them more willing to purchase it or willing to pay more for it. In effect, the trade mark influences the behaviour of consumers. A fourth reason is that a trade mark has an intrinsic aesthetic appeal to consumers. The Law-and-Economics analysis of trade mark law has tended to focus on the first of these reasons and has argued that this provides an economic rationale for the trade mark system.[21] This rationale justifies awarding property rights to trade mark owners to ensure that their trade marks are effective and reliable at guaranteeing and indicating origin, but does not justify extending them any further.

The leading Law-and-Economics analysts of trade mark law have argued that trade marks add value to products because they provide information that can reduce transaction costs and in particular 'search costs'.[22] Like much Law-and-Economics analysis, their work is based on the application of neo-classical economic theory, which rests on a stringent set of assumptions about the behaviour of economic actors and the operation of markets.[23] One way in which the law can improve economic efficiency is through mitigating the effect of transaction costs and other factors that distort the operation of markets.[24] In the neo-classical ideal of markets, parties are assumed to have information concerning the subject matter and other aspects of a potential transaction, and can transact

---

[20] Transaction costs are the various incidental costs that parties face or have to incur in order to enter a transaction. They include 'search costs', 'bargain costs' and 'enforcement costs'. See Ogus, *Regulation* 17, and Cooter and Ulen, *Law and Economics* 91–5.

[21] See W. Landes and R. Posner, 'Trademark Law: An Economic Perspective' (1987) 30 *Journal of Law & Economics* 265; W. Landes and R. Posner, *The Economic Structure of Intellectual Property Law* (Cambridge, Mass.: The Belknap Press of Harvard University Press, 2003); and N. Economides, 'The Economics of Trademarks' (1988) 78 *Trademark Reporter* 523. For a general survey, see G. Ramello, 'What's in a Sign? Trademark Law and Economic Theory' (2006) 20 *Journal of Economic Surveys* 547.

[22] Landes and Posner, 'Trademark Law'; Landes and Posner, *Economic Structure*.

[23] See generally Cooter and Ulen, *Law and Economics* Ch. 2, 'A Review of Microeconomic Theory'. Firms and individuals are, for example, treated as rational or consistent maximizers of their own benefit from transactions and other activity: see Cooter and Ulen, *Law and Economics* 15–17. There are variants within Law-and-Economics which depart from neo-classical economic analysis and relax some of its assumptions: see generally Mercuro and Medema, *Economics and the Law*.

[24] On transaction costs, see above, footnote 20.

accordingly. In practice, however, consumers and other parties often lack perfect information about the condition and quality of many of the products that they wish to buy and cannot acquire this information through inspection or other low-cost means. The law can therefore improve social welfare through combating this form of 'market failure'.

In neo-classical analysis, search costs are the costs of acquiring information about products or of having to incur the risks of uncertainty. They increase the total price that consumers pay for a product and reducing them is equivalent to reducing the product's sales price and a way of achieving a competitive advantage. The rise of the industrial economy increased the problem of search costs for consumers, with goods becoming more complex, and large-scale production increasing the distance between producers and consumers.[25] The scale of search costs depends on a number of variable factors, including the nature and complexity of the product; the characteristics of the relevant consumers; the relative importance to these consumers of 'hidden' attributes (positive and negative), such as quality, on which they lack information; the additional costs of supplying products with (or without) the hidden attributes; and the scale of the costs that might result from a deficient product. Search costs are therefore likely to be much greater when the product is complex, requiring specialist knowledge to examine properly, and where the notion of quality has to encompass such matters as reliability, durability and safety over time.[26]

The impact of search costs can be dynamic as well as static and therefore, through reducing or combating search costs, the law can improve efficiency at both these levels. Consumers might, for example, wish to acquire an improved version of a product, but be unable to distinguish it from an inferior version prior to purchase. Where improvements are costly to supply, producers and suppliers of an improved product would be at a competitive disadvantage in the absence of legal devices to overcome the information problem.[27] Such legal devices therefore encourage innovation, especially if consumers are viewed as highly risk-averse in relation to hidden attributes.[28] Depending on the relevance and effectiveness of alternative or additional legal devices such as consumer protection

---

[25] See M. Wilkins, 'The Neglected Intangible Asset: The Influence of the Trade Mark on the Rise of the Modern Corporation' (1992) 34 *Business History* 66.

[26] See Landes and Posner, 'Trademark Law' 280.

[27] See G. Akerlof, 'The Market for "Lemons": Quality Uncertainty and the Market Mechanism' (1970) 84 *Quarterly Journal of Economics* 488.

[28] On the economic significance of differing attitudes to risk, see Cooter and Ulen, *Law and Economics* 50–3.

248   *Andrew Griffiths*

regulation, consumers might be willing to pay a substantial premium in return for reassurance about the hidden attributes of certain products.

Economic analysts have recognized that a reputation for meeting consumers' expectations is one means of reducing search costs.[29] It brings the interests of the party that enjoys it into much closer alignment with the interests of those who lack information since the beneficiary has an incentive not to damage or lose the reputation. Trade marks enable undertakings to confer a distinctive identity on products that can transcend extensive distribution networks and remain under their exclusive control. This identity, because of its exclusivity, has the capacity to acquire a reputation and to achieve a closer alignment of interest. A legal device of this kind is of particular importance to companies since they have no physical presence or physical characteristics and their very existence is a matter of legal formality. It has been argued for this reason that trade marks were crucial to the evolution of the modern corporation.[30]

A trade mark's capacity for reducing search costs is based on the fact it can be used as both a product identifier and a reference point for acquiring information about products that have the origin it signifies. In some cases, it enables consumers to use their own experience as a source of information.[31] The key factor is the trade mark's capacity to acquire a reputation since its owner has an incentive to maintain or improve this. The owner has this incentive whether it has made the investment that has generated the reputation or has acquired the trade mark from another undertaking.[32] A good reputation can provide reassurance to consumers and reduce the risks and costs of a lack of information about the attributes of a product. Even if the party enjoying the reputation is otherwise

---

[29] See, for example, B. Klein and K. Leffler, 'The Role of Market Forces in Assuring Contractual Performance' (1981) 89 *Journal of Political Economy* 615; and S. Tadelis, 'What's in a Name? Reputation as a Tradeable Asset' (1999) 89 *American Economic Review* 548.
[30] See Wilkins, 'The Neglected Intangible Asset' 66.
[31] On the categorization of products into 'experience' and 'search' and the impact of this on the role of the trade mark, see P. Nelson, 'Information and Consumer Behaviour' (1970) 78 *Journal of Political Economy* 311; and Economides, 'The Economics of Trade Marks' 523.
[32] This rests on an assumption that companies and other firms act in 'their' interest in the same way as individuals, which means that their management and other agents are assumed to act in the best interests of their shareholders or owners. There is an extensive Law-and-Economics literature exploring this assumption and the extent to which agents are in fact likely to diverge from this goal and act in their own interests: see, for example, M. Jensen and W. Meckling, 'Theory of the Firm: Managerial Behaviour, Agency Costs and Capital Structure' (1976) 3 *Journal of Financial Economics* 305, and E. Fama and M. Jensen, 'Agency Problems and Residual Claims' (1983) 26 *Journal of Law and Economics* 327.

unknown to consumers, it still has an interest in not letting the reputation decline. In the Law-and-Economics analysis of trade marks, this alignment of interest has been portrayed as giving them a 'self-enforcing' aspect.[33]

A reputation focussed on a trade mark can replicate some of the effect of having personal knowledge of and trust in a human contracting party. It represents an asset that can be offered as a stake to consumers against the risk of disappointment. Further, a reputation of this kind is something that can be staked in new markets, depending on its strength and value. An undertaking can do this by using a familiar trade mark or one that, through its similarity to a familiar trade mark or its use of a common component, indicates a commercial link to an established reputation of a kind from which consumers can derive reassurance.[34] This can help undertakings to enter new markets where high search costs would otherwise represent a significant entry cost or barrier and provides an explanation for the trend whereby the distinctive identities that trade marks signify have become much broader and corporate in nature rather than being focussed on a specific kind of product.[35]

The Law-and-Economics analysis of trade marks provided an elegant reconciliation of their capacity to command premium prices with the ideal of competitive markets. It aimed to challenge the view of earlier analysts that trade marks distort the operation of the market and enable dominant firms to gain and consolidate excessive market power.[36] These analysts had argued that trade marks, in conjunction with advertising, provide a means of persuading consumers that products, which are essentially the same as lower-priced alternatives, are somehow superior and of charging them excessive prices accordingly.[37] In this earlier

---

[33] Landes and Posner, 'Trademark Law' 270.
[34] The ECJ has recognized this use of a trade mark in its ruling on what can constitute a 'likelihood of confusion' in the context of infringement: *Sabel BV* v *Puma AG and Rudolf Dassles Sport*, Case C-251/95 [1998] ETMR 1.
[35] See C. Lury, *Brands: The Logos of the Global Economy* (Oxford: Routledge, 2004) 28, on how corporate branding has come to eclipse product branding since the 1980s. On marketing practices that involve the use of the same trade mark for a variety of products, see also A. Ehrenberg, N. Barnard and J. Scriven, 'Differentiation or Salience' (1997) 37 *Journal of Advertising Research* 7, and Ramello, 'What's in a Sign?' 547.
[36] See also I. Png and D. Reitman, 'Why are Some Products Branded and Others Not?' (1995) 38 *Journal of Law and Economics* 207.
[37] See, for example, E. Chamberlin, *The Theory of Monopolistic Competition* (Cambridge, Mass.: Harvard University Press, 1933), and R. Brown, 'Advertising and the Public Interest: Legal Protection of Trade Symbols' (1948) 57 *Yale Law Journal* 1165, reprinted in (1999) 108 *Yale Law Journal* 1619. See generally F. Scherer and D. Ross, *Industrial Market Structure and Economic Performance* (Boston: Houghton-Mifflin, 1990) 571–611, and G. Lunney Jr, 'Trademark Monopolies' (1999) 48 *Emory Law Journal* 367, 367–73.

analysis, which reflects the third of the suggested reasons why trade marks can command premium prices, trade marks are not conducive to economic efficiency, but instead distort the effect of price-based competition and give the owners of familiar trade marks unfair market power. In the Law-and-Economics analysis, in contrast, all undertakings should be able to enjoy the benefit of premium prices through generating a good reputation for their trade marks and providing the same quality of reassurance.

The concept of 'search costs' could be stretched to explain substantial premium prices as reflecting a substantial risk of disappointment or the fact that consumers might attach great importance to hidden attributes such as safety, or the willingness of consumers to pay for reassurance on such hard-to-judge attributes as being fashionable or displaying good taste. Even so, it is still hard to accept that a capacity for reducing these provides the sole explanation of the power of all trade marks to attract consumers and command premium market prices. It does not explain, for example, why undertakings are willing to invest substantial time and resources in choosing their trade marks, which implies that some signs have the potential to achieve much greater value than others or to do so more easily.[38] And if a neo-classical assumption, namely that trade marks merely guide consumers towards the transactions that they would make in any event in an ideal world of perfect information, is relaxed and if consumers are treated as indecisive and open to persuasion, then there is room for trade marks to play a more active role in influencing their decision-making.[39]

If it is accepted that the economic role of trade marks goes beyond that of reducing search costs and that their value can far exceed anything explicable in this way, this does not mean that they should be viewed as operating against the public interest and it does not undermine the economic case for their legal protection.[40] However, it does mean that the pressure to extend their legal protection should be treated with caution since it cannot be assumed that it would improve social welfare. Whilst extending legal protection would clearly generate benefits for the owners of trade marks, an economic case for doing so requires account to be taken of the adverse impact on consumers and third parties, including that resulting from any restriction of competition.

[38] See generally S. Carter, 'The Trouble with Trademark' (1990) 99 *Yale Law Journal* 759.
[39] B. Beebe, 'Search and Persuasion in Trademark Law' (2005) 103 *Michigan Law Review* 2020.
[40] See, for example, W. Cornish and J. Phillips, 'The Economic Function of Trade Marks: An Analysis with Special Reference to Developing Countries' (1982) 13 IIC 41. See also Scherer and Ross, *Industrial Market Structure* 577–8.

It does seem to be the case that, for certain kinds of product, consumers attach disproportionate value to superficial differences and that some of the value-adding capacity of trade marks can be due to their contribution to such differentiation.[41] Such differentiation can be achieved through the packaging and presentation of the products, through their design and appearance and through giving them a distinctive image in advertising and other promotional material. A trade mark can contribute to such differentiation through its own distinctiveness as a sign, in which case its value derives, at least in part, from the extent of its difference from the trade marks and other features of rival products.[42] A trade mark's capacity to differentiate products in this way is something that goes beyond its capacity to enable consumers to distinguish products according to their origin.[43] It can give the trade mark a value that is vulnerable to erosion from similar signs that do not necessarily confuse consumers about origin.

The idea that some trade marks gain a selling power because they have a distinctive or even unique impact on the minds of consumers is associated in particular with the work of Frank Schechter.[44] He argued that such trade marks should be protected from signs that reduce or 'dilute' this capacity. In marketing, the power of some trade marks to catch the attention of consumers and attract them to products has been termed 'salience'.[45] It is the product of a number of factors including a trade mark's familiarity to consumers – which should be sustained through publicity and exposure – a high likelihood that consumers will notice and recall the trade mark, and a positive reputation.[46] A positive reputation might be due to the trade mark's triggering of positive associations in the minds of consumers and not necessarily due to having earned a good reputation for the quality and reliability of marked products. A trade mark's salience is therefore vulnerable to signs that can weaken the impact of any of these factors.

[41] For a sceptical depiction of such differentiation or 'gold-plating', see R. Sennett, *The Culture of the New Capitalism* (New Haven, Mass.: Yale University Press, 2006) 142–51. See also the comments of Lewison J concerning the market for mobile phones in *O2 Holdings* v *Hutchison 3G* [2006] EWHC 534, para. 5.
[42] B. Beebe, 'The Semiotic Analysis of Trademark Law' (2004) 51 *U.C.L.A. Law Review* 621.
[43] Beebe, 'Search and Persuasion' 2020; Ramello, 'What's in a Sign?' 547.
[44] F. Schechter, 'The Rational Basis of Trademark Protection' (1927) 40 *Harvard Law Review* 813, 819: 'The mark actually sells the goods. And, self-evidently, the more distinctive the mark, the more effective its selling power.'
[45] Ehrenberg *et al.*, 'Differentiation or Salience' 7. See generally Ramello, 'What's in a Sign?' 547, 556–9.
[46] Ehrenberg *et al.* 'Differentiation or Salience' 7, 9.

252   *Andrew Griffiths*

Whilst it is clear that trade mark owners have an incentive to ensure that their trade marks gain and retain this quality of salience, it is far from clear that the law would improve social welfare through enabling them to do so. It is arguable that the impact of a trade mark's salience on the decision-making of consumers is an example of what psychologists and behavioural economists have termed the 'availability heuristic'.[47] This is based on the view that people tend to simplify complex situations and rely on rules-of-thumb or 'heuristics' in their decision-making.[48] They tend to attach disproportionate weight to things that are 'cognitively available' to them, such as things with which they are familiar or which they can readily call to mind.[49] In the case of consumers seeking and purchasing products on the markets, they can attach disproportionate weight to salient trade marks as identifiers and reference points. This means that salient trade marks can acquire a disproportionate selling power, which is of great value to their owners, but weakens the impact of competition and thus reduces economic efficiency.

It is, however, arguable that the appeal of some salient trade marks to consumers is based on much more than their cognitive availability and that they engage with consumers at the emotional or psychological level. In effect, such a trade mark adds additional emotional or psychological attributes to marked products and represents a form of intangible output based on its reputation. Whilst such a reputation is normally founded upon the nature and quality of the products with which it has been used, it is also something that can be developed through advertising and imagery and can acquire an independent appeal to consumers.

The emotional or psychological appeal of a particular trade mark to consumers can take a variety of forms. It might simply reflect its capacity to persist over time and to provide an identity that can acquire history and tradition.[50] Or consumers might have come to the trade mark as signifying a certain social status so that acquiring marked products becomes a

---

[47] See, for example, D. Kahneman, P. Slovic and A. Tversky (eds.), *Judgment Under Uncertainty: Heuristics and Biases* (Cambridge: Cambridge University Press, 2002); T. Gilovich, D. Griffin and D. Kahneman (eds.), *Heuristics and Biases: The Psychology of Intuitive Judgment* (Cambridge: Cambridge University Press, 2002); and C. Sunstein, *Laws of Fear: Beyond the Precautionary Principle* (Cambridge: Cambridge University Press, 2005).

[48] D. Kahneman and S. Frederick, 'Representativeness Revisited: Attribute Substitution in Intuitive Judgment' in Gilovich *et al.* (eds.), *Heuristics and Biases*.

[49] A. Tversky and D. Kahneman, 'Judgment Under Uncertainty: Heuristics and Biases' in D. Kahneman, P. Slovic and A. Tversky (eds.), *Judgment Under Uncertainty*.

[50] See, for example, C. Hays, *Pop: Truth and Power at the Coca-Cola Company* (London: Arrow, 2005) 8–9: 'Fifty-seven years later, she still recalled the taste of that Coke on that summer day ... From then on, wherever she was, in a corner store or in a restaurant or on a plane, she always asked for Coca-Cola.'

way of achieving this status.[51] Their capacity to do so might depend much
less on the quality and condition of the marked products than on their
presentation and price. Such trade marks can turn products into symbols
of status even if this is not matched with any improvement in quality or
other characteristics. Some neo-classical analysts have argued that this
capacity contributes to social welfare through reducing the cost of satisfying a demand for social status.[52]

Some trade marks signify brands that purport to offer consumers a
means of self-expression or of declaring their allegiance to a set of 'brand
values'.[53] Others offer consumers the prospect of enjoying a sense of
community with a social grouping.[54] In *No Logo*, Naomi Klein depicted
this as the emergence of a new kind of product:

What was changing was the idea of what – in both advertising and branding – was
being sold. The old paradigm had it that all marketing was selling a product. In the
new model, however, the product always takes a back seat to the real product, the
brand, and the selling of the brand acquired an extra component that can only be
described as spiritual.[55]

The role of a trade mark that signifies such a brand goes far beyond that of
indicating the origin on which the brand is based.[56] It provides the means

[51] This reflects Thorstein Veblen's theory of 'conspicuous consumption': T. Veblen, *The
Theory of the Leisure Class: An Economic Study of Institutions* (London: Unwin Books,
1899, reprinted 1994 New York: Dover Publications). See also L. Bagwell and
B. Bernheim, 'Veblen Effects in a Theory of Conspicuous Consumption' (1996)
86 *American Economic Review* 349.
[52] See G. Becker and K. Murphy with E. Glaeser, 'Social Markets and the Escalation of
Quality: The World of Veblen Revisited' in G. Becker and K. Murphy (eds.), *Social
Economics: Market Behaviour in a Social Environment* (Cambridge, Mass.: Belknap Press,
2000) 97–8.
[53] Jerre B. Swann has presented trade marks as helping products to deliver an ascending
hierarchy of benefits, namely 'functional', 'emotional' and 'self-expressive': see
J. B. Swann, 'Trademarks and Marketing' (2001) 91 *Trademark Reporter* 787, 796–7.
See also D. Aaker and E. Joachimsthaler, *Brand Leadership: The Next Level of the
Brand Revolution* (New York: The Free Press, 2000) 48–9.
[54] On how creating 'atmosphere and a sense of community' and appealing to consumers'
'hearts as well as their heads' can enhance the experience of consuming coffee, see the
chapter on 'Howard Schultz and Starbucks Coffee Company' in N. Koehn, *Brand New:
How Entrepreneurs Earned Consumers' Trust from Wedgwood to Dell* (Boston: Harvard
Business School Press, 2001).
[55] N. Klein, *No Logo* 21.
[56] There is no legal definition of the term 'brand' and the precise nature of the relationship
between a trade mark and a brand is a matter of speculation: see, for example, J. Davis,
'The Value of Trade Marks: Economic Assets and Cultural Icons' in Y. Gendreau (ed.),
*Intellectual Property: Bridging Aesthetics and Economics – Propriété intellectuelle: entre l'art et
l'argent* (Montreal: Éditions Themis, 2006). In practice, there is likely to be more than
one trade mark signifying a brand of this kind. An undertaking might, for example, select
a variety of signs and features to present the brand and develop its image, not all of which

254   *Andrew Griffiths*

of linking products with the brand's image and for conferring upon these products the emotional or psychological attributes derived from this image.

Among other things, the evolution of an additional image-linking role for a trade mark can change the economic significance of the trade mark owner's power of control over its use to confer an identity on products. Depending on the relative importance of the link to the image compared to the quality and other tangible attributes of marked products, the evolution of an image-linking role can reduce the importance of the owner's power to exercise practical control over the quality and condition of marked products at the point of marketing. This in turn has implications for the trade mark's role as a structuring device. It can lead to much looser structures for the production and distribution of marked products whereby the owner retains its exclusive right to authorize the use of its trade mark for marketing purposes, but which are otherwise designed to minimize costs and maximize (or, depending on the image, optimize) output. The relative importance of the image can make such arrangements efficient even though they are likely to reduce the owner's practical control over the condition of the marked products. In entering such arrangements, the owner would have to balance the increased return against the risk of damage to the brand's image and reputation.

The economic role of a trade mark can therefore evolve from being a sign that indicates origin and that can acquire a reputation, thereby giving consumers some reassurance about the likely condition and quality of marked products, to being a link to a brand and a symbol of the brand's image, thereby conferring emotional or psychological attributes on marked products.[57] One consequence of this evolution is the use of trade marks in the commercial exploitation of fame and celebrity and the rise of the merchandising industry.[58] Here, there has not been a shift in emphasis so much as a reversal of the traditional evolution of the reputation focussed on a trade mark and this has led to tension in trade mark law.[59]

---

may be registrable as trade marks, and use varying combinations of these on marked products and in advertising and promotional material. See the use of a variety of images of bubbles according to a specified set of guidelines to develop the O2 brand: *O2 Holdings* v *Hutchison 3G* [2006] EWHC 534, [2006] RPC (29) 699 and [2006] EWCA Civ. 1656, [2007] RPC (16) 407.

[57] T. Drescher, 'The Transformation and Evolution of Trademarks: From Signals to Symbols to Myth' (1992) 82 *Trademark Reporter* 301.

[58] On merchandising, see H. Carty, 'Character Merchandising and the Limits of Passing Off' (1993) 13 *Legal Studies* 289; P. Jaffey, 'Merchandising and the Law of Trade Marks' [1998] IPQ 240; and S. L. Dogan and M. A. Lemley, 'The Merchandising Right: Fragile Theory or Fait Accompli?' (2005) 54 *Emory Law Journal* 461.

[59] See, for example, the issues arising in *Elvis Presley TMs* [1999] RPC 567 (CA); and *Arsenal Football Club plc* v *Matthew Reed*, Case C-206/01) [2003] ETMR (19) 227 and [2003] EWCA Civ. 696.

The capacity of trade marks to add value to products for reasons other than a reduction in search costs has implications for their legal protection. Trade marks with this capacity have the potential to achieve greater value because, among other reasons, the exploitation of their value is no longer constrained by any need to exercise practical control over the condition of marked products and to have the necessary expertise to do so. Further, insofar as marked products appeal to consumers for reasons that do not depend on their having a specific origin, they are vulnerable to damage and exploitation from signs that are not likely to mislead or confuse consumers about origin. However, whilst this combination increases the incentive for trade mark owners to seek extended protection, it does not mean that there is an economic case for extending it.

4   The economic role of trade mark law

The trade mark system enables undertakings to select and appropriate signs that they can then use to confer distinctive identities on designated categories of product, which also provides a basis for organizing their production and distribution. Trade mark law supports this system in two broad ways. First, it provides the mechanism whereby undertakings can select and appropriate signs for use as trade marks. Secondly, it protects a trade mark once registered from the unauthorized use of signs which conflict with or undermine its capacity to perform the function of a trade mark or which otherwise damage or exploit its value. It has already been noted in Section 2 that a trade mark can be used both actively to confer an identity (and, in effect, a specific origin) on marked products, and passively or nominatively to refer to marked products according to this identity. The owner of a trade mark needs at the very least the exclusive right to use it actively in relation to the designated products since this is essential to its capacity to guarantee a specific origin.

From an economic perspective, the trade mark system can be analysed and evaluated according to how far it improves economic efficiency, taking account of the resulting costs. As regards the registration of trade marks, the potential value that a sign might acquire as a trade mark has to be weighed against any meaning or other value that it already has as something freely available to all.[60] This provides an economic explanation for trade mark law's restriction of the registration of descriptive terms

---

[60] The standard of 'Pareto efficiency' would require signs appropriated in this way to have no existing value to other traders: see above, footnote 14. The Law-and-Economics analysis of trade mark law assumed that this would be the case: see Landes and Posner, 'Trademark Law'.

and other signs that other traders might legitimately wish to use and which therefore have value in the public domain.[61] It also explains the penalties for not making genuine use of a trade mark after registration.[62]

As regards the protection of registered trade marks, the law has to take account of both the exclusivity that is necessary for a trade mark to perform its essential function of guaranteeing a specific origin and the activities that can interfere with this function or can reduce the resulting benefits. A trade mark's owner does not, for example, necessarily need the right to prohibit third parties from using it in a nominative or origin-describing way to identify or refer to the owner's products.[63] This does not contradict the origin-guaranteeing message that a trade mark is supposed to convey as long as a third party uses it only to identify or refer to goods or services that the owner has marketed (or authorized to be marketed) under the trade mark. Such use might, however, create a misleading impression that there is an economic link of some kind between the third party and the trade mark or reduce the trade mark's value by impairing an image that it has acquired. This could occur, for example, where the third party is using the trade mark to promote and advertise goods that its owner has already marketed under the trade mark, but does so in a way that is not in keeping with a luxurious and prestigious image that the owner has developed for goods bearing the trade mark.[64] In such cases, it is necessary to take account of the overall balance of costs and benefits. For this reason, the potential benefit to trade mark owners of entitling them to prohibit the unauthorized nominative (and other collateral or derivative) use of their marks should be considered in relation to the costs that third parties would incur through being unable to make use of trade marks as a tool of communication. The ECJ has

---

[61] EC Directive, Art. 3; 1994 Act, s. 3. On the restriction on the use of descriptive terms and the like and the policy behind it, see the ECJ's judgments in *OHIM* v *W. M. Wrigley Jr Company*, Case C-191/01 [2003] ETMR 1068, and *Koninklijke KPN Nederland NV* v *Benelux-Merkenbureau*, Case C-363/99 [2004] ETMR 771.

[62] This policy is declared in the 8th recital to the EC Directive and set out in Arts. 10 and 11, and the ground of revocation under Art. 12.1. On the meaning of 'genuine use', see *La Mer Technology* v *Laboratoires Goemar*, Case C-259/02 [2004] ETMR 640; and *Alcon* v *OHIM*, Case C-192/03 [2005] ETMR (69) 860.

[63] In United States trade mark law, the judicial doctrine of 'nominative fair use' permits third parties to make use of a trade mark to identify its owner's products subject to certain conditions: *New Kids on the Block* v *News Am. Publishing* 971 F. 2d 302 (9th Cir. 1992). See further S. H. Klein and N. C. Norton, 'The Role of Trade Mark Use in US Infringement, Unfair Competition and Dilution Proceedings' in J. Phillips and I. Simon (eds.), *Trade Mark Use* (Oxford: Oxford University Press, 2005) 338.

[64] See, for example, *Parfums Christian Dior* v *Evora*, Case C-337/95 [1998] ETMR 26.

recognized that such costs conflict with the overriding goal of achieving a system of undistorted competition in the internal market.[65]

The economic case for awarding property rights to enable trade marks to perform their essential function is analogous to the economic case for awarding property rights over tangible resources such as land.[66] As noted in section 2, Law-and-Economics has drawn attention to the role that property rights can play in regulating conflicting or mutually incompatible uses of neighbouring resources so as to maximize the aggregate benefit from the resources.[67] This requires taking account of the relative value of the conflicting uses as well as the extent of the conflict. Trade mark law concerns an intangible resource, namely signs that can be appropriated and used to signify a specific origin. The law allocates this resource through awarding the owner of a sign registered as a trade mark the exclusive right to use it to guarantee that products of the designated kind have the origin that it signifies and thus to confer an origin-based identity upon such products.

However, the law goes further and protects trade marks once allocated from 'neighbouring resources': it restricts the rights of third parties to register or use the same sign as a trade mark for other kinds of product and to register or use a similar sign as a trade mark for products of the designated kind or of other kinds. Signs in these categories can be viewed as 'neighbouring signs' because they do not coincide with the owner's core exclusive right to use the trade mark to guarantee origin, but have the potential to weaken the trade mark's capacity to provide a clear signification of a specific origin or otherwise to reduce its value. Such signs can, for example, reduce the scope for using the trade mark in relation to different kinds of products and as a means of entering new markets. The range of neighbouring signs liable to affect a trade mark can also be extended to cover the use of the sign registered as a trade mark in relation to the products for which it has been registered, but in circumstances where it is not used to guarantee the origin of the products and thus again falls outside the owner's core exclusive right to use the trade mark for this purpose. Consumers might, for example, perceive such a sign as an embellishment or an incidental feature of a product, as where a card portraying a football player reproduces the logo on his shirt,[68] or a scale-model of a car

---

[65] *Bayerische Motor Werke AG* v *Deenik*, Case C-63/97 [1999] ETMR 339, para. 62; *Gerolsteiner Brunnen* v *Putsch*, Case C-100/02 [2004] ETMR 559, para. 16; *Gillette* v *LA-Laboratories Ltd*, Case C-228/03 [2005] ETMR 825, para. 29.

[66] Landes and Posner, 'Trademark Law' at 266. On the economic analysis of property rights, see Cooter and Ulen, *Law and Economics*, 74–114.

[67] See in particular Coase, 'The Problem of Social Cost' 1.

[68] *Trebor Bassett* v *The Football Association* [1997] FSR 211.

7

258   *Andrew Griffiths*

reproduces the logo on the original.[69] It also includes nominative use of the trade mark for origin-describing rather than origin-guaranteeing purposes since, although this does not necessarily conflict with the owner's core exclusive right, it might, as noted above, impair the trade mark's value.

The challenge for trade mark law is to strike an optimal balance in regulating the use of neighbouring signs. The Law-and-Economics analysis of trade marks has tended to endorse the traditional boundaries set on the property rights of trade mark owners, in particular the requirement that they should be entitled to prohibit only neighbouring signs that are likely to confuse consumers about origin.[70] Signs that have this effect weaken the capacity of trade marks to provide consumers with the means of recognizing and differentiating products according to their origin. Prohibiting such signs therefore secures the benefits attributable to this capacity, such as reducing search costs. The 'likelihood of confusion' requirement also reduces the costs of protection through taking account of the likely characteristics of relevant consumers, such as their expertise, attentiveness to detail and the extent to which they rely upon the trade mark as a source of information or reassurance.[71]

There is, however, a need to fine-tune the traditional boundaries of protection, to take account, for example, of the capacity of some trade marks to facilitate entry into new markets and the fact that trade marks can be used not merely to indicate a specific origin, but to indicate that this origin has a specific economic context in the sense of being linked to another origin or part of a wider economic organization.[72] For guidance on such issues, it is useful to examine more closely the potential costs and benefits of the property rights of trade mark owners.

As a general proposition, the benefits of property rights are likely to decrease and the costs increase once they extend beyond the boundary at which neighbouring signs cease to be likely to confuse consumers about

---

[69] *Adam Opel* v *Autec AG*, Case C-48/05 [2007] ETMR (33) 500.
[70] See, for example, Landes and Posner, 'Trademark Law' 300–9, and Landes and Posner, *Economic Structure* 201–9. These analysts have also presented a limited economic case for extending the protection of trade marks beyond that necessary to secure their capacity to signify and guarantee a specific origin and to include protection against those forms of 'dilution' termed 'blurring' and 'tarnishing'. This case applies where a strong trade mark provides a unique reference point in consumers' minds. A third party's use of the same sign in a different market would, at the least, damage the trade mark's 'communicative value' and increase consumers' 'imagination costs' (and thus their search costs) and might also reduce its appeal through introducing negative or inappropriate associations: 'Trademark Law' 306–9, and *Economic Structure* 206–9.
[71] See, for example, *Picasso* v *OHIM*, Case C-361/04 [2006] ECR I-643. See further J. Davis, 'Locating the Average Consumer: His Judicial Origins, Intellectual Influences and Current Role in European Trade Mark Law' [2005] IPQ 183.
[72] *Sabel* v *Puma*, Case C-251/95 [1998] ETMR 1, para. 16.

origin. Subject to this, the benefits of such legal protection should increase in proportion to the value of the trade mark. The benefits also depend on the degree of a trade mark's distinctiveness since this can render it vulnerable to damage and interference from a wider range of neighbouring signs. Thus, a wider range of similar signs are likely to remind consumers of a trade mark consisting of, for example, an arbitrary or coined word and thus to confuse them or affect or undermine an image that the trade mark has acquired in their minds.

The costs of legal protection depend on whether other traders have legitimate reasons for using neighbouring signs. Protecting a trade mark that makes use of descriptive terms or includes words that other traders might reasonably wish to use is more costly than protecting an unusual one or one consisting of coined or arbitrary words. In any event, there is less likely to be confusion (and less benefit from legal protection) where the similarity between a trade mark and a neighbouring sign is due to their having common components with some alternative significance or meaning to consumers, such as a place name, a descriptive term or a common surname. In *Reed Executive* v *Reed Business Information*,[73] the Court of Appeal considered two marks which included a common surname. Jacob LJ noted that, as with trade marks including a descriptive element, 'small differences may suffice to avoid confusion'.[74] He said that this was 'inherent in the nature of the public perception of trade marks' and was because the average consumer would expect others to use similar marks featuring such elements 'and thus be alert for detail which would differentiate one provider from another'.[75]

The EC Directive has provided that all registered trade marks should enjoy a standard zone of legal protection as well as a core zone of exclusivity, but a neighbouring sign must satisfy two requirements to fall within this zone and infringe a trade mark.[76] First, the sign must be used on goods or services that are similar to those for which the trade mark has been registered, though the ECJ has indicated that similarity in this context covers products that can be used together or are sold in proximate markets.[77] Secondly, the sign must give rise to a 'likelihood

---

[73] *Reed Executive* v *Reed Business Information* [2004] ETMR (56) 731.
[74] [2004] EWCA Civ. 159, para. 84, citing the judgment of Lord Simonds in *Office Cleaning Services* v *Westminster Window and General Cleaning* (1946) 63 RPC 30, 43.
[75] [2004] EWCA Civ. 159, paras. 85–6. Jacob LJ also noted the ECJ's linking of the absence of 'an element descriptive of the goods or services for which it has been registered' with a high level of 'distinctive character' in formulating its global appreciation approach to determining a likelihood of confusion: *Lloyd Schuhfabrik Meyer* v *Klijsen Handel BV*, Case C-342/97 [1999] ETMR 690, paras. 23 and 24.
[76] EC Directive, Art. 5.1(b); 1994 Act, s. 10(2).
[77] *Canon Kabushiki Kaisha* v *MGM* (Case C-39/97) [1999] RPC 117; *Hollywood* v *Souza Cruz* [2002] ETMR 705 (OHIM (3rd Bd App)).

of confusion', with 'confusion' meaning confusion about origin.[78] These two requirements reflect the traditional boundaries of trade mark protection and limit protection to that necessary to ensure that a trade mark can perform its essential function of guaranteeing a specific origin. For most trade marks, they also limit protection in a way that is likely to strike an optimal balance between the resulting costs and benefits. The EC Directive also qualifies legal protection through prescribing various defences and limitations, such as that permitting the use of descriptive terms and the like in accordance with 'honest practices'.[79]

The ECJ has interpreted the standard zone of protection in a way that appears to make it more sensitive to economic factors and ruled that there should be a 'global appreciation' of the trade mark and a neighbouring sign in order to determine infringement.[80] It has indicated that, in this exercise, weight should be given to the overall strength of the trade mark, this being the quality that results from its intrinsic 'distinctive character' as a trade mark or its level of recognition on the market or both of these factors. And the ECJ has indicated that a trade mark's standard protection should expand in proportion to its overall strength, though it based this proposition on an assumption that greater strength would give rise to a greater likelihood of confusion.[81] This assumption is not self-evident and has been disputed on the basis that, in practice, consumers are less likely to be confused where a neighbouring sign is similar to a trade mark that is both highly distinctive and very familiar to them.[82]

---

[78] This includes both 'direct confusion' about origin as such and 'indirect confusion' about the origin's economic context: see *Sabel* v *Puma*, Case C-251/95 [1998] ETMR 1, para. 16.

[79] EC Directive, Arts. 6 and 7; 1994 Act, ss. 11 and 12: see *Gerolsteiner Brunnen* v *Putsch*, Case C-100/02 [2004] ETMR 559; and *Gillette* v *LA-Laboratories Ltd*, Case C-228/03 [2005] ETMR 825.

[80] The ECJ developed this approach in its judgments in *Sabel* v *Puma*, Case C-251/95 [1998] ETMR 1; *Canon Kabushiki Kaisha* v *MGM*, Case C-39/97 [1999] RPC 117; *Lloyd Schuhfabrik Meyer* v *Klijsen Handel BV*, Case C-342/97 [1999] ETMR 690; and *Marca Mode* v *Adidas*, Case C-425/98 [2000] ETMR 723. See A. Griffiths, 'The Impact of the Global Appreciation Approach on the Boundaries of Trade Mark Protection' [2001] IPQ 326.

[81] See *Sabel* v *Puma* [1998] RPC 199, para. 24; *Canon* v *MGM* [1999] RPC 117, para. 18; and *Lloyd Schuhfabrik* [2000] FSR 77, para. 21.

[82] See the assertion of AG Colomer in the *Arsenal FC* case that consumers would be unlikely to confuse the sign COCO-COLO for COCA-COLA: 'By following the route of "likelihood of confusion", well-known trade marks may be left without protection against those using similar indications in order to distinguish identical or similar goods': *Arsenal FC plc* v *Matthew Reed*, Case C-206/01 [2002] ETMR 975, para. 33, fn. 22. And see the reservations that Jacob LJ expressed in *Reed Executive* v *Reed Business Information* [2004] EWCA Civ. 159, [2004] RPC (40) 767, paras. 78 and 83.

Despite the flexibility of the ECJ's global appreciation approach, the standard zone of protection alone is unlikely to be optimal for stronger trade marks for a number of reasons. One is that the limitation to neighbouring signs used for similar or identical kinds of product does not allow account to be taken of the potential that stronger trade marks can have to add value across a range of goods and services and, conversely, to suffer damage from the use of a neighbouring sign in a distant market. Another reason is that the 'likelihood of confusion' requirement has become too crude to strike an optimal balance in this context. As noted above, focussing on the actual perception of consumers could lead to a contraction of the standard zone for strong trade marks with a high level of distinctiveness since relevant consumers might prove to be alert to slight variations in detail between such trade marks and neighbouring signs. Moreover, leading brands tend to be presented to consumers through an array of trade marks, slogans and other features and consumers are likely to perceive these as an overall package.[83] A third party selling counterfeit versions of a familiar brand of product might even seek to argue that an identical sign would not mislead consumers about the origin of its products, though this would violate the owner's core exclusive right to use the sign as a trade mark.

The ECJ has so far glossed over these potential difficulties with applying the 'likelihood of confusion' requirement in relation to stronger trade marks. Its assertion that the standard zone should expand in proportion to a trade mark's strength could be taken to mean that the requirement should be treated as a matter of law rather than fact and that the required likelihood of confusion should be more readily presumed in the case of stronger marks.[84] The ECJ has, however, appeared to rule out this possibility in a later judgment in which it held that the owner of a strong trade mark must prove a genuine and properly substantiated likelihood of confusion to establish infringement under the standard zone and cannot rely on any presumption to that effect.[85]

There are other shortcomings of the EC Directive's specification of the standard zone of protection for stronger trade marks. The 'likelihood of

---

[83] See above, footnote 56.
[84] Such an approach would be consistent with the 'proxy deceptiveness' test that the British courts used for the equivalent ground of protection prior to the implementation of the EC Directive: see P. Jaffey, 'Likelihood of Association' [2002] EIPR 3.
[85] *Marca Mode* v *Adidas*, Case C-425/98 [2000] ETMR 723. The ECJ rejected an argument that a likelihood of confusion should be presumed where there is a likelihood of association between the trade mark and the neighbouring sign and the trade mark has a high level of distinctive character, in particular because of its reputation among consumers: [2000] ETMR 723, 731–2.

confusion' requirement does not allow for the possibility that the capacity of stronger trade marks to add value to products can be vulnerable to damage from neighbouring signs that do not give rise to a likelihood of confusion. Such trade marks can provide prominent or even unique reference points for consumers. This gives them a high communicative value,[86] but also makes them vulnerable to neighbouring signs that provide competing or distracting reference points. And if such a trade mark has also acquired the kind of image that engages with consumers at the emotional or psychological level, it is vulnerable to neighbouring signs that might sully this image by, for example, linking the trade mark in consumers' minds with inappropriate products. Also, where a strong trade mark has acquired market power due to its capacity to differentiate and its salience, it is vulnerable to neighbouring signs that reduce these qualities.

The EC Directive now permits, though it does not require,[87] Member States to provide an additional zone of protection to trade marks 'with a reputation' and this is specified in much more flexible terminology than the standard zone.[88] Its loose terminology provides much better scope for achieving an optimal level of protection, but also gives rise to a danger of over-protection. This 'additional protection' covers any neighbouring sign the use of which 'without due cause takes unfair advantage of, or is detrimental to, the distinctive character or the repute of the trade mark'. The ECJ has yet to provide detailed guidance on its scope,[89] but the references to detriment can be related to the federal law that protects 'famous' trade marks against 'dilution' in the United States.[90] The federal law targets two kinds of damage, namely 'blurring' and 'tarnishing'.[91]

There is a danger of the additional protection amounting to excessive protection if the costs that it imposes on third parties, including consumers, are not taken into account. These costs include the adverse impact on competition where a trade mark has salience and its owner is seeking to

---

[86] See above, footnote 70.

[87] The ECJ has ruled that Member States that provide this additional protection must do so on the terms specified in the EC Directive and in accordance with the ECJ's interpretation of this specification: *Adidas-Salomon AG* v *Fitnessworld Trading Ltd*, Case C-408/01 [2004] ETMR 129.

[88] EC Directive, Art. 5(2); 1994 Act, s. 10(3).

[89] It has, though, relaxed the zone's outer boundaries to give it greater flexibility: *General Motors Corpn* v *Yplon SA*, Case C-375/97 [1999] ETMR 950; *Davidoff* v *Gofkid*, Case C-292/00 [2003] ETMR 534; and *Adidas-Salomon* v *Fitnessworld*, Case C-408/01 [2004] ETMR 129.

[90] The Trade Mark Dilution Revision Act 2006 has extended this protection.

[91] See above, footnote 70. The High Court has made use of this terminology in, for example, *Premier Brands* [2000] FSR 767 and *Intel* v *CPM* [2006] EWHC 1878, [2006] ETMR (90) 1249.

protect one of the factors that give it this quality.[92] There is also a need for caution where the trade mark's owner is seeking to assert a monopoly over all commercial applications of the sign it has registered as a trade mark and to appropriate for itself all the benefit that can be derived from the sign. The EC Directive's specification of the core zone of exclusivity is also problematic in this respect because the ECJ has (so far) proved reluctant to state unequivocally that this zone should be confined to the use of identical signs as trade marks.[93]

In calibrating the scope of additional protection, the presence of the term 'unfair advantage' in its specification could lead to tribunals giving greater weight to a sense of fairness based on the private interests of trade mark owners than to any negative impact on social welfare. Some tribunals have indicated that it is enough to show that a neighbouring sign is 'free-riding' on the familiarity of a strong trade mark or 'reaping without sowing'.[94] It could also lead to the prohibition of certain nominative or other derivative uses of a strong trade mark, for example in comparative advertising, or of the imitation of the imagery of a trade mark to engage with or catch the attention of consumers. This would impose costs not only on other traders, but also on consumers since it would restrict the scope for using a familiar trade mark or its imagery as a general tool of communication.[95]

Where neighbouring signs can exploit the familiarity of a strong trade mark without confusing consumers about origin, the economic case for prohibiting them depends on there being damage of some kind to the trade mark's value-adding capacity that exceeds the benefit that others can derive from this. If this is not the case, prohibiting such neighbouring signs is not likely to improve social welfare unless it can be shown that exclusivity provides a necessary incentive for the production of a valuable intangible resource or can be justified by reference to some other principle or policy objective.

---

[92] See above, footnotes 44–9.
[93] See *Hölterhoff* v *Freiesleben*, Case C-2/00 [2002] ETMR (79) 917; *Arsenal FC* v *Matthew Reed*, Case C-206/01 [2003] ETMR (19) 227; *Anheuser-Busch, Inc.* v *Budejovicky Budvar*, Case C-245/02 [2005] ETMR 286; *Adam Opel* v *Autec*, Case C-48/05 [2007] ETMR (33) 500.
[94] See, for example, the judgment of the Office for Harmonisation in the Internal Market (First Board of Appeal) in *Mango Sport* v *Diknah* [2005] ETMR 25, para. 19. For criticisms of such reasoning, see M. Spence, 'Passing Off and the Misappropriation of Intangibles' (1996) 112 LQR 472; M. Lemley, 'The Modern Lanham Act and the Death of Common Sense' (1999) 108 *Yale Law Journal* 1687; and Lunney Jr, 'Trademark Monopolies' 367.
[95] The ECJ has recognized the significance of these costs in other contexts: see above, footnote 79.

The argument that the trade mark's owner should have a general right to prohibit unauthorized exploitation on the grounds that it amounts to free-riding treats the value-adding capacity of a strong trade mark as a form of intangible output that merits protection on the same basis as the patent and copyright systems. Whilst there might be some basis for treating trade marks that engage with consumers at the emotional or psychological level in this way, it would still entail a fundamentally different rationale for the trade mark system and require a different kind of balancing exercise. The patent and copyright systems award property rights that restrict the use of intangible output that can be exploited non-rivalrously and therefore amount to a form of monopoly. As with a monopoly, they increase market price and reduce social welfare in terms of the use, exploitation and development of the relevant resources. However, the economic case for imposing these costs rests on the view that exclusivity is a necessary incentive to encourage investment in the production of this output.[96] In effect, the benefits in terms of dynamic efficiency should exceed the costs in terms of allocative efficiency and improve social welfare overall.

To treat stronger trade marks as having a similar economic case for protection, it would have to be shown that exclusivity is a necessary incentive for the production of the intangible output that they represent and that encouraging this output would improve social welfare. Further, the beneficial effect of this incentive should outweigh the costs in terms of the adverse impact on competition. In this respect, account should be taken of the incentive that the law gives to trade mark owners in any event through its protection of their marks, including that against blurring and tarnishing, and of the market power that a familiar trade mark can acquire. Given these incentives and given the doubt as to how far the enhanced market power of the strongest trade marks represents an addition to social welfare rather than a distortion of competition, the case for having the further incentive of additional legal protection is yet to be made. In any event, as with the patent and copyright systems, the terms of any further incentive should be fine-tuned to minimize the adverse impact and maximize the overall contribution to social welfare.

---

[96] See, for example, C. Primo Braga, 'Guidance From Economic Theory' and 'The Developing Country Case For and Against Intellectual Property Protection' in W. Siebeck (ed.) *Strengthening Protection of Intellectual Property in Developing Countries* (World Bank Discussion Paper Series No. 112) (Washington, D.C.: World Bank, 1990); Scherer and Ross, *Industrial Market Structure*; and P. Menell, 'Intellectual Property: General Theories' in B. Bouckaert and G. De Geest (eds.), *Encyclopaedia of Law and Economics*, vol. II: *Civil Law and Economics* (Cheltenham: Edward Elgar, 2000) 129.

5   Conclusion

Products are presented to consumers with a great variety of distinctive identities or brands and some of these identities are now constructed through an array of signs, messages and imagery. In some cases the imagery and other trappings of the identity have greater appeal to consumers than the material attributes of the products they identify. Some branded products command very high premium prices on the market for this reason. Further, a complex and shifting network of production arrangements can lie behind an apparently familiar distinctive identity. A trade mark can help to shield such details from consumers and instead present them with an illusion of continuity, consistency or (as the case may be) product differentiation. The trade mark system is the legal institution that has provided the basis for both these developments.

The economic role of a trade mark has been largely based on its capacity to perform its essential function of guaranteeing a specific origin. This enables it to provide a focal point for goodwill and to secure the economic benefits of a reputation, which the Law-and-Economics analysis of trade marks has portrayed in terms of reducing search costs. To ensure that trade marks have and retain the capacity to perform their essential function, the law must give their owners a core zone of exclusivity over their use as trade marks and protect this zone with a right to prohibit the use of neighbouring signs that are likely to mislead or confuse consumers about origin.

However, the substantial value that some trade marks can acquire has led to pressure to extend their legal protection far beyond that necessary to ensure they can perform their essential function. There may be an economic case for some extension and the traditional 'likelihood of confusion' requirement has arguably become too crude to achieve an optimal level of protection for stronger trade marks. The EC Directive has made provision for such trade marks to enjoy additional protection, but has specified this in loose and flexible terminology. The extent of this protection is therefore contestable and there is a danger of trade mark owners achieving excessive protection. Whilst there is an economic case for protecting stronger trade marks from damage to their communicative value through blurring or tarnishing, this does not justify awarding their owners a general right to prohibit any activity that can be viewed as taking advantage of the familiarity of such trade marks and, in effect, free-riding upon them.

The danger of over-protection arises in part from treating stronger trade marks as a form of intangible output, equivalent to the subject matter of the patent and copyright systems, and as meriting broad protection against imitation and free-riding. Whilst this is a superficially attractive line of reasoning, it fails to take account of the costs that such a broad right would entail and the need to justify these costs as necessary to encourage the production of a worthwhile resource. It also fails to acknowledge the intricate balance that other forms of intellectual property right strike to minimize the adverse impact of the incentive.

The economic rationale of the property rights of trade mark owners within their traditional boundaries is different from that of the other forms of intellectual property right. It is analogous to the case for awarding property rights over tangible resources. Exclusive property rights ensure that undertakings can appropriate signs and give them a new meaning as trade marks. This generates the various benefits of having an effective and reliable means of guaranteeing that products have a specific origin and of identifying and differentiating products according to their origin. There is no economic case for extending legal protection beyond that necessary to ensure their effectiveness and reliability as trade marks unless the resulting benefits would outweigh the costs. The task for trade mark law is to define new boundaries for the legal protection of stronger trade marks that take these costs into account whilst avoiding a false analogy with other forms of intellectual property right.

12 The economic rationale of trade marks: an economist's critique

Jonathan Aldred

Introduction

I found Andrew Griffiths' chapter a fascinating read. As an economist previously unfamiliar with the foundations of trade mark law, I was surprised to learn of the dominant influence of 'Law-and-Economics'. One reason for my surprise is that Law-and-Economics rests on a very particular approach to economics, one arguably not shared by the majority of economists. Law-and-Economics rests on what might be loosely termed 'Chicago economics', which overlaps heavily, but does not coincide, with orthodox neo-classical economics. Thus Griffiths' tendency throughout to refer to the foundations of Law-and-Economics as 'neo-classical' economics is rather misleading. This is not the place to describe the distinctive features of Chicago economics in detail; I offer one here as an illustration. Chicago economics, and so Law-and-Economics, assumes that individuals are self-interested, in a narrow sense: individuals always maximize their own personal material benefit. Law-and-Economics, then, is the world of that caricature, *homo economicus*. I will return to exactly why it is a caricature later. In contrast, while neo-classical economics is well known for positing 'utility maximizing' agents, utility is defined in entirely formal terms as the numerical representation of individual preferences. Hence 'utility maximization' becomes merely 'maximization of preference satisfaction', or, more prosaically, 'doing what you want to do'. And if your preferences are best described as 'self-sacrificing' rather than 'self-interested', then so be it: 'The postulate that an agent is characterised by preferences rules out neither the saint nor Genghis Khan.'[1]

Griffiths seems to use Law-and-Economics both to explain, in a positive fashion, why trade mark law has developed in its present form, and also to justify, as a normative analysis, why trade marks are good for society. In their seminal paper, Landes and Posner state on the first

---

[1] F. Hahn and M. Hollis, *Philosophy and Economic Theory* (Oxford: Oxford University Press, 1979) 4.

268   *Jonathan Aldred*

page that 'This is an essay in positive rather than normative 'law and economics'. We use economics to try to explain the structure of trademark law rather than to change that law. Our overall conclusion is that trademark law, like tort law in general ... can best be explained on the hypothesis that the law is trying to promote economic efficiency.'[2] However, I find a strong normative purpose in Landes and Posner's analysis, even if they are not trying to change the law: by explaining the law in terms of economic efficiency, they justify it. But regardless of whether the appropriate label is 'positive' or 'normative', I take Griffiths' principal concern to be with the justification of trade mark law, and that is my focus in what follows.

I shall have nothing more to say about why trade mark law has developed as it has, save for the remark that, *if* the *homo economicus* worldview is granted, then it clears the way for a different positive economic analysis of trade marks, one not mentioned by Griffiths, although arguably closer to the understanding of most observers of the historical evolution of trade mark law. That analysis is rooted in public choice theory, the branch of economics which supposes that the development of political and legal institutions can best be understood as the outcome of competition among vested interests. In short, public choice theorists would look to the influence of powerful firms, who, through lobbying, campaign contributions and so forth, seek to persuade legislators to enact laws which will serve the firms' interests. Trade mark law seems a prima facie example worthy of investigation in this light.

I turn now to the normative justification of trade marks offered by Law-and-Economics.

Justifying trade mark protection

According to Griffiths, Law-and-Economics shows that trade marks bring two benefits to society: they convey information about the product, and they protect some kind of intangible output associated with the product but separate from it, and of value in itself.

Trade marks as information

The idea that trade marks convey useful information is the more developed argument, originating in Law-and-Economics with the work of Landes and Posner. They focus on the 'search costs' which consumers

---

[2] W. Landes, and R. Posner, 'Trademark Law: An Economic Perspective' (1987) 30 *Journal of Law and Economics* 265.

face when trying to decide which product to buy, if they have imperfect information about it. Trade marks are argued to reduce these search costs by conveying additional valuable information about the products which bear them. But what exactly is this valuable information? Classically, trade marks indicate trade origin. The European Court of Justice (ECJ) has stated that a trade mark is a 'guarantee of origin'. This is widely interpreted as a guarantee that the product originates from a process of production and distribution which is 'under the aegis of', or 'authorized by', the firm which controls the trade mark. In some sense the firm 'assumes responsibility' for the product. As an economist, I shall not attempt to analyse the richness of meaning captured by generations of legal interpretation. Instead, I persist in asking: What information is conveyed? What precisely is guaranteed to the consumer by a guarantee of origin? There is no guarantee regarding the product's function or fitness for purpose, nor that it has been made in a particular way or at a particular location. The firm 'authorizes' the product, but this conveys little information because authorization decisions, passive or active, are made by people, and the personnel of the firm may change rapidly. The 'responsibility' borne by the firm does not seem one which involves any kind of obligation, and, conversely, confers no rights on the consumer. To a cynical economist, it seems that the only thing *guaranteed* to the consumer is that the trade mark owner will take a share of the profits on the sale of the product. My central concern here is that there appears to be a trade-off between how much information is conveyed by the trade origin, and the degree to which 'trade origin' is a portable legal device carried from one set of production, distribution and after-sales arrangements to another. The commercial flexibility embodied in trade marks, so valuable to firms, limits the information that they can convey.

There is of course an obvious response to these worries. It is that a firm controlling a trade mark has a stronger incentive to maintain a good reputation, or goodwill. Assuming that products bearing a trade mark are more easily recognizable and memorable, consumer experience with such products is more likely to affect future sales. Since it is portable across diverse production arrangements, the trade mark helps a firm maintain a continuous identity, essential to building a reputation over time. Consumers will reward firms with a good reputation with repeat purchases, and punish those with a bad reputation by avoiding them. Griffiths cites Landes and Posner describing this incentive as the 'self-enforcing' aspect of trade marks.[3] The term 'self-enforcing' comes from

---

[3] A. Griffiths, Chapter 11 of this volume, 249.

game theory, and all reputation models in economics are ultimately built on game-theoretic analysis. Unfortunately, game-theoretic models are infamous for multiple equilibria. One (Nash) equilibrium may indeed be the state where the firm has an incentive to continue producing a high-quality product, in order to maintain its reputation, and the consumer has an incentive to continue buying it, even at a higher price, because quality can be relied upon. However, the state where the firm sells a mediocre product because it cannot command a high price, and consumers will not pay more because they know it is mediocre, but nevertheless buy it because it is 'good value', may also be an equilibrium outcome of the game. The reputation model alone does not tell us which equilibrium will occur. Both are 'self-enforcing'. Trade marks cease to convey useful information in this context because consumers do not know 'which equilibrium is being played'. In other words, a consumer does not know what information the trade mark conveys; in particular, a trade mark previously associated with high quality may no longer indicate that, because the firm is now playing the mediocre / 'good value' strategy. This seems especially plausible given that the same trade mark may mask major changes in management or production arrangements which trigger a change in strategy. Or a firm may switch to a different equilibrium strategy simply because it calculates that the short-run boost to profits from reducing product quality and hence cost (combined with high sales which reflect its good reputation built up previously) is large enough to outweigh the long-run deterioration in reputation and sales once consumers discover that product quality has declined. My discussion here is illustrative: the general point is not that trade marks fail to guarantee high quality, but that they do not ensure *consistency* of quality.[4]

To put the point in a legal context, Lord Nicholls refers to 'the proprietor of a trade mark having an economic interest in maintaining the value of his mark. It is normally contrary to a proprietor's self-interest to allow the quality of goods sold under his banner to decline.'[5] But the proprietor's self-interest is much more complex, because there is a trade-off between the cost savings from producing a lower-quality product with reduced marketing expenditure, set against the damage to reputation. It is more accurate to describe the firm's self-interest as involving building a good reputation at least cost. Often the best way of achieving this combination is through sophisticated marketing, rather than making

---

[4] I am grateful to Jane Ginsburg for advising that a producer who allows the quality of its product to slide is unlikely to be divested of its mark.

[5] [2001] ETMR 800 at para. 19, referring to the judgment of Laddie J in *Glaxo Group* v *Dowelhurst* [2000] FSR 529 at 540–1. (Cited in an earlier draft of Griffiths' chapter.)

high-quality products. Consumers come to *believe* the trade mark signals high quality, and may continue to do so even after purchase if the quality defects are hidden or debatable. As the central device in a marketing strategy, the trade-marked sign may be used by firms to mislead consumers rather than convey useful information, reputation arguments notwithstanding.

The argument for trade marks as useful information would be bolstered by supporting empirical evidence. If trade-marked signs provide an *aide-mémoire* for the brand, an opportunity to be remembered, then perhaps their holders take the opportunity to build a good reputation. Yet anecdotally, it does not seem that trade-marked, 'branded' goods are superior to their generic equivalents, whether in terms of quality, performance or reliability. This is hardly surprising, since, as noted above, the trade mark is entirely separate from the product bearing it and signals no particular mode of manufacture or person responsible. The separation is further illustrated by practices such as parallel importation. Two pairs of jeans may be identical, manufactured on the same day in the same factory, but one is allowed to bear the trade mark and the other is not, because the proprietor of the trade mark has not authorized their import.

From the Law-and-Economics perspective, there *is* evidence that trade-marked goods are superior, or at least 'reassuring', namely the willingness of consumers to pay more for them. This is probably the key claim in the Law-and-Economics rationale for trade marks, so I will postpone assessing it until the other putative explanation of higher consumer willingness-to-pay has been introduced – the argument that trade marks reflect the presence of a valuable intangible output in addition to the product itself.

I turn now to the supply side of the search costs argument. Landes and Posner make two standard assumptions: firms are profit maximizers, and the market structure is perfectly competitive. Griffiths mentions the first assumption, although it is worth elaborating on its importance for reputation arguments.[6] Leaving aside the problems raised already, firms only have an incentive to maintain a good reputation if the decision-maker within the firm is concerned about future profits. I have already suggested that a firm may sacrifice its long-run reputation for the sake of very high profits in the short run, and this possibility becomes much more likely if the firm's decision-maker is not a long-run profit maximizer. This is plausible if the firm's decision-maker is a manager acting to serve his own interests rather than those of shareholders. Performance-related pay

---

[6] Griffiths, Chapter 11 of this volume, 248, note 32.

and similar devices may help to align their interests in the short run, but are less successful in the long run, not least because by then the manager may have departed.

Following Landes and Posner, I understand that the Law-and-Economics of trade marks has always assumed the firm operates in a perfectly competitive market. I find this a wildly implausible assumption, but it raises such large issues that I can only sketch some of the reasons here. First, and most important, firms have a strong incentive to use the signs protected by trade marks to differentiate their product from others whenever they can. Product differentiation gives firms a degree of monopolistic power, allowing them to earn higher profits. The view that trade marks facilitate product differentiation and thus market power, higher profits and welfare losses has been a strand running through the trade mark literature since at least the beginning of the twentieth century, and continues today. Griffiths mentions this view, and offers no reason to reject it.[7]

Second, even if firms do not actively attempt product differentiation, imperfect competition emerges in another way from the Landes and Posner model. The information, the reassurance about product quality that trade marks provide, creates inertia amongst consumers. They stick with what they know. This gives the firm owning the trade mark a degree of market power, because it creates a barrier to entry for new firms entering the industry.

Third, the brands protected by trade marks may give rise to increasing returns to scale: there is an approximately fixed cost in establishing the brand, but the returns to the firm increase the more products are sold bearing the brand. Increasing returns to scale undermine the two fundamental theorems of welfare economics, on which much of Law-and-Economics is built. Increasing returns to scale are ruled out, by assumption, in the second theorem; and they make perfectly competitive markets virtually impossible, thus violating a key assumption of the first theorem.[8] Thus the theoretical arguments for assuming that market equilibria are efficient (the first theorem), and that policies concerned with efficiency can be separated from those concerned with distribution

---

[7] Ibid. 251.

[8] Intuitively, if there are increasing returns to scale, small firms will be unable to compete with larger ones, because they face higher unit costs. The tendency will be towards a few large firms, not the very large number of very small firms required by perfect competition. The link here can be demonstrated formally. For an introduction to some of these complex issues, although still not easy reading, see J. Stiglitz, *Whither Socialism?* (Cambridge, Mass.: MIT Press, 1994), where he introduces some of his Nobel Prize-winning work in this field.

(the second theorem), vanish altogether. The broader lesson is that trade marks are both a symptom of imperfect competition and a means for sustaining it; against this background, models based on perfect competition are irrelevant.[9]

Trade marks as protectors of intangible output

The other justification for trade marks suggested by Griffiths is that they protect some kind of intangible output associated with the product but separate from it, and of value in itself. The intangible output might take the form of a meaning, identity or status conferred on the buyer, and valued by the buyer, although wholly independent of the functional attributes of the product. So cars, trainers and perfume are bought not just for their function, but because they attempt to suggest the buyer is wealthy, athletic or sexually alluring.

This second role of trade marks is clearly important, and Griffiths suggests in various places that it is likely to become even more so. But if it is to justify supporting or extending trade mark protection, then it must be shown that these intangible outputs benefit society. Again, the willingness-to-pay (WTP) test seems pertinent. A consumer is willing to pay more for products which embody, or are associated with, certain meanings, identities or status, because such products give him an additional benefit, or so the argument runs. It requires two steps to succeed. First, in forming their preferences, individuals must pursue their own benefit, and second, in seeking to fulfil their preferences, individuals must not make mistakes in their choices, their expressions of willingness-to-pay. Rather than defend these claims, the Law-and-Economics approach discussed by Griffiths effectively assumes them away.

Regarding the first claim, Chicago economists adhere unwaveringly to the doctrine *de gustibus non est disputandum*.[10] Preferences are accepted at face value, no matter what their content or origin. On this account, it is a conceptual impossibility to argue that some preferences are mistaken or may make the individual worse off: preferences *define* what makes the individual better off. Regarding the second claim, it is held to be equally impossible to dispute observed choices as running counter to true preferences, at least in all practical cases, since observed choices provide the only reliable information about preferences: they 'reveal' preferences. In

---

[9] Again, see Stiglitz for a broader discussion showing that 'there are no general theorems ensuring the efficiency of market economies': ibid. 65.
[10] G. Stigler and G. Becker, 'De Gustibus Non Est Disputandum' (1977) 67 *American Economic Review* 76.

sum, observed choices define preferences and preferences define what makes the individual better off. This methodological position appears to be embraced by Griffiths, at least implicitly, because he refers uncritically to an argument of Chicago economists Becker, Murphy and Gleaser: '[T]rade marks can turn products into symbols of status even if this is not matched with any improvement in quality or other characteristics. Some neo-classical analysts have argued that this capacity contributes to social welfare through reducing the cost of satisfying a demand for social status.'[11]

The idea here appears to be that if the consumer is willing to pay more for a trade-marked product, then it must make him better off, even if he has only come to desire it because the firm's marketing strategy has successfully associated status attributes with the product. This process of stimulating new wants (for particular status attributes, etc.) and then satisfying them is held to be 'efficient' insofar as the same benefit to consumers can be secured at lower cost through marketing expenditure rather than improving the products themselves. This argument faces several objections. To begin with, products which confer status attributes on their owner tend to impose negative externalities on others. Although Ann feels better off because of her higher status derived from owning or consuming certain trade-marked products, Bill may feel worse off, because his status has fallen due to *not* owning them. Social welfare may not be increased by trade marks which facilitate status benefits because status is relative, and one person's gain is another's loss.

The second objection is more general and goes to the heart of the problem with any WTP test of benefit. The WTP test ignores a vast body of scientific evidence concerning how we choose, and what makes us better off. For example, 'stimulating new wants and then satisfying them' is not a good recipe for improving social welfare, as we have always known intuitively, because human happiness lies in narrowing the gap between what we have and what we want, at least that part of happiness concerned with material things. This intuition has been confirmed by recent research on happiness, suggesting, for example, that most television advertising makes people dissatisfied with their material circumstances, and therefore less happy.[12] An even more influential research development has been the growth of behavioural economics, which seeks

---

[11] Griffiths, Chapter 11 of this volume, 253, referring to G. Becker and K. Murphy with E. Glaeser, 'Social Markets and the Escalation of Quality: The World of Veblen Revisited' in G. Becker and K. Murphy (eds.), *Social Economics: Market Behaviour in a Social Environment* (Cambridge, Mass.: Belknap Press, 2000) 97–8.

[12] A recent study is L. Bruni and L. Stanca, 'Income Aspirations, Television and Happiness: Evidence from the World Values Survey' (2006) 59 *Kyklos* 209.

to supplant or supplement the rational choice account of neo-classical economics with realistic psychological models of choice. Behavioural economics addresses psychological phenomena such as availability bias, misprediction of future satisfaction, and self-control problems, all of which are supported by compelling empirical evidence but hard to reconcile with standard rational choice theory. Some examples must suffice here to suggest the impact of behavioural economics and happiness research taken together.

According to one history of American advertising, its most important development occurred in the 1930s.[13] Cigarette manufacturers discovered that smokers could not distinguish various cigarette brands on the basis of taste or smell alone. So manufacturers either had to change their product to make it truly distinctive, or make consumers *believe* it was distinctive, a generally easier and less costly strategy. Behind the argument mentioned above, that trade marks facilitate this less costly, and hence more efficient, second strategy, lurks a vision of sovereign consumers who are never deceived by marketing, and self-consciously buy certain brands of cigarette because of their association with glamorous living. But behavioural economics suggests we are easily led.

'Availability bias' concerns how readily some piece of information can be brought to mind – how available it is – and depends on how vivid, striking or distinctive the information is. More weight is attached to information merely because it is more available. Advertisers of SUVs can rest assured that one dramatic advert, showing a vehicle surviving a high-impact crash largely unscathed, will have more influence than well-publicized scientific research suggesting that SUVs are no safer for their occupants. Even if consumers know that the advert is unrepresentative, or downright manipulative, it still seems to exert its subconscious influence on choice. Brand recognition also relies on availability bias. Branding ensures an otherwise identical product becomes more familiar, and so more available to be brought to mind. This familiarity alone has been shown to breed approval of the product, again subconsciously. In one study, subjects were played different snippets of music, different numbers of times. On average, they preferred the snippets that were played more frequently, although their conscious verbal explanation of their preferences made no reference to frequency.[14] Griffiths discusses availability bias, but downplays its importance to the intangible output rationale for trade marks, arguing that availability bias is a 'cognitive' phenomenon,

---

[13] J. Twitchell, 'Lead us into Temptation: The Triumph of American Materialism' (New York: Columbia University Press, 1999).

[14] B. Schwartz, *The Paradox of Choice* (New York: Harper Collins, 2004) 54.

while in contrast 'the appeal of some salient trade marks to consumers is based on much more than their cognitive availability and they engage with consumers at the emotional or psychological level'.[15] For several reasons which must be confined to a footnote, I am unpersuaded by this argument.[16]

In any case, even without the distractions of availability or advertising, predictions concerning the satisfaction from future experiences are unreliable, so consumers fail to choose the best option.[17] In particular, predictions are biased by the consumer's current emotional state. Psychological evidence confirms the danger of buying more food than intended when shopping on an empty stomach.[18] Similarly, catalogue shoppers ordering by telephone seem overly influenced by the current weather: warm clothes ordered on cold days are more likely to be returned later.[19] And many people join gyms and health clubs which they subsequently barely use, because at the time of joining they focus on the health benefits, rather than how they will feel in the future when visiting the gym.[20]

Consumers may also fail to choose what will maximize their welfare because they lack the self-control at the heart of consumer sovereignty. Self-control problems are ubiquitous, and putative cases such as cigarette smoking, obesity and TV viewing have been analysed by behavioural economists, with testable implications.[21] For example, since they regard smoking as a self-control problem, behavioural economists predict that a cigarette price increase can lead to a rise in smokers' welfare. In contrast, Chicago economics unsurprisingly offers a model of 'rational addiction', implying that the welfare of smokers falls as cigarettes become more

---

[15] Griffiths, Chapter 11 of this volume, 253.

[16] I am not a psychologist, but understand availability bias to be broader than Griffiths' 'availability heuristic', not limited to dealing with complex decision-making situations where a simplifying 'heuristic' is required, and therefore potentially crossing into the 'emotional' realm. Besides, Griffiths offers no evidence that trade marks engage with consumers primarily at an emotional rather than cognitive level.

[17] See D. Kahneman and R. Thaler, 'Utility Maximisation and Experienced Utility' (2006) 20 *Journal of Economic Perspectives* 221, and G. Loewenstein, and D. Schkade, 'Wouldn't it be Nice? Predicting Future Feelings' in D. Kahneman, E. Diener and N. Schwarz (eds.), *Well-Being: The Foundations of Hedonic Psychology* (New York: Russell Sage, 1999).

[18] R. Nisbett and D. Kanouse, 'Obesity, Hunger, and Supermarket Shopping Behavior' (1968) 3 *Proceedings of the Annual Convention of the American Psychological Association* 683.

[19] Unpublished research cited in Kahneman and Thaler, 'Utility Maximisation' 224.

[20] S. DellaVigna and U. Malmendier, 'Paying Not to Go to the Gym' (2006) 96 *American Economic Review* 694.

[21] A. Offer, *The Challenge of Affluence* (Oxford: Oxford University Press, 2006), provides a rich historical survey.

expensive.[22] An opportunity to test these rival predictions arose in Canada, when tobacco taxes were increased in some provinces but not others. Happiness surveys across these provinces gave firm support to the self-control-based explanation.[23]

To sum up, just because a consumer is willing to pay (more) for a product, this does not imply the consumer obtains (more) benefit from it. Consumer preferences are easily manipulated by the marketing which trade marks facilitate; even if we pursue our true preferences unhindered, phenomena such as self-control problems and misprediction of future satisfaction suggest we may struggle to make the welfare-maximizing choice.

Behavioural economics has largely entered mainstream economic thought, as evidenced by the Nobel Prize in Economics recently awarded to one of its pioneers, Daniel Kahneman. Happiness research looks set to follow it shortly, because, after generations of scepticism, economists are increasingly persuaded that 'happiness', or some form of subjective well-being, can be meaningfully measured.[24] But whatever the merits of happiness research and behavioural economics, I believe that a better understanding of the influence of trade marks on consumers will be found in psychology, sociology and anthropology, rather than through the *homo economicus* worldview underpinning Law-and-Economics. Finally, even if we ignore happiness and behavioural economics, the methodological position of Chicago economics is hard to defend. A theoretical framework is needed in which it is possible to ask key questions without them being ruled out as conceptually incoherent, questions like 'Although the consumer is willing to pay more for it, does the trade-marked product offer any extra benefit?' and 'Was the consumer misled into choosing the product?' We may decide after reviewing the psychological evidence that the WTP test remains in many cases the best indicator of consumer benefit, but Law-and-Economics threatens to prevent that debate from even commencing.

---

[22] G. Becker and K. Murphy, 'A Theory of Rational Addiction' (1988) 96 *Journal of Political Economy* 675.

[23] A. Stutzer and B. Frey, 'What Happiness Research can Tell us about Self-Control Problems and Utility Misprediction' in B. Frey and A. Stutzer (eds.), *Economics and Psychology: A Promising New Cross-disciplinary Field* (Cambridge, Mass.: MIT Press, 2007).

[24] The most persuasive evidence is arguably the robust correlation between self-reported happiness (as measured in surveys) and objective measurements concerning particular patterns of brain activity. See, for instance, R. Layard, *Happiness: Lessons from a New Science* (London: Penguin, 2005), and C. Camerer, G. Loewenstein and D. Prelec, 'Neuroeconomics: How Neuroscience can Inform Economics' (2005) 43 *Journal of Economic Literature* 9.

278   *Jonathan Aldred*

The costs and benefits of trade marks

I have reviewed the two arguments discussed by Griffiths suggesting that trade marks provide social benefits. Griffiths rightly emphasizes that these arguments are at best incomplete: once the goal of social welfare maximization is assumed, a broader assessment of both the costs and benefits of trade mark law is required. This is an ambitious project which Griffiths introduces in section 4, but I have a number of worries about the way he frames the problem. First, it is unclear to me whether the two rationales for trade marks are simultaneously applicable. As already noted, the search costs rationale relies on perfect competition, while the intangible output rationale implies that products will be highly differentiated, this differentiation being essential for their ability to support distinctive meanings, identities or status attributes. But product differentiation and perfect competition do not mix.[25]

Second, Griffiths acknowledges that the costs of granting trade mark protection may fall on consumers as well as other traders, but I do not see how these costs can be properly analysed without acknowledging that consumers can be manipulated and misled – in other words, without dropping the sovereign consumer assumption that is implicit in Griffiths' repeated references to the 'value' of the intangible output.

Third, Griffiths misses some obvious but intractable difficulties with attempting any kind of cost–benefit analysis. When discussing the argument that 'the value-adding capacity of a strong trade mark as a form of intangible output merits protection on the same basis as the patent and copyright systems', Griffiths rightly notes that, for the analogy with patents and copyrights to make sense, the granting of trade mark protection must be 'a necessary incentive for the production of the intangible output'.[26] But he ignores the problem that, unlike copyrighted books and patented inventions, intangible outputs such as brand identities are hardly ever capable of independent existence. Thus they have no separate price in markets, on which a cost–benefit valuation could be based. (It would be interesting to see how much consumers might be willing to pay for a stick-on Nike 'Swoosh' that could be applied to unbranded clothing, but fraught with practical difficulties.)

Fourth, while Griffiths acknowledges that extending current patterns of trade mark protection might lead to overprotection, he seems curiously concerned to avoid *reducing* existing levels of protection. For instance, he

---

[25] A recent discussion which notes this tension is G. Ramello, 'What's in a Sign? Trademark Law and Economic Theory' (2006) 26 *Journal of Economic Surveys* 556.
[26] Griffiths, Chapter 11 of this volume 27.

objects to the 'likelihood of confusion' requirement on the grounds that 'focusing on the actual perception of consumers could lead to a contraction of the standard zone for strong trade marks', but does not explain why that would be an undesirable development in the law.[27] Of course, a full cost–benefit analysis of trade mark law is just as likely, a priori, to recommend reducing the scope of trade mark protection as expanding it. A suggestive example must suffice here. The economic analysis of trade mark infringement usually emphasizes the welfare losses from consumers bring misled, and ultimately the quality of all goods in the market deteriorating, because the original trade mark owner cannot afford to charge a premium following the loss of credibility of the sign. But if the counterfeiting production takes place abroad, economic models have suggested that the overall effect of trade mark infringement can be welfare-*enhancing*.[28]

There are also more fundamental problems with the calculus of cost–benefit analysis. I have alluded loosely to 'welfare' and 'social benefit' as its units of measurement. How does Law-and-Economics define these units? Griffiths is uninformative: 'Law-and-Economics is concerned with how legal rules can improve and increase social welfare or 'wealth'. . . . Allocative efficiency measures social welfare according to how far economic resources are allocated to those who value them most or who can derive the greatest return from them.'[29]

This is as close as Griffiths comes to defining social welfare. It suggests that social welfare is measured by actual or hypothetical willingness to pay, so that social welfare is maximized when resources are allocated to those willing to pay the most for them. There are several problems with this approach. To begin with, as already noted, 'utility maximization' for most economists means nothing more than 'doing what you want to do'. They prefer to keep economics neutral between different views about what will make a person's life go better, that is, increase that person's welfare. So they reject a definition of welfare which equates it to wealth, and, relatedly, a definition of welfare improvement in terms of willingness to pay. And other economists reach the same conclusion for different reasons: they endorse a more objective account of welfare, according to which some wealth changes, for some people in some situations, simply fail to correspond to welfare changes. For example, on Amartya Sen's capabilities approach, an improvement in educational opportunities for

[27] Ibid. 261.
[28] See Ramello, 'What's in a Sign?' 555, and G. Grossman and C. Shapiro, 'Counterfeit-product Trade' (1988) 78 *American Economic Review* 59.
[29] Griffiths, Chapter 11 of this volume, 243.

Ann might constitute a welfare improvement for Ann, regardless of whether she was actually or hypothetically able or willing to pay for them.

Setting these issues aside, individual welfare cannot be measured in terms of money (willingness to pay) and simply summed across individuals. Ignoring the flaws in consumer sovereignty mentioned earlier, monetary expressions of welfare are not in general comparable across individuals. Since the benefit from a marginal unit of money varies across individuals (usually it declines as wealth increases), different individuals may be willing to pay the same amount for some product, say £100, but this does not imply it yields them equal benefit, or provides equal welfare to them. An important consequence is that aggregate willingness-to-pay may not even track the direction of a welfare change, let alone its magnitude. For example, consider a policy which is favoured by a small number of rich people, but opposed by a much larger number of the poor. It might produce gains for the rich (whose positive willingness-to-pay valuations are 'inflated', since their marginal value of money is lower) and losses for the poor (whose negative valuations are correspondingly 'deflated'), such that the aggregate monetary valuation is positive, even though the policy reduces aggregate welfare. Accordingly, it is possible that a proposal to extend trade mark protection could pass a cost–benefit test, measured in terms of aggregate willingness-to-pay, while reducing aggregate welfare, because the beneficiaries are relatively much wealthier than the losers.[30]

Next, even supposing we have interpersonally comparable data on welfare, it should not be assumed without argument that social welfare is obtained just by adding up individual welfares. This may be an entirely uncontroversial assumption in the tradition of Law-and-Economics following Posner, but it is highly controversial among ethicists and welfare economists. Only Benthamite utilitarians define social welfare in this simplistic way. Other possibilities include social welfare as the weighted sum of individual welfares, the multiplication of them, or a Rawlsian social welfare function which gives priority to the worst-off individual.

Finally, it is worth noting in passing that ethical frameworks from Kantianism to libertarianism pay no attention to welfare maximization at all, or at least maintain that it must be balanced against other morally relevant considerations. These traditions appear to be very much alive in

---

[30] The Kaldor-Hicks compensation test does not offer a satisfactory resolution of the problem here. Following I. Little, *A Critique of Welfare Economics* (Oxford: Clarendon Press, 1950), most economists are now sceptical that a *potential* Pareto improvement has any normative significance per se. Besides, the Kaldor-Hicks 'test' has been proven to exhibit various internal inconsistencies and cycles (see J. Chipman and J. Moore, 'The New Welfare Economics 1939–74' (1978) 19 *International Economic Review* 547).

other areas of law, and so Griffiths' narrow focus on Benthamite utilitarianism needs justifying.[31]

Conclusion

Griffiths outlines two rationales for trade mark protection. The argument that trade marks protect valuable intangible output turns out to be dependent on many of the same economic presuppositions as the more standard search costs explanation. Both these rationales, as Griffiths lays them out, adopt a perspective on Law-and-Economics which relies heavily on a 'Chicago' view of economics. I remain surprised by the dominance of this economic worldview in thinking about trade mark law. Chicago economics no longer reflects mainstream economic thought (if it ever did), and the gap has recently widened with developments in behavioural economics, happiness research and our understanding of the ubiquitousness of increasing returns to scale. It is to be hoped that the economic analysis of trade mark law will soon be revised in light of these developments.

---

[31] Compare, for instance, M. White, 'A Kantian Critique of Law and Economics' (2006) 18 *Review of Political Economy* 235.

Part VII

Philosophy

13 Trade marks as property: a philosophical perspective

Dominic Scott, Alex Oliver and Miguel Ley-Pineda

In this chapter, we investigate the idea of trade marks as property. Three questions need to be answered. The first is a conceptual matter: are trade marks capable of being property or are they ruled out as a matter of conceptual necessity? The second is conceptual-*cum*-descriptive: is the current law's treatment of trade marks treatment of them as property? The third is normative: if the current law does in fact treat them as property, is it right to do so? The questions need to be tackled in turn.

1. Are trade marks capable of being property?

When we ask whether trade marks are capable of being property, we are of course assuming that it makes sense to speak of *things* (resources, assets) being property. In other words, we assume with the layman and the practising lawyer that it makes sense to speak of an owner of a thing, where the thing owned is the property. Admittedly, among legal theorists there is a long tradition going back to Bentham that ridicules this way of speaking.[1] It insists that property is best characterized not as the thing itself but as a bundle of normative relationships between people concerning the use of the thing. But, as Harris has rightly argued, this is a false opposition.[2] In particular, scepticism about the very idea of ownership of a thing is generally based on the thesis that ownership involves the right to use a thing in any way one pleases. There is indeed no such 'absolute' or 'totality' ownership. But it is common knowledge, even among laymen, that ownership is not like this, e.g. it is widely agreed that the owner of a knife is prohibited from using it to kill.

Given that it makes sense to conceive of things in general as property, does it make sense to speak of trade marks in particular as property? What must something be like to be capable of being property? Two authors,

---

[1] See J. Bentham, *An Introduction to the Principles of Morals and Legislation*, ed. J. H. Burns and H. L. A. Hart (Oxford: Clarendon Press, [1789] 1996) 211 n. 12.
[2] J. W. Harris, *Property and Justice* (Oxford: Clarendon Press, 1996) Ch. 8.

286   *Dominic Scott, Alex Oliver and Miguel Ley-Pineda*

Harris and Penner, have given broadly similar answers to this question, i.e. that there must be sufficient distance or separation between the owner and the object of their ownership. We shall discuss each in turn.

Harris claims that for something to count as property it must be 'reifiable as a person-independent resource': 'a human subject must be distanced from it in two ways. It must be something others could be accused of "taking" and something the subject himself could be seen to control or use as "owner"'.[3] On his reckoning, features of well-being such as friendship, joy or passion cannot count as property, since there could be no rules which *precisely* delimit trespassory actions. Sometimes specific trespassory rules are in place concerning a thing, yet the thing is still incapable of being property, since the subject cannot be literally conceived of as its owner. Harris' examples are personal reputations and information known only to single individuals. As for items of intellectual property, he evidently sees no conceptual bar to counting them as property. The law of intellectual property is rightly viewed as an extension of the property institution governing tangible entities: 'Only if the notions of using abstract things as one likes, and controlling use of them by others, were altogether incomprehensible would that extension not have occurred. Social intercourse is, however, replete with references to mental entities. Supposing the whole process to be justified, its property terminology is appropriate.'[4]

Harris' reasoning is cogent – up to a point. There does seem to be sufficient distance between human subjects and the objects of intellectual property. Specific trespassory rules can and have been formulated concerning, e.g, trade marks. And we can indeed conceive of owners of trade marks equipped with privileges of use, and powers of control and transmission. At the same time, however, there is a confusion in the variety of terminology that Harris uses (he is not alone) to characterize the subject matter of intellectual property law, terms for the kinds of thing that are intellectual property. In the passage just quoted, he talks of 'abstract things' and 'mental entities'. Elsewhere he uses 'ideas', 'ideational entities' and 'intangible things'. The term 'mental entities' is particularly problematic, for he himself declares that 'the contents of the human memory fail the distancing test which is a necessary, conceptual precondition of property'.[5] But aren't the contents of human memory 'mental entities'? If so, how can items of intellectual property characterized as mental entities be bona fide property?

---

[3] Ibid. 332.   [4] Ibid. 46.   [5] Ibid. 342.

In order to cut through this conceptual jungle, we suggest classifying things according to whether they are physical, mental or abstract (this is the ontologist's counterpart to 'animal, vegetable or mineral'). Physical things are material or tangible, things like chairs, clocks and cars. They can often be held, moved or touched, but they might be too large or too small or out of reach. Mental things are items within individual minds. They can be states, processes or events: a desire for ice-cream, a chain of reasoning or a headache. Like physical things, mental things have causes and effects: too much wine may prompt a headache which may itself prompt taking a pill. It is a vexed question whether all or any mental things are physical things. On the other hand, only panpsychists think that all physical things are mental.

As for abstract things, they form a motley crew. Mathematical objects, such as numbers and functions, are prime examples. They are usually characterized negatively: they do not have causes or effects. Thus they cannot be physical things, though physical things can represent them, e.g. a particular physical inscription of the numeral '1' stands for the abstract number 1. Abstract things are not mental either, since they are not within individual minds. Of course, we and you can think of the same number, but none of our thoughts *is* the number (which thought would it be?). No: the different thoughts are each *about* the same number.

We can now resolve the confusing ambiguity of Harris's 'idea' (and 'ideational entity'). To take a pertinent example, an inventor will have an idea of his invention. Co-inventors will have ideas of the same invention. As mental things, their ideas are different: they are within different minds. But they are ideas of the same thing. They are about the same thing. They have the same content. In another sense, then, the co-inventors come up with the same idea, since their different mental states have the same content. But in this second sense of 'idea', an idea is an abstract thing, the content of different mental vehicles. It is this ambiguity in 'idea' that results in Harris' slide from 'abstract' to 'mental' entities. He means to be talking about ideas in the abstract sense but confuses them with their mental vehicles.[6]

Now we turn to trade marks. What sort of thing are they? The simplest case is a word. But what is a word? Linguists and logicians distinguish between types and tokens. A word-token is a particular inscription or utterance, such as the two tokens 'cat' and 'cat' before your eyes. The two tokens are different physical things, but they are tokens or samples or embodiments of the same abstract type. (We may use quotation to pick out the type – 'cat' – but now we have to understand that types, not

[6] Harris himself hints at the distinction when he distinguishes the 'contents of human memory' from communicated information 'regarded as a distinct ideational entity': ibid.

tokens, are at issue.) The type cannot be the physical tokens, for they are many while it is one. The type is not on the page: it is not anywhere. It is another example of an abstract thing. The same distinction between types and tokens can be made for the other varieties of trade marks: pictures, sounds, shapes, gestures, etc.

Ordinary 'social discourse' (Harris' phrase) is indeed replete with reference to abstract things. Lawyers too, when they speak of trade marks, are actually speaking of abstract types, not physical tokens. When one registers a trade mark, one registers the one type, not its many tokens, nor any one of them (which one?). And when one seeks a graphic representation of a mark (singular 'a'), one is concerned with the abstract type, not a particular concrete token. It is still true to say that 'we are surrounded by and constantly interact with the subject matter of intellectual property law',[7] but it is true only under a roundabout interpretation. We are surrounded by trade marks in the sense that we are surrounded by tokens of them. We use a mark when we use a token of it. And we perceive a trade mark when we perceive one of its tokens. (When do two tokens count as tokens of the same mark or of similar or dissimilar ones? It is here that precision is needed if rules of infringement are to be specific. The task is complicated but not hopeless, and so trade marks cannot be ruled out as property in virtue of the inability to frame precise trespassory rules.)

Just as a trade mark cannot be a physical thing, so it cannot be a mental thing. We can of course think of a trade mark. Those that design one and contemplate its introduction think of it. So may consumers when they see it or imagine it. Producers and consumers each have different ideas – ideas as mental things – yet they have the same idea conceived as the abstract content. The single trade mark is obviously not each of these many mental ideas, but it is a good question whether the abstract content of their mental ideas is the same thing as the abstract type of physical tokens that we have just identified with a trade mark. For our purposes, however, we can leave the question undecided, since all that matters is that a trade mark is an abstract thing. In particular, it is not a mental thing, and so it does not violate Harris' necessary condition for a thing to qualify as property, that it be sufficiently distanced from a human subject.

Penner proposes a necessary condition for treating something as property that sounds similar to Harris' distancing condition,[8] although he uses

[7] L. Bently and B. Sherman, *Intellectual Property Law* (2nd edn, Oxford: Oxford University Press, 2004) 1.
[8] J. E. Penner, *The Idea of Property in Law* (Oxford: Clarendon Press, 1997).

it to draw the opposite conclusion that there cannot be intellectual property. Penner calls his condition the 'separability thesis': 'Only those "things" in the world which are contingently associated with any particular owner may be objects of property; as a function of the nature of this contingency, in theory nothing of normative consequence beyond the fact that the ownership has changed occurs when an object of property is alienated to another.'[9]

According to him, our talents, personalities, eyesight and friendship all violate the condition, since they are not 'separable from us in any straightforward way'; they have 'necessary links with particular persons'. This appears to be much like Harris' notion that, without sufficient distance between person and thing, there can be no notion of an ownership interest in the thing. But whereas Harris adds that precise trespassory rules need to be formulable, Penner omits this requirement and instead fleshes out the nature of the required contingent association between owner and thing: the nature of the relationship between the alleged owner and thing owned must not change when the owner changes. This is what drives him to a conclusion quite opposite to Harris'. For while apples and land may be owned, since 'we all stand to these objects in essentially the same way',[10] items of so-called 'intellectual property' fail the test. Like our talents, personalities, etc., they are not separable from us in the required way:

patents are not property rights in ideas, nor copyrights property rights in expressions, nor again trade marks property rights in symbols or words . . . the development of an idea or the creation of an artistic work can never be separated from the inventor or artist; it remains the inventor's or artist's forever. The light bulb is Edison's invention whoever makes use of it, and *Bleak House* is Dickens's whoever reads it.[11]

The underlying trouble with Penner's criterion is that there can be many particular relationships between a person and a given thing. Some of these may be unique to the person (even when the thing is an apple or land); others may be shared. His key notion of standing or failing to stand to things 'in essentially the same way' is quite indeterminate without some specification of 'essentially the same', i.e. we need to know when we can and when we cannot discount specific relationships to things that are unique to a given person. If Edison had also made a chair, why are we entitled to discount the special relationship between him and his chair, but not that between him and his invention?

---

[9] Ibid. 111.   [10] Ibid. 115.   [11] Ibid. 119.

As it happens and without argument, Penner refuses to discount the unique relationships holding between an inventor or artist and their idea or artistic work: it was they and they alone that developed or created it. But if this were sufficient to show that the idea and work are not separable in the required sense, it seems to have the absurd result that no man-made artefact could be property. For its maker would stand in a special relationship to it: they and they alone made it. It would be theirs, whoever made use of it. Perhaps Penner will say that the special relationship between maker and artefact can be discounted. But on what grounds can he distinguish it from those he refuses to discount?

We believe, on the contrary, that all of these special relationships can be discounted. As Harris argues, inventors' ideas and artists' works do have sufficient distance from the inventors and artists to be capable of being owned. The same goes for trade marks. (It is conspicuous that trade marks are not mentioned at the end of the passage quoted from Penner, even though they feature a few lines before. The reason is obvious. Since they need not be invented or created, he cannot always invoke special relationships of development or creation holding between a unique person and a trade mark in order to rule out a trade mark as a thing capable of being owned. So his argument against intellectual property is particularly weak in the case of trade marks.)

Of course, if one construed the objects of intellectual property as mental entities, one might be tempted to treat the maker/artefact relationship quite differently from the inventor/invention and artist/work relationships, and so to follow Penner towards his conclusion. But as soon as one realizes that the objects of intellectual property are not mental things but abstract things, this temptation should recede altogether.

2.   Does the law treat trade marks as property?

We agree with Bently and Sherman that the law of registered trade marks treats them as 'forms of property in their own right'.[12] Section 22 of the Trade Marks Act 1994 explicitly labels them 'personal property'. But it is not just a matter of a label. Registered trade marks do indeed display many of the standard incidents of ownership. They may be assigned without any transfer of business or goodwill. They may be licensed, be used as security for debts, and pass on death according to the laws of will or intestacy. The rules of infringement are, of course, still constrained but they have expanded in the direction of those governing tangible property

---

[12] Bently and Sherman, *Intellectual Property Law* 946.

(we shall be looking in particular at infringements under the heading of 'dilution'). Again, the exclusive rights to the use of trade marks may be lost by revocation on grounds of non-use or suspension of the mark, or its becoming generic or deceptive. Some of these limitations on use (or the lack of it) distinguish trade marks from tangible property, but we see no reason to think that this difference makes all the difference. The treatment of a thing as property is obviously not an all-or-nothing affair. If we take the law of tangible property as our paradigm of a property institution (allowing ourselves to ignore the differences among the various classes of tangibles), it is clear that the current law of trade marks treats them in such similar ways that the treatment can correctly be deemed treatment as property.

Someone who dissents from this view (as we might expect) is Penner,[13] though again he argues by way of patents and copyright (the extension to trade marks is obvious):

A true property right in an idea or an expression would constitute a right of exclusion from that idea or that expression itself. Subjects of the law would have a duty not to read about or understand an invention or take in the expression in a book or a painting (a funny notion since patents are published when granted, and a copyright is a right exclusively to disseminate).

If total exclusion from any kind of use by others is genuinely an incident of ownership, then indeed the current law treats neither ideas, expressions nor trade marks as property. But, as Penner himself notes, even owner-ship of land does not bring with it such exclusive control. Still, he thinks that land can be owned. So he tries to distinguish between the landowner and, e.g., the patent-holder with respect to the use-rights that are pro-tected by trespassory rules:

The landowner's use-rights are essentially indefinable, comprising every possible use of land. One cannot draw up an exhaustive list of them . . . The exact opposite is true of the patent-holder's use-rights. The patent is an exclusive right to a particular use of the invention or idea, that is, working it to produce goods for sale in the market . . . it is one use only.[14]

---

[13] Penner himself prefers to describe intellectual property rights as 'monopolies *defined* in terms of ideas and expressions and symbols' (Penner, *The Idea of Property in Law* 119). However, as Schechter remarked apropos the historical fear of monopoly, the owner of a trade mark 'obtains thereby no monopoly of goods or services; these may be freely sold on their own merits and under their own trade symbols' ('The Rational Basis of Trademark Protection' (1927) 40 *Harvard Law Review* 813–33, 833). And even if a product is conceived as a composite consisting of a good or service together with its trade mark, this is far from establishing the market power distinctive of a monopoly. Unlike trade marks, patents and copyright do yield control over particular goods or services them-selves, but again monopolistic market power is in no way guaranteed.

[14] Penner, *The Idea of Property in Law* 120.

292 Dominic Scott, Alex Oliver and Miguel Ley-Pineda

Of course, Penner is wrong to say that the landowner's use-rights comprise 'every possible use of land'. This is the chimera of absolute ownership. For example, independently of notions of ownership, the criminal law may prohibit some uses – burying someone alive – and, from within the institution of property, conservation laws may impose severe limits on use. As Callman pointed out long ago, in defence of treating trade marks as property, 'the property right, in any connection, has never been an *absolute* right in the sense that the owner can dispose thereof at his will'.[15]

Putting this objection to one side, we think that Penner is wrong to assert that the protected use-rights of the landowner are open-ended in a way that the rights of the patent-holder are not. *Both* are similarly open-ended. We cannot improve on Harris' remarks apropos of copyright:

a private domain is reserved. It consists of an open-ended set of use-privileges, control powers, and powers of transmission ... It is not specifically enacted that the copyright owner may (if he chooses) license only members of his family to make copies, or transact only with publishers whose politics match his own, or keep the work unpublished until some turn in public affairs which makes it topical and profitable, or read passages from it aloud at a charity bazaar. He may do these and countless other things with the work because he is its owner.[16]

The same goes, *mutatis mutandis*, for patents and trade marks.

2.1 Types of infringement

Having established that the law does indeed treat trade marks as property, we should now attempt to be more specific. As noted above, if anything is to count as property, it must be possible to formulate acts of infringement with precision. So as part of our answer to the descriptive question we need to discuss the types of action that the law treats as infringement of the trade mark owner's rights.

Where trade marks are concerned, the law currently divides infringement into two broad categories: confusion and dilution. Traditionally, it is confusion that has been the focus of infringement. This applies both to the law of passing-off and to statutory trade mark law. The law of passing-off concerns cases in which a trader already has goodwill with the public and where a second trader 'passes off' their goods as having been produced by the first. This is a form of misrepresentation (whether intentional or not) which may lead to confusion. Statutory trade mark law differs

---

[15] R. Callman, 'Unfair Competition Without Competition? The Importance of the Property Concept in the Law of Trade-marks' (1947) 95 *University of Pennsylvania Law Review* 443, 465.

[16] J. W. Harris, *Property and Justice* 46.

(in part) because the trader registers their mark, so that any infringement need not require that the trader has already built up any goodwill. But, traditionally, there is the same emphasis on proving misrepresentation. Construing infringement in terms of confusion connects to the informative function of trade marks, i.e. as indicators of the origin of the goods. The same could be said of the other type of infringement, dilution, to which we now turn. According to section 45 of the US Lanham Act:

the term 'dilution' means the lessening of the capacity of a famous mark to identify and distinguish goods or services, regardless of the presence or absence of
1. competition between the owner of the famous mark and other parties, or
2. likelihood of confusion, mistake or deception.[17]

In US law, dilution has been taken to come in two forms, blurring and tarnishment. According to the 2006 revision, dilution by blurring is defined as 'association arising from the similarity between a mark or trade name and a famous mark that impairs the distinctiveness of the famous mark'; dilution by tarnishment as 'association arising from the similarity between a mark or trade name and a famous mark that harms the reputation of the famous mark'. In either case, it could be argued that dilution (like confusion) is still essentially concerned with the informative function of the trade mark. Dilution in either of its two forms affects the capacity of the mark to inform the consumer about the origin and quality of the goods or services. Blurring causes the original mark to lose its capacity to summon up a particular class of goods. In a similar vein, 'tarnishment' may be thought of as setting the mark in a context that leads consumers to associate it with goods of questionable or inferior quality: i.e. after being exposed to the mark in the new context, consumers may cease to see it as pointing towards goods of a particular quality.

Thus conceived, dilution still relates to the capacity of the mark to provide information. The point is that this capacity can be undermined other than by confusion.[18] However, it has long been recognized that

[17] 15 USC §§ 1051 ff., first enacted 1946. For discussion, see Jane C. Ginsburg, Chapter 4 of this volume.
[18] Compare N. Economides, 'Trademarks' in P. Newman (ed.), *The New Palgrave Dictionary of Economics and the Law*, vol. III (London: Macmillan, 1998) 601, 603: 'Dilution by blurring prevents consumers from identifying a trademark or a tradename with a particular good or collection of goods, thereby diminishing the effectiveness of a trademark. Dilution by tarnishment does not allow the information about the quality level of the trademarked good or collection of goods to be correctly inferred. Thus, dilution interferes with the proper economic function of trademarks.' See also W. M. Landes and R. A. Posner, 'Trademark Law: An Economic Perspective' (1987) 30 *Journal of Law and Economics* 265, 307; M. A. Lemley, 'The Modern Lanham Act and the Death of Common Sense' (1999) 108 *Yale Law Journal* 1687, 1704; and T. Martino, *Trademark Dilution* (Oxford: Clarendon Press, 1996) 83.

trade marks also have a 'persuasive' function over and above that of providing information: the capacity to arouse certain positive associations in the consumer.[19] These may be the result of advertising, marketing and branding, as well as of the consumer's own experience of the product. The consumer may associate the trader's product with certain values or features that go beyond the purely functional qualities of the product.[20] At the extreme, a successful trade mark may conjure up a way of life. In such cases, the function of the trade mark is not just (or even primarily) to indicate to the consumer that a product comes from the same reliable source and will thus resemble previous purchases. It is to conjure up the brand values. The consumer may then make their purchase because these values are important to their sense of self, or because they want to express them to others or to show solidarity with others who share them. The list could go on. A successful brand explains why a consumer chooses one product rather than another, even though the two may be functionally very similar; and also why consumers are prepared to spend considerably more for their favoured choice.[21]

Once we introduce the persuasive function of trade marks the issue of dilution becomes more complex. Although we have just shown how the clauses about dilution (whether by blurring or tarnishment) might be invoked merely to protect the informative function of trade marks, they are increasingly being used to protect their persuasive function and ultimately the associated brand value, even in cases where there is no issue about misrepresentation.

The crux of the issue is that the law is currently being 'stretched'. It certainly treats trade marks as property in a very general sense. But once we start asking more specific questions about the types of associated infringement we find that, alongside the traditional concern with

---

[19] R. Brown, 'Advertising and the Public Interest: Legal Protection of Trade Symbols' (1948) 57 *Yale Law Journal* 1165.

[20] For an excellent example, see William Leith on NUROFEN in 'Confessions of a Ten-a-day Man' (*Guardian*, 26 April 2003): 'When it comes to headaches, ibuprofen is my drug of choice ... I also, I have noticed, have strong brand loyalty. When I go to the supermarket, my eye is drawn to the row of shiny silver packs with a chevron and a target design – Nurofen. Nurofen claims to be "targeted pain relief". Targeting a headache costs me around 20p a shot. On one level, I am aware that the active ingredient in a single Nurofen tablet, 200 mg of ibuprofen, is exactly the same as that in [various other brands]. On another level, Nurofen's targeting promise appeals to me. It feels hi-tech, almost environmentally sound. It makes me think of stealth bombers dropping smart bombs down the chimney of the building they want to destroy, with minimum collateral damage.'

[21] The distinction between the two functions is well captured by J. Davis, 'To Protect or Serve? European Trade Mark Law and the Decline of the Public Interest' (2003) 25 (4) EIPR 180: at one extreme, 'a trade mark is a badge of origin or source'; at another, it also serves to protect 'quality, reputation and, even in certain cases, a way of seeing life'.

misrepresentation (whether by confusion or dilution), there is a growing concern with brand protection. This constitutes a significant and controversial extension of trade mark law.

Turning to the UK Trade Marks Act 1994, we can see how it too may encourage moves to extend trade mark law into brand protection. Section 10(3) is particularly relevant:

> A person infringes a registered trade mark if he uses in the course of trade, in relation to goods or services, a sign which is identical with or similar to the trade mark, where the trade mark has a reputation in the United Kingdom and the use of the sign, being without due cause, takes unfair advantage of, or is detrimental to, the distinctive character or the repute of the trade mark.

'[D]etrimental to ... the distinctive character ... of the trade mark' is the UK Act's equivalent of blurring; 'detrimental to ... the repute of the trade mark', its equivalent to tarnishment.[22] As in the case of the Lanham Act, both kinds of detriment could be understood narrowly to mean merely undermining the informative function of the trade mark – i.e. undermining the association that consumers have between the mark and certain goods (of a certain quality). But this section of the Act also could mean something much broader: infringement occurs when the defendant uses the mark in such a way as to affect the public's perception of the plaintiff's brand (for the worse). Much of the debate currently surrounding the Act is about how far the law should be interpreted in this broader direction. If we interpret the Act in this broader sense, the point behind the detriment condition is to prevent the other party from somehow damaging the brand by alluding to the trade mark. The reference to 'unfair advantage' is designed to stop another party profiting from the brand that the trader has built up.

3.   What is wrong with dilution?

In this section we shall address the normative question of why the law should be used to prevent dilution. Before we do so, however, it is worth pausing to consider the much easier question of why the law should be used to prevent confusion. Here the justification is straightforwardly utilitarian. From the consumer's perspective, trade marks help reduce the risk and uncertainty of making a purchase. In the case of repeat purchases of the same products, or different products from the same producer, the mark gives crucial information to the consumer that cuts down substantially on search costs. In most manufacturing processes,

---

[22] Bently and Sherman, *Intellectual Property Law* 874.

there is an enormous gap between consumer and the source of the product, making the role of the trade mark all the more important. Consequently, it is not surprising that the traditional purpose of the law has been to stop traders misrepresenting the origin of their goods. Without such legal protection, there would be fewer incentives for traders to build up goodwill by making good-quality products; and, from the consumer side, the very function of trade marks would be seriously undermined. In all this, there seems no reason or need to question the fundamentals of the law, and there is little that philosophical analysis seems likely to add, except perhaps for some clarification (if lawyers and legal theorists need it) about the concepts of misrepresentation, confusion and imitation.

3.1   Utilitarian justifications for restricting dilution

If dilution is interpreted narrowly, i.e. with reference solely to the informative function of trade marks, the above argument can simply be deployed again. But this leaves open the question of why dilution should count as infringement when it is used to prevent damage to the brand, independently of concerns about information. Let us start by considering whether a utilitarian argument can be mounted here too. One might do so by pointing to the utility of having strong brands. These help product differentiation, facilitate consumer choice and incentivize purchasing. Furthermore, brands themselves become a product in their own right. In many cases consumers are purchasing the opportunity to express certain values or enjoy certain associations and emotions. More broadly still, brands have become part of our language and culture. Although they have their critics, one only has to think back to former Eastern bloc countries to see how dreary life without brands might be. The argument then claims that we need extended trade mark protection, because we need to incentivize businesses to build up strong brands. Allowing others to damage these brands, or to capitalize on them, would be to lower such incentives.

   This argument can be attacked from both inside and outside a utilitarian perspective. For a utilitarian, it might be very beneficial to allow the likes of Mr Reed to print the Arsenal logo on their merchandise as long as no one is confused about the origin of the merchandise, or thinks that Arsenal was commercially connected with Mr Reed.[23] Arsenal has already gained from the development of their mark, in that they run a successful football club, attracting huge numbers of loyal fans. Just for

[23] See Jennifer Davis, Chapter 3 of this volume.

this reason, they have every incentive to build up their brand. The question is why it is better to allow them to have the exclusive right to sell the associated merchandise and hence to exploit the surplus value of the trade mark,[24] i.e. value over and above the primary value that the trade mark brings to Arsenal. What is the social benefit of allowing only the company to capture this surplus value, especially when doing so may drive up prices and lower quality? By allowing free competition in the exploitation of this surplus value we benefit the consumer.

One could also argue that extending trade mark protection by restricting dilution is to undermine freedom of expression. This point could be made in an anti-utilitarian spirit: i.e. there is a clash between utility (especially as conceived in narrowly economic terms) and the rights to free speech. But more sophisticated utilitarians (or perhaps consequentialists) might claim that expressive autonomy is a component of well-being and that its value is diminished by expanded trade mark protection.

There is also a specifically linguistic version of this argument. Dreyfuss argues that trade marking has contributed many important words to our language, the removal of which could seriously inhibit our means of expression.[25] A good example is the way in which the US Olympics Committee managed to prevent a San Francisco gay rights group sponsoring their own 'Gay Olympic Games'. The Supreme Court ruled that they could perfectly well use the expression 'Gay Games'. Dreyfuss points out that 'Games' does not have the same associations as 'Olympic Games', which suggests the ideals of cooperation, mutual acceptance and international friendship.[26] None of this is to say that the utilitarian defence of expanding trade mark restrictions is doomed to failure. But we have reached something of a stalemate: the expansion may increase utility in some respects, but decrease it in others. As so often happens, the utilitarian defence offers too many hostages to empirical fortune. It is impossible to assert with any confidence – and without detailed, ongoing examination of the evidence – whether or not such expansion is justified on utilitarian grounds.

3.2   A Lockean justification

If one does not wish to offer hostages to fortune, one needs a different kind of justification for restricting dilution, based on a different principle altogether. Such a principle can be found in the Lockean idea that:

---

[24] See Andrew Griffiths, Chapter 11 of this volume.
[25] R. C. Dreyfuss, 'Expressive Genericity: Trademarks as Language in the Pepsi Generation' (1990) 65 *Notre Dame Law Review* 397.
[26] Ibid. 413.

'a person who labours upon resources that are either unowned or "held in common" has a natural property right to the fruits of his or her efforts'.[27]

It will help to express this so-called 'labour theory' schematically: if X labours on material Y to produce Z, then X owns Z as a matter of natural right (for our purposes, we can ignore the Lockean provisos[28]). In the case that interests us, X is a trade mark holder, and Z is the registered trade mark owned. Not any old trade mark, but one with a 'distinctive character' or 'repute' which may be diluted by blurring or tarnishment. For we are investigating just one incident of ownership embodied in current trade mark law, i.e. protection against dilution. We are imagining justifying it by appealing to ownership of the relevant trade mark as a matter of natural right, which is in turn based on labouring on some material to produce it. So we are not interested merely in the labour involved in the design or selection of a trade mark, but also in the extra labour that turns a trade mark into one that may then be diluted, namely the labour involved in producing quality products consistently and over an extended period, and the advertising and marketing that surrounds the trade mark. This extra labour creates something new, even if the trade mark itself is not invented. It is often said that the trade mark then comes to have valuable selling or drawing power, or commercial magnetism. This new feature may well be corrupted by the diluting actions of others, and so its protection appears to be justified via the natural property right we are supposing to exist. The magnetism may also be transferred to some other trader's identical or similar mark. To use the hackneyed phrase, the said trader is reaping where he has not sown. He has taken unfair advantage of the mark. He also infringes according to current law, and this too can be justified via the exclusive use that a natural property right would entail.

The labour theory is subject to serious criticism both in general and in its particular application to intellectual property.[29] A common complaint apropos of patents and copyright is that often there are other labourers besides the owner who ought to get a share. As Hettinger puts it: 'Invention, writing and thought in general do not operate in a vacuum;

---

[27] W. Fisher, 'Theories of Intellectual Property' in S. R. Munzer (ed.), *New Essays in the Legal and Political Theory of Property* (Cambridge: Cambridge University Press, 2001) 168, 170.

[28] They state (i) that, after acquisition, there should be 'enough and as good left in common', and (ii) that there should be no spoilage.

[29] Ibid. 184–9; E. C. Hettinger, 'The Justification of Intellectual Property' (1989) 18 *Philosophy and Public Affairs* 31, 36–40; S. V. Shiffrin, 'Lockean Arguments for Private Intellectual Property' in Munzer (ed.), *New Essays in the Legal and Political Theory of Property* 138–67.

intellectual activity is not creation *ex nihilo*. Given this vital dependence of a person's thoughts on the ideas of those who came before her, intellectual products are fundamentally social products.'[30] The same surely applies to trade marks; the development of their commercial magnetism will draw on the efforts of others besides the owner. But there is a more interesting point that applies to trade marks in particular. As Bently and Sherman put it: 'while the associations between the mark and a source or goodwill may be instigated and nurtured by the trader, they are as much created by the customers and the public'.[31] Their point is not the old one that many minds and hands may be involved in, e.g., marketing and advertising techniques featuring a trade mark. No: they seem to be saying that the relevant products of labour here are the networks of associations within various minds. And the creation of these associations is a two-sided affair: effort needs to be expended from without by the trade mark owner, but creative work also needs to be done from within by each member of the public. Why should the owner's labour count but not theirs?

Spence illustrates the point well by citing the case *Hogan and others* v *Pacific Dunlop Ltd*,[32] in which a company advertised shoes by reference to the character 'Mick Dundee'.[33] Spence argues that the product endorsement value of the bushman hero was in part created by the thousands who enjoyed the film *Crocodile Dundee*. That there may be multiple 'creators' at work, including consumers, can also be given a linguistic slant. According to Dreyfuss:

some words have core denotations (definitions that can be found in a dictionary), and a set of connotations that depend upon their history, derivation, and identification with users. These peripheral meanings are often highly individualized to the speaker, the listener, and possibly to the method by which they interact or perceive one another. When such words are used, they become infused with the listener's own associations, and their message is incorporated into the listener's own frame of reference. The result is that the expression as perceived can have much greater impact on the recipient's thinking than the words that were actually transmitted.[34]

In fact, Dreyfuss is making this point to bring out the harm done when a particular expression is withdrawn from use by over-zealous trademark protection. The value of an expression like 'Olympic Games' may lie in the associations that it triggers when registered in the minds of users. Another

---

[30] Hettinger, 'The Justification of Intellectual Property' 38.
[31] Bently and Sherman, *Intellectual Property Law* 699.
[32] (1989) 12 IPR 225 (Fed. Ct Australia).
[33] M. Spence, 'Passing Off and the Misappropriation of Valuable Intangibles' (1996) 112 *Law Quarterly Review* 472, 479–80.
[34] Dreyfuss, 'Expressive Genericity' 413–14.

word such as the plain 'Games', may have more or less the same core
definition, but has quite different associations in the minds of language
users, and therefore makes a very inadequate replacement. As such, this is
part of the linguistic attack on the utilitarian defence of expanded trade
mark protection discussed in the previous section (3.1). But the same point
can also be pressed into service to undermine the argument for expanded
trade mark protection based on the labour theory, because it brings out the
consumer's contribution in constructing the meaning of a trade mark
alongside the efforts of the trade mark proprietor.

In response to this line of argument, a defender of the Lockean
approach might object that the consumer's contribution to the meaning
of a trade mark is not as creative as has just been suggested, and that it
should not be counted as 'labour' alongside the activities of those
involved in the marketing and the advertising of the trade-marked product. One marketing theorist talks of such activities as 'programming' the
mind, which makes the consumer's role more passive than creative.[35]

Whatever the outcome of this debate – whether or not the consumer's
role can count as sufficiently creative to undermine the Lockean
argument – we wish to attack the argument from a different direction.
There is an oddity in the way in which the Lockean theory is applied in
this case: the product of labour has shifted from the trade mark to some
network of mental associations. Yet if this network were the product at
the beginning, the labour theory would not deliver what we want, since
the product is now different from the item owned, i.e. the trade mark.
This also raises a question that we have so far ignored, and which always
causes trouble for applications of the labour theory to intellectual property: what is the relevant raw material to which labour is applied?

In order to sort out this muddle, we return to the idea that a trade mark
may have a persuasive function and so come to possess a power or
magnetism. The language alludes to dispositional properties, properties
that have characteristic manifestations which are triggered in certain
circumstances: in general, if the circumstances occur, so does the manifestation. Fragility is a good example of a dispositional property. In
general, if a fragile thing is struck, it breaks. Here the manifestation is
displayed in the very object that has the dispositional property. But this
need not be so. The colour yellow belonging to surfaces of objects is a
disposition to produce a certain sensation in certain perceivers under
certain conditions. Here the manifestation is not in the yellow object
but in the perceivers. It is their response. Perhaps, then, we can think of

---

[35] T. Ambler, *Are Brands Good for Britain? British Brands Group Inaugural Lecture* (London:
British Brands Group, 2000) 4.

the magnetism of a trade mark on the model of colour. After all, the trade mark owner wants the trade mark to evoke responses in customers. These responses may be characterized in behavioural terms. A crude example: on seeing the trade mark on a product, the customer buys the product. Of course, a trade mark will evoke different behaviours in the same consumer in different circumstances. So the magnetism of a trade mark is better characterized as a bundle of dispositions. And different people will respond differently in the same circumstances: some will be switched off rather than on by the presence of a certain mark or even any mark. So there are different bundles of dispositions for different consumers. The trade mark owner will hope that enough bundles feature positive rather than negative behaviours, and that this will continue to be true over time.

Behavioural responses are not the only kind of response, however. We can instead move further back up the causal chain to the mental responses that lie behind the behavioural ones. It is here that we find the mental 'associations' concerning the trade mark. Researchers concerned with brands have catalogued the kinds of thing that may be called to mind on being presented with a trade mark, ranging from simple states of recognition, then thoughts about the source and functional qualities of a product, its price, the way it is used and its typical users, what it feels like to use it, whether it is prestigious or fashionable, right through to nebulous 'brand attitudes', quite general emotions or free-floating moods, perhaps a feeling of security or confidence.[36] The same point about variety of dispositions across observational circumstances and people applies.

[36] K. L. Keller, 'Conceptualizing, Measuring, and Managing Customer-Based Brand Equity' (1993) 57 *Journal of Marketing* 1. Often a brand is identified with a trade mark, and brand equity is then conceived either as identical to or as dependent on the mental associations involving the trade mark. Since the early 1990s, there has been a growing awareness that the marketing literature on the psychology of brands is of direct relevance to the law of trade marks, since blurring and tarnishment are forms of impairment of brand equity: see J. E. Moskin, 'Dilution or Delusion: The Rational Limits of Trademark Protection' (1993) 83 *Trademark Reporter* 122; A. F. Simonson, 'How and When Do Trademarks Dilute: A Behavioural Framework to Judge "Likelihood" of Dilution' (1993) 83 *Trademark Reporter* 149; J. B. Swann and T. H. Davis, 'Dilution, An Idea whose Time has Gone; Brand Equity as Protectible Property, the New/Old Paradigm' (1994) 84 *Trademark Reporter* 267; S. Hartman, 'Brand Equity Impairment – The Meaning of Dilution' (1997) 87 *Trademark Reporter* 418; and J. Jacoby, 'The Psychological Foundations of Trademark Law: Second Meaning, Genericism, Fame, Confusion and Dilution' (2001) 91 *Trademark Reporter* 1013. Armchair (or bench?) psychology is notoriously bad at understanding dilution. The literature on brand psychology promises something more than 'unreliable intuition' or 'junk science' (Jacoby, 'Psychological Foundations' 1068). Associative network memory models were first used to study unsuccessful brand extensions, a kind of self-dilution. These models are now being applied to explain dilution by others; for a state-of the-art investigation, see M. Morrin, J. Lee and G. M. Allenby, 'Determinants of Trademark Dilution' (2006) 33 *Journal of Consumer Research* 248.

So far, so good. But now there is a hitch. Abstract trade marks cannot themselves have any dispositional properties, since they have no effects and so cannot have the causal basis that a dispositional property needs (when a fragile cup is struck and breaks, its breaking is caused by the striking and some property of the cup, the causal basis of fragility; similarly, some causal basis in a yellow flower causes the relevant sensation when I look at it). So we must reconfigure what we have said by moving to the physical tokens of trade marks. They can supply the necessary causal bases for dispositions. Some terminology and simplification will help. Let us forget about different circumstances and different people and fix on one of each kind so that we can deal with a single disposition, rather than lots of bundles. And let us roll up the various mental responses of our given person P in the given observational circumstances C into one giant response R. Then we can spell out (a small part of) the magnetism of a given abstract trade mark: it is a dispositional property of its physical tokens. They are disposed to produce response R in person P in observational circumstances C.

What we have done is to try to give a sense in which the magnetism is in the trade mark itself. It is in the trade mark in the sense that the relevant dispositional property is in its physical tokens. A trade mark can gain magnetism in the sense that its tokens come to have the dispositional property; a trade mark's magnetism may be damaged in the sense that the disposition of its tokens to produce responses in consumers may change for the worse, through blurring or tarnishment. It seems, then, that we have a good candidate for the product produced by the labour of the trade mark owner. The advertising, marketing and production of quality goods or services produce a magnetic trade mark. Following the labour theory through, it follows that the magnetic trade mark is owned as a matter of natural right.

We have simplified enormously. We should properly speak of a trade mark having lots of bundles of dispositions to take into account the variety of responses across people and circumstances. Different bundles come into play as different people do, and the make-up of the bundles changes as people's dispositions to respond change over time. A trade mark's magnetism will thus not be fixed and all-or-nothing, but will be an indefinitely gradable affair in continual flux. These complications will, of course, affect the application of the labour theory. We are trying to justify a particular infringement rule that prohibits dilution, but only of marks that have reached a certain, rather vague level of magnetism. But labour will also be involved in producing marks that fall below, even well below, that level. The labour theory is unable, as it stands, to explain why owners of those marks should not be protected from dilution (and, we may add, the taking of unfair advantage).

We are interested in a different problem, however. The dispositional property of tokens we have described is controversial. Most writers on dispositions think that dispositions are an intrinsic matter.[37] To explain what this means, we need to distinguish between intrinsic and extrinsic properties. An *intrinsic* property is, roughly, one that has to do only with the thing that has it, e.g. being a certain mass. An *extrinsic* property concerns other things, e.g. being an uncle. Then dispositions are an intrinsic matter if any things that are alike in intrinsic properties must also share their dispositions, given the same laws of nature. But our disposition is extrinsic rather than intrinsic. For tokens of the same trade mark may be intrinsic duplicates while one has the given disposition and another a different one. Indeed, this is what happens on our account when a trade mark gains magnetism or loses it.

At this stage we can construct a dilemma. Suppose that our extrinsic dispositional property is ruled out. It will be replaced by its partner that resides in customers, not in the trade mark's tokens.[38] In other words, the disposition of tokens to produce response R in person P in observational circumstances C will be replaced by the bona fide *intrinsic* disposition of person P to respond with R to the tokens in the observational circumstances C. But this replacement frustrates any attempt to apply the labour theory. For then it really will be changes in people's minds that are brought about by the trade mark owner's labour. In which case the labour theory cannot be applied, since the product is different from the item owned.

Suppose on the other hand that extrinsic dispositions are accepted. After all, the case against them has not been made out. McKitrick[39] supplements the minuscule, extant argument against them but finds none of any force. And she gives a formidable array of examples of extrinsic dispositions. Most interesting for us are those she characterizes as dependent on social institutions and social context. Recognizability of people is her first case under this heading, and this obviously carries over to trade marks. She continues with others of similar relevance: 'A coupon is redeemable. A device is marketable. A position is enviable. An event is memorable. A statement is humorous, provocative, or inflammatory' (163).[40]

But even with extrinsic dispositions, the labour theory is still in trouble. Return to our dummy dispositional property of a trade mark token: the

---

[37] D. Lewis, 'Dispositional Theories of Value' (1989), reprinted in D. Lewis, *Papers in Ethics and Social Philosophy* (Cambridge: Cambridge University Press, 2000) 68–94.
[38] See Lewis, ibid. 80 fn. 16, for the idea of dispositional partners.
[39] J. McKitrick, 'The Case for Extrinsic Dispositions' (2003) 81 *Australasian Journal of Philosophy* 155.
[40] Ibid. 163.

disposition to produce response *R* in person *P* in observational circumstances *C*. Since it is extrinsic, two duplicate tokens may be differently disposed. One may have the disposition, the other not. What explains this difference? There is nothing about the tokens themselves that could do so, so the causal basis of the disposition cannot be an intrinsic property of a token. It must instead be an extrinsic property involving a person, namely the property of being present to a person who possesses a causal basis of the partner disposition to respond with *R* to tokens in the circumstances *C*. This extrinsic property of the token combines with the circumstances to cause a manifestation of the relevant disposition. But now ask how tokens get to have this extrinsic property. No labour is expended on *them*. It must be applied to people. The trade mark owner needs to change their minds. In which case, we have the same result as before. It follows that, whether or not extrinsic dispositions are admitted, the labour theory cannot be applied, since the relevant product is not the item owned.

In fact, the problem for the labour theory is much worse, for a reason we have so far glossed over. We have been trying to locate the magnetism of a trade mark in its tokens, by granting them a dispositional property based on an analogy with a colour property. They are both dispositions to evoke responses in spectators. But the value of a trade mark's magnetism goes beyond this kind of disposition. To take another simple example, brand recall is as significant for customer choice as brand recognition. A customer may well be contemplating buying a particular kind of product. His ability to retrieve the brand, to think of the trade mark, is evidently crucial to its selling power. But this ability is a disposition *in him* to recall. It cannot be conceived on the model of colours as a disposition of trade mark tokens to evoke a response, because that would get the matter the wrong way round. We are not moving from observed token to response, but rather from thoughts about a product category to thoughts concerning the trade mark. Trade mark owners expend labour on developing dispositions to recall. These dispositions reside in people's minds. The labour theory is in trouble again.

What we have shown is that the underlying idea of the labour theory that *X* owns *Z* if *X* produces *Z* through labour cannot be sustained if it is to be applied within the field of trade marks. It needs to be replaced by a quite different theory which allows that *X* may own *Z* if *X* produces *something else*, albeit associated with *Z*, through labour. Then ownership of magnetic trade marks could be justified via labour that produces a change in people's minds. But this new theory runs right against its Lockean roots. The driving idea of mixing labour with raw material to produce an owned product has simply vanished, since what is owned is not what is worked upon.

What too of our missing *Y*, the raw material to which labour is applied?
The Lockean idea is that this material should be unowned or 'held in
common'. There is considerable difficulty in characterizing it when the
labour theory is applied to other realms of intellectual property. One
sometimes reads of facts, languages or our cultural heritage, but most
often the commons is held to consist of some more or less extensive range
of ideas.[41] Not ideas in the sense of mental things, of course, for these are
within individual minds and could hardly be held in common, but rather
ideas conceived as the abstract contents of mental states. But even
granted that it makes sense to work on these abstract ideas, in the present
case of trade marks they cannot be the right raw material. After all, what
one is producing is a change in people's minds, so the raw material can
only be the previous state of their minds. But these mental things cannot
be held in common. So, once again, the original labour theory would need
a radical overhaul, if indeed it could be applied to the ownership of trade
marks at all.

4.   Conclusion

In section 1 of this chapter, we argued that there is no conceptual bar to
conceiving trade marks as property, and in section 2 showed that the law
does indeed do so. We then turned in section 3 to the question of whether
it is right to do so, in particular focussing on the specific rights and duties
embodied in rules of infringement. We found that protecting the informative function of trade marks could be straightforwardly justified by a
utilitarian argument. Much more difficult, however, was the attempt to
justify restricting dilution, where that involves protecting the brand value.
Utilitarian arguments failed to make the case. A Lockean defence can be
mounted but, as we have just seen, involves too radical a departure from
its traditional application to be likely to succeed. Trade marks throw up
peculiar and compelling philosophical difficulties for the defence in a way
that patents and copyright do not.

---

[41] Fisher, 'Theories of Intellectual Property' 186.

14 An alternative approach to dilution protection: a response to Scott, Oliver and Ley-Pineda

Michael Spence

Introduction

The chapter by Scott, Oliver and Ley-Pineda makes a powerful case against both utilitarian and Lockean justifications of the protection of trade marks against 'dilution' or, as I prefer it, protection against 'allusion' to the mark. In so doing, they reinforce a common scepticism about this type of protection. To that extent, the chapter makes a significant contribution to our understanding of trade mark law.

There are, of course, claims of detail in the chapter with which I disagree. For example, the authors' discussion of the object of an intellectual property right fails adequately to take account of either the structure of the relevant regimes, or the ways in which they develop. Thus section 60(1) of the Patent Act 1977 introduces a list of potentially infringing uses of an invention with the words '. . . a person infringes a patent if, but only if, . . . he does any of the following things'. Section 16(1) of the Copyright, Designs and Patents Act 1988 introduces a similar, but more specific, list with the words '[t]he owner of the copyright in a work has . . . the exclusive right to do the following acts in the United Kingdom'. The clear implication is that if a patent holder or copyright owner has 'an open-ended set of use-privileges, control powers and powers of transmission',[1] they relate, not to the invention or the work, but to the legal right that is the patent or the copyright. It is the legal right that is the object of the property. This understanding is also reflected in the development of intellectual property law in which there is inevitably debate about whether control over each new use of a particular

---

This chapter draws extensively on work also published as 'Restricting Allusion to Trade Marks: A New Justification' in G. Dinwoodie and M. Janis (eds.), *Trademark Law and Theory* (Northampton, Mass.: Edward Elgar, 2007) ch. 12.

[1] J. W. Harris, *Property and Justice* (Oxford: Clarendon Press, 1996) 46, cited in Dominic Scott, Alex Oliver and Miguel Ley-Pineda, Chapter 13 of this volume.

type of subject matter ought, or ought not, to be included within the ambit of the relevant right.[2]

Putting aside these issues of detail, my only objection to the chapter is that the contribution it makes to our understanding of dilution protection is essentially negative. It carefully explains why particular arguments cannot be used to justify such protection and concludes that '[t]rade marks throw up peculiar and compelling philosophical difficulties for the defence'. However, the intuition that trade mark owners ought sometimes to be protected against allusion to their marks, even in contexts in which no consumer confusion is involved, is remarkably powerful. And even in those legal systems, such as that of the UK, in which such protection is in some senses new, the intuition has long been given at least limited expression. For example, long before the enactment of section 10(3) of the Trade Marks Act 1994 giving protection against the use of signs that are identical or similar to a mark and, 'without due cause, [take] unfair advantage of, or [are] detrimental to, the distinctive character or the repute of the trade mark', section 4(1)(b) of the Trade Marks Act 1938 provided a type of protection against dilution in the form of protection against 'importing a reference' to a mark.[3] While scepticism about dilution protection is widespread, the power of the intuition that allusion to a trade mark is sometimes wrongful cannot easily be dismissed and it is imperative that we try to make sense of it.

In this response, I will therefore present an argument that seems to be a viable alternative to the justifications for dilution protection that Scott, Oliver and Ley-Pineda rightly reject.[4] This argument is grounded in the expressive autonomy of the trade mark owner and is one that I have made elsewhere. It is also an argument that can be used to justify certain aspects of the law of copyright, moral rights and so-called 'personality rights'. If it can be accepted, then there may be both good grounds for protecting trade marks against dilution, and greater commonality than Scott, Oliver and Ley-Pineda allow between the justification of such protection and the justification of at least some other intellectual property rights.

---

[2] Nevertheless, the astute reader will notice that throughout this chapter I refer to the 'trade mark owner' and 'her trade mark'. These expressions might be taken to reinforce the view that it is the mark itself that is the object of the property right. They are, however, intended as shorthand for the more accurate, but less elegant, expressions, 'the owner of the legal right to prevent the use of the trade mark in certain prescribed ways' and 'the trade mark in relation to which she enjoys that legal right'.

[3] For discussion in the UK, see J. Davis, 'Between a Sign and a Brand: Mapping the Boundaries of a Registered Trade Mark in European Union Trade Mark Law' in this volume, Ch. 3.

[4] See, for example, M. Spence, 'The Mark as Expression / The Mark as Property' (2005) 58 *Current Legal Problems* 491.

Protection against allusion to a trade mark and the expressive autonomy of the trade mark owner

The right to expressive autonomy arguably entails at least four claims, though the strength of those claims depends upon how the right is justified. In this response a justification grounded in speaker autonomy is assumed. First, freedom of speech entails freedom from unjustified speech restraint. Second, freedom of speech may entail a right to be heard, although the extent to which it does is highly contentious. Third, freedom of speech may entail freedom from compulsion to express a message not of the speaker's choosing. Fourth, freedom of speech may entail freedom from compulsion to subsidize a message with which the person from whom the subsidy is sought chooses not to be associated. It is upon the third and fourth of these claims that the argument of this chapter is built.

The third and fourth of these claims have been given expression in the free speech jurisprudence of the United States, though they have not long been carefully distinguished. In *Pacific Gas and Electric Company* v *Public Utilities Commission of California*,[5] the right to expressive autonomy was relied upon to prevent the compelled distribution with utility bills of a newsletter expressing views which the utility company did not endorse. In *Hurley* v *Irish-American Gay, Lesbian and Bisexual Group of Boston*,[6] it was relied upon to prevent the compelled inclusion of a gay rights group in a St Patrick's Day parade organized by a war veterans group. In *Boy Scouts of America* v *Dale*,[7] it was used to justify the dismissal of a Boy Scout leader who was openly gay, on the basis that his retention would 'force the organization to send a message, both to its young members and the world, that the Boy Scouts accepts homosexual conduct as a legitimate form of behaviour'[8] Finally, in *United States* v *United Foods Inc.*,[9] it was used to prohibit compelled contributions by growers to a mushroom advertising fund.

The principle that underpins each of these cases must be that expressive autonomy entails the ability to choose, not only which messages a speaker will herself convey or be taken to have conveyed, but also in the expression of which messages she will participate in the sense that she facilitates their communication. A concern to protect a person's expressive autonomy is not merely a concern that she should be free to determine how she is presented to others, but also a concern that she should be free to choose those messages that she wishes to promote. Participation

---

[5] 106 S. Ct 903 (1986).   [6] 115 S. Ct 2338 (1995).   [7] 120 S. Ct 2446 (2000).
[8] Ibid. at 2454.   [9] 121 S. Ct 2334 (2001).

in, and the promotion of, speech may consist in its financial subsidy. This is because choices about how to use our money are, in our culture, important autonomy-constituting choices (particularly as regards so personally important an issue as the meanings with which we are associated, whether by others or only by ourselves).[10] Participation in, and the promotion of, speech may also consist in the use of words with which we are associated, whether or not the use of those words gives rise to any suggestion that we have endorsed, or are even connected with, the message of which they become a part. This is because choices about the words we use are also, in our culture, important autonomy-constituting choices, as our commitment to expressive autonomy demonstrates. This may be what Madison means when, in relation to the fair use exceptions in copyright, he claims that allowing access to a work can be forcing its author to 'subsidize, with raw material, the speech of [the] ... second user'.[11] Of course, there is a difference between these two types of subsidy because I have a general claim to control the use of my money that I may not have in relation to my words, but the analogy does not seem too strained.

Quite so broadly expressed, this principle is potentially problematic, both as regards compelled speech and as regards the compelled subsidy of speech. As regards compelled speech, it is important to remember that communication is almost always difficult. There are many situations in which a speaker may be misrepresented as having expressed a particular point of view, been misquoted or poorly paraphrased, and legal redress ought not to be available. We would need to be very cautious, for example, in affording relief for non-defamatory misquotation. The chilling effect of such regulation would weigh against preventing the compulsion of speech to so great an extent: the usual remedy for misunderstanding is more speech. But that a principle ought not to be given legal expression in many circumstances does not mean that it ought never to be. If that were the case, then even protection against the restraint of speech might be difficult to justify. At least some level of protection against compelled speech is arguably a corollary of a commitment to protecting expressive autonomy.

Similarly, as regards the compelled subsidy of speech, the case of government speech exemplifies a situation in which an over-broad protection of expressive autonomy gives rise to particular difficulties. In the

[10] See also Howard M. Wasserman, 'Compelled Expression and the Public Forum Doctrine' (2002) 77 Tulane L. Rev 163.
[11] Michael J. Madison, 'Complexity and Copyright in Contradiction' (2000) 18 Cardozo Art & Ent. L. J. 125 at 166.

most recent Supreme Court case on the issue, *Johanns* v *Livestock Marketing Association* (*'Johanns'*), the Court was faced with the dilemma that allowing claimants to invoke the right to expressive autonomy whenever the subsidy of speech was compelled could effectively silence government: a complaint could be brought any time that tax revenues were used to propagate a message with which any individual tax payer disagreed.[12] This position was clearly unsustainable. The Supreme Court dealt with the problem by emphasizing the distinction between compelled speech and the compelled subsidy of speech, and by creating a further distinction between the compelled subsidy of government speech and the compelled subsidy of private speech. The majority in *Johanns* wrote:

> The principal dissent conflates the two concepts [of compelled speech and compelled subsidy] into something it describes as citizens' 'presumptive autonomy as speakers to decide what to say and what to pay for others to say' ... [T]here might be a valid objection if 'those singled out to pay the tax are closely linked with the expression' ... in a way that makes them appear to endorse the government message. But this compelled-speech argument ... differs substantively from the compelled-subsidy analysis. The latter invalidates an exaction not because being forced to pay for speech that is unattributed violates personal autonomy, but because being forced to fund someone else's private speech unconnected to any legitimate government purpose violates personal autonomy ... Such a violation does not occur when the exaction funds government speech.[13]

The Supreme Court's judgment has been rightly criticized.[14] But the distinction between the compelled subsidy of government speech and the compelled subsidy of private speech does have some merit. It is not that the compelled subsidy of government speech does not raise expressive autonomy concerns, but rather that the compelled subsidy of government speech through general taxation is not compelled subsidy of a type for which legal redress ought to be available. This is on a number of bases: government would otherwise be impossible; the sense in which a taxpayer 'participates' in government speech is clearly far more attenuated than the sense in which a member of a private organization 'participates' in the speech that she is compelled to subsidize; and participation in government activities is in any case moderated through the whole framework of representative democracy. Once again the problem seems to be, not with the general principle, but with the extent to which it might conceivably be given legal expression, a problem that marks every aspect of the law of free speech.

---

[12] 125 S. Ct 2055 (2005).   [13] Ibid. at 2065.

[14] See, for example, Robert Post, 'Compelled Subsidization of Speech: *Johanns* v *Livestock Marketing Association*' (2005) Sup. Ct Rev 195.

For our purposes it is important that, even when it was shown to create real difficulties and even in situations in which no implication of endorsement was raised, the Supreme Court in *Johanns* did not abandon the intuition that the subsidization of at least private speech raises issues of expressive autonomy. The basis of that intuition must be that subsidizing speech is participating in speech, even if the recipient of the speech does not identify it with all the subsidizing parties. Even though they distinguished between the two, the Supreme Court continued to affirm that protection against the compelled subsidy of speech ought to be afforded alongside protection against compelled speech.

If all this is right, then the implications for protection against allusion to a trade mark should be clear. When someone uses a sign that alludes to a mark, they may be involved either in compelling speech, or in an activity analogous to compelling a subsidy of speech. This consists either: in altering the meaning of a mark so that it subsequently bears a meaning with which the owner of the mark will be associated each time it is used, but from which she would wish to be disassociated; or in forcing the owner of the mark to participate in, or promote, speech with which she would disagree by providing the material upon which that speech is built.

Each of these possible wrongs is exemplified by the facts of the well-known American trade mark case *Girl Scouts of the United States of America v Personality Posters Manufacturing Co.*[15] This case concerned a poster with a picture of a pregnant Girl Scout wearing the uniform of the organization and marked with its trade mark. Her hands were clasped above her abdomen and next to her hands was the Girl Scouts' motto 'Be Prepared'. This use of the trade mark may have involved a type of compelled speech. Were this poster widely distributed, the Girl Scouts would have been forced either to abandon the use of their motto, a type of silencing, or to contend with the fact that they no longer controlled the message that it conveyed. It would be difficult, having seen the poster, ever to hear the motto again, or to receive the Girl Scouts' use of it, in quite the same way. If forcing the Boy Scouts to retain a gay Scout Leader constituted forcing them to express a message with which they might disagree, it must be at least conceivable that this use of the motto of the Girl Scouts also entailed a type of compelled speech. Further, this use of the trade mark might have involved an activity analogous to the compelled subsidy of speech. The Girl Scouts were effectively conscripted to express a message about sexual activity with which they might have

---

[15] 304 F. Supp. 1228 (DCNY 1969). Note, however, that in the case itself the dilution claim of the Girl Scouts was unsuccessful on the basis that New York law was said then to require a showing of confusion for a successful dilution claim.

312   *Michael Spence*

disagreed. Even if their use of the motto remained unaffected by the distribution of the poster, the Girl Scouts might have argued that the use of the motto forced them to participate in the expression of a message from which they would have wished to be disassociated. The claim to protect trade marks against allusive use then becomes a claim grounded in preserving autonomy of expression.

Objections to the argument from expressive autonomy

Before considering important qualifications to protection against allusion to a trade mark implied in this argument from expressive autonomy, we should briefly address the three most obvious objections to it.

The first of these objections is that in each of the free speech cases discussed in the preceding section it is the government that is responsible for compelling either speech or the subsidy of private speech. In the situation of allusion to a trade mark, it is a private party who has allegedly compelled either speech or its subsidy. In fact, it is hard to see why this distinction is of any importance. A government that is committed to expressive autonomy bears a responsibility to uphold it both in its own actions and in regulating the actions of private parties.

The second objection is that a trade mark is commercial speech and, in the usual course of events, the trade mark owner will be a corporation. The American cases dealing with compelled speech, and with corporate speech more generally, have been the subject of powerful criticism on this basis.[16] However, the fact that speech is commercial is not a reason for it to be denied protection altogether, although it may impact on the level of protection that it is given.[17] Protection of the expressive autonomy of a speaker must surely entail protecting the way in which a person chooses to be presented in inviting commercial transactions at least to some extent, given the importance of commercial transactions to our community life. But this reasoning, though it may justify the protection of commercial speech, highlights the difficulty regarding the corporate identity of most trade mark owners. It makes sense to protect the personal autonomy of

---

[16] See, for example, Randall P. Bezanson, 'Institutional Speech' (1994–5) 80 Iowa L. Rev 735; Alan Hirsch and Ralph Nader, '"The Corporate Conscience" and Other First Amendment Follies in *Pacific Gas & Electric*' (2004) 41 San Diego L. Rev 483; and C. Edwin Baker, 'Paternalism, Politics, and Citizen Freedom: The Commercial Speech Quandary in Nike' (2004) 54 Case W. Res. L. Rev 1161. For an opposing position, see Martin H. Redish and Howard M. Wasserman, 'What's Good for General Motors: Corporate Speech and the Theory of Free Expression' (1997–8) 66 Geo. Wash. L. Rev 235.
[17] *Central Hudson Gas & Electric Corporation* v *Public Service Commission of New York* (1980) 109 S. Ct 2343.

natural persons, but does it make sense to protect the personal autonomy of legal persons? This is an important question for many areas of the law, a full consideration of which is outside the scope of this response. However, a robust defence of the attribution of rights to corporations, including rights grounded in autonomy, can be made. For example, Finnis mounts a defence of the attribution of rights to corporations on the basis of the rights of the individuals who use a corporate vehicle to achieve their collective aims.[18] In doing so he builds upon classic arguments made by Hohfeld.[19]

The third objection to my argument is that infringement of a trade mark, whether infringement by causing confusion or by allusion, can in most trade mark systems only be constituted by the use of a sign in the course of trade. If protection against allusion is best understood as protection against a type of compelled speech or the compelled subsidy of speech, why ought that protection to be available only in these particular circumstances? Few marks, and certainly not those iconic marks to which allusion is most likely to be made, represent the unaltered speech of their owners. The meaning of a mark can be altered in a variety of ways, and in a variety of expressive acts from which its owner would wish to be disassociated, only some of such situations giving rise to the possibility of an infringement action because they constitute use in the course of trade. Moreover, it is appropriate that this should be the case. The law cannot, and should not, try to control all the ways in which vehicles of expression such as trade marks are used and acquire new meanings. Respect for the expressive autonomy of the trade mark owner does not require that the law give her such complete control over her mark. However, it may well be an appropriate way of evincing that respect to remove a powerful incentive for using and altering the meaning of speech, the incentive of potential economic advantage. It is the contention of this response that, subject to the qualifications outlined below, this is an appropriate alternative to offering the trade mark owner either no control, or complete control, over the meaning of her mark. If that is right, then the function of the requirement that an infringement occur in the course of trade is evident.

Limiting protection against allusion

On the basis of her right to expressive autonomy, then, there seems to be good reason for permitting the trade mark owner to control some

[18] John Finnis, 'The Priority of Persons' in Jeremy Horder (ed.), *Oxford Essays in Jurisprudence (Fourth Series)* (Oxford: Clarendon, 2000) 9–11.
[19] Wesley Newcomb Hohfeld, 'Nature of Stockholders' Individual Liability for Corporation Debts' (1909) 9 Columbia L. Rev 285.

allusions to her mark. The question that now arises is how that control ought to be limited. It is at this point that the expressive autonomy of the party who, free from legal restraint, would use the mark for an expressive purpose becomes relevant. The expressive autonomy claim of that other party is a very important way of limiting the availability of relief against allusion to a trade mark. There are at least two situations in which allusion to the mark ought to be permitted despite the expressive autonomy claims of the trade mark owner.

The first of these is the situation in which it is necessary to allude to the mark in order adequately to comment upon, or even identify, the mark, its owner or her goods or services. It is reasonable to allow allusion to the mark for this purpose because there may be no effective way in which to make such comments other than to use, and sometimes to alter the meaning of, the mark. Moreover, using a mark for this purpose does not undermine, but recognizes, the nexus between the mark and its owner. A speaker cannot object to compelled participation in an argument about her own activities.

Most trade mark systems include partial provision for this problem.[20] However, I would argue that the many systems have been insufficiently willing to allow allusive uses of the mark for this purpose. In particular, the courts seem suspicious of allowing allusive uses of a mark for one of the most commercially important purposes, that of signalling the substitutability of a product to consumers. Take, for example, the case of unauthorized fan merchandising, such as that bearing the names of sports teams. There is undoubtedly a market for such products. That market is defined by a very low cross-price elasticity of demand. Fans of one sports team are unlikely to purchase merchandising expressing support for a different sports team. Within that market, allowing a sports team to use its trade marks to prevent the production of unauthorized merchandise, even in contexts in which there is no possibility of confusion between authorized and unauthorized merchandise either at, or after, the point of sale, gives it a very powerful monopoly indeed.[21] If branding is not to become the powerful barrier to entry that some economists see it as, new entrants must be allowed to allude to trade marks to signal the substitutability of their products for those of the market leaders. This argument is also pertinent in fields such as 'me-too' marketing – allusion to the trade marks of market leaders by new entrants, often store-brand products, for the purpose of signalling substitutability.

---

[20] In the UK, section 11(2)(b) and (c).
[21] This example is built around the facts of *Arsenal Football Club Plc* v *Matthew Reed*, Case C-206/01 [2003] RPC 144 at 172.

The second situation in which it might be necessary to limit the expressive autonomy claim of a trade mark owner to prevent allusive uses of her mark is more problematic. This is the situation in which a mark has become a cipher for a range of meanings for which no adequate alternative vehicle of expression exists. In such circumstances it may be essential that it be available to other speakers. 'Barbie' as a cipher for a particular understanding of womanhood, is an example much discussed in the literature. The mark often operates as a shorthand for a view of women as the objects of sexual attraction, but lacking in either intelligence or personality. In the United States, the BARBIE mark has been the subject of litigation in cases such as *Mattel, Inc.* v *Walking Mountain Productions*[22] in which Barbie dolls were used in satirical photographs in which they were shown mutilated by various kitchen appliances, and *Mattel, Inc.* v *Universal Music International.*[23] concerning the satirical song 'Barbie Girl' by the Danish group Aqua. Indeed, Mattel themselves recognize this function of the BARBIE mark. When Barbie turned 35 the company supported the production of 100 images of the doll, most of which exploited this function of the mark, many in ways not too dissimilar from those over which Mattel has taken legal action.[24] If there genuinely exists no satisfactory alternative cipher for an idea or set of ideas – as there may not be in the case of 'Barbie' – then the mark itself should be available for use. To put it another way, the mark may have become a kind of public forum. It may have become a space for debate rather than a contribution to debate. This type of thinking seems to underpin the law of trade mark genericide, although that law is arguably inadequate to protect the relevant free speech interest. In the case of a limited range of marks which have become important cultural vehicles of expression, there may be good reason for only protecting them against confusion and not dilution. Such a response seems justified by a commitment to protecting the expressive autonomy, not only of the owner of the mark, but also of those who would allude to it.

Significantly, these two categories of case reflect the two categories of parody recognized in American copyright commentary, so-called 'target' and 'weapon' parody,[25] though situations of parody do not exhaust those in which the party who would allude to a trade mark has a claim of one or

---

[22] 353 F.3d 792 (9th Cir. 2003).
[23] 296 F.3d 894 (9th Cir. 2002). See further Jare C. Ginsburg at xxx in this volume, Ch 4.
[24] Craig Yoe (ed.), *The Art of Barbie* (New York: Workman, 1994) 72.
[25] The distinction between parodies that use a text to comment on the text itself or its author and parodies that use the text as vehicles for commenting on something else was drawn in *Campbell* v *Acuff-Rose Music, Inc.* (1994) 114 S. Ct 1164 at 1172, though the labels 'target' and 'weapon' parody were not actually used in the case. The distinction has been

316   *Michael Spence*

other of these two kinds. Indeed, the intuition of copyright law that weapon parody is usually more difficult to justify than target parody also seems sound on the arguments of this section. Framing contests between the trade mark owner and those who would allude to her mark as contests between competing claims to expressive autonomy seems far more analytically fruitful than the more usual approach of framing them as contests between a 'property' right and a right to freedom of expression. These are effectively arguments about who can be compelled to say, or to subsidize the saying of, what, and who can be silenced by whom.

Conclusion

If the argument of the preceding section can be accepted, then a powerful alternative to either a utilitarian or a Lockean justification of dilution protection exists. This is important because the absence of such a justification does not mean that dilution protection is not expanding in the legal systems of the world, but rather that it is expanding in an insufficiently principled way. The argument from expressive autonomy justifies such protection but, equally importantly, places important limits on its permissible scope. For this reason it may provide a helpful way of filling the lacuna arguably left open by the Scott, Oliver and Ley-Pineda rejection of alternative approaches to dilution protection.

widely criticized, but may find some justification on the reasoning of this chapter. See Michael Spence, 'Intellectual Property and the Problem of Parody' (1998) 114 *Law Quarterly Review* 594, 608–15.

Part VIII

Anthropology

15   An anthropological approach to transactions involving names and marks, drawing on Melanesia

*James Leach**

Introduction

Social Anthropology is the comparative study of social forms. Social anthropologists seek to understand the ongoing constitution of persons, institutions, values and cultures through a combination of in-depth analytic engagement with particular societies, and through a comparative methodology. Juxtaposing principles and assumptions discernible in one social and cultural situation with those in another yields understandings of the development and constitution of the social reality under scrutiny. It also exposes assumptions relevant to the constitution of the society of the analyst that otherwise might remain hidden. The ideal is to learn something about both other peoples' social and conceptual worlds, and simultaneously about one's own through this comparative method.

This chapter, written by a social anthropologist, seeks to throw light on the subject of trade marks. In it, I focus upon the generation of the value which trade marks have been designed to protect. I then look at how that protection (of the value generated) through the system of trade marks influences the form that transactions take, and how it inflects the outcomes (objects, persons) of these relations for the parties involved. My focus then is upon the ongoing generation of value in social processes, and how the law comes to shape that value. To achieve this end, comparative material on the ownership and transaction of names and marks relating to identity is introduced. This comparative material is drawn from Papua New Guinea. Close attention is paid to the transactions between persons,

*   Thanks to Jennifer Davis for her persistence while encouraging me to participate, and for her editorial and intellectual input; to Megan Richardson for her commentary; and to Fleur Rodgers, who talked through the initial analysis of trade marks and transaction with me. Katharina Schneider shared ideas to my benefit and Rebecca Empson kindly commented on a late draft. The inspiration I have taken from Simon Harrison's work should be obvious, as will be the influence of Marilyn Strathern.

319

and between groups, in which identities emerge and which result in proprietary control over names and marks.

Persons differ in their constitution depending on the objects they create and associate through. My task here is to show something of the constitution of persons which is specific to the working of trade marks in their wider socio-economic context. I do that by contrasting trade marks and the *relations they make possible* with a description of other kinds of person and their objects; that is, other possibilities for the emergence of persons, and marks associated with them, in a different socio-economic context. Examining trade marks through comparison tells us interesting things about the operation of these 'marks' in both instances. In analysing the specific ways names and marks are used in different transactional contexts, I show that we can learn about the emergence of particular kinds of social form, and how the law might be party to the construction of one form of personhood[1] rather than another. I point to contrasts between the kinds of relationships, and therefore the form persons take, in trade mark regimes, and the kinds of relationships and persons apparent in the Papua New Guinean material.

The chapter draws upon an analytic vocabulary developed within social anthropology, and particularly in relation to the ethnography of Melanesia.[2] That vocabulary speaks of transactions, and the constitution of kinds of persons in those transactions.[3] As mentioned, I also draw upon comparative material about names, value creation and its retention from that region of the world. My strategy is thus not primarily historical, but comparative and analytic. The Papua New Guinean materials upon which I draw are snapshots for purposes of comparison. More could be said about these examples and their transformation over time,[4] but that is not the endeavour for me here.

---

[1] 'Person' and 'personhood' are technical terms in social anthropology. To study 'the person' is to investigate how an entity must appear and how they must behave in a given social network in order that they are recognized as a person. The emergence of the person in these terms is thus a social issue, and the study of 'personhood' naturally draws in a study of social relations and their formative qualities both on social actors, and upon wider societal forms often approached under the rubric of 'political economy'.

[2] See A. Gell, 'Strathernograms' in *The Art of Anthropology: Essay and Diagrams*, ed. E. Hirsch (London: The Athlone Press, 1999); M. Strathern, *The Gender of the Gift. Problems with Women and Problems with Society in Melanesia* (Berkeley: University of California Press, 1988); M. Strathern, *Property, Substance and Effect* (London: Athlone Press, 1999).

[3] See M. Strathern, 'Transactions: An Analytical Foray' in E. Hirsch and M. Strathern (eds.), *Transactions and Creations. Property Debates and the Stimulus of Melanesia* (New York and Oxford: Berghahn Books, 2004).

[4] See S. Harrison, 'The Past Altered by the Present: A Melanesian Village after Twenty Years' (2001) 17 *Anthropology Today* 3–9; J. Leach, *Creative Land. Place and Procreation on the Rai Coast of Papua New Guinea* (Oxford and New York: Berghahn Books, 2003).

Outline of the argument

We are familiar with differences between personal names and those signs that name organizations and companies. Neither of these are necessarily quite the same as the distinguishing name or mark given to a commercial product. Yet as symbols denoting kinds of identity, they do have overlaps, or perhaps I should say 'underlaps', significant to how they achieve their effects.[5] The marks draw their associations from a common series of elements. How each comes to have distinctive value, while drawing upon common elements, is good anthropological subject matter.

In the first section of the chapter, I focus on names as signs which have particular value for dwellers on the north coast of Papua New Guinea with whom I am familiar, or for whom there is an extensive ethnographic literature. These signs both are items of transaction, and establish relations in which other transactions are appropriate. In other words, they participate in the formation of particular relations, and the persons who result. In both of the Papua New Guinean language groups to which I refer, names carry value, point to things and persons that are also perceived as having value, and, in doing so, participate in the establishment of particular forms of social relation and institutions. It is how that particularity (difference from aspects of trade mark regimes) comes into being that I seek to establish through detailed discussion of the cases.

What emerges is that people's appearance as persons of particular kinds (a brother, a clansman, an initiated man, a marriageable woman) is dependent upon the relationships in which they are enmeshed.[6] Transactions which establish, perpetuate and modify those relationships are foundational to the emergence of all persons there.[7] Each party to a relationship has ongoing interests in the future possibilities that relationship affords for identity (definition of the person), and for productivity. These reciprocal interests are dramatized by periodic exchanges of nurture, of food and wealth, and of people. My point will be that the 'future potential'[8] of the relationship is 'owned' by all parties to it. Their interest in acting upon those relationships is an interest in their very being, and its transformations, one might say. Identity then is wholly bound into the relations one has to others, and these relations, while not always equal, or,

---

[5] 'Underlaps' is to signify shared conceptual underpinnings.
[6] See also M. Strathern, *Kinship, Law and the Unexpected. Relatives are Always a Surprise* (Cambridge: Cambridge University Press, 2005) 157–60; and J. Leach, 'Drum and Voice. Aesthetics and Social Process on the Rai Coast of Papua New Guinea', (2002) 8 *Journal of the Royal Anthropological Institute* (n.s.) 713–34.
[7] As Strathern points out, persons are always particular, always one person, not another: Strathern, *Kinship, Law*.
[8] Or just 'future'.

indeed, peaceable, are clearly seen as core to the constitution of each party as an agentive social actor of one kind or another.

Moving on to a discussion of trade marks, I establish that from their basic definition[9] it is clear that registered trade marks do not directly reference relations to specific persons (unlike similar signs in the Papua New Guinean material). However, my suggestion is that, even though there is a clear separation (in the definition) between goods and sign, and although the person does not figure in the definition at all, these signs carry value *in relation to persons* in interesting ways, highlighted by the contrast with transactions in Papua New Guinea.

My starting point in the quoted passage from the Trade Mark Directive (footnote 9) is the designation of the sign in relation to a valued entity. There is a clear logical sequence apparent in the statement. Primary value lies in the good itself, in the service or substance that can be *used or consumed* by another party. This is interesting in its own right, as, despite the clear and arresting value of marks and indicators in themselves, their value in this construction is dependent upon, and derivative of, a transaction which involves the consumption of a tangible (and in a broad sense) consumable item. I am aware of other aspects of how the trade mark comes to hold value, how it is part of intangible and highly significant processes of identity creation in consumers, and so forth.[10] In fact, these are aspects to which I shall pay considerable attention later in the chapter. But my starting point is the distinction between the consumable element in a transaction involving trade marks, and the enduring or non-consumable element. I argue that consumers of trade-marked goods draw upon tropes both of interpersonal, and of autonomous, value creation. They are in pseudo-personal relationships to the kinds of person that a trade mark appears to delineate, but are able to consider themselves autonomous from those other persons for the purpose of making their own identity through the consumption of trade-marked goods.

Much of the value generated in transactions which involve trade-marked goods is shown to arise from the possibilities these goods allow for the formation of identity in relation to another person (the trader and the image he protects through the trade mark). Yet having approached

---

[9] First Council Directive 89/104/EEC of 21 December 1988 to approximate the laws of the Member States relating to trade marks (hereafter TM Directive), Art. 2: 'A trade mark consists of any sign capable of being represented graphically, particularly words, including personal names, designs, letters, numerals, the shape of goods or their packaging, provided that such signs are capable of distinguishing the goods or services of one undertaking from those of other undertakings.'

[10] See R. Coombe, *The Cultural Life of Intellectual Properties. Authorship, Appropriation, and the Law* (Durham, NC.: Duke University Press, 1998).

these transactions through the Melanesian cases, transactions involving trade marks come to look peculiar in that there is no ongoing relationship established with this other person. Here differences between notions of the person and notions of agency are significant. Autonomy and self-determination are ideologically significant for consumers in mass societies. Trade marks are shown to participate in the ongoing development of particular kinds of persons: those appropriate to a political economy of mass production and consumption where persons must forge relations with others while maintaining a particular image of self-determination and agency.

Implicit in establishing the difference between the Melanesian examples and those involving trade-marked goods are difficulties that the Melanesian people I discuss would have in adopting the principles of trade marks without disrupting existing creative social practices.[11] However, the chapter seeks to do more than point to a well-known incompatibility between Western and indigenous regimes of ownership. Instead, the focus is what we might learn about our own social form through looking at trade marks from the perspective of Papua New Guinea, and through a specific anthropological methodology.

I conclude by arguing that, in the Papua New Guinea material, what I describe as the 'future' of the relationship, which can be embodied by a name or a mark, is owned by both parties. They have a different, but oscillating and reciprocal interest in its potential. The relationship and its future is an aspect of the emergence of the person, or groups of persons, as identifiable social entities, entities for whom the ideals of autonomy and self-determination are subsumed by the need to appear as a particular person through their position in relation to other persons. It is this 'future' which both giver and receiver 'own' and which the mark embodies.

In the case of transactions involving trade-marked goods it appears that, although there is a 'future' to the relationship,[12] instantiated by and made concrete by the trade mark itself, power over crucial aspects of that future is owned by one party to the transaction. The emergence of the person in the transaction is thus constituted differently. Responsibility for

---

[11] As will become clear, these practices are based on different assumptions about the role of marks and names, in turn based upon different operational understandings of the relation of the signs, marks and performances. As shorthand, I have elsewhere argued that they do not operate with a representational theory of meaning (see, for example, Leach, *Creative Land*, Ch. 7, and 'Out of Proportion? Anthropological Description of Power, Regeneration and Scale on the Rai Coast of PNG' in S. Coleman and P. Collins (eds.), *Locating the Field. Space, Place and Context in Anthropology* (ASA Monograph 42) Oxford: Berg 2006) 149–62.

[12] And for this reason, these are fascinatingly different from standard commodity purchases.

324   *James Leach*

making the self appear, for forming an identity, lies with the purchaser/
consumer. It is made possible *in* the transaction *by* the form of the transaction itself. As I outline, transactions governed by trade marks thus have
a dual aspect for the consumer. A pseudo-interpersonal relationship
is established with the trader as if they were a person with whom the
consumer could have an ongoing and identity-defining relationship. Yet
at the same time, a sense of autonomy from relationships and thus a sense
of self-determination and individual character emerges through a relation
to an object, defined by the transaction as alienated from other people
and thus available, as it were, to be wholly incorporated into the consuming subject. This fosters the constitution of their identity *apparently* without reference to other persons. It is in this complex interplay of subject to
subject and subject to object relations that I locate the interesting aspect
of the social operation of trade marks.

Relations with constitutive effects. Names and marks on the Rai Coast of Papua New Guinea

Persons in Melanesia can be seen to be made up of the relations they have
to others. In what follows I seek to demonstrate that this ongoing constitution of personhood is made explicit through religious and exchange
practices. There is no emergence of an identity, or power or value, without the input of others, and, moreover, without their presence as registers
of the effect of a person's action. Marks and names can stand for these
relationships, and thus embody a future which all parties to their constitution have ongoing interests in and ownership of.

In the villages of Nekgini-speaking people, which lie on the Rai Coast
of Papua New Guinea,[13] names and marks are highly valued aspects of
places. 'Place' is a crucial term in my analysis. Places are complex entities

---

[13] The Rai Coast is the land that runs east from just south of Madang town on the north
coast of Papua New Guinea and extends to the border with Morobe Province. It is a
narrow land, hemmed in to the south by the massive and dramatic Finisterre mountain
range and is isolated by its extreme terrain. The area is densely populated in terms of
coastal Melanesia with multiple language groups living subsistence lifestyles based
around swidden horticulture ('gardening'), small-scale animal husbandry, and hunting.
All Rai Coast people have some access to the cash economy, and many have small cash-
cropping schemes, trade stores or cocoa buying and drying operations which produce
minimal returns in the vast majority of cases. Their access to print media, and certainly to
electronic media, is very limited, although local radio stations are popular when people
have money for and access to batteries. Common manufactured items present in these
hamlets around the turn of this century were kerosene lanterns, second-hand clothes,
steel knives and rice / tinned fish. The hamlets that make up Reite village lie between 300
and 700 metres above sea level, and between 7 and 11 km inland from the coast. Each
hamlet group comprises between 20 and 100 people.

comprising persons, spirits, knowledge, landforms, etc. Places are identified by, that is, called by, the name of the land on which they lie, after the people there have successfully attracted others to come and receive presentations of wealth grown upon this land, and given away in that location. Being known as a place is dependent then upon transactions with other places in whose emergent identity the donor's name has a significant role.

These presentations are always part of wider life-cycle processes. They are made at the time, or as a consequence, of birth and marriage. They rely upon all the residents of a hamlet contributing, but, more than this, they require the co-operation of spirits and ancestors that reside in the lands owned by these residents. Spirits and ancestors reside in the landforms, in the springs that water each area, and in bones placed strategically in the bush lands of their descendants. The presence and significance of spirits and ancestors is made apparent by their presence at exchange ceremonies, taking the form of musical voices, decorations and inscribed marks. It is these voices and the beauty of the marks that elicits the presence of the receivers, Rai Coast people say.

Successfully completing a payment has the radical consequence not only of putting the place and its inhabitants on the map, as it were, as a named entity, but also, as members of that newly emergent named entity, the residents of the hamlet become close kin with one another. Hamlet members share knowledge of how to make an area productive, they share spirits, forms of planting crops, myths and magic. But these are 'internal' specifications. They do not amount to an identity until someone from beyond the group recognizes and names the emergent place. The term for an emergent hamlet/kin group is *palem* in the Nekgini language, referring to the physical structure from which wealth is distributed, a named place in the landscape, and all those people who have given a presentation of wealth to others from there.

A peculiarity of kinship in the area is that all the children who grow up together in a hamlet are considered siblings whatever their previous relationship, and as a consequence may not inter-marry. To do so is likened to self-consumption, an unproductive self-closure. And this, I would argue, is because marriage is the archetypal form of making productive relations with outsiders.[14] Marriage results in the payments in the form of *palem* which at one and the same time name the hamlet *and* make its inhabitants 'one' (kinsmen). Identity is in essence a relational product. As Megan Richardson points out in her comments, trade marks were seen

---

[14] See C. Lévi-Strauss, *The Elementary Structures of Kinship*, trans. J. H. Bell, J. R. von Sturmer and R. Needham (Boston: Beacon Press, 1969).

as a means by which identities might be developed in the absence of the kinds of ongoing relationships apparent in Papua New Guinea by 'ordering commerce in a society where relationships, power, trust and intimacy could no longer be the sole basis of exchange'. But the consequences of the introduction of trade marks have, as I will come onto, been to obscure the possibility for this kind of identity formation by making concrete new a-symmetric relations.

Marks and designs in Reite

Among Nekgini speakers, each generation has the responsibility of making their presence and power known through generating named places. One sees a constant emergence of new named places, new spirits discovered in these places, new songs and designs associated with them, and new kinds of people (newly defined as from *this* place rather than *that*) as a constant efflorescence in the landscape. Nekgini people make a large claim in this context, and that is the ownership of the 'story' (*patuki*: myth, ancestor, inscribed marks and name) of the origin of differentiation (generative productivity) itself. As this is closely related to identifying marks, I recount their understanding briefly.

There was a time when there were only two brothers and one woman. She was mother, sister and wife to the men. There were no children, no in-laws, no gardens etc. at this time. One day, the younger brother tattooed his design onto the inner thighs of the woman. She became ashamed and hid herself, but the elder brother tricked her, and saw the design there. He was furious, but controlled his anger to discover who was responsible. He called for all the people to come to his hamlet, and carve their designs onto posts there. The very last to do so was his younger brother, and when the elder saw this mark, he knew who had tattooed the woman. He fought with his sibling in a drawn out and terrible battle. Eventually, the younger brother left, established himself with the woman at a distance from the original hamlet, and exchanged wealth items with his elder brother to make up for his initial actions and to establish his independence. In this move, plants and animal species came into being, and gardening and animal husbandry, as well as wealth items, were found (as ancestors of various kinds) in the landscape. The mark that he made on the woman is the 'public' mark of all Nekgini people. All have the right to carve and draw it onto their houses, decorative and ceremonial carvings, and dance ornaments. It is called Yandi'emung in the hamlets of Reite.

The man who first made the mark has a name that is known to many in Reite. They use the name, in conjunction with breath and tune, to achieve certain transformative effects on other people. Their mark is something that has direct effect on the bodies of others. Each *palem* group has its own store of ancestral names and marks. These are explicitly things generated by people in the past, or that emerge in one's own productive engagement in places with other people, and are elicited by the demands of kin from other places. Each generation is responsible for re-generating its position and name through effecting others, causing them to recognize their presence as the emergent generation through exchanging wealth items with them. New places, and new marks, emerge all the time, but they are explicitly seen as emergent from the inter-relations of affines.[15] Affines are the 'cause', the 'base' or 'origin' of generative and productive activity. Their presence elicits this activity, and thus marks and identities are not only relational, but jointly owned by groups connected by marriage. In the case of Yandi'emung, both places (established in the myth) have the right to use the mark. Its value is one generated by their relationship and it retains its value as an element in that and analogous relationships.

Among the Nekgini speakers I know, these marks are closely guarded, their use exclusive to those who are connected to the generative relations in which they emerged. But the idea that one party to the constitution of a valued mark might be excluded from its use undermines the logic of its value. These marks are valued and powerful because they reference a generative set of relations. In fact, they come to embody and carry that generative power. Others may appropriate them, but such acts are explicitly viewed as theft.[16]

Ideally there should be an oscillation of power in the relationships between affines in which persons, places and inscribed marks emerge.[17] However, one side is always in the ascendancy at any one time, as equality and balance would mean stasis. Power to effect others then is the power to give shape to the future of social and material forms, but doing this means acknowledging others' role in that process as co-creators, even if they are passive at the moment of creation.

[15] 'Affines' denotes those related through marriage rather than descent in the technical language of social anthropology.
[16] The punishment for this theft are 'fines' or death through sorcery. However, such fines can be interpreted not as a punishment as much as a demand for substantive proof, after the fact, of the user's claim to inclusion in the generative relations of the mark's production. Thieves of such marks, should they survive, are thus rehabilitated, they are retrospectively redefined though transactions of wealth items and thus included in the generative relations the producers enjoy (see M. Demian, 'Custom in the Courtroom, Law in the Village: Legal Transformations in Papua New Guinea' (2003) 9(1) *Journal of the Royal Anthropological Institute* 32–57; J. Leach, 'Modes of Creativity' in Hirsch and Strathern (eds.), *Transactions and Creations* 168.
[17] See R. Foster (ed.), *Nation Making. Emergent Identities in Postcolonial Melanesia* (Ann Arbor: University of Michigan Press, 1995); M. Mauss, 'Essai sur le don: forme et raison de l'échange dans les sociétés archaïques' (1925) 1 *Année Sociologique* (n.s.) 30–186.

Owning names in Reite

Among Nekgini speakers, names have a very puzzling element to them. A person there can live their whole life with a personal name, while remaining unaware that this name is also a powerful spell used by other people. Such spells are highly valued and closely guarded *as spells*. Yet the people who know of the power of the spell may well not own the name as one they could use to name their own children. Some people have a right to use a name for people, others have knowledge about how to make use of it for magic and ritual. Marks and names thus have value in particular relationships in which they are effective. Their power/value is not necessarily available outside those relations.

Nekgini spells are a combination of the use of a name, a particular purpose, a tune or rhythm,[18] and additional elements which may be best described as 'ingredients'. For example, when a gardener plants the central areas of his garden, the 'growing shoot' (*wating*) of the garden as it is called in Nekgini and which they describe as ensuring the growth of the whole garden, he uses certain secret names. This central ritual planting is said to encourage plants in the periphery by its vigour and example. These names must be sung, or hummed, in the tune of the animating spirit of the garden to which they ultimately refer. Plant matter, paints, other substances, and the gardener's own ritual preparations, are all essential here. The name on its own has no effect. It would not work for any other task either.

Merely having a name, even one attached to one as a personal name, is not to be in control of its power then. A named person might be a place marker, an unconscious keeper for others perhaps, of the possibilities of power. Such power resides in the combination of correct elements and procedures that surround a name and its purpose. And that combination in turn relies upon the correct relation to affinal kinsmen. The knowledge of these combinations is given to adolescents, during initiation rites, by their mother's brothers (affines of their father).

On this part of the Rai Coast, it is categorical that affines, that is, people directly related by a current marriage, live in separate named hamlets. So one's maternal kin live somewhere else. Mother's brothers, who take the lead in initiation sequences, are categorically not part of your family in Rai Coast terms (being affines, living elsewhere, not sharing bodily substances that make one close kin). It is from an external position that they perform the work of initiation, and in doing so effect the transformation of

---

[18] See also P. Lawrence, 'The Ngaing of the Rai Coast' in P. Lawrence and M. Meggitt (eds.), *Gods, Ghosts and Men in Melanesia* (Melbourne: Oxford University Press, 1965).

a child into an adult. Knowledge of how to achieve vital ends – successful gardening being a vital end in this economy – thus comes from an external other to oneself. Indeed, this is made explicit in that fathers also have stores of knowledge and names, magic and so forth. Yet they are not the ones who initiate their children.[19] In fact, *their* spells are given to their sister's children. One's own name may not be available to one as power without this input from other people, without making the relationship to them both the basis of one's productivity, and the receptive space in which that productivity will have its effect. By that, I mean that each party takes responsibility for the future of the relationship. In fact each 'owns' the relationship in that they have claims on its outcomes.

Productivity is demonstrated by the first obligation that an initiated man has on his emergence: that of giving garden food, meat and wealth items to his maternal kinsmen in return for his initiation. Achieving this amounts to the visible (by this I mean socially acknowledged)[20] emergent presence of that person in the world. The mother's brothers see their own power working elsewhere. They in turn acknowledge the emergence of the giver (situated in another place, with other kinsmen helping them) through receiving what has been grown and collected by the initiate. It is in these transactions themselves that the emergence of the person as a socially recognized entity occurs.

The complex relational nature of names and identities is further demonstrated by Nekgini technologies of communication. All Nekgini hamlets/places have spirits, and these manifest as musical voices. The voices are accompanied by a rhythm, a series of drum beats. In this area, large drums (actually idiophones – hollowed logs without membranes)[21] are used to communicate between hamlets. Complex messages can be sent as a combination of various series of beats. Naming people is an integral part of such a communication system. In a dramatic extension of the principle that one's identity (and its reality as others' recognition) is externally generated, all initiated men in these villages have a name which is a 'call sign', consisting of a series of drum beats, which is taken from one of the spirit songs which the mother's brother's family own. It is one of these unique beats which is given to the initiate by his mother's brother, and with which he can be identified for the rest of his life. A man's audible presence in the landscape is in the call sign his mothers' brothers allocate

---

[19] See Leach, *Creative Land* Ch. 5.   [20] Ibid.
[21] K. A. Gourlay, *Sound Producing Instruments in Traditional Society: A Study of Esoteric Instruments and their Role in Male–Female Relations* (New Guinea Research Bulletin 60) (Canberra: Australian National University, 1975); Leach, 'Drum and Voice'.

to him on initiation. It comes from the very heart of *their* power to effect others, to grow crops and so forth, which their spirits embody.

A Nekgini-speaking man's identity then is in a very real sense borrowed from others. In fact, the call sign reverts to the maternal kin on a man's death. They have it available then to use again in the future. Persons here appear as social entities through reference to the relations they have to others. There is no emergence of an identity, or power or value without the input of other persons, and, moreover, without these others' presence as registers for the effect of a person's action.[22] Initiates have a *right* to give wealth to their maternal kin just as much as those kin have a right to receive it. Establishing a valued social identity then is a process of mutual constitution – an often contested and even agonistic process – but one in which neither party has the option of denying the other side's 'ownership' of the potential (future) of the relationship. Each party's identity and power is dependent upon that relationship, and thus their future is wrapped up in it.

I suggest that thinking through this kind of material, and abstracting from it, if you like, the method used – that is, considering transactions and the ways in which persons emerge from their specificity – can be usefully applied to the transactions and kinds of persons which emerge around and in trade mark law. I begin though by delving deeper into the issue of names and by returning to the issue noted in the definition of a trade mark: that the sign itself is empty of value, and signifies value lying elsewhere.

'Stealing People's Names'

I mention the sign's 'emptiness' or representational status (it stands first and foremost in its trade mark definition as a token for value-in-substance elsewhere) in order to make a contrast. Simon Harrison's marvellous ethnography of Manambu-speaking people from Avatip village on the Sepik River in Papua New Guinea describes signs that are anything but empty.[23] These signs are the personal names of people. In this instance, one might even say that it is the person who is empty, and the name or sign that carries substance, power and value. People are attached to names rather than the other way around. Let me elaborate briefly.

Avatip people live through fishing and sago production, which needs to be supplemented through trade. This trade is with neighbouring groups,

[22] Harrison, 'The Past Altered'; Leach, *Creative Land* 151–7.
[23] S. Harrison, *Stealing People's Names. History and Politics in a Sepik River Cosmology* (Cambridge: Cambridge University Press, 1990).

who have different languages, with whom they routinely exchange fish for starch foods (sago and tubers). Manambu rituals and their cosmology have been viewed by outsiders as a kind of patchwork of parts of the cosmologies of their neighbours.[24] In common with other groups in the area, it seems that these rituals and symbols have been acquired piecemeal through trade. The trading of ceremonial goods and cultural or symbolic forms is well documented.[25] For Manambu and their neighbours such a trade is possible because each entertains reciprocal assumptions of a common totemic structure to the cosmos, and to human societies as an aspect of that cosmos. Each Manambu village such as Avatip, and, within Avatip, each sub-clan, had monopoly rights over the ritual goods obtained from trading partners because such goods were only transmitted between local descent groups who belonged to the same totemic category[26] in different villages and language groups.

Harrison tells us that *the* major resource in Avatip life was esoteric and ritual knowledge. Politics focussed on the struggle for control of this knowledge, not access to or control over material wealth. 'To Avatip people all ritual powers and attributes are held only contingently by particular descent groups, villages or tribal groups, and are ultimately the immemorial property of totemic categories conceived as transcending all social and cultural boundaries.'[27] One can usefully think of this as like a template. The whole world, social and physical, is divided into categories. These categories are repeated over and again. Thus Avatip people found trade partners in the same section of another society as the one they belonged to in their own. Material wealth had little political significance (unlike in other areas of Melanesia). Harrison instead describes an obsession with the ownership of names.[28] Major political events revolved around public debates over the ownership of names, and who had the right to use them.

---

[24] I. Bashkow and L. Dobrin, 'Pigs for Dance Songs': Reo Fortune's Empathetic Ethnography of the Arapesh Roads' (n.d.) *Histories of Anthropology Annual* 2; S. Harrison, 'Ritual as Intellectual Property' (1992) 27 *Man* (n.s.) 225–44; S. Harrison, 'The Commerce of Cultures in Melanesia' (1993) (28) *Man* (n.s.) 139–58; M. Mead, *The Mountain Arapesh: An Importing Culture* (Anthropological Papers no. 36) (Washington: American Museum of Natural History, 1938).

[25] See footnote 24.

[26] 'Totemic categories' refer to divisions between people which mirror divisions between animal species and other elements within the natural world which are grouped together as belonging to, or dependent upon, each other. To belong to the same totemic category as people in a different language group is thus to share with them an identification with and responsibility for certain behaviour in relation to those aspects of the world.

[27] Harrison, *Stealing People's Names* 23.

[28] See also A. Moutu, 'Names Are Thicker Than Blood' Ph.D.thesis, Cambridge University, Department of Social Anthropology, 2004.

Manambu are 'relentless totemic classifiers' according to Harrison.[29] They insist on placing everything in the world into their totemic categories, and the community is divided into three intermarrying patrilineal descent groups which follow from this principle. Each descent group owns hereditary functions in magic and ritual, and it is these that give them control over their part of the environment through weather magic, fertility magic and so forth. So the polity as a whole is held together by the interlocking of each descent group's cosmological powers. All three groups represent themselves as using their powers for each other's welfare and sustenance. Avatip is further divided into sixteen sub-clans and it is these that are important political units. Each has its own ward (area of the village), origin myths, land, totems, magic and sorcery, and hereditary functions in the male cult (exclusive responsibility for certain ritual procedures in the religious life of Avatip, which until the 1990s was a male theocracy).[30] The fundamental concept here is an Avatip one – *ndja'am* – which encapsulates the idea of total reciprocity between groups. This amounts to a closed system of archetypal categories forming an organic totality because of the transactions of power and effect between them that sustain the polity as a whole.

Sub-clans have a timeless existence. Rather than being defined by their current members, their exploits or achievements, they exist more significantly as funds of ritual power that are independent of the existence of their members. Each sub-clan has a store of names that are associated with particular ritual powers. These are both personal names carried by living people, and also the names of ancestors used as magical spells. This is a closed and finite universe: and thus men compete for names on the assumption that these are a limited resource.

Empty descent groups exist as conceptual classes. Harrison has recently argued that this is a common theme in the ethnography of lowland Melanesia:

In these societies, everyone was vulnerable to the violent theft of their name and kinship position, along with their soul-substance, life force, or vital principle. The new possessor of these personal attributes does not seem to have been viewed as some sort of 'impersonator' or counterfeit of an 'original'. Personal identity appears to have been conceived as transferable in a sense in which it is not in Western societies – where it can perhaps be imitated or counterfeited but not actually alienated or reassigned. But in some Melanesian societies it was as though

---

[29] Harrison, *Stealing People's Names* 18.
[30] S. Harrison, *The Mask of War* (Cambridge: Cambridge University Press, 1993); Harrison, 'The Past Altered'.

the person were imagined as a kind of miniature corporation sole ... capable of being bodily occupied by a series of position-holders.[31]

In Avatip, names are considered the source of all magical powers of the sub-clan. These are *personal names* borne through generations by members. People occupy, they 'are in' names, which are supposedly fixed forever. A set of names then is the past, present and future of the sub-clan, and clan categories are not dependent on personnel. They are timeless, basic properties of the world. Magical and ritual powers are made permanently available to people by the categories – filling one or another is a source of competition between people, hence the public debates over who has the right to use certain names.

The future is there in the past, we could reasonably say for Avatip. The power any person or group evinces is the same power as was there previously, and as peoples' identities and relations with one another are determined by the name (ritual position and powerful function) they hold, one might say that life and time are recursive, repetitive or regenerative. Harrison's ethnography is all about how Avatip people compete, in these circumstances, for the ownership of names and thus cosmological power in a stable and limited cosmos.[32]

The names which they are known by are separate from them, yet hold the power of their future relations to others. Avatip notions of the self take on a particular character in relation to the series of names and marks that put each person in a specific relation to others. And it is these positions that are transactable (or indeed, appropriable) by the transfer of personal names. Here then we see names as actual structural positions in which persons come to have value to one another. This value is not a value apart from this social positioning. The social position and abilities of persons are an aspect of their names.

The contrasting status of names and marks in two transactional contexts

The ethnographic material from Nekgini- and Manambu-speakers presents us with a complex series of suggestive analogies to, and differences from, what we know of transactions involving trade marks. I began by

[31] S. Harrison, *Fracturing Resemblances. Identity and Conflict in Melanesia and the West* (Oxford and New York: Berghahn Books, 2006).
[32] During the 1980s many Avatip people abandoned their totemic rituals and enthusiastically adopted evangelical Christianity. It is clear, however, that in doing so, much of the logic of a theocratic polity was maintained, and transferred onto the new form of religious authority and power: Harrison, 'The Past Altered'.

pointing out that, under trade marks, the name derives from value generated by transactions of other, 'real' or 'substantial' goods themselves.
Both Avatip names and trade marks have value because of their relation to
other sources of value. Yet Harrison points out that there is a contrast
between them. Avatip signs and names are valuable in themselves, they
embody or exist as positions of substance or power in their own right.
Their 'relational' element is in their contrast with other such positions or
powers.[33] That is, their particular definition is against other similar but
distinct positions. And the distinction lies in the particular effects of each
sign. Trade marks also have value because of their position, but the value
of the trade mark lies in its referential quality. Trade marks primarily have
value in relation to the objects which they denote or identify. Thus there
can be a fear of the counterfeit of trade-marked goods (inferior goods
assigned with a trade mark for superior goods) which cannot exist for
Avatip or Reite names. In Avatip, as we have seen, names can be appropriated, but, in appropriating them, the appropriator takes on the substance and value of the name. In Reite, the appropriator is forced to
demonstrate their connection to the powers which generated the mark
or name retrospectively. They are not in the position of counterfeiter, but
of a replacement of another's position as rightful holder of that name. The
sign carries with it the substance of its value in a direct, not a referential,
manner.

Following from this contrast, we might say that it is the cultural construction of the sign itself as empty, and of value primarily lying in the
substance to which it refers, that has the possible result of a fear of
counterfeit, as such, in trade mark regimes.[34] This in turn has the effect
of separating reputation from the person or object to which it refers.
Reputation itself becomes object-like. That is, it becomes a value or
good in its own right, which can then be appropriated and used as if it
were an object independent of the relationships in which it has come to
have value. Legal regimes sanctioning trade marks are put in place to
prevent this kind of appropriation of value.

From the point of view of anthropological analysis then, the law of
trade marks has a peculiar cultural logic. That logic begins with the
premise that signs are empty and denote or reference real things. Once
a sign comes to have value in its own right (the subject of trade mark
protection, generated through the work of trading particular qualities of

[33] Avatip names have an alternate function to, and thus different value from, other names
and signs of the same type.
[34] See also M. Jamieson, 'The Place of Counterfeits in Regimes of Value: An
Anthropological Approach' (1999) 5 *Journal of the Royal Anthropological Institute* 1–11.

goods), that value is transmuted into the value of an object which in turn makes it available for appropriation by others as (an inappropriate) name for another object. Reputation itself comes to have an object-like status: a thing, a value, embodied in an object (the mark) which can then be appropriated by a counterfeiter. There is a circularity here whereby the referential sign comes to refer to its own value rather than the value of what it references.

In both the Papua New Guinean cases here, other people are the register of effect. Thus, in Avatip, one's reciprocal responsibilities as part of a wider whole are essential for the maintenance of the cosmos. In Reite, by contrast, seeing one's effects on others shows the emergent capacities and powers of the complex whole that 'places' amount to. Marks, such as Yandi'emung condense that effect into images, 'icons of power'.[35] And these icons contain within them reference to their sources. They have the effects they do because of where they come from, and how they come into being. They are the markers of generative capacity itself, and that is not something any group can have without others.

Harrison begins his monograph on Avatip with the traffic in cultural forms, pointing to the Manambu tendency to import aspects of symbolism and ritual.[36] We have also seen the significance of transactions of symbols, wealth items, foods and persons in Reite. Through looking at the content and effect of transactions in their specific forms, it has been possible to begin to describe how persons come to have the capacities and identities they do, as aspects of a wider system of relations and transactions in which action in others is elicited as a way of coming to know the self.[37]

The fundamental point I wish to draw from this into another social, economic and political context is that the person, as a particular situated entity, comes into being in relation to others. This is a complex process, involving multiple and continuous transactions. I have attempted to show how marks, images and identities are central elements of this process in Melanesia, and, in doing so, follow many others.[38] The future of relationships, of productivity and, indeed, reproduction is shaped and made available through the forms people appear in, and the effects those forms have on other people. I have emphasized responsibility for action in each case: owning names in Avatip carries obligations to others in

---

[35] See N. Munn, *The Fame of Gawa. A Symbolic Study of Value Transformation in a Massim (Papua New Guinea) Society* (Durham, N.C.: Duke University Press, 1986).

[36] See footnote 27.   [37] Strathern, *The Gender of the Gift*.

[38] See footnote 35. Munn provides a classic Melanesian example which explicitly deals with 'qualisigns', marks of value which condense social understandings and logics and allow transformations in persons through their transaction. Other references abound.

reciprocal (not necessarily equal) relations. In Reite, putting a mark on a person, or giving them wealth items, has ongoing consequences in oscillations of power between the parties and the generation of certain kinds of personal identity, group identity and understandings of the self.

Armed with these principles, I return to the simplest aspect of a trade mark as a definition of a value sign. In what specific kinds of transactions between persons do they come to have their status and value, and how is that status and value related to emergent forms of those persons? How does a trade mark work to position persons in respect to one another and to things, and thus participate in the emergence of a particular social form?

The definition of a trade mark

A trade mark consists of any sign capable of being represented graphically, particularly words, including personal names, designs, letters, numerals, the shape of goods or their packaging, provided that such signs are capable of distinguishing the goods or services of one undertaking from those of other undertakings.[39]

As I pointed out in the introduction, in this definition, what is pointed to by the sign is something other than it (of course, that is what 'sign' means – although that perhaps means Avatip and Reite marks are not 'signs' in that sense).[40] That 'something other' is specifically goods/items/ services that are 'consumable'.[41] We might pause to consider here whether all values are based on consumable value. The response is obviously not, as even in the above formulation there is a secondary value there in the sign itself which becomes the object of protection. But notice the primary value of the sign (as a trade mark) is not in itself, but in reference to a tangible thing in the world, a service (labour) of others, or an item that is used/ consumed by its receiver.

This is a very particular kind of value; a value based on the incorporation of a 'good' into someone else's body (consumption), persona (also consumption as it is used for this purpose), project, etc. The transaction requires that the good itself is taken away, alienated from its trader or owner and incorporated into another person. To describe it thus makes it clear that there is another value here, and that is one in part created by or protected by, the legislation: the value of the sign, derivative of another

---

[39] Article 2, TM Directive.   [40] See footnote 11.
[41] A real difference from Melanesia. Consumable items are one aspect of what is generated by the mark Yandi'emung (gender relations, sexual productivity, the population of the lands with species). The mark activates a particular mode of productive relation itself.

kind of value, made apparent by the transaction of a consumable item. All well and good so far: being a sign, it cannot have value without pointing to something tangible and material.

What does the sign do in the context of registered trade marks? Well, it identifies a particular object's origin, gives it an identity above and beyond its actual value to the consumer as an item merely of use or consumption, through connecting it to that origin. The value of the sign itself then is a value placed on a mechanism (I think of the mechanism as a technology of a kind), a mechanism to persuade consumers to consume a particular iteration of something that might be more generally available. So we might say that while one owns what one produces as a consumable item, clearly once it is consumed by another, 'logic tells us' as Locke put it,[42] that the item then is part of that other person. It is this connecting mechanism that is owned. If the material goods are the alienable aspect in the transaction, there is an inalienable aspect that travels alongside the item itself. I suggest that this might be understood as one aspect of the future of the relationship. The future of the transaction is made into a 'right', a control or hold over certain actions of others. These rights do not circumscribe all of their actions. Thus, what I describe appears as the application in commerce of simple principles contained in the Enlightenment liberal political philosophy of John Locke and his followers.

Let us look a little closer at the alienation aspect. What the consumer gives the trader by purchasing the trade-marked product establishes no ongoing relationship.[43] The consumer's engagement in the relationship is a commodity relation. The transaction establishes no further formal obligation between the trader and himself[44] due to the trade marks, whereas the trader clearly has an additional element at his disposal generated specifically by the form of relationship the trade marks create. The trader has drawn the consumer into establishing a relationship with an image or form, separate from himself. A consumer cannot make a relationship to the trader of that form other than the one binding him (the consumer) into a contract giving the trader the value of that consumer agreeing to recognize the form of their mark in the future. This may sound a little extreme. The consumer is clearly able to purchase from other traders in the future. Yet in buying a consumable, that consumer agrees to

---

[42] J. Locke, *The Second Treatise of Civil Government: And A Letter Concerning Toleration* (Oxford: Basil Blackwell, 1946).
[43] Specifically under the terms of the trade mark, that is. There may well be other mechanisms to ensure the product is fit for purpose and so forth, but these are not specific to the individual marked item as an aspect of that marking.
[44] C. Gregory, *Gifts and Commodities* (London: Academic Press, 1982).

an identity, and an identity that has certain value for the trader, which he does not have a formal share in *the future of*. This then is very unlike a mother's brother giving a name, an inscribed mark or a call sign to their sister's son. In this latter case, the transaction of a sign ensures each party's future is bound to the actions of the other.

The value of the trade mark sign is something that *both* buyer and seller are making appear. It is a 'social value' that you as receiver/consumer are party to creating. But the traders claim this as theirs solely. Hence there is a distortion of the transaction given by the very form of the name or mark that is attached to the commodity. How this distortion comes to appear, and indeed, seem wholly reasonable is something we should consider.

Annette Weiner[45] has discussed how, in many exchange systems (even those seen as entailing balanced, reciprocal transactions), one can discern strategies aimed at withholding assets of an important type. These, which she dubs 'inalienable possessions', are elements which represent the identities of the transactors themselves. In Simon Harrison's most recent book, he makes an extension of Weiner's thesis by focussing on how 'the maintenance of identity often depends on maintaining an exclusive association with a distinctive set of symbolic objects', and this involves 'the power to prevent those defined as outsiders from reproducing these markers of identity'.[46] Weiner's thesis was that as an object moves and circulates in transactions it leaves a more fundamental possession intact: that is, something integral to the identity of the transactor.

This is a useful position, but I want to make use of the idea to underline a different aspect from that which Harrison highlights. That is, the transactions, rather than leaving something intact, have a dynamic or generative element. In the Nekgini material, it is the very act of transaction that precipitates and constitutes the identity of the transactors. This mechanism is equally clear when one thinks about the transactions around trade-marked goods. I propose that it is the movement of the consumable item that *makes* an identity which has value for the trader. It also makes apparent a static position, allows the perception of a stable identity (the seller as another entity) against which the movement of the object can be seen. This in turn has the effect of making that which has not been included in the transaction (what I described as the future of the relationship between the two parties) appear as the essence or internal specification of one of them. It seems then to follow naturally that this aspect

---

[45] A. Weiner, *Inalienable Possessions: The Paradox of Keeping-while-giving* (Berkeley: University of California Press, 1992).

[46] See Harrison, *Fracturing Resemblances* 7.

should be the trader's alone. (I come on below to the 'future' of the relationship as it is experienced by the consumer.)

Rosemary Coombe has described in detail how trade marks have a 'cultural life' as circulating images and symbols in which their value is constituted by the circulation and re-use of these marks by the public. This co-creation of value leads to conflicts between those who consume and transform goods and services while at the same time cleaving to the symbols and identities that the traders appear to offer alongside a consumable item.[47] As Harrison puts it, 'what is at issue . . . is the propriety of creating private property rights over public symbols and commoditizing valued public icons'.[48] These authors point to something we might conceive of as the common production of such value. And here the comparison with Melanesia becomes pertinent again.

Reite peoples' actions acknowledge that the power of their marks over other people exists in – is only perceivable in – their effects on those others. While one comes to know oneself through the responses of others, one retains a responsibility for those responses. The form the future of the relationship takes is not always in one's own hands. It is a connection never denied by either party. It is in taking responsibility for the effects of action that a palem's, or a person's, reputation is generated. Thus the social origin of value is kept in view. There are inequalities and distortions in the relations these people have with one another, but these do not take the form of denying the common production of value. That is something specific to our own form of political economy. To deny the relations of value generation in Reite would be to nullify the future effects of one's actions, as those effects only register in the further actions of others in respect to one's own. One's personhood is thus bound to this process of mutual effect. Autonomy is differently constituted, thus so is the self.

Now what trade mark law does is to protect something created as an aspect of a transaction between parties which amounts to the *commercially valuable* identity of one party to the transaction. (These are *trade* marks.) It assumes that persons are in some way coterminous with their images and representations.[49] Yet, in trade mark transactions, goods and sign pass to a consumer with the value of both (good and sign) apparently available, but, in fact, the mark or sign of the trader never is actually available for consumption and transformation. Thus the realization of this value is not something that can happen *in the* relationship with the trader for the consumer (unlike the other way around). The transaction adds value to the sign for the trader.

---

[47] Ibid. 7.   [48] Ibid. 32.   [49] Ibid.

To explore this aspect further, I turn to look at a common justification for the value of the trade mark system that potentially undermines the analysis I am here developing, certainly if that analysis is read as a critique of the system. That justification is that trade marks *do* give the consumer future value as well. They give the consumer that value in two ways. Firstly, trade marks help identify trusted sources of goods, and thus assist purchasing decisions. Secondly, they 'help to provide consumers with an identity'.[50] That is, the trader provides the consumer with an opportunity for 'brand loyalty'. I wish to elaborate on this in the following terms. 'Brand loyalty' operates as loyalty to an idea of the self (identity by differentiation)[51] and its desire for alienated objects (to be self-determining).[52]

By this I mean that there is a reciprocation, but a reciprocation which transforms the general future value of a sign for the seller into an opportunity for the consumer to add their own labour and imagination in developing an idea of themselves as a particular (differentiated) kind of person.[53] It is crucial to this dynamic that the object is just that, a commodity which can be wholly consumed, taken into the person, and which does not have any ongoing link to another person. That the object takes this social form is what makes the consumer able to imagine that they are acting autonomously of others, and thus engaging in an act of *self*-determination by their choice. To choose to consume one kind of object over another is to make one's agency apparent. But that only makes any sense when the objects that are available have a particularly constituted aspect of identity built into them which is not specifically the identity of any other person. The trade mark, or 'qualisign'[54] is then a floating signifier of identity which is available for transaction, but which is actually owned in its significant value-generating elements by another 'person' – the trader.

---

[50] L. Bently and B. Sherman, *Intellectual Property Law* (Oxford: Oxford University Press, 2001) 656–7.

[51] Purchasing one good rather than another is to differentiate oneself from other purchasers who make different choices.

[52] That is, objects which are alienable through purchase from their owners. These objects appear to have value apart from those owners. This value is wholly transferred to the purchaser on purchase. As the objects in question have an 'identity' or are associated with a particular 'identity', this is apparently also transferable to the purchaser. The act of purchase then appears as an autonomous act which defines the purchaser in relation to an object. Association with objects, and choice over that association, allows a purchaser to imagine that they determine their identity.

[53] It is another aspect of this 'labour' input that Rosemary Coombe points to as the justified basis for consumers to resist the total control over these signs by traders or corporations.

[54] See footnote 35.

Objects in this transaction appear as though they can become part of the self because they are shorn of obligation to others. Yet we have seen that, because of the mechanism of mediation that the sign allows, there is a connection to another 'person', that is, a corporation or trader who retains elements of the image of the person.[55] The relationship is modelled on the interpersonal, when the obligations that each party have to each other are very different.

The trader's obligation is also in some way 'to themselves'. They must continue to trade in recognizable goods. In a mirror of the self-realization of the consumer through the choice of goods, the trader too realizes his identity apparently through their own actions and agency, but, in fact, through their reception and recognition by others. This complex separation dynamic allows aspects of the person in a commodity economy to become part of the ongoing value-generation placed on the sign or image itself.

In essence then, to own a trade mark is to own an aspect of the future of a relationship with a consumer. The puzzle comes when one realizes that the mechanism works not to connect transactors in the same way as other marks or names do. With trade marks, we see a situation in which people are reciprocally constituting kinds of value for themselves – one side as economic actor, the other a self-determining consumer – but in which the future of the relationship established is particular because the logic of the sign-mechanism actually works to ensure that there is no person for the consumer to have a relationship with in the future. All they can do is continue to consume, and thus develop their own sense of self through the fantasy of self-determination. The obligations of the trader (reliable quality, easy identification) are a promise of the system of trade marks, when, in effect, it seems that the obligations are all on the side of the consumer. That obligation of the consumer is to imagine the development of a self through consuming goods which draw on tropes of value from relations to other persons, but which in reality are empty and require filling by their very need for self-realization. Unsurprisingly, the generation of a particular kind of self-determining individual is the outcome of a political economy in which trade marks make sense.

Conclusion

I have been looking here through the lens of, and utilizing a descriptive language derived from, a very different form of political economy. The

---

[55] Their identity is generated, just as it is protected, by appearing to offer a relationship, and thus a form of mutual constitution of identity.

forms of transaction and personhood that emerge within that description have given some purchase over the social significance of trade marks. As Davis shows clearly,[56] while the implementation of the law may well be instrumental, the policies which inform the law and thus give substance to the kinds of ownership (social relations) made possible, do have effects upon wider social forms as they emerge. Trade marks are particular technologies. They amount to objects which, when introduced into a relationship between persons, give structure to those relations in a way which makes certain realizations of the person as a social actor possible, and which, in doing so, obviate other possibilities.

The argument of this chapter has been that value and productivity are dependent upon others recognizing them. That is such a basic truth that I think we sometimes miss it. It also seems to be the case that *not* making it explicit, or, perhaps, making explicit certain elements while hiding others, is where value in trade marks comes from. So the economy in which trade marks make sense is one in which the social origin and the social value of signs and names are intricately manipulated. The idea of consistency and guaranteed quality is a version of an ongoing relationship modelled as if it were between persons of the same kind who come to know each other's character and trust that character. Only that is not quite right, as only one party to the transaction has to make this imaginative leap. These then are the 'underlaps' informing the status of names and marks of various kinds which I mentioned. I have pointed out how the idea of the self emerging in relation to others in Melanesia points up ways of making the self in an economy with trade marks as an element. Consumers are in pseudo-personal relationships to the kinds of person that a trade mark appears to delineate, but are able to consider themselves autonomous of those other persons for the purposes of making their own identity through the consumption of goods. It is little wonder that names and identifying marks are the form the technology takes. Abstracted and legally endorsed relations of commerce draw upon these tropes and understandings in the establishment of their value.

---

[56] J. Davis, 'European Trade Mark Law and the Enclosure of the Commons' (2002) 4 IPQ 342–67.

16 Traversing the cultures of trade marks: observations on the anthropological approach of James Leach

Megan Richardson*

Anthropology, we are told, involves the study of societies, so an anthropological perspective on trade marks, by definition, entails a search for social meaning. James Leach notes that a 'trade mark' is, in legal terms, a sign used to denote the source of a trader's goods or services in the market. The legislators' conception of a trade mark, reinforced by countless judicial statements and scholarly pronouncements, however, only gives a partial account of trade marks. In particular, it suggests that the central function of trade marks is to mediate between supply and demand in a mass market economy. This leads to a delimited role for trade marks, under which (as Dr. Leach says) 'the primary value of the sign is not in itself, but in reference to a real thing in the world, a service (labour) of others, or an item that is used/consumed by its receiver'. Or, in the words of Duncan Kerly from the first edition of his *Law of Trade Marks*, published in 1894,[1] a trade mark is 'a symbol ... applied or attached to goods ... offered for sale in the market ..., so as to distinguish them from similar goods, and to identify them with a particular trader ...',[2] the implication being that they have no other important function. Nevertheless, it may be questioned whether this conception fully accounts for the operation of trade marks in practice or even under law.

* Many thanks to Graeme Austin, Susy Frankel, Jane Ginsburg, Jonathan Griffiths, Janice Luck, Sam Ricketson and especially Jennifer Davis and James Leach for helpful advice and comments. Thanks also to those who organized and participated in the Cambridge Interdisciplinary Trade Marks Workshop 2006 for a fascinating and inspirational seminar on multidisciplinary aspects of trade marks and trade mark law. Information in this chapter is current as at the end of June 2007.
[1] D. M. Kerly, *The Law of Trade-Marks and Trade Name, and Merchandise Marks* (London: Sweet and Maxwell, 1894).
[2] Ibid. 25. This was Kerly's definition. There was no statutory definition of a 'trade mark' in the British Trade Marks Registration Act 1875 or the Patents, Designs and Trade Marks Acts of 1883 and 1888. However, Kerly's definition was adopted in much this form as the statutory definition in the Trade Marks Act 1905, s. 3.

I shall suggest that trade marks may have a social dimension beyond the consumption-based relationships and transactions discussed by Dr. Leach, although I generally agree that consumption has a role to play in the functioning of trade marks (something I shall come back to at the end of my comments). Dr. Leach shows how a traditional community uses symbols to tell stories, to entertain and enliven the humdrum of normal life, and to convey moral and other messages. I shall attempt to show that, even in a so-called 'sophisticated' society, trade marks may serve similar symbolic functions. However, the origin of meaning may be very different in a traditional community compared to our (post)modern society where we feel free to select our own symbols and meanings. Therefore, it is not surprising that conflicts arise when traditional symbols are selected by traders and offered to consumers for multiple purposes. Our post-colonial trade mark system seems ill equipped to handle the problem but perhaps a solution of sorts can be found in the (in this respect) neglected common law protection against passing-off.

Trade mark meaning in law and in practice

An obvious place to begin our examination of trade marks is the beginning of the British registered trade mark system in 1875.[3] For already at this stage it appears a rift was developing between the legal and social functions of trade marks. Early legislators may have conceived of trade marks as primarily signalling mechanisms designed to send trade in one direction or another in much the same way as the signal on a train line directed trains, ordering commerce in a society where relationships, power, trust and intimacy could no longer be the sole basis of exchange – even if they also thought that only some trade marks would be appropriate for registration under an intellectual property regime.[4] They may have maintained that the true value of trade marks could only come 'over time' through use in association with goods 'symbolized' and that, unlike designs, their purpose was not 'to please the market', as William Smith said in his evidence before the Select Committee on Trade Marks in

---

[3] With the Trade Marks Registration Act 1875 (38 & 39 Vict. c. 91) which established the British register.

[4] Their main concern, according to contemporaneous sources cited by Brad Sherman and Lionel Bently, was to prevent fraud: *The Making of Modern Intellectual Property Law* (Cambridge: Cambridge University Press, 1999) 172. If so, they chose a peculiar way to give it effect when they took as their model the designs and patents statutes of the period and set innovation thresholds for registration: see Megan Richardson, 'Trade Marks and Language' (2004) 26 Syd L Rev 193, 203–8. And see also Sherman and Bently, *The Making* 198–9: the result was to treat trade marks as a kind of intellectual property.

1862.[5] But traders could not resist employing their trade marks in a more ornamental fashion, taking their cue from the artists' and designers' marks that proliferated in the nineteenth century.[6] They commonly employed trade marks to enhance their products and, since the trade mark legislation did not preclude this, provided the trade mark was sufficiently distinctive to qualify for registration, the practice continued.

Many early registered trade marks had a strong visual, even pictorial, appeal and presumably were selected with this in mind. Examples are the striking eight-point star of tobacco company W. D. & H. O. Wills,[7] the simple yet attractive Bass ale red triangle[8] (the first registered trade mark, which also featured in Manet's painting *A Bar at Folies-Bergère*[9]), and a charming Portland vase trade mark[10] (one of several marks registered for the Wedgwood company which had been marking its wares since the late eighteenth century).[11] Also common were elaborate labels, such as those in Figure 16.1, whose 'flowery style, mass of information, engraved borders and decoration' have been characterized as 'typically Victorian' in a Patent Office centenary publication on the Trade Marks Registry.[12] The fact that food products, china, alcohol and tobacco featured as trade-marked products also says something about the tastes and means of ordinary Victorians.[13] A variety of evocative names and

[5] *Report from the Select Committee on Trade Marks Bill, and Merchandize Marks Bill* (London: House of Commons Papers, 1862) 27.
[6] For numerous examples, see Malcolm Haslam, *Marks and Monograms of the Modern Movement 1875–1930* (Guildford: Lutterworth, 1977).
[7] Wills' house mark was lodged when the register opened on 1 January 1876: Bernard Alford, *W. D. & H. O. Wills and the Development of the UK Tobacco Industry, 1786–1965* (London: Methuen, 1973) 129.
[8] This was the first trade mark registered under the 1875 Act, according to R. L. Moorby *et al.* for The Patent Office, *A Century of Trade Marks 1876–1976* (London: HMSO, 1976) 22–3.
[9] Paris, 1882: see Douglas Cooper, *The Courtauld Collection* (London: Athlone Press, 1954) 101.
[10] Trade Mark 8024 (lodged 8 July 1876) UK Patents Office. The image, which is still registered, can be viewed online at www.ipo.gov.uk/tm/t-find/t-find-number?details requested=C&trademark=8024.
[11] See L. Richard Smith, *A Guide to Wedgwood Marks* (Sydney: Wedgwood Press, 1977) 7 especially.
[12] Moorby *et al.*, *A Century* 41. Not just Victorian – elaborate representations could be found on the registers in France, Spain and the Netherlands in the late nineteenth century, and the first international trade mark registration (in 1893) was a pictorial device used by Russ Suchard et Cie for Swiss chocolate: see *The Madrid Agreement Concerning the International Registration of Marks from 1891 to 1991* (Geneva: International Bureau of Intellectual Property, 1991).
[13] See A. N. Wilson, *The Victorians* (London: Arrow Books, 2005) 198 (Britain a 'smoking nation'); Richard Wilson, 'Selling Beer in Victorian England' in Geoffrey Jones and Nicholas Morgan (eds.), *Adding Value: Brands and Marketing in Food and Drink* (London: Routledge, 1994) 103, 105 (large portion of working-class surplus income spent on alcohol); Megan Richardson and Lesley Hitchens, 'Celebrity Privacy and

Figure 16.1 Examples of elaborate labels (FISH SAUCE label,[14] OLD
ENGLAND SAUCE label[15]).

words were registered too, despite the fact that there were statutory
constraints imposed on the registration of words especially. The Act of
1875 specified that words could only be registered as trade marks in their
own right if they were 'special and distinctive' and in trade mark use
before the passing of the Act.[16] The Patents, Designs and Trade Marks
Act 1883 removed the need for prior trade mark use but stated instead
that only 'fancy' words that were not in 'common use'[17] could be registered on their own account, a standard slightly relaxed in 1888 to allow
registration of 'invented' words or words 'having no reference to the
character or quality of the goods and not being a geographical name'
(and in 1905 by inserting 'direct' before 'reference to the character or
quality' and 'according to ordinary signification' before 'geographical').[18]
Nevertheless, the statutory language was thought lenient enough to allow
registration of such subtly meaningful expressions as MAZAWATTEE (for

Benefits of Simple History' in Andrew T. Kenyon and Megan Richardson (eds.), *New
Dimensions in Privacy Law: International and Comparative Perspectives* (Cambridge:
Cambridge University Press, 2006) 250 (Victorians loved collectables).
[14] Moorby *et al.*, *A Century*, 42.　　[15] Ibid.
[16] Trade Marks Registration Act 1875 s. 10. Alternatively, words could be added to an
otherwise distinctive trade mark but then the words were part of the trade mark (as with
the examples shown in Figure 16.1 above).
[17] Patents, Designs and Trade Marks Act 1883 (46 & 47 Vict. c. 57), s. 64(1)(c).
[18] See Patents, Designs and Trade Marks Act 1888 (51 & 52 Vict. c. 50), s. 10; Trade
Marks Act 1905 (Edw. 7 c. 15), s. 9.

tea),[19] OOMOO (for wine)[20] and CALIFORNIA SYRUP OF FIGS (for medicine)[21] – paralleling the depictions of foreign people in native dress who
featured in a number of picture trade marks of the period.[22] The exoti-
cally romantic qualities of these examples give an insight into the British
psyche in these early days of international travel and adventures in far-off
lands.[23] More generally, the bizarre (for the audience) language of the
trade marks in question may have appealed in a society where innovation
was valued. So it is not surprising that traders preferred them.

Courts also seemed to be drawn to words of 'striking humour and
fancy'.[24] After some debate it was held that invented words need not
satisfy any additional standard (apart from being 'new and freshly
coined') of being 'obviously meaningless' in order to satisfy the inventive-
ness threshold of the Patents, Designs and Trade Marks Act 1888.[25] As
Lord Macnaghten said in the *Solio* case, 'invention is not so very common'.[26] Lord Herschell added that, although reward for merit is not the
basis of trade mark registration, invention takes a word from outside the
common language which the legislation's distinctiveness threshold pre-
serves for common use, and registration therefore 'deprives no member of
the community of the rights which he possesses to use the existing
vocabulary as he pleases'.[27] Interestingly, adoption of existing words as

---

[19] *Densham & Son's Trade Mark* (1895) 2 Ch 176 (CA). The word, registered as a trade mark
for tea in 1887, was coined from Hindi and Sinhalese words for 'luscious' and 'garden'.

[20] *Burgoyne's Trade Mark* (1889) 6 RPC 227. 'Oomoo' was a word in an Australian
Aboriginal language as noted further below, footnote 61 and accompanying text.

[21] The applicant applied for registration after some thirteen years local use and this contributed to the finding of distinctiveness under the 1905 Act: see *In re California Fig Syrup
Company* [1910] 1 Ch 130 (CA).

[22] For instance, the Aboriginal warrior symbol which featured in *Trade Mark of the Stock-
Owners' Meat Company of New South Wales* (1897) 14 RPC 783.

[23] As Disraeli proclaimed in 1862, '[i]t is a privilege ... to live in this age of brilliant and rapid
events. What an error to consider it a utilitarian age! It is one of infinite romance! Thrones
tumble down, and crowns are offered, like a fairy tale, and the more powerful people in the
world male and female, a few years past, were adventurers, exiles, demireps. Vive la
bagatelle': A. N. Wilson, *The Victorians* 262, although going on to point out that the view
may not have been shared by the poor and the children of the poor in Victorian England.

[24] The reference is from *Eastman Photographic Materials Co. Ltd v Comptroller-General of
Patents, Designs and Trade-Marks* [1898] AC 571, Lord Macnaghten, 583.

[25] Ibid. Thus SOLIO (with respect to photographic paper) was held to be an invented word
for purposes of the 1883 Act as amended in 1888, irrespective of whether those familiar
with Greek language might find some allusion to the sun.

[26] Ibid.

[27] Ibid. 581. Protecting the 'great open common of the English language' was seen as a
function of the distinctiveness standard: see ibid. Lord Macnaghten, 583, drawing a
parallel to nineteenth-century land enclosures and referring to *In re Dunn's Trade Marks*
(1889) 41 Chd 439, Fry LJ, 455. See also *Re Joseph Crosfield & Sons Ltd* [1910] 1 Ch 130
(CA), Cozens Hardy MR, 141, and compare Fletcher Moulton LJ, 148 (traders entitled
to 'bona fide description' of goods).

348 *Megan Richardson*

trade marks 'quite out of the common signification' was also enough to qualify as 'special and distinctive' under the 1875 Act[28] – equally satisfying the distinctiveness standards of the 1883 and 1888 Acts.[29] Well-known literary expressions and proverbs were therefore considered unobjectionable trade marks and the practice of using them was widespread according to a Board of Trade Committee Report in the late 1880s.[30] Examples are THREE CASTLES (from William Thackery's *The Virginians*)[31] and WESTWARD HO! (the title of Charles Kingsley's book),[32] registered as trade marks by W. D. & H. O. Wills in the late 1870s.[33] On the other hand, plainly descriptive terms such as 'Perfection' and 'Superfine' were considered insufficiently distinctive for trade mark registration (even if, through use, they had come to denote a particular trader's goods) on the policy of preserving the common language for common access.[34] Although judges' ideas about the common language as a depletive resource may be considered rather simplistic, given the fluid processes by which language appears to develop, the same may be said of historical linguistic theories of language that dominated at the time.[35]

In the twentieth century, trader activities went one step further in the trade mark sphere, aimed at forging an ongoing integral relationship between trade marks and popular culture. As Ralph Brown observed,[36] post-war advertisers began to see it as their task to respond to and affect consumers' desires to find a relationship between 'material reward and spiritual value'.[37] Using folk culture's techniques of 'repetition, a basic style, hyperbole and talk talk, folk verse and folk music' to convey advertising messages,[38] some trade marks developed into 'important cultural resources for the articulation of identity and community in Western

[28] Lewis Sebastian, *The Law of Trade Marks and Their Registration* (London: Stevens and Sons, 1878) 37.
[29] Lewis Sebastian, *The Law of Trade Marks and Their Registration* (2nd edn, London: Stevens and Sons, 1884) 58; (3rd edn, London: Stevens and Sons, 1890) 73.
[30] *Board of Trade Committee to Inquire into Duties, Organisation and Arrangements of Patent Office, as relates to Trade Marks and Designs Report, Minutes of Evidence, Appendices* (c.-5350) 81 *Parliamentary Papers* 37.
[31] William Thackery, *The Virginians* (London: Bradbury and Evans, 1858–9).
[32] Charles Kingsley, *Westward Ho!* (Cambridge: Macmillan and Co., 1855).
[33] Alford, *W. D. & H. O. Wills* 126, adding that both brands were highly successful.
[34] *In re Joseph Crosfield & Sons Ltd* above, footnote 27, Cozens-Hardy MR, 142–3.
[35] See Richardson, 'Trade Marks and Language' 207–8.
[36] 'Advertising and the Public Interest: Legal Protection of Trade Symbols' (1948) 57 Yale LJ 1165.
[37] Ibid. 1180.
[38] Daniel Boorstin, 'Advertising and American Civilization' in Yale Brozen (ed.), *Advertising and Society* (New York: New York University Press, 1974) 11, 22.

societies'.[39] COCA-COLA, PEPSI, MCDONALD'S, BARBIE and later HARRY POTTER and THE SIMPSONS (to name but a few) became the symbols of a modern culture which eschewed the traditional folk symbols of old in favour of a pop-language of its own. Of course, these trade marks retain important differences from traditional folk symbols. Daniel Boorstin, early on, pointed out that, in their case, cultural meaning is initiated through organized efforts by traders,[40] even if (as others have noted) audiences may participate in more or less active ways.[41] Rosemary Coombe argued in the late 1990s that traders' interests in controlling the use of their trade marks in public discourse may run counter to the abilities of audiences to recode 'commodified cultural forms' to suit their own agendas.[42] And James Leach notes that these trade marks forge relationships with traders, even if (it may be added) they also forge relationships between individuals who identify themselves as a community of Coca-Cola drinkers, McDonald's eaters, *The Simpsons* viewers, *Harry Potter* readers and so on. Nevertheless, I suggest that an important but largely overlooked change has occurred in the discourse of trade marks. Now, it seems, trade marks may, like folk symbols, tell stories.[43] They might, in the words of Brown, seem to offer little more than artificially romanticized 'illusion' if read to proclaim the merits of goods or services to which they happen to be applied.[44] There may be an element of 'not quite right', as Dr. Leach says, if the pretence is that the trade marks offer a guarantee of consistency and quality. But that is to under- and overestimate their meaning for their audience. As Burchett J of the Australian Federal Court framed it in *Pacific Dunlop Ltd v Hogan*,[45] '[n]o logic tells the consumer that boots are better because Crocodile Dundee wears them for a few seconds on the screen . . . but the boots *are* better in his eyes, worn by his idol' and '[t]he enhancement of the boots is not different in kind' from 'the effect produced when an alpine pass makes a grander impact on the tourist whose mind's eye captures a vision of

---

[39] Rosemary Coombe, *The Cultural Life of Intellectual Properties. Authorship, Appropriation, and the Law* (Durham, N. C.: Duke University Press, 1998) 57.
[40] Boorstin, 'Advertising and American Civilization' 23.
[41] See, for instance, Coombe, *The Cultural Life* 57 (a postmodern insight in stressing audience engagement in the 'construction' of reality as noted by Graeme Austin, 'Trademarks and the Burdened Imagination' (2004) 69 Brooklyn L Rev 827, 829 – but from the perspective of traders the starting point is still modernist: they establish the trend even if audiences embrace, redefine or critique it).
[42] *The Cultural Life* 57–8.
[43] See Megan Richardson, 'Copyright in Trade Marks? On Understanding Trade Mark Dilution' [2000] 1 IPQ 66.
[44] Brown, 'Advertising' (1948) 1181.   [45] *Pacific Dunlop Ltd v Hogan* (1988) 14 IPR 398.

Hannibal urging elephants and men to scale it'.[46] I would go further and say the boots are little more than a vehicle for cultural meaning, and what the consumer effectively purchases, 'consumes' (in the way of a reader of a book or a viewer of an artwork) and publicly displays is an association with Crocodile Dundee.

Such culturally charged trade marks pose challenges for legislators, courts and commentators accustomed to thinking of trade marks as signs that function, or *should* function, primarily to denote a trader's goods or services in the market.[47] While in extreme cases the development of cultural meaning has been treated as undermining distinctiveness (or rendering a previously districtive trade mark generic),[48] distinctiveness standards which are directed to preserving the already common language – and allow for appropriations from other sources – seem to have limited capacity to deal with 'expressive genericity'.[49] Thus the main focus has been on infringement. But here concepts such as trading by confusion and even trade mark dilution only go so far if courts maintain that the signalling function of trade marks must be implicated by a use that is calculated rather to tarnish or blur cultural meaning.[50] Limitations and exceptions to infringement have also been construed to allow certain public uses deemed socially valuable that would be unlikely to occur by consent, including uses in parody which in cleverly postmodern fashion

---

[46] Ibid. 429.

[47] See, for instance, Rochelle Cooper Dreyfuss, 'Expressive Genericity: Trademarks as Language in the Pepsi Generation' (1990) 65 Notre Dame L Rev 397 (expressive genericism should be a ground for denying or removing trade mark registration); Jessica Litman, 'Breakfast with Batman: The Public Interest in the Advertising Age' (1999) 108 Yale LJ 1717, 1735 ('neither incentive theory nor moral desert' offers a reason to protect from competition traders who 'sell the public on atmospherics'); Austin, 'Trademarks and the Burdened Imagination' 921 (modern trademark doctrine 'privileges those consumers who are concerned with the prestige value of their goods over those who care somewhat less, or not at all . . . [and] the latter group, of whom trademark law seems somewhat less solicitous, may actually be healthier').

[48] For instance, *Re 'Tarzan' Trade Mark* [1970] RPC 450; *Elvis Presley Trade Marks* [1999] RPC 567. See also *Davis v Commonwealth* (1988) 166 CLR 79 (Australian Bicentennial Authority's constitutional authority to regulate the trade mark use of '200 years' in conjunction with '1788', '1988' or '88').

[49] For the language of 'expressive genericity', see Dreyfuss, 'Expressive Genericity'. Interestingly, the judicial treatment of distinctiveness standards appears to have been little affected by legislative reforms in the 1990s which permit distinctiveness to be acquired through use without 'inherent' distinctiveness: see Richardson, 'Trade Marks and Language' at 200–2.

[50] As pointed out by Aldous LJ in *Arsenal Football Club plc v Matthew Reed* [2003] RPC (39) 696, 48 (CA), use of a trade mark for goods 'purchased and worn as badges of support, loyalty and affiliation' may jeopardize the trade mark's functions. See also *Campomar Soc. Ltd v Nike International Ltd* (2000) 202 CLR 45, 66–7 (High Ct of Australia) (interests of registered trade mark owners may go beyond indicating trade origin).

draw on a trade mark's imagery, distort it and turn it back on itself.[51] An example is the 'Barbie Girl' pop song which parodied the girl-as-commodity imagery associated with BARBIE.[52] The US Court of Appeals, Ninth Circuit, held that critical commentaries about pop icons entail First-Amendment privileged freedom of speech and should be exempted from liability under the Federal Trademark Dilution Act 1995: the use was declared 'noncommercial' for statutory purposes, notwithstanding that 'Barbie Girl' was a pop song worth some millions of dollars.[53] Some may take this reasoning to suggest that the new focus of 'commons' discourse in relation to trade marks will be on infringement rather than registration. If so, this would bring it closer to the idea of the English common land of the nineteenth century which, as Jennifer Davis has pointed out, was tradition-ally privately owned but 'there was a class of people, often very broadly defined, who had positive but differing rights to its fruits'.[54]

Trade marks and traditional symbols

That said, it must be remembered that one feature of a statutory system is that tradition need play no role in the way that rights are established and framed. Thus 'the common' in trade mark law can (although need not) mean 'raw elements of language' that are 'free for use and exploitation by all'.[55] Similarly, as we have seen, a trade mark can be 'invented' by a trader – including by acts of appropriation from other sources – rather than devel-oped and incorporated into reputation over time, as with the common law of passing-off.[56] The idea of innovation=appropriation sits easily with a

---

[51] For the cultural value of parody in providing a vehicle to challenge a trader's monopoly over meaning, see Jason Bosland, 'The Culture of Trade Marks: An Alternative Cultural Theory Perspective' (2005) 10 Media & Arts L Rev 99.

[52] *Mattel, Inc. v MCA Records Inc.* 296 F.3d 894 (9th Cir. 2002).

[53] Ibid. Kozinski J at 907. Since the case an explicit 'fair use' exception has been inserted into the Trademark Dilution Act: see the Trademark Dilution Revision Act 2006, s. 2.

[54] 'Protecting the Common: Delineating a Public Domain in Trade Mark Law' in Graeme Dinwoodie and Mark Janis (eds.), *Trademark Law and Theory: A Handbook of Contemporary Research* (Cheltenham: Edward Elgar Press, 2007).

[55] An 'unpropertised' common, as defined by Kevin Gray, 'Property in Thin Air' (1991) 50 Cambridge LJ 252, 256, 283.

[56] For instance, in the classic passing-off case of *Reddaway v Banham* [1896] AC 199 Lord Macnaghten described the process through which 'camel hair belting' became identified with plaintiff Reddaway's reputation in the following terms (at 217): '[o]wing to the excellence of his manufacture his belting became widely known all over the world. It was advertised as camel hair belting. It was ordered, sold and invoiced as such; and so camel hair belting came to mean Reddaway's belting, and nothing else. It was admitted at the trial that for about fourteen years no belting had been made or sold under the description of camel hair or camel hair belting except by Reddaway and certain persons whom he had

postmodern society. As Jeremy Waldron has pointed out, the 'cosmopolitan' (a term he prefers to 'postmodernist') 'refuses to think of himself as defined by his location or his ancestry or his citizenship or his language ... He is a creature of modernity, conscious of living in a mixed-up world and having a mixed-up self.'[57] But the contrast with those who live their lives by traditional customary standards is nicely illustrated by James Leach's comments on practices about names and signs among the Nekgini-speaking people of the Rai Coast of Papua New Guinea. As I understand it, names and signs may be 'invented' in Reite but, even so, their existence and ongoing symbolic meaning and power is determined by social context, relationships and experiences rather than established or re-established through acts of individual choice. In this respect, Aborigines in Australia and Māori in New Zealand appear to have similar ways of thinking about their traditional symbols.[58] Their understandings may to some extent be acknowledged under common law or equitable doctrines which share concerns with traditional values.[59] But they are not necessarily accommodated under a statutory, especially registration-based, intellectual property system, part of whose function is to define the very rules by which the system operates.

So what was the approach adopted to traditional symbols in the registered trade mark system? The original framers of the British legislation may have anticipated that traditional symbols would be treated as

promptly challenged and stopped ... Reddaway had no difficulty in holding the field against any interloper who hoped to find more profit and less trouble in trading on another man's reputation than on his own merits.'

[57] 'Minority Cultures and the Cosmopolitan Alternative' (1992) 25 Mich J L Ref 751, 754.

[58] See Brad Sherman and Leanne Wiseman, 'Towards an Indigenous Public Domain?' in Lucie Guibault and P. Bernt Hugenholtz (eds.), *The Future of the Public Domain: Identifying the Commons in Information Law* (Alphen aan den Rijn: Kluwer Law International, 2006) 259; Susy Frankel and Megan Richardson, 'Cultural Property and the Public Domain: Case Studies from New Zealand and Australia' forthcoming in Christoph Antons (ed.), *Traditional Knowledge, Traditional Cultural Expressions and Intellectual Property Law in the Asia-Pacific Region* (Alphen aande Rijn: Kluwer Law International, 2008).

[59] As, for instance, in *Bulun Bulun v R&T Textiles Pty Ltd* (1988) 157 ALR 193 (artist John Bulun Bulun's *Magpie Geese and Water Lilies at the Waterhole* (1980), made following the customs of the Ganalbingu People, allowing him to paint scenes featuring aspects of the Waterhole Dreaming, accepted to be his original copyright work under copyright law but subject to a fiduciary obligation on him to conserve the interests of the Ganalbingu People: per Von Doussa J at 194); *Foster v Mountford and Rigby Ltd* (1977) 14 ALR 71 (secret stories and rock drawings made by members of the Pitjantjarja community revealed to anthropologist Charles Mountford, at the instance of the Pitjantjara Council enjoined on the basis of the equitable breach of confidence doctrine from publication in the Northern Territory which, it was argued, 'may cause damage of a serious nature' disrupting the community's social system: Muirhead J at 74). The well-known passing-off case, *Erven Warnink BV and others v J. Townend & Sons (Hull) Ltd* [1979] AC 731 (HL), also concerned a kind of traditional knowledge, in this case the traditional Dutch method of producing the advocaat liqueur.

common rather than subject to trade mark rights. The Board of Trade stated that 'we think where any English word would be rejected as not entitled to registration no person ought to be permitted to register its translation into any other language'.[60] Yet traditional symbols, with their romantically foreign connotations, soon proved popular as trade marks. When cases got to court (after deliberation) English judges condoned the practice, deciding that the common language protected by the distinctiveness standard was the common English language. As Chitty J said with respect to OOMOO when its distinctiveness was questioned in *Burgoyne's Trade Mark*,[61] it was enough that for the 'ordinary Englishman' the word was 'a fancy word not in common use', although it might have been used to mean 'choice' in 'the aboriginal language of Australia'.[62] In Australia itself, among the first trade marks registered under the Trade Marks Act 1905 (Cth) were BOOMERANG[63] and BUNYIP.[64] DINGO, BILLABONG and KANGAROO came soon after.[65] Simple images of a kangaroo, boomerang and emu were also registered early on,[66] as shown in Figure 16.2, their style arguably reminiscent of the 'primitive' images common to Aboriginal art and artefacts which circulated in the colony and featured in its museums.[67] And it may be that indigenous Australians were not averse to the absorption [of their symbols]

---

[60] *Board of Trade Committee* xi.

[61] (1889) 6 RPC 227. The applicant claimed no connection with the Aboriginal people of Australia, or even Australia, having taken the name from a label used on Australian wine bottles exhibited at the 1886 Colonial Exhibition, 230.

[62] Ibid. 231–2.

[63] Trade Mark 454 (lodged 1906). BOOMERANG, originating in the Dharug (or Dharuk) language of the Sydney region, was only one of many possible words used for the implement in Australia: see Philip Jones, *Boomerang: Behind an Australian Icon* (Kent Town, South Australia: Wakefield Press, 1996) 80.

[64] Trade Mark 541 (lodged 1906). Charles Barrett, *The Bunyip and Other Mythical Monsters and Legends* (Melbourne: Reed and Harris, 1946) notes that, from early contacts with Aborigines, Europeans heard tales of the Bunyip (or 'Bunyup', 'Kajanprati', 'Katenpai', 'Tunapatam', 'Tumbate' or 'Toor-ru-dun', as it was also called) 8–10.

[65] Trade Marks 155444 (DINGO lodged 1917), 33112 (BILLABONG lodged 1922), 34531 (KANGAROO lodged 1922).

[66] Trade Marks 277 (Kangaroo image), 453 (Boomerang image), 600 (Emu image) – all lodged in 1906. The trade marks can be viewed online at http://pericles.ipaustralia.gov.au/atmoss/falcon.application_start.

[67] See Wally Caruana, 'Black Art on White Walls' in Sylvia Kleinert and Margo Neale (eds.), *The Oxford Companion to Aboriginal Art and Culture* (Melbourne: Oxford University Press, 2000) 454–5 especially; and, for examples of boomerangs, kangaroos and emus as featured in nineteenth-century Aboriginal art, Sylvia Kleinert, 'Art and Aboriginality in the South-East' in Kleinert and Neale (eds.), *The Oxford Companion to Aboriginal Art* 240 at 242–3. (Note that 'emu' itself is not an Aboriginal word.)

Figure 16.2 KANGAROO, BOOMERANG and EMU trade marks.[68]

into European culture, at least the more secular symbols,[69] even if they might have expected a more continuous and acknowledged connection to be maintained with their indigenous roots. By 2007 things have changed little as far as the register is concerned – there are still plenty of BOOMERANG, BUNYIP, KANGAROO, DINGO and BILLABONG trade marks and OOMOO has been registered by Hardy Wine Company Ltd (which claims a local tradition of use for its wines going back to the nineteenth century).[70]

Advocates of Aboriginal interests in Australia have argued that our trade mark law should be interpreted to prevent registration of culturally offensive trade marks[71] and suggested that a vehicle is the Registrar's obligation to deny registration to 'scandalous' trade marks under the Trade Marks Act 1995 (Cth).[72] Others might see this as a precedent for an overly censoring approach to trade mark registration, with implications for freedom of speech.[73] In any event, standards such as scandalousness, offensiveness[74] and even 'cultural offensiveness' (the

[68] See above, footnote 66.

[69] As said about the boomerang by Philip Jones, curator at the South Australian Museum and author of *Boomerang: Behind an Australian Icon*, correspondence, 17 April 2007: see Frankel and Richardson, 'Cultural Property'.

[70] Number 953036 (label/image) and 1099230 (word). The label, which dates back to the 1870s, was probably the one used by a 'Mr Hardy' at the Colonial Exhibition referred to above, note 61 at 230: see 'Original Bottle Discovered in Oomoo Revival', *Winestate*, 20 December 2003, www.winestate.com.au/newsletter/mailout/newsletter201203.htm.

[71] See, for instance, respected indigenous lawyer Terri Janke in her classic study *Our Culture: Our Future*, prepared for the Australian Institute of Aboriginal and Torres Strait Islander Studies and the Aboriginal and Torres Strait Islander Commission (Surry Hills, New South Wales: Michael Frankel and Company, 1999) 149.

[72] Section 42(a).

[73] Although US courts have held that the Lanham Act provisions barring registration of scandalous or disparaging trade marks (see below, note 74) do not violate the First Amendment since use is not precluded: see G. Austin, 'Trademarks and the Burdened Imagination' at 884.

[74] See §. 2(a) of the US Lanham Act 1946 (15 USC § 1052). This also proscribes trademarks that 'may disparage'.

statutory standard in New Zealand)[75] do little to address forms of behaviour which are *not* considered particularly scandalous or offensive by the community,[76] or a relevant section (in the New Zealand case, Māori – although there cultural offensiveness has served a useful educative exercise in raising awareness in the broader community about symbols that are offensive to some as registered trade marks).[77] And, so far, they have not generally been used on the ground that a person without any authentic connection to traditional culture is seeking to register a traditional symbol as a trade mark.[78] Nor has 'ownership', as shown by the Australian case of *Lomas* v *Winton Shire Council*[79] in which 'Waltzing Matilda', the name of a song regarded by many as an Australian folk song, was allowed to be registered as a trade mark by Brenda Lomas over objection of the Waltzing Matilda Centre and Winton Shire Council who maintained they were guardians of the 'Waltzing Matilda' heritage, but without evidence of trade could not establish ownership for trade mark law purposes.[80] Further, although the distinctiveness standard might better acknowledge that certain traditional symbols are not eligible for registration, it is most well suited to filter out those symbols that have

[75] Section 17(1)(c) of the Trade Marks Act 2002 (NZ) states that a trade mark must be refused registration if registration or use would in the Commissioner's opinion 'be likely to offend a significant section of the community, including Maori' (and s. 73(1) provides for cancellation of a registered trade mark). For a history, see Susy Frankel, 'Trade Marks and Traditional Knowledge and Cultural Intellectual Property Rights' in Dinwoodie and Janis (eds.), *Trademark Law and Theory*.

[76] As in the Washington Redskins case: on survey evidence 36.6–46.2 per cent of Americans considered 'Redskin(s)' to be offensive (interestingly, lower for Native Americans than for the general population), but this was insufficient for scandalousness which required a general feeling of outrage, as in 'shocking to the sense of truth, decency or propriety' of a 'substantial composite of the general population': *Harjo* v *Pro-Football Inc.* 50 USPQ 2d 1705 (TTAB, 1999) 154–6. A claim of disparagement succeeded but was set aside in *Pro-Football Inc.* v *Harjo* 284 F Supp. 2d 96 (DDC, 2003) as unsupported by substantial evidence and barred by laches after registrations of up to twenty-five years. For proceedings continued, see 415 F. 3d 44 (DC Cir. 2005). For 'Squaw' held disparaging, see *Re Squaw Development Co.* 80 USPQ 2d 1264 (TTAB, 2006).

[77] I am grateful to Simon Gallagher, Principal Trade Mark Examiner at the Intellectual Property Office of New Zealand (IPONZ) for this insight, based on experience of the New Zealand provisions.

[78] See also Trade Mark Practice Guideline Amendment T/2006/11 on the IPONZ website (Information Library) at www.iponz.govt.nz/pls/web/DBSSITEN.Main concerning the Pitau (Koru), stating that '[s]ince the threshold of offensiveness under the Trade Marks Act 2002 is much higher than that of appropriateness, and the cultural origins of designers and applicants are not part of the assessment process, processes under the Act cannot answer questions of this [i.e. appropriateness] type with regard to trade marks'.

[79] See *Lomas* v *Winton Shire Council* (2003) AIPC 91-839.

[80] Distinctiveness was not made an issue notwithstanding the Examiner's comment that the song had 'outgrown its origins' and 'belongs to and indicates Australia as a whole': *Winton Shire Council* v *Lomas* (2000) 51 IPR 174, 179.

fallen into common use – as, for instance, in New Zealand where an attempt by the Raukawa Marae Trust, claiming to act on behalf of the Ngāti Toa iwi, to register the words of the *Ka Mate* haka (long used by sports teams, schools and community groups as well as being the official haka of the national rugby team for some 100 years) has been the subject of objection by the Trade Marks Office which argues that this haka represents New Zealand as a whole and not a particular community or trader.[81] Finally, a difficulty with all registration thresholds is that they are essentially directed at trade mark *registration* rather than the *use* of traditional symbols in marketing which may continue irrespective of registration. Many do – especially in Australia where one only has to walk into a tourist shop in downtown Melbourne to be reminded of the words of anthropologist Chips Mackinolty in 1983 that:[82]

As a tourist item, the boomerang in its wonderful array of latter day permutations is arguably the most popular souvenir from Down Under; whether it is made of plastic, ply, laminate, metal or glass; whether made in Terrigal or Taiwan ... As the souvenir and advertising trades give commercial impetus, the image of the boomerang is readily subsumed into a nationalism that has only marginal reality to the first Australians.[83]

The prospect of trade mark law having much to say about these forms of conduct at present seems weak. Certainly there are possibilities. For instance, during the short life of the Australian 'label of authenticity' certification trade mark, a stylized boomerang symbol designed by indigenous artist Peter Yandana McKenzie served as a marker for authentic Aboriginal art.[84] Perhaps, had the label's use continued over time, there

---

[81] See Trade Marks (210) 305166, 305167, 305168 (in Abeyance) on the IPONZ website (Trade Marks Search) at www.iponz.govt.nz/pls/web/DBSSITEN.Main, and Frankel and Richardson, 'Cultural Property'. A hearing is scheduled.

[82] Chips Mackinolty, 'Whose Boomerang Won't Come Back?' in Peter Loveday and Peter Cooke (eds.), *Aboriginal Arts and Crafts and the Market* (Darwin: Australian National University North Australia Research Unit, 1983) 50.

[83] See Nelson Graburn, 'Introduction: Arts of the Fourth World' in Nelson Graburn (ed.), *Ethnic and Tourist Arts: Cultural Expressions from the Fourth World* (Berkeley: University of California Press, 1976) 29: 'Australia saturates its public institutions, its souvenir outlets, and its overseas exhibitions with its own aboriginal arts, crafts, motifs and color schemes'.

[84] The authenticity label has been the subject of extensive discussion and commentary: see, for instance, Sherman and Wiseman, 'Towards an Indigenous Public Domain?' 264; Matthew Rimmer, 'Authenticity Marks and Identity Politics' (2004) 3 Indig LJ 139; Terri Janke, *Case Studies on Intellectual Property and Traditional Cultural Expressions* prepared for WIPO (Geneva: WIPO, 2003) Case Study 8 (with an image at www.wipo. int/tk/en/studies/cultural/minding-culture/studies/finalstudy.pdf p.139); Terri Janke and Robynne Quiggin, *Indigenous Cultural and Intellectual Property: The Main Issues for the Indigenous Art Industry in 2006* prepared for the Australian and Torres Strait Islander Arts Board, Australia Council (Sydney: Aboriginal and Torres Strait Islander Arts Board, 2006) 31–2. Although generally the label seems to have been viewed as a good step for

might have developed a wider public understanding of the Aboriginality of the boomerang and not just the authenticity of the artworks to which the label was applied. More generally, traditional symbols might themselves be registered as trade marks by their traditional guardians, with the aim of using trade mark rights to prevent or delimit 'inappropriate' uses. That apparently was the purpose of the attempt in New Zealand to register the *Ka Mate* haka as a trade mark. But in some ways trade mark registration is fundamentally unsuited to traditional symbols. Even if I might question Dr. Leach's view of trade marks as concerned solely or primarily with consumption, I concede that trade mark law presupposes *some* trade and consumption in relation to registered trade marks and these may be anathema to traditional communities contemplating their traditional symbols.[85] In the longer term, passing-off, whose historical concern is honesty in trade,[86] which embraces deceptive uses of personal symbols for trading purposes,[87] and whose concept of 'reputation' is wide enough to allow for reputation to develop around traditional symbols,[88] may be better fitted than trade mark law to be a doctrine that generally polices the integrity of trading behaviour.

Aboriginal artists, there have been criticisms from within the Aboriginal community, including that an overly centralized model was used which meant that '[i]ndigenous people who did not know the artist, or the art, were signing off on the "authenticity"': Janke and Quiggin, *Indigenous Culture* 32. Since the demise of the label, along with its administering organization, standard trade marks as used, for instance, by Aboriginal Arts Centres and arts businesses in Australia have taken on a similar function. For examples, see Janke, *Case Studies* above, Case Studies 2 and 7.

[85] Trade marks which do not simply reproduce traditional symbols may be considered differently. But even here there can be a practical impediment to registration, as in Janke, *Case Studies*, Case Study 2 42–3 (giving examples where indigenous applications were not pursued after receiving an adverse report) – although Janke does conclude that there is 'strong evidence' that indigenous use of the trade mark system is increasing and supports this development.

[86] See, for instance, *Reddaway v Banham* above, footnote 56, Lord Macnaghten at 220–1: 'it is the fraud, not the manner of it, which calls for the interposition of the Court'; *Erven Warnink* [1979] AC 731, 742–3 per Lord Diplock: passing-off indicates (although does not fully encompass) 'what a moral code would censure as dishonest trading'.

[87] As in *Pacific Dunlop v Hogan* above, footnote 45 (claims for passing-off case and misleading/deceptive conduct under s. 52 of the Trade Practices Act 1974 (Cth) succeeded when Paul Hogan's character was spoofed in a television advertisement).

[88] As with the traditional recipe for advocaat: see *Erven Warnink* [1979] AC 731. Of course, this presupposes that reputation can be established (or in the case of the boomerang re-established) in traditional symbols.

Part IX

Geography

17 Geographical Indications: not all 'champagne and roses'

*Bronwyn Parry**

1 Introduction

The relationship between geography and trade mark law is, in many people's minds, most clearly evidenced in a specific type of intellectual property right (IPR) known as the 'geographical indication'. These instruments, which provide one kind of 'label of origin' for products, had their genesis in the agricultural and political milieu of eighteenth-century France. Perhaps because of this they have always been robustly championed by Europeans as exceptionally useful tools for defending the rights of local producers against the ever-present risk of the 'genericization' and 'passing-off' of their products by distant others. We now find ourselves, however, at a unique historical moment: one in which there is increasing pressure to universalize the use of geographical indications (GIs).[1]

This prospective universalization would be both geographical and epistemological in nature. Advocates from the European Union continue to argue vociferously within the World Trade Organization (WTO) that the globalization of production and consumption of specialty goods necessitates the development of a more extensive multilateral system for recognition of geographical indications. Compliance to such systems

* I would particularly like to thank the sponsors and organizers of the workshops held at Emmanuel College, University of Cambridge, in July 2005 and July 2006 – Lionel Bently, Jane Ginsburg and Jennifer Davis – for so generously providing me with the opportunity to 'do' interdisciplinarity the way it is in the movies. The terrific group of lawyers and colleagues from other disciplines at the workshop made it both a very fruitful and an exceptionally rewarding event for me. I must especially thank Dev Gangjee for being such a helpful, engaging and astute respondent, and my academic co-conspirators Sarah Franklin, Henrietta Moore, Juliet Davis, Catherine Nash, Simon Reid-Henry and Miles Ogborn for hearing endless ruminations on champagne before they actually got to drink any. Any errors remain my own.
1 WTO Secretariat, 'Discussions on the Establishment of a Multilateral System of Notification And Registration of Geographical Indications for Wines And Spirits: Compilation of Issues and Points' 23 May 2003 (TN/IP/W/7/Rev.1), available at http://docsonline. wto.org/DDFDocuments/t/tn/ip/W7R1.doc. All of the websites mentioned in this chapter's notes were accessed on 10 December 2007.

could be secured, they assert, through the creation and robust defence of a global registry of protected place names and associated products. They have also argued that the typology of goods that would attract the higher level of protection currently afforded only to wine and spirits be extended to include a range of other products including processed foods, beverages and even handicrafts. While their propositions have historically met with some resistance they have, nevertheless, recently succeeded in pushing forward their adoption by the WTO.[2]

These proposals have also been embraced by some developing country members of the WTO. They view geographical indications as a potential tool for protecting niche products (such as Darjeeling tea or Basmati rice) that have come to acquire a particular cachet in an increasingly consumer-led global marketplace. The move to expand their use appears to be gaining momentum. However, before GIs are clasped too tightly to the collective global bosom there may yet be time to pose of them some fundamental, if largely unexplored, questions. Firstly: what is the work we are asking GIs to do?; secondly, how do they do this work?; and thirdly, are they the most effective mechanism for achieving this work? In this chapter I cannot do more than offer a few speculations on the latter, which must ultimately be left up to the greater expertise of intellectual property rights lawyers to resolve. What I do hope to do, however, is to employ my disciplinary perspective on the history and role of geographical understandings of place and its significance to reveal the particular ways in which these concepts are mobilized in this form of intellectual property right. In so doing my intention is to point up, through a thoughtful, if preliminary, analysis some matters that might be taken into consideration in addressing the vexatious issue of the future of GIs.

The chapter is divided into four further sections. The first of these turns on the axes of the primary questions I have posed: what is the work we are asking GIs to do and how do they do it? In answering these questions I set about exposing and interrogating, at a conceptual level, the very particular 'geographical imaginary' to which the mechanism of GIs appeals. I then consider how this is employed to 'discipline' both the intellectual framework of GIs as a form of property right, and the various claims that are made of it. In considering these matters I pay careful attention to the way in which a very particular (and I would argue deeply essentialized and static) conception of 'place' is invoked to support

---

[2] W. New, 'WTO Meeting Reopens Discussions On Geographical Indications Register' *Intellectual Property Watch*, 12 December 2006, 1.

and prosecute appeals to 'authenticity'. In so doing, I ask the reader to consider how these rather flat-footed conceptions of place came to be so closely associated with GI law and why they have proven to be so resonant over time. By contrasting these conceptions with contemporary understandings of the fluid and progressive nature of place I intend to challenge some of the taken-for-granted assumptions about place that continue to underpin so much of GI law.

In answering the second question – how do GIs achieve their intended work – I turn in the third section to re-examine an iconic case study: the establishment of one of the earliest forms of geographical indication, the Appellation d'Origine Contrôlée (AOC) system that had its genesis in the Champagne riots of 1911. It may at first appear that there is little to be gained from any further analysis of this now rather well-worn and over-worked case study. I would argue, however, that a careful, if necessarily brief, analysis of the foundational concepts on which the system was premised reveals a great deal, most notably about the conceptions of place that were being appealed to in legitimating this new form of regulation. It also provides evidence that, although such conceptions were neither intellectually nor, it might even be argued, morally robust, they were warmly embraced at the time of their introduction and, moreover, continue to provide the philosophical underpinning of much of contemporary GI law. In order to understand something of the historiography of their usage it is helpful to situate this early twentieth-century thinking about place within wider intellectual movements that were in the ascendancy in the geographical academy at exactly that time, and I do this in section 4 of the chapter.

Returning in the fifth section of the paper to the twenty-first century, I here contemplate the legacy that these historical conceptualizations have had on current thinking about GI law and its application. Here I seek an answer to the question of whether GIs provide the most effective method for promoting (rather than protecting) local modes of production and products. I conclude that perhaps all that GIs currently serve to protect is a very parochial and occluded sense of place, one that fails to serve the interests of producers or consumers particularly well in an increasingly interconnected and interdependent global economy.

2   Concepts and ideals implicit in GIs

So to the first question: what is the work we want GIs to do? Geographical Indications, the World Intellectual Property Rights Organization (WIPO) suggests, play an important role in protecting products that have 'acquired valuable reputations which, if not adequately protected, may be misrepresented by dishonest commercial operators'.[3] This mis-representation of goods could, they argue, have detrimental effects for both consumers and legitimate producers. In their absence, the former 'would be deceived into believing they are buying a genuine product with specific qualities and characteristics, while they are, in fact, getting a worthless imitation ... [while] the latter would suffer damage because valuable business is taken away from them and the established reputation for their products is damaged'.[4] In this regard it is evident that the rationale for implementing GIs deviates little from that put forward to justify the prospective use of other instruments of trade mark law, such as brands or marks. These are also designed to prevent unscrupulous traders from 'passing-off', as 'genuine', inferior products reproduced without the permission of the licence-holder. Their work then is similar. What distinguishes GIs from these related forms of protection is the mechanism through which they intend to achieve this work. This is to be achieved by explicitly appealing to *place* (here construed as a unique assemblage of inhabitants, environment and associated cultural (artisanal) methods of production) to provide a guarantee of the quality of the products produced therein.

What is striking, and it must be said rather disturbing, to the contemporary geographer is the degree to which this project relies for its success on a production of another kind: the production of a highly constructed, deeply essentialized and static, conception of place. Nowhere is this more amply illustrated than in Article 22 (1) of the WTO's *Agreement on Trade Related Aspects of Intellectual Property Rights* which offers the following definition of Geographical Indications now utilized as a global standard: 'Geographical indications are, for the purposes of this Agreement, indications which identify a good as originating in the territory of a Member, or a region or locality in that territory, where a given quality, reputation or other characteristic of the good is *essentially attributable* to its geographical origin' (my italics).[5] Place, in this conception, is being asked to do a great deal of work in the service of IPRs. Firstly, and perhaps most problematically, what is being asserted here is that the quality, the reputation and, perhaps most significantly of all, the 'authenticity' of a product can be secured through reference to a place and the associated circumstances of its production. In other words, the 'authenticity' of the product is, in the WTO's equation, directly attributable to the 'authenticity' of the place

[3] WIPO website on Geographical Indications, available at www.wipo.int/about-ip/en/geographical_ind.html.
[4] Ibid.
[5] WTO, *Agreement on Trade Related Aspects of Intellectual Property Rights* Art. 22 (1).

from which it emanates. The reference to attribution in the WTO's description does not, in this context, seem entirely coincidental. Place is here characterized as the author of authenticity. However, for place to effectively 'go guarantor' for the 'authenticity' of products in this way, its authenticity must also be able to be guaranteed. This is where things get sticky.

Appealing to the 'authenticity' of places is a troubling and deeply political act. As the geographers Doreen Massey[6] and Tim Cresswell[7] argue, it usually involves the parochial and reactionary claiming of an imaginary, unchanging identity (of both place and its constituents), one that necessarily denies the myriad ways in which both are every day remade through productive engagement with local and global communities. In order to achieve this handiwork, place must first be made to 'sit still'. It must be apprehended like a butterfly pinned to a board so that its constituents and their essential character may be examined and known with absolute certainty. Such conceptions are underpinned by a number of troubling presuppositions. The first of these is that places have but one single, essentialized identity. Allied to this is a second more disturbing notion – the idea that this single essentialized identity can be excavated by 'delving into the past for internalised origins'.[8] Also implicit in this conception is the idea that places are made up only of individuals, practices and materials that exist within, and indeed are a product of, a particular bounded territory or locality. All of these conceptions actively sediment a very static and circumscribed sense of place, one that implies that places have a traditional, essential and unchanging identity, there to be unearthed, verified and known.

Such conceptions, as I shall illustrate, have their genesis in the environmental determinist tradition of the early twentieth century. That they could, at the commencement of the twenty-first century, be once again so warmly embraced is troubling but made explicable in the context of recent geopolitical developments. The emergence and acceleration of processes of cultural and economic globalization have transformed experiences of everyday life, radically altering individual and community understandings of the significance of place. As Massey notes: 'the search after the "real" meaning of places, the unearthing of heritages and so forth is, in part, a response to desire for fixity and for security of identity in the

[6] D. Massey, 'A Global Sense of Place' in T. Barnes and D. Gregory (eds.), *Reading Human Geography: The Politics and Poetics of Enquiry* (London: Arnold, 1994) 315–23.
[7] T. Cresswell, *Place: A Short Introduction* (Oxford: Blackwell, 2004); T. Cresswell and G. Vertstraete, *Mobilizing Place, Placing Mobilit: The Politics of Representation in a Globalized World* (Amsterdam: Rodopi, 2003).
[8] Massey, 'Global Sense of Place' 319.

middle of all the movement and change ... on this reading place and locality are foci for a form of romanticised escapism from the real business of the world'.[9]

To rely on place to provide the ballast that might anchor turbulent sentiments and postmodern anxieties about one's disposition in a changing world was always going to be a troublesome affair. This is because, as contemporary geographers know, place is, and always has been, fundamentally unreliable: mercurial, seditious and recalcitrant. Although we are wooed by the nostalgic fancy that places never change, this is a fiction that is all too readily exposed. Place has not sat still historically and it certainly is not going to sit still in this rapidly globalizing world. Places are neither hermetically sealed, nor immune to change. They are, and always have been, as Massey argues, 'porous', they are produced out of ongoing interactions and engagements with other people and places, both contiguous and distant. Places, I would argue, have always been a product of this process – one that has been in evidence in perpetuity but which has undoubtedly undergone an extreme process of acceleration in recent times as globalization brings people and places every day into closer and more interdependent relations.

The rural sociologist Elizabeth Barham has argued that the concept of *terroir* that underpins the operation of systems of Geographical Indications, and which idealizes the relationship between individuals and the specific geo-physical and cultural milieu in which they coexist, 'relates to a time of much less spatial mobility, when change occurred at a slower pace ... when terroir products resulted from long occupation of the same area and represented the interplay of human ingenuity and curiosity with the natural givens of place'.[10] The almost certainly unintentional suggestion here is that even if the authenticity of *terroir* is now more suspect, there perhaps existed a time in the recent historical past when its relationship with place was more secure – when *terroir* products were incontrovertibly, essentially, linked to the contained specificities of place. Barham also notes, presciently, that *terroir* now 'reflects a conscious and active social construction of the present by various groups concerned with rural areas in France who jostle for position in their efforts to recover and revalorize elements of the rural past ... in asserting a new vision of the rural future'.[11] In what may seem, even to the author, an act of sheer folly, I return now to perhaps the most iconic case in the history of the development

---

[9] Ibid.
[10] E. Barham, 'Translating Terroir: The Global Challenge of French AOC Labelling' (2003) 19 *Journal of Rural Studies* 127–38.
[11] Ibid. 132.

of the appellation d'Origine Contrôlée and Geographical Indications –
the Champagne case of 1911. I do so with the intention, firstly, of
challenging, through some small illustrative examples, the supposition
that there is such a thing as 'the natural givens of place' out of which *terroir*
is now, or indeed ever was, produced. By this I mean that I want to test the
presumption that there is anything 'natural', fixed or certain about the
character of places out of which a verifiably 'authentic' identity might be
produced. I then consider, secondly, how the idea that such 'authentic
identities' actually exist, let alone that they might provide the basis of a
mechanism of protection, came to acquire such purchase within GI law. I
shall then return in the final section of the paper to examine contemporary rationales for mobilizing them as mechanisms of economic and
cultural defence.

3   Revisiting Champagne

There remains some debate around the question of what *terroir* is and of
how its constituent elements might best be defined. Some advocates of
the Appellation d'Origine Contrôlée system have argued that the concept
of *terroir* should extend only to the biophysical elements of localities (soil,
microclimate, geology, aspect, etc.) that are characteristic of that particular *terre*. This seems the more defensible position since these elements
remain, as a consequence in part of their immobility, incontrovertibly
linked to specific places. This is not to say, however, that they are not also
subject to substantive change over time. The alternative (and ascendant
view) is that *terroir* should encompass not only these elements but also
further aspects of production – grape varietals, methods of vinification
and localized techniques of manufacture that are also portrayed as having
arisen 'organically' out of this interaction between inhabitants and their
environment. These techniques, it is agued, must also be afforded protection, as they too play a key role in imparting a unique and distinctive
quality to food and wines. What is not in dispute in either conception is
that the particular elements that are deemed to be constitutive of *terroir*
are to be found only in the particular bounded localities *of which they are a
product*.

The paradigmatic example of a *terroir* product, that most commonly
held up as an exemplar, is champagne. A great number of works, of which
I reference here but a few, have devoted many pages to outlining how the
particular specificities of the tightly circumscribed Champagne region of
France – its highly marginal northern continental climate, the slopes
generated by prehistoric earthquakes, the recession 70 million years ago
of a prehistoric sea which left in its wake a chalky calcite-laden soil, the

warmer friable topsoils and native vine stocks – have there been combined with generations of painstaking localized methods of production to create the world's premier sparkling wine.

A closer reading of the history of champagne production[12] is rewarding, however, not least for what it reveals about the degree to which winemaking practice, (*la méthode traditionelle*) was then, as it is now, informed by associations, interactions and cross-fertilizations between individuals, their scientific techniques and other craft practices, and even organisms and plants, that emanate far from this apparently discrete domain. While the biophysical environment of the Marne Valley and Aube district has undoubtedly provided the optimum growing conditions for the pinot grape varieties from which champagne is made, the method of production itself owes much more to the district's position at one of the most important crossroads of Europe. As McNie notes,[13] archaeological excavations have revealed that this area was a focal point for a trade in wine that extended from Rome across the Mediterranean and into the far north of Gaul. It is this trade that is thought to have first introduced the pinot grapes to the Champagne district. Indeed the excavations of chalk from this basin that the Romans undertook to create their network of roads were in time to create the 200- to 300-feet-deep chalk pits that are now said to act as 'natural' cellars for the maturing wine.[14]

Techniques for wine production also benefitted from trade of another kind – religious pilgrimage. For the production of champagne relied not only on the successful cultivation of Pinot grapes but also, crucially, on two early technological developments: the creation of an airtight cork and a stronger glass bottle. Both were essential in preventing the escape of carbon dioxide from the wine. Dom Perignon, a monk of the Abbey of Hautvilliers and the most celebrated early exponent of the *méthode traditionelle* is reported to have been unsuccessfully attempting to seal the wine with hemp dipped in oil when he was visited by two Spanish monks on a religious pilgrimage from Santiago de Compostella. They brought with them water skins that were stoppered with cork bark. On demonstration of their qualities, Perignon was said to have placed an order for an immediate consignment of the cork stoppers.[15]

---

[12] T. Stevenson, *Champagne* (London: Sotheby's Press, 1987); N. Faith *The Story of Champagne* (London: Hamish Hamilton, 1988); C. Ray, *Bollinger: The Story of a Champagne* (London: Peter Davies, 1971); N. McNie *Champagne* (London: Faber and Faber, 1999).
[13] McNie, *Champagne* 11.
[14] A. L. Simon, *The History of Champagne* (London: Ebury Press, 1962) 38.
[15] McNie, *Champagne* 21.

It is also evident that the development of champagne in Champagne was greatly facilitated by a series of events that emanated, curiously enough, in the English royal court of James 1, who, urged on by Sir Robert Mansell, Admiral of his Fleet, outlawed the burning of wood in glass furnaces, fearing the acceleration of consumption of oak that might otherwise be used for naval ship-building.[16] The use of sea coal[17] in the furnaces produced higher temperatures and more robust glass. The English were at that time importing light wines from the north of France and began to decant them from casks into these bottles in order to prolong their shelf life. Ironically, it is now thought that the champagne makers in France actually imported this technique and technology from the English before applying it to the production of highly carbonated wines.

The great champagne-producing families Clicquot, Pommery, Moet and so forth were able to acquire quite substantial estates in the late eighteenth century. Their relative size afforded them considerable advantages in production. This, in turn, provided the financial investment necessary to perfect important techniques such as *remuage* and disgorgement that further consolidated their position as Europe's pre-eminent *champenois*. Yet how did this estate-building process occur? Further analysis reveals it to have been the result not of immediate local events, but rather of economic and political developments that originated well beyond the mapped boundaries of the Champagne locality.

The extraordinarily complex internal tax regime that existed in pre-revolutionary France had allowed wines developed on ecclesiastical estates to pay lower duty on their entry into Paris. It was this concession that had greatly facilitated production at many abbeys throughout France, including Hautvilliers. Moreover, under the Ancien Régime, monasteries were allowed to own many vineyards, whereas small private *vignerons* were not.[18] This fomented discontent, not, curiously enough, in Champagne itself, where there was little evidence of widespread dissatisfaction with the ecclesiastical dominance of production, but primarily in other wine-producing areas of France. When discontent fomented into wide-scale revolution, this law was repealed. Vineyards were subsequently confiscated from the monasteries and aristocratic owners and forcibly redistributed amongst the oldest houses of the merchant producers. Although the impetus for this reformation did not have its genesis in the district of Champagne itself, the *champenois* of Champagne's merchant classes undoubtedly benefitted from it as it was this new

---

[16] Ibid. 20.
[17] Typically mineral coal washed up on shore or mined from sea-side rock faces.
[18] Faith, *The Story of Champagne* 50.

legislation that allowed them to consolidate their holdings substantially and, in so doing, to create their now-iconic estates.[19]

There is rarely any debate that techniques such as disgorgement (the deliberate and progressive release of sediment-laden gas from the inverted neck of the champagne bottle to create a perfectly clear wine) were invented in Champagne, but once again it was not a technique that was perfected in splendid isolation. As Simon argues, at the close of the eighteenth century 'the people of Champagne were still making sparkling wine more by guesswork than by safe scientific technique'.[20] Fermentation, which created the creaming mousse so valued in the highest-quality champagne, was highly unpredictable and often resulted in the explosion and breakage of up to 40 percent of the bottles, a loss so high that it threatened to undermine completely the economic foundations of the trade.

An important advancement in the resolution of this problem was offered to the *champenois* by Jean Antoine Chaptal, a professor of chemistry at the University of Montpellier (near the Mediterranean coast, far from the Champagne region of northeast France) and, later, Pasteur (in Paris). Both perfected methods for stabilizing sugar content in fermentation that were of key significance in reducing the volatility of the wine and consequent breakages.[21] The importation of these techniques into the Champagne district was particularly significant as these vineyards are so near to the northern limits beyond which grapes will not fully mature in the open. In such conditions an ability to stabilize sugar content through the fermentation process becomes exceptionally important, and, as Simon notes, 'the vineyards of Champagne benefited to a greater extent than most other French vineyards from Chaptel's initiative'.[22]

Ironically though, nowhere is the significance of *outside* influences on this apparently uniquely *localised terroir* more evident than in the catastrophic plague that actually created the impetus to establish the earliest form of GI – the Appellation d'Origine Contrôlée. Interestingly, while some may dismiss production techniques as an element that is tangential to, rather than implicit in, *terroir* there is a complete consensus that the vines themselves constitute a fundamental component of *terroir*. Very significantly however, in the case of champagne production, the pinot noir vine stock which continues to be celebrated (in the context of GI legislation) as one of the key 'naturally' occurring elements of this

[19] McNie, *Champagne* 40–1.   [20] A. L. Simon, *The History of Champagne* 80.
[21] NcNie, *Champagne* 31–2.
[22] A. L. Simon, *The History of Champagne* 81 The term 'chaptalisation' is still used to denote the addition of sugar to unfermented juice.

superior product prove, ironically enough, not even to be indigenous to this region. To understand how this could be so, it is necessary to return to the early nineteenth century to examine the crisis in champagne production that occurred at that time.

Once again it was events that emanated from outside the Champagne locality that were to induce this crisis in production. In the spring of 1911, in response to a shortage of locally grown grapes, Champagne was inundated: inundated with wine, of a purportedly inferior variety, from Aisne, from vineyards around Château Thierry (which was not then considered a part of viticultural Champagne) and from regions much further afield, from Chablis and even the Midi. It was the confirmation of rumours that this wine was to be used in the production of 'champagne' that incited the armed *vignerons* of Champagne to riot. They were incensed primarily by what they considered to be the highly deceptive practice of substituting wine from other localities in the manufacture of 'champagne' which they believed could only legitimately be described as such if it had been produced from grapes grown in their region.[23] It was this rioting that led directly to the promulgation of the first regulation that would attempt to demarcate physically (one might say *hermetically seal*) the boundaries of the place 'Champagne' which would in time come to act as a guarantor of the quality of the wine produced therein. The regulations were to constitute the very earliest form of Appellation d'Origine Contrôlée, the forerunner of most other types of the now rather more pernicious Geographical Indication.

But let us go back for a moment to investigate what had led to the failure in production of their 'native' crop that necessitated the substitution of wines from other districts. I do so here because the question of what happened to this crop – and of how the problem was remedied – speaks rather eloquently to the oft-cited assertion in *terroir* debates that it is the locality (this distinct locality alone, and events taking place within it – which are also oft characterized as 'natural' or 'organic') that in some way asserts its influence on the wine (through grape production and manufacture), making its presence known in the personality of the end product.

For, in this case, the collapse of the pinot crop (which had induced the need for wine substitution) was caused by a small insect pest – one that had clearly not been appraised of the apparent impermeability of place. Travelling from America to Europe via England, *phylloxera* arrived in France in 1860 and thence into the Marne Valley, decimating vineyards

[23] Ibid. 105–10.

and destroying grape production.[24] Curiously, and ironically enough, the salvation of the Champagne *vignerons* was also to arrive from foreign climes. Investigations in other parts of France had revealed that the celebrated native champagne grapes had a particularly vulnerable root-stock that offered little resistance to *phylloxera*. It also became apparent through international scientific experimentation that this disastrous problem could be remedied by grafting the vines onto *phylloxera*-resistant rootstocks. These rootstocks were only to be found, however, in America.[25] The *phylloxera*-resistant rootstocks, of course, remain a product of a locality and its specific environmental conditions, but that locality is not Champagne.

As Wilson notes, by the late 1870s French and American entomologists and viticulturalists were exchanging correspondence and visits to learn how best to replicate *phylloxera* resistance in French vines. The task of identifying those American rootstocks most suitable for grafting onto the pinot and chardonnay vines of Champagne was eventually undertaken by Thomas Munson, an eminent plant scientist of Denison, Texas. In recognition of his contribution, Munson was later proclaimed collo-quially as 'the Texan who saved the French vineyards' and honoured more formally by the French Government in 1889 through the award of the Légion d'Honneur for his assistance in remedying the *phylloxera* problem.[26] The vines that are now grown in Champagne are not a 'naturally occurring' or 'organic' product of Champagne but rather a scientifically constructed hybrid. Once again, the ability to secure the quality of the wine produced in Champagne had been brought about by interaction, cross-fertilization and exchange of scientific expertise and life-forms that originated a world away from what we are invited to imagine is an apparently self-contained, and self-sustaining, region.

Throughout the twentieth century, as industrialization has advanced, wholly new production techniques and technologies have, of course, found their way to Champagne. As McNie notes, the older pinot stock (pockets of which were unaffected by *phylloxera* and still remain in the Marne) grow in such an unruly and undisciplined manner that they would not now be reintroduced into the region, even if they could be, because this growth pattern would 'preclude mechanisation of any

---

[24] McNie, *Champagne* 41–3; A. L. Simon, *The History of Champagne* 100.
[25] J. E. Wilson (*Terroir: The Role of Geology, Climate and Culture in the Making of French Wines* (London: Mitchell Beazley, 1998) 49) reports that French experts believed resistance to *phylloxera* in American rootstocks to be probably 'a result of natural selection [there] and therefore a guarantee of the permanence of its resistance'.
[26] Ibid.

kind'.[27] Unsurprisingly, in this age of globalization, we continue to find evidence that the quality of the grapes and the production methods and techniques that are said to emanate from the district of Champagne (and which, therefore, could not possibly be reproduced anywhere else) remain, as they ever have, the product of ongoing interactions with other places and people. Even the task of picking and sorting the grapes, described as 'épluchage', once performed by highly skilled local women, is now undertaken, as I discovered through recent reading, by English university students working abroad on their gap years.[28]

4   Legitimizing the 'authenticity' of place: Ellen Semple and Social Darwinism

In thinking about why and how this rather static and essentialist notion of place came to inform both *terroir* and its legal instruments Appellation d'Origine Contrôlée and GIs, it is helpful to situate developments in Champagne within the broader context of ideas and debates that were informing public thinking about place at exactly this time. Some very influential work was being published by geographers in Europe and America at this time, including that undertaken by the prominent and respected American geographer Ellen Semple. Semple had travelled to Europe to study under the eminent German geographer Freidrich Ratzel whose work *Anthropogeographie* was then being adopted as one of the foundational texts of a new discipline, Human Geography. In this work, which draws on Darwin and Haeckel, Ratzel advances a biologically informed model of nationhood in which the primary unit of organization is an organic state – one predisposed to grow or contract in accordance with its current state of health. This, Ratzel argued, was determined by the strength of the spiritual bond between the land and its inhabitants. He postulated that once these were in harmonious union the state/organism (being consequently in rude good health) would begin to expand naturally in search of new territory, an expansion that was essential if a healthy 'living space' or 'Lebensraum' were to be maintained. It is unsurprising to discover that Ratzel's theories were later warmly adopted by Hitler's National Socialists to legitimate their progressive invasion of territories in Eastern Europe during the late 1930s.

In taking up Ratzel's work on the nature of this relationship between the state and its inhabitants, Semple became preoccupied with

[27] McNie, *Champagne* 13.
[28] S. Griffith, 'Work your way around France', *Independent Online*, 14 January 2006, http://travel.independent.co.uk/europe/article338402.ece.

374   *Bronwyn Parry*

theorizing the influence that environmental factors might have on individual, communal or national constitution and character. Her seminal work, *Influences of Geographic Environment*,[29] which was published in exactly the year that the Champagne riots occurred, conceives of place/environment as something that has an immutable and directly deterministic impact on its inhabitants. Semple was careful to impress on the reader that the geographic influences could not be reduced to climate, even though she believed the correspondence between climate and temperament to be a close one. She argued, for example, that it produced in the southern sub-tropical Mediterranean basin individuals who are 'easygoing, improvident except under pressing necessity, gay, emotional and imaginative', qualities that could, however, in more equatorial climes 'degenerate into grave racial faults'.[30] Despite these assertions, Semple believed that the relationship between environment and place and its inhabitants was, in fact, much more complex (if no less deterministic). As she noted: 'a blanket theory of climate cannot ... cover the case ... careful analysis supersedes it by a whole group of geographic factors working directly and indirectly'.[31]

Principal amongst these were the influences of land and soil: 'Man in his larger activities cannot be studied apart from the Land in which he inhabits ... in all cases the form and size of the social group, the nature of its activities, the trend and limit of its development will be strongly influenced by the size and nature of its habitat'.[32] The intelligent anthropo-geographer, she asserts, 'sees in the Land occupied by a primitive tribe or a highly organised state the underlying material bond holding society together, the ultimate basis of their fundamental social activities, which are therefore derivatives from the land'.[33] Taking this thesis to its full (il)logical conclusion, she is able to proceed so far as to attribute the presence or absence of artistic and poetic traits in European races to variances in topology. She argues, drawing on von Treischke, that, while the

absence of artistic and poetic development in Switzerland [is attributable] to the overwhelming aspect of Nature there, the majestic sublimity of which paralyses the mind ... conversely, areas where nature is gentle, stimulating, appealing and not overpowering have produced many poets and artists ... French men of letters, by the distribution of their birthplaces are essentially products of the fluvial valleys and plains, rarely of upland and mountain.[34]

[29] E. Semple, *Influences of Geographic Environment on the Basis of Ratzel's System of Anthropo-Geography* (New York and London: H. Holt and Co. 1911).
[30] Ibid. 620.   [31] Ibid. 20–1.   [32] Ibid. 54.   [33] Ibid. 53.   [34] Ibid.

I would argue that it is precisely this sort of theorizing about the synergistic and mutually reinforcing relationship between a particular bounded territory and the activities to which it is thought to give rise, the special 'spiritual bond' between land and inhabitant and its alleged influence on the very character of its outputs, that has historically informed the concept of *terroir*.

Having contextualized the development of this concept within the intellectual thinking about the relationship between place and environment that was in the ascendancy at this time (as promulgated by Ratzel and Semple), it becomes much easier to discern the historiography of this particular reading of *terroir* in many contemporary analyses of its purported effects. One example of this can be found in a recent, and award-winning, work by James Wilson, in which he states that *terroir* encompasses not only 'the measurable ecosystem' but, perhaps even more significantly, the additional dimension of 'the *spiritual aspect* that recognizes the joys, the heartbreaks, the pride, the sweat, and frustrations of [the vineyard's] history' (my italics).[35] Once again we see here evidence of the rather peculiar notion that it is the 'spiritual bond' that arises out of an essentialized, unchanging, 'natural' relationship between the land and its inhabitants that somehow becomes embodied in the corporeality, the character, of the wine itself. Unfortunately, it is also precisely in these arguments about the nature of *terroir* and its products that we see evidence of the kind of applied Social Darwinism which the theory and practice of GIs continue, whether intentionally or unintentionally, to subscribe and uphold.

5   The future of GIs: the role of place in a globalizing world

As contemporary geographers have noted, it is not productive to conceptualize place as an impermeable container – a kind of plastic bucket that contains a fixed number and type of constituent elements that one may rely on to remain consistent, and to which one may appeal in adjudging claims to authenticity. As Massey argues, what we need to develop and embrace is a 'progressive' sense of place – one that is 'not self-enclosing and defensive – but outward looking'.[36] As she also helpfully reminds us, 'place and community have only rarely been coterminous'[37] and this is surely the case in Champagne. As a closer examination of this case reveals, the unique community of persons, organisms, technologies, techniques and associations that have produced wines of such elegance in the Marne Valley are a product *not* of that specific closely

---

[35] J. E. Wilson, *Terroir* 55.   [36] Massey, *A Progressive Sense of Place* 315.   [37] Ibid.

bounded locality, but rather of the multiple interactions that occurred between it and an ostensibly 'outside' world. Processes of globalization are inevitably strengthening the degree of inter-relation and interdependence that exists between places. In light of this it seems a rather perverse moment to attempt to introduce a globally enforceable regime of GI protection that actively celebrates such an outdated, regressive and politically troublesome concept of place.

Given what we now know about *the kind of conception of place* to which GIs appeal – a very static, essentialized, deterministic conception – we must ask ourselves the question: does this seem the best mechanism through which to provide a guarantee of product quality for consumers? Unsurprisingly, I think not. This is for one very straightforward reason that I hope I have made evident in this chapter. Geographical Indications, like their precursor the Appellation d'Origine Contrôlée, attempt to provide the consumer with a guarantee of the quality of a product by linking the authenticity of the product to the authenticity of the specific places in which it is produced. For this to work, however, we must firstly be able to establish which places are, or are not, 'authentic'. This, it seems, can only be adjudged by reference to a number of specific (and, I would argue, essentialized) elements – be they biophysical or cultural – that are argued to be (forever) constitutive of that place. The guarantee can, therefore, only then retain its purchase if these constitutive elements remain the same, uncontaminated by exposure to other places, communities, individuals or processes that emanate from beyond its notional perimeter. As I have attempted to show here, places are never hermetically sealed but in fact brought into existence and every day re-made anew through a productive engagement with outside forces. It is therefore extremely difficult to ascertain what 'authenticity' can actually mean in this context, let alone how its existence may be verified in any court of law.

In my view there are several fundamental problems with GIs. The first is this: as 'authenticity' remains such an indeterminate and contested concept it seems that (at least) two eventualities may occur. The first of these is that everyone everywhere could claim that they come from an 'authentic place' and have therein generated 'authentic' products that are requisite of special IPR protection. GIs would then become very broad and meaningless. A review of some of the recent literature from WIPO produces the following list of products that Kenyan producers *alone* would wish to have recognized under an extended, internationally recognized regime of Geographical Indications:

In Kenya, the products that could benefit from GI extension include agricultural products such as Mt. Kenya coffee, Gathuthi tea, Kisii tea, Kericho tea, kangeta, miraa, meru potato, kikuyu grass, Mombasa mango, Machakos mango, Asembo mango, Muranga bananas and Kisii bananas. Livestock products that could benefit from GI extension include Molo lamb, Kitengela ostrich meat, Omena fish and Mursik milk. Other products are Keringeti mineral water and Victoria mineral water. Minerals such as Tsavonite and Magadi soda as well as industrial products such as the Kenyan kiondo. Other GI products include Naivasha wine, Kakamega papaya, Kakamega omukombera and Tilapia fish from Lake Victoria and Tilapia fish from Lake Turkana. Handicrafts would include Kisii soapstone, Akamba carvings, Maasai attire and beads. Enhanced protection of GI can also be used to protect small scale producers of Aloe Vera, Machakos Honey and Bixa.[38]

It is this latter point that perhaps speaks most eloquently to the true political impetus for implementing an internationally recognized system of GI. This impetus is, of course, precisely the same as that which first motivated the Champagne *vignerons* to argue for the establishment of a rudimentary system of Appellation d'Origine Contrôlée nearly 100 years ago: the desire to utilize GIs as a technology for protecting small-scale producers, their cultural heritage and 'traditional' ways of life. This is entirely understandable – as Massey put it, such moves reflect, both then and now, 'the desire for fixity and for security of identity in the middle of all the movement and change'.[39] However, it is not evident that GIs are necessarily the most effective tool for achieving such goals.

These rather crude mechanisms for artificially sustaining traditional activities are not only contentious but also, in many instances, unsuccessful. A prime example is agricultural subsidies. These are employed within the EU and in other countries, in many cases unashamedly, as a mechanism for protecting cultural heritage and 'traditional' ways of life. Their application within the European wine industry has allowed many French *vignerons* to continue to produce wine for which there is falling demand. This phenomenon has already led to the creation of a vast reserve of unsold wine, a so-called 'wine lake' that already constitutes more than one year's worth of total EU wine production. It has been estimated that as much as 15 per cent of total European wine production may go unsold by 2010.[40]

Such subsidies are also, as reports on the application of the EU's Common Agricultural Policy suggest, phenomenally expensive to implement and maintain. The same charge has recently been levelled at the proposal to implement and maintain a global register of GIs: that the

[38] J. Otieno-Odek, 'The Way Ahead – What Future for Geographical Indications?' WIPO conference paper, Parma, Italy, 27–29 June 2005.
[39] Massey, a 'Global Sense of Place' 319.
[40] BBC News, 'EU Wine Reform' 22 June 2006, available at http://news.bbc.co.uk/1/hi/world/europe/5107400.stm.

costs would create an undue financial and administrative burden for both local producers and the state.[41] Conversely, and this is a second concern, there is also a very real risk that specialized products that result from generations of development in communities that are nomadic or diasporic (in other words not rooted in or associated with a specific, bounded and named place) may find themselves ineligible for protection under the proposed new GI system. This also seems unfair.

It is not clear to me, nor indeed to many other trade mark commentators, why an indication of the quality of a product could not be secured as effectively through the application of a trade mark and an associated indication or certification of origin. The existing trade mark system is now extremely well characterized, its parameters and operation clearly established through precedent setting and case law. This system also already contains a clearly established system of certification marks (of both origin and quality) that appear to be functioning effectively. A certification mark offers an independent certification by its owner that the goods or services in relation to which it is used possess certain defined characteristics. Approval to register the certification mark is dependent on the establishment of the applicant's competence to certify the goods or services and to operate the scheme.

Collective marks may also be used to distinguish the goods or services of members of the association (which of course is a type of community, just not necessarily a spatially defined one) that owns the mark. Collective marks indicate commercial origin of goods or services just as ordinary trade marks do, but as collective marks they indicate origin in members of an association or group rather than origin in one place. The function of a collective mark, therefore, is to indicate who is entitled to use the mark, as opposed to the certification mark which indicates standards met by the goods or services on which the mark is used.[42] Both, it seems to me, might very effectively achieve the same ends as the much more complex and demanding proposed system of globally registered GI marks. This is, of course, already the case in the USA where products such as tequila and Ceylon tea are successfully protected through the application of these types of certification marks.[43]

[41] R. James, 'Burgundy Can't Agree on AOC Reform' (2004) *Decanter* available at www.decanter.com/news/56418.html.
[42] I am indebted to my commentator Dev Gangjee for providing me with this very helpful information.
[43] Further information on collective marks and certification marks and their use in the USA can be found at these sites: www.wipo.int/sme/en/ip_business/collective_marks/collective_marks.htm; www.wipo.int/sme/en/ip_business/collective_marks/certification_marks.htm and www.uspto.gov/web/offices/dcom/olia/globalip/gi_protection.htm#question5.

Some evidence is now emerging that suggests that even producers in countries such as Italy and France, which already provide robust systems of GI, are turning away from them as a preferred mechanism of protection, arguing that they actually limit their attempts to increase sales of their products by subjecting them to further and ever more complex layers of bureaucracy. As Anderson *et al.* have recently argued, onerous EU regulations are one of the reasons why Old World wine producers cannot respond as nimbly to changes in consumption patterns as they might otherwise do. As they note: 'despite the growth in UK and US demand, European suppliers have failed to respond due to myriad regulations such as restrictions on which grape varieties can be used in each appellation, on maximum yields and alcohol content, and on vine density and vine training systems'.[44]

6   Conclusion

It would appear then, in conclusion, that the very static and deterministic conception of place to which GIs appeal (which undoubtedly embodies a very regressive kind of determinism) is not only unattractive but may, in fact, also act to constrain in undesirable ways how goods are produced and consumed in a globalizing world. Even the champagne makers of the Marne Valley are discovering the limitations of the system that had its genesis in their historical past. As affluence increases, so does demand for their product. Their ability to meet this demand stagnates, however, as there is no more productive land to be found within the tightly delineated (but, of course, very arbitrarily established) boundaries of this artificially constructed place that is known as 'Champagne'.

The mechanism of the Geographic Indication could be justified at the time of its introduction by reference to a particular construction of place (fixed, static, unchanging, authentic and the product of particular national or regional environmental conditions) that contemporary geographers now understand to be completely outmoded – particularly in a rapidly globalizing world which serves to make place perhaps more porous than it ever has been before. By continuing to embrace GIs, we are collectively at risk of fragmenting claims of ownership to atomistic levels, creating with it a tendency for what might be termed a kind of 'acquisitive provincialism' – the promotion of the idea that community survival will come *not* through active and open engagement with other communities near and far, but instead through resort to a rather anxious,

[44] K. Anderson (ed.), *The World's Wine Markets: Globalization at Work* (Cheltenham: Edward Elgar, 2004) 5–6.

miserly claiming and vigilant defence of all that might, in some broad conception, be understood as having been produced out of a notionally 'self-sustaining' *terroir*. This, it seems, is a concept and a political practice that we might do well to resist in the interests of creating more outward-looking and progressive approaches to the protection of unique communal products.

18 (Re)Locating Geographical Indications: a response to Bronwyn Parry

*Dev Gangjee**

Introduction

A particular vision of geographical place has shaped much of the discourse and international legal architecture for the protection of Geographical Indications (GIs).[1] Dr Bronwyn Parry incisively demonstrates that this view is dangerously myopic as it makes several unsustainable assumptions. If the function of GIs is to guarantee the quality and authenticity of regional products such as Champagne, these desirable features rest on static, deterministic notions of place. Contemporary scholarship reveals place to be far more porous and dynamic, thereby throwing into doubt the very ontological foundations of GI protection. While acknowledging the value of this appraisal, this response frames it within historical legal and institutional responses, thereby drawing limits around its conclusions. The critique is potent but does not necessarily signal the end of GIs.

* Heartfelt thanks are due to the organizers of the interdisciplinary workshops held at Emmanuel College, University of Cambridge, in July 2005 and July 2006 – Lionel Bently, Jane Ginsburg and Jennifer Davis – for the opportunity to participate in a genuinely innovative and exciting project. Special thanks also to Jane Ginsburg for editorial polish where it was badly needed. A sincere thank you to Bronwyn Parry for the academic provocation and learning along the way. Bronwyn unerringly homed in on the weak arguments and exposed flanks; we agreed to disagree and had fun in the process. Finally, an old-fashioned doffing of the hat to Nikita for the help with Human Geography.
1 Geographical Indications are defined in Art. 22.1 of the Agreement on Trade-Related Aspects of Intellectual Property Rights (TRIPS) as 'indications which identify a good as originating in the territory of a Member, or a region or locality in that territory, where a given quality, reputation or other characteristic of the good is essentially attributable to its geographical origin'. Examples include 'Gorgonzola' cheese, 'Prosciutto di Parma' ham and 'Scotch' whisky, which function as valuable, collective brands. The term 'GI' is used in this paper to represent this umbrella concept. The World Intellectual Property Organisation (WIPO) provides a convenient summary in WIPO Secretariat *Document SCT/6/3: Rev. on Geographical Indications: Historical Background, Nature of Rights, Existing Systems for Protection and Obtaining Protection in Other Countries* (SCT/8/4) 2 April 2002, available from www.wipo.int/meetings/en/archive.jsp. All internet references are current as of 27 January 2007.

Instead, it helps to reposition the justification for this regime, placing it on a more durable foundation.

Through a formal challenge to the central premise of GI protection – that place can act as a guarantor for quality and authenticity – Dr Parry is asking whether GIs are 'fit for purpose'. Through the lens of a richer account of place, she interrogates this premise by asking: (i) what is the work GIs are being asked to do?; (ii) how they do this work; and (iii) whether more suitable alternatives exist. As a response to this, this response begins by both expanding the critique and qualifying it. The legal guarantee signified by an Appellation d'Origine Contrôlée (AOC) – the influential French kernel for much of present GI law – incorporates both verifiable qualities based upon circumscribed origin (*terroir* logic) and traditional or 'authentic' production methods (human factors). In continuing the conversation begun by Dr Parry, I address static notions of place found in both these interrelated aspects of product quality and authenticity. Classical *terroir* certainly rests on an essentialized and therefore problematic notion of place but the acknowledgment of human factors has weakened *terroir*'s hold. Increasing recognition of the human element in such traditional products has discreetly but progressively underlined the social construction of place. This story is told via the evolution of French law over the nineteenth and twentieth centuries, as its centre shifts away from pure *terroir* logic to progressively concede the value of skills and techniques. Dr Parry critiques this communal contribution as an unsustainable portrayal of enduring 'authenticity', but I opt for a historically informed and therefore contingent understanding of the term. Registered AOC specifications are grounded in place, fix best practices which have evolved over time from diverse sources, while in addition acting as a template to separate the genuine from the fake. Champagne production therefore represents collective, empirically tested traditional knowledge which is suited to the region rather than a timeless, fully formed and internal practice.

I conclude by briefly suggesting that, as a *sui generis* legal regime, GI law addresses issues which trade mark law cannot. I disagree with Dr Parry's conclusions that GIs are anachronistic in a globalized world, as they actively encourage differentiation based on practices suitable to embedded development. In the context of the politics of global food production, GIs may never have been more relevant as the Eurocentric bias fades. Trade mark law's priority-based registration system, principally territorial extent and aversion to peering behind applications which satisfy its bureaucratic logic mean that speed often trumps merit. This comment is therefore an appreciative response to Dr Parry's interdisciplinary provocation, as it forces some badly needed conceptual tidying up on the part of those who speak for the relevance of GIs.

Terroir in transition

According to 'Geographical Indications: Not all "Champagne and Roses"', static conceptions of place infuse both aspects of the legal guarantee in an AOC – *terroir* logic and authenticity. There is much to substantiate this accusation. Although Dr Parry focusses on authenticity in her chapter, the aim here is to test for this 'geographical imaginary' under each aspect, as they share a dyadic relationship.

A more grounded view of terroir

The French Appellation regime emerged as a registration-based system in the context of wine regulation, based on the notion of *terroir* and as a direct response to the *phylloxera* crisis of the nineteenth century. Each of these constitutive influences does much to explain how it defines the circle of legitimate users of an appellation and why it excludes outsiders. *Terroir* is a key ingredient in differentiating between wines by reference to a distinct origin.[2] The place of origin influences quality and in so doing shapes the reputation of the wine. Yet gauging a site's precise impact on the quality of the end product has been the subject of intense, unresolved debates.[3] There are at least three overlapping narratives that have arisen: *terroir* as (i) holistic and mystical, (ii) geographical and deterministic, and (iii) an evolving composite of natural and human factors. The first two assume static place, while the third begins to shake off its influence.

The first view holds *terroir* to be a 'much discussed term for the total natural environment of any viticultural site. No precise English equivalent exists for this quintessentially French term and concept.'[4] The influential wine expert Hugh Johnson says that it 'means much more than what goes on beneath the surface. Properly understood, it means the whole ecology of the vineyard ... not excluding the way the vineyard is tended, nor even the soul of the *vigneron*.'[5] Others believe that it extends beyond the chemical composition of the soil to indicate 'the coming

---

[2] This introduces the parallels with trade mark logic, which seeks to guarantee the commercial (as opposed to geographical) source of a product, thereby guaranteeing consistent (as opposed to specific) quality.

[3] Robert E. White, *Soils for Fine Wines* (New York: Oxford University Press, 2003) 3 ('evokes passion in any discussion'); J. Robinson (ed.), *The Oxford Companion to Wine* (2nd edn, Oxford: Oxford University Press, 1999) 700 ('central to philosophical and commercial differences').

[4] Robinson (ed.), *Oxford Companion* 700.

[5] See the Foreword to J. E. Wilson, *Terroir: The Role of Geology, Climate, and Culture in the Making of French Wines* (London: Mitchell Beazley, 1998) 4.

together of the climate, the soil and the landscape'.[6] Considered by some
as 'a mythic and holistic concept, terroir refers to the distinctive and
inimitable environment of a specific vineyard'.[7] Thus conceived, *terroir*
reaffirms the uniqueness of place. It implicitly assumes that the people–
place connection is static.

Dr Parry traces this 'spiritual bond' to environmental determinism as a
plausible suspect. I would agree with the thrust of the argument – why this
is problematic – but not with its proposed intellectual origins. Instead, the
conscious promotion of such mythical product–place relationships has
been traced back to the politics of the early days of the French Republic,
when a modern nation-building project was underway. Post-revolutionary
France required symbols around which to coalesce, and regional special-
ities became an important part of this process. These became 'closely
associated with the creation of a national identity based upon the notion
of regional and local diversity'.[8] The idea of a culinary heritage and the
emergence of gastronomy as an art form were located in the politics of
preserving 'local customs, language and folklore against the centralising
pressure of the Third Republic'.[9] The Industrial Revolution and improved
transportation led to national markets, which in turn fuelled the sales of
reputed regional speciality foods.[10] As a prominent part of this culinary
heritage, 'wine consumption and *terroir* were fundamental references that
the collective "France" elaborated for itself in the late nineteenth century'.[11] The authentic France was an organic entity constituted by the
symbiotic relationship between landscape and those who lived in it.
Conceived as a 'land of treasures' where the environment determined a
way of life, France became unique as a nation, as opposed to others such as
Germany that were premised upon an ethnic ideal.[12] Products of the vine
were undeniably influenced by place and located between an art and a

[6] B. Prats, 'The Terroir is Important' (1983) 8 *Decanter* 16, cited in T. Unwin, *Wine and the Vine: An Historical Geography of Viticulture and the Wine Trade* (London: Routledge, 1991) 45.
[7] W. Zhao, 'Understanding Classifications: Empirical Evidence from the American and French Wine Industries' (2005) 33 *Poetics* 179, 185.
[8] M. Demossier, 'Culinary Heritage and *Produits de Terroir* in France: Food for Thought' in S. Blowen, M. Demossier and J. Picard (eds.), *Recollections of France: Memories, Identities and Heritage in Contemporary France* (New York: Berghahn Books, 2000) 141, 145.
[9] Ibid. 146.
[10] X. de Planhol, *An Historical Geography of France*, trans. J. Lloyd (Cambridge: Cambridge University Press, 1994) 374.
[11] Koleen M. Guy, 'Rituals of Pleasure in the Land of Treasures: Wine Consumption and the Making of French Identity in the Late Nineteenth Century' in W. J. Belasco and P. Scranton, *Food Nations: Selling Taste in Consumer Societies* (London: Routledge, 2002) 34, 36.
[12] Ibid. 43.

craft, making them exemplary symbols for this purpose. Wine thus continues to play a prominent part in constituting identity at the national or regional level.[13] This also provides the backdrop as to why *terroir* products were considered inimitable and the legal discourse appears to have adopted this characterization.

By contrast, the second iteration of *terroir* focusses on its physical, empirically verifiable elements. Once again, the inference is that the complex blend of natural conditions produces a unique place of origin. Thus it is referred to as:

A plot of land or site, with its own individual fingerprint, made up of geological features, soil composition and structure, mineral content, exposure to general weather conditions, micro-climates, rainfall and drainage, sunshine, degree and variation in orientation, slope, all of which may vary in content and make-up throughout the site, and which has been so used for the growing of the vine through generations resulting in the land being composed of its natural constituents for that purpose.[14]

Amongst the various elements, geological formation is given great importance, as illustrated by the soil of Burgundy, formed by the gradual disintegration of mountain slopes. This is not only a crucial source of minerals and nutrients but also regulates the optimal drainage of rainwater.[15] Soil is said to have four prominent attributes – it holds up the vine, supplies moisture, warms up and cools down at a variable rate and supplies nutrients.[16] The geographically deterministic view of *terroir* also rests on an immutable notion of place that finds traction with courts:

The two features of Champagne of prime importance for its uniqueness are the soil and climate in which the grapes are grown, and the method of manufacture by skilled personnel. The first of those elements cannot be exactly duplicated anywhere in the world, but the second can. It apparently is generally recognised among wine experts that the precise geographical location (i.e. soil and climate) for the growing of a vine is the outstanding, unchanging factor which governs the final product. Hence the predominance of place names for appellations.[17]

Both these conceptions of *terroir* suggest a unique product as the end result. Yet the emphasis on the mystical or natural de-emphasizes a crucial dimension, giving rise to a third account. This more balanced

---

[13] For example, see Ch. 15 of M. J. Gannon, *Understanding Global Cultures* (3rd edn., Thousand Oaks, Calif.: Sage, 2004). Wine is the (stereotypical) metaphor chosen to depict French culture and society.

[14] A. Biss and O. Smith, *The Wines of Chablis* (Bournemouth: Writers International, 2000) 49.

[15] A. Hanson, *Burgundy* (London: Mitchell Beazley, 2003) 58–9.

[16] C. Foulkes (ed.), *Larousse Encyclopedia of Wine* (2nd edn, London: Hamlyn, 2001) 130.

[17] *Comité Interprofessionnel du Vin de Champagne* v *Wineworths Group Ltd* [1991] 2 NZLR 432 at 10 (Wellington HCt).

notion of *terroir* encompasses a 'combination of natural factors such as the quality and nature of the soils, climate, and location and orientation factors such as the slope and sunshine exposure of the vineyards. To these *terroir* quality attributes are added others that pertain to traditional winemaking processes.'[18] This introduces the human element as good grapes must be turned into fine wine, so the 'mastery of vinification techniques is just as important'.[19] There is a recognition that each wine maker 'builds on local traditions, legal requirements, and his or her own skills and experience to create a particular style of wine'.[20] Thus Wilson writes that, while geology had prepared the land, it would be up to human ingenuity in 'good time to make France a wine country'.[21] Movement begins to appear across the canvas of static place.

Yet for several decades deterministic *terroir* was to be found buttressing arguments for the legal protection of GIs. It was explicitly mobilized as a counterweight to the argument that often geographical names for regional products would become generic for the type of product, regardless of origin. This logic appears during negotiations leading up to the Madrid Agreement for the Repression of False Indications of Source of 1891.[22] As the title suggests, the agreement sought to prohibit the use of false indications of source on products, and a controversy arose as to whether generic terms for products of the vine should be exempted from this. The countervailing argument, suggested by the Portuguese delegate, was that all agricultural products should be excluded from this generic exception as they could never truthfully slide into genericide. He distinguished between industrial or manufactured products such as eau de Cologne or Russian leather which referred to a type or class of goods and agricultural products such as the wines of Bordeaux, which could only originate in a particular region.[23] The argument was pursued during subsequent negotiations as well. In 1900 M. Pelletier, the French delegate, acknowledged the practice of adopting generic names for manufactured articles such as suede gloves, but suggested that 'nature' itself placed limits upon such use for viticultural products:

[18] E. Auriol *et al.*, 'France' in K. Anderson (ed.), *The World's Wine Markets: Globalization at Work* (Cheltenham: Edward Elgar, 2004) 64.
[19] Unwin, *Historical Geography* 50.
[20] Ibid. See also J. Halliday and H. Johnson, *The Art and Science of Wine* (London: Mitchell Beazley, 1994) 19–20.
[21] J. E. Wilson, *Terroir* 15.
[22] Madrid Agreement for the Repression of False or Deceptive Indications of Source on Goods, 14 Apr. 1891, 828 UNTS 389 (hereinafter, the Madrid Agreement). Also at www.wipo.org/treaties/ip/madrid/.
[23] See *Procès Verbaux de la Conférence de Madrid de 1890 de Union Pour la Protection de la Propriété Industrielle* (Madrid: Bureau International de l'Union, 1892) 87.

Ici il est impossible d'admettre les appellations génériques, puisque le nom du produit évoque nécessairement l'idée de son origine. Donc, si l'on cherche à se rendre un compte exact de la portée de l'article 4, on ne tarde pas à comprendre que les produits vinicoles n'ont pas été exceptés par hasard. Cette exception était imposée par la nature même des produits.

[In this case, it is impossible to acknowledge the use of generic appellations, since the name of the product necessarily evokes the idea of its origin. Therefore, if one seeks to establish precisely the scope of article 4, one rapidly understands that the products of the vine were not exempted arbitrarily. This exception was imposed by the very nature of such products.][24]

Strategically, arguing that a fixed place has a uniquely deterministic influence on products has enormous importance as it insulates indications of origin such as 'Bordeaux'. Usually protection is contingent upon a sign's communicative ability and, if generic use is established, such use is not considered misleading as to origin. The *terroir* argument was deployed here – suggesting that there could only be one true product – to ensure that GIs were shielded against the semantic cross-winds that otherwise buffet an indication used in international commerce.

To this extent, there is evidence to support Dr Parry's concerns about the static construction of place under the *terroir* rubric. The place of origin was assumed to be neatly definable and deterministically influential, while timeless *terroir* was informed by the French nation-building project. This notion was then deployed for strategic purposes at international negotiations. However, the following pages trace the unravelling of this construct within GI discourse over the twentieth century.

Phylloxera *and the response to fraud*

While *terroir* provided the conceptual basis, the impetus for a dedicated legal regime was fraud. Certain products enjoy a positive image and reputation on the basis of their region of origin. In the case of wines, the idea that geography is fundamentally related to quality is well established, dating back to at least Greek and Roman times, and had become a widespread belief by the nineteenth century.[25] Since place of origin plays a crucial role in quality assurance,[26] it is an obvious target for fraudulent adoption by outsiders. What opened the floodgates was, as Dr Parry

[24] See *Actes de la Conférence de Bruxelles 1897 et 1900* (Berne: Bureau International de l'Union, 1901) 268. I am grateful to Jane Ginsburg and Essie Maglo for assistance with the translation.
[25] Leo A. Loubére, *The Wine Revolution in France – The Twentieth Century* (Princeton, N.J.: Princeton University Press, 1990) 114.
[26] The continued relevance of environmental factors is evident as both the USA and Australia have organized their wine labelling regulations along 'place of origin' lines.

notes, *phylloxera*. This tiny sap-sucking, aphid-like, root-louse feeds on the roots and leaves of grapevines. Native to the United States, it was accidentally introduced into Europe in the 1860s when vines from the East coast of America were sent to France as museum specimens.[27] The consequences were devastating. As the roots of infected vines become distorted, the regeneration of new roots is inhibited thereby affecting the root system's ability to absorb water and minerals.[28] After several attempts, including chemical responses and hybridization of vine varieties, the solution which finally emerged was to graft European vines on to American rootstock that had a natural resistance to the pest.[29] This was not the only misfortune to beset French vineyards around that period. It also saw the onset of fungal diseases such as oidium or powdery mildew, which swept through European vineyards in the 1840s and 1850s, proving extremely difficult to control.[30] While the output from the traditional vineyards of Europe slumped during this period, demand did not. Ideal conditions were created not only for the fraudulent misrepresentation of origin but for cutting corners and compromising on quality. One source wryly observes that the merchants of Burgundy were attempting to repeat the miracle at Cana. While not quite turning water into wine, they were certainly re-labelling Algerian reds as Burgundy originals.[31] This was part of a trend to fill the vacuum left by dwindling supplies of authentic wines from reputed French regions. The epidemic also resulted in indiscriminate replanting, leading to low-grade wines flooding the market. The relative value of wine to the French economy entered a decline and the Government was forced to intervene. The task before it was therefore to address fraud as to origin while ensuring quality.[32]

Is deterministic terroir sufficient to guarantee quality?

The Parliamentary response to this crisis reveals the extent to which *terroir*, in the deterministic sense, was considered a necessary or sufficient condition to guarantee wine quality. The episodes that follow demonstrate that

---

See, respectively, the Approved Viticultural Area regime at www.ttb.gov/appellation/index.shtml, and the Geographical Indications regime at www.wineaustralia.com/australia/Default.aspx?tabid=246.

[27] M. G. Mullins *et al.*, *The Biology of the Grapevine* (Cambridge: Cambridge University Press, 1992) 183.

[28] Ibid.

[29] For an engaging social history on the campaign to find a solution, see C. Campbell, *Phylloxera: How Wine was Saved for the World* (London: Harper Perennial, 2004).

[30] Unwin, *Historical Geography* 283–4.   [31] Foulkes (ed.), *Larousse Encyclopedia* 131.

[32] See Charles K. Warner, *The Winegrowers of France and the Government since 1875* (New York: Columbia University Press, 1960) 26–9.

guaranteeing truthful origin labelling is an insufficient condition, as (i) defining the region of origin is often a political, contentious act, leading to large geologically and climatically diverse places being specified, while (ii) the legal regime increasingly recognized the importance of the human element in ensuring wine quality by imposing controls on production standards. Both these developments undermined the proposition that physical place was solely or predominantly responsible for the quality of the end product.

While there were some attempts in the late nineteenth century to address fraudulent practices that affected quality,[33] it is with the 1905 law[34] that a systematic response began to take shape. This aimed at discouraging fraud in general and there were no specific rules relating to demarcated wine regions. It penalized 'anyone who attempts to deceive the contracting party as to the nature, substantial qualities, composition and content of productive principles of any goods, either with regard to their variety or their origin, when, according to conventions or customs, the designation of a falsely attributed variety or origin is to be considered as the main cause for the sale'.[35] This naturally poses the difficulty of establishing benchmarks for genuine products, starting with defining the authentic place of origin. Under Article 11, the establishment of individual product specifications was left to local administrative bodies. This may have been a well-intentioned remedy to improve quality but the result was a disaster.

The history of this period indicates that: (i) establishing boundary limits was not simply based on 'objective' geographical criteria but was a politically charged process; (ii) areas specified were therefore fluid compromises in the early stages and not necessarily homogeneous; this directly challenges the proposition that distinct geographical places guarantee quality. A series of decrees were promulgated between 1908 and 1912 establishing administrative commissions to define formally the regions of production for 'Champagne', 'Bordeaux' and 'Cognac'. But on what basis were these bodies to demarcate regions? The three contenders were:

A. existing administrative boundaries, such as the extent of a *département*;
B. historical production areas;
C. a region sharing similar geographical and climatic features.

[33] Such as the Loi Griffe passed in 1889 which, *inter alia*, regulated the watering of wine. See ibid. 39–40.
[34] Loi du 1er août 1905 sur les Fraudes et Falsifications en Matière de Produits ou de Services (5 août 1905) Journal Officiel 4813.
[35] As translated by A. Stanziani, 'Wine Reputation and Quality Controls: The Origin of the AOCs in 19th Century France' (2004) 18(2) *European Journal of Law and Economics* 149, 159.

The act of prioritizing one over the others led to contentious conclusions. Reverting to Dr Parry's case study, for Champagne the decree of 17 September 1908 resulted in Aube's exclusion, despite the claims that there was a history of production in this region, that geographical conditions were favourable and that for centuries their wines had been bought by the merchants (négociants) of Reims and Épernay as true Champagne wines.[36] This led to demonstrations throughout 1911. In one notorious incident, 5,000 protestors marched on Ay and then Épernay, which led to the dispatch of 15,000 troops to put down the violent protest.[37] Unrest continued until the law of 22 July 1927 allowed seventy-one communes in the Aube region to bear this appellation and specified the three permissible varieties of grapes to be used.[38] A similar problem arose with the commission set up for Bordeaux. While it consisted of a mix of local administrators, regional representatives, wine makers and négociants, as the number of wine growers' associations increased the commission finally resorted to an administrative solution. The Bordeaux production region was assimilated within the department of Gironde, triggering protests by those who were excluded.[39] Attempts were then made to redress this with subsequent delimitations by new commissions set up after a law passed in 1908. Here it was a committee of 'technicians, archivists and professors of agriculture', moving towards a more acceptable compromise.[40] Even this synopsis suggests that appellation regions were often born out of compromises between administrative delimitations, geographically homogeneous regions and historical areas of production. They are constructed rather than found. Dr Parry's critique is in alignment with other geographers who are suspicious of such 'static place' claims. Warren Moran notes that 'the manner in which assumptions about natural environmental influences are used to assert and justify political and territorial control, and thereby influence the distribution of the industry, has received little attention'.[41]

Joseph Capus, the most influential architect of the modern French AOC regime, doggedly maintained that this regulatory response rested on the flawed assumption that, by regulating the truthful use of geographical origin on labels, problems associated with product quality

---

[36] A. L. Simon, The History of Champagne (London: Ebury Press, 1962) 109–10.

[37] Unwin, Historical Geography 315.

[38] Loi du 22 juillet 1927 Modifie La Loi du 6 mai 1919 (Protection des Appellations D'Origine) (27 fuillet 1927) Journal Official 7762.

[39] Stanziani, 'Origin of the AOCs' 160.   [40] Loubére, Wine Revolution 116.

[41] W. Moran, 'The Wine Appellation as Territory in France and California' (1993) 83 Annals of the Association of American Geographers 694, 694.

would fall into line.[42] Origin alone was simply insufficient as a warranty and he spent the better part of three decades arguing that recognizing existing best practices associated with established places and organizing production along these lines was a crucial complement to geography. Thus the link between quality based on origin and authenticity (or the human contribution) emerges.

'Authenticity': from the AO to the AOC

The law of 1919: the insufficiency of origin

A partial response to these shortcomings was the law of 1919.[43] Attempts were made to incorporate concerns regarding the fairness of boundary determinations by laying out a general principle for determining the place of origin as well as shifting the decision-making powers from administrative committees to the judiciary. Most significantly, the law introduced the Appellation d'Origine (AO) as the conceptual vector which represented this qualitative link between product and place. The AO is presently defined in Article L. 115–1 of the French Code de la Consommation as the name of a region or locality serving to designate a product which originates from there and whose quality or characteristics are due to its geographical origin, comprising of both natural and human factors.[44]

Thus if a sign (directly or indirectly) falsely indicated the origin of the product or went against local, loyal and constant usages, remedial action was possible.[45] These three stipulations attempt to capture authentic production practices. One author interprets them as follows: local in contrast to individual, suggesting a collective interest; loyal is honest, as opposed to clandestine, practices; and constant implies consistent,

---

[42] See, generally, J. Capus, *L'Évolution de la Législation sur les Appellations d'Origine: Genèse des Appellations Contrôlées* (Paris: Institut National des Appellations d' Origine 1947). The text is available at: www.inao.gouv.fr/public/home.php.

[43] *Loi du 6 mai 1919 Relative à la Protection des Appellations d'Origine* (8 mai 1919) Journal Officiel 4726. The full text is available at www.wipo.int/clea/docs_new/pdf/fr/fr/fr030fr.pdf.

[44] Article L. 115–1 of the Code de la Consommation reads : 'Constitue une appellation d'origine la dénomination d'un pays, d'une région ou d'une localité servant à désigner un produit qui en est originaire et dont la qualité ou les caractères sont dus au milieu géographique, comprenant des facteurs naturels et des facteurs humains.'

[45] Article 1 of the law of 1919 reads: 'Toute personne qui prétendra qu'une appellation d'origine est appliquée à son préjudice direct ou indirect et contre son droit à un produit naturel ou fabriqué et contrairement à l'origine de ce produit, ou à des usages locaux, loyaux et constants, aura une action en justice pour faire interdire l'usage de cette appellation.'

tried and tested techniques.[46] Yet under this law the emphasis remained restricted to setting out regions of origin and regulating their truthful use on labels. The focus was on place rather than practice. Capus draws on legal decisions interpreting this to show that while 'usages locaux, loyaux et constants' was sensibly interpreted by some courts as mandating the need to define collective production practices, it was interpreted by others as a safety valve for working out the contours of historical entitlement to use the name. For instance, was longstanding, customary use of an appellation by those in a contiguous administrative department a defensible use of the region's name? By de-emphasizing production conditions, vintners located in a famous region or otherwise traditionally entitled to the use of the name would technically be able to use an appellation signifying a high-quality wine despite using inferior-quality, high-yield vines. And, by the same token, contiguous vintners on the wrong side of the boundary of the *département* making high-quality wines would not be able to use the appellation. Further issues arose from the manner in which *négociants* made use of geographical names. Should a wine merchant in a reputed region be permitted to use its name despite sourcing the grapes from elsewhere? Complications arose due to the custom of producing *mélanges* or blending wine from different regions.[47] Often the merchant's interests (e.g. favouring imports or using high-yielding vines and techniques) would conflict with producers' interests (e.g. favouring exports and using reliable methods). Therefore the porosity of place was very much a backdrop when trying to determine what constituted authentic use of an appellation. The solution was to opt for tried and tested best practices, which may have originated from a variety of sources, both internal and external, but which came together and were widely adopted at the place in question.

The law of 1935: origin and quality assured

It soon became apparent under the law of 1919 that, while judges could define geographical boundaries, 'they were not competent to specify other production criteria for an appellation. All kinds of areas could be, and were, declared to be appellations, the outcome being a host of appellations of origin throughout the wine industry.'[48] Successive legislative attempts

---

[46] H. L. Pinner (ed.), *World Unfair Competition Law: An Encyclopedia*, vol. II (Leyden: Sijthoff, 1965) 637.
[47] Stanziani 'Origin of the AOCs' 156.
[48] OECD, *Appellations of Origin and Geographical Indications in OECD Member Countries: Economic and Legal Implications* (COM/AGR/APM/TD/WP(2000)15/FINAL) 58.

such as the law of 1927[49] put an end to the Champagne boundary-setting
controversy and moved closer to the ideal of directly ensuring minimum
standards of quality by establishing permissible vines and grape varieties,
while banning hybrids.[50]

Finally, on 30 July 1935, the law creating the Appellation d'Origine
Contrôlée (AOC) regime was promulgated.[51] The AOC is defined essentially as an official seal of approval.[52] Not only areas of production but
detailed product specifications are collectively established via Decree
and then regulated, thereby guaranteeing both origin and quality.[53] The
co-ordinating body is the Institut National des Appellations d'Origine
(INAO). It has a broad mandate, but its primary function remains to
improve quality by regulating production conditions (including overpro-
duction) and fraudulent labelling nationally and internationally, as well as
by facilitating registration according to acceptable established criteria.[54]
This leads to a contemporary understanding of 'Produits de Terroir'
that embraces the human element. These are considered to be: '(L)ocal
and traditional food products or produce with a unique and identifiable character based upon specific historical, cultural or technical components. The definition includes the accumulation and transmission of
savoir-faire';[55] or '(L)ocal agricultural products and foodstuffs whose
qualities cross time and space and are anchored in a specific place and
history . . . (and) depend on the shared savoir-faire of a given community
and its culture'.[56] Anthropologists explore how this technical culture
evolved, is shared and also transmitted between generations, thereby
creating spaces for innovation and improvement. There is little evidence
to suggest that local communities legally claim internalized origins for
all these innovations but they do put them to work. Authenticity is the
accumulated result of collective historical experimentation but is by no
means an unproblematic concept. In this process, a number of actors
including producers, consumers, local groups and political institutions

---

[49] Above, note 38, Loi du 22 juillet 1927.
[50] N. Olszak, *Droit des Appellations d'Origine et Indications de Provenance* (Paris: TEC &
DOC, 2001) 43.
[51] *Décret-loi du 30 juillet 1935 Relatif à la Défense du Marché des Vins et au Régime Économique
de l'Alcool* (31 juillet 1935) Journal Officiel 8314.
[52] See Art. L 112–2 of the Code de la Consommation.
[53] The idea of self-imposed collective standards had been a possibility for some time.
A modern pioneer in this regard was Baron Pierre Le Roy de Boiseaumarie who was
instrumental in establishing the detailed guidelines for the appellation 'Châteauneuf-
du-Pape' in the southern Rhône wine region. See A. L. Simon, *The History of Champagne*
118–19.
[54] See www.inao.gouv.fr/public/home.php.   [55] Demossier, 'Culinary Heritage' 146.
[56] L. Bérard and P. Marchenay, 'A Market Culture: *Produits de Terroir* or the Selling of
Culture' in Blowen *et al.* (eds.), *Recollections of France* 154.

394   Dev Gangjee

come together to construct the heritage around a product. On occasion, tensions arise between this constructed tradition and the need for innovation, such as disputed decisions about raw materials or methods of production.[57] Moreover, while events leading up to the original product specification may have incorporated innovations along the way, why should one presume that at the time of 'fixing' they were the last word? Therefore, it is possible, but difficult, to modify an AOC specification, recognizing the tension between permitting ongoing innovation while retaining the cachet of authentic production methods.[58]

The incorporation of 'authenticity' as *savoir faire* poses another puzzle, as the subject matter for GI protection has been expanding. Dr Parry expresses unease with the diversity of suggested Kenyan products in her example, along with the charge that 'authenticity' has become an empty vessel within which anything fits. While the appropriate subject matter for appellation protection is a legitimate concern, this wide array does not represent the breakdown of 'authenticity' as a meaningful organizing concept. Cheese fits within the appellation paradigm for local flora is influenced by climate and geology. The diet of the sheep in the La Mancha region of Spain is translated, via their thick aromatic milk, into the flavour of 'Manchego' cheese.[59] Yet human know-how plays an important role in the production of traditional cheese as well. For instance, in the case of Roquefort, a court has acknowledged that 'the historic methods and usages of production, curing and development'[60] play a decisive part. Going beyond this, one increasingly finds craft and textile products on GI registers.[61] 'Authenticity', defined as *savoir faire*,

---

[57] Ibid. 163.

[58] For example, Gade records the evolution of the 'Cassis' AOC specifications, noting that '(a)ppellation rules are not inflexible'. See D. W. Gade, 'Tradition, Territory, and Terroir in French Viniculture: Cassis, France, and Appellation Contrôlée', (2004) 94 *Annals of the Association of American Geographers* 848, 853.

[59] J. Harbutt, *Cheese: A Complete Guide to Over 300 Cheeses of Distinction* (Minoqua: Willow Creek Press, 1999) 13.

[60] The cumulative and collective human element recognized in *Community of Roquefort v William Faehndrich* 303 F.2d 494, 495 (2nd Cir. 1962) (Kaufman, J). The case held that 'Roquefort', which was protected as a certification trade mark in the USA, had not become a generic term and could not be applied to blue cheese imported from Hungary and Italy.

[61] For examples drawn from the Lisbon Register for Appellations of Origin, see Czech Jablonec ware for ornamental jewellery and decorative glass (Registration Nos. 62 and 64); Hungarian Halas lace (Registration No. 738); Mexican Olinalá wood handcrafted objects (Registration No. 732). Under the Indian Geographical Indications Act of 1999, the majority of registrations have been for craft and textile products such as the Aranmula Kannadi metal mirror (Application No. 3); Pochampally Ikat textiles (Application No. 4); Mysore Silk (Application No. 11); Channapatna toys (Application No. 23). The product specifications are available in the GI Journal at www.girindia.in.

is common to all these products. If cheese represents an intermediate point on the spectrum between physical geographical influences and human skills, then surely crafts must lie at one end of it. As the effect of place is muted, what is to stop communities of traditional crafts producers from moving out of the regions which have made these products well known? Would their products still fit within the appellation paradigm and therefore should they qualify for GI protection? This response is not the appropriate platform for developing these ideas, but issues concerning the definition of authenticity have arisen in the context of indigenous crafts, such as the 'Label of Authenticity' in Australia.[62] If the relevant community (the identification of which is often politically contentious) can establish that production in a specific region is necessary for the way in which an authentic craft is defined, the appellation model may continue to apply. Again GI law would benefit from the insights of those who study the interplay between place and identity.

Conclusion

When sited within this historical context, the concept of 'authenticity' is not as simplistic or flat as it is made out to be. Human skill and know-how associated with traditional products is neither timeless, nor self-contained. Instead, this *savoir faire* was the result of a collective investment, based on much experimentation and empirically tested methods but tied to local geographical conditions. Place thus becomes the catchment area for production techniques and not the fount. Yet Dr Parry does not set up a straw man, for the legal discourse is replete with precisely the allusions to authenticity that she wishes to puncture.[63] Even legislative wording does not avoid this myth making, as illustrated by Article 4(2)(e) of EC Regulation 510/2006 on the Protection of Geographical Indications.[64] At the time of registration, appellation product specifications must contain

---

[62] For a summary of the US, Australian and New Zealand experiences in verifying authenticity via a label, see WIPO Secretariat, 'The Protection of Traditional Cultural Expressions / Expressions of Folklore: Overview of Policy Objectives and Core Principles' 20 Aug. 2004 (WIPO/GRTKF/IC/7/3) at Annex II [38–41].

[63] An apt illustration is provided by Advocate General Colomer during the *Feta* litigation in *Canadane Cheese Trading* v *Hellenic Republic*, C. 317/95 [1997] ECR I-4681 at [13] (AGO) ('This cultural context may to some degree be relevant to a case such as that now before the Court because, so far as cheeses are concerned, what matters is the natural element, *the rest being mystery and patience*: they have more to do with *immemorial custom* and traditional flavours than with recipes which, like the law, can be improvised' (emphasis added)).

[64] Council Regulation (EEC) No. 510/2006 of 20 March 2006 on the Protection of Geographical Indications and Designations of Origin for Agricultural Products and Foodstuffs [2006] OJ No. L93/12.

'a description of the method of obtaining the agricultural product or foodstuff and, if appropriate, *the authentic and unvarying local methods*'. This somewhat misleading appeal to authenticity must be considered in light of the *phylloxera* crisis and the fraud that ensued. The objective was to preserve hard-earned regional reputations by setting down tried and tested methods which resulted in high-quality products, rather than appealing to changeless practices with internalized origins.

This insight leads on to why it may make sense to have GIs as a distinct *sui generis* regime. The purpose of GIs is in part to acknowledge this inter-generational investment that is sited in a particular place. Therefore, one should not be restricted to an evaluation according to the same market efficiency logic of trade mark law,[65] in isolation from the *savoir faire* and cultural heritage elements.[66] As part of a broader research agenda, I have considered the continued relevance of the distinction between these two species of intellectual property rights in signs. Protecting GIs as Collective or Certification marks is certainly a pragmatic compromise in countries where a separate protection regime does not exist, but there are hidden consequences. For a start, the US 'Tequila' Certification mark[67] referred to in Dr Parry's paper has to coexist with 263 other live applications or registrations which include 'Tequila', making the ability to communicate a clear message of Mexican origin doubtful.[68] Trade mark doctrine continues to view a geographical term either as a descriptive expression open to all or as capable of individual appropriation through acquired distinctiveness, but is uncomfortable with a collective, geographical yet 'brand'-like and distinctive usage. Collective or Certification marks are viewed as a non-exclusive concession in these circumstances. Furthermore, trade mark law manages conflicts between signs by resorting to principles such as 'First in Time, First in Right'.[69] This leads to inequitable results where a swift trade mark registrant manages to trump the GI collective at the registry.[70] Given the jurisdictional limits of registered trade mark law and the consequent

---

[65] See the contributions on the economic analysis of trade marks in this volume.
[66] For a sketch of some of these additional dimensions, see L. Bently and B. Sherman, *Intellectual Property Law* (2nd edn, Oxford: Oxford University Press, 2004) 970–1.
[67] 'Tequila' has been applied for as a Certification by the Consejo Regulador del Tequila in 2003 (Serial No. 78286762).
[68] Some of the more charming entries include 'Legal Alien Tequila' (S No. 78896769) and 'T&T Tacos Tequila' (S No. 78950338): search conducted on the US PTO Trademark Electronic Search System (TESS) on 25 Feb. 2007. Available at www.uspto.gov/main/trademarks.htm.
[69] I have explored this in greater length elsewhere. See D. Gangjee, 'Quibbling Siblings: Conflicts Between Trade Marks and GIs' (2007) 82 *Chicago-Kent Law Review* 1253.
[70] This led the EU to adopt a coexistence-based model in the case of a prior trade mark – subsequent GI conflict. On the issue of whether this is TRIPS compatible, see *European*

territorial division of rights, it is possible for traditional producers to discover that their designation belongs to someone else.[71] Therefore *sui generis* GI regimes have crafted specific responses to issues such as setting a high threshold for generic status[72] or have established principles of coexistence between prior trade marks and subsequent GIs, rather than permitting an outright trump.

I finally return to the themes of porosity and osmosis. Thanks to TRIPS debates, GIs are no longer solely about French farmers and state subsidies. At the risk of generalizing, the reason why GIs have struck a chord with several developing countries is because they concern products which are relevant for their producer communities, who have been excluded from the formal intellectual property system thus far.[73] While postmodern critiques of place have tremendous analytical value, they tend to get co-opted by forces in favour of globalized food production. These tend to be arrayed against movements such as Fair Trade, or those in support of organic food, Eco-labels or non-GMO production, emphasizing the politics of consumption. Place continues to matter for many traditional or artisanal producers and consumers as well, as the evidence indicates.[74] If *sui generis* GI protection is also about recognizing traditional skills and innovations, then protecting the appellation while leaving the production practices to flow freely across national borders and boundaries may be the most balanced response to that investment. Spanish sparkling wine producers drew on French appellation methods to produce what is today Cava. They're doing pretty well with it and that may be an appropriately celebratory note on which to end this comment.

Communities – Protection of Trademarks and Geographical Indications for Agricultural Products and Foodstuffs (WT/DS174/R) 15 Mar. 2005. Panel Report and Written Submissions at www.wto.int/english/news_e/news05_e/panelreport_174_290_e.htm.

[71] A prominent example is 'Kobe' beef from Japan. It has already been registered as a trade mark by producers based outside of Japan in the USA, Australia and Canada: D. Gangjee, *Protecting Geographical Indications as Trademarks: The Prospects and Pitfalls* (Tokyo: Institute of Intellectual Property, 2006) 35–9. A draft of the report is available at www.lse.ac.uk/collections/law/staff/gangjee/Gangjee_IIP%20Report%202006.pdf.

[72] See D. Gangjee, 'Say Cheese! A Sharper Image of Genericuse through the Lens of Feta' (2007) 29 EIPR 172.

[73] On the mismatch between traditional knowledge and mainstream intellectual property regimes, see generally the WIPO *Report on Fact-finding Missions on Intellectual Property and Traditional Knowledge* (1998–9) www.wipo.int/tk/en/tk/ffm/report/index.html.

[74] For an overview of various European surveys, see D. Skuras and E. Dimara, 'Regional Image and the Consumption of Regionally Denominated Products' (2004) 41 (4) *Urban Studies* 801; K. Van Ittersum *et al.*, 'The Influence of the Image of a Product's Region of Origin on Product Evaluation' (2003) 56 *Journal of Business Research* 215. More generally, see B. Krissoff, M. Bohman and J. A. Caswell, *Global Food Trade and Consumer Demand for Quality* (New York: Kluwer, 2002).

Bibliography

(1875) 23 *Journal of the Society of Arts* 567.

(1876) *Solicitors' Journal* 402 (18 Mar. 1876).

(1879) 23 *Solicitors' Journal* 819 (16 Aug. 1879).

Aaker, D., and E. Joachimsthaler, *Brand Leadership: The Next Level of the Brand Revolution* (New York: The Free Press, 2000).

Actes de la Conférence de Bruxelles 1897 et 1900 (Berne: Bureau International de l'Union, 1901).

Adams, F. M., *A Treatise on the Law of Trade Marks* (London: George Bell and Sons, 1874).

A Treatise on the Law of Trade-Marks: With the Trade-Marks Registration Act of 1875 and Rules (London: Butterworths, 1876).

Adams, J., *The Doctrine of Equity* (London: William Benning and Co., 1850).

Adams, J. N., 'Court Endorses Rent Seeking: Arsenal Football Club v Reed (Adidas-Salomon AG v Fitness Trading Ltd en passant)' (2004) 1 *Intellectual Property Quarterly* 114–20.

Adams, J. N., and K. V. Prichard Jones, *Franchising* (4th edn, London: Butterworths, 1997).

'Advertisements' (1855) 97 *Quarterly Review* 183–225.

Aitchison, Jean, *Words in the Mind: An Introduction to the Mental Lexicon*. (3rd edn, Oxford: Blackwell, 2003).

Akerlof, G., 'The Market for "Lemons": Quality Uncertainty and the Market Mechanism' (1970) 84 *Quarterly Journal of Economics* 488–500.

Alford, Bernard, *W. D. and H. O. Wills and the Development of the UK Tobacco Industry, 1786–1965* (London: Methuen, 1973).

Allen, T., and J. Simmons, 'Visual and Verbal Identity' in R. Clifton and J. Simmons (eds.), *Brands and Branding* (Princeton, N. J.: Bloomberg, 2003).

Ambler, T., *Are Brands Good for Britain? British Brands Group Inaugural Lecture* (London: British Brands Group, 2000).

Anderson, Kim (ed.), *The World's Wine Markets: Globalization at Work* (Cheltenham: Edward Elgar, 2004).

Arnheim, Rudolf, *The Dynamics of Architectural Form* (Berkeley: University of California Press, 1977).

Arvidsson, A., *Brands: Meaning and Value in Media Culture* (London: Routledge, 2006).

'Associated Chambers of Commerce' *The Times*, 24 Sept. 1873, p. 12c.

'Association in Birmingham' (1866) 14 *Journal of the Society of Arts* 131.

'Association of Chambers of Commerce' *The Times*, 7 Feb. 1861, p. 12f.

Auriol, E. *et al.*, 'France' in Kim Anderson (ed.), *The World's Wine Markets: Globalization at Work* (Cheltenham: Edward Elgar, 2004).

Austin, Graeme, 'The Story of Steele v. Bulova: Trademarks on the Line' in Jane C. Ginsburg and Rochelle Cooper Dreyfuss (eds.), *Intellectual Property Stories* (New York: Foundation Press, 2005).

'Trademarks and the Burdened Imagination' (2004) 69 *Brooklyn Law Review* 827–922.

Austin, J. L., *Philosophical Papers*, ed. J. O. Urmson and G. J. Warnock (Oxford: Oxford University Press, 1979).

Ayling, R. (1999) 'British Airways Brand Leadership Results from being True to our Long-term Vision' in F. Gilmore (ed.), *Brand Warriors: Corporate Leaders Share Their Winning Strategies* (London: HarperCollins Business, 1999).

Bagwell, L., and B. Bernheim, 'Veblen Effects in a Theory of Conspicuous Consumption' (1996) 86 *American Economic Review* 349–73.

Baker, C. Edwin, 'Paternalism, Politics, and Citizen Freedom: The Commercial Speech Quandary in Nike' (2004) 54 *Case Western Reserve Law Review* 1161.

Barham, E., 'Translating Terroir: The Global Challenge of French AOC Labelling' (2003) 19 *Journal of Rural Studies* 127–38.

Barrett, Charles, *The Bunyip and Other Mythical Monsters and Legends* (Melbourne: Reed and Harris, 1946).

Barwise, P., A. Dunham and M. Ritson, 'Ties that Bind: Consumers and Businesses' in J. Pavitt (ed.), *Brand.new* (London: V&A Publications, 2000).

Bashkow, I., and L. Dobrin, 'Pigs for Sance Songs': Reo Fortune's Empathetic Ethnography of the Arapesh Roads' (n.d.) *Histories of Anthropology Annual* 2.

Baudrillard, J., 'The Evil Demon of Images and the Precession of Simulacra' in T. Docherty (ed.), *Postmodernism: A Reader* (Hemel Hempstead, Herts.: Harvester, 1993).

BBC news, 'EU Wine Reform' 22 June 2006, available at http://news.bbc.co.uk/1/hi/world/europe/5107400.stm.

Becker, G., and K. Murphy, 'A Theory of Rational Addiction' (1988) 96 *Journal of Political Economy* 675–700.

(eds.), *Social Economics: Market Behaviour in a Social Environment* (Cambridge, Mass.: Belknap Press, 2000).

Beebe, Barton, 'An Empirical Study of the Multifactor Tests for Trademark Infringement' (2006) 94 *California Law Review* 1581–654.

'Search and Persuasion in Trademark Law' (2005) 103 *Michigan Law Review* 2020–72.

'The Semiotic Analysis of Trademark Law' (2004) 51 *U.C.L.A. Law Review* 621–704.

Beier, F. K., and A. Preimer, 'Preparatory Study for the Establishment of a Uniform International Trademark Definition' (1955) 45 *Trademark Reporter* 1266.

Bentham, J., *An Introduction to the Principles of Morals and Legislation* ed. J. H. Burns and H. L. A. Hart (Oxford: Clarendon Press, [1789] 1996).

Bently, Lionel, 'From Communication to Thing: Historical Aspects of the Conceptualisation of Trade Marks as Property' in Graeme Dinwoodie and Mark Janis (eds.), *Trademark Law and Theory: A Handbook of Contemporary Research* (Cheltenham: Edward Elgar, 2008).

Bently, Lionel, and Brad Sherman, *Intellectual Property Law* (Oxford: Oxford University Press, 2001; 2nd edn, Oxford: Oxford University Press, 2004).

Bérard, L., and P. Marchenay, 'A Market Culture: Produits de Terroir or the Selling of Culture' in S Blowen (ed.), *Recollections of France: Memories, Identities and Heritage in Contemporary France* (New York: Berghahn Books, 2000).

Berg, Donna Lee, *A Guide to the Oxford English Dictionary* (Oxford: Oxford University Press, 1993).

Berger, John, *Ways of Seeing* (London: Penguin, 1972).

Best, J. 'Orange and easyMobile Go to War over Colour', 21 Feb. 2005. http://networks.silicon.com/mobile/0.39024665.39128035.00.htm.

Bezanson, Randall P., 'Institutional Speech' (1994–5) 80 *Iowa Law Review* 735.

Birks, P. (ed.), *The Classification of Obligations* (Oxford: Clarendon Press, 1997).

'Birmingham Chamber of Commerce' *The Times*, 2 Aug. 1872, p. 12e.

Biss, A., and O. Smith, *The Wines of Chablis* (Bournemouth: Writers International, 2000).

Blackett, T., *Trademarks* (London: Macmillan Business and Interbrand, 1998).

Blakemore, Diane, *Understanding Utterances: An Introduction to Pragmatics* (Oxford: Blackwell, 1992).

Bone, Robert G., 'Enforcement Costs and Trademark Puzzles' (2004) 90 *Virginia Law Review* 2099–186.

Boorstin, Daniel, 'Advertising and American Civilization' in Yale Brozen (ed.), *Advertising and Society* (New York: New York University Press, 1974).

Borgerson, Janet L., and Jonathan E. Schroeder, 'Identity in Marketing Communications: An Ethics of Visual Representation' in Allan J. Kimmel (ed.), *Marketing Communications: Emerging Trends and Developments* (Oxford: Oxford University Press, 2005).

Borgerson, Janet L., Jonathan E. Schroeder, Britta Blomberg and Erika Thorssén, 'The Gay Family in the Ad: Consumer Responses to Non-Traditional Families in Marketing Communications' (2006) 22 *Journal of Marketing Management* 955–78.

Bosland, Jason, 'The Culture of Trade Marks: An Alternative Cultural Studies Perspective' (2005) 10 *Media and Arts Law Review* 99–116.

Bouckaert, B., and G. De Geest (eds.), *Encyclopaedia of Law and Economics* (Cheltenham: Edward Elgar, 2000).

Bourdieu, Pierre, *Distinction – A Social Critique of the Judgment of Taste* (Cambridge, Mass.: Harvard University Press, 1984).

Bragg, R., *Trade Descriptions* (Oxford: Clarendon Press, 1991).

Branson, R., 'Virgin: The Virtues of a Diversified Brand' in F. Gilmore (ed.), *Brand Warriors: Corporate Leaders Share Their Winning Strategies* (London: HarperCollins Business, 1999).

Brown, R., 'Advertising and the Public Interest: Legal Protection of Trade Symbols' (1948) 57 *Yale Law Journal* 1165–206, reprinted in (1999) 108 *Yale Law Journal* 1619–59.

Bruni, L., and L. Stanca, 'Income Aspirations, Television and Happiness: Evidence from the World Values Survey' (2006) 59 *Kyklos* 209–29.

Bryce, J., *The Trade Marks Registration Acts 1875 and 1876* (London: William Maxwell and Sons, 1877).

Bucheim, C., 'Aspects of XIXth Century Anglo-German Trade Rivalry Reconsidered' (1981) 10 *Journal of European Economic History* 273–89.

Burrell, R., and M. Handler, 'Making Sense of Trade Mark Law' (2003) 1(4) *Intellectual Property Quarterly* 388–409.

Cable, D. M., and M. E. Graham, 'The Determinants of Job Seekers' Reputation Perceptions' (2000) 21 *Journal of Organisational Behaviour* 929–47.

Calabresi, G., and D. Melamed, 'Property Rules, Liability Rules and Inalienability: One View of the Cathedral' (1972) 85 *Harvard Law Review* 1089–128.

Calleja, R., 'R. v Johnstone [2003] UKHL 28: Bootlegging and Legitimate Use of an Artist's Trade Mark' (2003) 14(7) *Entertainment Law Review* 186–8.

Callman, R., 'Unfair Competition Without Competition? The Importance of the Property Concept in the Law of Trade-marks' (1947) 95 *University of Pennsylvania Law Review* 443–67.

Callon, M., C. Meadel and V. Rabehariosa, 'The Economy of Qualities' (May 2002) 31(2) *Economy and Society* 194–217.

Camerer, C., G. Loewenstein and D. Prelec, 'Neuroeconomics: How Neuroscience can Inform Economics' (2005) 43 *Journal of Economic Literature* 9–64.

Caminiti, S., 'Ralph Lauren: The Emperor has Clothes' (11 Nov. 1998) 137(9) *Fortune* 80–9.

Campbell, C., *Phylloxera: How Wine was Saved for the World* (London: Harper Perennial, 2004).

Capus, J., *L'Évolution de la législation sur les Appellations d'Origine: genèse des Appellations Contrôlées* (Paris: Institut National des Appellations d'Origine, 1947).

Carboni, Anna, 'Distinctive Character Acquired through Use: Establishing the Facts' in Jeremy Phillips and Ilanah Simon (eds.), *Trade Mark Use* (Oxford: Oxford University Press, 2005).

'Two Stripes and You're Out: Added Protection for Trade Marks With a Reputation' (2004) 5 *European Intellectual Property Review* 229–33.

Carroll, Lewis, *Through the Looking-glass and What Alice Found There*, illus. Helen Oxenbury (London: Walker Books, [1871] 2005).

Carter, Ronald, *Language and Creativity: The Art of Common Talk* (London: Routledge, 2004).

Carter, Stephen, 'Does it Matter Whether Intellectual Property is Property?' (1993) 68 *Chicago-Kent Law Review* 715–23.

'The Trouble with Trademark' (1990) 99 *Yale Law Journal* 759–800.

Carty, Hazel, 'Character Merchandising and the Limits of Passing Off' (1993) 13 *Legal Studies* 289–307.

Caruana, Wally, 'Black Art on White Walls' in Sylvia Kleinert and Margot Neale (eds.), *The Oxford Companion to Aboriginal Art and Culture* (Melbourne: Oxford University Press, 2000).

Casperie-Kerdel, S. 'Dilution Disguised: Has the Concept of Trade Mark Dilution Made its Way into the Laws of Europe?' (2001) *European Intellectual Property Review* 185.

Caton, Charles E. (ed.), *Philosophy and Ordinary Language* (Urbana: University of Illinois Press, 1970).

Caves, R. E., and W. F. Murphy, 'Franchising: Forms, Markets and Intangible Assets' in F. Hoy and J. Murphy (eds.), *Franchising: An International Perspective* (London: Routledge, 2003).

Chamberlin, E., *The Theory of Monopolistic Competition* (Cambridge, Mass.: Harvard University Press, 1933).

Chandler, A. D., *Scale and Scope: The Dynamics of Industrial Capitalism* (Cambridge, Mass.: Harvard University Press, 1990).

Chapman, Siobhan, *Philosophy for Linguists* (London: Routledge, 2000).

Charters, Steve, 'Aesthetic Products and Aesthetic Consumption: A Review' (2006) 9 *Consumption Markets and Culture* 3 235–55.

Chipman, J., and J. Moore, 'The New Welfare Economics 1939–74' (1978) 19 *International Economic Review* 547–84.

Church, R., 'Advertising Consumer Goods in Nineteenth-Century Britain: Reinterpretations' (2000) 53(4) *Economic History Review* 621–45.

'New Perspectives on the History of Products, Firms, Marketing and Consumers in Britain and the United States Since the Mid-Nineteenth Century' (1999) 52 *Economic History Review* 405–35.

Clarke, Nancy L., 'Issues in the Federal Registration of Flavors as Trademarks for Pharmaceutical Products' (1993) *University of Illinois Law Review* 105–32.

Coase, R., 'The Problem of Social Cost' (1960) *Journal of Law and Economics* 1–23.

Cohen, Felix, 'Transcendental Nonsense and the Functional Approach' (1935) 35 *Columbia Law Review* 809–49.

Committee Appointed by the Board of Trade to Inquire into the Duties, Organisation, and Arrangements of the Patent Office Under the Patents, Designs and Trade Marks Act, 1883, So Far as it Relates to Trade Marks and Designs, Report (London: HMSO, 1888).

Conway, Hazel, and Rowan Roenisch, *Understanding Architecture* (London: Routledge, 2005).

Coombe, Rosemary, *The Cultural Life of Intellectual Properties. Authorship, Appropriation, and the Law* (Durham, N. C.: Duke University Press, 1998).

'Objects of Property and Subjects of Politics: Intellectual Property Laws and Democratic Dialogue' (1991) 69 *Texas Law Review* 1853–80.

Cooper, Douglas, *The Courtauld Collection* (London: Athlone Press, 1954).

Cooter, R., and T. Ulen, *Law and Economics* (4th edn, London: Pearson Addison Wesley, 2004).

Corley, T. A. B., *Quaker Enterprise in Biscuits: Huntley and Palmers of Reading, 1822–1972* (London: Hutchinson, 1972).

Cornish, W., and J. Phillips, 'The Economic Function of Trade Marks: An Analysis with Special Reference to Developing Countries' (1982) 13 *International Review of Intellectual Property and Competition Law* 41–56.

Crafts, N., 'Long-run Growth' in R. Floud and P. Johnson (eds.), *The Cambridge Economic History of Modern Britain*, vol. II: *Economic Maturity, 1860–1939* (Cambridge: Cambridge University Press, 2004).

Cresswell, T., *Place: A Short Introduction* (Oxford, Blackwell, 2004)

Cresswell, T., and G. Vertstraete, *Mobilizing Place, Placing Mobility: The Politics of Representation in a Globalized World* (Amsterdam: Rodopi, 2003).

Croft, William, and D. A. Cruse, *Cognitive Linguistics* (Cambridge Textbooks in Linguistics) (Cambridge: Cambridge University Press, 2004).

Crystal, David, *A Dictionary of Linguistics and Phonetics* (5th edn, Oxford: Blackwell, 2003).

Cummings, Louise, *Pragmatics: An Interdisciplinary Perspective* (Edinburgh: Edinburgh University Press, 2005).

Cutler, J., *On Passing Off; Or Illegal Substitution of the Goods of One Trader for the Goods of Another Trader* (London, 1904).

Daniel, E. M., *The Trade Mark Registration Act* (London: Stevens and Haynes, 1876).

Davis, Jennifer, 'A European Constitution for IPRs? Competition, Trade Marks and Culturally Significant Signs' (2004) 41 *Common Market Law Reports* 1005–26.

'European Trade Mark Law and the Enclosure of the Commons' (2002) 4 *Intellectual Property Quarterly* 342–67.

Intellectual Property Law (2nd edn, London: Butterworths, 2003).

'Locating the Average Consumer: His Judicial Origins, Intellectual Influences and Current Role in European Trade Mark Law' (2005) *Intellectual Property Quarterly* 2 183–203.

'Protecting the Common: Delineating a Public Domain in Trade Mark Law' in Graeme Dinwoodie and Mark Janis (eds.), *Trademark Law and Theory: A Handbook of Contemporary Research* (Cheltenham: Edward Elgar, 2007).

'To Protect or Serve? European Trade Mark Law and the Decline of the Public Interest' (2003) 25(4) *European Intellectual Property Review* 180–7.

'The Value of Trade Marks: Economic Assets and Cultural Icons' in Y. Gendreau (ed.), *Intellectual Property: Bridging Aesthetics and Economics – Propriété intellectuelle: entre l'art et l'argent* (Montreal: Éditions Themis, 2006).

Day, J. 'Easy Brand's Future may not be Orange' *Guardian*, 16 Aug. 2004.

de Planhol, X., *An Historical Geography of France*, trans. J. Lloyd (Cambridge: Cambridge University Press, 1994).

Deakin, S., and A. Hughes, 'Economic Efficiency and the Proceduralisation of Company Law' (1999) *Company Financial and Insolvency Law Review* 169–89.

DellaVigna, S., and U. Malmendier, 'Paying Not to Go to the Gym' (2006) 96 *American Economic Review* 694–719.

Demian, M., 'Custom in the Courtroom, Law in the Village: Legal Transformations in Papua New Guinea' (2003) 9 (1) *Journal of the Royal Anthropological Institute* 32–57.

Demossier, M., 'Culinary Heritage and Produits de Terroir in France: Food for Thought' in S. Blowen, M. Demossier and J. Picard (eds.), *Recollections of*

France: Memories, Identities and Heritage in Contemporary France (New York: Berghahn Books, 2000).

Denicola, Robert C., 'Trademarks as Speech: Constitutional Implications of the Emerging Rationales for the Protection of Trade Symbols' (1982) *Wisconsin Law Review* 158–207.

Dinwoodie, Graeme B., 'The Death of Ontology: A Teleological Approach to Trademark Law' (1999) 84 *Iowa Law Review* 611–752.

'Reconceptualizing the Inherent Distinctiveness of Product Design Trade Dress' (1997) 75 *North Carolina Law Review* 471–606.

'The Story of *Kellogg Co. v. National Biscuit Co.*: Breakfast with Brandeis' in Jane C. Ginsburg and Rochelle Cooper Dreyfuss (eds.), *Intellectual Property Stories* (New York: Foundation Press, 2005).

Trademark Law and Social Norms (Working Paper, March 2007), available at www.ssrn.com.

'Trademarks and Territoriality: Detaching Trademark Law from the Nation-State' (2004) 41 *Houston Law Review* 885–973.

Dinwoodie, Graeme B., and Mark D. Janis, 'Confusion over Use: Contextualism in Trademark Law' (2007) 92 *Iowa Law Review* 1597.

'Lessons from the Trademark Use Debate' (2007) 92 *Iowa Law Review* 1703.

Trademarks and Unfair Competition: Law and Policy (New York: Aspen Publishers, 2004).

Dogan, Stacey L., and Mark A. Lemley, 'The Merchandising Right: Fragile Theory or Fait Accompli?' (2005) 54 *Emory Law Journal* 461–506.

'Trademark and Consumer Search Costs on the Internet' (2004) 41 *Houston Law Review* 777–839.

'What the Right of Publicity can Learn from Trademark Law' (2006) 58 *Stanford Law Review* 1161–220.

Dollinger, M. J., P. A. Golden and T. Saxton, 'The Effect of Reputation on the Decision to Joint Venture' (1997) 18(2) *Strategic Management Journal* 127–40.

Drescher, T., 'The Transformation and Evolution of Trademarks: From Signals to Symbols to Myth' (1992) 82 *Trademark Reporter* 301–40.

Drewry, Charles Stewart, *The Law of Trade Marks* (London: Knight, 1878).

Dreyfuss, Rochelle Cooper, 'Expressive Genericity: Trademarks as Language in the Pepsi Generation' (1990) 65 *Notre Dame Law Review* 397–424.

'We are Symbols and Inhabit Symbols, So Should We Be Paying Rent? Deconstructing the Lanham Act and Rights of Publicity' (1996) 20 *Columbia-VLA Journal of Law and the Arts* 123–56.

Dryberg, P., and M. Skylv, 'Does Trade Mark Infringement Require that the Infringing Use be Trade Mark Use and if so, what is "Trade Mark Use"?' (2003) 5 *European Intellectual Property Review* 229–33.

Duguid, P., 'Developing the Brand: The Case of Alcohol, 1800–1880' (2003) 4 *Enterprise and Society* 405–41.

Duxbury, Neil, *Patterns of American Jurisprudence* (paperback edn, Oxford: Clarendon Press, 1997).

Easthope, A., 'Postmodernism and Critical and Cultural Theory' in S. Sim (ed.), *The Icon Dictionary of Postmodern Thought* (Cambridge: Icon Books, 1998).

Economides, N., 'Economics of Trademarks' (1988) 78 *The Trademark Reporter* 523–39.

'Trademarks' in P. Newman (ed.), *The New Palgrave Dictionary of Economics and Law*, vol. III (London: Macmillan, 1998).

Ehrenberg, A., N. Barnard and J. Scriven, 'Differentiation or Salience' (1997) 37 *Journal of Advertising Research* 7.

Ellwood, L. A., 'The Industrial Property Convention and the "Telle Quelle" Clause' (1956) 46 *Trademark Reporter* 36–52.

Empson, William, *The Structure of Complex Words* (London: Chatto and Windus, [1951] 1979).

Evans-Jackson, J. E., 'The Law of Trade Marks' (1899) 47 *Journal of Society of Arts* 563–70.

Faith, N., *The Story of Champagne* (London: Hamish Hamilton, 1988).

Fama, E., and M. Jensen, 'Agency Problems and Residual Claims' (1983) 26 *Journal of Law and Economics* 327–49.

Felstead, A., *The Corporate Paradox: Power and Control in the Business Franchise* (London: Routledge, 1993).

Finnis, John, 'The Priority of Persons' in Jeremy Horder (ed.), *Oxford Essays in Jurisprudence (Fourth Series)* (Oxford: Clarendon Press, 2000).

Fisher, W., 'Theories of Intellectual Property' in Stephen R. Munzer (ed.), *New Essays in the Legal and Political Theory of Property* (Cambridge: Cambridge University Press, 2001).

Fitzgerald, R., 'Rowntree and Market Strategy, 1897–1939' (1989) 18 *Business and Economic History* 47–8.

Rowntree and the Marketing Revolution, 1862–1969 (Cambridge: Cambridge University Press, 1995).

Fleischer, V., 'Brand New Deal: The Branding Effect of Corporate Deal Structures' (2006) 104 *Michigan Law Review* 1581–637.

Floud, R., 'Britain, 1860–1914: A Survey' in R. Floud and D. N. McCloskey (eds.), *The Economic History of Britain Since 1700* (2nd edn, Cambridge: Cambridge University Press, 1994).

Folliard-Monguiral, A., 'Distinctive Character Acquired through Use: The Law and the Case Law' in Jeremy Phillips and Ilanah Simon (eds.), *Trade Mark Use* (Oxford: Oxford University Press, 2005).

Foster, R. (ed.), *Nation Making. Emergent Identities in Postcolonial Melanesia* (Ann Arbor: University of Michigan Press, 1995).

Foulkes, C. (ed.), *Larousse Encyclopedia of Wine* (2nd edn, London: Hamlyn, 2001).

Frankel, Susy, 'Trade Marks and Traditional Knowledge and Cultural Intellectual Property Rights' in Graeme Dinwoodie and Mark Janis (eds.), *Trademark Law and Theory: A Handbook of Contemporary Research* (Cheltenham: Edward Elgar, 2007).

Frankel, Susy, and Megan Richardson, 'Cultural Property and the Public Domain: Case Studies from New Zealand and Australia' in Christoph Antons (ed.), *Traditional Knowledge, Traditional Cultural Expressions and Intellectual Property Law in the Asia-Pacific Region* (Alphen aar de Rijn: Kluwer Law International, 2008).

Gade, D. W., 'Tradition, Territory, and Terroir in French Viniculture: Cassis, France, and Appellation Contrôlée' (2004) 94 *Annals of the Association of American Geographers* 848–67.

Gaines, J., *Contested Culture: The Image, the Voice and the Law* (London: bfi Publishing, 1991).

Gangjee, D., *Protecting Geographical Indications as Trademarks: The Prospects and Pitfalls* (Tokyo: Institute of Intellectual Property, 2006).

'Quibbling Siblings: Conflicts between Trade Marks and GIs' (2007) 82 *Chicago-Kent Law Review* 1253.

'Say Cheese: A Snapshot of Genericide through the Feta Dispute' (2007) *European Intellectual Property Review* (forthcoming).

Gannon, M. J., *Understanding Global Cultures* (3rd edn, Thousand Oaks, Calif.: Sage, 2004).

Gell, A., *The Art of Anthropology: Essay and Diagrams*, ed. E. Hirsch (London: The Athlone Press, 1999).

Gendreau, Y. (ed.), *Intellectual Property: Bridging Aesthetics and Economics* (Montreal: Éditions Themis, 2006).

Gibbs Jr, Raymond, *Intentions in the Experience of Meaning* (Cambridge: Cambridge University Press, 1999).

Gilmore, F. (ed.), *Brand Warriors: Corporate Leaders Share Their Winning Strategies* (London: HarperCollins Business, 1999).

Gilovich, T., D. Griffin and D. Kahneman (eds.), *Heuristics and Biases: The Psychology of Intuitive Judgment* (Cambridge: Cambridge University Press, 2002).

Ginsburg, Jane C., 'Of Mubarh Copyrights, Mangled Trademarks, and Babie's Bereficence: The Influence of Copyright on Trademark Law' in Graeme Dinwoodie and Mark Janis (eds.), *Trademark Law and Theory: A Hardbook of Contemporary Research* (Chelferhan: Edward Elgar, forthcoming 2008).

Ginsburg, Jane C., Jessica Litman and Mary L. Kevlin, *Trademark and Unfair Competition Law* (4th edn, New York: Foundation Press, 2007).

Godson, R., *A Practical Treatise on the Law of Patents for Inventions and of Copyright* (London: Butterworth, 1823).

Goldman, L., *Science, Reform, and Politics in Victorian Britain: The Social Science Association, 1857–1886* (Cambridge: Cambridge University Press, 2002).

'The Social Science Association, 1857–1886: A Context for Mid-Victorian Liberalism' (1986) 101 *English Historical Review* 95–134.

Gombrich, Ernst, *The Uses of Images: Studies in the Social Function of Art and Visual Communication* (London: Phaidon, 1999).

Gourlay, K. A., *Sound Producing Instruments in Traditional Society: A Study of Esoteric Instruments and their Role in Male–Female Relations* (New Guinea Research Bulletin 60) (Canberra: Australian National University, 1975).

Gower, L. C. B., *The Principles of Modern Company Law* (London: Stevens and Sons, 1954; 3rd edn, London: Stevens and Sons, 1969).

Graburn, Nelson, 'Introduction: Arts of the Fourth World' in Nelson Graburn, (ed.), *Ethnic and Tourist Arts: Cultural Expressions from the Fourth World* (Berkeley: University of California Press, 1976).

Granovetter, M., 'Economic Action and Social Structure: The Problem of Embeddedness' (1985) 91(3) *American Journal of Sociology* 481–510.

Gray, Kevin, 'Property in Thin Air' (1991) 50 *Cambridge Law Journal* 252–37.

Greenawalt, Kent, *Speech, Crime and the Uses of Language* (Oxford: Oxford University Press, 1989).

Greenbaum, Arthur J., Jane C. Ginsburg and Steven M. Weinberg, 'A Proposal for Evaluating Genericism after "Anti–Monopoly"' (1983) 73 *Trademark Reporter* 101.

Gregory, C., *Gifts and Commodities* (London: Academic Press, 1982).

Griffith, S., 'Work your Way around France' *Independent Online*, 14 Jan. 2006, http://travel.independent.co.uk/europe/article338402.ece.

Griffiths, Andrew, 'The Impact of the Global Appreciation Approach on the Boundaries of Trade Mark Protection' (2001) *Intellectual Property Quarterly* 326–60.

'Modernising Trade Mark Law and Promoting Economic Efficiency: An Evaluation of the Baby-Dry Judgement and its Aftermath' (2003) 1 *Intellectual Property Quarterly* 1–37.

Grossman, G., and C. Shapiro, 'Counterfeit-product Trade' (1988) 78 *American Economic Review* 59–75.

Guthey, Eric, and Brad Jackson, 'CEO Portraits and the Authenticity Paradox' (2005) 42 *Journal of Management Studies* July 1057–82.

Guy, Koleen M., 'Rituals of Pleasure in the Land of Treasures: Wine Consumption and the Making of French Identity in the Late Nineteenth Century' in W. J. Belasco and P. Scranton (eds.), *Food Nations: Selling Taste in Consumer Societies* (London: Routledge, 2002).

Haan, Sarah C., 'The "Persuasion Route" of the Law: Advertising and Legal Persuasion' (2000) 100 *Columbia Law Review* 1281–326.

Hahn, F., and M. Hollis, *Philosophy and Economic Theory* (Oxford: Oxford University Press, 1979).

Haigh, D., *Brand Valuation: Understanding, Exploiting and Communicating Brand Values* (London: Financial Times, 1998).

Hall, Stuart (ed.), *Representation: Cultural Representation and Signifying Practices* (London: Sage, 1997).

Halliday, J., and H. Johnson, *The Art and Science of Wine* (London: Mitchell Beazley, 1994).

Handler, Milton, 'Are the State Antidilution Laws Compatible With the National Protection of Trademarks?' (1985) 75 *Trademark Reporter* 269–87.

Handler, Milton, and Charles Pickett, 'Trade-marks and Trade Names – An Analysis and Synthesis' (1930) 30 *Columbia Law Review* 168–201.

Hanson, A., *Burgundy* (London: Mitchell Beazley, 2003).

Hanson, Jon, and Douglas A. Kysar, 'Taking Behavioralism Seriously: Some Evidence of Market Manipulation' (1999) 112 *Harvard Law Review* 1420–572.

Harbutt, J., *Cheese: A Complete Guide to Over 300 Cheeses of Distinction* (Minoqua, Wis.: Willow Creek Press, 1999).

Harris, J. W., *Property and Justice* (Oxford: Clarendon Press, 1996).

Harris, R., and T. J. Taylor, *Landmarks in Linguistic Thought, vol. I: The Western Tradition from Socrates to Saussure* (2nd edn, London: Routledge, 1997).

Harrison, S., 'The Commerce of Cultures in Melanesia' (1993) (28) *Man* (n.s.) 139–58.

Fracturing Resemblances. Identity and Conflict in Melanesia and the West (Oxford and New York: Berghahn Books, 2006).

The Mask of War (Cambridge: Cambridge University Press, 1993).

'The Past Altered by the Present: A Melanesian Village after Twenty Years' (2001) 17 *Anthropology Today* 3–9.

'Ritual as Intellectual Property' (1992) 27 *Man* (n.s.) 225–44.

Stealing People's Names. History and Politics in a Sepik River Cosmology (Cambridge: Cambridge University Press, 1990).

Hartman, S., 'Brand Equity Impairment – The Meaning of Dilution' (1997) 87 *Trademark Reporter* 418–35.

Haslam, Malcolm, *Marks and Monograms of the Modern Movement 1875–1930* (Guildford: Lutterworth, 1977).

Hays, C., *Pop: Truth and Power at the Coca-Cola Company* (London: Arrow, 2005).

Hays, T., 'Distinguishing Use versus Functional Use: Three Dimensional Marks' in Jeremy Phillips and Ilanah Simons (eds.), *Trade Mark Use* (Oxford: Oxford University Press, 2005).

Heilbrunn, Benoît, 'Cultural Branding between Utopia and A-topia' in Jonathan E. Schroeder and Miriam Salzer-Mörling (eds.), *Brand Culture* (London: Routledge, 2006).

Henry, M., 'Trade Marks' (1862) 10 *Journal of the Royal Society of Arts* 255.

Hettinger, E. C., 'The Justification of Intellectual Property' (1989) 18 *Philosophy and Public Affairs* 31–52.

Higgins, D. M., '"Made in Sheffield?": Trade Marks, the Cutlers' Company and the Defence of "Sheffield" in C. Binfield and D. Hey (eds.), *Mesters to Masters: A History of the Company of Cutlers in Hallamshire* (Oxford: Oxford University Press, 1997).

'Mutton Dressed as Lamb? The Misrepresentation of Australian and New Zealand Meat in the British Market, c. 1890–1914' (2004) 44 *Australian Economic History Review* 161–84.

Higgins, D. M., and T. James, *The Economic Importance of Trade Marks in the UK (1973–1992): A Preliminary Investigation* (London: The Intellectual Property Institute, 1996).

Higgins, D. M., and G. Tweedale, 'Asset or Liability? Trade Marks in the Sheffield Cutlery and Tool Trades' (1995) 37 *Business History* 1–27.

'The Trade Marks Question and the Lancashire Cotton Industry, 1870–1914' (1996) 27 *Textile History* 207–28.

Hindmarch, W. M., *A Treatise on the Law Relating to Patent Privileges* (London: Stevens, 1846).

Hirsch Alan, and Ralph Nader, '"The Corporate Conscience" and Other first Amendment Follies in *Pacific Gas of Electric*' (2004) *San Diego Law Review* 483.

Hoffman, David, 'The Best Puffery Article Ever' (Temple University Legal Studies Research Paper No. 2006–11, 2006).

Hoffman, R. J. S., *Great Britain and the German Trade Rivalry, 1875–1914* (New York: Russell and Russell, 1964).

Hohufeld, Wesley Newcomb, 'Nature of Shockholders' Individual Liability for Corporation Desk' (1909) 9 *Columbia Law Review* 285.

Holt, D. B., *How Brands Become Icons: The Principles of Cultural Branding* (Boston: Harvard Business School Press, 2004).

Hoy, F., and J. Starworth (eds.), *Franchising: An International Perspective* (London: Routledge, 2003).

Ilersic, A. R., and P. F. B. Liddle, *Parliament of Commerce: The Story of the Association of British Chambers of Commerce, 1860–1960* (London: Association of British Chambers of Commerce and Newman Neame, 1960).

In, Sung, 'Death of a Trademark: Genericide in the Digital Age' (2002) 21 *Review of Litigation* 159–89.

Indemaur, J., *A Manual of the Principles of Equity* (2nd edn, London: Geo Barber 'Law Students' Journal' Office, 1890).

International Bureau of Intellectual Property, *The Madrid Agreement Concerning the International Registration of Marks from 1891 to 1991* (Geneva: WIPO, 1991).

Jackson, Howard, *Lexicography: An Introduction* (London: Routledge, 2002).

Jackson, P., M. Lowe, D. Miller and F. Mort (eds.), *Commercial Cultures: Economies, Practices, Spaces* (Oxford: Berg, 2000).

Jacoby, J., 'The Psychological Foundations of Trademark Law: Second Meaning, Genericism, Fame, Confusion and Dilution' (2001) 91 *Trademark Reporter* 1013–71.

Jaffey, Peter, 'Likelihood of Association' (2002) *European Intellectual Property Review* 3–8.

'Merchandising and the Law of Trade Marks' (1998) *Intellectual Property Quarterly* 240–66.

James, R., 'Burgundy Can't Agree on AOC Reform' (2004) *Decanter*, available at www.decanter.com/news/56418.html.

Jamieson, M., 'The Place of Counterfeits in Regimes of Value: An Anthropological Approach' (1999) 5 *Journal of the Royal Anthropological Institute* 1–11.

Janke, Terri, *Case Studies on Intellectual Property and Traditional Cultural Expressions* prepared for WIPO (Geneva: WIPO, 2003).

Our Culture: Our Future (Surry Hills, New South Wales: Michael Frankel and Company, 1999).

Janke, Terri, and Robynne Quiggin, *Indigenous Cultural and Intellectual Property: The Main Issues for the Indigenous Art Industry in 2006* prepared for the Australian and Torres Strait Islander Arts Board, Australia Council (Sydney: Aboriginal and Torres Strait Islander Arts Board, 2006).

Jensen, M., and W. Meckling, 'Theory of the Firm: Managerial Behaviour, Agency Costs and Capital Structure' (1976) 3 *Journal of Financial Economics* 305–60.

Johnson, E., 'Trade Marks' (1881) 29 *Journal of the Society of Arts* 493–506.

Jones, E., 'Marketing the Nettlefold Woodscrew by GKN 1850–1939' in R. P. T Davenport-Hines (ed.), *Markets and Bagmen: Studies in the History of Marketing and British Industrial Performance, 1830–1939* (Aldershot: Gower, 1986).

Jones, Philip, *Boomerang: Behind an Australian Icon* (Kent Town, South Australia: Wakefield Press, 1996).

Kahneman, D., P. Slovic and A. Tversky (eds.), *Judgment Under Uncertainty: Heuristics and Biases* (Cambridge: Cambridge University Press, 2002).

Kahneman, D., and R. Thaler, 'Utility Maximisation and Experienced Utility' (2006) 20 *Journal of Economic Perspectives* 221–34.

Keller, K. L., 'Conceptualizing, Measuring, and Managing Customer-Based Brand Equity' (1993) 57 *Journal of Marketing* 1–22.

Kerly, D. M. *The Law of Trade-Marks and Trade Name, and Merchandise Marks* (London: Sweet and Maxwell, 1894).

Kingsley, Charles, *Westward Ho!* (Cambridge: Macmillan and Co., 1855).

Kintsch, Walter, *Comprehension: A Paradigm for Cognition* (Cambridge: Cambridge University Press, 1998).

Kitchin, D., D. Llewelyn, J. Mellor, R. Meade, T. Moody-Stuart and R. Jacob, *Kerly's Law of Trade Marks and Trade Names* (13th edn, London: Sweet and Maxwell, 2001).

Kitchin, D., D. Llewelyn, J. Mellor *et al.*, *Kerly's law of Trade Marks and Trade Names* (14th rev. edn, London: Sweet and Maxwell, 2005).

Klein, B., and K. Leffler, 'The Role of Market Forces in Assuring Contractual Performance' (1981) 89 *Journal of Political Economy* 615–41.

Klein, Naomi, *No Logo* (London: Flamingo, 2000).

Kleinert, Sylvia, 'Art and Aboriginality in the South-East' in Sylvia Kleinert and Margot Neale (eds.), *The Oxford Companion to Aboriginal Art and Culture* (Melbourne: Oxford University Press, 2000).

Knick Harley, C., 'Trade, 1870–1919: From Globalisation to Fragmentation' in R. Floud and P. Johnson (eds.), *The Cambridge Economic History of Modern Britain, vol. II: Economic Maturity, 1860–1939* (Cambridge: Cambridge University Press, 2004).

Koehn, N., *Brand New: How Entrepreneurs Earned Consumers' Trust from Wedgwood to Dell* (Boston: Harvard Business School Press, 2001).

Kozinsky, Alex, 'Trademarks Unplugged' (1993) 68 *New York University Law Review* 960, 961–75.

Krissoff, B., M. Bohman and J. A. Caswell, *Global Food Trade and Consumer Demand for Quality* (New York: Kluwer, 2002).

Ladas, S. P., *Patents, Trademarks, and Related Rights: National and International Protection* (Cambridge, Mass.: Harvard University Press, 1975).

Landau, Sidney, *Dictionaries: The Art and Craft of Lexicography* (Cambridge: Cambridge University Press, 1984).

Landes, William M., and Richard A. Posner, *The Economic Structure of Intellectual Property Law* (Cambridge, Mass.: The Belknap Press of Harvard University Press, 2003).

'Trademark Law: An Economic Perspective' (1987) 30 *Journal of Law and Economics* 265–309.

Lane, Shelley, 'Goodwill Hunting: Assignments and Licences in Gross after *Scandecor*' [1999] 2 *Intellectual Property Quarterly* 264–79.

Lange, D., 'Recognizing the Public Domain' (1981) 44 *Law and Contemporary Problems* 147–77.

Lash, Scott, and John Urry, *The Economies of Sign and Space* (London: Sage, 1994).

Lass, Roger, *Phonology: An Introduction to Basic Concepts*. (Cambridge Textbooks in Linguistics) (Cambridge: Cambridge University Press, 1984).

Lawrence, P., 'The Ngaing of the Rai Coast' in P. Lawrence and M. Meggitt (eds.), *Gods, Ghosts and Men in Melanesia* (Melbourne: Oxford University Press, 1965).

Layard, R., *Happiness: Lessons from a New Science* (London: Penguin, 2005).

Leach, J., *Creative Land. Place and Procreation on the Rai Coast of Papua New Guinea* (Oxford and New York: Berghahn Books, 2003).

'Drum and Voice: Aesthetics and Social Process on the Rai Coast of Papua New Guinea' (2002) 8 *Journal of the Royal Anthropological Institute* 713–34.

'Modes of Creativity' in E. Hirsch and M. Strathern (eds.), *Transactions and Creations. Property Debates and the Stimulus of Melanesia* (Oxford and New York: Berghahn Books, 2004).

'Out of Proportion? Anthropological Description of Power, Regeneration and Scale on the Rai Coast of PNG' in S. Coleman and P. Collins (eds.), *Locating the Field. Space, Place and Context in Anthropology*. ASA Monograph 42. (Oxford: Berg, 2006).

Leff, Arthur A., *Swindling and Selling* (New York: Free Press, 1977).

Leiss, William, Stephen Kline, Sot Jhally and Jacqueline Botterill, *Social Communication in Advertising: Consumption in the Mediated Marketplace* (New York, Routledge, 2005).

Lemley, Mark A., 'The Modern Lanham Act and the Death of Common Sense' (1999) 108 *Yale Law Journal* 1687–715.

'Property, Intellectual Property, and Free Riding' (2005) 83 *Texas Law Review* 1031–75.

Leval, Pierre N., 'Trademark: Champion of Free Speech' (2004) 27 *Columbia Journal of Law and the Arts* 187–210.

Levi, L., 'An International Commercial Code', *The Times*, 27 August 1878, p. 6f. *International Commercial Law* (London: V. and R. Stevens, 1863).

'On Trade Marks' (1859) 7 *Journal of the Society of Arts* 262–70.

Lévi-Strauss, C., *The Elementary Structures of Kinship*, trans. J. H. Bell, J. R.von Sturmer and R. Needham (Boston: Beacon Press, 1969).

Levinson, Stephen, *Pragmatics*. (Cambridge Textbooks in Linguistics) (Cambridge: Cambridge University Press, 1983).

Levitt, Theodore, *The Marketing Imagination* (expanded edn, New York: Free Press, 1986).

Lewis, D., 'Dispositional Theories of Value' (1989), reprinted in D. Lewis, *Papers in Ethics and Social Philosophy* (Cambridge: Cambridge University Press, 2000).

'Finkish Dispositions' (1997), reprinted in D. Lewis, *Papers in Metaphysics and Epistemology* (Cambridge: Cambridge University Press, 1999).

Litman, Jessica, 'Breakfast with Batman: The Public Interest in the Advertising Age' (1999) 108 *Yale Law Journal* 1717–35.

Little, I., *A Critique of Welfare Economics* (Oxford: Clarendon Press, 1950).

Lloyd, E. 'On the Law of Trade Marks No. V' (1861) *Solicitors' Journal and Reporter* 614.

Locke, J., *The Second Treatise of Civil Government: And a Letter Concerning Toleration* (Oxford: Basil Blackwell, 1946).

Loewenstein, G., and D. Schkade, 'Wouldn't it be Nice? Predicting Future Feelings' in D. Kahneman, E. Diener and N. Schwarz (eds.), *Well-Being: The Foundations of Hedonic Psychology* (New York: Russell Sage, 1999).

Loubére, Leo A., *The Wine Revolution in France – The Twentieth Century* (Princeton, N.J.: Princeton University Press, 1990).

Ludlow, H., and H. Jenkins, *A Treatise on the Law of Trade-Marks and Trade-Names* (London: W. Maxwell and Son, 1873).

Lunney, Glynn S., Jr, 'Trademark Monopolies' (1999) 48 *Emory Law Journal* 367–487.

Lury, Celia, *Brands: The Logos of the Global Economy* (Oxford: Routledge, 2004).

Consumer Culture (Cambridge: Polity Press, 1996).

Cultural Rights: Technology, Legality and Personality (London: Routledge, 1993).

'Portrait of the Artist as a Brand' in D. McClean and K. Schubert (eds.), *Dear Images: Art, Copyright and Culture* (London: Ridinghouse and ICA, 2002).

'Trade Mark Style as a Way of Fixing Things', paper presented at the Trade Marks Workshop, University of Cambridge (3 July 2006).

Lury, G., *Brandwatching* (Dublin: Blackhall Publishing, 1998).

Lyons, Christopher, *Definiteness* (Cambridge: Cambridge University Press, 1999).

Lyons, John, *Linguistic Semantics: An Introduction* (Cambridge: Cambridge University Press, 1995).

Mackinolty, Chips, 'Whose Boomerang Won't Come Back?' in Peter Loveday and Peter Cooke (eds.), *Aboriginal Arts and Crafts and the Market* (Darwin: Australian National University North Australia Research Unit, 1983).

Madison, Michael J., 'Complexity and Copyright in Contradiction' (2000) 18 *Carchozo Art & Entertainment Law Journal* 125.

The Madrid Agreement Concerning the International Registration of Marks from 1891 to 1991 (Geneva: International Bureau of Intellectual Property, 1991).

Martino, T., *Trademark Dilution* (Oxford: Clarendon Press, 1996).

Massey, D., 'A Global Sense of Place' in T. Barnes and D. Gregory (eds.), *Reading Human Geography: The Politics and Poetics of Enquiry* (London: Arnold, 1994).

Mauss, M., 'Essai sur le don: forme et raison de l'échange dans les sociétés archaïques' (1925) 1 *Année Sociologique* (n.s.) 30–186.

McCarthy, J. Thomas, *Trademarks and Unfair Competition* (4th edn, Rochester, N.Y.: Lawyers Co-operative Pub. Co., 2002).

McClean, D., and K. Schubert (eds.), *Dear Images: Art, Copyright and Culture* (London: Ridinghouse and ICA, 2002).

McEnerney, Thomas W., 'Note: Fraudulent Material is Entitled to Copyright Protection in Action for Injunctive Relief and Damages' (1974) 74 *Columbia Law Review* 1351–9.

McKitrick, J., 'The Case for Extrinsic Dispositions' (2003) 81 *Australasian Journal of Philosophy* 155–74.

McNie, N., *Champagne* (London: Faber and Faber, 1999).

Mead, M., *The Mountain Arapesh: An Importing Culture* (American Museum of Natural History, Anthropological Papers no. 36, 1938).

'The Merchandise Marks Act, 1887' (5 Nov. 1887) *Solicitors' Journal* 3–4, 20–1, 40–1, 56.

Mercuro, N., and S. Medema, *Economics and the Law: From Posner to Postmodernism* (Princeton, N.J.: Princeton University Press, 1997).

Moorby, R. L. *et al.* for The Patent Office, *A Century of Trade Marks 1876–1976* (London: HMSO, 1976).

Moore, C., 'Streets of Style: Fashion Retailing Within London and New York' in P. Jackson, M. Lowe, D. Miller and F. Mort (eds.), *Commercial Cultures: Economies, Practices, Spaces* (Oxford: Berg, 2000).

Moran, W., 'The Wine Appellation as Territory in France and California' (1993) 83 *Annals of the Association of American Geographers* 694–717.

Morico, Paul, 'Protecting Color Per Se in the Wake of Qualitex v. Jacobson' (1995) 77 *Journal of the Patent and Trademark Office Society* 571–82.

Morrin, M., J. Lee, and G. M. Allenby, 'Determinants of Trademark Dilution' (2006) 33 *Journal of Consumer Research* 248–57.

Moskin, J. E., 'Dilution or Delusion: The Rational Limits of Trademark Protection' (1993) 83 *Trademark Reporter* 122–48.

Mostert, Frederick W., 'Well-Known and Famous Marks: Is Harmony Possible in the Global Village?' (1996) 86 *Trademark Reporter* 103–41.

Moutu, A., 'Names Are Thicker Than Blood' (Ph.D. thesis, Cambridge University, Department of Social Anthropology, 2004).

Mozley, L. B., *Trade Marks Registration. A Concise View of the Law and Practice* (London: 1877).

Mullins, M. G. *et al.*, *The Biology of the Grapevine* (Cambridge: Cambridge University Press, 1992).

Munn, N., *The Fame of Gawa. A Symbolic Study of Value Transformation in a Massim (Papua New Guinea) Society* (Durham, N.C.: Duke University Press, 1986).

Murphy, J., 'What is Branding?' in S. Hart and J. Murphy (eds.), *Brands* (Macmillan: Basingstoke, 1998).

Musson, A. E., *Enterprise in Soap and Chemicals: Joseph Crosfield and Sons Ltd, 1815–1965* (Manchester: Manchester University Press, 1965).

Myers, Gary, 'Trademark Parody: Lessons From the Copyright Decision in Campbell v. Acuff-Rose Music, Inc.' (1996) 59 *Journal of Law and Contemporary Problems* 181–211.

Myers, Greg, *Words in Ads* (London: Arnold, 1994).

Nelson, P., 'Information and Consumer Behaviour' (1970) 78 *Journal of Political Economy* 311–29.

Nevett, T. R., *Advertising in Britain: A History* (London: Heinemann / History of Advertising Trust, 1982).

New, W., 'WTO Meeting Reopens Discussions On Geographical Indications Register' *Intellectual Property Watch*, 12 December 2006, 1.

'The New Patents, Designs and Trade-Marks Bills' (7 Apr. 1883) *Solicitors' Journal* 374.

'The New Patents, Designs and Trade-Marks Bills II' (5 May 1883) *Solicitors' Journal* 444.

Ng, Catherine, 'The Dilution of the Law of Passing-off: Toward a Rational Basis for Irrational Trade Mark protection' (D. Phil. thesis, University of Oxford, 2004).

'The Limits of Comparative Advertising in Civil Actions: Just When you Dare to Compare' (1998) 15 *Canadian Intellectual Property Review* 143–66; (1999) 16 *Canadian Intellectual Property Review* 149–70.

Nisbet, Robert, 'Men and Money: Reflections by a Sociologist' in Robert Nisbet, Susan Wagg and Anne W. Tucker (eds.), *Money Matters: A Critical Look at Bank Architecture* (New York: McGraw Hill, 1990).

Nisbett, R., and D. Kanouse, 'Obesity, Hunger, and Supermarket Shopping Behavior' (1968) 3 *Proceedings of the Annual Convention of the American Psychological Association* 683–4.

Norman, Helen, 'Time to Blow the Whistle on Trade Mark Use' (2004) 1 *Intellectual Property Quarterly* 1–34.

'Trade Mark Licences in the United Kingdom: Time for Bostitch to be Reevaluated' (1994) 16(4) *European Intellectual Property Review* 154–8.

'Note: The Besmirched Plaintiff and the Confused Public: Unclean Hands in Trademark Infringement' (1965) 65 *Columbia Law Review* 109–22.

O'Gorman, James F., *A B C of Architecture* (Philadelphia: University of Pennsylvania Press, 1998).

O'Reilly, Daragh, 'Cultural Brands/Branding Cultures' (2005) 21 *Journal of Marketing Management* 573–88.

OECD, *Appellations of Origin and Geographical Indications in OECD Member Countries: Economic and Legal Implications* (COM/AGR/APM/TD/WP(2000)15/FINAL).

Offer, A., *The Challenge of Affluence* (Oxford: Oxford University Press, 2006).

Ogden, C. K., and I. A. Richards, *The Meaning of Meaning* (London: Routledge and Kegan Paul, 1923).

Ogus, A., 'Economics and Law Reform: Thirty Years of Law Commission Endeavour' (1995) 111 *Law Quarterly Review* 407–20.

Regulation: Legal Form and Economic Theory (Oxford: Clarendon Press, 1994).

Oldham, J., *English Common Law in the Age of Mansfield* (Chapel Hill: University of North Carolina Press, 2004).

Olszak, N., *Droit des Appellations d'Origine et Indications de Provenance* (Paris: TEC and DOC, 2001).

'On Fraudulent Trade Marks' (1861) *Solicitors' Journal and Reporter* 820.

Onians, John, *Bearers of Meaning: The Classical Orders in Antiquity, the Middle Ages, and the Renaissance* (Princeton, N.J.: Princeton University Press, 1988).

Ostertag, Gary (ed.), *Definite Descriptions: A Reader* (Cambridge, Mass.: MIT Press, 1998).

Otieno-Odek, J., 'The Way Ahead – What Future for Geographical Indications?', paper presented at the WIPO conference, Parma, Italy (27–29 June 2005).

Panesar, S., *General Principles of Property Law* (Harlow: Pearson Education, 2001).

Parness, Hillel, 'Note: The Curse of the Pink Panther: The Legacy of the Owens-Corning Fiberglass Dissent and Its Role in the Qualitex Supreme Court Appeal' (1994) 18 *Columbia VLA Journal of Law and the Arts* 327–84.

Pattishall, Beverly W., 'Dawning Acceptance of the Dilution Rationale for Trademark–Trade Identity Protection' (1984) 74 *Trademark Reporter* 289–310.

Pavitt, J. (ed.), *Brand.new* (London: VandA Publications, 2000).

Payne, P. L., *British Entrepreneurship in the Nineteenth Century* (London: Macmillan, 1974).

Pendergrast, Mark, *For God, Country and Coca-Cola* (revised updated edn, New York: Thomson Texere, 2000).

Penner, J. E., *The Idea of Property in Law* (Oxford: Clarendon Press, 1997).

Perry, N., *Hyperreality and Global Culture* (London: Routledge, 1998).

Phillips, Jeremy, *Trade Mark Law: A Practical Anatomy* (Oxford: Oxford University Press, 2003).

Phillips, Jeremy, and Ilanah Simon (eds.), *Trade Mark Use* (Oxford: Oxford University Press, 2005).

Pinner, H. L. (ed.), *World Unfair Competition Law: An Encyclopedia*, vol. II (Leyden: Sijthoff, 1965).

Png, I., and D. Reitman, 'Why are Some Products Branded and Others Not?' (1995) 38 *Journal of Law and Economics* 207–24.

Poland, H. B., *The Merchandise Marks Act 1862* (London: J. Crockford, 1862).

Posner, R., *Economic Analysis of Law* (6th edn, New York: Aspen Publishing, 2002).

Post, Robert, 'Compelled Subsidization of Speech: *Johams v Livestock Marketing Association*' (2005) Sup. Ct Rev. 195.

Poulter, A., 'What is "Use": Reconciling Divergent Views on the Nature of Infringing Use' (December 2003 / January 2004) 163 *Trademark World* 23–4.

Preston, Ivan L., *The Tangled Web They Weave: Truth, Falsity and Advertisers* (Madison: University of Wisconsin Press, 1994).

Procès Verbaux de la Conférence de Madrid de 1890 de Union Pour la Protection de la Propriété Industrielle (Madrid: Bureau International de l'Union, 1892).

'Proposed Alterations in the law of Trade Marks' (1861) *Solicitors' Journal and Reporter* 2.

Rahmatian, A., 'Music and Creativity as Perceived by Copyright Law' (2005) 3 *Intellectual Property Quarterly* 267–93.

Ramello, G., 'What's in a Sign? Trademark Law and Economic Theory' (2006) 20 *Journal of Economic Surveys* 547–65.

Rampley, Matthew (ed.), *Exploring Visual Culture: Definitions, Concepts, Contexts* (Edinburgh: Edinburgh University Press, 2005).

Ramsey, Lisa P., 'Descriptive Trademarks and the First Amendment' (2003) 70 *Tennessee Law Review* 1095–176.

Rawkins, Jason, 'Entry Denied: Visa for Condoms Rejected in the UK' (2002) *Trade Mark World* 22.

Ray, C., *Bollinger: The Story of a Champagne* (London: Peter Davies, 1971).

Redish, Martin H., and Heward M. Wassman, 'What's Good fer General motors: Corporate Speech and the Theory of Free Expression' (1997–8) 66 *George Washington Law Review* 235.

'The Registration of Trade Marks' (1861) *Solicitors' Journal and Reporter* 839.

'Registration of Trade Marks – Notes on the Register' (20 June 1885) *Solicitors' Journal* 550–2, 569–70, 586.

'Registration of Trade-Marks: The Three-Mark Rule' (25 April 1885) *Solicitors' Journal* 414–15, 432–3.

Richards, T., *The Commodity Culture of Victorian England: Advertising and Spectacle, 1851–1914* (London: Verso, 1991).

Richardson, Megan, 'Copyright in Trade Marks? On Understanding Trade Mark Dilution' (2000) 1 *Intellectual Property Quarterly* 66–83.

'Trade Marks and Language' (2004) 26 *Sydney Law Review* 193–220.

Richardson, Megan, and Lesley Hitchens, 'Celebrity Privacy and Benefits of Simple History' in Andrew T. Kenyon and Megan Richardson (eds.), *New Dimensions in Privacy Law: International and Comparative Perspectives* (Cambridge: Cambridge University Press, 2006).

Rimmer, Matthew, 'Authenticity Marks and Identity Politics' (2004) 3 *Indigenous Law Journal* 139–79.

Ritzer, George, *The McDonaldization of Society* (Boston: Pine Forge Press, 2000).

Robertson, W., 'On Trade Marks' (1869) 14 *Journal of the Society of Arts* 414–17.

Robinson, Jancis (ed.), *The Oxford Companion to Wine* (2nd edn, Oxford: Oxford University Press, 1999).

Rogers, Edward S., 'The Lanham Act and the Social Function of Trademarks' (1949) 14 *Law and Contemporary Problems* 173–84.

Ross, A. (ed.), *No Sweat: Fashion, Free Trade, and the Rights of Garment Workers* (New York: Verso, 2000).

Rowe, R. C., 'Bile Beans: For Inner Health' (2003) 17(3–4) *International Journal of Pharmaceutical Medicine* 137–40.

Royle, T., *Working for McDonald's in Europe: The Unequal Struggle?* (London: Routledge, 2000).

Ryland, A., 'The Fraudulent Imitation of Trade Marks' (1859) *Transactions of the National Association for the Promotion of Social Science* 229.

Salaman, J. S., *A Manual of the Practice of Trade Mark Registration* (London: Shaw and Son, 1876).

Sampson, J., 'Brand Valuation Today and Tomorrow' in R. Perrier (ed.), *Brand Valuation* (London: Interbrand, 1997).

Schechter, Frank I., *The Historical Foundations of the Law Relating to Trade-Marks* (New York: Columbia University Press, 1925).

'The Rational Basis of Trademark Protection' (1927) 40 *Harvard Law Review* 813–33.

Schechter, Roger E., and John R. Thomas, *Intellectual Property: The Law of Copyrights, Patents and Trademarks* (St Paul, Minn.: Thomson West, 2003).

Scherer, F., and D. Ross, *Industrial Market Structure and Economic Performance* (Boston: Houghton-Mifflin, 1990).

Schroeder, Jonathan E., 'Architectural Expression in the Electronic Age' in Linda M. Scott and Rajeev Batra (eds.), *Persuasive Imagery: A Consumer Response Perspective* (Mahwah, N.J.: Lawrence Erlbaum, 2003).

'The Artist and the Brand' (2005) 39 *European Journal of Marketing* 1291–305.

'Critical Visual Analysis', in Russell W. Belk (ed.), *Handbook of Qualitative Research Methods in Marketing* (Cheltenham: Edward Elgar, 2006).

Visual Consumption (London: Routledge, 2002).

Schroeder, Jonathan E., and Janet L. Borgerson, 'An Ethics of Representation for International Marketing' (2005) 22 *International Marketing Review* 578–600.

Schroeder, Jonathan E., and Miriam Salzer-Mörling (eds.), *Brand Culture* (London: Routledge, 2006).

Schroeder, Jonathan E., and Detlev Zwick, 'Mirrors of Masculinity: Representation and Identity in Advertising Images' (2004) 7 *Consumption Markets and Culture* 21–52.

Schwartz, B., *The Paradox of Choice* (New York: Harper Collins, 2004).

Searle, G. R., *Entrepreneurial Politics in Mid-Victorian Britain* (New York: Oxford University Press, 1993).

Sebastian, Lewis, *A Digest of Cases of Trade Mark, Trade Name, Trade Secret ... decided in the courts of the United Kingdom, India, the Colonies and the United States of America* (London: Stevens and Sons, 1879).

The Law of Trade Marks and their Registration (London: Stevens and Sons, 1878; 2nd edn, 1884; 3rd edn, 1890).

Semple, E., *Influences of Geographic Environment on the Basis of Ratzel's System of Anthropo-Geography* (New York and London: H. Holt and Co., 1911).

Sennett, R., *The Culture of the New Capitalism* (New Haven, Mass.: Yale University Press, 2006).

Sherman, Brad, and Lionel Bently, *The Making of Modern Intellectual Property Law – The British Experience, 1760–1911* (Cambridge: Cambridge University Press, 1999).

Sherman, Brad, and Leanne Wiseman, 'Towards an Indigenous Public Domain?' in Lucie Guibault and P. Bernt Hugenholtz (eds.), *The Future of the Public Domain: Identifying the Commons in Information Law* (Alphen aan den Rijn: Kluwer Law International, 2006).

Shiffrin, S. V., 'Lockean Arguments for Private Intellectual Property' in Stephen R. Munzer (ed.), *New Essays in the Legal and Political Theory of Property* (Cambridge: Cambridge University Press, 2001).

Shuy, Roger, *Language Crimes: The Use and Abuse of Language Evidence in the Courtroom* (Oxford: Blackwell, 1993).

Linguistic Battles in Trademark Disputes (Basingstoke: Palgrave, 2002).

Siebeck, W. (ed.), *Strengthening Protection of Intellectual Property in Developing Countries* (World Bank Discussion Paper no 112, 1990).

Simmons, D. A., *Schweppes: The First 200 Years* (London: Springwood Books, 1983).

Simon, A. L., *The History of Champagne* (London: Ebury Press, 1962).

Simon, I., 'Dilutive Trade Mark Applications: 'Trading on Reputations or Just Playing Games' (2004) *European Intellectual Property Review* 26(2), 67–74.

Simonson, A. F., 'How and When Do Trademarks Dilute: A Behavioural Framework to Judge "likelihood" of Dilution' (1993) 83 *Trademark Reporter* 149–74.

Simpson, J., 'Selling to Reluctant Drinkers: The British Wine Market, 1860–1914' (2004) 57 *Economic History Review* 80–108.

Skuras, D., and E. Dimara, 'Regional Image and the Consumption of Regionally Denominated Products' (2004) 41(4) *Urban Studies* 801–15.

Smith, G. V., *Trade Mark Valuation* (New York: J. Wiley and Sons, 1997).

Smith, L. Richard, *A Guide to Wedgwood Marks* (Sydney: Wedgwood Press, 1977).

Smith, P., 'Tommy Hilfiger in the Age of Mass Customization' in A. Ross (ed.), *No Sweat: Fashion, Free Trade, and the Rights of Garment Workers* (New York: Verso, 2000).

Spence, Michael, 'Intellectual Property and the Problem of Parody' (1998) 114 *Law Quarterly Review* 594.

'The Mark as Expression / The Mark as Property' (2005) 58 *Current Legal Problems* 491.

Spence, M., 'Passing Off and the Misappropriation of Valuable Intangibles' (1996) 112 *Law Quarterly Review* 472–98.

Sperber, Dan, and Deirdre Wilson, 'Irony and the Use–Mention Distinction' in P.Cole (ed.), *Radical Pragmatics* (New York: Academic Press, 1981).

Relevance: Communication and Cognition (2nd edn, Oxford: Blackwell, 1995).

Spirits: Compilation of Issues and Points 23 May 2003 (TN/IP/W/7/Rev.1), available at http://docsonline.wto.org/DDFDocuments/t/tn/ip/W7R1.doc.

Stanziani, A., 'Wine Reputation and Quality Controls: The Origin of the AOCs in 19th Century France' (2004) 18(2) *European Journal of Law and Economics* 149–67.

'State of Trade' *The Times*, 3 December 1860, p. 4f.

Stadler, Sara K., 'The Wages of Ubiquity in Trademark Law' (2003) 88 *Iowa Law Review* 731.

Stern, Barbara B., and Jonathan E. Schroeder, 'Interpretive Methodology from Art and Literary Criticism: A Humanistic Approach to Advertising Imagery' (1994) 28 *European Journal of Marketing* 114–32.

Stern, Barbara B., George M. Zinkhan and Morris Holbrook, 'The Netvertising Image: Netvertising Image Communication Model (NICM) and Construct Definition' (2002) 31 *Journal of Advertising Fall* 15–28.

Stevenson, T., *Champagne* (London: Sotheby's Press, 1987).

Stigler, G., and G. Becker, 'De Gustibus Non Est Disputandum' (1977) 67 *American Economic Review* 76–90.

Stiglitz, J., *Whither Socialism?* (Cambridge, Mass.: MIT Press, 1994).

Strathern, M., *The Gender of the Gift. Problems with Women and Problems with Society in Melanesia* (Berkeley: University of California Press, 1988).

Kinship, Law and the Unexpected. Relatives are Always a Surprise (Cambridge: Cambridge University Press, 2005).

Property, Substance and Effect: Anthropological Essays on Persons and Things (London: Athlone Press, 1999).

Transactions: An Analytical Foray' in E. Hirsch and M. Strathern (eds.), *Transactions and Creations. Property Debates and the Stimulus of Melanesia* (New York and Oxford: Berghahn Books, 2004).

Stubbs, Michael, *Corpus Studies of Lexical Semantics* (Oxford: Blackwell, 2002).

Stutzer, A., and B. Frey, 'What Happiness Research can Tell us about Self-control Problems and Utility Misprediction' in B. Frey and A. Stutzer (eds.), *Economics and Psychology: A Promising New Cross-disciplinary Field* (Cambridge, Mass.: MIT Press, 2007).

Sumroy, R., and C. Badger, 'Infringing "Use in the Course of Trade": Trade Mark Use and the Essential Function of a Trade Mark' in Jeremy Phillips and Ilanah Simon (eds.), *Trade Mark Use* (Oxford: Oxford University Press, 2005).

Sunstein, C., *Laws of Fear: Beyond the Precautionary Principle* (Cambridge: Cambridge University Press, 2005).

Sutton, G. B., 'The Marketing of Ready Made Footwear in the Nineteenth Century: A Study of the Firm of C. and J. Clark' (1964) 6 *Business History* 93–112.

Swann, J. B., 'Trademarks and Marketing' (2001) 91 *Trademark Reporter* 787–832.

Swann, J. B., and T. H. Davis, 'Dilution, An Idea Whose Time has Gone; Brand Equity as Protectible Property, the New/Old Paradigm' (1994) 84 *Trademark Reporter* 267–99.

Sweetser, Eve, *From Etymology to Pragmatics: Metaphorical and Cultural Aspects of Semantic Change* (Cambridge: Cambridge University Press, 1990).

Tadelis, S., 'What's in a Name? Reputation as a Tradeable Asset' (1999) 89 *American Economic Review* 548–63.

Thackery, William, *The Virginians* (London: Bradbury and Evans, 1858–9).

Thomas, Jenny, *Meaning in Interaction: An Introduction to Pragmatics* (London: Longman, 1995).

Thompson, A., and G. Magee, 'A Soft Touch? British Industry, Empire Markets, and the Self-Governing Dominions, c.1870–1914' (2003) 56 *Economic History Review* 689–717.

The Times, 10 Sept. 1875, p. 8a.

   24 Sept. 1873, p. 12c.

Torremans, P., *Holyoak and Torremans Intellectual Property Law* (4th edn, Oxford: Oxford University Press, 2005).

'Trade Marks' (1858) 6 *Journal of the Society of Arts* 595–7 (20 August 1858).

'Trade Marks and Property Marks' (1861) 14 *Solicitors' Journal and Reporter* 3.

Traugott, Elizabeth Closs, and Richard Dasher, *Regularity in Semantic Change* (Cambridge: Cambridge University Press, 2002).

Tumbridge, J., 'Trade Marks: The Confusion of "Use"' (2004) 9 *European Intellectual Property Review* 431–4.

Turban, D. B., and D. W. Greening, 'Corporate Social Performance and Organisational Attractiveness to Prospective Employees' (1996) 40(3) *Academy of Management Journal* 658–72.

Turner-Kerr, P., 'Trade Mark Tangles: Recent Twists and Turns in EC Trade Mark Law' (2004) 29(3) *European Law Review* 345–65.

Tweedale, G., *Steel City: Entrepreneurship, Strategy, and Technology in Sheffield, 1743–1993* (Oxford: Oxford University Press, 1995).

Twitchell, J., *Lead us into Temptation: The Triumph of American Materialism* (New York: Columbia University Press, 1999).

Tzonis, Alexander, and Liane Lefaivre, *Classical Architecture: The Poetics of Order* (Cambridge, Mass.: MIT Press, 1986).

Underdown, E. M., *The Law of Artistic Copyright* (London: John Crockford, 1863).

'On the Piracy of Trade Marks' (1866) 14 *Journal of the Society of Arts* 370–4.

'The United States Trademark Association Trademark Review Commission Report and Recommendations to USTA President and Board of Directors" (1987) 77 *Trademark Reporter* 375.

Unwin, T., *Wine and the Vine: An Historical Geography of Viticulture and the Wine Trade* (London: Routledge, 1991).

Upton, Francis H., *A Treatise on the Law of Trade Marks, With a Digest and Review of the English and American Authorities* (Albany: W. C. Little, 1860).

Urry, J., *Global Complexity* (Cambridge: Polity, 2003).

van Ittersum, K., *et al.*, 'The Influence of the Image of a Product's Region of Origin on Product Evaluation' (2003) 56 *Journal of Business Research* 215–26.

van Leeuwen, Theo, and Carey Jewitt (eds.), *Handbook of Visual Analysis* (London: Sage, 2001).

Vaver, D., 'Does Intellectual Property have Personality?' in R. Zimmerman and N. Whitty (eds.), *Rights of Personality in Scots Law: a Comparative Perspective* (Dundee: University of Dundee Press, 2007, forthcoming).

Veblen, T., *The Theory of the Leisure Class: An Economic Study of Institutions* (London: Unwin Books, 1899; reprinted New York: Dover Publications, 1994].

Venkatesh, Alladi, and Laurie Meamber, 'Arts and Aesthetics: Marketing and Cultural Production' (2006) 6 *Marketing Theory* March 11–39.

Wadlow, C., *The Law of Passing Off: Unfair Competition by Misrepresentation* (3rd edn, London: Sweet and Maxwell, 2004).

Waldron, Jeremy, 'Minority Cultures and the Cosmopolitan Alternative' (1992) 25 *Michigan Journal of Law Reform* 751–93.

Waldrop, M., *Complexity* (London: Penguin, 1994).

Warner, Charles K., *The Winegrowers of France and the Government since 1875* (New York: Columbia University Press, 1960).

Wasserman, Howard M., 'Compelled Expression and the Public Forum Doctrine' (2002) 77 *Tulare Law Review* 163.

Weiner, A., *Inalienable Possessions: The Paradox of Keeping-while-giving* (Berkeley: University of California Press, 1992).

Wells Fargo Bank 1999 Annual Report (San Francisco: Wells Fargo, 2000).

White, H. *Markets from Networks: Socioeconomic Models of Production* (Princeton and Oxford: Princeton University Press, 2002).

White, M., 'A Kantian Critique of Law and Economics' (2006) 18 *Review of Political Economy* 235–52.

White, Robert E., *Soils for Fine Wines* (New York: Oxford University Press, 2003).

Whittle, J. Lowry, 'The Late Earl Cairns' (1885–6) 11 *Law Magazine and Law Review* (5th ser.) 133.

Wierzbicka, Anna, *English: Meaning and Culture* (Oxford: Oxford University Press, 2006).

Wilkins, M., 'The Neglected Intangible Asset: The Influence of the Trade Mark on the Rise of the Modern Corporation' (1992) 34 *Business History* 66–95.

Wilkof, N. J., and D. Burkitt, *Trade Mark Licensing* (2nd edn, London: Sweet and Maxwell, 2005).

Williams, E. E., *Made in Germany* (London: Heinemann, 1896).

Williamson, Judith, *Decoding Advertisements: Ideology and Meaning in Advertising* (reprint, London and New York: Marion Boyers, 2002).

Wilson, A. N., *The Victorians* (London: Arrow Books, 2005).

Wilson, C., 'Economy and Society in Late Victorian Britain' (1965) 18 *Economic History Review* 183–98.

The History of Unilever: A Study in Economic Growth and Social Change, vol. I (London: Cassell, 1954).

Wilson, J. E., *Terroir: The Role of Geology, Climate, and Culture in the Making of French Wines* (London: Mitchell Beazley, 1998).

Wilson, Richard, 'Selling Beer in Victorian England' in Geoffrey Jones and Nicholas Morgan (eds.), *Adding Value: Brands and Marketing in Food and Drink* (London: Routledge, 1994).

WIPO, *Report on Fact-finding Missions on Intellectual Property and Traditional Knowledge* (1998–9).

Secretariat Document SCT/6/3: Rev. on Geographical Indications: Historical Background, Nature of Rights, Existing Systems for Protection and Obtaining Protection in Other Countries (SCT/8/4) 2 Apr. 2002.

Web Site on Geographical Indications, available at www.wipo.int/about-ip/en/geographical_ind.html.

WIPO Secretariat, 'The Protection of Traditional Cultural Expressions/ Expressions of Foelzlore: Overview of Policy Objectives and Core Principles' 20 Aug. 2004 (WIPO/GRTKF/IC/7/3) at Annex II [38–41].

Wittgenstein, Ludwig, *Philosophical Investigations*, trans. G. E. M Anscombe (Oxford: Blackwell, 1953).

Wood, J. B., *The Law of Trade Marks* (London: Stevens, 1876).

'Words as Trade-Marks' (1900) 44 *Solicitors' Journal* 548–9 (23 June 1900).

Wray, Alison, Kate Trott and Aileen Bloomer, *Projects in Linguistics: A Practical Guide to Researching Language* (London: Arnold, 1998).

WTO, *Agreement on Trade Related Aspects of Intellectual Property Rights* Article 22 (1)

WTO Secretariat, 'Discussions on the Establishment of a Multilateral System of Notification And Registration of Geographical Indications for Wines And Spirits: Compilation of Issues and Points' 23 May 2003 (TN/IP/W/7/Rev.1) available at www.dsgiplc.com 12 Jan. 2007; www.orange.com, 3 March 2006.

Yoe, Craig (ed.), *The Art of Barbie* (New York, Workman, 1994).

Zaichowsky, Judith Lynne, *The Psychology behind Trademark Infringement and Counterfeiting* (Mahwah, N.J.: Lawrence Erlbaum, 2005).

Zhao, W., 'Understanding Classifications: Empirical Evidence from the American and French Wine Industries' (2005) 33 *Poetics* 179–200.

PARLIAMENTARY PAPERS AND LEGISLATIVE DOCUMENTS

(1862) *Minutes of Evidence of the Select Committee to whom the Trade Marks Bill, and the Merchandise Marks Bill were Referred* XII.

(1862) *Report from the Select Committee on Trade Marks Bill, and Merchandize Marks Bill* (London: House of Commons Papers, 1862).

(1862) *Select Committee on Trade Marks Bill and Merchandize Marks Bill, Report, Proceedings and Minutes of Evidence* 12 *Parliamentary Papers* 431

(1872) *Reports Relative to Legislation in Foreign Countries on the Subject of Trade Marks* C. 596 54 *Parliamentary Papers* 585.

(1872) *Treaty Stipulations Between Great Britain and Foreign Powers on the Subject of Trade Marks* C. 633 54 Parliamentary Papers 673.

(1875) *Declaration for extending to German Empire Stipulations in Commercial Treaty Between Great Britain and Zollverein, May 1865, for Protection of Trade Marks, London, April 1875* C. 1207 82 Parliamentary Papers 585.

(1878) *Declaration between Great Britain and United States for Protection of Trade Marks* C. 1901 80 Parliamentary Papers 439.

(1878) *Reports of the Commissioners of Patents for Inventions* (C. 335) 26 Parliamentary Papers 809.

(1879) *Reports Relative to Legislation in Foreign Countries on the Subject of Trade Marks* C. 2284 73 Parliamentary Papers 469

(1880) *Declaration between Great Britain and Denmark for the Protection of Trade Marks, Copenhagen, November 28, 1879* C. 2463 78 Parliamentary Papers 295

(1884) *International Convention for the Protection of Industrial Property*, C. 4043.

(1887) *Special Report from the Select Committee on Merchandise Marks Act (1862) Amendment Bill* C. 203 10 Parliamentary Papers 357.

(1888) *Correspondence Relative to the Protection of Industrial Property*, C. 5521.

(1888) *Extracts from Treaties and Declarations Now in Force Between Great Britain and Foreign Powers Relating to Trade Marks, Designs and Industrial Property* (C. 5554) 98 Parliamentary Papers 745.

(1888) *Report of a Commission Appointed by the Board of Trade to Inquire into the Duties, Organisation and Arrangements of the Patent Office under the Patents, Designs and Trade Marks Act 1883, so far as relates to Trade Marks and Designs,* C. 5350 81 Parliamentary Papers 37.

(1888) *Report of the Committee Appointed by the Board of Trade to Inquire into the Duties, Organisation, and Arrangements of the Patent Office*, C. 5350.

(1890) *Papers and Correspondence Relative to the Recent Conference at Madrid on the Subject of Industrial Property and Merchandise Marks* C. 6023.

(1890) *Report from the Select Committee on Merchandise Marks Act, 1887* C. 334 15 Parliamentary Papers 19.

(1893) *Report from the Select Committee on Marking of Foreign Meat* C. 214 12 Parliamentary Papers 341.

(1897) *Report and Special Report from the Select Committee on the Agricultural Produce (Marks) Bill* C. 365 8 Parliamentary Papers 227.

(1897) *Report from the Select Committee on Merchandise Marks* C. 346 11 Parliamentary Papers 29.

(1900) *Reports from Her Majesty's Representatives Abroad on Trade-Marks Laws and Regulations* Cd 104 1900 Parliamentary Papers 269.

(1905) *Report and Special report from the Select Committee on the Trade Marks Bill* Cd 231 8 Parliamentary Papers 257.

(1934) Board of Trade, *Report of the Departmental Committee on the Law and Practice Relating to Trade Marks*, Cmd 4568.

(1974) Under-Secretary of State for Trade, *Report of the Committee to Examine British Trade Mark Law and Practice*, Cmnd 5601.

(1990) The Secretary of State for Trade and Industry, *White Paper on Reform of Trade Marks Law*, Cm 1203.

Index

mirrors, 166–7, 184
Moët, 369
Moffatt, George, MP, 9
monopolies, 216, 235, 263, 264, 272
Montenegro, 18
Moore, C., 208, 215–16
Moran, Warren, 390
Morris, John, 20
Moulton, Fletcher, 60
Mountford, Charles, 352
Mozley, Lionel, 13, 30
Muller, Max, 39
Munson, Thomas, 372
Murphy, K., 274

Nader, Ralph, 102, 104
names. *See* personal names
National Association for the Protection of
   Social Science, 8
neighbouring signs, 184, 257–62, 263–4, 279
Nekgini-speaking people, 324–36
neo-classical economics, 246–7, 250, 267,
   274, 275
neologisms, 76
NESCAFÉ, 218
Nestlé, 203, 217
Netherlands, 26, 40, 55, 89
Nettleford and Chamberlain, 43
New Zealand, 218, 352, 356, 357
News International, 218
news reporting, 102, 134, 135–6, 154
newspapers, stamp duty, 11
Ngati Toa iwi, 356
Nike, 220
Nissan, 215
NOKIA, 218
non-trade mark use
   Community Trade Marks, 152–3, 256
   descriptive fair use, 155–6, 256
   Joy of Six case, 135–6, 156
   linguistics and, 142, 155–6
   non-liability, 154
   UK 1994 changes, 211
   United States, 102–3, 133–6, 145–7,
      152–3
   nominative fair use, 256
non-use of trade marks
   1883 Act, 346
   EU penalties, 256
Norman, H., 88
NORTH POLE, 74, 79, 115
NUROFEN, 294

O2, 186–8, 190
odours, 71–2, 73

Ogden, C. K., 115
Olympic Games, 297, 299
onomatopoeia, 72
Opel, 88
orange colour, 65–7, 72, 78
Orange Communications, 65–7, 78,
   81, 90
origins of products
   See also geographical indications
   ECJ jurisprudence, 86–7
   neighbouring signs and, 257–9
   non-trade mark use and, 256–7
   rationale of trade marks, 86–7, 243,
      244–5, 265, 269–71
OXO, 52

Pacific Dunlop, 218
packaging, 79, 190, 202, 251
Page-Wood, William, 10, 11, 12
Palmer, Roundell, 12
Papua New Guinea
   marks and designs, 326–7
   names and marks, 324–6
   owning names, 328–30
   stealing people's names, 330–3
   transactions and marks, 333–6
parallel imports, 271
Paris Convention (1883)
   definition of trade marks, 41
   original signatories, 4, 55
   origins, 15
   provisions, 55–6
   revisions, 56
Parma ham, 182
parodies, 103–4, 137–9, 146, 315, 350
passing-off
   Coloma case, 188–91
   common law, 21, 34, 226–7, 230
   deceitful claimants, 194
   infringement action or, 150
   licensing as passing-off, 207
   meaning, 292–3
   Orange case, 65
   origins, 227–8
   scope, 187, 231, 235–6, 237
   traditional symbols and, 357
   unfair competition, 182
patents, 23, 264, 278, 291, 298, 306
Peak Frean, 44
Peirce, Charles, 115
Pelletier, M., 386–7
Penner, J. E., 286, 288–90, 291–2
Pepsi, 178–9, 180, 349
Perignon, Dom, 368
Pernod Ricard, 218

432   Index

personal names
  common names, 144
  historical trade mark debate, 20–3
  Papua New Guinea, 328–33
  registration, 22–3
  reputation, 234–6
  secondary meanings, 144
  US trade mark law, 144–5
  use as trade marks, 225
personality rights, 21
personhood, 320, 324
persons, meaning, 320
pharmaceuticals, quack medicines, 193–7
Philip Morris, 213, 217
phonology, 119
photography, 163
phylloxera, 371–3, 388
pictures. *See* images
Pitjantjarja people, 352
place
  authenticity and, 364–5, 373–5, 376
  concept, 364–7, 397
  globalization and, 375–9
  terroir, 366–73, 375, 383–91, 393–5
Poland, Harry Bodkin, 13
POLO Jeans, 207
Polson, John, 24
Pommery, 369
Portugal, 55
Posner, R., 267, 268, 269, 272, 280
postmodernism, 71, 351, 366, 397
Potter, Edmund, MP, 9, 21, 28
Presley, Elvis, 234–5
producer markets, 201–22
product differentiation, 272, 275
product liability, 197
productive efficiency, 244
PRONTAPRINT, 204
property rights
  absolute ownership, 285, 292
  copyright, 264, 278, 291, 292, 298
  economic efficiency and, 244
  patents, 264, 278, 291, 298
  theory of property
    bundle of rights, 285
    Locke, 297–305
    reifiability, 286–8
    separability thesis, 288–90
  trade marks, 255–64
    1994 Act, 290
    economic rationale, 246
    extension, 245, 262–4
    neighbouring signs, 257–62, 263–4
    rights *in rem*, 227
    Scotland and England, 229

trade marks as property
  competence, 285–90
  dilution of marks, 295–305
  trade mark law treatment, 290–5
Prussia, 18, 46–7
psychological harm, 180
psychology, 252–4, 275
public choice theory, 268
public interest, Community Trade Marks
  and, 75–6, 77, 79

quack medicines, 193–7
quality guarantees, 212–13, 376, 387,
  388–91
quality maintenance, 269–72
quality profiles, 208–9, 213–14

Ralph Lauren, 206, 207, 215–16
Rank Hovis McDougall, 218
Ratzel, Friedrich, 373, 375
Rawls, John, 280
Reckitt, 44
Redditch, 32, 46
registration
  See also definition of trade marks
  advantages, 228
  historic debate, 17
  legal effect. *See* property rights
  linguistics and, 150
  nineteenth-century statistics, 49–51
  objective, 66
  personal names, 22–3
  prima facie evidence, 42, 53
  registrability threshold, 211–09
  shapes and get-ups, 24
reputation
  development by advertising, 252
  extension of protection, 262–4
  Geographical Indications, 364, 387
  maintaining, 269–72
  Papua New Guinea, 334–5
  passing-off, 357
  personal names, 234–6
  trade marks, 248–9
  triggers, 251
Revlon, 192
Richards, I. A., 115
risqué terms, 127, 197
Roebuck, John Arthur, MP, 9, 28
Roenisch, Rowan, 168
ROLLS ROYCE, 52
Rolt, John, 12
Roman law, 3
Romania, 18
Romans, 368

Titles in the series (formerly known as *Cambridge Studies in Intellectual Property Rights*)

Brad Sherman and Lionel Bently *The Making of Modern Intellectual Property Law*
978 0 521 56363 5

Irini A. Stamatoudi *Copyright and Multimedia Products: A Comparative Analysis*
978 0 521 80819 4

Pascal Kamina *Film Copyright in the European Union*
978 0 521 77053 8

Huw Beverly-Smith *The Commercial Appropriation of Personality*
978 0 521 80014 3

Mark J. Davison *The Legal Protection of Databases*
978 0 521 80257 4

Robert Burrell and Allison Coleman *Copyright Exceptions: The Digital Impact*
978 0 521 84726 1

Huw Beverly-Smith, Ansgar Ohly and Agnès Lucas-Schloetter *Privacy, Property and Personality: Civil Law Perspectives on Commercial Appropriation*
978 0 521 82080 6

Philip Leith *Software and Patents in Europe*
978 0 521 86839 6

Lionel Bently, Jennifer Davis and Jane C. Ginsburg *Trade Marks and Brands: An Interdisciplinary Critique*
978 0 521 88965 0